Collins

# Collins
# Welsh
# Dictionary

**HarperCollins Publishers**
Westerhill Road
Bishopbriggs
Glasgow
G64 2QT
Great Britain

**Second Edition 2006**

Previously published as Collins
Spurrell Pocket Welsh Dictionary

© William Collins Sons & Co. Ltd. 1960
© HarperCollins Publishers 1991, 2006

ISBN-13 978-0-00-722395-4
ISBN-10 0-00-722395-1

www.collins.co.uk

A catalogue record for this book is
available from the British Library

Typeset by Thomas Callan

Printed in Italy by Rotolito Lombarda
SpA

**Acknowledgements**
We would like to thank those authors
and publishers who kindly gave
permission for copyright material to
be used in the Collins Word Web. We
would also like to thank Times
Newspapers Ltd for providing
valuable data.

*Revised in collaboration with/*
*Diwygiwyd mewn cydweithrediad â'r*

Dr. David A. Thorne and the
Department of Welsh Language and
Literature, St David's University
College, Lampeter

Dr. David A. Thorne ac Adran Iaith a
Llenyddiaeth Cymru, Coleg Prifysgol
Dewi Sant, Llanbedr Pont Steffan

EDITOR/GOLYGYDD
Anne Convery

# CONTENTS

## INTRODUCTION

The first Spurrell Welsh-English dictionary appeared in 1848 published by William Spurrell (1813–89) the Carmarthen printer and publisher. One of his sons, Walter Spurrell (1858–1934), joined his father in the business and the family firm published a series of distinguished Welsh-English, English-Welsh dictionaries and influential Welsh grammars during the latter part of last century and the first half of the present century. William Spurrell was advised by and well-acquainted with Daniel Silvan Evans (1818–1903), one of the father figures of Welsh lexicography, sometime lecturer in Welsh at St David's University College, Lampeter and the first professor of Welsh to be appointed by the University of Wales.

The Collins-Spurrell Welsh Dictionary was first published in 1960 and quickly became an essential tool of general reference for Welsh learners as well as those anxious to interpret literature. It was edited by Henry Lewis, Professor of Welsh Language and Literature at University College, Swansea. The staff of the Department of Welsh Language and Literature at St David's University College, Lampeter are happy to cooperate with the editorial staff at Collins to produce this latest edition of a famous dictionary.

D A THORNE

## NOTES ON THE PRONUNCIATION OF WELSH

### VOWELS

They are sounded, long or short, as the vowels in the English words given.

| | |
|---|---|
| A | p*a*lm, p*a*t. |
| E | g*a*te (without dipthongization), g*e*t. |
| I | f*ee*t, f*i*t. |
| O | m*o*re, n*o*t. |
| U (1) | North Wales: like French *u* or German *ü* without rounding lips. |
| (2) | South Wales: as I. |
| W | c*oo*l, f*u*ll. |
| Y (1) | In monosyllables generally, and in final syllables, as U (the 'clear' sound). |
| (2) | In all but final syllables, and in **y, yr** (the), **fy** (my), **dy** (thy), **yn, yng, ym** (in), the adverbial **yn**, the preverbal and relative particle **y, yr** (**y'm, y'th** etc), **syr** (sir), **nyrs** (nurse), as English f*u*n, (the 'obscure' sound). |

### DIPHTHONGS

1    Falling diphthongs, in which the second sound is consonantal: the two vowels have the sound noted above: **ae, oe, ai, oi,** the diphthong **ei** as English *by*, **aw, ew, iw, ow, uw, ŵy, yw.**

2    Rising diphthongs, in which the first sound is consonantal: **ia, ie, io, iw, iy,** ('obscure' y); **wa, we, wi, wo, wy,** ('clear' y), **wy,** ('obscure' y).

## CONSONANTS

Only such as differ from English need be noted.

| | |
|---|---|
| CH | (following C in the alphabet), as Scottish lo*ch*. |
| DD | (following D in the alphabet), as *th* in English *this*, brea*the*. |
| F | as English *v*. |
| FF | as English *f*. |
| G | always as in English *go*. |
| NG | (following G in the alphabet), as in English si*ng*. In some words (e.g. **dangos**), however, it is sounded *ng-g*, as in English lo*ng*er. Alphabetically this follows after N. |
| LL | produced by placing the tongue to pronounce *l*, then emitting breath without voice. |
| PH | (following P in the alphabet), as English *f*. |
| TH | always as th in English *thin*. |

## ACCENT

Welsh words are generally accented on the last syllable but one. There are certain exceptions:

1. The reduplicated personal pronouns **myfi, tydi, efe, efô, hyhi, nyni, chwychwi, hwynt-hwy**, accented on the final syllable.
2. Verbs in **–(h)au, -(h)oi, -eu**, accented on the final syllable.
3. A few dissyllabic words beginning **y** + consonant, accented on the final syllable.
4. Certain polysyllabic words with a diphthong resulting in contraction in the final syllable, such as **Cymraeg**.
5. Some late borrowings accented as in the language of origin, generally English.

## INITIAL MUTATIONS

Certain initial consonants are mutated under certain conditions, as shown in the following table. Only the radical form is given in the dictionary.

| SOUNDS | | EXAMPLES | | |
|---|---|---|---|---|
| | Radical | Soft | Nasal | Spirant |
| **p** | *p*ren | *b*ren | *mh*ren | *ph*ren |
| **t** | *t*ad | *d*ad | *nh*ad | *th*ad |
| **c** | *c*am | *g*am | *ngh*am | *ch*am |
| **b** | *b*aich | *f*aich | *m*aich | |
| **d** | *d*yn | *dd*yn | *n*yn | |
| **g** | *g*ŵr | *-*ŵr | *ng*ŵr | |
| **ll** | *ll*ais | *l*ais | | |
| **rh** | *rh*es | *r*es | | |
| **m** | *m*am | *f*am | | |

vi

| | | |
|---|---|---|
| abbreviation | *abbr* | byrfodd |
| adjective | *adj* | ansoddair |
| adverb | *adv* | adferf |
| collective noun | *coll n* | enw torfol |
| colloquial | *col* | tafodieithol |
| conjunction | *conj* | cysylltiad |
| contraction | *contr* | cywasgiad |
| demonstrative | *dem* | dangosol |
| dual noun | *dn* | enw deuol |
| emphatic | *emphat* | pwyslais |
| exclamation | *excl* | ebychiad |
| feminine | *f* | benywaidd |
| grammatical | *gram* | gramadegol |
| imperative | *imper* | gorchmynnol |
| masculine | *m* | gwrywaidd |
| mutation | *mut* | treiglad |
| noun dual | *nd* | enw deuol |
| plural | *pl* | lluosog |
| pronoun | *pron* | rhagenw |
| preposition | *prep* | arddodiad |
| relative | *rel* | perthynol |
| singular | *sg* | unigol |
| verb | *vb* | berf |
| intransitive verb | *vi* | berf gyflawn |
| transitive verb | *vt* | berf anghyflawn |

William Collins' dream of knowledge for all began with the publication of his first book in 1819. A self-educated mill worker, he not only enriched millions of lives, but also founded a flourising publishing house. Today, staying true to this spirit, Collins books are packed with inspiration, innovation, and practical expertise. They place you at the centre of a world of possibility and give you exactly what you need to explore it.

Language is the key to this exploration, and at the heart of Collins Dictionaries is language as it is really used. New words, phrases, and meanings spring up every day, and all of them are captured and analysed by the Collins Word Web. Constantly updated, and with over 2.5 billion entries, this living language resource is unique to our dictionaries.

Words are tools for life. And a Collins Dictionary makes them work for you.

**Collins. Do more.**

# WELSH - ENGLISH
# CYMRAEG - SAESNEG

# a

**a** *interrogative particle; preverbal particle; rel pron* who, that, which
**a, ac** *conj* and
**â, ag** *conj* as
**â, ag** *prep* with
**a** *excl* ah, oh
**ab, ap** *nm* son (*before name, in place of surname, like 'Mac', and 'Fitz'*)
**abad (-au)** *nm* abbot
**abadaeth (-au)** *nf* abbacy, abbotship
**abades (-au)** *nf* abbess
**abatir (-oedd)** *nm* abbey-land
**abaty (abatai)** *nm* abbey
**aber (-oedd, ebyr)** *nm* confluence; mouth of river, estuary; brook, stream
**aberfa (-oedd)** *nf* mouth of river, estuary
**abergofiant** *nm* forgetfulness, oblivion
**aberth (-au, ebyrth)** *nm* sacrifice
**aberthged** *nf* oblation; offering of fruits
**aberthol** *adj* sacrificial
**aberthu** *vb* sacrifice
**aberthwr (-wyr)** *nm* sacrificer
**aberu** *vb* flow into, disembogue
**abid** *nm/f* apparel; dress of religious order

**abiéc** *nm/f* alphabet
**abl** *adj* able; well-off
**abladol** *adj* ablative
**abledd** *nm* ability; plenty
**abrwysg** *adj* clumsy, drunken
**absen** *nm* absence; slander
**absennol** *adj* absent
**absennu** *vb* backbite, slander
**absennwr (absenwyr)** *nm* backbiter
**absenoldeb** *nm* absence
**absenoli** *vb* absent
**absenoliaeth (-au)** *nm* absenteeism
**abwyd, -yn (-od)** *nm* worm; fishing-bait
**ac, a** *conj* and
**academaidd** *adj* academic
**academi (-ïau)** *nm* academy
**acen (-ion)** *nf* accent
**aceniad** *nm* accentuation
**acennod** *nf* accent mark
**acennu** *vb* accent, stress
**acenyddiaeth** *nf* accentuation
**acer (-i)** *nf* acre
**acrilig** *adj* acrylic
**act (-au)** *nf* act
**actio** *vb* act
**actor (-ion)** *nm* actor
**actores (-au)** *nf* actress

**acw** *adv* there, yonder

**ach** *excl* ugh

**ach** (-au, -oedd) *nf* degree of kinship; (*pl*) pedigree, ancestry

**aches** *nm* tide, flood; eloquence

**achlân** *adv* wholly, entirely

**achles** (-oedd) *nf* succour, protection; manure

**achlesol** *adj* succouring

**achlesu** *vb* succour, cherish; manure

**achlod** *nm* shame, disgrace

**achlust** *nm* rumour ▷ *adj* attentive

**achlysur** (-on) *nm* occasion

**achlysuro** *vb* occasion

**achlysurol** *adj* occasional

**achos** (-ion) *nm* cause, case

**achos** *conj* because, for

**achosi** *vb* cause

**achres** (-i, -au) *nf* genealogical table

**achub** *vb* seize, snatch; save, rescue; **~ y blaen** forestall; **~ y cyfle** seize the opportunity

**achubiaeth** *nf* salvation

**achubol** *adj* saving

**achubwr** (-wyr), **-ydd** (-ion) *nm* saviour, rescuer

**achul** *adj* thin, emaciated

**achwre, ach(f)re** *n* under-thatch, protection; covering, garment

**achwyn** *vb* complain ▷ (-ion) *nm* complaint, plaint

**achwyngar** *adj* querulous

**achwyniad** (-au) *nm* complaint, accusation

**achwynwr** (-wyr) *nm* complainer, complainant, plaintiff

**achwynyddes** (-au) *nf* complainant

**achydd** (-ion) *nm* genealogist

**achyddiaeth** *nf* genealogy

**achyddol** *adj* genealogical

**ad-** *prefix* very; second; bad, re-

**adail** *nf* building, edifice, structure

**adain, aden** (adenydd) *nf* wing; fin; spoke

**adamant** *nm* adamant, diamond

**adamantaidd** *adj* adamantine

**adar** *npl* (*nm* aderyn) birds, fowls; **~ drudwy, ~ yr eira** starlings; **~ y to** sparrows

**adara** *vb* catch birds, fowl

**adardy** (-dai) *nm* aviary

**adareg** *nf* ornithology

**adargi** (-gwn) *nm* retriever, setter, spaniel

**adargraffiad** (-au) *nm* reprint

**adarwr** (-wyr) *nm* fowler

**adarwriaeth** *nf* fowling

**adarydd** (-ion) *nm* ornithologist

**adaryddiaeth** *nf* ornithology

**ad-dalu** *vb* repay, requite

**ad-drefnu** *vb* rearrange

**adeg** (-au) *nf* time, occasion, opportunity

**adeilad** (-au) *nm/f* building, edifice

**adeiladaeth** *nf* building; edification, construction

**adeiladol** *adj* edifying, constructive

**adeiladu** *vb* build, edify

**adeiladwr** (-wyr), **-ydd** (-ion) *nm* builder

**adeiledd** *nm* structure

**adeiniog** *adj* winged

**aden** (-ydd, edyn) *nf* wing (adain)

**adenedigaeth** *nf* regeneration

**adeni** *vb* regenerate

**adennill** *vb* regain, recover

**aderyn** (adar) *nm* bird

**adfach** (-au) *nm* barb; liver-fluke

**adfail** (-feilion) *nm* ruin

**adfeddiannu** *vb* repossess

**adfeiliad** *nm* decay, ruin

**adfeiliedig** *adj* decayed, in ruins

**adfeilio** *vb* decay, moulder

**Adfent** *nm* Advent

**adfer, -u, -yd** *vb* restore

**adferf** (-au) *nf* adverb

**adferfol** *adj* adverbial

**adferiad** *nm* restoration

**adferol** *adj* restorative; remedial

**adferwr** (-wyr) *nm* restorer

**adflas** *nm* after-taste, bad taste

**adfyd** *nm* adversity
**adfydus** *adj* adverse, miserable
**adfynach** *nm* renegade monk
**adfyw** *adj* half alive, half dead
**adfywhau** *vb* revive, reanimate
**adfywiad (-au)** *nm* revival
**adfywio** *vb* revive, resuscitate
**adfywiol** *adj* refreshing
**adg-** *see* **atg-**
**adiad** *nm* drake
**adio** *nm* addition ▷ *vb* add
**adiolyn (adiolion)** *nm* additive
**adladd, adlodd** *nm* aftermath
**adlais (-leisiau)** *nm* echo
**adlam (-au)** *nm* home; rebound; **cic**
**~ drop-kick**
**adlamu** *vb* rebound
**adleisio** *vb* resound
**adlewyrch, -iad (-au)** *nm*
reflection
**adlewyrchu** *vb* reflect
**adlewyrchydd (-ion)** *nm* reflector
**adlog (-au)** *nm* compound interest
**adloniadol** *adj* of or for
entertainment
**adloniant** *nm* recreation,
entertainment
**adlonni** *vb* entertain, refresh
**adlunio** *vb* remodel, reconstruct
**adnabod** *vb* know, recognize
**adnabyddiaeth** *nf* knowledge,
acquaintance
**adnabyddus** *adj* known, familiar
**adnabyddwr** *nm* knower
**adnau (adneuon)** *nm* deposit,
pledge; **ar ~ on deposit**
**adneuo** *vb* deposit
**adneuol** *adj* depositing
**adneuwr (-wyr)** *nm* depositor
**adnewyddiad (-au)** *nm* renewal,
renovation
**adnewyddu** *vb* renew, renovate
**adnewyddwr (-wyr)** *nm* renewer,
renovator
**adnod (-au)** *nf* verse
**adnoddau** *npl* resources
**adolygiad (-au)** *nm* review

**adolygu** *vb* review
**adolygydd (-ion)** *nm* reviewer
**adran (-nau)** *nf* division, section,
department
**adref** *adv* homewards, home
**adrodd** *vb* relate, recite
**adroddgan (-au)** *nf* recitative
**adroddiad (-au)** *nm* report;
recitation
**adroddwr (-wyr)** *nm* narrator,
reciter
**ads-** *see* **ats-**
**aduniad** *nm* reunion
**aduno** *vb* reunite
**adwaith (-weithiau)** *nm* reaction
**adweithiol** *adj* reactionary
**adweithydd (-ion)** *nm* reactor
**adwr** *nm* coward, churl
**adwy (-au, -on)** *nf* gap, breach; pass
**adwyth (-au)** *nm* evil, misfortune,
illness
**adwythig** *adj* cruel; evil, baneful;
sore, sick; harmful
**adyn (-od)** *nm* wretch
**adysgrif (-au)** *nf* copy, transcript
**adysgrifio** *vb* copy, transcribe
**addas** *adj* suitable, proper
**addasiad (-au)** *nm* adjustment,
adaptation
**addasrwydd** *nm* suitableness,
fitness
**addasu** *vb* suit, adapt, fit
**addawol** *adj* promising
**addef** *vb* acknowledge, own, admit
**addefiad** *nm* admission,
confession
**addewid (-ion)** *nf* promise
**addfain** *adj* slender, shapely
**addfed** *see* **aeddfed**
**addfwyn** *adj* gentle, meek, mild
**addfwynder** *nm* gentleness,
meekness
**addien** *adj* fair, beautiful
**addo** *vb* promise
**addod** *nm*: **wy ~ nest-egg**
**addoed** *nm* death, hurt
**addoedi** *vb* delay, postpone,

prorogue
**addoediad** *nm* prorogation
**addoer** *adj* sad, cruel; chilling
**addoldy** (**-dai**) *nm* place of worship
**addolgar** *adj* devout, reverent
**addolgarwch** *nm* devoutness,
reverence
**addoli** *vb* worship, adore
**addoliad** *nm* worship
**addolwr** (**-wyr**) *nm* worshipper
**adduned** (**-au**) *nf* vow
**addunedu** *vb* vow
**addurn** (**-au, -iadau**) *nm* ornament,
adornment
**addurnedig** *adj* decorated
**addurniad** *nm* ornamentation
**addurno** *vb* adorn, ornament
**addurnol** *adj* ornamental,
decorative
**addurnwr** (**-wyr**) *nm* decorator
**addysg** *nf* education, instruction
**addysgiadol** *adj* instructive,
educational
**addysgiaeth** *nf* instruction,
training
**addysgol** *adj* educational
**addysgu** *vb* educate, instruct
**addysgwr** (**-wyr**), **-ydd** (**-ion**) *nm*
educator, instructor, tutor
**aeddfed** *adj* ripe, mature
**aeddfedrwydd** *nm* ripeness,
maturity
**aeddfedu** *vb* ripen; mature
**ael** (**-iau**) *nf* brow
**aele** *adj* sad, wretched
**aelgerth, -geth** *see* **elgeth**
**aelod** (**-au**) *nm* member, limb; **A-
Seneddol** Member of Parliament
**aelodaeth** *nf* membership
**aelodi** *vb* become a member; enrol
**aelwyd** (**-ydd**) *nf* hearth, fireside
**aer** (**-ion**) *nm* heir
**aer** *nm* air
**aeres** (**-au**) *nf* heiress
**aerfa** *nf* slaughter, battle
**aerglo** *nm* air-lock
**aeron** *npl* fruit, fruits, berries

**aerwy** (**-au, -on**) *nm* collar, torque;
neck-chain
**aes** *nf* shield
**aestheteg** *nf* aesthetics
**aesthetig** *adj* aesthetic
**aeth** *nm* pain, grief, fear, shock
**aethnen** *nf* aspen, poplar
**aethus** *adj* poignant, grievous,
severe
**afal** (**-au**) *nm* apple
**afaleua** *vb* gather apples
**afallen** (**-nau**) *nf* apple-tree
**afan** *npl* (**nf-en**) raspberries
**afanc** (**-od**) *nm* beaver
**afiach** *adj* unwell, unhealthy,
morbid
**afiachus** *adj* sickly; unwholesome
**afiaith** *nm* zest, mirth, glee
**afiechyd** (**-on**) *nm* disease, malady
**afieithus** *adj* mirthful, gleeful
**aflafar** *adj* harsh, unmelodious
**aflan** *adj* unclean, polluted, foul
**aflawen** *adj* fierce; sad, cheerless,
dismal; awful
**aflednais** *adj* immodest, indelicate
**afledneisrwydd** *nm* immodesty,
indelicacy
**aflem** *adj* obtuse
**aflendid** *nm* uncleanness; pollution
**aflêr** *adj* untidy, slovenly
**aflerwch** *nm* untidiness,
slovenliness
**afles** *nm* disadvantage, hurt
**aflesol** *adj* disadvantageous,
unprofitable
**afliwiog** *adj* pale, colourless
**aflonydd** *adj* unquiet, restless
**aflonyddu** *vb* disquiet, disturb,
molest
**aflonyddwch** *nm* disturbance,
unrest
**aflonyddwr** (**-wyr**) *nm* disturber
**afloyw** *adj* turbid; opaque
**afluniaidd** *adj* mis-shapen,
deformed
**aflunio** *vb* disfigure, deform
**aflwydd** *nm* misfortune, calamity

**aflwyddiannus** *adj* unsuccessful
**aflwyddiant** *nm* failure
**aflwyddo** *vb* fail
**aflywodraeth** *nf* misrule, anarchy
**aflywodraethus** *adj*
 ungovernable, uncontrollable
**afon** (-ydd) *nf* river
**afonig** *nf* rivulet, streamlet, brook
**afradlon** *adj* wasteful, prodigal
**afradlonedd** *nm* prodigality
**afradloni, afradu** *vb* waste,
 lavish, squander
**afraid** *adj* unnecessary, needless
**afrasol** *adj* graceless, impious
**afreidiau** *nm* superfluity
**afreidiol** *adj* needless, superfluous
**afreol** *nf* misrule, disorder
**afreolaidd** *adj* irregular; disorderly
**afreoleidd-dra** *nm* irregularity
**afreolus** *adj* unruly, disorderly
**afreswm** *nm* absurdity
**afresymol** *adj* unreasonable
**afresymoldeb** *nm*
 unreasonableness
**afrifed** *adj* innumerable
**afrllad, -en** (-au, -ennau) *nf* wafer
**afrosgo** *adj* clumsy, unwieldy
**afrwydd** *adj* difficult, stiff,
 awkward
**afrwyddineb** *nm* difficulty
**afrwyddo** *vb* obstruct, hinder
**afrywiog** *adj* perverse,
 crossgrained, improper
**afrywiogrwydd** *nm* churlishness,
 roughness
**afu** liver *nm/f*: **~ (g)las** gizzard
**afwyn** (-au) *nf* rein
**affeithiad** *nm* affection (in
 grammar)
**afflau** *nm* grip, hug, embrace
**affliw** *nm* shred, particle
**Affrica** *nf* Africa
**affwysol** *nm* abysmal
**ag** *conj* as ▷ *prep* with; *see* **â**
**agen** (-nau) *nf* cleft, chink, fissure
**agendor** *nm/f* gulf, abyss
**agennu** *vb* split, crack

**ager, agerdd** *nm* steam, vapour
**agerfad** (-au) *nm* steamboat
**agerlong** (-au) *nf* steamship,
 steamer
**ageru** *vb* steam, evaporate
**agerw** *adj* bitter, fierce
**agor, -yd** *vb* open, expand
**agorawd** (-au) *nf* overture
**agored** *adj* open; liable
**agorfa** (-oedd) *nf* opening, orifice
**agoriad** (-au) *nm* opening; key
**agoriadol** *adj* opening, inaugural
**agorwr** (-wyr), **-ydd** (-ion) *nm*
 opener
**agos** *adj* near, nigh
**agosaol** *adj* approaching
**agosatrwydd** *nm* intimacy
**agosáu** *vb* draw near, approach
**agosrwydd** *nm* nearness,
 proximity
**agwedd** (-au) *nf* form; aspect;
 attitude
**agweddi** *nm* dowry, marriage gift
**agwrdd** *adj* strong, mighty
**angall** *adj* unwise, foolish
**angau** *nm/f* death
**angel** (**angylion, engyl**) *nm* angel
**angen** (**anghenion**) *nm* need, want
**angenrheidiol** *adj* necessary,
 needful
**angenrheidrwydd** *nm* necessity
**angerdd** *nm* heat; passion; force
**angerddol** *adj* ardent, intense,
 passionate
**angerddoldeb** *nm* vehemence,
 intensity
**anghaffael** *nm* mishap; defect,
 flaw
**anghallineb** *nm* unwisdom,
 imprudence
**angharedig** *adj* unkind
**angharedigrwydd** *nm*
 unkindness
**anghelfydd** *adj* unskilful, clumsy
**anghenfil** (**angenfilod**) *nm*
 monster
**anghenraid** (**angenrheidiau**) *nm*

necessity

**anghenus** adj needy, necessitous, indigent

**angheuol** adj deadly, mortal, fatal

**anghlod** nm dispraise, dishonour

**anghoelio** vb disbelieve

**anghofiedig** adj forgotten

**anghofio** vb forget

**anghofrwydd** nm forgetfulness

**anghofus** adj forgetful, oblivious

**anghred** nf unbelief, infidelity

**anghredadun** (anghredinwyr) nm unbeliever

**anghrediniaeth** nf unbelief, infidelity

**anghrediniol** adj unbelieving

**anghredu** vb disbelieve

**anghrefyddol** adj irreligious

**anghrist** (-iau) nm antichrist

**anghryno** adj incompact, prolix

**anghwrtais** adj discourteous

**anghwrteisi** nm discourtesy

**anghydbwysedd** nm imbalance

**anghydfod** nm disagreement, discord

**Anghydffurfiaeth** nf Nonconformity

**Anghydffurfiwr** (-wyr) nm Nonconformist

**anghydnaws** adj uncongenial

**anghydsynio** vb dissent, disagree

**anghydweddol** adj incompatible

**anghyfaddas** adj unsuitable, unfit

**anghyfaddasu** vb unfit, disqualify

**anghyfamodol** adj uncovenanted

**anghyfanhedd-dra** nm desolation

**anghyfanheddle** (-aneddleoedd) nm desolate place

**anghyfanheddol** adj desolating; desert

**anghyfannedd** adj uninhabited, desert

**anghyfansoddiadol** adj unconstitutional

**anghyfartal** adj unequal, uneven

**anghyfartaledd** nm disparity

**anghyfarwydd** adj unfamiliar, unskilled

**anghyfeillgar** adj unfriendly

**anghyfiaith** adj foreign, alien

**anghyfiawn** adj unjust, unrighteous

**anghyfiawnder** nm injustice

**anghyflawn** adj incomplete

**anghyfleus** adj inconvenient

**anghyfleustra** (-terau) nm inconvenience

**anghyflogaeth** nm unemployment

**anghyfnewidiol** adj immutable

**anghyfraith** nf transgression, crime

**anghyfranogol** adj incommunicable

**anghyfreithlon** adj unlawful, illegal, illegitimate

**anghyfrifol** adj irresponsible

**anghyffredin** adj uncommon, rare

**anghyffwrdd** adj intangible

**anghyffyrddus** adj uncomfortable

**anghymedrol** adj immoderate

**anghymen** adj rash, coarse, untidy

**anghymeradwy** adj unacceptable

**anghymeradwyo** vb disapprove

**anghymesur** adj inordinate

**anghymharol** adj incomparable

**anghymharus** adj ill-matched

**anghymhendod** nm foolishness, indelicacy, untidiness

**anghymhwyso** vb unfit, disqualify

**anghymhwyster** nm incapacity, disqualification

**anghymodlon** adj implacable

**anghymwys** adj unfit, unsuitable

**anghynefin** adj unfamiliar

**anghynefindra** nm unfamiliarity

**anghynhyrchiol** adj unproductive

**anghynnes** adj odious, loathsome

**anghysbell** adj out-of-the-way; remote

**anghyson** adj inconsistent

**anghysondeb, -der** (-au) nm

inconsistency

**anghysur** (-on) *nm* discomfort

**anghysuro** *vb* discomfort

**anghysurus** *adj* uncomfortable

**anghytbwys** *adj* unbalanced, lopsided

**anghytgord** (-iau) *nm* discord, dissension

**anghytûn** *adj* not agreeing, discordant

**anghytundeb** *nm* disagreement

**anghytuno** *vb* disagree

**anghywair** *adj* ill-equipped; discordant ▷ *nm* disrepair

**anghyweithas** *adj* froward, uncivil

**anghywir** *adj* incorrect, inaccurate, false

**anghywirdeb** (-au) *nm* inaccuracy, falseness

**anghywrain** *adj* unskilful; slovenly

**angladd** (-au) *nm/f* burial, funeral

**angladdol** *adj* funereal

**angof** *nm* forgetfulness, oblivion

**angor** (-au, -ion) *nm* anchor

**angorfa** (-oedd, -feydd) *nf* anchorage

**angori** *vb* anchor

**angylaidd** *adj* angelic

**angyles** (-au) *nf* female angel

**ai** *adv* is it? what?; **ai e**? is it so?

**ai** *conj* or; either; if

**aidd** *nm* zeal, ardour, zest

**Aifft: yr A~** *nf* Egypt

**aig, eigiau** *nf* host, shoal

**aig** *nf* (late corrupt form) sea, ocean

**ail** *adj* second ▷ *adv* a second time, again

**ailadrodd** *vb* repeat

**ailadroddiad** (-au) *nm* repetition

**ailenedigaeth** *nf* rebirth

**aileni** *vb* bear again, regenerate

**Ailfedyddiwr** (-wyr) *nm* Anabaptist

**ail-law** *adj* second-hand

**aillt** *nm* vassal, villain, slave

**ais** *npl* (*nf* eisen) laths; ribs

**alaeth** *nm* wailing, lamentation, grief

**alaethu** *vb* lament

**alaethus** *adj* mournful, lamentable

**alarch** (-od, elyrch) *nm* swan

**alaru** *vb* surfeit; loathe

**alaw** (-on) *nf* lily; air, melody, tune

**Alban: yr A~** *nf* Scotland

**Albanwr** (-wyr) *nm* Scot

**alcali** (-ïau) *nm* alkali

**alcam** *nm* tin

**alcohol** *nm* alcohol

**alch** (-au, eilch) *nf* grate, grill

**ale** (-au, -on) *nf* aisle; gangway; alley

**algebra** *nm* algebra

**Algeria** *nf* Algeria

**Almaen: yr A~** *nf* Germany

**Almaeneg** *nf* German

**Almaenwr** (-wyr) *nm* German

**almon** *nm* almond

**aloi** (aloeon) *nm* alloy

**Alpau: yr** *npl* the Alps

**allan** *adv* out

**allanol** *adj* outward, external

**allblyg** *adj* extrovert

**allforio** *vb* export

**allfro** *nm* foreigner; foreign land

**allfudwr** (-wyr) *nm* emigrant

**allgarwch** *nm* altruism

**allor** (-au) *nf* altar

**allt** (elltydd) *nf* hill; cliff; wood

**alltud** (-ion) *nm* alien; exile

**alltudiaeth** *nf* banishment, exile

**alltudio** *vb* banish, exile

**allwedd** (-au, -i) *nf* key, clef (music)

**am** *prep* round, about; for; at; on ▷ *conj* for, because; so long as

**am** *see* **ym**

**amaeth** *nm* husbandman; agriculture

**amaethdy** (-dai) *nm* farm-house

**amaethu** *vb* farm, till

**amaethwr** (-wyr) *nm* farmer

**amaethwraig** *nf* farm-wife

**amaethyddiaeth** *nf* agriculture

**amaethyddol** *adj* agricultural

**amarch** *nm* disrespect, dishonour

**amau** vb doubt, suspect ▷ (**-heuon**) nm doubt

**ambell** adj occasional; **~ waith** sometimes

**amcan** (**-ion**) nm purpose, aim; guess; **ar ~** at random, approximately, at a guess

**amcangyfrif** vb estimate ▷ (**-on**) nm estimate

**amcanu** vb purpose; aim; guess

**amdo** (**-oeau**) nm shroud, winding-sheet

**amdoi** vb shroud, enshroud

**amdorch** (**-dyrch**) nf chaplet, wreath

**amddifad** adj destitute, orphan

**amddifadrwydd** nm destitution, privation

**amddifadu** vb bereave, deprive

**amddifaty** (**-tai**) nm orphanage

**amddifedi** nm destitution, privation

**amddiffyn** vb defend, protect, shield ▷ (**-ion**) nm defence

**amddiffynfa** (**-feydd**) nf fortress

**amddiffyniad** nm protection, defence

**amdiffynnwr** (**-ynwyr**), **-ynnydd** (**-ynyddion**) nm defender, protector

**amddfrwys** adj mighty, rugged; marshy

**America Ladin** nf Latin America

**Amerig: yr A~** nf America

**amfesur** (**-au**) nm perimeter

**amgáu** vb enclose, shut in

**amgen** adj, adv other, else, otherwise; different; **nid ~** that is to say, namely

**amgenach** adj, adv otherwise; better

**amgueddfa** (**-feydd**) nf museum

**amgyffred** vb comprehend, comprise ▷ (**-ion**) nm comprehension

**amgyffrediad** nm comprehension

**amgylch** (**-oedd**) nm circuit; environs, surroundings; **o (oddi) ~** round about, about

**amgylchedd** nm circumference; environment

**amgylchfyd** nm environment

**amgylchiad** (**-au**) nm circumstance; occasion

**amgylchiadol** adj circumstantial

**amgylchu** vb surround

**amgylchynol** adj surrounding

**amgylchynu** vb surround

**amharchu** vb dishonour, disrespect

**amharchus** adj disrespectful, disreputable

**amhariad** nm impairment, damage

**amharod** adj unprepared, unready

**amharodrwydd** nm unreadiness

**amharu** vb impair, harm, injure, damage

**amhendant** adj indefinite, vague

**amhenderfynol** adj irresolute

**amhenodol** adj indefinite

**amherchi** vb dishonour, insult

**amherffaith** adj imperfect

**amherffeithrwydd** nm imperfection

**amhersonol** adj impersonal

**amherth(y)nasol** adj irrelevant

**amheuaeth** nf doubt, scepticism

**amheugar** adj suspicious; sceptical

**amheuol** adj doubting, doubtful

**amheus** adj doubting, doubtful, dubious

**amheuthun** adj dainty, savoury ▷ (**-ion**) nm dainty, delicacy, treat

**amheuwr** (**-wyr**) nm doubter, sceptic

**amhlantadwy** adj childless, barren

**amhleidiol, amhleitgar** adj impartial

**amhoblog** adj sparsely populated

**amhoblogaidd** adj unpopular

**amhosibl** adj impossible

**amhriodol** *adj* improper
**amhrisiadwy** *adj* priceless
**amhrofiadol** *adj* inexperienced
**amhrydlon** *adj* unpunctual
**amhûr** *adj* impure, foul
**amhwrpasol** *adj* irrelevant
**amhwyllo** *vb* lose one's senses, go mad
**aml** *adj* frequent, abundant ▷ *adv* often
**amlder, amldra** *nm* abundance
**amldduwiad** (-iaid) *nm* polytheist
**amldduwiaeth** *nf* polytheism
**amleiriog** *adj* wordy, verbose, prolix
**amlen** (-ni) *nf* envelope, wrapper
**amlhad** *nm* increasing, increase
**amlhau** *vb* increase, multiply
**amlinelliad** (-au) *nm* outline
**aml-lawr** *adj* multi-storey
**amlochrog** *adj* many-sided
**amlosgfa** *nf* crematorium
**amlosgi** *vb* cremate
**amlwg** *adj* plain, clear, manifest, evident, prominent
**amlwreigiaeth** *nf* polygamy
**amlwreigiwr** (-wyr) *nm* polygamist
**amlygiad** (-au) *nm* manifestation
**amlygrwydd** *nm* prominence, limelight
**amlygu** *vb* manifest, reveal, evince
**amnaid** (-neidiau) *nf* beck, nod
**amneidio** *vb* beckon, nod
**amnest** (-au) *nm* amnesty
**amod** (-au) *nm/f* condition
**amodi** *vb* covenant, stipulate
**amodol** *adj* conditional
**amrant** (-au, -rannau) *nm* eyelid
**amrantiad** *nm* wink, twinkling, second
**amreiniol** *adj* unprivileged
**amrwd** *adj* uncooked, raw, crude
**amryddawn** *adj* versatile
**amryfal** *adj* sundry, manifold
**amryfus** *adj* erroneous, inadvertent

**amryfusedd** (-au) *nm* error, oversight
**amryliw** *adj* variegated; multicoloured
**amryw** *adj* several, sundry, various
**amrywiad** (-au) *nm* variant
**amrywiaeth** *nm* variety, diversity
**amrywio** *vb* vary, differ
**amrywiol** *adj* sundry
**amser** (-oedd, -au) *nm/f* time
**amseriad** (-au) *nm* timing, dating, date
**amserlen** (-ni) *nf* time-table
**amserol** *adj* timely; temporal
**amseru** *vb* time, date
**amserydd** (-ion) *nm* chronologist
**amseryddiaeth** *nf* chronology
**amseryddol** *adj* chronological
**amwisg** (-oedd) *nf* covering, shroud
**amwisgo** *vb* enwrap, shroud
**amwys** *adj* ambiguous
**amwysedd** *nm* ambiguity
**amyn** *conj, prep* unless, except, but
**amynedd** *nm* patience
**amyneddgar** *adj* patient
**an-** *prefix* un-, in-, de-, dis-
**anabl** *adj* disabled
**anabledd** *nm* disability
**anad** *adj*: **yn ~** above all, more than
**anadferadwy** *adj* irreparable
**anadl** (-au, -on) *nf/m* breath
**anadliad** *nm* breath, breathing
**anadlu** *vb* breathe
**anadnabyddus** *adj* unknown
**anaddas** *adj* unfit, unsuitable
**anaddasu** *vb* unfit, disqualify
**anaeddfed, anaddfed** *adj* unripe, immature
**anaeddfedrwydd** *nm* unripeness, immaturity
**anaele** *adj* awful, direful; incurable
**anaesthetig** *adj* anaesthetic
**anaf** (-au) *nm* blemish, defect; wound
**anafu** *vb* blemish, maim, hurt
**anafus** *adj* maimed, disabled

**anair** (-eiriau) *nm* ill report, slander
**anallu** *nm* inability
**analluog** *adj* unable
**analluogi** *vb* disenable; disable
**anaml** *adj* infrequent, rare ▷ *adv* rarely, seldom
**anamlwg** *adj* obscure, inconspicuous
**anamserol** *adj* untimely, mistimed
**anap** (-hapon) *nm/f* mischance, mishap
**anarchiaeth** *nm* anarchy
**anarchydd** (-ion) *nm* anarchist
**anarferol** *adj* unusual, extraordinary
**anarfog** *adj* unarmed
**anchwiliadwy** *adj* unsearchable
**ancr** *nm/f* anchorite, anchoress
**ancwyn** (-ion) *nm* dinner, supper; delicacy
**andras** *nm* curse; devil, deuce
**andwyo** *vb* spoil, ruin, undo
**andwyol** *adj* harmful, ruinous
**anedifeiriol** *adj* impenitent
**aneddfa** *see* **anheddfa**
**aneffeithiol** *adj* ineffectual
**aneglur** *adj* indistinct; illegible
**aneirif** *adj* innumerable
**anelu** *vb* bend, aim
**anenwog** *adj* unrenowned, ignoble, mean
**anerchiad** (-au) *nm* salutation, address
**anesboniadwy** *adj* inexplicable
**anesgusodol** *adj* inexcusable
**anesmwyth** *adj* uneasy, restless
**anesmwythder, -dra** *nm* uneasiness, unrest
**anesmwytho** *vb* be or make uneasy
**anesmwythyd** *nm* uneasiness, disquiet
**anewyllysgar** *adj* unwilling
**anfad** *adj* wicked, nefarious
**anfadrwydd** *nm* wickedness, villainy
**anfadwaith** *nm* villainy; crime

**anfadwr** (-wyr) *nm* villain, scoundrel
**anfaddeugar** *adj* unforgiving
**anfaddeuol** *adj* unpardonable
**anfantais** (-teision) *nf* disadvantage
**anfanteisiol** *adj* disadvantageous
**anfarwol** *adj* undying, immortal
**anfarwoldeb** *nm* immortality
**anfedrus** *adj* unskilful
**anfedrusrwydd** *nm* unskilfulness
**anfeidrol** *adj* infinite
**anfeidroldeb** *nm* infinity
**anferth** *adj* huge, monstrous
**anferthedd** *nm* hugeness, monstrosity
**anfodlon** *adj* unwilling
**anfodloni** *vb* discontent, dissatisfy
**anfodlonrwydd** *nm* discontent
**anfodd** *nm* unwillingness, displeasure
**anfoddio** *vb* displease, disoblige
**anfoddlon** *etc see* **anfodlon**
**anfoddog** *adj* discontented, dissatisfied
**anfoddogrwydd** *nm* discontentment
**anfoesgar** *adj* unmannerly, rude
**anfoesgarwch** *nm* rudeness, incivility
**anfoesol** *adj* immoral
**anfoesoldeb** *nm* immorality
**anfon** *vb* send, transmit, dispatch
**anfoneddigaidd** *adj* ungentlemanly
**anfonheddig** *adj* ignoble, discourteous
**anfoniad** *nm* sending, transmission
**anfri** *nm* disrespect, dishonour
**anfucheddol** *adj* immoral
**anfuddiol** *adj* unprofitable
**anfwriadol** *adj* unintentional
**anfwyn** *adj* unkind, ungentle, uncivil
**anfynych** *adj* infrequent, seldom, rare

**anffaeledig** *adj* infallible
**anffaeledigrwydd** *nm* infallibility
**anffafriol** *adj* unfavourable
**anffawd** (-ffodion) *nf* misfortune
**anffodus, anffortunus** *adj* unfortunate
**anffrwythlon** *adj* unfruitful, barren
**anffurfio** *vb* disfigure, deform
**anffurfiol** *adj* informal
**anffyddiaeth** *nf* atheism
**anffyddiwr** (-wyr) *nm* infidel, atheist
**anffyddlon** *adj* unfaithful
**anhaeddiannol** *adj* unmerited, undeserved
**anhaeddiant** *nm* demerit, unworthiness
**anhapus** *adj* unhappy, unlucky
**anhardd** *adj* unhandsome, unseemly, ugly
**anhawdd** *adj* hard, difficult
**anhawddgar** *adj* unamiable, unlovely
**anhawster** (anawsterau) *nm* difficulty
**anheddfa** (aneddfaoedd) *nf*, **-le** (aneddleoedd) *nm/f* dwelling-place
**anhepgor** (-ion) *nm* essential
**anhepgorol** *adj* indispensable
**anhoffter** *nm* hatred, dislike
**anhraethadwy** *adj* unutterable
**anhraethol** *adj* unspeakable, ineffable
**anhrefn** *nm* disorder, confusion
**anhrefnu** *vb* disorder, disarrange
**anhrefnus** *adj* disorderly, untidy
**anhreiddiol** *adj* impervious, impenetrable
**anhreuliedig** *adj* undigested; unspent
**anhrugarog** *adj* unmerciful, merciless
**anhuddo** *vb* cover (a fire)
**anhunedd** *nm* wakefulness, disquiet

**anhwyldeb** *nm* disorder, complaint, illness
**anhwylustod** *nm* inconvenience
**anhyblyg** *adj* inflexible, stiff, rigid
**anhydawdd** *adj* insoluble
**anhyder** *nm* distrust, diffidence
**anhyderus** *adj* diffident
**anhydrin** *adj* unmanageable
**anhydyn** *adj* intractable, obstinate
**anhyddysg** *adj* unversed, ignorant
**anhyfryd** *adj* unpleasant
**anhyfrydwch** *nm* unpleasantness
**anhygar** *adj* unpleasant, unamiable
**anhygoel** *adj* incredible
**anhygyrch** *adj* inaccessible
**anhylaw** *adj* unhandy, unwieldy
**anhynod** *adj* indistinctive; uncertain
**anhysbys** *adj* unknown; unversed
**anhywaith** *adj* intractable, refractory
**anial** *adj* desert, wild ▷ *nm* wilderness
**anialwch** *nm* wilderness
**anian** (-au) *nf* nature, instinct, genius
**anianawd** *nm* temperament, disposition
**anianol** *adj* natural
**anianyddol** *adj* physical
**anifail** (-feiliaid) *nm* animal, beast
**anifeilaidd** *adj* beastly, brutish
**anifeileiddio** *vb* animalize, brutalize
**anlwc** *nm* bad luck, misfortune
**anlwcus** *adj* unlucky
**anllad** *adj* wanton, lascivious, lewd
**anlladrwydd** *nm* wantonness, lewdness
**anlladu** *vb* wanton
**anllygredig** *adj* incorrupt, incorruptible
**anllygredigaeth** *nf* incorruption
**anllythrennog** *adj* illiterate
**anllywodraeth** *nf* misrule, anarchy

**annaearol** *adj* unearthly, weird
**annatodol** *adj* indissoluble, that cannot be undone
**annaturiol** *adj* unnatural
**annealladwy** *adj* unintelligible
**anneallus** *adj* unintelligent
**annedwydd** *adj* unhappy, miserable
**annedwyddwch** *nm* unhappiness
**annedd** (anheddau) *nf* dwelling
**anneddfol** *adj* lawless
**annefnyddiol** *adj* useless; immaterial
**annel** (anelau) *nm/f* trap; purpose, aim
**annelwig** *adj* shapeless, unformed; vague
**anner** (aneirod, -i, -au) *nf* heifer
**annerbyniol** *adj* unacceptable
**annerch** *vb* salute, greet, address ▷ (anerchion) *nm* salutation, greeting
**annewisol** *adj* ineligible, undesirable, unwelcome
**annhebyg** *adj* unlike, dissimilar
**annhebygol** *adj* unlikely, improbable
**annhebygolrwydd** *nm* improbability
**annhebygrwydd** *nm* unlikeness, unlikelihood
**annheg** *adj* unfair
**annhegwch** *nm* unfairness
**annheilwng** *adj* unworthy
**annheilyngdod** *nm* unworthiness
**annherfynol** *adj* endless; infinitive, infinite
**annhirion** *adj* ungentle, cruel
**annhosturiol** *adj* pitiless, ruthless
**annhuedd** *nf* disinclination
**annhueddol** *adj* disinclined, indisposed
**anniben** *adj* untidy, slovenly
**annibendod** *nm* untidiness
**annibyniaeth** *nf* independence
**annibynnol** *adj* independent
**Annibynnwr** (-ynwyr) *nm* Independent

**annichellgar** *adj* guileless, simple
**annichon, -adwy** *adj* impossible
**anniddan** *adj* comfortless, miserable
**anniddig** *adj* peevish, irritable, fretful
**anniddigrwydd** *nm* peevishness
**anniddos** *adj* leaky, comfortless
**annifeiriol** *adj* innumerable, countless
**anniflanedig** *adj* unfading, imperishable
**annifyr** *adj* miserable, wretched
**annifyrrwch** *nm* misery
**anniffoddadwy** *adj* unquenchable
**annigonedd** *nm* insufficiency
**annigonol** *adj* insufficient, inadequate
**annigonolrwydd** *nm* inadequacy
**annileadwy** *adj* indelible, ineffaceable
**annilys** *adj* unauthentic, spurious, insincere
**annillyn** *adj* inelegant, clumsy
**annioddefol** *adj* unbearable, intolerable
**anniogel** *adj* unsafe, insecure
**anniolchgar** *adj* unthankful, ungrateful
**anniolchgarwch** *nm* ingratitude
**annirnadwy** *adj* incomprehensible
**annisgrifiadwy** *adj* indescribable
**annisgwyliadwy** *adj* unexpected
**anniwair** *adj* unchaste, incontinent, lewd
**anniwall** *adj* insatiable
**anniweirdeb** *nm* unchastity, incontinence
**anniwylliedig** *adj* uncultured
**annoeth** *adj* unwise, imprudent
**annoethineb** *nm* unwisdom, folly
**annog** *vb* incite, urge; exhort
**annormal** *adj* abnormal
**annos** *vb* incite, set (a dog) on
**annosbarthus** *adj* unruly, disorderly

**annuw, -iad** (-iaid) nm atheist
**annuwiaeth** nf atheism
**annuwiol** adj ungodly, godless
**annuwioldeb** nm ungodliness
**annwn, annwfn** nm the underworld; hell
**annwyd** (anwydau, -on) nm cold
**annwyl** adj dear, beloved
**annyledus** adj undue, wrongful
**annymunol** adj unpleasant, disagreeable
**annynol** adj inhuman, cruel
**annysgedig** adj unlearned
**anobaith** nm despair
**anobeithio** vb despair
**anobeithiol** adj hopeless
**anochel, -adwy** adj unavoidable, inevitable
**anodd** adj hard, difficult
**anoddefgar** adj impatient, intolerant
**anogaeth** (-au) nf exhortation
**anolrheinadwy** adj untraceable
**anolygus** adj unsightly
**anonest** adj dishonest
**anonestrwydd** nm dishonesty
**anorchfygol** adj irresistible; unconquerable
**anorfod** adj insuperable; unavoidable
**anorffen** adj endless, unending
**anorffenedig** adj incomplete, unfinished
**anorthrech** adj invincible
**anrasol** adj graceless
**anrhaith** (-rheithiau) nf prey, spoil, booty
**anrheg** (-ion) nf present, gift
**anrhegu** vb present, give
**anrheithio** vb prey, spoil, plunder
**anrheithiwr** (-wyr) nm spoiler, pillager
**anrhydedd** (-au) nm honour
**anrhydeddu** vb honour
**anrhydeddus** adj honourable
**anrhydeddwr** (-wyr) nm honourer
**ansad** adj unsteady, unstable

**ansadrwydd** nm instability
**ansafadwy** adj unstable; fickle
**ansathredig** adj untrodden, unfrequented
**ansawdd** (-soddau) nm/f quality, state
**ansefydlog** adj unsettled, unstable; fickle
**ansefydlogi** vb unsettle
**ansicr** adj uncertain, doubtful
**ansicrwydd** nm uncertainty, doubt
**ansoddair** (-eiriau) nm adjective
**ansoddeiriol** adj adjectival
**ansyber** adj untidy, slovenly
**Antartica** nf the Antarctic
**anterliwt** (-iau) nm/f interlude
**anterth** nm meridian, zenith, prime
**antur** (-iau) nm attempt, venture; adventure; enterprise; **ar ~** at random
**anturiaeth** (-au) nf adventure, enterprise
**anturiaethus** adj adventurous, enterprising
**anturiaethwr** (-wyr) nm adventurer
**anturio** vb venture, adventure
**anturus** adj adventurous
**anthem** (-au) nf anthem
**anudon** (-au) nm false oath, perjury
**anudoniaeth** nf perjury
**anudonwr** (-wyr) nm perjurer
**anufudd** adj disobedient
**anufudd-dod** nm disobedience
**anufuddhau** vb disobey
**anundeb** nm disunion
**anunion** adj crooked; unjust
**anuniondeb** nm injustice, iniquity
**anurddo** vb spoil, mar, disfigure
**anwadal** adj unstable, fickle, changeable
**anwadalu** vb waver, vacillate
**anwadalwch** nm fickleness
**anwar** adj wild, barbarous, savage
**anwaraidd** adj uncivilized, barbarous

**anwarddyn** (-**wariaid**) *nm* barbarian, savage
**anwareidd-dra** *nm* barbarity
**anwastad** *adj* uneven, unstable, fickle
**anwe** (-**oedd**) *nf* woof
**anwedd** *nm* vapour, steam
**anweddaidd** *adj* unseemly, indecent
**anweddus** *adj* improper, indecent
**anweledig** *adj* unseen, invisible
**anwes** *nm* indulgence; caress
**anwesog** *adj* pampered, affectionate
**anwesu** *vb* fondle, caress, pamper, indulge
**anwir** *adj* untrue, lying, false; wicked
**anwiredd** (-**au**) *nm* untruth; iniquity
**anwireddu** *vb* falsify
**anwireddus** *adj* untruthful, false, lying
**anwr** (-**wyr**) *nm* wretch, coward
**anwybod** *nm* ignorance
**anwybodaeth** *nf* ignorance
**anwybodus** *adj* ignorant
**anwybyddu** *vb* ignore
**anwydog** *adj* cold, chilly; having a cold
**anwydwst** *nf* influenza
**anwyldeb** *nm* belovedness, dearness
**anwyliaid** *npl* beloved ones, favourites
**anwylo** *vb* cherish, fondle, caress
**anwylyd** (-**liaid**) *nm* beloved
**anwylyn** *nm* favourite
**anwythiad** *nm* induction
**anwytho** *vb* induce
**anwythol** *adj* inductive
**anymarferol** *adj* impractical, impracticable
**anymddiried** *vb, nm* mistrust, distrust
**anymwybodol** *adj* unconscious
**anymwybyddiaeth** *nf* unconsciousness
**anynad** *adj* peevish, petulant; brawling
**anysgrifenedig** *adj* unwritten
**anysgrythurol** *adj* unscriptural
**anystwyth** *adj* stiff, rigid
**anystwytho** *vb* stiffen
**anystyriaeth** *nf* heedlessness, rashness
**anystyriol** *adj* heedless, reckless, rash
**anystywallt, -ell** *adj* unmanageable
**apêl** (**apelion**) *nm/f*, **apeliad** (-**au**) *nm* appeal
**apelio** *vb* appeal
**apostol** (-**ion**) *nm* apostle
**apostolaidd, -ig** *adj* apostolic
**apostoliaeth** *nf* apostleship
**apwyntiad** (-**au**) *nm* appointment
**apwyntio** *vb* appoint
**âr** *nm* ploughed land, tilth; ground
**ar** *prep* on, upon, over
**arab** *adj* facetious, merry, pleasant
**arabedd** *nm* facetiousness, wit
**arabus** *adj* witty
**aradr** (**erydr**) *nm* plough
**araf** *adj* slow, soft, gentle, still
**arafu** *vb* slow; quiet; moderate
**arafwch** *nm* slowness; moderation
**arail** *vb* guard, care for, foster ▷ *adj* attending, careful
**araith** (**areithiau**) *nf* speech
**arall** (**eraill**) *adj, pron* another, other; else
**aralleg** (-**au**) *nf/m* allegory
**aralleiriad** (-**au**) *nm* paraphrase
**aralleirio** *vb* paraphrase
**araul** *adj* sunny, sunlit; serene
**arawd** *nf* speech, oration
**arbed** *vb* spare, save
**arbediad** (-**au**) *nm* save, salvage
**arbedol** *adj* sparing, saving
**arbenigaeth** *nf* expertise; specialisation
**arbenigo** *vb* specialise
**arbenigrwydd** *nm* speciality,

prominence
**arbenigwr (-wyr)** *nm* specialist
**arbennig** *adj* special
**arbrawf (arbrofion)** *nm* experiment
**arbrofi** *vb* experiment
**arbrofol** *adj* experimental
**arch (eirchion)** *nf* request, petition; bidding
**arch (eirch)** *nf* ark, coffin; trunk, waist
**archaeoleg** *nf* archaeology
**archangel (-ylion)** *nm* archangel
**archddiacon (-iaid)** *nm* archdeacon
**archeb (-ion)** *nf* order
**archebu** *vb* order
**archen** *nf*, **-ad** *nm* shoe; clothing
**archesgob (-ion)** *nm* archbishop
**archesgobaeth (-au)** *nf* archbishopric
**archfarchnad (-oedd)** *nf* supermarket
**archiad** *nm* bidding
**archif (-au)** *nm* archive
**archifdy (-dai)** *nm* record office
**archifydd (-ion)** *nm* archivist
**archoffeiriad (-iaid)** *nm* high priest
**archoll (-ion)** *nf* wound
**archolli** *vb* wound
**archwaeth** *nm* taste, appetite
**archwaethu** *vb* taste, savour
**archwilio** *vb* examine, audit; explore
**archwiliwr (-wyr)** *nm* examiner, auditor; explorer
**ardal (-oedd)** *nf* region, district
**ardalydd (-ion)** *nm* marquis
**ardreth (-i)** *nf* rent
**ardrethu** *vb* rent
**ardystiad (-au)** *nm* pledge, attestation
**ardystio** *vb* pledge, attest
**arddangos** *vb* show, exhibit, indicate
**arddangosfa (-feydd)** *nf* show, exhibition

**arddegol** *adj* teenage
**arddel** *vb* avow, own
**arddeliad** *nm* claim, avowal; unction
**ardderchog** *adj* excellent, noble, splendid
**ardderchowgrwydd** *nm* excellency
**arddodi** *vb* prefix; impose
**arddodiad (-iaid)** *nm* preposition
**arddu** *vb* plough (*properly* aredig)
**arddull (-iau)** *nf* style
**arddulleg** *nf* stylistics
**ardduniant** *nm* sublimity
**arddunol** *adj* sublime
**arddwr (-wyr)** *nm* ploughman
**arddwrn (-ddyrnau)** *nm* wrist
**arddywediad (-au)** *nm* dictation
**aredig** *vb* plough
**areitheg** *nf* rhetoric
**areithio** *vb* speak, make a speech
**areithiwr (-wyr)** *nm* speaker, orator
**areithyddiaeth** *nf* oratory; elocution
**arel** *nm* laurel
**aren (-nau)** *nf* kidney; (*pl*) reins
**arestio** *vb* arrest
**arf (-au)** *nm/f* weapon; (*pl*) arms; tool
**arfaeth (-au)** *nf* purpose; decree
**arfaethu** *vb* purpose, intend
**arfbais (-beisiau)** *nf* coat of arms
**arfdy (-dai)** *nm* armoury
**arfer** *vb* use, accustom ▷ **(-ion)** *nf/m* use, custom, habit
**arferiad** *nm/f* use, custom, habit
**arferol** *adj* usual, customary
**arfod** *nf* stroke of a weapon, fight; armour; opportunity
**arfog** *adj* armed
**arfogaeth** *nf* armour
**arfogi** *vb* arm
**arfoll (-au)** *nm* pledge, oath
**arfordir (-oedd)** *nm* coast
**arforol** *adj* maritime

**arffed** (-au) *nf* lap

**argae** (-au) *nm* dam, embankment; enclosed place

**argeisio** *vb* seek

**argel** *nm/f* concealment, refuge ▷ *adj* hidden, occult

**arglwydd** (-i) *nm* lord

**arglwyddaidd** *adj* lordly

**arglwyddes** (-au) *nf* lady

**arglwyddiaeth** (-au) *nf* lordship, dominion

**arglwyddiaethu** *vb* have dominion

**argoed** (-ydd) *nm* enclosure of trees

**argoel** (-ion) *nf* sign, token, omen

**argoeli** *vb* betoken, portend, augur

**argoelus** *adj* ominous

**argraff** (-ion, -au) *nf* print, impression

**argraffdy** (-dai) *nm* printing-house

**argraffiad** (-au) *nm* impression; edition

**argraffu** *vb* print, impress

**argraffwaith** *nm* print, typography

**argraffwasg** *nf* printing-press

**argraffwr** (-wyr), **-ydd** (-ion) *nm* printer

**argrwm, -wn** *adj* convex

**argyfwng** (-yngau, -yngoedd) *nm* crisis

**argyhoeddi** *vb* reprove; convince, convict

**argyhoeddiad** (-au) *nm* conviction

**argyhoeddiadol** *adj* convincing

**argymell** *vb* urge, recommend

**argymhelliad** *nm* recommendation

**arholi** *vb* examine

**arholiad** (-au) *nm* examination

**arholwr** (-wyr) *nm* examiner

**arhosfa** *nf* abode; (*bus*) stopping-place

**arhosiad** *nm* staying, stay

**arhosol** *adj* abiding, permanent

**arial** *nm/f* vigour, mettle

**arian** *nm* silver ▷ *coll n* money, cash; **~ breiniol** currency; **~ byw** mercury; **~ gleision** silver; **~ parod** cash; **~ pen** exact money; **~ treigl** current money

**ariandy** (-dai) *nm* bank

**ariangar** *adj* fond of money, avaricious

**ariangarwch** *nm* love of money, avarice

**ariannaid** *adj* silver, silvern

**ariannaidd** *adj* silvery

**arianneg** *nm/f* finance

**Ariannin** *nf* Argentina

**ariannog** *adj* moneyed, wealthy, rich

**ariannol** *adj* financial, monetary

**ariannu** *vb* silver; finance/fund

**ariannydd** (arianyddion) *nm* banker, investor, financier

**arlais** (-leisiau) *nf* temple

**arloesi** *vb* clear, prepare the way, pioneer

**arloesydd** (-wyr) *nm* pioneer

**arluniaeth** *nf* portraiture, painting

**arlunio** *vb* draw, paint, portray

**arlunydd** (-wyr) *nm* artist

**arlwy** (-au, -on) *nm/f* provision, feast, menu

**arlwyaeth** (-au) *nf* catering

**arlwyo** *vb* prepare, provide; cook

**arlywydd** (-ion) *nm* president

**arlywyddiaeth** *nf* presidency

**arlywyddol** *adj* presidential

**arlliw** (-iau) *nm* varnish, tint, shade, trace

**arlliwio** *vb* colour, tint, paint

**arllwys** *vb* pour out, empty

**arllwysfa** *nf* outfall, outlet, vent

**armel** *nm* second milk

**armes** *nf* prophecy; calamity

**arobryn** *adj* worthy, prize-winning

**arofun** *vb* intend, purpose

**arogl** (-au), **aroglau** (-euon) *nm* scent, smell

**arogl-darth** *nm* incense

**arogldarthu** *vb* burn incense

**arogli, arogleuo** vb scent; smell
**arogliad** nm smelling, sense of smell
**arolwg** nm survey
**arolygiaeth** nf superintendency
**arolygu** vb superintend
**arolygwr (-wyr), -ydd (-ion)** nm superintendent, inspector
**aros** vb wait, await, stay, stop, tarry, abide, remain
**arswyd** nm dread, terror, horror
**arswydo** vb dread; shudder
**arswydus** adj fearful, terrible, dreadful
**arsyllfa (-feydd)** nf observatory
**arsylwi** vb observe
**artaith (-teithiau)** nf torture, torment, pang
**arteithio** vb torture, rack
**arteithiol** adj racking, excruciating
**arth (eirth)** nm/f bear
**arthes (-au)** nf she-bear
**arthio, -u** vb bark, growl
**Artig: yr A-** nf the Arctic
**artistig** adj artistic
**aruchel** adj lofty, sublime
**arucheledd** nm loftiness, sublimity
**aruthr** adj marvellous, strange
**aruthredd** nm amazement, horror
**aruthrol** adj huge, prodigious
**arwahanrwydd** nm uniqueness, individuality
**arwain** vb conduct, lead, guide, carry
**arwedd (-au, -ion)** nf bearing, aspect
**arweddu** vb bear
**arweddwr (-wyr)** nm bearer
**arweiniad** nm guidance; introduction
**arweiniol** adj leading, introductory
**arweinydd (-ion)** nm guide, leader; conductor
**arweinyddiaeth** nf leadership
**arwerthiant (-iannau)** nm auction
**arwerthu** vb sell by auction

**arwerthwr (-wyr)** nm auctioneer
**arwisgiad** nm investiture
**arwisgo** vb enrobe, array, invest
**arwr (-wyr)** nm hero
**arwraidd** adj heroic, epic
**arwres (-au)** nf heroine
**arwrgerdd (-i)** nf epic poem
**arwriaeth** nf heroism
**arwrol** adj heroic, gallant
**arwybod** nm awareness
**arwydd (-ion)** nm/f sign, signal; ensign
**arwyddair (-eiriau)** nm motto
**arwyddlun (-iau)** nm emblem, symbol
**arwyddluniol** adj emblematic, symbolic
**arwyddnod (-au)** nm mark, token
**arwyddo** vb sign; signify
**arwyddocâd** nm signification, significance
**arwyddocaol** adj significant
**arwyddocáu** vb signify, denote
**arwyl (-ion)** nf funeral, funeral rites
**arwylo** vb mourn over the dead
**arwynebedd** nm surface, superficies
**arwynebol** adj superficial
**arwyrain** nm/f praise, panegyric
▷ vb rise, extol
**arwystlo** vb pledge, mortgage
**arysgrif (-au), -en (-nau)** nf inscription, epigraph
**asb (-iaid)** nf asp
**asbri** nm animation, vivacity, spirits
**asen (-nau)** nf rib
**asen (-nod)** nf she-ass
**asesu** vb assess
**aseth** nf stake, spar, lath
**asgell (esgyll)** nf wing, fin; **~ fraith** chaffinch
**asgellog** adj winged
**asgellwr (-wyr)** nm wing, outside-forward
**asglod, asglodion** npl (nm ~yn) chips
**asgre** nf bosom, heart

**asgwrn** (**esgyrn**) *nm* bone
**asiad** (**-au**) *nm* joint, weld
**asiant** (**-au**) *nm* agent
**asio** *vb* join, weld; solder; cement
**astell** (**estyll, ystyllod**) *nf* plank, shelf
**astroleg** *nf* astrology
**astrus** *adj* abstruse, difficult
**astud** *adj* attentive
**astudiaeth** (**-au**) *nf* study
**astudio** *vb* study
**astudrwydd** *nm* attentiveness
**aswy** *adj* left
**asyn** (**-nod**) *nm* he-ass
**asynnaidd** *adj* asinine
**at** *prep* to, towards; for; at; by
**atafaeliad** *nm* confiscation, distraint
**atafaelu** *vb* distrain, confiscate
**atal** *vb* stop, hinder, withhold ▷ (**-ion**) *nm* hindrance, impediment; **~ dweud** stammering
**ataleb** (**-au**) *nf* injunction
**atalfa** (**-feydd**) *nf* check; stoppage
**ataliad** (**-au**) *nm* stoppage
**ataliol** *adj* preventive
**atalnod** (**-au**) *nf* stop, point
**atalnodi** *vb* point, punctuate
**atblygol** *adj* reflexive
**ateb** *vb* answer, reply ▷ (**-ion**) *nm* answer
**atebol** *adj* answerable, responsible
**ateg** (**-ion**) *nf* prop, stay, support
**ategiad** (**-au**) *nm* affirmation
**ategol** *adj* confirming; auxiliary
**ategu** *vb* support
**atgas** *adj* odious, hateful
**atgasedd** *nm* hatred
**atgasrwydd** *nm* odiousness, hatefulness
**atgenhedliad** *nm* regeneration
**atgenhedlu** *vb* regenerate
**atgno** (**-oeau, -oeon**) *nm* remorse
**atgof** (**-ion**) *nm* remembrance, reminiscence
**atgofio** *vb* recollect, remember, remind

**atgofus** *adj* reminiscent
**atgoffa** *vb* recall, remind
**atgyfnerthion** *npl* reinforcements
**atgyfnerthu** *vb* reinforce
**atgyfodi** *vb* rise, raise again
**atgyfodiad** *nm* resurrection
**atgynhyrchu** *vb* reproduce
**atgyweiriad** (**-au**) *nm* repair
**atgyweirio** *vb* repair, mend
**atgyweiriwr** (**-wyr**) *nm* repairer, mender
**Athen** *nf* Athens
**atig** (**-au**) *nm/f* attic
**atodi** *vb* add, append, affix
**atodiad** (**-au**) *nm* addition, appendix
**atodlen** (**-ni**) *nf* supplement; schedule
**atodol** *adj* supplementary
**atolwg, atolygu** *vb* pray, beseech
**atom** (**-au**) *nm/f* atom
**atomfa** (**-feydd**) *nf* nuclear power station
**atomig** *adj* atomic
**atsain** (**-seiniau**) *nf* echo
**atseinio** *vb* resound, echo
**atwf** (**atyfion**) *nm* second growth
**atyniad** (**-au**) *nm* attraction
**atyniadol** *adj* attractive
**atynnu** *vb* attract
**athletau** *npl* athletics
**athrawes** (**-au**) *nf* teacher, governess
**athrawiaeth** (**-au**) *nf* doctrine
**athrawiaethol** *adj* doctrinal
**athrist** *adj* very sad, pensive, sorrowful
**athro** (**-athrawon**) *nm* teacher, master
**athrod** (**-ion**) *nm* slander, libel
**athrodwr** (**-wyr**) *nm* slanderer, libeller
**athrofa** (**-feydd**) *nf* college, academy, institute
**athrofaol** *adj* academic
**athroniaeth** *nf* philosophy
**athronydd** (**-ion, -wyr**) *nm*

philosopher
**athronyddol** *adj* philosophical
**athronyddu** *vb* philosophize
**athrylith** (-oedd) *nf* genius
**athrylithgar** *adj* of genius, talented
**athrywyn** *nm* mediation, intervention ▷ *vb* mediate, arbitrate
**aur** *nm* gold
**awch** *nm* edge; ardour, zest; relish, appetite
**awchlym** *adj* sharp, keen, acute
**awchlymu** *vb* sharpen, whet
**awchus** *adj* sharp, keen; eager; greedy
**awdl** (-au, odlau) *nf* ode
**awdur** (-on, -iaid) *nm* author
**awdurdod** (-au) *nm/f* authority
**awdurdodedig** *adj* authorised
**awdurdodi** *vb* authorize
**awdurdodol** *adj* authoritative
**awdures** (-au) *nf* authoress
**awduriaeth** *nf* authorship
**awel** (-on) *nf* breeze, wind
**awelog** *adj* breezy, windy
**awen** (-au) *nf* muse
**awen** (-au) *nf* rein
**awenydd** (-ion) *nm* poet
**awenyddiaeth** *nf* poetry, poesy
**awenyddol** *adj* poetical
**awenyddu** *vb* poetize
**awgrym** (-au, -iadau) *nm* hint, suggestion
**awgrymiadol** *adj* suggestive
**awgrymog** *adj* suggestive
**awgrymu** *vb* hint, suggest
**awr** (oriau) *nf* hour
**Awst** *nm* August
**Awstralia** *nf* Australia
**Awstria** *nf* Austria
**awtistig** *adj* autistic
**awydd** (-au) *nm* desire, eagerness
**awyddfryd** *nm* vehement desire, zeal
**awyddu** *vb* desire
**awyddus** *adj* desirous, eager,

zealous
**awyr** *nf* air, sky
**awyrdrom** (-au) *nf* aerodrome
**awyren** (-nau, -ni) *nf* balloon, aeroplane
**awyrendy** (-dai) *nm* hangar
**awyrgylch** (-au, -oedd) *nm/f* atmosphere
**awyriad** *nm* ventilation
**awyrlong** (-au) *nf* airship
**awyro, -u** *vb* air, ventilate

# b

**baban** (-od) *adj* baby
**babanaidd** *adj* babyish
**babandod** *nm* babyhood, infancy
**babi** *nm/f* baby
**bacas** (bacs(i)au) *nf* footless stocking; hair on horse's fetlocks
**baco** *nm* tobacco
**bacwn** *nm* bacon
**bach** (-au) *nm* hook; **~au petryal** square brackets
**bach** *adj* little, small
**bachell** (-au, -ion) *nf* nook, corner; snare
**bachgen** (bechgyn) *nm* boy
**bachgendod** *nm* boyhood
**bachgennaidd** *adj* boyish
**bachgennyn** (bechgynnos) *nm* little boy
**bachigyn** (bachigion) *nm* little bit,

diminutive
**bachog** adj hooked
**bachu** vb hook, grapple
**bachwr** (-wyr) nm (Rugby) hooker
**bad** (-au) nm boat; **~ achub** lifeboat
**badwr** (-wyr) nm boatman
**badd** (-au), **baddon** (-au) nm bath
**bae** (-au) nm bay
**baedd** (-od) nm boar
**baeddu** vb beat, buffet; soil
**baetio** vb bait, maltreat
**bag** (-iau) nm bag
**bagad** (-au) nm cluster; troop, multitude
**bagl** (-au) nf crook; crutch; leg
**baglor** (-ion) nf bachelor
**bagloriaeth** nf bachelorship
**baglu** vb entangle, ensnare, trip
**bai** (beiau) nm fault, vice; defect; blame
**baich** (beichiau) nm burden, load
**bais** nm bottom, ford; walking
**bala** nm efflux of river from lake
**balch** adj proud; glad
**balchder** nm pride
**balchdra** nm joy, gladness
**balchïo** vb pride
**baldordd** nm babble, balderdash
**baldorddi** vb babble
**bale** nm ballet
**baled** (-i) nf ballad
**baledwr** (-wyr) nm ballad-monger
**balm** nm balm
**balmaidd** adj balmy
**balog** (-au, -ion) nf fly, cod-piece; flap
**balleg** nf hamper, net, purse
**ballegrwyd** (-au) nf drag-net
**ban** (-nau) nm/f peak; horn; corner; stanza
**banadl** npl (nf-badlen) broom
**banc** (-iau) nm bank
**banc** (bencydd) nm bank, mound, hill
**bancaw** (-iau) nm band, tuft
**baner** (-au, -i) nf banner, flag
**banerog** adj with banners,

bannered
**banerwr** (-wyr) nm standard-bearer; ensign
**banffagl** (-au) nf bonfire, blaze
**bangaw** adj eloquent, melodious, skilful
**bangor** (-au, bangyr) nf/m upper row of rods in wattle fence; monastery
**baniar** (-ieri) nm/f shout; banner
**banllawr** (-lloriau) nm platform
**banllef** (-au) nf loud shout
**bannod** (banodau) nf article
**bannog** adj elevated, conspicuous; horned
**bar** (-rau) nm bar
**bâr** nm fury, greed
**bara** nm bread
**barbaraidd** adj barbarous
**barbareidd-dra** nm barbarity
**barbareiddio** vb barbarize
**barbariad** (-iaid) nm barbarian
**barbariaeth** nm barbarism
**barbwr** (-wyr) nm barber
**barcer** (-iaid) nm tanner
**barclod** (-iau) nm apron
**barcud** (-iaid), **barcutan** (-od) nm kite
**bardd** (beirdd) nm bard, poet
**barddas** nm/f bardism
**barddol** adj bardic
**barddoni** vb compose poetry, poetize
**barddoniaeth** nf poetry, verse
**barddonol** adj poetic, poetical
**barf** (-au) nf beard, whiskers
**barfog** adj bearded
**bargeinio, bargenna** vb bargain
**bargen** (-einion) nf bargain
**bargod** (-ion) nm eaves
**bargyfreithiwr** (-wyr) nm barrister
**bariaeth** nf/m evil, grief, wrath; greed
**baril** (-au) nf barrel
**barilaid** (-eidiau) nf barrelful
**bario** vb bar, bolt

**barlad** *nm* drake
**barlys** *nm* barley
**barn** (-au) *nf* judgment; opinion; sentence
**barnais** *nf* varnish
**barnedigaeth** (-au) *nf* judgment
**barneisio** *vb* varnish
**barnol** *adj* judicial, condemnatory, annoying
**barnu** *vb* judge
**barnwr** (-wyr) *nm* judge
**baromedr** *nm* barometer
**barrug** *nm* hoar-frost
**barugo** *vb* cast hoar-frost
**barugog** *adj* white with hoar-frost
**barus** *adj* voracious, greedy
**barwn** (-iaid) *nm* baron
**barwnes** (-au) *nf* baroness
**barwniaeth** (-au) *nf* barony
**barwnig** (-iaid) *nm* baronet
**bas** *adj* shallow ▷ (**bais, beis**) *npl* shallows
**bas** *adj*, *nm* bass
**basged** (-i, -au) *nf* basket
**basgedaid** (-eidiau) *nf* basketful
**basgedwr** (-wyr) *nm* basket-maker
**basn** (-au, -ys) *nm* basin
**bastard** (-iaid) *nm* bastard
**bastardiaeth** *nf* bastardy
**batri** *nm* battery
**bath** (-au) *nm* kind, sort; stamp; coin
**bathdy** (-dai) *nm* mint
**bathodyn** (-odau) *nm* medal, badge
**bathol** *adj* coin, coined
**bathu** *vb* coin
**baw** *nm* dirt, mire, dung, filth
**bawaidd** *adj* dirty, vile; sordid, mean
**bawd** (**bodiau**) *nf* thumb, toe
**bechan** *adj f of* **bychan**
**bechgynnos** *npl* little boys, youngsters
**bedw** *npl* (*nf*-**en**) birch
**bedydd** *nm* baptism
**bedyddfa** (-fâu, -feydd) *nf* baptistry

**bedyddfaen** (-feini) *nm* font
**bedyddio** *vb* baptize
**bedyddiol** *adj* baptismal; baptized
**Bedyddiwr** (-wyr) *nm* Baptist
**bedd** (-au) *nm* grave, tomb, sepulchre
**beddargraff** (-iadau) *nm* epitaph
**beddfaen** (-feini) *nm* tombstone
**beddgell** (-oedd) *nf* vault, catacomb
**beddrod** (-au) *nm* tomb, sepulchre
**Beibl** (-au) *nm* Bible
**Beiblaidd** *adj* Biblical
**beichio** *vb* burden; low; sob
**beichiog** *adj* pregnant
**beichiogi** *vb* conceive
**beichus** *adj* burdensome, oppressive
**beicio** *vb* cycle
**beiddgar** *adj* daring, audacious
**beiddgarwch** *nm* daring, audacity
**beiddio** *vb* dare, presume
**beili** (~aid) *nm* bailiff
**beio** *vb* blame, censure
**beirniad** (-iaid) *nm* adjudicator; critic
**beirniadaeth** (-au) *nf* adjudication; criticism
**beirniadol** *adj* critical
**beirniadu** *vb* adjudicate; criticize
**beisgawn** (-au) *nf* stack, heap of corn sheaves
**beiston** *nf* sea-shore, beach; surf
**beius** *adj* faulty; blameworthy
**bellach** *adv* now, at length
**bendigaid, bendigedig** *adj* blessed
**bendigedigrwydd** *nm* blessedness
**bendith** (-ion) *nf* blessing, benediction
**bendithio** *vb* bless
**bendithiol** *adj* conferring blessings
**benthyca, -io** *vb* borrow, lend
**benthyciwr** (-wyr) *nm* borrower, lender

**benthyg** nm loan
**benyw** adj female ▷ (-od) nf female, woman
**benywaidd** adj feminine; effeminate
**benywol** adj feminine, female
**ber** adj f of **byr**
**bêr** (**berau, -i**) nm spear; roasting-spit
**bera** nf/m rick; pyramid
**berdys** npl (nm -yn, nf -en) shrimps
**berf** (-au) nf verb; ~ **anghyflawn** transitive verb; ~ **gyflawn** intransitive verb
**berfa** (-fâu, -feydd) nf barrow
**Berlin** nf Berlin
**berth** adj beautiful, valuable
**berthog** adj wealthy, fair
**berw** nm, adj boiling, seething, ebullition
**berwedig** adj boiling
**berwedydd** (-ion) nm boiler
**berwedd-dy** (-dai) nm brewery
**berweddu** vb brew
**berwi** vb boil, seethe, effervesce
**berwr** coll n cress
**betgwn** nm/f bedgown
**betws** nm oratory, chapel; birch grove
**beudy** (-dai) nm cow-house, byre
**beunoeth, beunos** adv nightly, every night
**beunydd** adv daily, every day, always
**beunyddiol** adj daily, quotidian
**bidog** (-au) nf dagger; bayonet
**bil** (-iau) nm bill
**bilidowcar** nm cormorant
**bilwg** (-ygau) nm billhook
**bing** (-oedd) nm alley, bin
**biocemeg** nm/f biochemistry
**bir** (-oedd) nm beer
**biswail** nm dung
**blaen** adj fore, foremost, first; front ▷ (-au, -ion) nm point, end, top, tip; front, van, priority, precedence; edge

**blaenasgellwr** (-wyr) nm wing-forward
**blaenbrawf** (-brofion) nm foretaste
**blaendal** nm prepayment, deposit
**blaendarddu** vb sprout
**blaenddalen** (-nau) nf title page
**blaenddodi** vb prefix
**blaenddodiad** (-iaid) nm prefix
**blaenffrwyth** nm first-fruits
**blaengar** adj prominent, progressive
**blaengroen** (-grwyn) nm foreskin
**blaenllaw** adj forward, prominent
**blaenllym** adj sharp, keen
**blaenllymu** adj sharpen, whet
**blaenor** (-iaid) nm leader; elder
**blaenori** vb lead, precede
**blaenoriaeth** nf preference; precedence
**blaenorol** adj previous, antecedent
**blaenu** vb point; outrun; precede
**blaenwr** (-wyr) nm leader; forward
**blagur** coll n sprouts, buds, shoots
**blaguro** vb sprout, bud; flourish
**blaguryn** nm sprout, bud, shoot
**blaidd** (**bleiddiaid, bleiddiau**) nm wolf
**blas** nm taste, savour, relish
**blasio, -u** vb taste
**blasus** adj tasty, savoury, delicious
**blawd** (**blodion, -iau**) nm flour, meal
**blêr** adj untidy, slovenly
**blerwm** nm blabberer; blab-blab
**blew** npl (nm -yn) hairs; hair; fur
**blewog** adj hairy, shaggy
**bliant** nm lawn, fine linen
**blif** (-iau) nm catapult
**blingo** vb skin, flay
**blin** adj tired, weary; peevish, irritable
**blinder** (-au) nm weariness; trouble
**blinderog, -derus** adj wearisome
**blinfyd** nm tribulation
**blino** vb tire, weary; trouble, vex
**blith** (-ion) nm milk ▷ adj milch

**blith draphlith** *adv* helter-skelter
**blodeugerdd** (-i) *nf* anthology
**blodeuglwm** *nm* bunch, nosegay
**blodeuo** *vb* flower, bloom, flourish
**blodeuog** *adj* flowery; flourishing
**blodeuyn, blodyn** (blodau) *nm*
  flower
**blodiog** *adj* floury, mealy
**bloddest** *nf* rejoicing, acclamation
**bloedd** (-iau, -iadau) *nf* shout
**bloeddio, -ian** *vb* shout, cry
**bloeddiwr** (-wyr) *nm* shouter
**bloesg** *adj* lisping, faltering,
  indistinct
**bloesgi** *vb* lisp, falter, speak
  indistinctly
**bloneg** *nm*, **-en** *nf* lard, grease
**blwch** (blychau) *nm* box
**blwng** *adj* angry, sullen, cheerless
  ▷ *nm* anger
**blwydd** (-au, -i) *nf, adj* year of age;
  year-old
**blwydd-dal** *nm* annuity, pension
**blwyddiad** (-iaid) *nm* yearling,
  annual
**blwyddiadur** (-on) *nm* yearbook,
  annual
**blwyddyn** (blynyddoedd) *nf* year
**blychaid** (-eidiau) *nm* boxful
**blynedd** *nplf* years (*after numerals*)
**blynyddol** *adj* annual, yearly
**blys** (-iau) *nm* craving, lust
**blysig** *adj* greedy, lustful
**blysigrwydd** *nm* greediness
**blysio** *vb* crave, lust
**bocs** (-ys) *nm* box
**bocsach** *nm* vaunt, boast, brag
**boch** (-au) *nf* check
**bochgoch** *adj* rosy-cheeked
**bod** *vb* be, exist ▷ (-au) *nm* being,
  existence; **Y Bod Mawr** *nm* God
**boda** *nm/f* buzzard
**bodio** *vb* thumb, finger
**bodlon** *adj* content, willing
**bodloni** *vb* satisfy, content; be
  content
**bodlonrwydd** *nm* contentment

**bodolaeth** *nf* existence
**bodoli** *vb* exist
**bodd** *nm* pleasure, will, consent
**boddfa** *nf* flood, drenching
**boddhad** *nm* pleasure, satisfaction
**boddhaol** *adj* pleasing, satisfactory
**boddhau** *vb* please, satisfy
**boddhaus** *adj* pleased
**boddi** *vb* drown; flood
**boddio** *vb* please, satisfy
**boddlon** *etc see* **bodlon**
**bogail** (-eiliau) *nm/f* navel; boss,
  hub
**boglwm** (-lymau), **-lyn** (-lynnau)
  *nm* boss, knob, stud, bud, bubble
**bol, bola** (-iau) *nm* belly
**bolaid** (-eidiau) *nm* bellyful
**bolera** *vb* gorge, guzzle; (*fig*) sponge
**bolerwr** (-wyr) *nm* sponge, parasite
**bolgi** (-gwn) *nm* gourmand, glutton
**bolgno** *nm*, **-fa** *nf* gripes, colic
**bolheulo** *vb* bask in the sun
**bolio** *vb* belly, gorge
**boliog** *adj* big-bellied, corpulent
**boloch** *nm* pain, anxiety,
  destruction
**bolrwth** *adj* gluttonous, greedy
**bolrwym** *adj* costive, constipated
**bollt** (-au, -ydd, byllt) *nf* bolt
**bolwst** *nf/m* gripes, colic
**bol(y)sothach** *nm* hotchpotch;
  jargon
**bom** (-iau) *nm/f* bomb
**bomio** *vb* bomb
**bôn** (bonau, bonion) *nm* bottom;
  stump
**boncath** (-od) *nm* buzzard
**bonclust** (-iau) *nm* box on the ear
**boncyff** (-ion) *nm* stump, trunk,
  stock
**bondigrybwyll** *adv* forsooth ▷ *adj*
  hardly mentionable
**bondo** *nm* eaves
**bonedd** *nm* gentility, nobility
**boneddigaidd** *adj* noble;
  gentlemanly
**boneddigeiddrwydd** *nm*

gentlemanliness

**boneddiges** (-au) *nf* lady

**bonesig** *nf* lady; Miss

**bonet** (-i) *nf* bonnet

**bongam** *adj* bandy-legged

**bonheddig** *adj* noble, gentle, gentlemanly ▷ (**boneddigion**) *nmpl* gentlemen

**bonheddwr** (-wyr) *nm* gentleman

**bonllef** (-au) *nf* shout

**bonllwm** *adj* bare-bottomed, breechless; bare-backed

**Bonn** *nf* Bonn

**bonyn** (**bonion**) *nm* stump

**bord** (-ydd, -au) *nf* table, board

**bore** (-au) *nm* morning ▷ *adj* early

**boreddydd** *nm* day-break, morning

**borefwyd** *nm* breakfast

**boreol** *adj* morning

**bors** *nf* hernia

**bos** *nf* palm of the hand, fist

**bost** (-iau) *nm* boast, brag

**bostio** *vb* boast, brag

**botas, en** (-asau) *nf* boot

**botwm** (-ymau) *nm* button

**botymog** *adj* buttoned

**botymu** *vb* button

**both** (-au) *nf* nave of wheel; boss

**brac** *adj* free, frank, talkative

**bracso** *vb* wade, paddle

**bracty** (-tai) *nm* malt-house, brewery

**brad** (-au) *nm* treason; plot

**bradfwriadu** *vb* plot, conspire

**bradlofrudd** (-ion) *nm* assassin

**bradlofruddiaeth** (-au) *nf* assassination

**bradlofruddio** *vb* assassinate

**bradwr** (-wyr) *nm* traitor

**bradwriaeth** (-au) *nf* treason, treachery

**bradwrus** *adj* traitorous, treacherous

**bradychu** *vb* betray

**braen** *adj* rotten, corrupt

**braenar** (-au) *nm* fallow

**braenaru** *vb* fallow, pioneer

**braenu** *vb* rot, putrify

**braf** *adj* fine

**brag** *nm* malt

**bragad** *nf* army, battle; offspring

**bragaldian** *vb* jabber, gabble, prate

**bragio** *vb* brag, boast

**bragiwr** (-wyr) *nm* bragger, boaster

**bragod** (-au, -ydd) *nm* bragget

**bragu** *vb* malt, brew

**bragwair** *nm* moorland hay, coarse grass

**bragwr** (-wyr) *nm* maltster, brewer

**braich** (**breichiau**) *nf* arm; branch, handle; headland

**braidd** *adv* rather, somewhat

**braint** (**breintiau**) *nf* privilege

**braisg** *adj* gross, thick, large; pregnant

**braith** *adj f of* **brith**

**brân** (**brain**) *nf* crow, rook, raven

**bras** (**breision**) *adj* fat; coarse; rich; luxuriant

**brasáu** *vb* grow fat or gross

**brasbwytho** *vb* baste, tack

**brasgamu** *vb* stride

**Brasil** *nf* Brazil

**braslun** (-iau) *nm* sketch, outline

**braslunio** *vb* sketch, outline

**brasnaddu** *vb* rough-hew

**braster** *nm* fat

**brasterog** *adj* fat, greasy

**brat** (-iau) *nm* rag, clout; pinafore

**bratiaith** *nf* debased language

**bratiog** *adj* ragged, tattered

**brath** (-au) *nm* stab, wound; sting; bite

**brathog** *adj* that bites; biting

**brathu** *vb* stab, wound; sting; bite

**brau** *adj* brittle, frail, fragile; kindly; prompt

**braw** (-iau) *nm* terror, dread, fright

**brawd** (**brodyr**) *nm* brother; friar

**brawd** (**brodiau**) *nf* judgment

**brawdgarwch** *nm* brotherly love

**brawdle** (-oedd) *nf/m* judgement-seat

**brawdlys** (-oedd) *nf/m* assize-

court
**brawdmaeth** *nm* foster-brother
**brawdol** *adj* brotherly, fraternal
**brawdoliaeth** (-au) *nf* brotherhood, fraternity
**brawddeg** (-au) *nf* sentence
**brawddegu** *vb* construct sentences
**brawl** *nm* boast, brag; gabble, tattle
**brawychu** *vb* frighten, terrify
**brawychus** *adj* frightful, terrible
**bre** (-on, -oedd) *nf* hill, highland
**brebwl** (-yliaid) *nm* blockhead; prattler
**breci** *nm* wort; spree
**brecwast** (-au) *nm/f* breakfast
**brecwasta** *vb* breakfast
**brech** *nf* eruption, pox
**brech** *adj f of* **brych**
**brechdan** (-au) *nf* slice of bread and butter
**brechiad** (-au) *nm* inoculation, vaccination
**brechu** *vb* vaccinate, inoculate
**bredych** (-au, -ion) *nm* betrayal; fear; rascal
**bref** (-iadau) *nf* lowing; bleat; bray
**breferad** (-au) *nm* bellowing
**brefiad** (-au) *nm* lowing; bleating
**brefu** *vb* low; bleat; bray
**breg** *nm* guile, blemish, breach ▷ *adj* fragile, faulty
**bregliach** *vb* jabber
**bregus** *adj* frail, brittle, rickety
**breichled** (-au) *nf* bracelet
**breichrwy(f)** (-au) *nm/f* bracelet
**breinio** *vb* privilege, enfranchise
**breiniol** *adj* privileged, free
**breinlen** (-ni) *nf* charter
**breintal** *nm* bonus; royalty
**breintiedig** *adj* patented, patent
**breintio** *vb* privilege, favour
**brenhinaidd** *adj* kingly, regal
**brenhindod** *nm* royalty
**brenhindref** (-i) *nf* royal city
**brenhindy** (-dai) *nm* royal palace
**brenhines** (breninesau) *nf* queen

**brenhinfainc** *nf* throne
**brenhiniaeth** (breniniaethau) *nf* kingdom
**brenhinol** *adj* royal, regal
**brenin** (-hinoedd) *nm* king
**brest** (-iau) *nf* breast, chest
**bresych** *npl* (*nf-en*) cabbages
**brethyn** (-nau) *nm* cloth
**brethynnwr** (-ynwyr) *nm* clothier; cloth-worker
**breuan** (-au) *nf* quern; print of butter
**breuder** *nm* brittleness, frailty
**breuddwyd** (-ion) *nm/f* dream; ~ **gwrach** wishful thinking
**breuddwydio** *vb* dream
**breuddwydiol** *adj* dreaming, dreamy
**breuddwydiwr** (-wyr) *nm* dreamer
**brëyr, brehyr** (brehyrion, -iaid) *nm* nobleman, chief, baron
**bri** *nm* honour, renown, distinction
**briallu** *npl* (*nf briallen*) primroses
**bribys** *npl* fragments, scraps
**brifo** *vb* hurt
**brig** (-au) *nm* top; (*pl*) twigs
**brigâd** (-au) *nf* brigade; ~ **dân** fire-brigade
**briger** (-au) *nm* hair of head; top
**brigo** *vb* top; branch
**brigog** *adj* branching; flourishing
**brigwyn** *adj* white-topped, white-crested
**brigyn** (brigau) *nm* twig
**brith** (*f* braith) *adj* mottled, speckled
**britho** *vb* mottle, speckle; dazzle
**Brithwr** (-wyr) *nm* Pict
**brithyll** (-od, -iaid) *nm* trout
**briw** *adj* broken, bruised, sore ▷ (-iau) *nm* wound, sore
**briwfwyd** *nm* crumbs, mince
**briwlaw** *nm* drizzling rain
**briwlio** *vb* broil
**briwo** *vb* wound, hurt
**briwsion** *npl* (*nm-yn*) crumbs, fragments.

**briwsioni** vb crumble

**briwsyn** (**briwsion**) nm crumb, morsel

**bro** (**-ydd**) nf land; region; vale

**broch** nm badger

**broch** nm froth, anger, tumult

**brochi** vb chafe, fume; bluster

**brochus** adj fuming; blustering

**brodio** vb embroider; darn

**brodor** (**-ion**) nm native; fellow countryman

**brodorol** adj native, indigenous

**broga** (**-od**) nm frog

**brol** nf boast, brag

**brolio** vb boast, brag, vaunt

**broliwr** (**-wyr**) nm boaster, braggart

**bron** (**-nau, -nydd**) nf breast; hillside

**bron** adv almost, nearly; **o'r ~** completely, in succession

**bronfraith** (**-freithod**) nf thrush

**brongoch** (**-iaid**) nf/m robin redbreast

**bronwen** nf weasel

**bru** nm womb

**brud** (**-iau**) nm chronicle; divination

**brudio** vb prognosticate, divine

**brudiwr** (**-wyr**) nm wizard, soothsayer

**brwd** adj hot, fervent ▷ nm boil, heat

**brwdfrydedd** nm ardour, enthusiasm

**brwdfrydig** adj ardent, enthusiastic

**brwmstan** nm brimstone, sulphur

**brwmstanaidd** adj brimstony, sulphury

**brwnt** (f **bront**) adj foul, nasty, dirty; harsh

**brwyd** (**-au**) nm embroidering frame; skewer

**brwyd** adj variegated; bloodstained; shattered

**brwydo** vb embroider; tear, consume

**brwydr** (**-au**) nf battle, combat

**brwydro** vb battle, combat

**brwydrwr** (**-wyr**) nm fighter, combatant

**brwydwaith** nm embroidery

**brwylio** vb broil

**brwyn** nm grief, sadness

**brwynen** (**brwyn**) nf rush

**brwynog** adj rushy

**brwysg** adj drunk; vigorous

**brycan, brecan** (**-au**) nf/m blanket, rug

**brych** (f **brech**) adj mottled, brindled, freckled ▷ nm the after-birth of a cow

**brychau** npl (nm **-euyn**) spots, freckles

**brycheulyd** adj spotted, brindled

**brychni** nm spots, freckles

**brychu** vb spot, freckle

**bryd** nm mind, heart, will

**brydio** vb burn, inflame, boil, throb

**brygawthan** vb jabber, prate, rant

**bryn** (**-iau**) nm hill

**bryncyn** (**-nau**) nm hillock

**bryniog** adj hilly

**brynti, bryntni** nm filthiness, filth

**brys** nm haste, hurry

**brysio** vb hasten, hurry

**brysiog** adj hurried, hasty

**bryslythyr** (**-au**) nm dispatch

**brysneges** (**-au**) nf telegram

**brytheirio** vb belch; utter oaths, threats etc

**Brython** (**-iaid**) nm Briton, Welshman

**Brythoneg** nf British language, Welsh

**brythwch** nm storm, tumult; groan

**bryweddu** vb brew

**brywes** nm brewis

**bual** (**buail**) nm buffalo, drinking horn

**buan** adj fast, quick, swift, fleet; soon

**buander, -dra** nm swiftness, speed

**buandroed** adj swift-footed

**buarth** (**-au**) nm yard

**buchdraeth** (-au) *nf* biography, memoir
**buchedd** (-au) *nf* life, conduct
**bucheddol** *adj* right-living, virtuous
**bucheddu** *vb* live, flourish
**buches** (-au) *nf* herd of cows
**buchfrechu** *vb* vaccinate
**budr** *adj* dirty, filthy, foul, vile
**budreddi** *nm* filthiness, filth
**budro** *vb* dirty, soil, foul
**budd** (-ion) *nm* benefit, profit, gain
**buddai** (-eiau) *nf* churn
**buddel** (-wydd) *nm/f* cow-house post, pillar
**buddiant** (-iannau) *nm* interest
**buddio** *vb* profit, avail
**buddiol** *adj* profitable, beneficial, useful
**buddioldeb** *nm* profitableness, expediency
**buddsodd** (-ion), **-iad** (-au) *nm* investment
**buddsoddi** *vb* invest
**buddugol** *adj* winning, victorious
**buddugoliaeth** (-au) *nf* victory
**buddugoliaethus** *adj* victorious, triumphant
**buddugwr** (-wyr) *nm* winner, victor
**bugail** (-eiliaid) *nm* shepherd; pastor
**bugeiles** (-au) *nf* shepherdess
**bugeiliaeth** (-au) *nf* pastorate
**bugeilio, -a** *vb* watch, shepherd
**bugeiliol** *adj* pastoral
**bugunad** *nm* bellowing, roar
**bun** *nf* maid, maiden
**burgyn** (-nod, iaid) *nm* carcass, carrion
**burman, burum** *nm* barm, yeast
**busnes** (-ion) *nm/f* business
**busnesa** *vb* interfere, meddle
**busnesgar, busneslyd** *adj* meddlesome
**bustach** (-tych) *nm* bullock, steer
**bustachu** *vb* buffet about, bungle

**bustl** *nm* gall, bile
**bustlaidd** *adj* like gall; bitter as gall
**buwch** (buchod) *nf* cow; **~ goch gota** ladybird
**bwa** (bwâu) *nm* bow; arch
**bwaog** *adj* arched, vaulted
**bwbach** (-od) *nm* bugbear, bogey, scarecrow
**bwced** (-i) *nm/f* bucket
**bwci** (-ïod) *nm* bugbear, bogey, ghost
**bwcl** (byclau) *nm* buckle
**bwcled** (-au) *nf* buckler
**bwch** (bychod) *nm* buck; **~ dihangol** scapegoat; **~ gafr** he-goat
**bwgan** (-od) *nm* bogey, ghost, scarecrow
**bwgwl** (bygylau) *nm* threat, menace
**bwgwth** *see* **bygwth, bygythio**
**bwhwman** *vb* beat about; vacillate
**bŵl** (bylau) *nm* globe, ball, knob
**bwlch** (bylchau) *nm* gap; pass; notch
**bwled** (-i) *nf* bullet
**bwn** (bynnoedd, byniaid) *nm* bittern
**bwndel** (-i) *nm* bundle
**bwngler** (-iaid) *nm* bungler
**bwnglera** *vb* bungle
**bwngleraidd** *adj* bungling, clumsy
**bwnglerwaith** *nm* bungle, botch
**bwnglerwch** *nm* clumsiness
**bwr** (byr) *adj* fat, big, strong
**bwrdais** (-deisiaid) *nm* burgess
**bwrdeistref** (-i) *nm* borough
**bwrdd** (byrddau) *nm* table; deck; board; **~ du** black-board
**bwriad** (-au) *nm* purpose, intention
**bwriadol** *adj* intentional
**bwriadu** *vb* purpose, intend
**bwrlwm** (byrlymau) *nm* bubble; gurgling
**bwrn** (byrnau) *nm* burden, incubus; bale
**bwrw** *vb* cast, shed; strike; imagine, suppose; spend ▷ *nm* cast, throw;

woof

**bwtler** (-iaid) *nm* butler

**bwtri** *nm* buttery, pantry, dairy

**bwth** (bythod) *nm* hut, booth, cot

**bwthyn** (bythynnod) *nm* cottage, cabin, hut

**bwyall, -ell** (-eill, -yll) *nf* axe

**bwyd** (-ydd) *nm* food

**bwyda, bwydo** *vb* feed

**bwyd-offrwm** (-ymau) *nm* meat-offering

**bwydwr** (-wyr) *nm* feeder

**bwygilydd** *adv* (from one) to the other

**bwylltid** (-au) *nm* swivel

**bwyllwr(w)** (-yriau) *nf* provisions for journey

**bwysel** (-au, -i) *nm* bushel

**bwystfil** (-od) *nm* (wild) beast

**bwystfilaidd** *adj* beastly, brutish

**bwystfiles** (-au) *nf* beast

**bwyta** *vb* eat; corrode

**bwytadwy** *adj* eatable, edible

**bwytawr** (-wyr) *nm* eater

**bwyteig** *adj* greedy, voracious

**bwyty** (-tai, -tyau) *nm* restaurant

**bychan** (fbechan) *adj* little, small

**bychander, -dra** *nm* littleness, smallness

**bychanu** *vb* belittle, minimize

**bychanus** *adj* derogatory

**byd** (-oedd) *nm* world; state; life

**bydaf** (-au) *nm/f* beehive

**bydio** *vb* live, fare

**bydol** *adj* worldly, secular

**bydolddyn** (-ion) *nm* worldling

**bydolrwydd** *nm* worldliness

**bydwraig** (-wragedd) *nf* midwife

**bydwreigiaeth** *nf* midwifery

**bydysawd** *nm* universe

**byddag** (-au) *nf* running knot, noose

**byddar** *adj* deaf ▷ (-iaid, byddair) *nm* deaf person

**byddardod** *nm* deafness

**byddarol** *adj* deafening

**byddaru** *vb* deafen, stun

**byddin** (-oedd) *nf* army, host

**byddino** *vb* set army in array, embattle

**byddinog** *adj* with armies

**bygwth** *vb* threaten, menace ▷ (-ython, -ythiau) *nm* threat, menace

**bygythiad** (-au) *nm* threat

**bygythio** *vb* threaten, menace

**bygythiol** *adj* threatening, menacing

**byl** (-au) *nm/f* edge, brim (of vessel); **hyd y fyl** to the brim

**bylb** (-au) *nm* bulb

**bylchog** *adj* gapped, gappy; notched

**bylchu** *vb* make a gap, breach; notch

**byngalo** (-s, -au) *nm* bungalow

**bynnag** *pron* -ever, -soever

**byr** (fber) *adj* short, brief

**byrbryd** (-iau) *nm* luncheon, snack

**byrbwyll** *adj* impulsive, rash

**byrbwylltra** *nm* impulsiveness

**byrder, -dra** *nm* shortness, brevity

**byrdwn** *nm* burden, refrain, chorus

**byrddaid** (-eidiau) *nm* tableful

**byrddio** *vb* board

**byrddiwr** (-wyr) *nm* boarder

**byrfyfyr** *adj* impromptu

**byrgorn** *adj* shorthorn

**byrhau** *vb* shorten, abridge

**byrhoedlog** *adj* short-lived

**byrlymu** *vb* bubble, gurgle

**byrllysg** (-au) *nm/f* mace

**byrnio** (-u) *vb* bale, bundle

**byrnwr** (-wyr) *nm* baler

**bys** (-edd) *nm* finger; toe; hand of dial, latch

**bysaid** (-eidiau) *nm* pinch

**byseddu** *vb* finger

**bysled(r)** (-au) *nm* finger-stall

**byth** *adv* ever, for ever ▷ *nm* eternity

**bytheiad** (-aid) *nm* hound

**bytheirio** *vb* belch, threaten

**bythfywiol** *adj* everliving

**bythgofiadwy** *adj* memorable

**bythol** *adj* everlasting, eternal, perpetual
**bytholi** *vb* perpetuate
**bytholwyrdd** (-ion) *adj, nm* evergreen
**bythynnwr** (-ynwyr) *nm* cottager
**byw** *vb* live ▷ *adj* alive, living, quick ▷ *nm* life
**bywgraffiad** (-au) *nm* biography
**bywgraffiadol** *adj* biographical
**bywgraffiadur** (-on) *nm* biographical dictionary
**bywgraffydd** (-ion) *nm* biographer
**bywgraffyddol** *adj* biographical
**bywhau, bywiocáu** *vb* animate, vivify, quicken
**byw(i)ad** *nm* soft part of bread
**bywiog** *adj* lively, animated, vivacious
**bywiogi** *vb* enliven, animate
**bywiol** *adj* living, animate
**bywoliaeth** (-iolaethau) *nf* living
**bywyd** (-au) *nm* life
**bywydeg** *nf* biology
**bywydegwr** (-wyr) *nm* biologist
**bywydfad** (-au) *nm* lifeboat
**bywydol** *adj* of life, vital
**bywyn** (-nau) *nm* pith, core

# C

**cabaets** *npl* (*nf*~en) cabbage
**caban** (-au) *nm* cabin

**cabidwl** *nm* consistory, chapter
**cabl** (-au) *nm* blasphemy, reviling
**cabledd** (-au) *nm* blasphemy
**cableddus** *adj* blasphemous
**cablu** *vb* blaspheme, revile
**cablwr** (-wyr), **-ydd** (-ion) *nm* blasphemer
**caboli** *vb* polish
**cacamwci** *nm* burdock
**cacen** (-nau, -ni) *nf* cake
**cacwn** *npl* (*nf* cacynen) wasps; wild bees
**cachfa** (-feydd) *nf* excretion; closet
**cachgi** (-gwn) *nm* coward; sneak
**cachiad** *nm* excretion, jiffy; coward
**cachlyd** *adj* befouled, dirty
**cachu** *vb* defecate
**cachwr** (-wyr) *nm* coward; sneak; one who excretes
**cad** (-au, -oedd) *nf* battle; army, host
**cadach** (-au) *nm* cloth, kerchief, clout
**cadair** (-eiriau) *nf* chair, seat; cradle; udder
**cadarn** (cedyrn) *adj* strong, mighty; firm
**cadarnhad** *nm* affirmation, confirmation
**cadarnhaol** *adj* affirmative
**cadarnhau** *vb* strengthen, confirm
**cadeirfardd** (-feirdd) *nm* chaired bard
**cadeirio** *vb* chair
**cadeiriog** *adj* chaired
**cadeiriol** *adj* pertaining to a chair, cathedral
**cadeirydd** (-ion) *nm* chairman
**cadernid** *nm* strength; stability
**cadfarch** (-feirch) *nm* war-horse
**cadfridog** (-ion) *nm* general
**cadfwyall** (-eill, -yll) *nf* battleaxe
**cadlas** (-lesydd) *nf* close, enclosure
**cadlong** (-au) *nf* warship, battleship
**cadlys** (-oedd) *nf* camp, headquarters

cadno (~id, cadnawon) nm fox
cadnöes, cadnawes (-au) nf vixen
cadoediad (-au) nm armistice, truce
cadofydd (-ion) nm tactician, strategist
cadofyddiaeth nf tactics, strategy
cadofyddol adj tactical, strategic
cadw vb keep, preserve, save; hold
cadwedig adj saved
cadwedigaeth nf salvation
cadw-mi-gei nm money-box
cadwraeth nf keeping; observance; conservation
cadwyn (-au, -i) nf chain
cadwyno vb chain
cadwynog adj chained, in chains
caddug nm darkness; mist, fog
caddugo vb darken, obscure
cae (-au) nm field; fence, hedge; brooch
caead (-au) nm cover, lid ▷ adj shut, closed
caeadle (-oedd) nm enclosure
caeëdig adj closed, fenced
cael vb have; get; find
caen (-au) nf surface; peel; coating
caenen (-nau) nf layer, film, flake
caentach (-au) nf wrangle, grumbling ▷ vb wrangle, grumble
caenu vb coat, finish
caer (-au, ceyrydd) nf wall; castle; city
Caerdydd nf Cardiff
Caeredin nf Edinburgh
caeriwrch nm roebuck
caerog adj walled, fortified; brocaded
Caersalem nf Jerusalem
caeth adj bound, captive, confined ▷ (-ion) nm bondman, slave
caethder nm strictness; restraint; asthma
caethfab (-feibion) nm slave
caethfasnach nf slave-trade
caethferch (-ed) nf slave

caethforwyn (-forynion) nf slave
caethglud nf captivity
caethgludiad (-au) nm captivity
caethgludo vb lead captive
caethiwed nm slavery, bondage, captivity, detention
caethiwo vb bind, confine, enslave
caethiwus adj confining; confined, tied
caethlong (-au) nf slave-ship
caethwas (-weision) nm slave
caethwasanaeth, -wasiaeth nm slavery
cafell (-au) nf cell; sanctuary, oracle
cafn (-au) nm trough, gutter
cafnedd nm concavity
cafnio, -u vb hollow out, scoop, gouge
cafod see cawod
caffael vb get, obtain
caffaeledd nm availability; acquisitiveness
caffaeliad (-au) nm acquisition, asset; prey, spoil
caffe, -i (-s) nm café, restaurant
caffio vb snatch, grapple
cafflo vb cheat; entangle
cagl nm clotted dirt
caglu vb befoul, bedraggle
cangell (-hellau) nf chancel
cangelloriaeth nf chancellorship
cangen (-hennau) nf branch, bough
canghellor (cangellorion) nm chancellor
canghennog adj branching
canghennu vb branch, ramify
caib (ceibiau) nf pickaxe, mattock
cail (ceiliau) nf sheepfold, flock of sheep
caill (ceilliau) nf testicle
cain adj fair, fine, elegant
cainc (cangau, ceinciau) nf branch; strand; strain
cais (ceisiadau) nm application; attempt; try
cal(a) (-iau) nf penis

calan (-nau) nm first day of month;
  **Dydd C~** New Year's Day
calch nm lime
calchaidd adj calcareous
calchbibonwy nm stalactite
calchbost (-byst) nm stalagmite
calchen nf limestone; lump of lime
calchfaen (-feini) nm limestone
calcho, calchu vb lime
calcwlws (calcwli) nm calculus
caled adj hard; severe; harsh; dry
caledfwrdd nm hardboard
caledi nm hardness; hardship
caledu vb harden, dry
caledwch nm hardness
calen (-nau, -ni) nf whetstone; bar
calendr nm calendar
calennig nm/f New Year's gift
calon (-nau) nf heart
calondid nm encouragement
calon-dyner adj tender-hearted
calon-galed adj hard-hearted
calon-galedwch nm hard-
  heartedness
calonnog adj hearty; high-spirited
calonogi vb hearten, encourage
calori (-ïau) nm calorie
call adj wise, sensible, rational
callestr (cellystr) nf flint
callineb nm wisdom, sense
calsiwm nm calcium
cam (-au) nm step
cam adj crooked, wry; wrong ▷ (-au)
  nm injury, wrong
cam- prefix wrong, mis-
camarfer vb misuse, abuse ▷ (-ion)
  nm/f misuse, malpractice
camargraff nf/m wrong
  impression
camarwain vb mislead
camarweiniol adj misleading
Cambodia nf Cambodia
cambren (-ni) nm swingletree
camchwarae nm foul play
camdafliad (-au) nm foul throw
camdaflu vb foul throw
camder, -dra nm crookedness

cam-drefn nf disorder
camdreuliad nm indigestion
camdreulio vb mis-spend
cam-drin vb ill-treat, abuse
camdriniaeth (-au) nf ill-
  treatment
camdystiolaeth (-au) nf false
  witness
camdystiolaethu vb bear false
  witness
camddeall vb misunderstand
camddealltwriaeth nm
  misunderstanding
camddefnydd nm misuse
camddefnyddio vb misuse
camedd nm bend, curvature; **~ y
  droed** instep; **~ y gar** knee-joint
cameg (-au, cemyg) nf felloe
camel (-od) nm camel
camenw (-au) nm misnomer
camenwi vb misname
camfa (-feydd) nf stile
camfarnu vb misjudge
camgred (-oau, -au) nf misbelief,
  heresy
camgredu vb misbelieve
camgredwr (-wyr) nm heretic
camgwl nm penalty, fine; blame
camgyfrif vb miscalculate
camgyhuddiad (-au) nm false
  accusation
camgyhuddo vb accuse falsely
camgymeriad (-au) nm mistake
camgymryd vb mistake, err
camlas (-lesi, -lesydd) nf/m canal
camliwio vb misrepresent
camochri vb be offside
camog (-au) nf felloe
camp (-au) nf feat, exploit; game;
  prize
campfa (-feydd) nf gymnasium
campus adj excellent, splendid,
  grand
campwaith (-weithiau) nm
  masterpiece, feat
campwr (-wyr) nm champion
camre nm walk, footstep(s)

**camsyniad** (-au) nm mistake
**camsynied** vb mistake
**camsyniol** adj mistaken
**camu** vb bow, bend, stoop
**camu** vb step, stride
**camwedd** (-au) nm iniquity, transgression
**camweddu** vb transgress
**camwri** nm injury, wrong
**camymddwyn** vb misbehave
**camymddygiad** (-au) nm misconduct
**cân** (caniadau, caneuon) nf song
**can** adj white ▷ nm flour
**Canada** nf Canada
**cancr** nm canker; cancer
**cancro** vb canker, corrode
**candryll** adj shattered, wrecked
**canfasio** vb canvass
**canfed** adj hundredth
**canfod** vb see, perceive, behold
**canfyddadwy** adj perceptible
**canfyddiad** nm perception
**canhwyllbren** (canwyllbrenni, -au) nm/f candlestick
**canhwyllwr** (canhwyllwyr) nm chandler
**caniad** nm singing; ringing; crowing
**caniad** (-au) nf song, poem
**caniadaeth** nf singing, psalmody
**caniatâd** nm leave, permission, consent
**caniataol** adj permissive; granted
**caniatáu** vb permit, allow
**caniedydd** (-ion) nm singer, songster; song-book
**canlyn** vb follow, pursue
**canlyniad** (-au) nm consequence, result
**canlynol** adj following, consequent
**canlynwr** (-wyr) nm follower
**canllaw** (-iau) nf/m hand-rail, parapet, aid
**canmlwyddiant** nm centenary
**canmol** vb praise, commend

**canmoladwy** adj praiseworthy
**canmoliaeth** (-au) nf praise, commendation
**canmoliaethus** adj eulogistic, complimentary
**cannaid** adj white, bright, luminous
**cannu** vb whiten, bleach
**cannwr** (canwyr) nm bleacher
**cannwyll** (canhwyllau) nf candle
**canol** adj, (-au) nm middle, centre, midst
**canolbarth** (-au) nm middle part, midland
**canolbwynt** (-iau) nm centre, focus
**canolbwyntio** vb centre, concentrate
**canoldir** (-oedd) nm inland region
**canolddydd** nm mid-day, noon
**canolfan** (-nau) nm/f centre
**canoli** vb centre; arbitrate; centralize
**canolig** adj middling
**canoloesol** adj mediaeval
**canolog** adj central
**canolradd** (-ol) adj intermediate
**canolwr** (-wyr) nm mediator, referee; centrehalf, centre; **~ blaen** centreforward
**canon** (-au) nf/m, (-iaid) nm canon
**canonaidd** adj canonical
**canoneiddio** vb canonize
**canoniaeth** (-au) nf canonry
**canonwr** (-wyr) nm canon, canonist
**canradd** (-au) adj, nf centigrade, percentile
**canran** (-nau) nm percentage
**canrif** (-oedd) nf century
**cansen** (-ni) nf cane
**canser** nm cancer
**canslo** vb cancel
**cant** (-au) nm circle, ring, rim; tyre
**cant** (cannoedd) nm hundred
**cantel** (-au) nm rim, brim
**cantîn** (cantinoedd) nf canteen

**cantor** (-ion) *nm* singer
**cantores** (-au) *nf* songstress, singer
**cantref** (-i, -ydd) *nm* hundred
**cantwr** (-orion) *nm* singer, songster
**cantwraig** *nf* songstress, singer
**canu** *vb* sing, chant; play; crow; ring;
  **~ gwlad** country music
**canŵ** (-od) *nm* canoe
**canŵo** *vb* canoe
**canwr** (-wyr) *nm* singer
**canwriad** (-iaid) *nm* centurion
**canwyr** (-au, -ion) *nm* (*in carpentry*) plane
**canys** *conj* because, for
**cap** (-iau) *nm* cap
**capan** (-au) *nm* cap; lintel
**capel** (-i, -ydd, -au) *nm* chapel
**capelwr** (-wyr) *nm* chapel-goer
**caplan** (-iaid) *nm* chaplain
**caplaniaeth** (-au) *nf* chaplaincy
**capteiniaeth** *nf* captaincy
**capten** (-einiaid) *nm* captain
**car** (ceir) *nm* car; **~ campau** sports car
**câr** (ceraint) *nm* friend; relation
**carafán** (-au) *nf* caravan
**carbohydrad** (-au) *nm* carbohydrate
**carbon** (-au) *adj, nm* carbon
**carbwl** *adj* clumsy, awkward
**carco** *vb* take care
**carcus** *adj* solicitous, anxious, careful
**carchar** (-au) *nm* prison; restraint
**carchardy** (-dai) *nm* prison-house
**carchariad** *nm* imprisonment
**carcharor** (-ion) *nm* prisoner
**carcharu** *vb* imprison
**carden** (cardiau) *nf* card
**cardigan** (-au) *nf* cardigan
**cardod** (-au) *nf* charity, alms, dole
**cardota** *vb* beg
**cardotyn** (-wyr) *nm* beggar
**cardydwyn, -odwyn - wen** *nf* weakest of brood or litter
**caredig** *adj* kind

**caredigrwydd** *nm* kindness
**caregog** *adj* stony
**caregu** *vb* stone; petrify; gather stones
**carennydd** *nm* friendship; kinship
**caretsen** (carets) *nf* carrot
**carfaglog** *adj* clumsy
**carfan** (-au) *nf* beam; swath; party, faction
**cariad** (-au) *nm* love
**cariad** (-au, -on) *nm/f* lover, sweetheart
**cariadfab** *nm* lover, sweetheart
**cariadferch** *nf* sweetheart, mistress
**cariadlawn** *adj* full of love, loving
**cariadus** *adj* loving, beloved, dear
**caridým** (-s) *nm* ragamuffin
**cario** *vb* carry, bear
**carismatig** *adj* charismatic
**carlam** (-au) *nm* prance, gallop
**carlamu** *vb* prance, gallop
**carlwm** (-lymod) *nm* ermine, stoat
**carn** (-au) *nm* hoof; hilt, haft, handle
**carn** (-au), **carnedd** (-au) *nf* cairn
**cárnifal** *nm* carnival
**carniforus** *adj* carnivorous
**carnog, -ol** *adj* hoofed
**carol** (-au) *nm/f* carol
**carp** (-iau) *nm* clout, rag
**carped** (-au, -i) *nm* carpet
**carpiog** *adj* ragged, tattered
**carrai** (careiau) *nf* lace, thong
**carreg** (cerrig) *nf* stone
**cart** (ceirt) *nm/f* cart
**cartaid, certaid** (-eidiau) *nm* cartful
**cartilag** (-au) *nm* cartilage
**cartref** (-i, -ydd) *nm* home, abode
**cartrefle** (-oedd) *nm* abode
**cartreflu** *nm* militia
**cartrefol** *adj* homely, domestic, home; civil
**cartrefu** *vb* make one's home, settle
**cartŵn** (cartwnau) *nm* cartoon
**cartwnydd** (-ion) *nm* cartoonist

**carth** (-ion) *nm* tow, oakum; off-scouring
**carthen** (-ni, -nau) *nf* Welsh blanket, coverlet
**carthffos** (-ydd) *nf* sewer
**carthffosaeth** *nf* sewage
**carthu** *vb* cleanse, purge, scavenge
**caru** *vb* love; like; court
**caruaidd** *adj* loving, kind
**carw** (ceirw) *nm* stag, deer
**carwden** (-ni) *nf* back-chain; tall awkward fellow
**carwr** (-wyr) *nm* lover, wooer
**carwriaeth** (-au) *nf* courtship
**cas** *adj* hateful, odious; nasty, disagreeable ▷ *nm* hatred, aversion
**cas** (~eion) *nm* hater, foe, enemy
**casáu** *vb* hate, detest, abhor
**casbeth** (-au) *nm* aversion, nuisance
**caseg** (cesig) *nf* mare
**casét** (-iau) *nm* cassette
**casgen** (-ni, casgiau) *nf* cask
**casgl** *nf/m* collection
**casgliad** (-au) *nm* collection; gathering
**casglu** *vb* collect, gather; infer
**casglwr** (-wyr), **-ydd** (-ion) *nm* collector
**casineb** *nm* hatred
**cast** (-iau) *nm* vice, knack
**castan** (-au) *nf* chestnut
**castanwydd** *npl* (*nf-en*) chestnut-trees
**castell** (cestyll) *nm* castle
**castellog** *adj* castled, castellated
**castellu** *vb* castle, encamp
**castio** *vb* trick, cheat; cast, calculate
**castiog** *adj* full of tricks, tricky
**casul** (-(i)au) *nm/f* chasuble, cassock
**caswir** *nm* unpalatable truth
**casyn** (casiau) *nm* case, casing
**cat** (-iau) *nm* bit, piece, fragment; pipe
**catalog** (-au) *nm* catalogue
**catalogio** *vb* catalogue

**catalydd** (-ion) *nm* catalyst
**categori** (-ïau) *nm* category
**catel** *coll n* chattels; cattle
**catgor** (-(i)au) *nm* ember day(s)
**catrawd** (-rodau) *nf* regiment
**cath** (-od, -au) *nf* cat
**cathl** (-au) *nf* melody, hymn, lay
**cathlu** *vb* sing, hymn
**cathod** (-au) *nf* cathode
**catholig** *adj* catholic
**Catholigiaeth** *nf* Catholicism
**catholigrwydd** *nm* catholicity
**cau** *adj* hollow, concave
**cau** *vb* shut, close, enclose
**caul** (ceulion) *nm* maw; rennet; curd
**caw** (-(i)au) *nm* band, swaddling-clothes
**cawdel** *nm* hotchpotch, mess
**cawell** (cewyll) *nm* hamper, basket, cradle
**cawellaid** (-eidiau) *nm* hamperful
**cawellwr** (-wyr) *nm* basket-maker
**cawg** (-iau) *nm* basin, bowl, pitcher
**cawl** *nm* broth, soup; hotchpotch
**cawn** *npl* (*nf-en*) reeds
**cawod** (-ydd) *nf* shower
**cawodi** *vb* shower
**cawodog** *adj* showery
**cawr** (cewri) *nm* giant
**cawraidd** *adj* gigantic
**cawres** (-au) *nf* giantess
**caws** *nm* cheese; curd
**cawsai, cawsi** *nf/m* causeway
**cawsaidd** *adj* cheesy, caseous
**cawsellt** (-ydd, -i, -au) *nm* cheese-vat
**cawsio** *vb* curd, curdle
**cawsiog** *adj* curdled
**cecian** *vb* stammer
**cecren** (-nod) *nf* shrew, scold, cantankerous woman
**cecru** *vb* wrangle, bicker
**cecrus** *adj* cantankerous, quarrelsome
**cecryn** (-nod) *nm* wrangler, brawler
**cedor** *nm/f* pubic hair
**cedrwydd** *npl* (*nf-en*) cedars

cefn (-au) nm back; support

cefndedyn nm mesentery; diaphragm, pancreas

cefnder (-dyr) nm first cousin

cefndir (-oedd) nm background

cefnen (-nau) nf ridge

cefnfor (-oedd) nm main sea, ocean

cefngrwm adj hump-backed

cefnog adj well-off, well-to-do

cefnogaeth nf encouragement, support

cefnogi vb encourage, support

cefnogol adj encouraging

cefnu vb back, turn the back, forsake

cefnwlad (-wledydd) nf hinterland

cefnwr (-wyr) nm back, full-back

ceffyl (-au) nm horse

ceg (-au) nf mouth

cega vb mouth, prate

cegaid (-eidiau) nf mouthful

cegen (-nau) nf gullet, windpipe

cegid, -en (-au) nf green woodpecker, jay

cegin (-au) nf kitchen

cegrwth adj gaping

cegyr npl hemlock

cengl (-au) nf band; girth; hank

cenglu vb hank; girth; wind

cei (-au) nm quay

ceibio vb pick with pickaxe

ceidwad (-aid) nm keeper, saviour

ceidwadaeth nf conservatism; conservancy

ceidwadol adj conservative

Ceidwadwr (-wyr) nm Conservative

ceiliagwydd (-au) nm gander

ceiliog (-od) nm cock; ~ rhedyn grasshopper

ceinach (-od) nf hare

ceincio vb branch out, ramify

ceinciog adj branched, branching

ceinder nm elegance, beauty

ceiniog (-au) nf penny

ceiniogwerth (-au, -i) nf pennyworth

ceinion npl beauties, gems

ceintach vb grumble, croak

ceintachlyd adj querulous

ceintachwr (-wyr) nm grumbler, croaker

ceirch (nf-en) coll n oats

ceirios npl (nf-en) cherries

ceisbwl (-byliaid) nm catchpole, bailiff

ceisio vb seek; ask; try, attempt, endeavour; fetch, get

cêl adj hidden, concealed ▷ nm concealment ▷ npl kale

celain (celanedd) nf dead body

celanedd coll nf carnage, slaughter

celc nm/f concealment; hoard

celf (-au) nf art, craft

celfi npl (nm-cyn) tools, gear; furniture

celfydd adj skilled, skilful

celfyddgar adj ingenious; artistic

celfyddwr (-wyr) nm artificer, artist

celfyddyd (-au) nf art, craft; skill; ~au graffig graphic arts

celfyddydol adj relating to art/the Arts

celu vb hide, conceal

celwrn (-yrnau) nm tub, bucket, pail

celwydd (-au) nm lie, falsehood, untruth

celwyddog adj lying, mendacious; false

celwyddwr (-wyr) nm liar

celyn npl (nf-nen) holly

cell (-oedd, -au) nf cell, chamber; ~oedd cenhedlu germ cells; ~oedd enyniad y ~oedd cellulitis

celli (cellïau, -ïoedd) nf grove

cellog adj cellular

cellwair vb jest, trifle ▷ nm fun

cellweiriwr (-wyr) nm jester, trifler

cellweirus adj playful, jocular

cemeg nm chemistry

cemegol adj chemical

cemegwr, -ydd (-wyr) nm chemist

**cemegyn** (cemegau) *nm* chemical
**cen** *coll n* skin, peel, scales, scurf, film, lichen
**cenadwri** *nf* message
**cenau** (cenawon) *nm* cub, whelp; rascal
**cenedl** (-hedloedd) *nf* nation; gender
**cenedlaethol** *adj* national
**cenedlaetholdeb** *nm* nationalism
**cenedlaetholi** *vb* nationalize
**cenedlaetholwr** (-wyr) *nm* nationalist
**cenedl-ddyn** (-ion) *nm* gentile
**cenfaint** (-feiniau) *nf* herd
**cenfigen** (-nau) *nf* envy, jealousy
**cenfigennu** *vb* envy
**cenfigennus, -enllyd** *adj* envious, jealous
**cenhadaeth** (cenadaethau) *nf* mission
**cenhadol** *adj* missionary
**cenhadu** *vb* permit; propagate, conduct a mission
**cenhadwr** (-hadon) *nm* missionary
**cenhedlaeth** (cenedlaethau) *nf* generation
**cenhedlig** *adj* gentile, pagan
**cenhedlu** *vb* beget, generate
**cenllif** *nm* flood, torrent, deluge
**cenllysg** *coll nm* hailstones, hail
**cennad** (-hadau, -hadon) *nf* leave; messenger
**cennin** *npl* (*nf*-hinen) leeks
**cennog** *adj* scaly, scurfy
**cennu** *vb* scale, scurf
**cêr** *nf* gear, tools, trappings
**cerameg** *nm/f* ceramics
**ceramig** *adj* ceramic
**cerbyd** (-au) *nm* chariot, coach, car
**cerbydwr** (-wyr) *nm* coachman
**cerdyn** (cardiau) *nm* card
**cerdd** (-i) *nf* song, poem; music, poetry
**cerddbrenni** *npl* woodwinds
**cerddbresi** *npl* brass section (orchestra)

**cerdded** *vb* walk; go; travel
**cerddediad** *nm* walking, going; pace
**cerddgar** *adj* harmonious, musical
**cerddin, cerdin** *npl* (*nf*-en) rowan
**cerddor** (-ion) *nm* singer, musician
**cerddorfa** (-feydd) *nf* orchestra
**cerddorfaol** *adj* orchestral
**cerddoriaeth** *nf* music
**cerddorol** *adj* musical
**cerddwr** (-wyr) *nm* walker
**cerfddelw** (-au) *nf* graven image, statue
**cerfio** *vb* carve
**cerflun** (-iau) *nm* statue; engraving
**cerfluniaeth** *nf* sculpture
**cerflunydd** (-lunwyr) *nm* sculptor
**cerfwaith** *nm* carving, sculpture
**cern** (-au) *nf* cheek, jaw
**cernod** (-iau) *nf* buffet
**cernodio** *vb* buffet, clout
**cerpyn** (carpiau) *nm* clout, rag
**cerrynt** *nm/f* course, road; current
**cert** (-i) *nf* cart
**certiwr** (-wyr) *nm* carter
**certh** *adj* right; awful
**cerub, ceriwb** (-iaid) *nm* cherub
**cerwyn** (-i) *nf* tub; vat; winepress
**cerydd** (-on) *nm* correction, chastisement; rebuke, reproof, censure
**ceryddol** *adj* chastising, chastening
**ceryddu** *vb* correct, chastise; rebuke
**ceryddwr** (-wyr) *nm* chastiser; rebuker
**cesail** (-eiliau) *nf* arm-pit; bosom
**cesair** *npl*, *coll n* hailstones, hail
**cest** (-au) *nf* belly, paunch
**cestog** *adj* corpulent
**cetyn** (catiau) *nm* piece, bit; pipe
**cethin** *adj* dark, fierce, ugly
**ceubren** (-nau) *nm* hollow tree
**ceubwll** (-byllau) *nm* pit
**ceudod** *nm* cavity; abdomen; thought, heart

**ceuffordd** (-ffyrdd) nf tunnel
**ceuffos** (-ydd) nf drain, ditch
**ceugrwm** adj concave
**ceulan** (-nau, -lennydd) nf bank, brink
**ceulo** vb curdle, coagulate
**ceunant** (-nentydd) nm ravine, gorge
**cewyn** (-nau, cawiau) nm napkin
**ci** (cŵn) nm dog, hound
**cïaidd** adj dog-like, houndish; brutal
**cib** (-au) nm pod, husk
**cibddall** adj purblind
**cibo** vb frown, scowl
**cibog** adj scowling
**cibws, cibwst** nf kibes, chilblains
**cibwts** (-au) nm kibbutz
**cibyn** (-nau) nm shell; husk; half a bushel
**cic** (-iau) nm/f kick
**cicio** vb kick
**ciciwr** (-wyr) nm kicker
**cidwm** (-ymiaid, -ymod) nm wolf; rascal
**cieidd-dra** nm houndishness, brutality
**cig** (-oedd) nm flesh, meat
**cigfran** (-frain) nf raven
**cignoeth** adj touching to the quick, caustic
**cigog** adj fleshy
**cigwain** (-weiniau) nf flesh-hook
**cigydd** (-ion) nm butcher
**cigyddiaeth** nf butchery
**cigysol** adj carnivorous
**cigysydd** (-ion) nm carnivore
**cil** (-iau, -ion) nm back; retreat; corner
**cilagor** vb open partly
**cilagored** adj ajar
**cilbost** (cilbyst) nm gate-post
**cilchwyrn** npl (nf-en), nm (-au, -od) glands
**cildrem** (-iau) nf leer
**cildremio** vb leer
**cildroi** vb reverse
**cildwrn** nm tip, bribe

**cildyn** adj obstinate, stubborn
**cildynnu** vb be obstinate
**cildynnus** adj obstinate, stubborn
**cildynrwydd** nm obstinacy
**cilddant** (-ddannedd) nm molar
**cilfach** (-au) nf nook; creek, bay
**cilfilyn** (-filod) nm ruminant
**cilgnoi** vb chew the cud, ruminate
**cilgwthio** vb simper, shove, jostle
**cilgynnyrch** (-gynhyrchion) nm by-product
**cilio** vb retreat, recede, swerve
**cilocalori** (-ïau) nm kilocalorie
**cilogram** (-au) nm kilogram
**cilomedr** (-au) nm kilometre
**cilwen** (-au) nf half smile
**cilwenu** vb simper, smile, leer
**cilwg** (-ygon) nm frown, scowl
**cilydd** (-ion) nm fellow, companion
**cilyddol** adj reciprocal
**cimwch** (-ychiaid) nm lobster
**cingroen** nf stink-horn
**ciniawa** vb dine
**cinio** (ciniawau) nm dinner
**cip** (-ion) nm pluck, snatch; glimpse
**cipdrem** (-iau) nf/m glance, glimpse
**cipedrych** vb glance, glimpse
**cipio** vb snatch
**cipiwr** (-wyr) nm snatcher
**cipolwg** nm/f glance, glimpse
**ciprys** vb, nm scramble
**cis** (-iau) nm/f buffet; slap, touch
**cist** (-iau) nf chest, coffer, box; bin
**ciw** (-iau) nm cue, queue
**ciwb** nm cube
**ciwed** coll nf rabble, mob, crew
**ciwrad** (-iaid) nm curate
**ciwt** adj cute, clever, ingenious
**claddedigaeth** (-au) nf/m burial
**claddfa** (-feydd) nf burial-ground, cemetery
**claddu** vb bury
**claear** adj lukewarm, tepid; mild; cool
**claearineb** nm lukewarmness
**claearu** vb make mild or tepid;

soothe
**claer** adj clear, bright, shining
**claerder** nm clearness, brightness
**claf (cleifion)** adj sick, ill ▷ nm sick person, patient
**clafdy (-dai)** nm hospital, infirmary
**clafr** nm itch, mange
**clafrllyd** adj mangy
**clafychu** vb sicken, fall ill
**clai (cleiau)** nm clay
**clais (cleisiau)** nm stripe; bruise
**clamp (-iau)** nm mass, lump; monster
**clap (-iau)** nm lump
**clapgi (-gwn)** nm telltale
**clapio** vb lump; strike; gossip
**clapiog** adj lumpy
**clas** nm monastic community, cloister, college
**clasur (-on)** nm classic
**clasurol** adj classical
**clau** adj quick, swift, soon; true; audible
**clawdd (cloddiau)** nm hedge; dyke, embankment
**clawr (cloriau)** nm face, surface; cover, lid; board
**clebar, cleber** nf/m idle talk, gossip, tattle
**clebran** vb chatter, gossip, tattle
**clebryn** nm, **clebren** nf tattler
**clec (-iau, -s)** nf click; clack; crack; gossip
**cleci (-cwn)** nm telltale
**clecian** vb click; clack; crack, snap
**clecyn** nm, **clecen** nf gossip, telltale
**cledr (-au)** nf pole; rail; palm (of hand)
**cledren (-nau, -ni)** nf pale, pole, rail
**cleddyf, cleddau, cledd (~au)** nm sword; brace
**cleddyfwr (-wyr)** nm swordsman
**clefyd (-au)** nm disease; fever; ~ melys diabetes
**clegar** vb clack, cluck, cackle
**clegyr, clegr** nm rock; cairn,

stony place
**cleiog** adj clayey
**cleiriach** nm decrepit one
**cleisio** vb bruise
**cleisiog** adj bruised
**clem (-iau)** nf notion, idea; look, gaze ▷ pl grimaces
**clep (-iau)** nf clack, clap; gossip
**clepgi (-gwn)** nm babbler; telltale
**clepian** vb clap; slam; blab
**clêr** coll nf itinerant minstrels; bards
**clêr** npl (nf cleren) flies
**clera** vb stroll as minstrels
**clerc (-od)** nm clerk
**clercio** vb serve as clerk
**clerigol** adj clerical
**clerigwr (-wyr)** nm clergyman
**clerwr (-wyr)** nm itinerant minstrel
**clerwriaeth** nf minstrelsy
**clewt (-iau)** nm clout
**clewtian** vb clout
**clic (~iau)** nm clique
**clicied (-au)** nf clicket; trigger
**cliciedu** vb latch, fasten
**clindarddach** vb crackle ▷ nm crackling
**clinig (-au)** nm clinic
**clir** adj clear
**clirio** vb clear
**clo (~eau, ~eon)** nm lock, conclusion
**clobyn** nm, **cloben** nf monster
**cloc (-iau)** nm clock
**clocian** vb cluck
**clocsiau** npl (nf clocsen) clog
**cloch (clych, clychau)** nf bell; **o'r/ar gloch** o'clock
**clochaidd** adj sonorous, noisy
**clochdar** vb cluck, cackle
**clochdy (-dai)** nm belfry, steeple
**clochydd (-ion)** nm bell-man; sexton
**clod (-ydd)** nm/f praise, fame, renown
**clodfori** vb praise, extol
**clodwiw** adj commendable, praiseworthy
**cloddfa (-feydd)** nf quarry, mine

**cloddio** *vb* dig, delve; quarry, mine
**cloddiwr (-wyr)** *nm* digger, navvy
**cloëdig** *adj* locked, closed
**cloer (-(i)au)** *nm/f* locker; niche, embrasure; pigeon-hole
**cloff** *adj* lame
**cloffi** *vb* lame, halt ▷ *nm* lameness
**cloffni** *nm* lameness
**cloffrwym (-au)** *nm* fetter, hobble;
 **~ y cythraul, ~ y mwci** great bindweed
**clog (-au)** *nm/f* cloak
**clog (-au)** *nf* rock, precipice
**clogfaen (-feini)** *nm* boulder
**clogwyn (-i)** *nm* cliff, crag, precipice
**clogwynog** *adj* craggy, precipitous
**clogyn (-nau)** *nm* cloak, cape
**clogyrnaidd** *adj* rough, rugged, clumsy
**cloi** *vb* lock
**clonc** *nf* clank; gossip ▷ *adj* addled
**clopa (-âu)** *nf/m* noddle; knob; club
**cloren (-nau)** *nf* rump, tail
**clorian (-nau)** *nm/f* pair of scales
**cloriannu** *vb* weigh, balance
**clorin** *nm* chlorine
**clorinio, -adu** *vb* chlorinate
**clos (-ydd)** *nm* yard
**clos (~au)** *nm* pair of breeches
**clòs** *adj* close
**closio** *vb* close, near
**cludadwy** *adj* portable
**cludair (-eiriau)** *nf* heap, load, wood-pile
**cludiad** *nm* carriage
**cludiant (-nnau)** *nm* transport, haulage
**cludo** *vb* carry, convey
**cludwr (-wyr), -ydd (-ion)** *nm* porter
**clul (-iau)** *nm* knell
**clun (-iau)** *nf* hip, haunch, thigh, leg; moor
**cluro** *vb* rub, smear
**clust (-iau)** *nf/m* ear; handle
**clustfeinio** *vb* prick up the ears; eavesdrop

**clustfys** *nm* little finger
**clustffôn (-ffonau)** *nm* earphone
**clustlws (-lysau)** *nm* earring
**clustnod (-au)** *nm* earmark
**clustog (-au)** *nf/m* cushion, pillow
**clwb (clybiau)** *nm* club
**clwc** *adj* addled
**clwcian** *vb* cluck
**clwm (clymau)** *nm* knot, tie
**clwpa (-od)** *nm* knob, boss; club; dolt
**clws (f clos)** *adj* pretty, nice
**clwstwr (clystyrau)** *nm* cluster
**clwt (clytiau)** *nm* patch, clout, rag
**clwyd (-au, -i, -ydd)** *nf* hurdle; gate; roost
**clwydo** *vb* roost
**clwyf (-au)** *nm* wound; disease
**clwyfo** *vb* wound
**clwyfus** *adj* wounded; sore; sick
**clybodeg** *nf* acoustics
**clybodig** *adj* acoustic
**clyd** *adj* warm, sheltered, snug, cosy
**clydwch, clydwr** *nm* warmth, shelter
**clyfar** *adj* clever; pleasant, agreeable
**clymblaid (-bleidiau)** *nf* clique, cabal
**clymog** *adj* knotty, entangled
**clymu** *vb* knot, tie
**clytio** *vb* patch, piece
**clytiog** *adj* patched; ragged
**clytwaith (-weithiau)** *nm* patchwork
**clyw** *nm* sense of hearing
**clywadwy** *adj* audible
**clywed** *vb* hear; feel; taste; smell
**clywedigaeth** *nf* hearing
**clywedol** *adj* aural
**clywedydd (-ion)** *nm* hearer, auditor
**clyweled** *adj* audio-visual
**cnaf (-on, -iaid)** *nm* knave, rascal
**cnafaidd** *adj* knavish, rascally
**cnaif (cneifion)** *nm* shearing, fleece
**cnap (-iau)** *nm* lump, knob, boss

**cnapan** (-au) *nm* ball, bowl, kind of ball game

**cnapiog** *adj* lumpy

**cnau** *npl* (*nf* **cneuen**) nuts

**cnawd** *nm* flesh

**cnawdol** *adj* carnal, fleshly, fleshy

**cneifio** *vb* shear, fleece

**cneifiwr** (-wyr) *nm* shearer

**cneua** *vb* knock

**cneuen** (cnau) *nf* nut

**cnewyllyn** (cnewyll) *nm* kernel, nucleus

**cnith** (-iau, -ion) *nm* slight touch, blow; pluck

**cno** *nm* bite, chewing, gnawing

**cnoc** (-iau) *nm/f* knock

**cnocio** *vb* knock

**cnofa** (-feydd) *nf* gnawing, pang

**cnofil** (-od) *nm* rodent

**cnoi** *vb* gnaw, chew, bite; ache

**cnot** (-iau) *nm* knot, bunch

**cnu** (-au), **cnuf** (-iau) *nm* fleece

**cnud** (-oedd) *nf* (of wolves etc) pack

**cnùl, cnul** (-iau) *nm* knell

**cnwd** (cnydau) *nm* crop; covering

**cnydfawr** *adj* fruitful, productive

**cnydio** *vb* crop, yield increase

**cnydiog** *adj* fruitful, productive

**cob** (~au) *nf* coat, cloak, robe

**còb** (-iau) *nm* embankment; miser; wag; cob

**coban** (-au) *nf*: ~ **nos** nightshirt

**coblyn** (-nod) *nm* sprite, goblin, imp

**cocos** *npl* cogs; **olwyn gocos** cog-wheel

**cocos, cocs** *npl* (*nf* **cocsen**) cockles

**coch** *adj, nm* red

**coch-gam** *nf* robin

**cochi** *vb* redden, blush

**cochi, cochder** *nm* redness

**cochl** (-au) *nm/f* mantle, cloak

**cod** (-au) *nf* bag, pouch

**codaid** (-eidiau) *nf* bagful

**codi** *vb* rise, raise, lift, erect

**codiad** (-au) *nm* rise, rising; erection

**codog** *adj* baggy ▷ (-ion) *nm/f* rich man; miser

**codwm** (codymau) *nm* fall, tumble

**codwr** (-wyr) *nm* riser; raiser, lifter; ~ **canu** precentor

**codymu** *vb* wrestle

**codymwr** (-wyr) *nm* wrestler

**codded** *nm* anger; grief

**coddi** *vb* anger, offend

**coed** (-ydd) *coll nm* wood, timber, trees

**coeden** (coed) *nf* tree

**coedio** *vb* timber

**coediog** *adj* wooded, woody

**coedwig** (-oedd) *nf* wood, forest

**coedwigaeth** *nf* forestry

**coedwigwr** (-wyr) *nm* woodman, forester

**coedd** *adj* public

**coeg** *adj* empty, vain; one-eyed, blind

**coegddyn** (-ion) *nm* fop, coxcomb, fool

**coegedd** *nm* emptiness, silliness

**coegen** (-nod) *nf* minx, coquette

**coegennaidd** *adj* coquettish

**coegfalch** *adj* vain, foppish

**coegi** *vb* jeer at, mock

**coeglyd** *adj* vain, sarcastic

**coegni** *nm* vanity; spite; sarcasm

**coegwr** (-wyr) *nm* fool

**coegwych** *adj* gaudy, garish, tawdry

**coegyn** (-nod) *nm* coxcomb

**coel** (-ion) *nf* belief, trust, credit

**coelbren** (-nau, -ni) *nm* lot

**coelcerth** (-i) *nf* bonfire, blaze

**coelgrefydd** (-au) *nf* superstition

**coelgrefyddol** *adj* superstitious

**coelio** *vb* believe, credit, trust

**coes** (-au) *nf* leg, shank ▷ *nm/f* handle; stem, stalk

**coetgae** *nm* hedge; enclosure

**coetmon** (-myn) *nm* lumberjack

**coetref** *nf* woodland, homestead

**coeth** *adj* fine, refined; elegant

**coethder** *nm* refinement, elegance

**coethi** vb refine; chastise; babble
**coethwr** (-wyr) nm refiner
**cof** (-ion) nm memory; remembrance
**cofadail** (-eiladau) nf monument
**cofeb** (-ion) nf memorandum; memorial
**cofgolofn** (-au) nf monument
**cofiadur** (-on, -iaid) nf recorder
**cofiadwy** adj memorable
**cofiannydd** (-anyddion) nm biographer
**cofiant** (-iannau) nm memoir, biography
**cofio** vb remember, recollect
**cofl** (-au) nf embrace; bosom
**coflaid** (-eidiau) nf armful; bundle
**coflech** (-au) nf memorial tablet
**cofleidio** vb embrace, hug
**coflyfr** (-au) nm record, chronicle
**cofnod** (-ion) nm memorandum, minute
**cofnodi** vb record, register
**cofrestr** (-au) nf register, roll
**cofrestrfa** nf registry
**cofrestru** vb register
**cofrestrydd** (-ion) nm registrar
**cofus** adj mindful
**cofweini** vb prompt
**cofweinydd** (-ion) nm prompter
**coffa** vb remember ▷ nm remembrance
**coffâd** nm remembrance
**coffadwriaeth** nf remembrance, memory
**coffadwriaethol** adj memorial
**coffáu** vb remember; remind; commemorate
**coffi** nm coffee
**coffr** (-au) nm coffer, trunk, chest
**cog** (-au) nf cuckoo
**cog** (-au) nm cook
**coginiaeth** nf cookery
**coginio** vb cook
**cogio** vb cog; sham, feign, pretend
**cogiwr** (-wyr) nm pretender, swindler

**cogor** vb chatter, caw, croak ▷ nm chattering
**cogwrn** (-yrnau, cegyrn) nm knob, cone; cock (of corn); shell
**cogydd** (-ion) nm, **cogyddes** (-au) nf cook
**cogyddiaeth** nf cookery
**congl** (-au) nf corner
**côl** nf bosom, embrace
**col** (-ion) nm awn, beard
**coladu** vb collate
**coledd, -u** vb cherish, foster
**coleddwr** (-wyr) nm cherisher, fosterer, patron, supporter
**coleg** (-au) nm college
**colegol** adj collegiate
**colegwr** (-wyr) nm collegian
**coler** (-i) nf/m collar
**colfen** (-nau, -ni) nf bough, branch; tree
**colofn** (-au) nf column, pillar
**colomen** (-nod) nf dove, pigeon
**colomendy** (-dai) nm dove-cot
**colomennaidd** adj dove-like
**coluddion** npl (nm-yn) bowels
**colur** (-au) nm make-up, colour
**coluro** vb make-up, paint; conceal
**colwyn** (-od) nm puppy
**colyn** (-nau) nm pivot; sting; tail
**colynnog** adj stinging; hinged
**colynnu** vb sting
**coll** (-iadau) nm loss; failing, defect
**colladwy** adj perishable
**collddail** adj deciduous
**colled** (-ion) nm/f loss
**colledig** adj lost, damned
**colledigaeth** nf perdition
**colledu** vb occasion loss
**colledus** adj fraught with loss
**colledwr** (-wyr) nm loser
**collen** (cyll) nf hazel
**collfarn** (-au) nf doom, condemnation
**collfarnu** vb condemn
**colli** vb lose; be lost, perish; spill, shed
**collnod** (-au) nm apostrophe

**collwr** (-wyr) nm loser
**côma** (comâu) nm coma
**coma** (-s) nm comma
**comed** (-au) nf comet
**comedi** (-ïau) nf/m comedy
**comig** adj comic, comical ▷ nm comic (paper)
**comisiwn** (-iynau) nm commission
**comisiynu** vb commission
**comiwnydd** (-ion) nm communist
**comiwnyddiaeth** nf communism
**comiwnyddol** adj communist
**conach** vb grumble
**conclaf** nm conclave
**concro** vb conquer
**concwerwr** (-wyr) nm conqueror
**concwest** (-au) nf conquest, victory
**condemniad** nm condemnation
**condemnio** vb condemn
**confensiwn** (-iynau) nm convention
**conffederasiwn** (-asïynau) nm confederation
**conffirmasiwn** nm confirmation
**conffirmio** vb confirm
**conifferaidd** adj coniferous
**cono** nm rascal; wag; old fogey
**consesiwn** (-iynau) nm concession
**consuriaeth** nf conjuring
**consurio** vb conjure
**consuriwr** (-wyr) nm conjurer
**conwydd** npl (nf-en) coniferous trees
**cop, copyn** (-nod, -nau) nm spider
**copa** (-âu) nf top, crest; head
**copi** (-ïau) nm copy; copy-book
**copïo** vb copy, transcribe
**copïwr** (-wyr) nm copyist, transcriber
**copr** nm copper
**côr** (corau) nm choir; stall, pew; ~ **feistr** choirmaster
**cor** (-rod) nm dwarf; spider
**corachaidd** adj dwarfish, stunted
**corawl** adj choral
**corbwll** (-byllau) nm whirlpool; puddle

**corcyn** (cyrc) nm cork
**cord** (-iau) nm cord; chord
**cordeddu** vb twist, twine
**corddi** vb churn; turn; agitate
**corddiad** (-au) nm churning
**corddwr** (-wyr) nm churner
**cored** (-au) nf weir, dam
**coreograffiaeth** nf choreography
**corfan** (-nau) nm metrical foot
**corff** (cyrff) nm body
**corfflu** (-oedd) nm corps
**corffol** adj corpulent; physical
**corffolaeth** nf bodily form; stature
**corfforaeth** (-au) nf corporation
**corffori** vb embody, incorporate
**corfforiad** (-au) nm embodiment
**corfforol** adj bodily, corporeal, corporal
**corgan, côr-gân** (-au) nf chant
**corganu** vb chant
**corgi** (-gwn) nm cur, corgi
**corgimwch** (-ychiaid) nm prawn
**corhwyad** (-aid) nf teal; moorhen
**corlan** (-nau) nf fold
**corlannu** vb fold
**corn** (cyrn) nm horn; pipe, tube; roll; corn; stethoscope; ~ **gwddw(f)**, ~ **gwynt** windpipe; ~ **siarad** loudspeaker
**cornant** (-nentydd) nm brook, rill
**cornboer** nm phlegm
**cornchwiglen** (-chwiglod) nf lapwing
**cornel** (-i, -au) nf/m corner
**cornelu** vb corner
**cornicyll** (-od) nm lapwing, plover, peewit
**cornio** vb horn, butt; examine with a stethoscope
**corniog** adj horned
**cornwyd** (-ydd) nm boil, abscess, sore
**coron** (-au) nf crown
**coroni** vb crown ▷ nm coronation
**coroniad** nm coronation
**coronog** adj crowned

**corpws** nm (facetious) body
**corrach** (corachod) nm dwarf, pygmy
**corryn** (corynnod) nm spider
**cors** (-ydd) nf bog, swamp
**corsen** (-nau, cyrs) nf reed; stem, stalk; cane
**cortyn** (-nau) nm cord, rope
**corun** (-au) nm crown of the head; tonsure
**corwg(l)** (-yg(l)au) nm coracle
**corws** nm chorus
**corwynt** (-oedd) nm whirlwind
**cosb** (-au) nf punishment, penalty; **~ ddihenydd** capital punishment
**cosbadwy** adj punishable
**cosbedigaeth** nf punishment
**cosbi** vb punish
**cosbol** adj punitive, penal
**cosbwr** (-wyr) nm punisher
**cosfa** (-feydd) nf itch, itching; thrashing
**cosi** vb scratch, itch ▷ nm itching
**cosmetigau** npl cosmetics
**cosmig** adj cosmic
**cost** (-au) nf cost, expense
**costiad** (-au) nm costing
**costio** vb cost
**costiwm** (-tiymau) nm/f costume
**costog** (-ion) nm mastiff; cur ▷ adj surly
**costowci** (-cwn) nm mastiff, mongrel
**costrel** (-au, -i) nf bottle
**costrelaid** (-eidiau) nf bottleful
**costrelu** vb bottle
**costus** adj costly, expensive
**cosyn** (-nau, -nod) nm a cheese
**côt, cot** (cotiau) nf coat
**cotwm** nm cotton
**cowlas** (-au) nm/f bay of building; hay-mow
**cownter** (-au, -i) nm counter
**cowntio** vb count, account, esteem
**crac** (-iau) nm crack
**cracio** vb crack
**craciog** adj cracked

**crach** npl (nf -en) scabs ▷ adj scabby; petty; **-ach** npl snobs
**crachboer** nm phlegm
**crachfardd** (-feirdd) nm poetaster
**crachfeddyg** (-on) nm quack doctor
**crachfonheddwr** (-wyr) nm snob
**crafangio, -u** vb claw, grab
**crafanc** (-angau) nf claw; talon; clutch
**crafiad** (-au) nm scratch
**crafog** adj cutting, sarcastic
**crafu** vb scrape; scratch ▷ nm itch
**crafwr** (-wyr) nm scraper
**craff** adj close; keen; sagacious ▷ nm hold, grip
**craffter** nm keenness, sagacity
**craffu** vb look closely, observe intently
**craffus** adj keen, sagacious
**cragen** (cregyn) nf shell
**crai** adj new, fresh, raw
**craidd** (creiddiau) nm middle, centre
**craig** (creigiau) nf rock
**crair** (creiriau) nm relic
**craith** (creithiau) nf scar
**cramen** (-nau) nf crust, scab
**cranc** (-od) nm crab
**crand** adj grand
**crandrwydd** nm grandeur, finery
**crap** (-iau) nm hold; smattering
**crapio** vb grapple; pick up
**cras** (creision) adj parched, dry; harsh
**crasiad** nm baking
**craslyd** adj harsh, grating
**craster** nm dryness; harshness
**crasu** vb parch, scorch; bake
**crau** (creuau) nm hole, eye, socket
**crau** nm/f blood, gore
**crau** (creuau) nm sty; stockade
**crawcian, crawcio** vb croak, caw
**crawen** (-nau) nf crust
**crawn** nm matter, pus
**crawni** vb gather, suppurate
**crawnllyd** adj purulent

**cread** nm creation
**creadigaeth (-au)** nf creation
**creadigol** adj creative
**creadur (-iaid)** nm creature; animal
**creadures (-au)** nf female creature
**creawdwr (-wyr)** nm creator
**crebach** adj shrunk, withered
**crebachlyd** adj crabbed, wrinkled
**crebachu** vb shrink, shrivel,
wrinkle, pucker
**crebwyll (-ion)** nm invention,
understanding, fancy
**crecian** vb cluck; crackle
**crechwen** nf loud laughter, guffaw
**crechwenu** vb laugh loud, guffaw
**cred (-au)** nf belief; trust; pledge,
troth
**credadun (credinwyr)** nm believer
**credadwy** adj credible
**crediniaeth** nf belief
**crediniol** adj believing
**credo (-au)** nm/f creed, belief
**credu** vb believe
**credwr (-wyr)** nm believer
**credyd (-on)** nm credit
**credydu** vb credit
**cref** adj f of **cryf**
**crefu** vb crave, beg, implore
**crefydd (-au)** nf religion
**crefydda** vb profess or practise
religion
**crefyddol** adj religious, pious
**crefyddolder** nm religiousness,
piety
**crefyddwr (-wyr)** nm religioner,
religionist
**crefft (-au)** nf handicraft, trade
**crefftus** adj skilled, workmanlike
**crefftwaith** nm craftwork
**crefftwr (-wyr)** nm craftsman
**cregyn** npl (nf cragen) shells
**creider** nm freshness
**creifion** npl scrapings
**creigiog** adj rocky
**creigiwr (-wyr)** nm quarryman
**creigle (-oedd)** nm rocky place
**creinio** vb wallow, lie or fall down;
cringe

**creision** npl flakes, crisps
**crempog (-au)** nf pancake
**crensio** vb grind (the teeth)
**crepach** adj numb ▷ nf numbness
**crest** nm crust, scurf
**Creta** nf Crete
**creu** vb create
**creulon** adj cruel
**creulondeb (-derau)** nm cruelty
**crëwr (crewyr)** nm creator
**crëyr (crehyrod)** nm heron
**cri (-au)** nm cry, clamour
**cri** adj new, fresh, raw; unleavened
**criafol, -en** nf mountain ash
**crib (-au)** nf/m comb, crest; ridge
**cribddeilio** vb grab, extort
**cribddeiliwr (-wyr)** nm
extortioner; speculator
**cribin (-iau)** nf/m rake; skinflint
**cribinio** vb rake
**cribo** vb comb; card
**criced** nm cricket
**cricedwr (-wyr)** nm cricketer
**crimog (-au)** nf, **crimp (-(i)au)**
nm shin
**crin** adj withered, sear, dry
**crino** vb wither, dry up
**crintach, -lyd** adj niggardly, stingy
**crintachrwydd** nm niggardliness
**crintachu** vb scrimp, skimp, stint
**crio** vb cry, weep
**cripio** vb scratch; climb, creep
**cris-groes** nf criss-cross
**crisial (-au)** nm, adj crystal
**crisialu** vb crystallise
**Cristion (-ogion), Cristnogion**
nm Christian
**Cristionogaeth** nf Christianity
**Cristionogol** adj Christian
**criw (-iau)** nm crew
**crïwr (-wyr)** nm crier
**crocbont (-ydd)** nf suspension
bridge
**crocbren (-ni)** nm/f gallows, gibbet
**crocbris (-iau)** nm exorbitant price
**croch** adj loud, vehement

**crochan** (-au) *nm* pot, cauldron
**crochanaid** (-eidiau) *nm* potful
**crochenydd** (-ion) *nm* potter
**crochenwaith** (-weithiau) *nm*
pottery
**croen** (crwyn) *nm* skin; hide;
peel, rind
**croendenau** *adj* thin-skinned
**croeni, -io** *vb* form skin, skin over
**croes** (-au) *nf* cross ▷ *nm* transept
**croes** (-ion) *adj* cross, contrary
**croesair** (-eiriau) *nm* crossword
**croesawgar** *adj* hospitable
**croesawiad** *nm* welcome,
reception
**croesawu** *vb* welcome
**croesawus** *adj* hospitable
**croesbren** (-nau) *nm/f* cross
**croesddweud** *vb* contradict
**croesfan** (-nau) *nf* crossing
**croesffordd** (-ffyrdd) *nf* crossroad
**croesgad** (-au) *nf* crusade
**croesgadwr** (-wyr) *nm* crusader
**croeshoeliad** *nm* crucifixion
**croeshoelio** *vb* crucify
**croesholi** *vb* cross-examine
**croesholiad** (-au) *nm* cross-
examination
**croesi** *vb* cross
**croeso** *nm* welcome
**croesymgroes** *adj* criss-cross;
vice-versa
**crofen** (-nau, -ni) *nf* rind, crust
**crog** (-au) *nf* cross, rood ▷ *adj*
hanging
**crogi** *vb* hang, suspend
**croglath** (-au) *nf* springe, snare,
gibbet
**Croglith** *nm/f*: **Dydd Gwener y**
**Groglith** Good Friday
**croglofft** (-ydd, -au) *nf* garret;
rood-loft
**crogwr** (-wyr) *nm* hangman
**cronglwyd** (-ydd) *nf*: **tan fy**
**nghronglwyd** under my roof
**crombil** (-iau) *nf* crop; gizzard;
bowels

**cromen** (-ni, -nau) *nf* dome
**cromfach** (-au) *nf* bracket,
parenthesis
**cromlech** (-au, -i) *nf* cromlech
**cromosom** (-au) *nm* chromosome
**cron** *adj f of* **crwn**
**cronfa** (-feydd) *nf* reservoir; fund
**cronicl** (-au) *nm* chronicle
**croniclo** *vb* chronicle
**cronnell** (cronellau) *nf* sphere,
globe
**cronni** *vb* collect, hoard; dam
**cronolegol** *adj* chronological
**cropian** *vb* creep, crawl, grope
**crosiet** (-au, -i) *nm* crotchet
**croth** (-au) *nf* womb; calf (*of leg*)
**croyw** *adj* clear, plain, distinct; fresh
**croywder** *nm* clearness; freshness
**croywi** *vb* clear; freshen
**crud** (-au) *nm* cradle
**crug** (-iau) *nm* hillock; tumulus;
heap; multitude; abscess, blister
**cruglwyth** (-i) *nm* heap, pile
**cruglwytho** *vb* heap, pile up;
overload
**crugo** *vb* fester, vex, plague
**crwban** (-od) *nm* tortoise, turtle
**crwca** *adj* crooked, bowed, bent
**crwm** (*f* crom) *adj* convex, curved,
bowed
**crwn** (*f* cron) *adj* round; complete
**crwner** (-iaid) *nm* coroner
**crwsâd** (-adau) *nm/f* crusade
**crwst** (crystiau) *nm* crust
**crwt** (cryts) *nm* boy, lad
**crwth** (crythau) *nm* crowd, fiddle;
purring; hump
**crwybr** *nm* honeycomb; mist;
hoarfrost
**crwydr** *nm* wandering; **ar grwydr**
astray
**crwydro** *vb* wander, stray, roam
**crwydrol, crwydrus** *adj*
wandering
**crwydrwr** (-wyr) *nm* wanderer,
rover
**crwydryn** (-riaid) *nm* vagrant,

tramp

**crwys** *nf, npl* cross, crucifix; **dan ei grwys** laid out for burial

**crybwyll** *vb* mention ▷ **(-ion)** *nm* mention

**crybwylliad** *nm* mention, notice

**crych** *adj* rippling; curly; quavering ▷ **(-au)** *nm* crease, ripple, wrinkle

**crychlais** (-leisiau) *nm* trill, tremolo

**crychlyd** *adj* wrinkled, puckered

**crychnaid** (-neidiau) *nf* leap, gambol

**crychneidio** *vb* skip, frisk

**crychni** *nm* curliness; wrinkle

**crychu** *vb* wrinkle, pucker; ruffle, ripple

**cryd** (-iau) *nm* shivering; fever; ague

**crydd** (-ion) *nm* cobbler, shoemaker

**crydda** *vb* cobble

**cryf** (f cref) *adj* strong

**cryfder, -dwr** *nm* strength

**cryfhaol** *adj* strengthening

**cryfhau** *vb* strengthen; grow strong

**cryg** (f creg) *adj* hoarse

**cryglyd** *adj* hoarse, raucous

**crygni** *nm* hoarseness

**crygu** *vb* hoarsen

**cryman** (-au) *nm* reaping-hook, sickle

**crymanwr** (-wyr) *nm* reaper

**crymu** *vb* bow, bend, stoop

**cryn** *adj* considerable, much

**crŷn, cryn** *nm, adj* shivering

**crynder** *nm* roundness

**cryndod** *nm* trembling, shivering

**crynedig** *adj* trembling, tremulous

**crynfa** (-feydd) *nf* tremble, tremor

**crynhoad** (-noadau) *nm* collection, digest

**crynhoi** *vb* gather together, collect

**cryno** *adj* compact; neat, tidy

**crynodeb** (-au) *nm* summary

**crynswth** *nm* mass, bulk, whole

**crynu** *vb* shiver, tremble, quake

**Crynwr** (-wyr) *nm* Quaker

**crys** (-au) *nm* shirt

**crysbaid** (-beisiau) *nf* jacket, jerkin

**crystyn** (crystiau) *nm* crust

**crythor** (-ion) *nm* fiddler, violinist

**cryw** (-iau) *nm* creel; weir

**cu** *adj* dear, fond, kind

**cuchio** *vb* scowl, frown

**cuchiog** *adj* scowling, frowning

**cudyll** (-od) *nm* hawk

**cudyn** (-nau) *nm* lock (of hair), tuft

**cudd** *adj* hidden, concealed

**cuddfa** (-feydd) *nf* hiding-place; hoard

**cuddiad** *nm* hiding

**cuddiedig** *adj* hidden, concealed

**cuddio** *vb* hide, conceal

**cufydd** (-au) *nm* cubit

**cul** (-ion) *adj* narrow, lean

**culfor** (-oedd) *nm* strait

**culhau** *vb* narrow; grow lean

**culni** *nm* narrowness

**cun** *adj* dear, beloved; lovely

**cunnog** (cunogau) *nf* pail

**cur** *nm* throb, ache, pain; care, trouble

**curad** (-iaid) *nm* curate

**curadiaeth** (-au) *nf* curacy

**curfa** (-feydd) *nf* beating, flogging

**curiad** (-au) *nm* beat, throb, pulse

**curio** *vb* pine, waste

**curlaw** *nm* pelting rain

**curn** (-au), **curnen** (-nau) *nf* mound, core, rick

**curnennu** *vb* heap, stack

**curo** *vb* beat, strike, knock; throb; clap

**curwr** (-wyr) *nm* beater

**curyll** (-od) *nm* hawk

**cusan** (-au) *nf/m* kiss

**cusanu** *vb* kiss

**cut** (-iau) *nm* hovel, shed, sty

**cuwch** (cuchiau) *nm* scowl, frown

**cwafrio** *vb* quaver, trill

**cwar** (-rau) *nm* quarry

**cwb** (cybiau) *nm* kennel, coop, sty

**cwbl** *adj, nm* all, whole, total

**cwblhad** *nm* fulfilment

**cwblhau** vb fulfil, complete, finish
**cwcer** (-au) nm cooker
**cwcw** nf cuckoo
**cwcwallt** (-iaid) nm cuckold
**cwcwalltu** vb cuckold
**cwcwll** (cycyllau) nm hood, cowl
**cwch** (cychod) nm boat; hive; **~ gwyllt** speed boat
**cwd** (cydau) nm pouch, bag
**cweir** (-iau) nm thrashing, hiding
**cweryl** (-on) nm quarrel
**cweryla** vb quarrel
**cwerylgar** adj quarrelsome
**cwest** (-au) nm inquest
**cwestiwn** (-iynau) nm question
**cwestiynu** vb question
**cwffio** vb fight, box
**cwgn** (cygnau) nm knot; knuckle; joint
**cwilt** (-iau) nm quilt
**cwlbren** (-ni) nm bludgeon
**cwlff, -yn** (cylffiau) nm chunk
**cwlwm** see **clwm**
**cwlltwr** (cylltyrau) nm coulter
**cwm** (cymau, cymoedd) nm valley
**cwman** nm rump; stoop; churn
**cwmanu** vb stoop
**cwmni** (-ïau, -ïoedd) nm company
**cwmnïaeth** nf companionship
**cwmpas** (-oedd) nm round; **wmpasgwmpas** about
**cwmpasog** adj round about, circuitous
**cwmpasu** vb round, wind, surround
**cwmpawd** (-odau) nm compass
**cwmpeini, cwmpni** nm company
**cwmwd** (cymydau) nm commot
**cwmwl** (cymylau) nm cloud
**cŵn** see **ci**
**cwndid** (-au) nm song, carol
**cwningen** (-ingod) nf rabbit
**cwnsel** (-au, -oedd, -i) nm council; counsel, advice, secret
**cwnsela** vb counsel
**cwnsler** (-iaid) nm counsellor
**cwnstabl** (-iaid) nm constable

**cworwm** nm quorum
**cwota** (-au) nm quota
**cwpan** (-au) nm/f cup, goblet; chalice
**cwpanaid** (-eidiau) nm/f cupful
**cwpl** (cyplau) nm couple; tie beam
**cwplâd, cwpláu** see **cwblhad, cwblhau**
**cwpled** (-i, -au) nm couplet
**cwplws** (cyplysau) nm coupling; brace
**cwpwrdd** (cypyrddau) nm cupboard
**cwr** (cyrrau) nm edge, border, skirt
**cwrcwd** nm stooping; squatting
**cwrdd** (cyrddau) nm meeting
**cwrdd, cwrddyd** vb meet, touch
**cwrel** nm coral
**cwricwlwm** (cwricwla) nm curriculum
**cwrlid** (-au) nm coverlet
**cwrs** (cyrsiau) nm course; fit
**cwrt** (cyrtiau) nm court
**cwrtais** adj courteous
**cwrteisi, cwrteisrwydd** nm courtesy
**cwrw** (cyrfau) nm ale, beer
**cwrwg(l)** see **corwg(l)**
**cwsg** nm sleep
**cwsmer** (-iaid) nm customer
**cwsmeriaeth** nf custom
**cwstard** (-iau) nm custard
**cwstwm** (cystymau) nm custom, patronage
**cwt** (cytiau) nf/m tail, skirt, queue
**cwt** (cytiau) nm hut, sty
**cwta** adj short, curt
**cwter** (-i, -ydd) nf gutter, channel
**cwtogi** vb shorten, curtail
**cwthr** (cythrau) nm anus, rectum
**cwthwm** (cythymau) nm puff of wind, storm
**cwymp** (-au) nm fall, tumble
**cwympo** vb fall; fell
**cwyn** (-ion) nm/f complaint, plaint
**cwynfan** vb complain, lament
**cwynfanllyd** adj querulous

**cwynfanus** *adj* plaintive, mournful
**cwyno** *vb* complain, lament
**cwyr** *nm* wax
**cwyro** *vb* wax
**cwys** (-au, -i) *nf* furrow-slice, furrow
**cybôl** *nm* nonsense, rubbish
**cybolfa** *nf* hotchpotch, medley
**cyboli** *vb* muddle; talk nonsense;
mess, bother
**cybydd** (-ion) *nm* miser, niggard
**cybydda** *vb* stint, hoard
**cybydd-dod, -dra** *nm* miserliness
**cybyddlyd** *adj* miserly
**cycyllog** *adj* hooded, cowled
**cychaid** (-eidiau) *nm* boatful;
hiveful
**cychwr** (-wyr) *nm* boatman
**cychwyn** *vb* rise, stir, start
**cychwynfa** *nf* start, starting-point
**cychwyniad** (-au) *nm* start,
beginning
**cyd** *adj* joint, united, common;
fellow ▷ *prefix* together
**cydadrodd** *vb* to recite together
**cydaid** (-eidiau) *nm* bagful
**cydbwysedd** *nm* balance
**cyd-destun** (-au) *nm* context
**cydfod** *nm* agreement, concord
**cydfodolaeth** *nf* coexistence
**cydfyned** *vb* go with, concur, agree
**cydfyw** *vb* cohabit
**cydffurfio** *vb* conform
**cydgordio** *vb* agree, harmonize
**cydgwmni** (-ïau) *nm* consortium
**cydiedig** *adj* adjoined
**cydio** *vb* join; bite; take hold
**cydnabod** *vb* acknowledge ▷ *nm*
acquaintance
**cydnabyddiaeth** *nf*
acquaintance; recognition
**cydnabyddus** *adj* acquainted;
familiar
**cydnaws** *adj* congenial
**cydnerth** *adj* well set
**cydol** *nf/m, adj* whole
**cydradd** *adj* equal
**cydraddoldeb** *nm* equality

**cyd-rhwng** *prep* between
**cydsyniad** *nm* consent
**cydsynio** *vb* consent
**cydwastad** *adj* level (with), even
**cydweddog** *adj* conjugal
**cydweddu** *vb* accord, agree
**cydweithfa** (-feydd) *nf* co-
operative
**cydweithrediad** *nm* co-operation
**cydweithredol** *adj* co-operative
**cydweithredu** *vb* co-operate
**cydweled** *vb* agree
**cydwladol** *adj* international
**cyd-wladwr** (-wyr) *nm* compatriot
**cydwybod** (-au) *nf* conscience
**cydwybodol** *adj* conscientious
**cydwybodolrwydd** *nm*
conscientiousness
**cydymaith** (cymdeithion) *nm*
companion
**cydymdeimlad** *nm* sympathy
**cydymdeimlo** *vb* sympathize
**cydymffurfiad** *nm* conformity
**cydymffurfio** *vb* conform
**cydymgais** *nm* competition,
rivalry, joint effort
**cydymgeisydd** (-wyr) *nm* rival
**cyddwysiad** (-au) *nm*
condensation
**cyfadran** (-nau) *nf* faculty (*in
college*), period (*in music*)
**cyfaddas** *adj* fit, suitable,
convenient
**cyfaddasiad** (-au) *nm* adaptation
**cyfaddaster** *nm* fitness, suitability
**cyfaddasu** *vb* fit, adapt
**cyfaddawd** (-odau) *nm*
compromise
**cyfaddawdu** *vb* compromise
**cyfaddef** *vb* confess, own, admit
**cyfaddefiad** (-au) *nm* confession,
admission
**cyfaenad** *nm, adj* harmonious song
**cyfagos** *adj* near, adjacent,
neighbouring
**cyfaill** (-eillion) *nm* friend
**cyfair** (-eiriau) *nm* acre

**cyfair, -er** *nm* direction; **ar** for; opposite
**cyfalaf** *nm* capital
**cyfalafiaeth** *nf* capitalism
**cyfalafol** *adj* capitalistic
**cyfalafwr (-wyr)** *nm* capitalist
**cyfamod (-au)** *nm* covenant
**cyfamodi** *vb* covenant
**cyfamodol** *adj* federal; covenanted
**cyfamodwr (-wyr)** *nm* covenanter
**cyfamser** *nm* meantime
**cyfamserol** *adj* timely; synchronous
**cyfan** *adj, nm* whole
**cyfandir (-oedd)** *nm* continent
**cyfandirol** *adj* continental
**cyfanfor (-oedd)** *nm* main sea, ocean
**cyfanfyd** *nm* whole world, universe
**cyfangorff** *nm* whole, bulk, mass
**cyfan gwbl** *adj*: **yn gyfan gwbl** altogether, complete
**cyfanheddol** *adj* habitable, inhabited
**cyfanheddu** *vb* dwell, inhabit
**cyfannedd** *adj* inhabited ▷ **(-anheddau)** *nf* inhabited place, habitation
**cyfannol** *adj* integrated, integral
**cyfannu** *vb* make whole, complete
**cyfanrwydd** *nm* wholeness, entirety
**cyfansawdd** *adj* composite, compound
**cyfansoddi** *vb* compose, constitute
**cyfansoddiad (-au)** *nm* composition; constitution
**cyfansoddiadol** *adj* constitutional
**cyfansoddwr (-wyr)** *nm* composer
**cyfansoddyn (-ion)** *nm* constituent, compound
**cyfanswm (-symiau)** *nm* total
**cyfantoledd (-au)** *nm* equilibrium
**cyfanwaith (-weithiau)** *nm* complete composition, whole

**cyfarch** *vb* greet, salute, address
**cyfarchiad (-au)** *nm* greeting, salutation
**cyfaredd (-ion)** *nf* charm, spell
**cyfareddol** *adj* enchanting
**cyfareddu** *vb* charm, enchant
**cyfarfod** *vb* meet ▷ **(-ydd)** *nm* meeting
**cyfarfyddiad (-au)** *nm* meeting
**cyfarpar** *nm* provision, equipment; diet; **~ rhyfel** munitions of war
**cyfarparu** *vb* equip
**cyfartal** *adj* equal, even
**cyfartaledd** *nm* proportion, average
**cyfartalu** *vb* proportion, equalize
**cyfarth** *vb, nm* bark
**cyfarwydd** *adj* skilled; familiar ▷ **(-iaid)** *nm* storyteller
**cyfarwyddo** *vb* direct; become familiar
**cyfarwyddwr (-wyr)** *nm* director
**cyfarwyddyd (-iadau)** *nm* direction, instruction
**cyfatal** *adj* unsettled, hindering
**cyfateb** *vb* correspond, agree, tally
**cyfatebiaeth (-au)** *nf* correspondence, analogy
**cyfatebol** *adj* corresponding, proportionate
**cyfathrach (-au)** *nf* affinity; intercourse
**cyfathrachu** *vb* have intercourse
**cyfathrachwr (-wyr)** *nm* kinsman
**cyfathreb (-au)** *nm* communication
**cyfathrebu** *vb* communicate
**cyfddydd** *nm* day-break, dawn
**cyfeb, cyfebr** *adj* pregnant (of mare, ewe)
**cyfebol** *adj* in foal
**cyfeddach (-au)** *nf* carousal
**cyfeddachwr (-wyr)** *nm* carouser
**cyfeiliant** *nm* musical accompaniment
**cyfeilio** *vb* accompany
**cyfeiliorn** *nm* error; wandering,

lost (*person etc*); **ar gyfeiliorn** astray
**cyfeiliornad** (-au) *nm* error, heresy
**cyfeiliorni** *vb* err, stray
**cyfeiliornus** *adj* erroneous, mistaken
**cyfeilydd** (-ion) *nm* accompanist
**cyfeillach** (-au) *nf* fellowship; fellowship-meeting
**cyfeillachu** *vb* associate
**cyfeilles** (-au) *nf* female friend
**cyfeillgar** *adj* friendly
**cyfeillgarwch** *nm* friendship
**cyfeiriad** (-au) *nm* direction; reference; (postal) address
**cyfeiriannu** *nm* orienteering
**cyfeirio** *vb* point; direct; refer; address (letter)
**cyfeirnod** (-au) *nm* mark of reference; aim; direct (in music)
**cyfeirydd** (-ion) *nm* indicator, guide
**cyfenw** (-au) *nm* surname; namesake
**cyfenwi** *vb* surname
**cyfer** *nm*: **ar gyfer** for; opposite
**cyferbyn** *adj* opposite
**cyferbyniad** (-au) *nm* contrast
**cyferbyniol** *adj* opposing, opposite, contrasting
**cyferbynnu** *vb* contrast, compare
**cyfethol** *vb* co-opt
**cyfiaith** *adj* of the same language
**cyfiawn** *adj* just, righteous
**cyfiawnder** (-au) *nm* justice, righteousness
**cyfiawnhad** *nm* justification
**cyfiawnhau** *vb* justify
**cyfieithiad** (-au) *nm* translation, version
**cyfieithu** *vb* translate, interpret
**cyfieithydd** (-wyr) *nm* translator, interpreter
**cyfisol** *adj* of the present month, instant
**cyflafan** (-au) *nf* outrage; massacre
**cyflafareddiad** *nm* arbitration
**cyflafareddu** *vb* arbitrate

**cyflafareddwr** (-wyr) *nm* arbitrator
**cyflaith** *nm* toffee
**cyflawn** *adj* full, complete
**cyflawnder** *nm* fullness; abundance
**cyflawni** *vb* fulfil, perform, commit
**cyflawniad** (-au) *nm* fulfilment, performance
**cyfle** (-oedd) *nm* place; chance, opportunity
**cyfled** *adj* as broad as
**cyflegr** (-au) *nm* gun, cannon, battery
**cyflegru** *vb* bombard
**cyflenwad** (-au) *nm* supply
**cyflenwi** *vb* supply
**cyfleu** *vb* place, set; convey
**cyfleus** *adj* convenient
**cyfleustra** (-terau) *nm* opportunity, convenience
**cyflin** *adj* parallel
**cyfliw** *adj* of the same colour
**cyflo** *adj* in calf
**cyflog** (-au) *nm/f* hire, wage, wages
**cyflogaeth** *nf* employment
**cyflogedig** (-ion) *nm* employee
**cyflogi** *vb* hire; engage in service
**cyflogwr** (-wyr) *nm* hirer, employer
**cyflwr** (-lyrau) *nm* condition; case
**cyflwyniad** *nm* presentation; dedication
**cyflwyno** *vb* present; dedicate
**cyflwynydd** (-ion) *nm* compère, presenter
**cyflychwr, -wyr** *nm* evening twilight, dusk
**cyflym** *adj* quick, fast, swift
**cyflymder, -dra** *nm* swiftness, speed
**cyflymu** *vb* speed, accelerate
**cyflynu** *vb* stick together
**cyflyru** *vb* condition
**cyflythreniad** (-au) *nm* alliteration
**cyfnerthu** *vb* confirm; aid, help
**cyfnerthydd** (-ion, -wyr) *nm*

strengthener, booster

**cyfnesaf (-iaid, -eifiaid)** *nm/f* next of kin, kinsman ▷ *adj* next, nearest

**cyfnewid** *vb* change, exchange

**cyfnewidfa (-oedd, -feydd)** *nf* exchange

**cyfnewidiad (-au)** *nm* change, alteration

**cyfnewidiol** *adj* changeable

**cyfnewidiwr (-wyr)** *nm* changer, trader

**cyfnither (-oedd)** *nf* female cousin

**cyfnod (-au)** *nm* period

**cyfnodol** *adj* periodic(al); ▷ **-yn (-ion)** *nm* periodical publication

**cyfnos** *nm* evening twilight, dusk

**cyfochredd** *nm* parallelism

**cyfochrog** *adj* parallel

**cyfodi** *vb* rise, arise; raise

**cyfodiad** *nm* rise, rising

**cyfoed** *adj* contemporary, of the same age ▷ **(-ion)** *nm* contemporaries

**cyfoes** *adj* contemporary

**cyfoesi** *vb* be contemporary

**cyfoeswr (-wyr)** *nm* contemporary

**cyfoeth** *nm* power; riches, wealth

**cyfoethog** *adj* powerful; rich, wealthy

**cyfoethogi** *vb* make or grow rich

**cyfog** *nm* sickness

**cyfogi** *vb* vomit

**cyfor** *nm* flood, abundance; rim, brim, edge ▷ *adj* entire, brim-full

**cyforiog** *adj* brim-full, overflowing

**cyfosodiad** *nm* apposition

**cyfradd (-au)** *nf* rate; **~ llog** rate of interest ▷ *adj* of equal rank

**cyfraid (-reidiau)** *nm* necessity

**cyfraith (-reithiau)** *nf* law

**cyfran (-nau)** *nf* part, portion, share

**cyfranc (-rangau)** *nf/m* meeting; combat; incident; story, tale

**cyfrandaliad (-au)** *nm* share

**cyfrandaliwr (-wyr)** *nm* shareholder

**cyfraniad (-au)** *nm* contribution

**cyfrannog** *adj* participating, partaking

**cyfrannol** *adj* contributing

**cyfrannu** *vb* contribute; impart

**cyfrannwr (-anwyr)** *nm* contributor

**cyfranogi** *vb* participate, partake

**cyfranogwr (-wyr)** *nm* partaker

**cyfredol** *adj* current, concurrent

**cyfreithio** *vb* go to law, litigate

**cyfreithiol** *adj* legal

**cyfreithiwr (-wyr)** *nm* lawyer

**cyfreithlon** *adj* lawful, legitimate

**cyfreithlondeb** *nm* lawfulness

**cyfreithloni** *vb* legalize; justify

**cyfreithus** *adj* legitimate

**cyfres (-i)** *nf* series

**cyfresol** *adj* serial

**cyfresu** *vb* serialise

**cyfresymiad (-au)** *nm* syllogism

**cyfresymu** *vb* syllogise

**cyfrgolli** *vb* lose utterly; damn

**cyfrif** *vb* count, reckon; account; impute ▷ **(-on)** *nm* account, reckoning

**cyfrifeg** *nm/f* accountancy

**cyfrifiad (-au)** *nm* counting; census

**cyfrifiadur (-on)** *nm* computer

**cyfrifiadureg** *nf* computer science

**cyfrifianell** *nf* calculator

**cyfrifol** *adj* of repute; responsible

**cyfrifoldeb (-au)** *nm* responsibility

**cyfrifydd (-ion)** *nm* statistician, accountant

**cyfrin** *adj* secret, subtle

**cyfrinach (-au)** *nf* secret

**cyfrinachol** *adj* secret, private, confidential

**cyfrinfa** *nf* lodge of friendly society or trade union

**cyfrin-gyngor (-nghorau)** *nm* privy council

**cyfriniaeth** *nf* mystery; mysticism

**cyfriniol** *adj* mysterious, mystic

**cyfriniwr (-wyr)** *nm* mystic

**cyfrodedd** *adj* twisted, twined

**cyfrodeddu** *vb* twist, twine

**cyfrol** (-au) *nf* volume
**cyfrwng** (-ryngau) *nm* medium, means
**cyfrwy** (-au) *nm* saddle
**cyfrwyo** *vb* saddle
**cyfrwys** *adj* cunning
**cyfrwystra** *nm* cunning
**cyfrwywr** (-wyr) *nm* saddler
**cyfryngdod** *nm* mediation, intercession; mediatorship
**cyfryngiad** *nm* mediation; intervention
**cyfryngol** *adj* mediatorial
**cyfryngu** *vb* mediate; intervene
**cyfryngwr** (-wyr) *nm* mediator
**cyfryngwriaeth** *nf* mediatorship
**cyfryw** *adj* like, such
**cyfuchlinedd** (-au) *nm* contour
**cyfuchliniau** *npl* contours
**cyfundeb** (-au) *nm* union; connexion
**cyfundebol** *adj* connexional; denominational
**cyfundrefn** (-au) *nf* system
**cyfundrefnol** *adj* systematic
**cyfundrefnu** *vb* systematize
**cyfuniad** (-au) *nm* combination
**cyfuno** *vb* unite, combine
**cyfunol** *adj* united
**cyfunrywiol** *adj* homosexual
**cyfuwch** *adj* as high
**cyfweld** *vb* interview
**cyfweliad** (-au) *nm* interview
**cyfwerth** *adj* equivalent
**cyfwng** (-yngau) *nm* space; interval
**cyfwrdd** *vb* meet
**cyfyng** *adj* narrow, confined
**cyfyngder** (-au) *nm* trouble, distress
**cyfyngdra** *nm* narrowness; distress
**cyfyngedig** *adj* confined, restricted, limited
**cyfyng-gyngor** *nm* perplexity
**cyfyngu** *vb* narrow, confine, limit
**cyfyl** *nm* neighbourhood; **ar ei gyfyl** near him

**cyfyrder** (-dyr) *nm* second cousin
**cyfystlys** *adj* side by side
**cyfystyr** *adj* synonymous
**cyfystyron** *npl* synonyms
**cyff** (-ion) *nm* stock
**cyffaith** (-ffeithiau) *nm* confection
**cyffelyb** *adj* like, similar
**cyffelybiaeth** (-au) *nf* likeness, similitude
**cyffelybiaethol** *adj* figurative
**cyffelybrwydd** *nm* likeness, similarity
**cyffelybu** *vb* liken, compare
**cyffes** (-ion) *nf* confession
**cyffesgell** (-oedd) *nf* confessional
**cyffesu** *vb* confess
**cyffeswr** (-wyr), **-ydd** (-ion) *nm* confessor
**cyffin** (-iau, -ydd) *nf/m* border, confine
**cyffindir** (-oedd) *nm* frontier, march
**cyffio** *vb* stiffen; fetter, shackle; beat
**cyffion** *npl* stocks
**cyffordd** (-ffyrdd) *nf* junction
**cyffredin** *adj* common; general
**cyffredinedd** *nm* mediocrity, banality
**cyffredinol** *adj* general, universal
**cyffredinoli** *vb* universalize, generalize
**cyffredinolrwydd** *nm* universality
**cyffredinwch** *nm* commonness
**cyffro** (-adau) *nm* motion, stir; excitement
**cyffroi** *vb* move, excite; provoke
**cyffrous** *adj* exciting; excited
**cyffur** (-iau) *nm/f* ingredient, drug
**cyffuriwr** (-wyr) *nm* apothecary, druggist
**cyffwrdd** *vb* meet, touch
**cyffylog** (-od) *nm* woodcock
**cyffyrddiad** (-au) *nm* touch, contact
**cyffyrddus** *adj* comfortable
**cygnog** *adj* knotted, gnarled

**cyngaf, cyngaw** *nm* burdock; burs
**cyngan** *adj* suitable, harmonious
**cynganeddol** *adj* in *cynghanedd*
**cynganeddu** *vb* form *cynghanedd*; harmonize
**cynganeddwr (-wyr)** *nm* writer of *cynghanedd*
**cyngaws (cynghawsau, -ion)** *nm* lawsuit, action; trial; battle
**cyngerdd (-ngherddau)** *nm/f* concert
**cynghanedd (cynganeddion)** *nf* music, harmony; Welsh metrical alliteration
**cynghori** *vb* counsel, advise; exhort
**cynghorwr (-wyr)** *nm* councillor; counsellor; exhorter
**cynghrair (-eiriau)** *nm/f* alliance, league
**cynghreiriad (-iaid)** *nm* confederate, ally
**cynghreirio** *vb* league, confederate
**cynghreiriwr (-wyr)** *nm* confederate, ally
**cyngor (-nghorion)** *nm* counsel, advice ▷ **(-nghorau)** *nm* council; **C~ Bro** Community Council; **C~ Tref** Town Council; **C~ Sir** County Council
**cyngres (-au, -i)** *nf* congress
**cyngresydd (-wyr)** *nm* congressman
**cyngwystl (-(i)on)** *nm/f* wager, pledge
**cyhoedd** *adj, nm* public
**cyhoeddi** *vb* publish, announce
**cyhoeddiad (-au)** *nm* publication; announcement; (preaching) engagement
**cyhoeddus** *adj* public
**cyhoeddusrwydd** *nm* publicity
**cyhoeddwr (-wyr)** *nm* publisher
**cyhuddiad (-au)** *nm* accusation, charge
**cyhuddo** *vb* accuse, charge
**cyhuddwr (-wyr)** *nm* accuser
**cyhwfan** *vb* wave, heave

**cyhyd** *adj* as long, so long
**cyhydedd** *nm* equator
**cyhydeddol** *adj* equatorial, equinoctial
**cyhyr (-au)** *nm* flesh, muscle
**cyhyrog** *adj* muscular
**cylch (-au, oedd)** *nm* round, circle, sphere, hoop
**cylchdaith (-deithiau)** *nf* circuit
**cylchdro (-eon, -adau)** *nm* orbit
**cylchdroi** *vb* rotate, revolve
**cylched (-au)** *nm* coverlet, blanket
**cylchedd (-au)** *nm/f* compass, circle, circuit
**cylchgrawn (-gronau)** *nm* magazine
**cylchlythyr (-au)** *nm* circular
**cylchredeg** *vb* circulate
**cylchrediad** *nm* circulation
**cylchres (-i)** *nf* round, rota
**cylchwyl (-iau)** *nf* anniversary, festival
**cylchynol** *adj* surrounding
**cylchynu** *vb* surround, encompass
**cylion** *npl* (*nm* -yn, *nf* -en) flies, gnats
**cylymu** *vb* knot, tie
**cyll** *npl* (*nf* collen) hazel-trees
**cylla (-on)** *nm* stomach
**cyllell (-yll)** *nf* knife
**cyllid (-au)** *nm* revenue, income
**cyllideb (-au)** *nf* budget
**cyllidol** *adj* financial, fiscal
**cyllidwr (-wyr), cyllidydd (-ion)** *nm* taxgatherer, revenue or excise officer, financier
**cymaint** *adj* as big, as much, as many; so big *etc*
**cymal (-au)** *nm* joint; (*Gram*) clause
**cymalwst** *nf* rheumatism
**cymanfa (-oedd)** *nf* assembly; festival
**cymantoledd (-au)** *nm* equilibrium
**cymanwlad** *nf* commonwealth
**cymar (-heiriaid)** *nm* fellow, partner

**cymathiad** *nm* assimilation
**cymathu** *vb* assimilate
**cymdeithas** (-au) *nf* society, association; **C~ yr laith Gymraeg** The Welsh Language Society
**cymdeithaseg** *nf/m* sociology
**cymdeithasegol** *adj* sociological
**cymdeithasgar** *adj* sociable
**cymdeithasol** *adj* social
**cymdeithasu** *vb* associate
**cymdogaeth** (-au) *nf* neighbourhood
**cymdogol** *adj* neighbourly
**cymedr** (-au) *nm* mean (*maths*), average
**cymedrol** *adj* moderate, temperate
**cymedroldeb** *nm* moderation, temperance
**cymedroli** *vb* moderate
**cymedrolwr** (-wyr) *nm* moderator; moderate drinker
**cymell** *vb* urge, press, persuade, induce
**cymen** *adj* wise, skilful, neat, becoming
**cymer** (-au) *nm* confluence
**cymeradwy** *adj* acceptable, approved, commendable
**cymeradwyaeth** *nf* approval; applause
**cymeradwyo** *vb* approve; recommend
**cymeradwyol** *adj* commendatory
**cymeriad** (-au) *nm* character, reputation
**cymesur** *adj* proportionate, symmetrical
**cymesuredd** *nm* proportion, symmetry
**cymesurol** *adj* commensurate, proportionate
**cymhareb** (cymarebau) *nf* ratio
**cymhariaeth** (cymariaethau) *nf* comparison
**cymharol** *adj* comparative
**cymharu** *vb* pair; compare
**cymhathu** *vb* assimilate

**cymhelliad** (-hellion) *nm* motive, inducement
**cymhelliant** (-nnau) *nm* motivation
**cymhendod** *nm* knowledge; proficiency; tidiness; eloquence; affection
**cymhennu** *vb* put in order, trim; scold, reprove
**cymhercyn** *adj* limping, infirm ▷ *nm* valetudinarian
**cymhleth** (-au) *adj* complex, complicated
**cymhlethdod** (-au) *nm* complexity
**cymhlethu** *vb* complicate
**cymhorthdal** (cymorthdaloedd) *nm* subsidy, grant
**cymhwysiad** *nm* application, adjustment
**cymhwyso** *vb* apply, adjust
**cymhwyster** (cymwysterau) *nm* fitness, suitability; (*pl*) qualifications
**cymod** *nm* reconciliation
**cymodi** *vb* reconcile; be reconciled
**cymodol** *adj* reconciliatory, propitiatory
**cymodwr** (-wyr) *nm* reconciler
**cymon** *adj* orderly, tidy; seemly
**cymorth** *vb* assist, aid, help ▷ *nm* assistance, aid, help
**Cymraeg** *nf/m*, *adj* Welsh
**Cymraes** *nf* Welshwoman
**cymrawd** (-odyr) *nm* comrade, fellow
**Cymreictod** *nm* Welshness
**Cymreig** *adj* Welsh
**Cymreigaidd** *adj* Welshy
**Cymreiges** (-au) *nf* Welshwoman
**Cymreigio** *vb* translate into Welsh
**Cymreigiwr** (-wyr) *nm* one versed or skilled in Welsh; Welsh-speaking Welshman
**Cymro** (Cymry) *nm* Welshman
**cymrodedd** *nm* arbitration; compromise
**cymrodeddu** *vb* compromise,

reconcile

**cymrodor** (-ion) *nm* consociate, fellow

**cymrodoriaeth** *nf* fellowship

**Cymru** *nf* Wales

**cymrwd** *nm* mortar, plaster

**Cymry** *see* **Cymro**

**cymryd** *vb* take, accept; **~ ar** pretend

**cymun, -deb** *nm* communion, fellowship

**cymuned** *nf* community

**cymunedol** *adj* community

**cymuno** *vb* commune

**cymunwr** (-wyr) *nm* communicant

**cymwy** (-au) *nm* affliction

**cymwynas** (-au) *nf* kindness, favour

**cymwynasgar** *adj* obliging, kind

**cymwynasgarwch** *nm* obligingness, kindness

**cymwynaswr** (-wyr) *nm* benefactor

**cymwys** *adj* fit, proper, suitable; exact

**cymwysedig** *adj* applied

**cymwysiadol** *adj* applicable

**cymydog** (cymdogion, *f* cymdoges) *nm* neighbour

**cymylog** *adj* cloudy, clouded

**cymylu** *vb* cloud, dim, obscure

**cymyndod** *nm* committal

**cymynnu** *vb* bequeath

**cymynrodd** (-ion) *nf* legacy, bequest

**cymynroddi** *vb* bequeath

**cymynu** *vb* hew, fell

**cymynwr** (-wyr) *nm* hewer, feller

**cymysg** *adj* mixed

**cymysgedd** *nm/f* mixture

**cymysgfa** *nf* mixture, medley, hotchpotch

**cymysgliw** *adj* motley

**cymysglyd** *adj* muddled, confused

**cymysgryw** *adj* mongrel; heterogeneous

**cymysgu** *vb* mix, blend; confuse

**cymysgwch** *nm* mixture, jumble

**cymysgwr** (-wyr) *nm* mixer, blender

**cyn** *prefix* before, previous, first, former, pre-, ex-

**cyn** *adv*: **~ wynned â** as white as

**cŷn** (cynion) *nm* wedge, chisel

**cynadledda** *vb* meet in conference

**cynaeafu** *vb* harvest

**cynamserol** *adj* premature, untimely

**cynaniad** *nm* pronunciation

**cynanu** *vb* pronounce

**cyndad** (-au) *nm* forefather, ancestor

**cynderfynol** *adj* semi-final

**cyndyn** *adj* stubborn, obstinate

**cyndynnu** *vb* be obstinate

**cyndynrwydd** *nm* stubborness, obstinacy

**cynddaredd** *nf* madness; rabies

**cynddeiriog** *adj* mad, rabid

**cynddeiriogi** *vb* madden, enrage

**cynddeiriogrwydd** *nm* rage, fury

**cynddrwg** *adj* as bad

**cynddydd** *nm* day-break, dawn

**cynefin** *adj* acquainted, accustomed, familiar ▷ *nm* haunt, habitat

**cynefindra** *nm* use, familarity

**cynefino** *vb* get used, become accustomed

**cynefinol** *adj* usual, accustomed

**cynfas** (-au) *nf/m* (bed) sheet; canvas

**cynfyd** *nm* primitive world, antiquity

**cynffon** (-nau) *nf* tail; tang

**cynffonna** *vb* fawn, toady, cringe

**cynffonnwr** (-onwyr) *nm* toady, sycophant; sneak

**cyn-geni** *adj* antenatal

**cynhadledd** (cynadleddau) *nf* conference

**cynhaeaf** (cynaeafau) *nm* harvest

**cyn(h)aeafa** *vb* dry in the sun

**cyn(h)aeafu** *vb* harvest

**cyn(h)aeafwr** (-wyr) *nm* harvester
**cynhaliaeth** *nf* maintenance, support
**cynhaliol** *adj* sustaining
**cynhaliwr** (-wyr) *nm* supporter, sustainer
**cynhanesiol** *adj* prehistoric
**cynhebrwng** (-yngau) *nm* funeral
**cynhenid** *adj* innate
**cynhennu** *vb* contend, quarrel
**cynhennus** *adj* contentious, quarrelsome
**cynhennwr** (-henwyr) *nm* wrangler
**cynhesol** *adj* agreeable, amiable
**cynhesrwydd** *nm* warmth
**cynhesu** *vb* warm, get warm
**cynhorthwy** (cynorthwyon) *nm* help, aid
**cynhwynol** *adj* natural, congenital, innate
**cynhwysedd** (cynwyseddau) *nm* capacity, capacitance
**cynhwysfawr** *adj* comprehensive
**cynhwysiad** *nm* contents
**cynhyrchiad** (-au) *nm* production
**cynhyrchiol** *adj* productive
**cynhyrchu** *vb* produce
**cynhyrchydd** (-ion, cynhyrchwyr) *nm* producer, generator
**cynhyrfiad** (cynyrfiadau) *nm* stirring, agitation
**cynhyrfiol** *adj* stirring, thrilling
**cynhyrfu** *vb* stir, agitate
**cynhyrfus** *adj* agitated; exciting
**cynhyrfwr** (-wyr) *nm* agitator, disturber
**cynhysgaeth** *nf* dower, portion, fortune
**cyni** *nm* anguish, distress, adversity
**cynifer** *adj, nm* as many, so many
**cynigiad** (-au) *nm* proposal, motion
**cynigiwr** (-wyr), **-ydd** (-ion) *nm* proposer, mover
**cynildeb** *nm* frugality, economy
**cynilion** *npl* savings
**cynilo** *vb* save, economise

**cynio** *vb* chisel, gouge
**cyniwair** *vb* go to and fro, frequent
**cyniweirfa** (-feydd) *nf* resort, haunt
**cyniweirydd** *nm* wayfarer
**cynllun** (-iau) *nm* pattern; plan
**cynllunio** *vb* plan, design
**cynllunydd** (-ion, -wyr) *nm* designer
**cynllwyn** *vb* plot, conspire ▷ (-ion) *nm* plot
**cynllwynio** *vb* conspire, plot
**cynllwynwr** (-wyr) *nm* conspirator
**cynnal** *vb* hold, uphold, support, sustain
**cynnar** *adj* early
**cynnau** *vb* kindle, light
**cynneddf** (cyneddfau) *nf* quality, faculty
**cynnen** (cynhennau) *nf* contention, strife; **asgwrn y gynnen** bone of contention
**cynnes** *adj* warm
**cynnig** *vb* offer; attempt; propose, move; bid; apply ▷ (cynigion) *nm* offer; attempt; motion
**cynnil** *adj* economical; delicate
**cynnor** (cynhorau) *nf* door-post
**cynnud** *nm* firewood, fuel
**cynnull** *vb* collect, gather, assemble
**cynnwrf** *nm* stir, commotion, agitation
**cynnwys** *vb* contain, include, comprise, comprehend ▷ *nm* content(s)
**cynnydd** *nm* increase, growth, progress
**cynnyrch** (cynhyrchion) *nm* produce, product; (*pl*) productions
**cynoesol** *adj* primeval
**cynorthwyo** *vb* help, assist
**cynorthwyol** *adj* auxiliary; assistant
**cynorthwywr** (-wyr) *nm* helper, assistant
**cynradd** *adj* primary
**cynrhon** *npl* (*nm* -yn) maggots

**cynrhoni** vb breed maggots
**cynrhonllyd** adj maggoty
**cynrychioladol** adj representative
**cynrychiolaeth** nf representation
**cynrychioli** vb represent
**cynrychiolwr (-wyr), -ydd (-ion)** nm representative, delegate
**cynt** adj earlier, sooner, quicker
  ▷ adv see **gynt**
**cyntaf** adj, adv first
**cyntedd (-au)** nm court; porch, foyer
**cyntefig** adj prime, primitive
**cyntun** nm nap
**cynulleidfa (-oedd)** nf congregation
**cynulleidfaol** adj congregational
**cynulliad (-au)** nm gathering
**cynuta** vb gather fuel
**cynyddol** adj increasing, growing
**cynyddu** vb increase
**cynysgaeddu** vb endow, endue
**cyplad** nm copula
**cypladu** vb copulate
**cyplu, cyplysu** vb couple
**cyraeddadwy** adj attainable
**cyraeddiadau** npl attainments
**cyrbibion** npl atoms, smithereens
**cyrcydu** vb squat, cower
**cyrch (-au)** nm attack
**cyrchfa (-feydd)** nf resort
**cyrchu** vb go, resort, repair
**cyrhaeddgar** adj telling, incisive
**cyrhaeddiad (cyraeddiadau)** nm reach, attainment
**cyrliog** adj curly
**cyrraedd** vb reach, attain; arrive
**cyrren** npl (nf cyrensen) currants
**cyrydiad** nm corrosion
**cyrydu** vb corrode
**cysawd (-odau)** nm system; constellation
**cysefin** adj original, primordial
**cysegr (-au, -oedd)** nm sanctuary
**cysegredig** adj consecrated, sacred
**cysegredigrwydd** nm sacredness
**cysegriad (-au)** nm consecration

**cysegr-ladrad** nm sacrilege
**cysegr-lân** adj holy
**cysegru** vb consecrate, dedicate, devote
**cyseinedd** nm alliteration
**cysetlyd** adj fastidious
**cysgadrwydd** nm sleepiness, drowsiness
**cysgadur (-iaid)** nm sleeper
**cysglyd** adj sleepy
**cysgod (-au, -ion)** nm shade, shadow; shelter; type
**cysgodi** vb shadow, shade; shelter
**cysgodol** adj shady, sheltered
**cysgu** vb sleep
**cysgwr (-wyr)** nm sleeper
**cysidro** vb consider
**cysodi** vb set type, compose
**cysodydd (-ion, -wyr)** nm compositor
**cyson** adj consistent, constant
**cysondeb** nm consistency; regularity
**cysoni** vb harmonize; reconcile
**cysonwr (-wyr), -ydd (-ion)** nm harmonist
**cystadleuaeth (-au)** nf competition
**cystadleuol** adj competitive
**cystadleuwr, -ydd (-wyr)** nm competitor
**cystadlu** vb compete; compare
**cystal** adj as good, so good ▷ adv as well, so well
**cystrawen (-nau)** nf construction, syntax
**cystudd (-iau)** nm affliction; illness
**cystuddiedig** adj afflicted, contrite
**cystuddio** vb afflict, trouble
**cystuddiol** adj afflicted
**cystuddiwr (-wyr)** nm afflicter, oppressor
**cystwyo** vb chastise, castigate, trounce
**cysur (-on)** nm comfort, consolation

**cysuro** vb comfort, console
**cysurus** adj comfortable
**cysurwr** (-wyr) nm comforter
**cyswllt** (-ylltiadau) nm joint, junction
**cysylltiad** (-au) nm conjunction; joining, connexion
**cysylltiol** adj connecting; connected
**cysylltnod** (-au) nm ligature, hyphen
**cysylltu** vb join, connect
**cysylltydd** (-ion) nm connector, contact
**cysyniad** (-au) nm concept
**cytbell** adj equidistant
**cytbwys** adj of equal weight
**cytbwysedd** nm balance
**cytew** nm batter
**cytgan** (-au) nm/f chorus
**cytgord** nm concord
**cytir** (-oedd) nm common
**cytras** adj allied, related; cognate
**cytsain** (-seiniaid) nf consonant
**cytûn** adj agreed, of one accord, unanimous
**cytundeb** (-au) nm agreement, consent
**cytuno** vb agree, consent
**cythlwng** nm fasting, fast, hunger
**cythraul** (-euliaid) nm devil, demon
**cythreuldeb** nm devilment
**cythreulig** adj devilish, fiendish
**cythru** vb snatch, rush
**cythruddo** vb annoy, provoke, irritate
**cythrwfl** nm uproar, tumult
**cythryblu** vb trouble, agitate
**cythryblus** adj troubled, agitated
**cyw** (-ion) nm young bird, chick, chicken; baby
**cywain** vb convey, carry; garner
**cywair** (-eiriau) nm order; key; tune
**cywaith** (-weithiau) nm collective work, project
**cywarch** nm hemp

**cywasg, -edig** adj compressor, diminished
**cywasgiad** (-au) nm contraction, compression
**cywasgu** vb contract, compress
**cywasgydd** (-ion) nm compressor
**cyweiriad** (-au) nm repair
**cyweiriadur** (-on) nm modulator
**cyweirio** vb set in order; prepare, dress
**cyweirnod** (-au) nm key-note
**cywen** (-nod) nf pullet, young hen
**cywerth** adj equivalent
**cywilydd** nm shame; shyness
**cywilydd-dra** nm shamefulness
**cywilyddgar** adj bashful, shy
**cywilyddio** vb shame; be ashamed
**cywilyddus** adj shameful, disgraceful
**cywir** adj correct, accurate, true, faithful
**cywirdeb** nm correctness; integrity
**cywiriad** (-au) nm correction
**cywiro** vb correct; make good; perform
**cywirwr** (-wyr) nm corrector
**cywladu** vb naturalize
**cywrain** adj skilful; curious
**cywreinbeth** (-au, -einion) nm curiosity
**cywreindeb** nm skill, ingenuity
**cywreinrwydd** nm skill; curiosity
**cywydd** (-au) nm alliterative Welsh poem
**cywyddwr** (-wyr) nm composer of *cywyddau*

# ch

actor, performer

**chwaraeydd** (-ion) *nm* actor
**chwarddiad** (-au) *nm* laugh
**chwarel** (-au, -i, -ydd) *nf* quarry
**chwarelwr** (-wyr) *nm* quarryman
**chwareus** *adj* playful
**chwarren** (-arennau) *nf* gland; kernel
**chwart** (-iau) *nm* quart
**chwarter** (-i, -au) *nm* quarter
**chwarterol** *adj* quarterly
**chwarterolyn** (-olion) *nm* quarterly (magazine)
**chwarteru** *vb* quarter
**chwe** *adj* six (*before a noun*)
**chweban** (-nau) *nm* sestet, sextain
**chwech** *adj* six ▷ (-au) *nm* six; sixpence
**chwechawd** (-au) *nm* sextet
**chwedl** (-au) *nf* story, tale
**chwedleua** *vb* talk, gossip
**chwedleuwr** (-wyr) *nm* story-teller
**chwedloniaeth** *nf* mythology
**chwedlonol** *adj* mythical, mythological
**chwedlonydd** (-wyr) *nm* mythologist
**chwedyn** *adv*: **na chynt na chhwedyn** neither before nor after
**Chwefror, Chwefrol** *nm* February
**chwennych, chwenychu** *vb* covet, desire
**chwenychiad** (-au) *nm* desire
**chweongl** (-au) *nm* hexagon
**chwephlyg** *adj* sixfold
**chwerthin** *vb* laugh ▷ *nm* laughter
**chwerthiniad** (-au) *nm* laugh
**chwerthinllyd** *adj* laughable, ridiculous
**chwerthinog** *adj* laughing, merry
**chwerw** *adj* bitter
**chwerwder, -dod** *nm* bitterness
**chwerwedd** *nm* bitterness
**chwerwi** *vb* grow bitter, embitter
**chwi** *pron* you
**chwib** (-iau) *nm* whistle
**chwiban** *vb*, *nm* whistle

**Chile** *nf* Chile
**China** *nf* China
**chwa** (-on) *nf* puff, gust, breeze
**chwaer** (chwiorydd) *nf* sister
**chwaeroliaeth** *nf* sisterhood
**chwaeth** (-au, -oedd) *nf* taste
**chwaethu** *vb* taste
**chwaethus** *adj* tasteful; decent
**chwaith** *adv* nor either, neither
**chwâl** *adj* scattered, loose
**chwalfa** (-feydd) *nf* upset, rout
**chwalu** *vb* scatter, spread
**chwalwr** (-wyr) *nm* scatterer, demolisher
**chwaneg** *adj*, *nm* more
**chwanegiad** (-au) *nm* addition
**chwanegol** *adj* additional
**chwanegu** *vb* add, augment, increase
**chwannen** (chwain) *nf* flea
**chwannog** *adj* desirous; addicted; prone
**chwant** (-au) *nm* desire, craving, lust
**chwantu** *vb* desire, lust
**chwap** *nm* sudden blow, moment ▷ *adv* instantly
**chwarae, chware** *vb* play ▷ (-on) *nm* play
**chwaraedy** (-dai) *nm* playhouse, theatre
**chwaraefa** (-feydd) *nf* pitch, playground
**chwaraegar** *adj* playful, sportive
**chwaraewr** (-wyr) *nm* player,

**chwibaniad** nm whistling, whistle
**chwibanogl** (-au) nf whistle, flute
**chwibanu** vb whistle
**chwibon** (-iaid) nm curlew, stork
**chwifio** vb wave, flourish, brandish
**chwiff** (-iau) nf whiff, puff
**chwiffiad** nm whiff, jiffy
**chwil** (-od) nm/f beetle, chafer
**chwil** adj whirling, reeling
**chwilboeth** adj scorching, piping hot
**chwildroi** vb whirl, spin
**chwilen** (chwilod) nf beetle
**chwilenna** vb rummage; pry; pilfer
**chwiler** (-od) nm chrysalis, pupa
**chwilfriw** adj smashed to atoms
**chwilfriwio** vb smash, shatter
**chwilfrydedd** nm curiosity
**chwilfrydig** adj curious, inquisitive
**chwilgar** adj curious, inquisitive
**chwilgarwch** nm inquisitiveness
**chwiliad** (-au) nm search, scrutiny
**chwilibawa(n)** vb dawdle, trifle
**chwilio** vb search; examine
**chwiliwr** (-wyr) nm searcher
**chwil-lys** nm inquisition
**chwilmantan** vb pry, rummage
**chwilolau** (-oleuadau) nm searchlight
**chwilota** vb rummage, pry
**chwilotwr** (-wyr) nm searcher, rummager
**chwim** adj nimble, quick, agile
**chwimder, -dra** nm nimbleness
**chwimio** vb move, stir, accelerate
**chwimwth** adj nimble, brisk
**chwinc** nm wink
**chwinciad** nm twinkling, trice
**chwiorydd** see **chwaer**
**chwip** (-iau) nf whip; whipping
**chwipiad** (-au) nm whipping
**chwipio** vb whip
**chwipyn** adv instantly
**chwirligwgan** nf whirligig
**chwisgi** nm whisky
**chwisl** (-au) nm whistle

**chwistrell** (-au, -i) nf squirt, syringe
**chwistrelliad** (-au) nm injection
**chwistrellu** vb squirt, syringe, inject
**chwit-chwat** adj fickle, inconstant
**chwith** adj left; wrong; sad; strange
**chwithau** pron conj you (on your part), you also
**chwithdod, -dra** nm strangeness
**chwithig** adj strange, wrong, awkward
**chwithigrwydd** nm awkwardness
**chwiw** (-iau) nf fit, attack, malady
**chwiwgar** adj fickle
**chwychwi** pron you yourselves
**chwŷd, chwydiad** nm vomit
**chwydu** vb vomit, spew
**chwydd, chwyddi** nm swelling
**chwyddiant** (-nnau) nm inflation; inflammation
**chwyddo** vb swell, increase, magnify
**chwyddwydr** (-au) nm microscope
**chwŷl** (chwylion) nm/f turn, rotation
**chwyldro** (-ion) nm rotation; orbit
**chwyldroad** (-au) nm revolution
**chwyldroadol** adj revolutionary
**chwyldroadwr** (-wyr) nm revolutionary
**chwyldroi** vb whirl, revolve, rotate
**chwyldrowr** see **chwyldroadwr**
**chwylolwyn** (-ion) nf flywheel
**chwyn** (nm ~nyn) coll n, npl weeds
**chwynladdwr** nm weed-killer
**chwynnu** vb weed
**chwyrligwgan** (-od) nm spinning top, whirligig
**chwyrlïo** vb whirl, spin, speed
**chwyrlwynt** (-oedd) nm whirlwind
**chwyrn** adj rapid, swift
**chwyrnellu** vb whirl, whiz
**chwyrnu** vb hum; snore; snarl
**chwyrnwr** (-wyr) nm snorer; snarler

**chwys** nm sweat, perspiration
**chwysfa** (-feydd) nf sweating
**chwysiant** nm exudation
**chwysigen** (-igod) nf blister,
vesicle
**chwyslyd** adj sweaty
**chwystyllau** npl pores
**chwysu** vb sweat, perspire; exude
**chwyswr** (-wyr) nm sweater
**chwyth, chwythad** nm breath
**chwythbib** (-au) nf blowpipe
**chwythbrenni** npl woodwinds
**chwythell** (-i) nf jet
**chwythiad** (-au) nm blow, blast
**chwythu** vb blow, blast; breathe;
hiss
**chwythwr** (-wyr) nm blower

# d

**da** adj good, well ▷ (-oedd) nm good;
goods; stock, cattle
**da-da** nm sweets
**dacw** adv there is, are; behold there
**dad-, dat-** prefix un-, dis-re-, back
**dadansoddi** vb analyse
**dadansoddiad** (-au) nm analysis
**dadansoddol** adj analytic(al)
**dadansoddwr** (-wyr) nm analyst
**dadansoddydd** (-wyr) nm
analyser
**dadchwyddiant** (-nnau) nm
deflation

**dad-ddyfrio** vb dehydrate
**dadebriad** nm resuscitation
**dadebru** vb resuscitate, revive
**dadelfeniad** (-au) nm
decomposition
**dadelfennu** vb decompose; refine
**dadeni** vb regenerate, reanimate
▷ nm rebirth, renascence,
renaissance
**dadfachu** vb unhook
**dadfathiad** nm dissimulation
**dadfeiliad** nm decay
**dadfeilio** vb fall to ruin, decay
**dadflino** vb rest (after exertion)
**dadl** (-euon) nf debate; doubt; plea
**dadlaith** vb thaw; dissolve
**dadlau** vb argue, debate; plead
**dadleniad** (-au) nm disclosure,
exposure
**dadlennol** adj revealing,
disclosing, exposing
**dadlennu** vb disclose, expose
**dadleoli** vb dislocate
**dadleoliad** (-au) nm dislocation
**dadleuaeth** nf polemics,
controversy
**dadleugar** adj argumentative
**dadleuol** adj controversial,
polemical
**dadleuwr** (-wyr), **-ydd** (-ion) nm
debater, controversialist; advocate
**dadluddedu** vb rest (after
exertion)
**dadlwytho** vb unload, unburden
**dadlygru** vb decontaminate
**dadmer** vb thaw; dissolve
**dadnitreiddiad** nm denitrification
**dadolwch** nm propitiation ▷ vb
worship, seek forgiveness
**dadorchuddio** vb unveil, uncover
**dadreolaeth** nf decontrol
**dadrewlifiant** nm deglaciation
**dadrithiad** (-au) nm
disillusionment
**dadrithio** vb disillusion
**dadsefydlu** vb disestablish
**dadwaddoli** vb disendow

**dadwaddoliad** *nm* disendowment
**dadwneuthur, dadwneud** *vb* undo, unmake
**dadwrdd** *nm* noise, uproar, hubbub
**dadymchwel, -yd** *vb* overturn, overthrow
**daear (-oedd)** *nf* earth, ground, soil
**daeardy (-dai)** *nm* dungeon
**daeareg** *nf* geology
**daearegol** *adj* geological
**daearegwr (-wyr), -ydd (-ion)** *nm* geologist
**daearen** *nf* the earth; land, country
**daearfochyn (-foch)** *nm* badger
**daeargell (-oedd)** *nf* dungeon, vault
**daeargi (-gwn)** *nm* terrier
**daeargryd (-iau)** *nm* earth tremor
**daeargryn (-fâu)** *nm/f* earthquake
**daearol** *adj* terrestrial, earthly, earthy
**daearu** *vb* earth; inter
**daearyddiaeth** *nf* geography
**daearyddol** *adj* geographical
**daearyddwr (-wyr)** *nm* geographer
**dafad (defaid)** *nf* sheep; wart
**dafaden (-ennau)** *nf* wart
**dafn (-au)** *nm* drop
**dafnu** *vb* trickle
**dagr (-au)** *nm* dagger, bayonet, dirk
**dagrau** *npl* (*nm* deigryn) tears
**dagreuol** *adj* tearful, sad
**dangos** *see* **dan-**
**dail** *npl* (*nf* dalen, deilen) leaves
**daioni** *nm* goodness, good
**daionus** *adj* good; beneficial; beneficent
**dal, -a** *vb* hold; catch; arrest; last
**dalen (-nau, dail)** *nf* leaf
**dalfa (-feydd)** *nf* hold; arrest, custody; prison
**dalgylch (-oedd)** *nm* catchment area
**daliad (-au)** *nm* holding; tenet; spell
**daliwr (-wyr)** *nm* jig, catcher
**dall (deillion)** *adj* blind

**dallbleidiaeth** *nf* bigotry
**dallbleidiol** *adj* bigoted
**dallbleidiwr (-wyr)** *nm* bigot
**dallineb** *nm* blindness
**dallu** *vb* blind; dazzle
**damcaniaeth (-au)** *nf* theory
**damcaniaethol** *adj* theoretical
**damcaniaethwr (-wyr)** *nm* theorist
**damcanu** *vb* theorize, speculate
**dameg (-hegion)** *nf* parable
**damhegol** *adj* parabolic(al), allegorical
**damhegwr (-wyr)** *nm* allegorist
**damnedig** *adj* damned, damnable
**damnedigaeth** *nf* damnation, condemnation
**damnio** *vb* damn
**damniol** *adj* damning, damnatory
**damsang** *vb* tread, trample
**damwain (-weiniau)** *nf* accident, chance, fate
**damweinio** *vb* befall, happen
**damweiniol** *adj* accidental, casual
**dan** *see* **tan**
**danadl** *npl* (*nf* danhadlen) nettles
**danas** *coll n* deer; **bwch ~** buck
**danfon** *vb* send, convey; escort
**dangos** *vb* show
**dangoseg (-ion)** *nf* index; indication
**dangosol** *adj* indicative, demonstrative
**danheddog** *adj* jagged, serrated, toothed
**dannod** *vb* reproach, upbraid, taunt, twit
**dannoedd** *nf* toothache
**dansoddol** *adj* abstract
**dant (dannedd)** *nm* tooth
**danteithfwyd (-teithion)** *nm* dainty
**danteithiol** *adj* dainty, delicious
**danteithion** *npl* delicacies
**darbodus** *adj* provident, thrifty
**darbwyllo** *vb* persuade, convince
**darfod** *vb* finish, end; perish;

happen

**darfodadwy** *adj* transitory, perishable

**darfodedig** *adj* perishable, transient

**darfodedigaeth** *nm* consumption

**darfudiad** (-au) *nm* convection

**darfudol** *adj* convectional

**darganfod** *vb* discover

**darganfyddiad** (-au) *nm* discovery

**darganfyddwr** (-wyr) *nm* discoverer

**dargludedd** *nm* conductivity

**dargludo** *vb* conduct

**dargludydd** (-ion) *nm* conductor

**dargyfeiredd** *nm* divergence

**dargyfeirio** *vb* diverge, divert

**darlith** (-iau, -oedd) *nf* lecture

**darlithfa** (-feydd) *nf* lecture room

**darlithio** *vb* lecture

**darlithiwr** (-wyr), **-ydd** (-ion) *nm* lecturer

**darlun** (-iau) *nm* picture

**darluniad** (-au) *nm* portrayal, description

**darluniadol** *adj* pictorial, illustrated

**darluniaeth** *nf* imagery

**darlunio** *vb* portray, depict, describe

**darluniol** *adj* pictorial

**darllediad** (-au) *nm* broadcast

**darlledu** *vb* broadcast

**darlledwr** (-wyr) *nm* broadcaster

**darllen** *vb* read

**darllenadwy** *adj* readable, legible

**darllenfa** (-feydd) *nf* reading room; reading-desk; lectern

**darllengar** *adj* fond of reading, studious

**darlleniad** (-au) *nm* reading

**darllenwr** (-wyr), **-ydd** (-ion) *nm* reader

**darn** (-au) *nm* piece, fragment, part

**darnguddio** *vb* conceal or withhold a part

**darniad** (-au) *nm* fragmentation

**darnio** *vb* cut up, hack

**darn-ladd** *vb* beat mercilessly

**darogan** *vb* predict, foretell, forebode ▷ (-au) *nf* prediction, foreboding

**daroganu** *vb* predict, foretell

**daroganwr** (-wyr) *nm* predictor, prophet, soothsayer, forecaster

**darostwng** *vb* lower; subdue; subject, humiliate

**darostyngiad** *nm* humiliation; subjection

**darpar** (-ion, -iadau) *nm* preparation, provision ▷ *adj* intended, elect

**darpariaeth** (-au) *nf* preparation, provision

**darparu** *vb* prepare, provide

**darparwr** (-wyr) *nm* provider

**darwden** *nf* ringworm

**das** (-au, **deisi**) *nf* rick, stack

**dat-** *prefix see* **dad-**

**data** *nm* data

**datblygiad** (-au) *nm* development, evolution

**datblygol** *adj* nascent, developing

**datblygu** *vb* develop, evolve

**datblygus** *adj* developmental

**datblygydd** (-ion) *nm* developer

**datchwyddiant** *nm* deflation

**datgan** *vb* declare; recount; render

**datganiad** (-au) *nm* declaration; rendering

**datganoli** *vb* devolve, decentralize

**datganoli(ad)** *nm* devolution

**datganu** *vb* declare; sing, render

**datgeliad** (-au) *nm* detection; revelation

**datgelu** *vb* detect; reveal

**datgloi** *vb* unlock

**datglymu** *vb* unhitch, undo

**datgorffori** *vb* dissolve (*parliament*)

**datgorfforiad** *nm* dissolution

**datguddiad** (-au) *nm* revelation, disclosure

**datguddio** *vb* reveal, disclose

**datgyffesiad** *nm* recantation

**datgyffesu** vb recant
**datgymalu** vb dislocate, dismember
**datgysylltiad** nm disestablishment
**datgysylltu** vb disconnect; disestablish
**datod** vb undo, untie, dissolve
**datrannu** vb dissect
**datro** vb change; undo
**datru** vb de-code
**datrys** vb solve
**datrysiad** (-au) nm solution, resolution
**datseinio** vb resound, reverberate
**datsgwar** (-au) nm square root
**datysen** (datys) nf date
**dathliad** (-au) nm celebration
**dathlu** vb celebrate
**dau** (f dwy) adj, nm two
**dau-, deu-** prefix two, bi-
**dauddyblyg** adj twofold, double
**daufiniog** adj double-edged
**dauwynebog** adj two-faced
**dawn** (doniau) nm/f gift, talent
**dawns** (-iau) nf dance
**dawnsio** vb dance
**dawnsiwr** (-wyr) nm dancer
**dawnus** adj gifted, talented
**de** see **deau**
**De Affrica** nf South Africa
**deall** vb understand ▷ nm understanding, intellect, intelligence
**dealladwy** adj intelligible
**deallgar** adj intelligent
**deallol** adj intellectual
**dealltwriaeth** (-au) nf understanding, intelligence
**deallus** adj understanding, intelligent
**deallusion** npl intelligentsia
**deallusrwydd** nm intelligence
**deau** adj, nm right; south
**debentur** (-on) nm debenture
**debyd** (-au) nm debit
**debydu** vb debit

**dec** (-iau, -s) nm deck
**decilitr** (-au) nm decilitre
**decimetr** (-au) nm decimetre
**decstros** nm dextrose
**dectant** nm ten-stringed instrument, psaltery
**dechrau** vb begin ▷ nm beginning
**dechreuad** (-au) nm beginning
**dechreunos** nf nightfall, dusk
**dechreuol** adj initial
**dechreuwr** (-wyr) nm beginner
**dedfryd** (-au) nf verdict; sentence
**dedfrydu** vb sentence
**dedwydd** adj happy, blessed
**dedwyddwch, -yd** nm happiness, bliss
**deddf** (-au) nf law, statute, act
**deddfeg** nf jurisprudence
**deddfegwr** (-wyr) nm jurist
**deddfol** adj legal, lawful
**deddfu** vb legislate, enact
**deddfwr** (-wyr) nm legislator
**deddfwriaeth** nf legislation, legislature
**deddfwriaethol** adj legislative
**deddflyfr** (-au) nm statute book
**defni** vb drip, trickle
**defnydd** (-iau) nm material, stuff; use
**defnyddio** vb use, utilize, employ
**defnyddiol** adj useful
**defnyddioldeb** nm usefulness, utility
**defnyddiwr** (-wyr) nm user, consumer
**defnyn** (-nau) nm drop
**defnynnu** vb drop, drip, dribble, distil
**defod** (-au) nf custom; rite, ceremony
**defodaeth** nf ritualism
**defodol** adj ritualistic
**defosiwn** (-ynau) nm devotion
**defosiynol** adj devotional, devout
**deffiniad, -io** see **diff-**
**deffro, deffroi** vb rouse; wake
**deffroad** (-au) nm awakening

**deg** *adj* ten ▷ (-au) *nm* ten
**degawd** (-au) *nm* decade
**degaidd** *adj* denary
**degiad** (-au) *nm* decimal
**degol** (-ion) *nm, adj* decimal
**degoli** *vb* decimalise
**degoliad** *nm* decimalisation
**degolyn** (degolion) *nm* decimal
**degwm** (-ymau) *nm* tenth, tithe
**degymu** *vb* tithe
**deng** *adj* ten (*before certain words*)
**dehau, deheu** *see* **deau**
**deheubarth, -dir** *nm* southern
  region, south
**deheuig** *adj* dexterous, skilful
**deheulaw** *nf* right hand
**deheuol** *adj* southern
**deheurwydd** *nm* dexterity, skill
**deheuwr** (-wyr) *nm* southerner,
  southman
**deheuwynt** *nm* south wind
**dehongli** *vb* interpret
**dehongliad** (-au) *nm*
  interpretation
**dehonglwr** (-wyr), -ydd (-ion) *nm*
  interpreter
**dehydrad** (-au) *nm* dehydration
**dehydru** *vb* dehydrate
**deial** (-au) *nm* dial
**deialog** (-au) *nm/f* dialogue
**deialu** *vb* dial
**deifio** *vb* singe, scorch; blast; dive
**deifiol** *adj* scorching, scathing
**deifiwr** (-wyr) *nm* diver
**deigryn** (dagrau) *nm* tear
**deilbridd** *nm* humus
**deildy** (-dai) *nm* bower, arbour
**deilen** (dail) *nf* leaf
**deilgoll** *adj* deciduous
**deiliad** (-on, deiliaid) *nm* tenant;
  subject
**deiliant** (-nnau) *nm* foliage
**deilio** *vb* leaf
**deiliog** *adj* leafy
**deillio** *vb* proceed, emanate, issue
**deinameg** *nf/m* dynamics
**deinamig** *adj* dynamic

**deinamo** (-s, -au) *nm* dynamo
**deincod** *nm* teeth on edge
**deincryd** *nm* chattering or
  gnashing of teeth
**deintio** *vb* nibble
**deintrod** (-au) *nf* cog
**deintydd** (-ion) *nm* dentist
**deintyddiaeth** *nf* dentistry
**deintyddol** *adj* dental
**deiseb** (-au) *nf* petition
**deisebu** *vb* petition
**deisebwr, -ydd** (-wyr) *nm*
  petitioner
**deisyf, deisyfu** *vb* desire, wish;
  beseech, entreat
**deisyfiad** (-au) *nm* request,
  petition
**del** *adj* pretty, neat
**delfryd** (-au) *nm* ideal
**delfrydiaeth** *nf* idealism
**delfrydol** *adj* ideal
**delfrydwr** (-wyr) *nm* idealist
**delff** *nm* churl, oaf, dolt, rascal
**delio** *vb* deal
**delw** (-au) *nf* image; form, mode,
  manner
**delwedd** (-au) *nf* image
**delweddaeth** *nf* imagery
**delweddu** *vb* portray
**delwi** *vb* be wool-gathering; pale, be
  paralysed with fright.
**dellni** *nm* blindness
**dellt** *npl* (*nf* -en) laths, lattice,
  splinters
**democratiaeth** (-au) *nf*
  democracy
**democratig** *adj* democratic
**demograffeg** *nf* demography
**demograffig** *adj* demographic
**dengar** *adj* attractive
**dengarwch** *nm* attractiveness
**deniadau** *npl* attractions,
  allurements
**deniadol** *adj* attractive
**Denmarc** *nf* Denmark
**denu** *vb* attract, allure, entice
**deon** (-iaid) *nm* dean

**deondy** (-dai) *nm* deanery
**deoniaeth** (-au) *nf* deanery
**deor** *vb* brood, hatch, incubate
**deorfa** (-fâu, -feydd) *nf* hatchery
**deorydd** (-ion) *nf* incubator
**derbyn** *vb* receive; accept; admit
**derbyniad** (-au) *nm* receipt; reception
**derbyniadwy** *adj* admissible
**derbyniol** *adj* acceptable
**derbyniwr** (-wyr), **-nnydd**
**derbynneb** (-ynebau, -ynebion) *nf* receipt, voucher
**derbynnydd** (-ynyddion) *nm* receiver
**deri** *npl* (*nf* dâr) oak-trees, oak
**dernyn** (-nau) *nm* piece, scrap
**derwen** (derw, deri) *nf* oak-tree, oak
**derwydd** (-on) *nm* druid
**derwyddiaeth** *nf* druidism
**derwyddol** *adj* druidic(al)
**desg** (-iau) *nf* desk
**desgant** (-au) *nm* descant
**desibel** (-au) *nm* decibel
**destlus** *adj* neat
**destlusrwydd** *nm* neatness
**detector** (-au) *nm* detector
**dethol** *vb* select, pick, choose ▷ *adj* select
**detholedd** *nm* selectivity
**detholiad** (-au, detholion) *nm* selection, anthology
**deu-** *see* **dau-**
**deuawd** (-au) *nm/f* duet
**deublyg** *adj* double, twofold
**deuddeg** *adj*, *nm* twelve
**deufin** *adj* two-edged
**deuffocal** *adj* bifocal
**deugain** *adj*, *nm* forty
**deugraff** *nm* digraph
**deunaw** *adj*, *nm* eighteen
**deunydd** (-iau) *nm* stuff, material
**deuocsid** *nm* dioxide
**deuod** (-au) *nm* diode, binary
**deuol** *adj* dual
**deuoliaeth** *nf* dualism, duality

**deuparth** *nd* two-thirds
**deuris** *adj* two-tier
**deurudd** *nd* the cheeks
**deuryw** *adj* bisexual
**deusain** *nd* diphthong
**deutu** *nd*: **o d~** about
**dewin** (-iaid) *nm* diviner, magician, wizard
**dewines** (-au) *nf* witch, sorceress
**dewiniaeth** *nf* divination, witchcraft
**dewinio** *vb* divine
**dewin(i)ol** *adj* prophetic, divinatory
**dewis** *vb* choose, select ▷ *nm* choice
**dewisiad** *nm* choice, option
**dewisol** *adj* choice, desirable
**dewr** *adj* brave ▷ (-ion) *nm* brave man, hero
**dewrder** *nm* bravery, valour
**di-** *neg prefix* without, not, un-, non-, -less
**diabetig** *adj*, *nm/f* diabetic
**diacon** (-iaid) *nm* deacon
**diacones** (-au) *nf* deaconess
**diaconiaeth** *nf* diaconate
**diadell** (-au, -oedd) *nf* flock
**diaddurn** *adj* unadorned, plain, rude
**diaelodi** *vb* dismember; expel a member
**diafael** *adj* slippery, careless
**diafol** (diefyl, dieifl) *nm* devil
**diaffram** (-au) *nm* diaphragm
**diagnosis** *nm* diagnosis
**diangen** *adj* unnecessary, free from want
**dianghenraid** *adj* unnecessary, needless
**di-ail** *adj* unequalled, unrivalled
**dial** *vb* avenge, revenge ▷ *nm* vengeance, revenge
**dialedd** (-au) *nm* vengeance, nemesis
**dialgar** *adj* revengeful, vindictive
**dialgarwch** *nm* vindictiveness
**di-alw-amdano** *adj* redundant,

uncalled for
**dialwr (-wyr), -ydd (-ion)** *nm* avenger
**diamau** *adj* doubtless
**diamcan** *adj* aimless, purposeless
**diamedr (-au)** *nm* diameter
**diamedral** *adj* diametral
**diamheuol** *adj* undoubted, indisputable
**diamod** *adj* unconditional, absolute
**diamodol** *adj* unconditional, unqualified
**diamwys** *adj* unambiguous
**diamynedd** *adj* impatient
**dianc** *vb* escape
**dianwadal** *adj* unwavering, immutable
**dianwadalwch** *nm* immutability
**diarddel** *vb* expel, excommunicate
**diarddeliad** *nm* expulsion, excommunication
**diarfogi** *vb* disarm
**diarfogiad** *nm* disarmament
**diarffordd** *adj* out of the way, inaccessible
**diargyhoedd** *adj* blameless
**diarhebol** *adj* proverbial
**diaroglydd (-ion)** *nm* deodorant
**diarwybod** *adj* unawares
**diasbad** *nf* cry, scream
**diasbedain** *vb* resound, ring
**diatreg** *adj* immediate
**diau** *adj* true, certain; doubtless
**diawl (-iaid)** *nm* devil
**diawledig** *adj* devilish
**di-baid, dibaid** *adj* unceasing, ceaseless
**di-ball, diball** *adj* unfailing, infallible, sure
**diben (-ion)** *nm* end, purpose, aim
**di-ben-draw** *adj* endless
**dibeniad (-au)** *nm* ending, conclusion, predicate
**di-benllanw** *adj* off-peak
**dibennu** *vb* end, conclude, finish
**diberfeddu** *vb* disembowel,

eviscerate
**dibetrus** *adj* unhesitating
**dibl (-au)** *nm* border, edge
**diboblogaeth** *nf* depopulation
**diboblogi** *vb* depopulate
**dibrin** *adj* abundant, plentiful
**dibriod** *adj* unmarried, single
**dibris** *adj* reckless, contemptuous
**dibrisio** *vb* depreciate, despise
**dibristod** *nm* depreciation, contempt
**dibwys** *adj* trivial, unimportant
**dibwysiant (-nnau)** *nm* depression
**dibyn (-nau)** *nm* steep, precipice
**dibynadwy** *adj* reliable
**dibynadwyedd** *nm* reliability
**dibyniad** *nm* dependence
**dibyniant** *nm* dependence
**dibynnedd** *nm* reliability
**dibynnol** *adj* depending; subjunctive
**dibynnu** *vb* depend, rely
**dibynnydd (dibynyddion)** *nm* dependant
**dicllon** *adj* wrathful, angry
**dicllonrwydd** *nm* wrath, indignation
**dicotomi (-ïau)** *nm* dichotomy
**dicra** *adj* squeamish, fastidious, slow
**dicter** *nm* anger, wrath, displeasure
**dichell (-ion)** *nf* wile, craft, guile
**dichellgar** *adj* wily, crafty, cunning
**dichlyn** *vb* choose, pick ▷ *adj* careful, circumspect, exact
**dichon** *vb* be able; it may be
**di-dact** *adj* tactless
**didactig** *adj* didactic
**didaro** *adj* unaffected, unconcerned, cool
**di-daw** *adj* ceaseless, clamant
**diden (-nau)** *nf* nipple, teat
**diderfyn** *adj* unlimited
**didoli** *vb* separate, segregate
**didoliad** *nm* separation, segregation
**didolnod (-au)** *nm/f* diæresis

**di-dor, didor** adj unbroken, uninterrupted

**didoreth** adj shiftless, silly, fickle

**didoriad** adj unbroken, untamed, rough

**di-drais, didrais** adj non-violent, meek

**diduedd** adj impartial, unbiassed

**didwyll** adj guileless, sincere

**didwylledd** nm guilelessness, sincerity

**di-ddadl** adj unquestionable, indisputable

**diddan** adj amusing, diverting, pleasant

**diddanion** npl pleasantries, jokes

**diddanu** vb amuse, divert; comfort

**diddanwch** nm comfort, consolation

**diddanwr** (-wyr), **-ydd** (-ion) nm comforter

**diddarbod** adj shiftless

**di-dderbyn-wyneb** adj outspoken

**diddig** adj contented, pleased

**diddigrwydd** nm contentment, placidity

**diddim** adj, nm void

**diddordeb** nm interest

**diddori** vb interest

**diddorol** adj interesting

**diddos** adj watertight, sheltered; snug

**diddosi** vb shelter

**diddosrwydd** nm shelter, safety

**di-dduw, didduw** adj ungodly
  ▷ nm atheist

**di-ddweud** adj taciturn, stubborn

**diddwythiad** nm deduction

**diddwytho** vb deduce

**diddyfnu** vb wean

**diddymdra** nm nothingness, void

**diddymiad, -iant** nm annihilation

**diddymu** vb annihilate, abolish

**dieflig** adj devilish, diabolical, fiendish

**diegwyddor** adj unprincipled

**dieisiau** adj unnecessary, needless

**dieithr** adj strange, alien, foreign
  ▷ (-iaid) nm stranger

**dieithrio** vb estrange, alienate

**dieithrwch** nm strangeness

**dienaid** adj soulless, senseless

**dienyddiad** (-au) nm execution

**dienyddio** vb put to death, execute

**dienyddiwr** (-wyr) nm executioner

**dieuog** adj guiltless, innocent

**difa** vb consume, destroy; devour

**di-fai, difai** adj blameless, faultless

**difalch** adj humble

**difancoll** nf total loss, perdition

**difaol** adj consuming, devouring

**difater** adj indifferent, unconcerned

**difaterwch** nm indifference, apathy

**difeddiannu** vb dispossess, deprive

**di-feind** adj heedless

**difenwad** (-au) nm defamation

**difenwi** vb revile, abuse, belittle

**diferlif** nm stream, issue

**diferol** adj dripping, dropping

**diferu** vb drip, drop, dribble, distil

**diferyn** (-nau, **diferion**) nm drop

**difesur** adj huge, immeasurable, unstinted

**di-feth, difeth** adj infallible, certain

**difetha** vb destroy, spoil, waste

**difethwr** (-wyr) nm destroyer

**Difiau** nm Thursday

**difidend** (-au) nm dividend

**diflanbwynt** nm vanishing point

**diflanedig** adj evanescent, fleeting

**diflannu** vb vanish, disappear

**di-flas** adj tasteless

**diflas** adj insipid, dull, wearisome

**diflastod** nm disgust

**diflasu** vb disgust; weary, surfeit

**diflin, -o** adj untiring, indefatigable

**difodi** vb annihilate, exterminate

**difodiad, -iant** nm annihilation

**di-foes, difoes** adj rude,

unmannerly
**difreiniad** *nm* disfranchisement
**difreinio** *vb* disfranchise, deprive
**difrïaeth** *nf* abuse, calumny
**difrif** *nm* seriousness, earnestness
**difrifddwys** *adj* solemn
**difrifol** *adj* serious, earnest, solemn, grave
**difrifoldeb** *see* **difrifwch**
**difrifoli** *vb* sober, solemnize
**difrifwch** *nm* seriousness, earnestness, solemnity
**difrïo** *vb* scold, abuse, malign
**difrod** *nm* waste, havoc, damage
**difrodi** *vb* waste, spoil, ravage
**difrodol** *adj* destructive
**difrodwr** (-wyr) *nm* spoiler, devastator
**difrycheulyd** *adj* spotless, immaculate
**di-fudd, difudd** *adj* unprofitable, useless, futile
**di-fwlch, difwlch** *adj* without a break, continuous
**difwyniad** (-au) *nm* adulteration, pollution
**difwyniant** *nm* defilement
**difwyno** *vb* mar, soil, sully, defile
**difyfyr** *adj* impromptu
**difynio** *vb* dissect, vivisect
**difyr** *adj* pleasant, diverting, amusing
**difyrion** *npl* diversions, amusements
**difyrru** *vb* divert, amuse, beguile
**difyrrus** *adj* diverting, amusing
**difyrrwch** *nm* diversion, amusement, fun
**difyrrwr** (-yrwyr) *nm* entertainer
**difyrwaith** (-weithiau) *nm* hobby
**difywyd** *adj* inert
**diffaith** *adj* waste, desert; base, mean ▷ (-ffeithydd) *nm* wilderness, desert
**diffeithdra** *nm* dereliction
**diffeithio** *vb* lay waste
**diffeithwch** (-ychau) *nm* desert, wilderness

**diffiniad** (-au) *nm* definition
**diffinio** *vb* define
**diffodd, -i** *vb* quench, extinguish
**diffoddiad** *nm* quenching, extinction
**diffoddwr** (-wyr), **-ydd** (-ion) *nm* quencher
**diffrwyth** *adj* barren; numb, paralysed
**diffrwythder, -dra** *nm* barrenness; numbness
**diffrwytho** *vb* make barren; paralyse
**diffuant** *adj* unfeigned, sincere, genuine
**diffuantrwydd** *nm* genuineness
**di-ffurf** *adj* amorphous
**diffwys** *adj* wild, waste; high, steep; huge, awful
**diffyg** (-ion) *nm* defect, want, lack; eclipse
**diffygiant** *nm* deficiency
**diffygio** *vb* fail; faint, weary
**diffygiol** *adj* defective; faint, weary
**diffyndoll** (-au) *nf* tariff
**diffyndollaeth** *nf* protectionism
**diffynnydd** (-ynyddion) *nm* defendant
**dig** *adj* angry, wrathful ▷ *nm* anger, wrath
**digalon** *adj* disheartened, depressed, dejected, sad
**digalondid** *nm* depression, dejection
**digalonni** *vb* dishearten, discourage
**digamsyniol** *adj* unmistakable
**digasedd** *nm* hatred, enmity
**digid** (-au) *nm* digit
**digidiad** (-au) *nm* digitation
**digidol** *adj* digital
**digio** *vb* anger, offend; take offence
**di-glem** *adj* inept
**digllon** *see* **dicllon**
**digofaint** *nm* anger, wrath, indignation

**digofus** adj angry, indignant

**digolledu** vb indemnify, compensate

**digon** nm, adj, adv enough; done (of cooking)

**digonedd** nm abundance, plenty

**digoni** vb suffice; satisfy; cook

**digonol** adj satisfying; sufficient, adequate; satisfied

**digonolrwydd** nm sufficiency, abundance

**digornio** vb dehorn

**di-gred** adj infidel

**di-grefft, digrefft** adj unskilled

**digrif, -ol** adj mirthful, funny

**digriflun** (-iau) nm caricature, cartoon

**digrifwas** (-weision) nm clown, buffoon

**digrifwch** nm mirth, fun

**digroeso** adj inhospitable

**digwydd** vb befall, happen, occur

**digwyddiad** (-au) nm happening, occurrence, event

**digyfnewid** adj unchangeable

**digyffelyb** adj incomparable

**digymysg** adj unmixed

**digyswllt** adj incoherent

**digywilydd** adj impudent

**digywilydd-dra** nm impudence

**dihafal** adj unequalled, peerless

**dihangfa** (diangfâu) nf escape

**dihangol** adj escaped, safe

**dihareb** (diarhebion) nf proverb

**dihatru** vb strip, undress

**dihefelydd** adj unequalled

**diheintio** vb disinfect

**diheintydd** (-ion) nm disinfectant, sterilizer

**di-hid(io)** adj heedless, indifferent, reckless

**dihidlo** vb drop, distil; shed

**dihidrwydd** nm indifference, recklessness

**dihiryn** (-hirod) nm rascal, scoundrel

**dihoeni** vb languish, pine

**dihuno** vb wake, rouse

**di-hwyl** adj out of sorts

**dihyder** adj lacking confidence

**dihydradu** vb dehydrate

**dihysbydd** adj inexhaustible

**dihysbyddu** vb empty, exhaust

**dil** (-iau) nm: ~ **mêl** honeycomb

**dilead** nm abolition, deletion

**dilechdid** nm dialectic

**diledryw** adj pure, genuine

**dileu** vb blot out, delete; abolish

**dilewyrch** adj dismal; unprosperous

**dilorni** vb abuse, revile

**di-lun** adj slovenly

**diluw** see **dilyw**

**dilyffethair** adj unencumbered, unfettered

**dilyn** vb follow, pursue; imitate

**dilyniad** nm following; imitation

**dilyniant** (-nnau) nm sequence, progression

**dilynol** adj following; consequent

**dilynwr** (-wyr) nm follower; imitator

**dilys** adj sure, certain; genuine

**dilysiant** (-nnau) nm validation

**dilysnod** (-au) nm hallmark

**dilysrwydd** nm genuineness

**dilysu** vb certify, warrant, guarantee

**dilyw** nm flood, deluge

**dillad** (nm **dilledyn**) npl clothes, clothing

**dilladu** vb clothe

**dilledydd** nm clothier

**dilledyn** nm garment

**dim** adj any (with negative understood); no ▷ nm anything; none, nothing

**dimensiwn** (-iynau) nm dimension

**dimensiynol** adj dimensional

**di-nam, dinam** adj faultless

**dinas** (-oedd) nf city

**dinasol** adj municipal

**dinasyddiaeth** nf citizenship

**dincod** see **deincod**

**dinesig** adj civil, civic
**dinesydd** (**dinasyddion**) nm citizen
**dinistr** nm destruction
**dinistrio** vb destroy
**dinistriol** adj destroying, destructive
**dinistriwr** (**-wyr**) nm destroyer
**dinistrydd** (**-ion**) nm destroyer
**diniwed** adj harmless, innocent
**diniweidrwydd** nm innocence
**di-nod, dinod** adj insignificant, obscure
**dinodedd** nm insignificance, obscurity
**dinoethi** vb bare, denude, expose
**diod** (**-ydd**) nf drink, beverage
**diodi** vb give drink
**dioddef** vb suffer, bear; wait
 ▷ (**-iadau**) nm suffering
**dioddefaint** nm suffering, passion
**dioddefgar, -efus** adj patient
**dioddefgarwch** nm patience
**dioddefwr, -ydd** (**-wyr**) nm sufferer, patient
**di-oed, dioed** adj without delay, immediate
**diofal** adj careless
**diofalwch** nm carelessness
**diog** adj slothful, indolent, lazy
**diogel** adj safe, secure; sure, certain
**diogelu** vb make safe, secure
**diogelwch** nm safety, security
**diogi** vb be lazy, idle ▷ nm laziness
**dioglyd** adj lazy, sluggish, indolent
**diogyn** nm lazy one, idler, sluggard
**diolch** vb thank, give thanks
 ▷ (**-iadau**) nm thanks, thanksgiving
**diolchgar** adj thankful, grateful
**diolchgarwch** nm thankfulness, gratitude, thanksgiving
**diolwg** adj ugly
**diorseddu** vb dethrone, depose
**di-os** adj without doubt
**diosg** vb undress, put off, strip, divest
**diota** vb tipple

**diotwr** (**-wyr**) nm boozer, drunkard
**dioty** (**-tai**) nm ale-house, public-house
**diploma** (**-âu**) nm/f diploma
**diplomateg** nf diplomacy
**diplomydd** (**-ion**) nm diplomat
**diplomyddol** adj diplomatic
**dipton** (**-au**) nf diphthong
**dir** adj certain, necessary
**diraddiad** (**-au**) nm degradation
**diraddio** vb degrade
**diraddiol** adj degrading
**di-raen** adj shabby, dull
**dirboeni** vb torture, excruciate
**dirdyniad** (**-au**) nm convulsion
**dirdynnol** adj excruciating
**dirdynnu** vb rack, torture
**direidi** nm mischievousness, mischief
**direidus** adj mischievous
**direol** adj unruly, disorderly
**direwydd** nm defroster
**direwyn** nm antifreeze
**dirfawr** adj vast, huge, immense, enormous
**dirgel** adj secret ▷ (**-ion**) nm secret
**dirgeledig** adj hidden, secret; mystical
**dirgeledigaeth** (**-au**) nm/f mystery
**dirgelu** vb secrete, conceal, hide
**dirgelwch** nm secrecy, mystery, secret
**dirgryniad** (**-au**) nm tremor, vibration
**dirgrynol** adj vibrating
**dirgrynu** vb tremble, vibrate
**diriaethol** adj concrete
**dirlawn** adj saturated
**dirmyg** nm contempt, scorn
**dirmygu** vb despise, scorn
**dirmygus** adj contemptuous; contemptible
**dirnad** vb discern, comprehend
**dirnadaeth** nf discernment, comprehension
**dirnadwy** adj discernible

**dirprwy (-on)** *nm* deputy; delegate
**dirprwyaeth (-au)** *nf* commission; deputation
**dirprwyo** *vb* deputise, delegate
**dirprwyol** *adj* vicarious
**dirprwywr (-wyr)** *nm* commissioner
**dirwasgiad (-au)** *nm* depression
**dirwest** *nm/f* abstinence, temperance
**dirwestol** *adj* temperate
**dirwestwr (-wyr)** *nm* abstainer
**dirwy (-on)** *nf* fine
**dirwyn** *vb* wind, twist, twine
**dirwynwr (-wyr)** *nm* winder
**dirwyo** *vb* fine
**di-rym** *adj* powerless, void
**dirymu** *vb* nullify, annul, cancel
**diryw** *adj* neuter
**dirywiad** *nm* degeneration, deterioration
**dirywiaeth** *nf* degeneracy
**dirywiedig** *adj* degenerate
**dirywio** *vb* degenerate, deteriorate
**dirywiol** *adj* decadent, retrograde
**dis (-iau)** *nm* die, dice
**di-sail** *adj* groundless, baseless
**disbaddu** *vb* castrate, geld, spay
**disbaddwr (-wyr)** *nm* castrator
**disberod** *nm*: **ar d~** wandering, astray
**disbyddedig** *adj* exhausted
**disbyddu** *vb* empty, exhaust
**disbyddwr** *nm* exhaust
**disco (-au)** *nm* disco
**diserch** *adj* sullen, sulky, loveless
**disg (-iau)** *nm* disk, record
**disgen (disgiau)** *nf* discus
**disglair** *adj* bright, brilliant
**disgleirdeb, -der** *nm* brightness, brilliance
**disgleirio** *vb* shine, glitter
**disgloff** *adj* free from lameness
**disgownt (-iau, -s)** *nm* discount
**disgrifiad (-au)** *nm* description
**disgrifiadol** *adj* descriptive
**disgrifio** *vb* describe

**disgwyl** *vb* look, expect, wait
**disgwylfa (-feydd)** *nf* watch-tower
**disgwylgar** *adj* watchful, expectant
**disgwyliad (-au)** *nm* expectation
**disgybl (-ion)** *nm* disciple, pupil
**disgyblaeth** *nf* discipline
**disgyblu** *vb* discipline
**disgyblwr (-wyr)** *nm* disciplinarian
**disgyn** *vb* descend; fall, drop; let down
**disgynfa (-feydd)** *nf* descent, declivity; landing place
**disgyniad (-au)** *nm* descent
**disgynnol** *adj* descending
**disgynnydd (-ynyddion)** *nm* descendant
**disgyrchedd** *nm* gravitation
**disgyrchiad, -iant** *nm* gravity; **craidd ~** centre of gravity
**disgyrchu** *vb* gravitate
**di-sigl** *adj* unshaken, steadfast, firm
**disiog** *adj* diced
**disodli** *vb* trip up, supplant
**dist (-iau)** *nm* joist, beam
**distadl** *adj* insignificant, low, base, mean
**distadledd** *nm* insignificance, obscurity
**distain (-einiaid)** *nm* steward
**distaw** *adj* silent, quiet
**distawrwydd** *nm* silence, quiet
**distewi** *vb* silence; calm, quiet
**distryw** *nm* destruction
**distrywgar** *adj* destructive, wasteful
**distrywio** *vb* destroy
**distrywiwr (-wyr)** *nm* destroyer
**distyll** *nm*, **-iad** distillation
**distyllio** *vb* distil
**di-sut** *adj* unwell; small
**diswta** *adj* sudden, abrupt
**diswyddiad (-au)** *nm* dismissal
**diswyddo** *vb* dismiss from office, discharge
**disychedu** *vb* quench thirst
**di-syfl** *adj* immovable, impregnable

**disyfyd** *adj* sudden, instantaneous
**disyml** *adj* simple, artless, ingenuous
**disymwth** *adj* sudden, instantaneous
**disynnwyr** *adj* senseless
**ditectif** (-s) *nm* detective
**diwahân** *adj* inseparable, indiscriminate
**diwair** *adj* chaste
**di-waith, diwaith** *adj* unemployed, idle
**diwall** *adj* satisfied, full, perfect
**diwallu** *vb* satisfy, supply
**diwarafun** *adj* unforbidden, ungrudging
**diwasgedd** (-au) *nm* depression (*weather*)
**diwedydd** (-iau) *nm* evening, eventide
**diwedd** *nm* end, conclusion
**diweddar** *adj* late, modern
**diweddaru** *vb* modernize
**diweddarwch** *nm* lateness
**diweddeb** *nf* cadence
**diweddglo** *nm* conclusion
**diweddu** *vb* end, finish, conclude
**diweirdeb** *nm* chastity
**diweithdra** *nm* unemployment
**diwelfa** (-feydd) *nf* watershed
**diwethaf** *adj* last
**diwinydd** (-ion) *nm* divine, theologian
**diwinyddiaeth** *nf* divinity, theology
**diwinyddol** *adj* theological
**diwreiddio** *vb* uproot, eradicate
**diwrnod** (-iau) *nm* day
**diwrthdro** *adj* inexorable
**diwyd** *adj* diligent, industrious
**diwydianfa** *nf* industrial estate
**diwydiannaeth** *nf* industrialization, industrialism
**diwydiannol** *adj* industrial
**diwydiannwr** (-ianwyr) *nm* industrialist
**diwydiant** (-iannau) *nm* industry

**diwydrwydd** *nm* diligence, industry
**diwyg** *nm* form, dress, garb
**diwygiad** (-au) *nm* reform, reformation; revival
**diwygiadol** *adj* reformatory; revivalistic
**diwygiedig** *adj* reformed; revised
**diwygio** *vb* amend, reform, revise
**diwygiol** *adj* reformatory
**diwygiwr** (-wyr) *nm* reformer; revivalist
**diwylliadol** *adj* cultural
**diwylliannol** *adj* cultural
**diwylliant** (-nnau) *nm* culture
**diwylliedig** *adj* cultured
**diwyllio** *vb* cultivate
**diymadferth** *adj* helpless
**diymadferthedd** *nm* helplessness
**diymdroi** *adj* without delay
**diymhongar** *adj* unassuming
**diymod** *adj* steadfast, immovable
**diymwad** *adj* undeniable, indisputable
**diysgog** *adj* steadfast, firm, stable
**diystyr** *adj* contemptuous; contemptible; meaningless
**diystyrllyd** *adj* contemptuous, disdainful
**diystyru** *vb* disregard, despise
**diystyrwch** *nm* contempt, disdain, scorn
**do** *adv* yes (*to questions in preterite tense*)
**doc** (-iau) *nm* dock
**docfa** (-feydd) *nf* berth
**docio** *vb* shorten; dock, berth
**doctor** (-iaid) *nm* doctor
**doctora** *vb* doctor
**dod** *see* **dyfod**
**dodi** *vb* put, place; give
**dodrefn** *npl* (*nm-yn*) furniture
**dodrefnu** *vb* furnish
**dodrefnwr** (-wyr) *nm* furnisher
**dodwy** *vb* lay eggs
**doe** *adv* yesterday
**doeth** (-ion) *adj* wise

**doethineb** nm/f wisdom
**doethinebu** vb discourse wisely, pontificate
**doethor** (-iaid) nm doctor (of university)
**doethur** (-iaid) nm doctor (of university)
**doethuriaeth** (-au) nf doctorate
**dof** adj tame, domesticated; garden
**dofednod** npl fowls, poultry
**dofi** vb tame, domesticate; assuage
**dofn** adj f of **dwfn**
**Dofydd** nm God
**dogfen** (-ni, -nau) nf document
**dogfennaeth** nf documentation
**dogfennen** (-ennau) nf documentary
**dogfennol** adj documentary
**dogn** (-au) nm share, portion; dose
**dogni** vb ration
**doili** nm doyley
**dol** (-iau) nf doll
**dôl** nm dole
**dôl** (dolydd, dolau) nf meadow
**dolbridd** (-oedd) nm alluvium, meadow soil
**doldir** (-oedd) nm meadow-land
**dolef** (-au) nf cry
**dolefain** vb cry out
**dolefus** adj wailing, plaintive
**dolen** (-nau) nf loop, link, ring, bow
**dolennog** adj ringed, looped; winding
**dolennu** vb loop; wind, meander
**doler** (-i) nf dollar
**dolffin** nm dolphin
**dolur** (-iau) nm sore; ailment; grief
**dolurio** vb hurt, wound; grieve
**dolurus** adj sore
**dominyddu** vb dominate
**donio** vb endow, gift
**doniol** adj gifted; witty, humorous
**donioldeb, -wch** nm wit, humour
**dôr** (dorau) nf door
**dos** (-ys, -au) nf dose
**dosbarth** (au, -iadau) nm reason; class; district

**dosbarthiad** nm distribution
**dosbarthu** vb class, classify; distribute
**dosbarthwr** (-wyr) nm distributor
**dosio** vb dose
**dosran** (-nau) nf division, section
**dosrannu** vb separate, analyse
**dot** (-iau) nm/f dot
**dot** nf giddiness, vertigo
**dotio** vb dote
**drachefn** adv again
**dracht** (-iau) nm draught (of liquor)
**drachtio** vb drink deep
**draen** (-iau) nm drain
**draen** (drain) nf prickle, thorn
**draen, -en** (drain) nf thorn
**draeniad** (-au) nm drainage
**draenio** vb drain
**draenog** (-od) nm hedgehog
**drafft** (-iau) nm draft, draught
**draffts** npl draughts
**dragio** vb drag, tear, mangle
**draig** (dreigiau) nf dragon
**drain** see **draen, draenen**
**drama** (dramâu) nf drama
**dramateiddio** vb dramatize
**dramatig** adj dramatic
**dramodiad** (-au) nm dramatization
**dramodwr** (-wyr) nm dramatist
**draw** adv yonder, away
**dreflan** vb dribble
**dreng** adj morose, surly, sullen, harsh
**dresel, -er** (-i, -ydd) nm dresser
**drewdod** nm stink, stench
**drewi** vb, nm stink
**drewllyd** adj stinking
**driblo** vb dribble
**drifft** (-iau) nm drift
**dril** (-iau) nm drill
**drilio** vb drill
**dringad** vb, nm climb
**dringfa** (-feydd) nf climb, ascent
**dringo** vb climb
**dringwr** (-wyr) nm climber
**dripsych** adj dripdry

**drôr** (drors) *nm* drawer

**dros** *see* **tros**

**drud** *adj* dear, precious, costly; reckless

**drudfawr** *adj* costly, expensive

**drudwen** *nf*, **drudwy** *nm* starling

**drwg** *adj* evil, bad, naughty, wicked ▷ (drygau) *nm* evil, harm, hurt

**drwgdybiaeth** (-au) *nf* suspicion

**drwgdybio** *vb* suspect

**drwgdybus** *adj* suspicious

**drwglosgiad** *nm* arson

**drwgweithredwr** (-wyr) *nm* evildoer

**drwm** (drymiau) *nm* drum

**drws** (drysau) *nm* door

**drwy** *see* **trwy**

**drycin** (-oedd) *nf* foul weather

**drycinog** *adj* stormy

**drych** (-au) *nm* spectacle; mirror; object, pattern

**drychfeddwl** (-yliau) *nm* idea

**drychiolaeth** (-au) *nf* apparition, phantom

**drygair** *nm* ill report; scandal

**dryganadl** *nm* halitosis

**drygfyd** *nm* adversity

**drygioni** *nm* badness, wickedness

**drygionus** *adj* bad, wicked

**drygu** *vb* hurt, harm, injure

**dryll** (-iau) *nm* piece; part ▷ *nm/f* gun, rifle

**drylliad** (-au) *nm* breaking; wreck

**drylliedig** *adj* broken

**dryllio** *vb* break in pieces, shatter

**drylliog** *adj* broken, contrite

**drysi** *npl* (nf-ïen) thorns, briers

**dryslwyn** (-i) *nm* thicket

**dryslyd** *adj* perplexing; confused

**drysu** *vb* tangle; perplex; be confused

**dryswch** *nm* tangle; perplexity; confusion

**dryw** (-od) *nm/f* wren

**du** *adj*, *nm* black

**duc, dug** (-iaid) *nm* duke

**dugiaeth** *nf* duchy

**dull** (-iau) *nm* form, manner, mode

**dullwedd** (-au) *nm* mannerism

**Dulyn** *nf* Dublin

**duo** *vb* black, blacken

**dur** *nm* steel

**duw** (-iau) *nm* god; **D~** God

**düwch** *nm* blackness

**duwdod** *nm* godhead, divinity, deity

**duwies** (-au) *nf* goddess

**duwiol** (-ion) *adj* godly, pious

**duwioldeb** *nm* godliness, piety

**duwiolfrydedd** *nm* godliness, piety

**duwiolfrydig** *adj* god-fearing, pious

**dwbio** *vb* daub, plaster

**dwbl** *adj* double

**dweud, dweyd** *see* **dywedyd**

**dwfn** (f dofn) *adj* deep, profound

**dwfr, dŵr** (dyfroedd) *nm* water

**dwl** *adj* dull, stupid, foolish

**dwlu** *vb* dote

**dwmbwr-dambar** *adv* helter-skelter

**dwndwr** *nm* din, babble, hubbub

**dwnsiwn** (-iynau) *nm* dungeon

**dŵr** *see* **dwfr**

**dwrdio** *vb* scold

**dwrn** (dyrnau) *nm* fist; knob, handle, hilt

**dwsin** (-inau) *nm* dozen

**dwst** *nm* dust, powder

**dwster** (-i) *nm* duster

**dwthwn** *nm* day

**dwy** *see* **dau**

**dwyfol** *adj* divine

**dwyfoldeb** *nm* divinity, deity

**dwyfoli** *vb* deify

**dwyfron** (-nau) *nf* breast, chest

**dwyfronneg** *nf* breastplate

**dwyieithedd** *nm* bilingualism

**dwyieitheg** *nf* study of bilingualism

**dwyieithog** *adj* bilingual, duoglot

**dwyieithrwydd** *nm* bilingualism

**dwylaw, -lo** *nd*, *pl* two hands,

hands
**dwyn** vb bear; bring; steal
**dwyochredd** nm bilateralism
**dwyochrol** adj bilateral
**dwyradd** adj quadratic, two-tier
**dwyrain** nm, adj east; **D~ yr Almaen** East Germany
**dwyraniad** nm dichotomy
**dwyrannu** vb bisect
**dwyreiniol** adj easterly, eastern, oriental
**dwyreiniwr** (-wyr) nm easterner, oriental
**dwys** adj dense, grave, deep, intense
**dwysáu** vb deepen, intensify
**dwysbigo** vb prick, sting
**dwysedd** (-au) nm density
**dwyster** nm gravity, solemnity
**dwythell** (-au) nf duct
**dwywaith** adv twice
**dy** pron thy, thine
**dyblu** vb double; repeat
**dyblyg** adj twofold, double
**dyblygiad** (-au) nm duplication, duplicate
**dyblygu** vb double, fold
**dyblygydd** (-ion) nm duplicator
**dybryd** adj sore, dire; flagrant
**dychan** (-au) nf lampoon, satire
**dychangerdd** (-i) nf satirical poem, satire
**dychanol** adj satirical
**dychanu** vb lampoon, satirize, revile
**dychanwr** (-wyr) nm satirist
**dychmygadwy** adj imaginable
**dychmygol** adj imaginary
**dychmygu** vb imagine
**dychmygus** adj imaginative, inventive
**dychryn** (-iadau) nm fright, terror ▷ vb frighten
**dychrynllyd** adj frightful, terrible
**dychrynu** vb frighten, be frightened
**dychweledig** adj returned
**dychweliad** (-au) nm return; conversion
**dychwelyd** vb return
**dychymyg** (dychmygion) nm imagination, fancy; riddle, device
**dydd** (-iau) nm day; **~iau cŵn** silly season
**dyddfu** vb flag, pine, faint
**dyddiad** (-au) nm date
**dyddiadur** (-on) nm diary, journal
**dyddiedig** adj dated
**dyddio** vb become day, dawn; date
**dyddiol** adj daily
**dyddlyfr** (-au) nm diary, journal
**dyddodyn** (-odion) nm deposit
**dyfais** (-feisiau) nf device, invention
**dyfal** adj diligent
**dyfalbarhad** nm perseverance
**dyfalbarhau** vb persevere
**dyfaliad** (-au) nm guess, conjecture
**dyfalu** vb guess, conjecture
**dyfalwch** nm diligence, assiduity
**dyfarniad** (-au) nm decision, verdict
**dyfarnu** vb adjudge
**dyfarnwr** (-wyr) nm judge, umpire
**dyfeisio** vb devise, invent, imagine; guess
**dyfeisiwr** (-wyr) nm inventor
**dyfnant** (-nentydd) nf ravine
**dyfnder** (-au, -oedd) nm deep, depth
**dyfnhau** vb deepen
**dyfod, dod** vb come, become
**dyfodfa** nf access, entrance
**dyfodiad** nm coming, arrival, advent
**dyfodiad** (-iaid) nm incomer, stranger
**dyfodol** adj coming, future ▷ nm future
**dyfradwy** adj watered; watering
**dyfredig** adj irrigated
**dyfrffos** (-ydd) nm canal, watercourse
**dyfrgi** (-gwn) nm otter
**dyfrhad** nm irrigation

**dyfrhau, dyfrio** *vb* water
**dyfrllyd** *adj* watery
**dyfyniad** (-au) *nm* citation, quotation
**dyfynnod** (-ynodau) *nm* quotation mark
**dyfynnol** *adj* citatory, summoned
**dyfynnu** *vb* cite, quote; summon
**dyffryn** (-noedd) *nm* valley
**dyffryndir** (-oedd) *nm* low country; vale
**dygn** *adj* hard, severe, grievous, dire
**dygnu** *vb* strive, persevere
**dygnwch** *nm* perseverance, assiduity
**dygwyl** *nm* holiday, feast day
**dygymod** *vb* agree (with), put up (with)
**dyhead** (-au) *nm* aspiration
**dyheu** *vb* pant; long, yearn, aspire
**dyhiryn** *see* **dihiryn**
**dyladwy** *adj* due
**dylanwad** (-au) *nm* influence
**dylanwadol** *adj* influential
**dylanwadu** *vb* influence
**dyled** (-ion) *nf* debt, obligation
**dyledog** *adj* in debt, indebted
**dyledus** *adj* due
**dyledwr** (-wyr) *nm* debtor
**dyletswydd** (-au) *nf* duty, obligation
**dylif** *nm* flood, deluge ▷ *nf* warp
**dylifo** *vb* flow, stream, pour
**dylni** *nm* stupidity, dullness
**dyluniad** (-au) *nm* design, drawing
**dylunio** *vb* design
**dylunydd** (-ion) *nm* designer
**dylyfu gên** *vb* yawn, gape
**dylluan** *see* **tylluan**
**dyma** *adv* here is, here are; this is, these are
**dymchweliad** *nm* overthrow
**dymchwelyd** *vb* overthrow, upset, subvert
**dymuniad** (-au) *nm* wish, desire
**dymuno** *vb* wish, desire
**dymunol** *adj* desirable, agreeable, pleasant
**dyn** (-ion) *nm* man, person
**dyna** *adv* there is, there are; that is, those are
**dynad** *npl* nettles
**dyndod** *nm* manhood, humanity
**dyneiddiaeth** *nf* humanism
**dyneiddiol** *adj* humanistic
**dyneiddiwr** (-wyr) *nm* humanist
**dynes** *nf* woman
**dynesiad** *nm* approach
**dynesu** *vb* draw near, approach
**dyngar** *adj* humane
**dyngarol** *adj* philanthropic
**dyngarwch** *nm* philanthropy
**dyngarwr** (-wyr) *nm* philanthropist
**dyniawed** (-iewaid) *nm* yearling, steer
**dyn-laddiad** *nm* manslaughter
**dynodi** *vb* denote, signify
**dynodiad** (-au) *nm* denotation
**dynol** *adj* human; man-like; manly
**dynoliaeth** *nf* humanity
**dynoliaethau** *npl* humanities
**dynolryw** *coll n* mankind
**dynwared** *vb* imitate, mimic
**dynwarededd** *nm* mimicry
**dynwarediad** (-au) *nm* imitation, mimicry
**dynwaredol** *adj* imitative
**dynwaredwr** (-wyr) *nm* imitator, mimic
**dyraddiant** *nm* degradation
**dyraniad** (-au) *nm* allocation
**dyrchafael** *vb* rise, ascend ▷ *nm* ascension
**dyrchafedig** *adj* exalted
**dyrchafiad** *nm* elevation, promotion
**dyrchafol** *adj* elevating
**dyrchafu** *vb* raise, elevate; rise, ascend
**dyri** (-ïau), **dyrif** (-au) *nf* ballad, lyric
**dyrnaid** (-eidiau) *nm* handful
**dyrnio** *vb* punch

**dyrnod** (-iau) *nm/f* blow, stroke
**dyrnu** *vb* thump; thresh
**dyrnwr** (-wyr) *nm* thresher
**dyrnwr medi** *nm* combine harvester
**dyrys** *adj* tangled; difficult; perplexing
**dyryslyd, dyrysu, dyryswch** *see* **dryslyd, drysu, dryswch**
**dysg** *nm/f* learning
**dysgedig** (-ion) *adj* learned
**dysgeidiaeth** *nf* teaching, doctrine
**dysgl** (-au) *nf* dish
**dysglaid** (-eidiau) *nf* dishful, dish
**dysgu** *vb* learn, teach
**dysgwr** (-wyr) *nm* learner, teacher
**dywalgi** (-gwn) *nm* tiger
**dywediad** (-au) *nm* saying
**dywedwst** *adj* taciturn ▷ *nm* taciturnity
**dywedyd** *vb* say, speak, tell
**dyweddi** (-ïau) *nf* betrothal, fiancé(e) ▷ *n coll* betrothed
**dyweddïad** *nm* betrothal
**dyweddïo** *vb* betroth

# e

**eang** *adj* wide, broad, immense
**eangder, eangu** *see* **ehangder, ehangu**
**eangfrydedd** *nm* magnanimity

**eangfrydig** *adj* broad-minded, magnanimous
**eb, ebe, ebr** *vb* said, quoth
**ebargofiant** *nm* oblivion
**ebill** (-ion) *nm* auger, borer; peg
**ebillio** *vb* bore
**ebol** (-ion) *nm* colt, foal
**eboles** (-au) *nf* foal, filly
**eboni** *nm* ebony
**ebran** (-nau) *nm* provender, fodder
**Ebrill** *nm* April
**ebrwydd** *adj* quick, swift, soon
**ebwch** (-ychau) *nm* gasp
**ebychiad** (-au) *nm* interjection, ejaculation
**ebychu** *vb* gasp, interject, ejaculate
**eciwmenaidd** *adj* ecumenical
**ecliptig** *adj, nm* ecliptic
**ecoleg** (-au) *nf/m* ecology
**ecolegol** *adj* ecological
**ecolegwr** (-wyr) *nm* ecologist
**economaidd** *adj* economic
**economeg** *nf* economics
**economegol** *adj* economic
**economegwr** (-wyr) *nm* economist
**economegydd** (-ion) *nm* economist
**economi** (-ïau) *nm* economy
**economydd** *nm* economist
**ecsbloetio** *vb* exploit
**ecsbloetiwr** (-wyr) *nm* exploiter
**ecseis** *nm* excise
**ecseismon** (-myn) *nm* exciseman
**ecsema** *nm* eczema
**ecsentredd** (-au) *nm* eccentricity
**ecsentrig** *adj* eccentric (*maths*)
**ecstasi** *nm* ecstasy
**ecstatig** *adj* ecstatic
**echblyg** *adj* explicit, outward
**echblygol** *adj* extrovert
**echdoe** *adv* day before yesterday
**echdoriad** (-au) *nm* eruption
**echel** (-au) *nf* axle, axletree; axis
**echelin** (-au) *nm* axis
**echnos** *adv* night before last
**echrydus** *adj* fearful, frightful,

shocking
**echwyn** (-ion) *nm* loan
**echwynna** *vb* borrow, lend
**echwynnwr** (-wynwyr) *nm* lender, creditor
**edau** (edafedd) *nf* thread; (*pl*) yarn, wool
**edfryd** *vb* restore
**edifar** *adj* penitent, sorry
**edifarhau, -faru** *vb* repent, be sorry
**edifarus, -feiriol** *adj* repentant, penitent
**edifeirwch** *nm* repentance, penitence
**edliw** *vb* upbraid, reproach, taunt
**edmygedd** *nm* admiration
**edmygol** *adj* admiring
**edmygu** *vb* admire
**edmygwr, -ydd** (-wyr) *nm* admirer
**edrych** *vb* look, examine
**edrychiad** *nm* look
**edrychwr** (-wyr) *nm* beholder, spectator
**edwi, edwino** *vb* fade, wither, decay
**eddi** *npl* thrums; fringe, nap
**ef, efe** *pron* he, him; it
**efallai** *adv* perhaps, peradventure
**efengyl** (-au) *nf* gospel
**efengylaidd** *adj* evangelical
**efengyleiddio** *vb* evangelize
**efengyles** (-au) *nf* female evangelist
**efengylu** *vb* evangelize
**efengylwr, -ydd** (-wyr) *nm* evangelist
**efelychiad** (-au) *nm* imitation
**efelychiadol** *adj* imitative
**efelychu** *vb* imitate
**efelychwr** (-wyr) *nm* imitator
**efelychydd** (-ion) *nm* simulator
**eferw** *adj* effervescent
**eferwad** (-au) *nm* effervescence
**eferwi** *vb* effervesce
**efo** *prep* with

**efô** *pron* he, him; it
**efrau** *npl* tares
**Efrog Newydd** *nf* New York
**efrydiaeth** (-au) *nf* study
**efrydu** *vb* study
**efrydydd** (-ion, -wyr) *nm* student
**efydd** *nm* bronze, copper, brass
**effaith** (-eithiau) *nf* effect
**effeithio** *vb* effect, affect
**effeithiol** *adj* effectual, effective, efficient
**effeithioli** *vb* render effectual
**effeithiolrwydd** *nm* efficacy
**effeithlon** *adj* efficient
**effeithlonedd** *nm* efficiency (*of machines etc*)
**effeithlonrwydd** *nm* efficiency
**effro** *adj* awake, vigilant
**eger** (-au) *nm* bore, eagre
**egin** *npl* (*nm*-yn) germs, sprouts
**eginhad, eginiad** (-au) *nm* germination, sprouting
**egino** *vb* germinate, shoot, sprout
**eginol** *adj* germinal, shooting
**eginyn** (egin) *nm* sprout
**eglur** *adj* clear, plain, evident
**eglurdeb, -der** *nm* clearness
**eglureb** (-au) *nf* illustration
**eglurhad** *nm* explanation, demonstration
**eglurhaol** *adj* explanatory
**egluro** *vb* make clear, explain
**eglwys** (-i, -ydd) *nf* church
**eglwysig** *adj* church, ecclesiastical
**eglwyswr** (-wyr) *nm* churchman
**eglwyswraig** (-wragedd) *nf* churchwoman
**egni** (-ïon) *nm* effort, might, energy
**egnïo** *vb* endeavour, make an effort
**egnïol** *adj* energetic
**egnïoli** *vb* energise
**ego** *nm* ego
**egoistiaeth** *nm* egoism
**egosentrig** *adj* egocentric
**egöydd** *nm* egoist
**egr** *adj* sharp, sour; severe; savage; cheeky

**egroes** npl (nf -en) hips
**egwan** adj weak, feeble
**egwyd** (-ydd) nf fetlock; fetter
**egwyddor** (-ion, -au) nf rudiment; principle; alphabet
**egwyddorol** adj high-principled
**egwyl** nf lull, respite; opportunity
**enghraifft** (-eifftiau) nf example, instance
**enghreifftiol** adj exemplary, illustrative
**englyn** (-ion) nm Welsh alliterative stanza
**englyna, -u** vb compose englynion
**englynwr** (-wyr) nm composer of englynion
**engyl** see **angel**
**ehangder** (eangderau) nm breadth, immensity
**ehangu** vb enlarge, extend
**ehedeg** vb fly; run to seed
**ehedfa** (-feydd) nf flight
**ehedfan** vb hover, fly
**ehediad** (-au) nm flight
**ehediad** (-iaid) nm fowl, bird
**ehedog** adj flying
**ehedydd** (-ion) nm lark
**ehofndra** nm fearlessness, boldness
**ei** pron his, hers; its
**eich** pron your
**Eidal**: **yr Eidal** Italy
**eidion** (-nau) nm ox
**eiddew** coll n ivy
**eiddgar** adj zealous, ardent
**eiddgarwch** nm zeal, ardour
**eiddigedd** nm jealousy; zeal
**eiddigeddu** vb be jealous, envy; have zeal
**eiddigeddus** adj jealous, envious
**eiddigus** adj jealous; zealous
**eiddil** adj slender, feeble
**eiddilwch** nm slenderness, feebleness
**eiddiorwg** coll n ivy
**eiddo** nm property, possessions
▷ pron his etc

**eidduno** vb desire, wish, pray
**Eifftaidd** adj Egyptian
**Eifftiwr** (-wyr), **Eifftiad** (-iaid) nm Egyptian
**eigion** nm depth, ocean
**eigioneg** nf/m oceanography
**eigionol** adj pelagic
**eingion** (-au) nf anvil
**Eingl** npl Angles, Englishmen
**Eingl-Gymro** (-Gymry) nm Anglo-Welshman
**Eingl-Sais** (-Saeson) nm Anglo-Saxon
**Eingl-Seisnig** adj Anglo-Saxon
**eil-** prefix second (**ail**)
**eilchwyl** adv again
**eiliad** (-au) nm/f second, moment
**eiliadur** (-on) nm alternator
**eilio** vb weave, plait; sing; second
**eiliwr** (-wyr) nm seconder
**eilradd** (-ol) adj secondary, inferior
**eilrif** (-au) nm even number
**eilun** (-od) nm image, idol
**eilunaddolgar** adj idolatrous
**eilunaddoli** vb worship idols
**eilunaddolwr** (-wyr) nm idolator
**eilwaith** adv again
**eilydd** (-ion) nm seconder, reserve
**eillio** vb shave
**eilliwr** (-wyr) nm shaver, barber
**ein** pron adj our
**einioes** nf life, lifetime
**einion** (-au) nf anvil
**eira** nm snow
**eirchion** see **arch**
**eirias** adj burning, glowing, fiery
**eirin** npl (nf -en) plums; **~ gwlanog** peaches; **~ duon** damsons; **~ duon bach** sloes; **~ Mair** gooseberries
**eiriol** vb plead, pray, intercede
**eiriolaeth** nf intercession
**eiriolwr** (-wyr) nm intercessor, mediator
**eirlaw** nm sleet
**eirlin** (-iau) nm snowline
**eirlithrad** (-au) nm avalanche
**eirlys** (-iau) nm snowdrop

**eironi** nm irony
**eisen** (ais) nf rib; lath
**eisglwyf** nm pleurisy
**eisiau** nm want, need, lack
**eisin** coll n bran, husk
**eising** nm icing
**eisio** vb ice
**eisoes** adv already
**eistedd** vb sit, seat
**eisteddfa** (-oedd, -fâu) nf seat
**eisteddfod** (-au) nf session;
  eisteddfod
**eisteddfodol** adj eisteddfodic
**eisteddfodwr** (-wyr) nm
  frequenter of eisteddfodau
**eisteddfota** vb frequent
  eisteddfodau
**eisteddiad** (-au) nm sitting,
  session
**eisteddle** (-oedd) nm seat, sitting,
  pew
**eitem** (-au) nf item
**eithaf** (-ion) adj, nm extreme;
  superlative ▷ adv very, quite
**eithafbwynt** (-iau) nm extremity;
  apogee
**eithafiaeth** nf extremism
**eithafion** npl extremes, extremities
**eithafol** adj extreme
**eithafwr** (-wyr) nm extremist
**eithin** npl (nf -en) furze, gorse
**eithinog** adj furzy
**eithr** prep except; besides ▷ conj but
**eithriad** (-au) nm exception
**eithriadol** adj exceptional
**eithrio** vb except, exclude
**elastig** adj, nm elastic
**elastigedd** nm elasticity
**electromagneteg** nf/m
  electromagnetism
**electromedr** (-au) nm
  electrometer
**electron** (-au) nm electron
**electroneg** nf/m electronics
**electronig** adj electronic
**elegeiog** adj elegiac, mournful
**eleni** adv this year

**elfen** (-nau) nf element
**elfennig** adj elemental
**elfennol** adj elementary
**eli** (elïoedd) nm ointment, salve
**elifiant** (-nnau) nm effluence
**elifyn** (elifion) nm effluent
**eliffant** (-od, -iaid) nm elephant
**eliffantaidd** adj elephantine
**elin** (-au, -oedd) nf elbow; angle,
  bend
**elips** (-au) nm ellipse
**eliptig** adj elliptical
**elor** (-au) nf bier
**elusen** (-nau) nf alms
**elusendy** (-dai) nm almshouse
**elusengar** adj charitable,
  benevolent
**elusengarwch** nm charity,
  benevolence
**elusennol** adj eleemosynary
**elusennwr** (-enwyr) nm almoner
**elw** nm possession, gain, profit
**elwa** vb gain, profit
**elwlen** (-wlod) nf kidney
**ellyll** (-on) nm fiend; goblin
**ellyllaidd** adj fiendish; elfish
**ellylles** (-au) nf fury, she-goblin
**ellyn** (-au, -od) nm razor
**embryo** nm embryo
**embryoleg** nf embryology
**emosiwn** (-iynau) nm emotion
**emosiynol** adj emotional
**empeiraeth** nf empiricism
**empeiraidd** adj empirical
**empirig** adj empirical
**emrallt** nm emerald
**emyn** (-au) nm hymn
**emyn-dôn** (-au) nf hymn-tune
**emyniadur** (-on) nm hymnal
**emynwr** (-wyr) nm hymnist
**emynydd** (-ion, -wyr) hymnist
**emynyddiaeth** nf hymnody,
  hymnology
**enaid** (eneidiau) nm life, soul
**enamel** (-au) nm enamel
**enamlio** vb enamel
**enbyd, -us** adj dangerous, perilous

**enbydrwydd** *nm* peril, danger, jeopardy

**encil (-ion)** *nm* retreat, flight

**encilfa (-feydd)** *nf* retreat

**enciliad (-au)** *nm* retreat; desertion

**encilio** *vb* retreat; desert

**enciliwr (-wyr)** *nm* retreater; deserter

**enclitig** *adj* enclitic

**encôr** *nm* encore

**encyd** *nm* space; while

**enchwythu** *vb* inflate

**endemig** *adj* endemic

**endid** *nm* entity, existence

**endothermig** *adj* endothermic

**eneidiog** *adj* animate

**eneidiol** *adj* animate, living

**eneiniad (-au)** *nm* anointing, unction

**eneinio** *vb* anoint

**Eneiniog** *nm* The Messiah, Christ

**eneiniog** *adj, nm* anointed

**enfawr** *adj* enormous, huge, immense

**enfys (-au)** *nf* rainbow

**engiriol** *adj* nefarious, cruel, terrible

**engrafiad (-au)** *nm* engraving

**engrafu** *vb* engrave

**enhuddo** *see* **anhuddo**

**enigma** *nm* enigma

**enigmatig** *adj* enigmatic

**enillfawr** *adj* lucrative, remunerative

**enillgar** *adj* gainful; winsome

**enillion** *npl* profits, earnings

**enillwr, -ydd (-wyr)** *nm* gainer, winner

**enllib (-ion, -iau)** *nm* slander, libel

**enllibaidd** *adj* slanderous, libellous

**enllibio** *vb* slander, libel

**enllibiwr (-wyr)** *nm* slanderer, libeller

**enllibus** *adj* slanderous, libellous

**enllyn** *nm* relish eaten with bread

**ennaint (eneiniau)** *nm* ointment

**ennill** *vb* gain, win, earn ▷ **(enillion)**

*nm* gain, profit; *(pl)* earnings

**ennyd** *nm/f* while, moment

**ennyn** *vb* kindle, burn, inflame; excite

**ensyniad (-au)** *nm* insinuation

**ensynio** *vb* insinuate

**entrych (-ion)** *nm* firmament, height, zenith

**enw (-au)** *nm* name; noun

**enwad (-au)** *nm* denomination, sect

**enwadaeth** *nf* sectarianism

**enwadol** *adj* sectarian; nominative

**enwadwr (-wyr)** *nm* sectarian, sectary

**enwaediad** *nm* circumcision

**enwaedu** *vb* circumcise

**enwebai (-eion)** *nm* nominee

**enwebiad (-au)** *nm* nomination

**enwebu** *vb* nominate

**enwedig** *adj:* **yn ~** particularly, especially

**enwi** *vb* name

**enwog (-ion)** *adj* famous, renowned, noted

**enwogi** *vb* make famous

**enwogrwydd** *nm* fame, renown

**enwol** *adj* nominal, nominative

**enwyn** *nm:* **llaeth ~** buttermilk

**enynfa** *nf* inflammation; itching

**enyniad (-au)** *nm* inflammation

**enynnol** *adj* inflammatory; inflamed

**eofn** *adj* fearless, bold

**eog (-iaid)** *nm* salmon

**eos (-au)** *nf* nightingale

**eosaidd** *adj* like a nightingale

**epa (-od)** *nm* ape, monkey

**epidemig** *adj, nm* epidemic

**epig** *nf* epic

**epiglotis (-au)** *nm* epiglottis

**epigram (-au)** *nm* epigram

**epil** *nm* offspring, brood

**epilepsi** *nm* epilepsy

**epilgar** *adj* prolific, teeming

**epiliad (-au)** *nm* reproduction

**epilio** *vb* bring forth, teem, breed

**epilog** *nm* epilogue
**episeicloid** (-au) *nm* epicycloid
**epistol** (-au) *nm* epistle
**eples** *nm* leaven, ferment
**eplesiad** *nm* fermentation
**eplesu** *vb* leaven, ferment
**er** *prep* for, in order to; since ▷ *conj* though
**eraill** *see* **arall**
**erbyn** *vb* receive, meet ▷ *prep* against, by
**erch** *adj* speckled; frightful
**erchi** *vb* ask, pray, command, demand
**erchwyn** (-ion) *nm* side, bed-side
**erchyll** *adj* hideous, horrible
**erchyllter** (-au) *nm* atrocity
**erchylltod, -tra** *nm* hideousness, horror
**eres** *adj* wonderful, strange
**erestyn** *nm* minstrel, buffoon
**erfin** *npl* (*nf*-en) turnips
**erfyn** *vb* beg, pray, implore, expect
**erfyniad** (-au) *nm* prayer, petition
**ergyd** (-ion) *nm/f* blow, stroke; shot; cast
**ergydio** *vb* strike; throw, cast
**ergydiwr** (-wyr) *nm* striker
**erial** (-au) *nm* aerial
**erioed** *adv* ever
**erledigaeth** (-au) *nf* persecution
**erlid** *vb* persecute ▷ (-iau) *nm* persecution
**erlidiwr** (-wyr) *nm* persecutor
**erlyn** *vb* pursue, prosecute
**erlyniad** *nm* prosecution
**erlynydd** (-ion) *nm* prosecutor
**ern, ernes** (-au) *nf* earnest, pledge, deposit
**ers** *prep* since (**er ys**)
**erthwch** *nm* grunt, pant
**erthygl** (-au) *nf* article
**erthyl** (-od) *nm* abortion
**erthylaidd** *adj* abortive
**erthyliad** (-au) *nm* abortion, miscarriage
**erthylu** *vb* abort, miscarry

**erw** (-au) *nf* acre
**erwain** *npl* meadow-sweet
**erwydd** *npl* stave (in music)
**erydiad** (-au) *nm* erosion
**erydol** *adj* erosive
**erydu** *vb* erode
**erydydd** (-ion) *nm* erosive agent
**eryr** (-od) *nm* eagle; shingles
**eryraidd** *adj* eagle-like, aquiline
**esblygiad** (-au) *nm* evolution
**esblygiadaeth** *nf* evolutionism
**esboniad** (-au) *nm* explanation; commentary
**esboniadaeth** *nf* exposition, exegesis
**esboniadol** *adj* expository, explanatory
**esbonio** *vb* explain, expound
**esboniwr** (-wyr) *nm* expositor, commentator
**esbonydd** (-ion) *nm* exponent
**esbonyddol** *adj* exponential
**escaladur** (-on) *nm* escalator
**esgair** (-eiriau) *nf* shank, leg; ridge
**esgeirlwm** *adj* exposed, wind-swept
**esgeulus** *adj* neglectful, negligent
**esgeuluso** *vb* neglect
**esgeulustod, -tra** *nm* negligence
**esgid** (-iau) *nf* boot, shoe
**esgob** (-ion) *nm* bishop
**esgobaeth** (-au) *nf* bishopric, see, diocese
**esgobyddiaeth** *nf* episcopalianism
**esgoli** *vb* escalate
**esgor** *vb* bring forth, bear
**esgud** *adj* quick, swift, active
**esgus** (-ion, -odion) *nm* excuse, pretext
**esgusodi** *vb* excuse
**esgusodol** *adj* excusable, excused
**esgymun** *adj* execrable, excommunicate
**esgymuno** *vb* excommunicate
**esgyn** *vb* ascend, rise
**esgynbren** (-nau) *nm* perch

**esgynfa** (**-feydd**) *nf* ascent, rise
**esgynfaen** *nm* horse-block
**esgyniad** *nm* ascension
**esgynneb** (**esgynebau**) *nf* climax
**esgynnol** *adj* ascending
**esgyrn** *see* **asgwrn**
**esgyrnog** *adj* bony
**esiampl** (**-au**) *nf* example
**esmwyth** *adj* soft, smooth; easy
**esmwythâd** *nm* ease, relief
**esmwytháu** *vb* soothe, ease
**esmwythder, -dra** *nm* ease
**esmwytho, -áu** *vb* ease, soothe, soften
**esmwythyd** *nm* ease, luxury
**estron** (**-iaid**) *nm* foreigner, alien
**estron** *adj* foreign, strange, alien
**estrones** (**-au**) *nf* alien woman
**estronol** *adj* strange, foreign, alien
**estrys** (**-od**) *nm/f* ostrich
**estyll** *npl* (*nf*-**en**) planks, boards
**estyn** *vb* extend, reach; stretch, prolong
**estynadwy** *adj* extensible
**estyniad** *nm* extension, prolongation
**estheteg** *nm/f* aesthetics
**esthetig** *adj* aesthetic
**etifedd** (**-ion**) *nm* heir, inheritor
**etifeddeg** *nm/f* heredity
**etifeddes** (**-au**) *nf* heiress
**etifeddiaeth** (**-au**) *nf* inheritance
**etifeddol** *adj* hereditary
**etifeddu** *vb* inherit
**eto** *conj* yet, still ▷ *adv* again; yet, still
**ether** *nm* ether
**ethnig** *nm* ethnic
**ethnoleg** *nf* ethnology
**ethol** *vb* elect
**etholaeth** (**-au**) *nf* constituency
**etholedig** (**-ion**) *adj* elect
**etholedigaeth** *nf* election (*theol*)
**etholiad** (**-au**) *nm* election
**etholiadol** *adj* electoral, elective
**etholwr** (**-wyr**) *nm* elector, voter
**ethos** *nm* ethos

**eu** *pron* their
**euog** *adj* guilty
**euogrwydd** *nm* guiltiness, guilt
**euraid, -aidd** *adj* golden, (of) gold
**euro** *vb* apply or bestow gold; gild
**eurych** (**-od**) *nm* goldsmith
**ewig** (**-od**) *nf* hind
**ewin** (**-edd**) *nm/f* nail, talon, claw; hoof
**ewino** *vb* claw
**ewinog** *adj* having nails or claws
**ewinrhew** *nf* frost-bite
**Ewrop** *nf* Europe
**Ewropead** (**-aid**) *nm* European
**Ewropeaidd** *adj* European
**ewyllys** (**-iau**) *nf* will
**ewyllysio** *vb* will, wish
**ewyn** *nm* foam, froth, surf
**ewynnog** *adj* foaming, foamy, frothy
**ewynnu** *vb* foam, froth
**ewythr** (**-edd**) *nm* uncle

# f

**fagddu** *nf*: **y ~** gross darkness
**falf** (**-iau**) *nf* valve
**fan** (**-iau**) *nf* van
**fandal** (**-iaid**) *nm* vandal
**fandaleiddio** *vb* vandalise
**fandaliaeth** *nf* vandalism
**farnais** (**-eisiau**) *nm* varnish
**farneisio** *vb* varnish

**fe** *pron* he, him ▷ *preverbal particle*
**feallai** *adv* perhaps, peradventure
**fel** *adv, conj, prep* so, as, that, thus, like; how
**felly** *adv* so, thus
**festri** (-ïoedd) *nf* vestry
**ficer** (-iaid) *nm* vicar
**ficerdy** (-dai) *nm* vicarage
**finegr** *nm* vinegar
**fiola** (-s) *nf* viola
**firws** (-au, fira) *nm* virus
**fitamin** (-au) *nm* vitamin
**folt** (-iau) *nf* volt
**foltamedr** (-au) *nm* voltameter
**foltedd** (-au) *nm* voltage
**foltmedr** (-au) *nm* voltmeter
**fortais** (-eisiau) *nm* vortex
**fory** *adv* tomorrow (y~)
**fry** *adv* above, aloft
**fwltur** (-iaid) *nm* vulture
**fy** *pron* my
**fyny** *adv* up, upwards

**ffa** *npl* (nffäen, ffeuen) beans; **~'r gors** buckbeans; **~ pob** baked beans
**ffabrigo** *vb* fabricate
**ffacbys** *npl* fitches, vetches
**ffactor** (-au) *nm/f* factor; **f~ cyffredin mwyaf** highest common factor; **f~ cysefin** prime factor
**ffactori, -o** *vb* factorize
**ffactri** (-ïoedd) *nf* factory, mill

**ffaeledig** *adj* fallible, ailing
**ffaeledigrwydd** *nm* fallibility
**ffaeledd** (-au) *nf* failing, defect.
**ffaelu** *vb* fail
**ffafr** (-au) *nf* favour
**ffafraeth** *nf* favouritism
**ffafrio** *vb* favour
**ffafriol** *adj* favourable
**ffagl** (-au) *nf* blaze, flame; torch
**ffair** (ffeiriau) *nf* fair, exchange; **~ sborion** jumble sale
**ffaith** (ffeithiau) *nf* fact
**ffald** (-au) *nf* fold; pound
**ffals** (ffeilsion) *adj* false, deceitful
**ffalsedd** *nm* falsehood, deceit
**ffalster** *nm* deceitfulness, cunning
**ffalwm** *nm* whitlow
**ffan** (-nau) *nf* fan
**ffanatig** *nm* fanatic
**ffansi** *nf* fancy
**ffansïo** *vb* fancy
**ffansïol** *adj* fanciful
**ffanatigiaeth** *nf* fanaticism
**ffantasi(a)** (-ïau) *nf/m* fantasy
**ffarm** (ffermydd) *nf* farm
**ffarmio** *vb* farm
**ffarmwr** (ffermwyr) *nm* farmer
**ffarmwraig** (-wragedd) *nf* farmwoman
**ffârs** (-iau) *nf* farce
**ffarwél** *nf* farewell
**ffarwelio** *vb* bid farewell
**ffas** (-ys, -au) *nf* face, coal-face
**ffasâd** (ffasadau) *nm* facade
**ffasiwn** (-iynau) *nm* fashion
**ffasiynol** *adj* fashionable
**ffasner** (-i) *nm* fastener
**ffasnin** (-au) *nm* fastening
**ffasno** *vb* fasten
**ffasnydd** (-ion) *nm* fastener
**ffatri** (-ïoedd) *nf* factory, mill
**ffatrïaeth** *nf* manufacturing
**ffau** (ffeuau) *nf* den
**ffawd** (ffodion) *nf* fortune, fate
**ffawdheglu** *vb* hitch-hike
**ffawdheglwr** (-wyr) *nm* hitch-hiker

**ffawna** nf fauna
**ffawydd** npl (nf-en) beech trees
**ffederal** adj federal
**ffederaliaeth** nf federalism
**ffederasiwn** (-iynau) nm federation
**ffed(e)reiddio** vb federate
**ffefryn** (-nau) nm favourite
**ffeil** nf file
**ffein, ffeind** adj fine
**ffeirio** vb barter, exchange
**ffelt** nm felt
**ffelwm** nm whitlow
**ffemwr** (ffemora) nm femur
**ffendir** nm fenland
**ffenestr** (-i) nf window
**ffenigl** nm fennel
**ffenomen** (-au) nf phenomenon
**ffens** (-ys) nf fence
**ffensio** vb fence
**ffêr** (fferau) nf ankle
**fferdod** nm numbness
**fferi** (-ïau) nf ferry
**fferins** npl sweets
**fferm** (-ydd) nf farm
**ffermdy** (-dai) nm farm-house
**ffermio** vb farm
**ffermwr** (-wyr) nm farmer
**fferru** vb congeal, freeze; perish with cold
**fferyllfa** (-feydd) nf dispensary
**fferylliaeth** nf pharmacy
**fferyllol** adj chemical, pharmaceutical
**fferyllydd** (-wyr) nm chemist, pharmacist
**ffesant** (-s, -au) nm pheasant
**ffest** adj fast
**ffest** nf feast
**ffetan** (-au) nf sack, bag
**ffi** (-oedd) nf fee
**ffiaidd** adj loathsome, abominable
**ffibr** (-au) nm fibre
**ffibrog, -us** adj fibrous
**Ffichtiad** (-iaid) nm Pict
**ffidil** (ffidlau) nf fiddle
**ffidlan** vb fiddle, dawdle

**ffidler** (-iaid) nm fiddler
**ffidlo** vb fiddle
**ffieiddbeth** (-au) nm abomination
**ffieidd-dra** nm abomination
**ffieiddio** vb loathe, abominate
**ffigur** (-au) nf figure, type
**ffigurol** adj figurative
**ffigys** npl (nf-en) figs
**ffigysbren** (-nau) nm fig-tree
**ffiled** (-au, -i) nf fillet
**ffilharmonig** adj philharmonic
**ffilm** (-iau) nf film
**ffilmio** vb film
**ffiloreg** nf rigmarole, nonsense
**ffilter** (-au, -i) nm filter
**ffin** (-iau) nf boundary, limit
**Ffindir:** y nf Finland
**ffindir** (-oedd) nm borderland
**ffinio** vb border (upon), abut
**ffiniol** adj bordering
**ffiol** (-au) nf vial; cup
**ffiseg** nm physics
**ffisegol** adj physical
**ffisegwr** (-wyr) nm physicist
**ffisig** nm physic, medicine
**ffisigwr** (-wyr) nm physician
**ffisigwriaeth** nm physic, medicine
**ffisioleg** nf/m physiology
**ffit** adj fit ▷ (-iau) nf fit, paroxysm
**ffit-ffatio** vb flip-flop
**ffitrwydd** nm fitness
**ffiwdal** adj feudal
**ffiwg** (-iau) nf fugue
**ffiws** (-iau) nm fuse
**ffiwsio** vb fuse
**fflach** (-iau) nf, **fflachiad** (-au) nm flash
**fflachio** vb flash
**fflachiog** adj flashing
**fflag** (-iau) nf flag
**fflagen** (-ni) nf flagon, flag-stone
**fflangell** (-au) nf scourge
**fflangelliad** (-au) nm flagellation
**fflangellu** vb scourge, whip, flog
**fflam** (-au) nf flame
**fflamadwy** adj (in)flammable
**fflamio** vb flame, blaze

**fflamllyd** *adj* flaming, blazing
**fflan** (-iau) *nm* flan
**fflap** (-iau) *nm* flap
**fflasg** (-iau) *nf* flask, basket
**fflat** *adj* flat (-iau) ▷ *nm* flat-iron
  ▷ (-au, -iau) *nf* a flat
**fflatio** *vb* flat, flatten
**fflatwadn** *adj* flatfooted
**fflecs** (-ys) *nm* flex
**fflêm, fflem** *nf* phlegm
**fflint** *nm* flint
**ffliwt** (-iau) *nf* flute
**ffloch** (-au) *nm* floe; **~ iâ** ice floe
**fflodiad, -iart** *nf* floodgate
**ffo** *nm* flight
**ffoadur** (-iaid) *nm* fugitive, refugee
**ffodus** *adj* fortunate, lucky
**ffoëdigaeth** *nf* flight
**ffoi** *vb* flee
**ffôl** *adj* foolish, silly ▷ (**ffols**) *nf* fall
  (in a slate quarry)
**ffoledd** *nm* foolishness, folly, fatuity
**ffolen** (-nau) *nf* buttock
**ffoli** *vb* infatuate, dote; fool
**ffolineb** *nm* foolishness, folly
**ffon** (**ffyn**) *nf* stick, staff
**ffonnod** (**ffonodiau**) *nf* stroke,
  blow, stripe
**ffonodio** *vb* cudgel, beat
**fforc** (**ffyrc**) *nf* (table) fork
**fforch** (-au, **ffyrch**) *nf* fork
**fforchi** *vb* fork
**fforchog** *adj* forked, cleft, cloven
**ffordd** (**ffyrdd**) *nf* way, road;
  distance
**fforddio** *vb* afford
**fforddol** (-ion) *nm* wayfarer,
  passer-by
**fforest** (-ydd, -au) *nf* forest
**fforffedu** *vb* forfeit
**ffortiwn** (-iynau), **-un** (-au) *nf*
  fortune
**fforwm** (-ymau) *nm* forum
**ffos** (-ydd) *nf* ditch, trench
**ffosffad** (-au) *nm* phosphate
**ffosil** (-au) *nm* fossil
**ffracsiwn** (-iynau) *nm* fraction

**ffrae** (-au) *nf* quarrel
**ffraeo** *vb* quarrel
**ffraeth** *adj* fluent; witty, facetious
**ffraetheb** (-ion) *nf* joke, witticism
**ffraethineb** *nm* wit, facetiousness
**Ffrangeg** *nf* French (language)
**Ffrainc** *nf* France
**ffrâm** (**fframiau**) *nf* frame
**fframio** *vb* frame
**fframwaith** *nm* framework
**Ffrances** (-au) *nf* Frenchwoman
**Ffrancwr** (-wyr, **Ffrancod**) *nm*
  Frenchman
**Ffrengig** *adj* French; **llygod
  fffrengig** rats
**ffres** *adj* fresh
**ffresgo** (-au) *nm* fresco
**ffresni** *nm* freshness
**ffretwaith** *nm* fretwork
**ffreutur** *nf* refectory
**ffrewyll** (-au) *nf* whip, scourge
**ffridd** (-oedd) *nf* mountain pasture
**ffrimpan** (-au) *nf* frying pan
**ffrind** (-iau) *nm* friend
**ffrio** *vb* fry; hiss
**ffrîs** (-iau) *nf* frieze
**ffrit** (-iau) *nm* frit, flop ▷ *adj*
  worthless, unsubstantial
**ffrith** (-oedd) *nf* mountain pasture
**ffrithiant** (-nnau) *nm* friction
**ffroch, ffrochwyllt** *adj* furious
**ffroen** (-au) *nf* nostril; muzzle
  (of gun)
**ffroenell** (-au) *nf* nozzle
**ffroeni** *vb* snort, snuff, sniff
**ffroenuchel** *adj* haughty,
  disdainful
**ffroes** *npl* (*nf*-en) pancakes
**ffrog** (-iau) *nf* frock
**ffrom** *adj* angry, irascible, testy,
  touchy
**ffromi** *vb* fume, chafe, rage
**ffrostgar** *adj* boastful
**ffrwd** (**ffrydiau**) *nf* stream, torrent
**ffrwgwd** (**ffrygydau**) *nm* squabble
**ffrwst** *nm* hurry, haste, bustle
**ffrwtian** *vb* splutter

**ffrwydriad** (-au) *nm* explosion

**ffrwydro** *vb* explode

**ffrwydrol** *adj* explosive

**ffrwydryn** (-nau, ffrwydron) *nm* mine, explosive

**ffrwyn** (-au) *nf* bridle

**ffrwyno** *vb* bridle, curb

**ffrwyth** (-au, -ydd) *nm* fruit; vigour, use

**ffrwythlon** *adj* fruitful, fertile

**ffrwythlondeb, -der** *nm* fruitfulness, fertility

**ffrwythloni** *vb* become fruitful; fertilize

**ffrwytho** *vb* bear fruit

**ffrydio** *vb* stream, gush

**ffrydlif** *nm/f* stream, flood, torrent

**ffug** *adj* fictitious, false, sham ▷ (-ion) *nm* fiction, sham

**ffug-bas** (-ys) *nf* dummy (pass)

**ffugbasio** *vb* dummy

**ffugenw** (-au) *nm* pseudonym

**ffugiad** (-au) *nm* forgery

**ffugio** *vb* feign; forge

**ffugiwr** (-wyr) *nm* impostor; forger

**ffuglen** *nf* fiction

**ffugliw** (-iau) *nm* camouflage

**ffugliwio** *vb* camouflage

**ffunud** *nm* form, manner; **yr un ~ â** exactly like

**ffured** (-au) *nf* ferret

**ffureta** *vb* ferret

**ffurf** (-iau) *nf* form, shape

**ffurfafen** *nf* firmament, sky

**ffurfdro** (-eon) *nm* inflection

**ffurfeb** (-au) *nf* formula

**ffurfiad** (-au) *nm* formation

**ffurfiant** (-nnau) *nm* accidence; formation

**ffurfio** *vb* form

**ffurfiol** *adj* formal

**ffurfiolaeth** *nf* formalism

**ffurfioldeb** *nm* formality, formalism

**ffurflen** (-ni) *nf* form (*to fill*)

**ffurflin** (-iau) *nm* formline

**ffurfwasanaeth** (-au) *nm* liturgy

**ffurfwedd** (-au) *nf* configuration

**ffust** (-iau) *nf* flail

**ffustio, -o** *vb* beat

**ffwdan** *nf* fuss, bustle, flurry

**ffwdanllyd** *adj* fussy, bustling

**ffwdanu** *vb* fuss, bustle

**ffwdanus** *adj* fussy, fidgety, flurried

**ffwng** (ffyngoedd, ffyngau) *nm* fungus

**ffwngleiddiad** (-au) *nf* fungicide

**ffŵl** (ffyliaid) *nm* fool

**ffwlbart** (-iaid) *nm* polecat

**ffwlbri** *nm* fudge, nonsense, tomfoolery

**ffwlcyn** *nm* fool, ninny, nincompoop

**ffwndro** *vb* founder, become confused

**ffwndrus** *adj* confused, bewildered

**ffwndwr** *nm* confusion, hurly-burly

**ffwr** *nm* fur

**ffwrdd** *nm* way; **I f~** away

**ffwrn** (ffyrnau) *nf* furnace, oven

**ffwrnais** (-eisiau) *nf* furnace

**ffwrwm** (ffyrymau) *nf* form, bench

**ffydd** *nf* faith

**ffyddiog** *adj* strong in faith, trustful

**ffyddlon** *adj* faithful

**ffyddlondeb** *nm* faithfulness, fidelity

**ffyddloniaid** *npl* faithful ones

**ffynhonnell** (ffynonellau) *nf* fount, source

**ffyniannus** *adj* prosperous

**ffyniant** *nm* prosperity

**ffynidwydd** *npl* (*nf-en*) fir-trees, pine-trees

**ffynnon** (ffynhonnau) *nf* fountain, well, spring

**ffynnu** *vb* prosper, thrive

**ffyrf** (fferf) *adj* thick, stout

**ffyrfder** *nm* thickness, stoutness

**ffyrling** (-au, -od) *nf* farthing

**ffyrnig** *adj* fierce, savage, ferocious

**ffyrnigo** *vb* grow fierce; enrage

**ffyrnigrwydd** *nm* fierceness, ferocity

# g

**gadael, gadu** vb leave, forsake; let, allow

**gaeaf (-au, -oedd)** nm winter

**gaeafaidd, -ol** adj wintry

**gaeafu** vb winter, hibernate

**gafael, -yd** vb hold, grasp ▷ nm (-ion) nf hold, grasp

**gafaelgar** adj gripping, tenacious

**gafl (-au, geifl)** nf fork, groin

**gafr (geifr)** nf goat

**gafrewig (-od)** nf gazelle, antelope

**gagendor** see **agendor**

**gaing (geingau)** nf chisel; **~ gau** gouge

**gair (geiriau)** nm word

**galanas (-au)** nf murder, massacre

**galanastra** nm slaughter; mess

**galar** nm mourning, grief, sorrow

**galarnad (-au)** nf lamentation

**galarnadu** vb bewail, lament

**galaru** vb mourn, grieve, lament

**galarus** adj mournful, lamentable, sad

**galarwr (-wyr)** nm mourner

**galw** vb call ▷ nm call, demand

**galwad (-au)** nm/f call, demand

**galwedigaeth (-au)** nf occupation, vocation, calling

**galwyn (-i)** nm gallon

**gallt (gelltydd)** nf wooded slope; hill, rise

**gallu** vb be able ▷ (-oedd) nm power, ability

**galluog** adj able, powerful, mighty

**galluogi** vb enable, empower

**gan** prep with; by; of, from

**gar (-rau)** nf/m thigh, shank

**garan (-od)** nf heron, crane

**Garawys** nm Lent

**gardas, -ys (-ysau)** nm/f garter

**gardd (gerddi)** nf garden; garth, yard

**garddio** vb garden ▷ nm gardening

**garddwr (-wyr)** nm gardener

**garddwriaeth** nf horticulture

**gargam** adj knock-kneed

**garlant (-au)** nm garland

**garlleg** npl (nf-en) garlic

**gartref** adv at home (mutation); of **cartref**

**garth** nm hill; enclosure

**garw (geirwon)** adj coarse, rough, harsh

**garwedd** nm roughness

**garwhau** vb roughen; ruffle

**gast (geist)** nf bitch

**gau** adj false; hollow

**gefail (-eiliau)** nf smithy

**gefel (-eiliau)** nf tongs, pincers

**gefell (-eilliaid)** n coll twin

**gefelldref (-i)** nf twinned town

**gefyn (-nau)** nm fetter, shackle

**gefynnu** vb fetter, shackle

**geingio** vb chisel, gouge

**geilwad (-waid)** nm caller

**geirfa (-oedd)** nf vocabulary, glossary

**geiriad** nm wording, phraseology

**geiriadur (-on)** nm dictionary, lexicon

**geiriadurol** adj lexicographical

**geiriadurwr (-wyr)** nm lexicographer

**geirio** vb word, phrase

**geirlyfr (-au)** nm word-book, dictionary

**geirwir** adj truthful, truth-speaking

**geirwiredd** nm truthfulness

**gelau, gelen (gelod)** nf leech

**gelyn (-ion)** nm foe, enemy

**gelyniaeth** nf enmity, hostility

**gelyniaethus** adj hostile, inimical

**gelynol** *adj* hostile, adverse
**gellyg** *npl* (*nf* -**en**) pears
**gem** (-**au**) *nf* gem, jewel
**gêm** (~**au**) *nf* game
**gemog** *adj* gemmed, jewelled
**gemydd** (-**ion**) *nm* jeweller
**gên** *nf* jaw, chin
**genau** (-**euau**) *nm* mouth, orifice
**genau-goeg, geneuoeg** (-**ion**) *nf* lizard; newt
**genedigaeth** (-**au**) *nf* birth
**genedigol** *adj* native
**Genefa** *nf* Geneva
**geneth** (-**od**) *nf* girl
**genethaidd** *adj* girlish
**genethig** *nf* little girl, maiden
**geni** *vb* be born
**genni** *vb* be contained
**genwair** (-**eiriau**) *nf* fishing-rod
**genweirio** *vb* angle, fish
**genweiriwr** (-**wyr**) *nm* angler
**ger** *prep* by, near
**gêr** *coll n* gear, tackle
**gerbron** *prep* before (*place*); in the presence of
**gerfydd** *prep* by
**geri** *nm* bile, gall; ~ **marwol** cholera morbus
**geriach** *coll n* gear, odds and ends
**gerllaw** *prep* near ▷ *adv* at hand
**gerwin** *adj* rough, severe, harsh
**gerwindeb, -der** *nm* roughness, severity
**gerwino** *vb* roughen
**gewyn** (-**nau**, **gïau**) *nm* sinew, tendon
**gewynnog** *adj* sinewy
**Ghana** *nf* Ghana
**gïach** (-**od**) *nm* snipe
**Gibralter** *n* Gibraltar
**gieuwst** *nf* neuralgia
**gildio** *vb* yield; gild
**gilydd** *nm*: **ei ~** each other; **gyda'i ~** together
**gimbill** *nf* gimlet
**glafoerio** *vb* drivel, slobber
**glafoerion** *npl* drivel, slobber

**glaif, gleifiau** *nm* lance, sword, glaive
**glain** (**gleiniau**) *nm* gem, jewel; bead
**glan** (-**nau**, **glennydd**) *nf* bank, shore
**glân** *adj* clean; holy; fair, beautiful
**glanhad** *nm* cleansing, purification
**glanhaol** *adj* cleansing, purging
**glanhau** *vb* cleanse, purify
**glaniad** *nm* landing, disembarkation
**glanio** *vb* land, disembark
**glanwaith** *adj* clean, tidy
**glanweithdra** *nm* cleanliness
**glas** (**gleision**) *adj* blue, green, grey, silver ▷ *nm* blue
**glasgoch** *adj, nm* purple
**glaslanc** (-**iau**) *nm* youth, stripling
**glasog** (-**au**) *nf* crop, gizzard
**glastwr** *nm* milk and water
**glastwraidd** *adj* watered down, feeble; muddled
**glasu** *vb* become blue, green or grey; turn pale
**glaswellt** *coll n* grass
**glaswelltyn** *nm* blade of grass; tigridia
**glaw** (-**ogydd**) *nm* rain
**glawiad** (-**au**) *nm* rainfall
**glawio** *vb* rain
**glawlen** (-**ni**) *nf* umbrella
**glawog** *adj* rainy
**gleisiad** (-**iaid**) *nm* sewin
**gleision** *npl* whey
**glendid** *nm* cleanness; fairness, beauty
**glesni** *nm* blueness, verdure
**glew** (-**ion**) *adj* brave, daring; astute
**glewdra, -der** *nm* courage, resource
**glin** (-**iau**) *nm* knee
**glo** *nm* coal
**gloddest** (-**au**) *nm* carousal, revelling
**gloddesta** *vb* carouse, revel
**gloddestwr** (-**wyr**) *nm* reveller

**gloes** (-au, -ion) nf pang; qualm
**glofa** (-feydd) nf colliery
**glöwr** (-wyr) nm collier
**glowty** (-tai) nm cow-house, shippon
**glöyn** nm coal; ~ **byw** butterfly
**gloyw** (-on) adj bright, clear; shiny, glossy
**gloywder** nm brightness, clearness
**gloywi** vb brighten, polish
**glud** (-ion) nm glue; bird-lime
**gludio** vb glue
**gludiog** adj sticky
**glwth** (glythau) nm couch
**glwth** (glythion) adj gluttonous ▷ nm glutton
**glwys** adj fair; holy
**glyn** (-noedd) nm glen, valley
**glynu** vb stick, adhere, cleave
**glythineb, glythni** nm gluttony
**glythinebu, glythu** vb glut, gormandize
**go** adv rather, somewhat
**goachul** adj lean; puny; sickly, poorly
**gobaith** (-eithion) nm hope
**gobeithio** vb hope
**gobeithiol** adj hopeful
**gobeithlu** (-oedd) nm Band of Hope
**gobennydd** (-enyddiau) nm bolster, pillow
**goblygu** vb fold, wrap
**gochel** see **gochelyd**
**gocheladwy** adj avoidable
**gochelgar** adj wary, cautious
**gocheliad** nm avoidance; **ar ei ocheliad** on his guard
**gochelyd** vb avoid, shun
**godidog** adj excellent, splendid
**godidowgrwydd** nm excellence
**godineb** nm adultery
**godinebu** vb commit adultery
**godinebus** adj adulterous
**godinebwr** (-wyr) nm adulterer
**godre** (-on) nm skirt, border, edge
**godriad** (-au) nm milking

**godro** vb milk
**goddaith** (-eithiau) nf fire, bonfire
**goddef** vb bear, suffer, allow, permit
**goddefgar** adj forbearing, tolerant
**goddefgarwch** nm forbearance, tolerance
**goddefiad** (-au) nm licence; toleration
**goddefol** adj tolerable; passive
**goddiweddyd, goddiwes** vb over-take
**goddrych** nm subject (in grammar)
**goddrychol** adj subjective
**gof** (-aint) nm smith
**gofal** (-on) nm care, charge
**gofalu** vb care, mind, take care
**gofalus** adj careful
**gofaniaeth** nf smith's craft
**gofer** (-oedd, -ydd) nm overflow of well; rill
**gofid** (-iau) nm grief, sorrow, trouble
**gofidio** vb afflict, grieve, vex
**gofidus** adj grievous, sad
**gofod** nm space; **llong ofod** nf spaceship
**gofodwr** (-wyr) nm astronaut
**gofyn** vb ask, demand, require ▷ (-ion) nm demand, requirement
**gofyniad** (-au) nm question, query
**gofynnod** (-ynodau) nm note of interrogation, question-mark
**gofynnol** adj necessary, requisite; interrogative (pronoun etc)
**gogan** nf defamation, satire
**goganu** vb defame, satirize, lampoon
**goganwr** (-wyr) nm satirist
**goglais** vb, nm tickle
**gogledd** nm, adj north
**Gogledd, Iwerddon** nf Northern Ireland
**gogleddol** adj northern
**gogleddwynt** nm north wind
**gogleddwr** (-wyr) nm northman; North Walian
**gogleisio** vb tickle
**gogleisiol** adj tickling, titillating,

amusing
**gogoneddu** vb glorify
**gogoneddus** adj glorious
**gogoniant** nm glory
**gogor** (-ion) nf fodder, provender
**gogr** (-au) nm sieve, riddle
**gogri, gogrwn, gogryn** vb
sift, riddle
**gogwydd** nm slant, inclination,
bent
**gogwyddiad** (-au) nm inclination
**gogwyddo** vb incline, slope, lean
**gogyfer** adj opposite; for, by
**gogyfuwch** adj, prep of equal
height
**gogyhyd** adj of equal length
**gogymaint** adj equal in size
**gohebiaeth** (-au) nf
correspondence
**gohebol** adj corresponding
**gohebu** vb correspond (by letter
etc); reply
**gohebydd** (-wyr) nm
correspondent, reporter
**gohiriad** (-au) nm postponement
**gohirio** vb delay, postpone, defer
**golau** adj, nm, vb light
**golau-leuad** nm moonlight
**golch** (-ion) nm wash; coating; lye
**golchdy** (-dai) nm wash-house,
laundry
**golchfa** nf wash; lathering
**golchi** vb wash; coat
**golchiad** (-au) nm washing;
plating, coating
**golchion** npl slops; suds
**golchwr** (-wyr), **-ydd** (-ion) nm
washer
**golchwraig** (-wragedd) nf
washerwoman
**golchyddes** (-au) nf laundress
**goledd(f)** nm slant, slope
**goledd(f)u** vb slant, slope
**goleuad** (-au) nm light, luminary
**goleudy** (-dai) nm lighthouse
**goleuni** nm light
**goleuo** vb light, enlighten,

illuminate
**golosg** nm coke, charcoal
**golud** (-oedd) nm wealth, riches
**goludog** adj wealthy, rich
**golwg** (-ygon) nf/m sight, look;
(pl) eyes
**golwr** (-wyr) nm goalkeeper
**golwyth** (-ion) nm chop, slice, cut
**golygfa** (-feydd) nf scene, view;
(pl) scenery
**golygiad** (-au) nm view
**golygu** vb view; mean; edit
**golygus** adj slightly, comely,
handsome
**golygwedd** (-au) nf feature, aspect
**golygydd** (-ion, -wyr) nm editor
**golygyddiaeth** nf editorship
**golygyddol** adj editorial
**gollwng** vb drop, release, let go;
discharge; dismiss; leak
**gollyngdod** nm release; absolution
**gomedd** vb refuse
**gomeddiad** nm refusal, omission
**gonest, onest** adj honest
**gonestrwydd** nm honesty
**gôr** nm pus
**gor-** prefix over-, super-
**gorau** (-euon) adj best; **o'r ~**
very well
**gorawen** nf joy, ecstasy
**gorblu** npl immature feathers
**gorboblogi** vb overpopulate
**gorbwyso** vb outweigh, overweigh
**gorchest** (-ion) nf feat, exploit
**gorchestol** adj excellent, masterly
**gorchfygu** vb overcome, conquer
**gorchfygwr** (-wyr) nm victor;
conqueror
**gorchudd** (-ion) nm cover,
covering, veil
**gorchuddio** vb cover
**gorchwyl** (-ion) nm task,
undertaking
**gorchymyn** vb command
▷ (gorchmynion) nm command,
commandment
**gordoi** vb overspread, cover

**gordyfu** vb overgrow
**gordd (gyrdd)** nf sledge-hammer, mallet
**gordderch (-adon)** nf concubine; lover; bastard
**goresgyn** vb overrun, invade; conquer
**goresgyniad** nm invasion; conquest
**goresgynnydd** nm invader; conqueror
**goreuro** vb gild
**gorfod** vb be obliged ▷ nm obligation, necessity
**gorfodaeth** nf obligation, compulsion
**gorfodi** vb oblige, compel
**gorfodol** adj obligatory, compulsory
**gorfoledd** nm joy, rejoicing, triumph
**gorfoleddu** vb rejoice, triumph
**gorfoleddus** adj jubilant, triumphant
**gorffen** vb finish, complete, conclude
**gorffeniad** nm finishing, finish
**Gorffennaf** nm July
**gorffennol** adj, nm past
**gorffwyll** adj mad, frenzied
**gorffwyllo** vb rave
**gorffwyllog** adj mad, insane
**gorffwylltra** nm madness, insanity
**gorffwys** vb, nm rest, repose
**gorffwysfa (-oedd)** nf resting-place, rest
**gorffwysiad (-au)** nm rest, pause
**gorffwyso, gorffwystra** see **gorffwys**
**gorhendaid** nm great-great-grandfather
**gorhennain** nf great-great-grandmother
**gori** vb hatch
**gorifyny** nm ascent, hill, steep climb

**goris** prep below, beneath, under
**goriwaered** nm descent, declivity
**gorlawn** adj superabundant
**gorlenwi** vb overfill
**gorliwio** vb colour too highly, exaggerate
**gorllewin** nm west; **G~ yr Almaen** West Germany
**gorllewinol** adj westerly, western
**gorllewinwr (-wyr)** nm westerner
**gormes** nm oppression, tyranny
**gormesol** adj oppressive, tyrannical
**gormesu** vb oppress, tyrannize
**gormeswr (-wyr), -ydd (-ion)** nm oppressor, tyrant
**gormod (-ion)** nm too much, excess
**gormodedd** nm excess, superfluity
**gormodiaith** nf hyperbole, exaggeration
**gormodol** adj excessive
**gormwyth** nm catarrh
**gornest, ornest (-au)** contest, match
**goroesi** vb outlive, survive
**goroesiad (-au)** nm survival
**goroeswr (-wyr)** nm survivor
**goror (-au)** nm border, coast, frontier
**gorsaf (-oedd)** nf station
**gorsedd (-au)** nf, **gorseddfa**
**gorseddu** vb throne, enthrone, install
**gorsin, gorsing (-au)** nf door-post
**gorthrech** nm oppression; coercion
**gorthrechu** vb oppress; coerce
**gorthrwm** nm oppression
**gorthrymder** nm oppression, tribulation
**gorthrymedig** adj oppressed
**gorthrymu** vb oppress
**gorthrymus** adj oppressive
**gorthrymwr, -ydd (-wyr)** nm oppressor
**goruchaf** adj most high, supreme
**goruchafiaeth** nf supremacy;

triumph

**goruchel** *adj* high, exalted

**goruchwyliaeth** (-au) *nf* oversight, supervision; dispensation

**goruchwylio** *vb* oversee, supervise

**goruchwyliwr** (-wyr) *nm* supervisor, steward

**goruwch** *prep* above, over

**goruwchnaturiol** *adj* supernatural

**goruwchreoli** *vb* overrule

**gorwedd** *vb* lie

**gorweddfa** (-oedd), **-fan** (-nau) *nf* bed, couch

**gorweddian** *vb* lounge, loll

**gorweiddiog** *adj* bedridden

**gorwel** (-ion) *nm* horizon

**gorwych** *adj* gorgeous

**gorwyr** (-ion) *nm* great-grandson

**gorwyres** (-au) *nf* great-granddaughter

**gorymdaith** (-deithiau) *nf* procession

**gorymdeithio** *vb* walk in procession

**gorynys** (-oedd) *nf* peninsula

**gosber** (-au) *nm* vespers

**gosgedd** (-au) *nm* form, figure

**gosgeiddig** *adj* comely, graceful

**gosgordd** (-ion) *nf* retinue, train, escort

**gosgorddlu** (-oedd) *nm* bodyguard

**goslef** (-au) *nf* tone, intonation (**oslef**)

**gosod** *vb* put, place, set; let ▷ *adj* false, artificial

**gosodiad** (-au) *nm* proposition, statement

**gosteg** (-ion) *nf* silence; (*pl*) banns

**gostegu** *vb* silence, still, quell

**gostwng** *vb* lower, reduce; bow; put down, humble

**gostyngedig** *adj* humble

**gostyngeiddrwydd** *nm* humility

**gostyngiad** *nm* reduction; humiliation

**gowt** *nm* gout

**gradell** (-gredyll) *nf* griddle

**gradd** (-au) *nm/f* grade, degree, stage

**graddedigion** *npl* graduates

**graddfa** (-feydd) *nf* scale

**graddio** *vb* graduate

**graddol** *adj* gradual

**graddoli** *vb* grade, graduate

**graean** *coll n*, **greyenyn** *nm* gravel

**graeanu** *vb* granulate

**graeanwst** *nf* gravel (*complaint*)

**graen** *nm* grain, gloss, lustre

**graenus** *adj* of good grain, glossy, sleek

**graff** (-iau) *nm* graph

**gramadeg** (-au) *nm* grammar

**gramadegol** *adj* grammatical

**gramadegwr**, **-ydd** (-wyr) *nm* grammarian

**gran** (-nau) *nm* cheek

**gras** (-au, -usau) *nm* grace

**graslawn**, **-lon** *adj* full of grace, gracious

**graslonrwydd** *nm* graciousness, grace

**grasol**, **grasusol** *adj* gracious

**grât** (gratiau) *nm* grate

**grawn** *npl* (*nm* **gronyn**) grain; grapes; roe

**grawnfwyd** (-ydd) *coll n* cereal

**grawnwin** *npl* grapes

**Grawys** *nm* Lent

**gre** (-oedd) *nf* stud, flock

**greddf** (-au) *nf* instinct, intuition

**greddfol** *adj* instinctive, intuitive, rooted

**greddfu** *vb* become ingrained

**grefi** *nm* gravy

**gresyn** *nm* pity

**gresyni**, **-dod** *nm* misery, wretchedness

**gresynu** *vb* commiserate, pity

**gresynus** *adj* miserable, wretched

**gridyll** (-au) *nm/f* griddle

**griddfan** *vb* groan, moan ▷ (-nau) *nm* groan

**grillian, -io** vb squeak, creak; chirp; crunch

**gris (-iau)** nm step, stair

**grisial** nm crystal

**grisialaidd** adj crystal, crystalline

**gro** coll n (nm **gröyn**) gravel, pebbles

**Groeg** nf Greek language; Greece ▷ adj Greek

**Groegaidd** adj Grecian, Greek

**Groeges (-au)** nf Greek woman

**Groegwr (-wyr, -iaid)** nm Greek

**gronell (-au)** nf roe

**Grønland** nf Greenland

**gronyn (-nau)** nm grain, particle; while

**grot (-iau)** nm groat, fourpence

**grual** nm gruel

**grud** nm grit

**grudd (-iau)** nf cheek

**gruddfan** see **griddfan**

**grug** nm heather

**grugiar (-ieir)** nf moor-hen, grouse

**grugog** adj heathery

**grwgnach** vb grumble, murmur

**grwgnachlyd** adj given to grumbling

**grwgnachwr (-wyr)** nm grumbler

**grwn (grynnau)** nm ridge (in ploughing)

**grŵn, grwndi** nm purr

**grwnan** vb croon, purr

**grwndwal (-au)** nm foundation

**grydian** vb murmur; grunt

**grym (-oedd)** nm force, power, might

**grymial** vb mutter, murmur, grumble

**grymus** adj strong, powerful, mighty

**grymuso** vb strengthen

**grymuster, -tra** nm power, might

**gwacáu** vb empty

**gwacsaw** adj trivial, frivolous

**gwacsawrwydd** nm levity, vanity

**gwacter** nm emptiness, vacuity

**gwachul** see **goachul**

**gwad, gwadiad** nm denial, disavowal

**gwadn (-au)** nm sole

**gwadnu** vb sole; foot it

**gwadu** vb deny, disown; renounce, forsake

**gwadwr (-wyr)** nm denier

**gwadd (-od)** nf mole

**gwadd** see **gwahodd**

**gwaddod (-ion)** nm sediment, lees, dregs

**gwaddodi** vb deposit sediment

**gwaddol (-ion, -iadau)** nm endowment; dowry

**gwaddoli** vb endow

**gwae (-au)** nm/f woe

**gwaed** nm blood

**gwaedlif, gwaedlyn** nm hæmorrhage, dysentery

**gwaedlyd** adj bloody, sanguinary

**gwaedoliaeth** nf blood, consanguinity

**gwaedu** vb bleed

**gwaedd (-au)** nf cry, shout

**gwaeddi** see **gweiddi**

**gwaeg (~au)** nf buckle, clasp

**gwael** adj poor, vile; poorly, ill

**gwaelder, -dra** nm poorness, vileness

**gwaeledd** nm illness

**gwaelod (-ion)** nm bottom; (pl) sediment

**gwaelodi** vb settle, deposit sediment

**gwaelu** vb sicken

**gwaell (gwëyll, gweill)** nf knitting-needle

**gwaered** nm descent; **I waered** down

**gwaeth** adj worse

**gwaethwaeth** adj worse and worse

**gwaethygu** vb worsen

**gwaew** see **gwayw**

**gwag (gweigion)** adj empty, vacant, vain

**gwagedd** nm vanity

**gwagelog** adj wary, circumspect

**gwagen** (-i) *nf* waggon
**gwagenwr** (-wyr) *nm* waggoner
**gwagfa** (-feydd) *nf* vacuum
**gwagle** (-oedd) *nm* space, void
**gwagu** *vb* empty
**gwahadden** (gwahaddod) *nf* mole
**gwahan, gwahân** *nm*: **ar** apart, separately
**gwahangleifion** *npl* lepers
**gwahanglwyf** *nm* leprosy
**gwahanglwyfus** *adj* leprous ▷ *nm* leper
**gwahaniaeth** (-au) *nm* difference
**gwahaniaethol** *adj* distinguishing
**gwahaniaethu** *vb* differ; distinguish
**gwahanol** *adj* different
**gwahanu** *vb* divide, part, separate
**gwahardd** *vb* forbid, prohibit
**gwaharddiad** (-au) *nm* prohibition, veto
**gwahodd** *vb* invite
**gwahoddedigion** *npl* guests
**gwahoddiad** (-au) *nm* invitation
**gwahoddwr** (-wyr) *nm* inviter, host
**gwain** (gweiniau) *nf* sheath, scabbard
**gwair** (gweiriau) *nm* hay
**gwaith** (gweithiau) *nm* work
**gwaith** (gweithiau) *nf* time, turn
**gwal** (-iau, gwelydd) *nf* wall
**gwâl** (gwalau) *nf* couch, bed; lair
**gwala** *nf* enough, plenty
**gwalch** (gweilch) *nm* hawk; rogue, rascal
**gwaled** (-au) *nf* wallet
**gwalio** *vb* wall, fence
**gwall** (-au) *nm* defect, want; mistake, error
**gwallgof** *adj* mad, insane
**gwallgofdy** (-dai) *nm* madhouse, lunatic asylum
**gwallgofddyn** (-gofiaid) *nm* madman

**gwallgofi** *vb* go mad, rave
**gwallgofrwydd** *nm* madness, insanity
**gwallt** (-iau) *nm*, *coll n* hair of the head
**gwalltog** *adj* hairy
**gwallus** *adj* faulty, incorrect, inaccurate
**gwamal** *adj* fickle, frivolous
**gwamalio, -u** *vb* waver; behave frivolously
**gwamalrwydd** *nm* frivolity, levity
**gwan** (gweiniaid, gweinion) *adj* weak, feeble
**gwanaf** (-au) *nf* layer; row, swath
**gwanc** *nm* greed, voracity
**gwancus** *adj* greedy, voracious
**gwaneg** (-au, gwenyg) *nf* wave, billow
**gwangalon** *adj* faint-hearted
**gwangalonni** *vb* lose heart
**gwanhau** *vb* weaken, enfeeble
**gwanllyd, gwannaidd** *adj* weakly, delicate
**gwant** *nm* caesura; division
**gwantan** *adj* unsteady, fickle; feeble, poor
**gwanu** *vb* pierce, stab
**gwanwyn** (-au) *nm* spring
**gwanwynol** *adj* vernal, spring-like
**gwanychu** *vb* weaken, enfeeble
**gwar** (-rau) *nm/f* (nape of) neck
**gwâr** *adj* civilised, tame, gentle
**gwaradwydd** (-iadau) *nm* shame, disgrace
**gwaradwyddo** *vb* shame, disgrace
**gwaradwyddus** *adj* shameful, disgraceful
**gwarafun** *vb* forbid, refuse, grudge
**gwaraidd** *adj* gentle, civilized
**gwarant** (-au) *nf* warrant
**gwarantu** *vb* warrant, guarantee
**gwarchae** *vb* besiege ▷ *nm* siege
**gwarcheidiol** *adj* guardian, tutelary
**gwarcheidwad** (-waid) *nm*

guardian
**gwarchod** vb watch, ward, mind
**gwarchodaeth** nf ward, custody
**gwarchodlu** (-oedd) nm garrison, guards
**gward** (-iau) nm/f ward
**gwarden** (-deiniaid) nm warden
**gwared** vb rid; deliver, redeem
**gwaredigaeth** (-au) nf deliverance
**gwaredigion** npl redeemed, ransomed
**gwaredu** vb save, deliver, redeem; rid
**gwaredwr** (-wyr), **-ydd** (-ion) nm saviour
**gwaredd** nm mildness, gentleness
**gwareiddiad** nm civilization
**gwareiddiedig** adj civilized
**gwareiddio** vb civilize
**gwargaled** adj stiffnecked, stubborn
**gwargaledwch** nm stubbornness
**gwargam** adj stooping
**gwargamu** vb stoop
**gwarged** nm remains
**gwargrwm** adj round-shouldered
**gwargrymu** vb stoop
**gwario** vb spend
**gwarogaeth** see **gwrogaeth**
**gwarth** nm shame, disgrace
**gwarthaf** nm top, summit; **ar warthaf** on top of, upon
**gwarthafl** (-au) nf stirrup
**gwartheg** npl cows, cattle
**gwarthnod** (-au) nm stigma
**gwarthnodi** vb stigmatize
**gwarthol** (-ion) nf stirrup
**gwarthrudd** nm shame, disgrace
**gwarthruddo** vb shame, disgrace
**gwarthus** adj shameful, disgraceful
**gwas** (gweision) nm lad; servant
**gwasaidd** adj servile, slavish
**gwasanaeth** (-au) nm service
**gwasanaethferch** (-ed) nf handmaid

**gwasanaethgar** adj serviceable; obliging
**gwasanaethu** vb serve, minister
**gwasanaethwr** (-wyr) nm manservant, servant
**gwasanaethwraig** (-wragedd) nf maidservant
**gwasanaethydd** (-ion) nm servant
**gwasanaethyddes** (-au) nf handmaid
**gwaseidd-dra** nm servility
**gwasg** (-au, -oedd, gweisg) nf press ▷ nm waist; bodice
**gwasgar** nm dispersion; **ar wasgar** scattered, dispersed
**gwasgaredig** (-ion) adj scattered
**gwasgarog** adj scattered; divided
**gwasgaru** vb scatter, disperse; spread
**gwasgarwr** (-wyr) nm scatterer; spreader
**gwasgfa** (-feydd, -feuon) nf squeeze; fit
**gwasgod** (-au) nf waistcoat
**gwasgu** vb press, squeeze, crush, wring
**gwasod** adj in heat (of a cow)
**gwastad** adj level, flat; even; constant, continual
**gwastadedd** (-au) nm plain
**gwastadol** adj continual, perpetual
**gwastadrwydd** nm evenness
**gwastatáu** vb make even, level; settle
**gwastatir** (-oedd) nm level ground, plain
**gwastraff** nm waste, extravagance
**gwastraffu** vb waste, squander
**gwastraffus** adj wasteful, extravagant
**gwastrawd** (-odion) nm groom, ostler
**gwastrodaeth, -odi** vb grooming; discipline
**gwatwar** vb mock; mimic ▷ nm

mockery

**gwatwareg** *nf* sarcasm, satire, irony

**gwatwarus** *adj* mocking, scoffing

**gwatwarwr** (-wyr) *nm* mocker, scoffer

**gwau** *vb* knit, weave

**gwaun** (gweunydd) *nf* moor, meadow

**gwawch** (-iau) *nf*, **-io** *vb* scream, yell

**gwawd** *nm* scoff, scorn, ridicule

**gwawdiaeth** *nf* ridicule

**gwawdio** *vb* mock, scoff, jeer, ridicule

**gwawdiwr** (-wyr) *nm* mocker, scoffer

**gwawdlyd** *adj* mocking, jeering, sneering

**gwawl** *nm* light

**gwawn** *nm* gossamer

**gwawr** *nf* dawn, day-break; hue, nuance

**gwawrio** *vb* dawn

**gwayw** (gwewyr) *nm* pang, pain, stitch

**gwaywffon** (-ffyn) *nf* spear

**gwden** (-ni, gwdyn) *nf* withe

**gwdihŵ** *nm* owl

**gwddf** (gyddfau) *nm* neck, throat

**gwe** (-oedd) *nf* web; texture

**gwead** *nm* weaving, knitting; texture

**gwedd** (-au) *nf* aspect, form; appearance

**gwedd** (-oedd) *nf* yoke; team

**gweddaidd** *adj* seemly, decent

**gweddeidd-dra** *nm* seemliness, decency

**gwedder** (gweddrod) *nm* wether; **cig ~** mutton

**gweddgar** *adj* plump, sleek

**gweddi** (-ïau) *nm* prayer

**gweddigar** *adj* prayerful

**gweddill** (-ion) *nm* remnant, remainder, rest; (*pl*) remains

**gweddillio** *vb* leave spare, leave

a remnant

**gweddïo** *vb* pray

**gweddïwr** (-ïwyr) *nm* one who prays

**gweddol** *adj* fair, fairly

**gweddu** *vb* suit, become, befit

**gweddus** *adj* seemly, decent, proper

**gweddustra** *nm* decency, propriety

**gweddw** *adj* single; widow, widowed; **gŵr ~** widower ▷ (-on) *nf* widow

**gweddwdod** *nm* widowhood

**gweddwi** *vb* widow

**gwefl** (-au) *nf* lip (*usu.* of animal)

**gwefr** *nm* thrill, excitement; charge

**gwefreiddio** *vb* electrify, thrill

**gwefreiddiol** *adj* thrilling

**gwefus** (-au) *nf* (human) lip

**gwefusol** *adj* of the lip, labial

**gwegi** *nm* vanity, levity

**gwegian** *vb* sway, totter

**gwegil** *nm* back of head

**gwehelyth** *nm/f* lineage, pedigree

**gwehilion** *npl* refuse, trash, riffraff

**gwehydd** (-ion) *nm* weaver

**gwehynnu** *vb* draw, pour, empty

**gweiddi** *vb* cry, shout

**gweilgi** *nf* sea, torrent

**gweili** *adj* empty, idle

**gweini** *vb* serve, minister; be in service

**gweinidog** (-ion) *nm* minister, servant

**gweinidogaeth** (-au) *nf* ministry, service

**gweinidogaethol** *adj* ministerial

**gweinidogaethu** *vb* minister

**gweinio** *vb* sheathe

**gweinyddes** (-au) *nf* attendant, nurse; waitress

**gweinyddiaeth** (-au) *nf* administration

**gweinyddol** *adj* administrative

**gweinyddu** *vb* administer, officiate

**gweirglodd** (iau) *nf* meadow
**gweitied, -io** *vb* wait
**gweithdy** (-dai) *nm* workshop
**gweithfa** (-oedd, -feydd) *nf* works
**gweithfaol** *adj* industrial
**gweithgar** *adj* hard-working, industrious
**gweithgaredd** (-au), **-garwch** *nm* activity
**gweithio** *vb* work; ferment; purge
**gweithiwr** (-wyr) *nm* workman, worker
**gweithred** (-oedd) *nf* act, deed, work
**gweithrediad** (-au) *nm* action, operation
**gweithredol** *adj* active, actual, virtual
**gweithredu** *vb* act, work, operate
**gweithredwr** (-wyr) *nm* doer
**gweithredydd** (-ion) *nm* doer, factor, agent
**gweladwy** *adj* perceptible, visible
**gweled, gweld** *vb* see, perceive
**gwelediad** *nm* sight, appearance
**gweledig** *adj* seen, visible
**gweledigaeth** (-au) *nf* vision
**gweledydd** (-ion) *nm* seer
**gwelw** *adj* pale
**gwelwi** *vb* pale
**gwely** (-au, gwelâu) *nm* bed; river basin; sea bed; stratum; flat surface
**gwell** *adj* better, superior
**gwella** *vb* better, mend, improve, recover
**gwellau, gwellaif** (-eifiau) *nm* shears
**gwellen** (gweill) *nf* knitting-needle
**gwellhad** *nm* recovery, improvement
**gwellhau** *vb* better, improve
**gwelliant** (-iannau) *nm* amendment, improvement
**gwellt** *coll n* grass; sward; straw
**gwelltglas** *nm* grass, greensward
**gwelltog** *adj* grassy, green
**gwelltyn** *nm* blade of grass; a straw

**gwellwell** *adv* better and better
**gwen** *adj f of* **gwyn**
**gwên** (gwenau) *nf* smile
**gwenci** (-ïod) *nf* stoat, weasel
**gwendid** (-au) *nm* weakness, frailty
**Gwener** *nf* Venus; **Dydd ~** Friday
**gwenerol** *adj* venereal
**gwenfflam** *adj* blazing, ablaze
**gweniaith** *nf* flattery
**gwenieithio** *vb* flatter
**gwenieithiwr** (-wyr) *nm* flatterer
**gwenieithus** *adj* flattering
**gwenith** *npl* (*nf-en*) wheat
**gwenithfaen** *nm* granite
**gwennol** (gwenoliaid) *nf* swallow, martin; shuttle
**gwenu** *vb* smile
**gwenwisg** (-oedd) *nf* surplice
**gwenwyn** *nm* poison, venom; jealousy
**gwenwynig, -wynol** *adj* poisonous, venomous
**gwenwynllyd** *adj* peevish; jealous
**gwenwyno** *vb* poison; fret; be jealous
**gwenyn** *npl* (*nf-en*) bees
**gwep** *nf* visage, grimace
**gwêr** *nm* tallow, suet *etc*
**gŵer** *nm* shade
**gwerchyr** *nm* cover, lid, valve
**gwerdd** *adj f of* **gwyrdd**
**gwerin** *coll nf* men, people; democracy; crew
**gweriniaeth** (-au) *nf* democracy; republic
**Gweriniaeth, Iwerddon** *nf* Eire
**gwerinlywodraeth** (-au) *nf* republic
**gwerinol** *adj* plebian, vulgar
**gwerinos** *coll nf* the rabble, the mob
**gwerinwr** (-wyr) *nm* democrat
**gwern** (-i, -ydd) *nf* swamp, meadow; alder-grove
**gwern** *npl* (*nf-en*) alder-trees
**gwerog** *adj* tallowy, suety
**gwers** (-i) *nf* verse; lesson

**gwersyll** (-oedd) *nm* camp, encampment

**gwersyllu, -a** *vb* encamp

**gwerth** *nm* worth, value; **ar werth** for sale

**gwerthfawr** *adj* valuable, precious

**gwerthfawredd** *nm* preciousness

**gwerthfawrogi** *vb* appreciate

**gwerthfawrogiad** *nm* appreciation

**gwerthu** *vb* sell

**gwerthwr** (-wyr) *nm* seller

**gwerthyd** (-au) *nf* spindle, axle

**gweryd** (-au) *nm* earth, soil; sward ⊳ *nf* groin

**gweryriad** *nm* neighing

**gweryru** *vb* neigh

**gwestai** (-eion) *nm* guest

**gwesty** (-au, -tai) *nm* inn, hotel

**gweu** *vb* weave, knit

**gwewyr** *nm* anguish

**gwg** *nm* frown, scowl; disapproval

**gwgu** *vb* frown, scowl, lower

**gwialen** (gwiail) *nf* rod, switch

**gwialennod** (-enodiau) *nf* stroke, stripe

**gwialenodio** *vb* beat with a rod

**gwib** *nf* wandering, jaunt ⊳ *adj* wandering

**gwibdaith** (-deithiau) *nf* excursion

**gwiber** (-od) *nf* viper

**gwibio** *vb* flash, flit, dart, wander

**gwibiog** *adj* flitting, darting, wandering

**gwiblong** (-au) *nf* cruiser

**gwich** *nf* squeak; creak; wheeze, wheezing

**gwichiad** (-iaid) *nm* periwinkle

**gwichian** *vb* squeak, squeal; creak; wheeze

**gwichlyd** *adj* creaking; wheezy

**gwiddon** (-od) *nf* witch

**gwiddon** *npl* mites

**gwif** (-iau) *nm* lever, crowbar

**gwig** (-oedd) *nf* wood

**gwingo** *vb* wriggle, fidget; writhe; kick, struggle

**gwin** (-oedd) *nm* wine

**gwinau** *adj* bay, brown, auburn

**gwinc** (-od) *nf* chaffinch

**gwinegr** *nm* vinegar

**gwinllan** (-noedd, -nau) *nf* vine-yard

**gwinllannwr, -nydd** *nm* vine-dresser

**gwinwryf** (-oedd) *nm* wine-press

**gwinwydd** *npl* (*nf* -en) vines

**gwir** *adj* true ⊳ *nm* truth

**gwireb** (-au, -ion) *nf* truism, axiom

**gwireddu** *vb* verify, substantiate

**gwirfodd** *nm* goodwill; own accord

**gwirfoddol** *adj* voluntary, spontaneous

**gwirfoddolwr** (-wyr) *nm* volunteer

**gwirio** *vb* verify

**gwirion** (-iaid) *adj* innocent; silly

**gwiriondeb** *nm* innocence; silliness

**gwirionedd** (-au) *nm* truth, verity, reality

**gwirioneddol** *adj* true, real, genuine

**gwirioni** *vb* infatuate, dote

**gwirionyn** *nm* simpleton

**gwirod** (-ydd) *nm* liquor, spirits

**gwisg** (-oedd) *nf* dress, garment, robe

**gwisgi** *adj* brisk, lively, nimble; ripe

**gwisgo** *vb* dress; wear

**gwisgwr** (-wyr) *nm* wearer

**gwiw** *adj* fit, meet; worthy

**gwiwer** (-od) *nf* squirrel

**gwlad** (gwledydd) *nf* country, land

**gwladaidd** *adj* countrified, rustic

**Gwlad Belg** *nf* Belgium

**Gwlad yr Iâ** *nf* Iceland

**Gwlad Thai** *nf* Thailand

**gwladfa** (-oedd) *nf* colony, settlement

**gwladgar** *see* **gwlatgar**

**gwladgarol** *adj* patriotic

**gwladgarwch** *nm* patriotism

**gwladgarwr** (-wyr) *nm* patriot

**gwladol** *adj* of a country, civil, state
**gwladoli** *vb* nationalize
**gwladweiniaeth** *nf* statesmanship
**gwladweinydd** (-ion, -wyr) *nm* statesman
**gwladwr** (-wyr) *nm* countryman, peasant
**gwladwriaeth** (-au) *nf* state
**gwladwriaethol** *adj* state, political
**gwladychfa** (-oedd) *nf* settlement, colony
**gwladychu** *vb* inhabit, settle, colonize; rule
**gwladychwr** (-wyr) *nm* settler, colonist
**gwlân** (gwlanoedd) *nm* wool
**gwlana** *vb* gather wool
**gwlanen** (-ni) *nf* flannel
**gwlanog** *adj* woolly
**gwlatgar** *adj* patriotic
**gwlaw** *see* **glaw**
**gwledig** *adj* countrified, country, rural
**gwledd** (-oedd) *nf* feast, banquet
**gwledda** *vb* feast
**gwleddwr** (-wyr) *nm* feaster
**gwleidydd** (-ion) *nm* politician, statesman
**gwleidyddiaeth** *nf* politics
**gwleidyddol** *adj* political
**gwleidyddwr** (-wyr) *nm* politician
**gwlith** (-oedd) *nm* dew
**gwlitho** *vb* dew, bedew
**gwlithog** *adj* dewy; inspiring
**gwlithyn** *nm* dewdrop
**gwlyb** (-ion) *adj* wet, fluid, liquid ▷ *nm* fluid, liquid
**gwlybaniaeth** *nm* wet, moisture
**gwlybwr** *nm* wet, moisture, liquid, fluid
**gwlybyrog** *adj* wet, damp, rainy
**gwlych** *nm* wet; **rhoi yng n~** steep
**gwlychu** *vb* wet, moisten; get wet; dip
**gwlydd** *npl, coll n* (*nm* -yn) haulm

**gwn** (gynnau) *nm* gun
**gŵn** (gynau) *nm* gown
**gwndwn** *see* **gwyndwn**
**gwneud, gwneuthur** *vb* do, make
**gwneuthuriad** *nm* make, making
**gwneuthurwr** (-wyr) *nm* maker, doer, manufacturer
**gwnïad** *nm* sewing, stitching, seam
**gwniadur** (-iau, on) *nm/f* thimble
**gwniadwraig** *nf* stitcher, seamstress
**gwniadyddes** (-au) *nf* seamstress
**gwnïo** *vb* sew, stitch
**gwnïyddes** (-au) *nf* seamstress
**gwobr** (-au) *nf/m*, **gwobrwy** (-au, -on) *nm* reward, prize
**gwobrwyo** *vb* reward
**gwobrwywr** (-wyr) *nm* rewarder
**gŵr** (gwŷr) *nm* man; husband
**gwra** *vb* seek *or* marry a husband
**gwrach** (-ïod, -od) *nf* hag, witch; **breuddwyd ~** wishful thinking
**gwrachïaidd** *adj* old-womanish
**gwraidd** (gwreiddiau) *coll n* roots
**gwraig** (gwragedd) *nf* woman; wife
**gwrandaw** *see* **gwrando**
**gwrandawiad** *nm* listening, hearing
**gwrandawr** (-wyr) *nm* listener, hearer
**gwrando** *vb* listen, hearken
**gwrcath** (-od) *nm* tom-cat
**gwregys** (-au) *nm* girdle, belt, truss; zone
**gwregysu** *vb* girdle, gird
**gwrêng** *nm, coll n* (one of the) common people
**gwreica** *vb* seek ▷ *or* marry a wife
**gwreichion** *npl* (*nf*-en) sparks
**gwreichioni** *vb* emit sparks, sparkle
**gwreiddio** *vb* root
**gwreiddiol** *adj* radical, rooted; original
**gwreiddioldeb** *nm* originality

**gwreiddyn** (gwreiddiau) *nm* root

**gwres** *nm* heat, warmth

**gwresfesurydd** (-ion) *nm* thermometer

**gwresog** *adj* warm, hot; fervent

**gwresogi** *vb* warm, heat

**gwrhyd** (-oedd), **gwryd** *nm* fathom

**gwrhydri** *nm* exploit; valour

**gwrid** *nm* blush, flush

**gwrido** *vb* blush, flush

**gwridog, gwritgoch** *adj* rosy-cheeked, ruddy

**gwrogaeth** *nf* homage

**gwrogi** *vb* do homage

**gwrol** *adj* brave, courageous

**gwroldeb** *nm* bravery, courage

**gwroli** *vb* hearten

**gwron** (-iaid) *nm* hero

**gwroniaeth** *nf* heroism

**gwrtaith** (-teithiau) *nm* manure, fertiliser

**gwrteithiad** *nm* cultivation, culture

**gwrteithio** *vb* manure; cultivate, culture

**gwrth-** *prefix* counter-, contra-, anti-

**gwrthban** (-au) *nm* blanket

**gwrthblaid** *nf* (party in) opposition

**gwrthbrofi** *vb* disprove, refute

**gwrthbwynt** *nm* counterpoint

**gwrthdaro** *vb* clash, collide

**gwrthdrawiad** (-au) *nm* collision

**gwrthdystiad** (-au) *nm* protest

**gwrthdystio** *vb* protest

**gwrthddadl** (-euon) *nf* objection

**gwrthddadlau** *vb* object, controvert

**gwrthddywediad** (-au) *nm* contradiction

**gwrthddywedyd** *vb* contradict

**gwrthgiliad** (-au) *nm* backsliding

**gwrthgilio** *vb* backslide, secede

**gwrthgiliwr** (-wr) *nm* backslider, seceder

**gwrthglawdd** (-gloddiau) *nm* rampart

**gwrthgyferbyniad** (-au) *nm* contrast, antithesis

**gwrthgyferbynnu** *vb* contrast

**gwrthnaws** *nm* antipathy ▷ *adj* repugnant

**gwrthnysig** *adj* obstinate, stubborn

**gwrthod** *vb* refuse, reject

**gwrthodedig** *adj* rejected, reprobate

**gwrthodiad** *nm* refusal, rejection

**gwrthodwr** (-wyr) *nm* refuser, rejecter

**gwrthol** *nm*, *adv* back; **ôl a ~** to and fro

**gwrthrych** (-au) *nm* object; subject (*of biography*)

**gwrthrychol** *adj* objective

**gwrthryfel** (-oedd) *nm* rebellion, mutiny

**gwrthryfela** *vb* rebel

**gwrthryfelgar** *adj* rebellious, mutinous

**gwrthryfelwr** (-wyr) *nm* rebel, mutineer

**gwrthsafiad** *nm* resistance

**gwrthsefyll** *vb* withstand, resist

**gwrthun** *adj* repugnant, odious, absurd

**gwrthuni** *nm* odiousness, absurdity

**gwrthuno** *vb* mar, deform, disfigure

**gwrthweithio** *vb* counteract

**gwrthwyneb** *nm* opposite, contrary

**gwrthwynebiad** (-au) *nm* objection

**gwrthwynebol** *adj* opposed

**gwrthwynebu** *vb* resist, oppose

**gwrthwynebus** *adj* repugnant; antagonistic

**gwrthwynebwr, -ydd** (-wyr) *nm* opponent, adversary

**gwrych** (-oedd) *nm* hedge

gwrych *npl, coll n* (*nm* -yn) bristles
gwryd *see* **gwrhyd**
gwryf (-oedd) *nm* press
gwrym (-iau) *nm* seam; wale
gwrysg *npl* (*nf*-en) stalks, haulm
gwryw *adj* male ▷ (-od) *nm* male
gwrywaidd, -ol *adj* masculine
gwrywgydiaeth *nm* homosexuality
gwrywgydiol *adj* homosexual
gwrywgydiwr (-wyr) *nm* homosexual
gwth *nm* push, thrust, shove; gust
gwthio *vb* push, thrust, shove
gwthiwr (-wyr) *nm* pusher
gwyar *nm* gore, blood
gwybed *npl* (*nm*-yn) flies
gwybod *vb* know ▷ (-au) *nm* knowledge; ~au studies
gwybodaeth (-au) *nf* knowledge
gwybodeg *nm* epistemology
gwybodus *adj* knowing, well-informed
gwybyddus *adj* known, aware of
gwych *adj* fine, splendid, brilliant
gwychder *nm* splendour, pomp
gwŷd (gwydiau) *nm* vice
gwydn *adj* tough
gwydnwch *nm* toughness
gwydr (-au) *nm* glass
gwydraid (-eidiau) *nm* glassful, glass
gwydro *vb* glaze
gwydrwr (-wyr) *nm* glazier
gwydryn (gwydrau) *nm* drinking-glass
gwŷdd *nm* presence
gwŷdd (gwyddau) *nm* goose
gwŷdd (gwehyddion, gwyddion) *nm* loom; plough
gwŷdd *npl* (*nf* gwydden) trees
gwyddbwyll *nf* chess
Gwyddel (-od, Gwyddyl) *nm* Irishman
Gwyddeleg *nf* Irish language
Gwyddeles (-au) *nf* Irishwoman
Gwyddelig *adj* Irish

gwyddfa *nf* tumulus, grave
gwyddfid *nm* honeysuckle
gwyddfod *nm* presence
gwyddoniadur (-on) *nm* encyclopædia
gwyddoniaeth *nf* science
gwyddonol *adj* scientific
gwyddonydd (-wyr) *nm* scientist
gwyddor (-ion) *nf* rudiment; science; **yr wyddor** the alphabet
gwyddori *vb* instruct, ground
gwyfyn (-od) *nm* moth
gwŷg *coll n* vetch
gŵyl *adj* bashful, modest
gŵyl (-iau) *nf* holiday, feast, festival
gwylaidd *adj* bashful, modest
gwylan (-od) *nf* sea-gull
gwylder *nm* bashfulness, modesty
gwyleidd-dra *nm* bashfulness, modesty
gwylfa (-fâu, -feydd) *nf* watch; lookout
gwyliadwriaeth *nm* watchfulness, caution ▷ (-au) *nf* watch; guard
gwyliadwrus *adj* watchful, cautious
gwyliedydd (-ion) *nm* watchman, sentinel
gwylio *vb* watch, mind, beware
gwyliwr (-wyr) *nm* watchman, sentinel
gwylmabsant (-au) *nf* wake
gwylnos (-au) *nf* watch-night, wake, vigil
gwyll *nm* darkness, gloom
gwylliad (-iaid) *nm* robber, bandit
gwyllt *adj* wild, savage, mad; rapid ▷ (-oedd) *nm* wild
gwylltineb *nm* wildness; rage, fury
gwylltio, -u *vb* frighten; fly into a passion
gwymon *nm* seaweed
gwyn (f gwen) *adj* white; blessed
gwŷn (gwyniau) *nm/f* ache, smart; lust
gwynder, -dra *nm* whiteness

**gwyndwn** nm unploughed land
**gwyneb** see **wyneb**
**gwynegon** nm rheumatism
**gwynegu** vb throb, ache
**gwynfa** nf paradise
**gwynfyd** (-au) nm blessedness, bliss; (pl) beatitudes
**gwynfydedig** adj blessed, happy, beatific
**gwyngalch** nm whitewash
**gwyngalchog** adj whitewashed
**gwyngalchu** vb whitewash
**gwyniad** (-iaid) nm whiting
**gwynias** adj white-hot
**gwyniedyn** nm sewin
**gwynio** vb throb, ache
**gwynnu** vb whiten, bleach
**gwynnwy** nm white of egg
**gwynt** (-oedd) nm wind; breath; smell
**gwyntell** (-i) nf round basket without handle
**gwyntio** vb smell
**gwyntog** adj windy
**gwyntyll** (-au) nf fan
**gwyntylliad** nm ventilation
**gwynytyllio, -u** vb ventilate, winnow
**gŵyr** adj crooked, oblique, sloping
**gwyr** see **gŵr**
**gwyrdraws** adj perverse
**gwyrdro** (-ion) nm perversion
**gwyrdroi** vb pervert, distort
**gwyrdd** (-ion) adj, nm green
**gwyrddlas** adj green, verdant
**gwyrddlesni** nm verdure
**gwrddni** nm greenness, verdure
**gwyrgam** adj crooked
**gwyrni** nm crookedness, perverseness
**gwyro** vb swerve; slope; stoop; tilt; deviate
**gwyrth** (-iau) nf miracle
**gwyrthiol** adj miraculous
**gwyry, gwyryf** (~fon) nf virgin
**gwyryfdod** nm virginity
**gwyryfol** adj virgin

**gwŷs** (gwysion) nf summons
**gwysio** vb summon
**gwystl** (-on) nm pledge; hostage
**gwystlo** vb pledge, pawn
**gwystno** vb dry, wither, flag
**gwythïen** (gwythi, gwythiennau) nf vein, blood vessel, artery; **cwlwm gwythi** cramp
**gwyw** adj withered, faded, sere
**gwywo** vb wither, fade
**gyda, -g** prefix with
**gyddfol** adj guttural
**gyferbyn** prefix over against, opposite
**gylfin** (-od) nm bill, beak
**gylfinir** nm curlew
**gynfad** (-au) nm gunboat
**gynnau** adv a little while ago, just now
**gynt** adv formerly, of yore
**gyr** (-roedd) nm drove
**gyrfa** (-oedd, -feydd) nf race; course; career
**gyriedydd** (-ion) nm driver
**gyrru** vb drive; send; work, forge
**gyrrwr** (gyrwyr) nm driver; sender
**gyrwynt** (-oedd) nm hurricane, tornado
**gysb** nm staggers

# h

**ha** *excl* ha
**hac** (-iau) *nf* cut, notch, hack
**hacio** *vb* hack
**had** (-au) *nm, coll n* (*nm* hedyn) seed
**hadlif** *nm* seminal fluid
**hadog** *nm* haddock
**hadu** *vb* seed
**hadyd** *coll n* seed-corn
**haearn** (heyrn) *nm* iron; **~ bwrw** cast iron; **~ gyr** wrought iron
**haearnaidd** *adj* like iron
**haeddiannol** *adj* meritorious; merited
**haeddiant** (-iannau) *nm* merit, desert
**haeddu** *vb* deserve, merit
**hael** *adj* generous, liberal
**haelfrydedd** *nm* liberality
**haelfrydig** *adj* generous, free
**haelioni** *nm* generosity
**haelionus** *adj* generous, liberal
**haen** (-au) *nf* layer, stratum; seam
**haenen** (-nau) *nf* layer, film
**haenu** *vb* stratify
**haeriad** (-au) *nm* assertion
**haerllug** *adj* importunate; impudent
**haerllugrwydd** *nm* importunity; impudence
**haeru** *vb* affirm, assert
**haf** (-au) *nm* summer
**hafaidd** *adj* summer-like, summery
**hafal** *adj* like, equal
**hafaliad** *nm* equation
**hafan** *nf* haven

**hafn** (-au) *nf* hollow, gorge, ravine
**hafod** (-ydd) *nf* summer dwelling, upland farm
**hafog** *nm* havoc
**hafoty** (-tai) *nm* summer residence
**hagr** *adj* ugly
**hagru** *vb* mar, disfigure
**hagrwch** *nm* ugliness
**haid** (heidiau) *nf* swarm, drove, horde
**haidd** (heiddiau) *nm, coll n* (*nf* heidden) barley
**haig** (heigiau) *nf* shoal
**haint** (heintiau) *nm/f* pestilence; faint
**hala** *vb* send, spend
**halen** *nm* salt, brine
**halog, -edig** *adj* defiled, polluted
**halogi** *vb* defile, profane, pollute
**halogrwydd** *nm* defilement, pollution
**halogwr** (-wyr) *nm* defiler, profaner
**hallt** *adj* salt, salty; severe
**halltedd, -rwydd** *nm* saltness, saltiness
**halltu** *vb* salt
**halltwr** (-wyr) *nm* salter
**hambwrdd** (-byrddau) *nm* tray
**hamdden** *nf* leisure, respite
**hamddenol** *adj* leisurely
**hanerob** (-au) *nf* flitch of bacon
**haneru** *vb* halve
**hanes** (-ion) *nm* history, story, account
**hanesydd** (-wyr) *nm* historian
**hanesyddol** *adj* historical
**hanesyn** (-nau) *nm* anecdote
**hanfod** *vb* descend from, issue ▷ *nm* essence
**hanfodol** *adj* essential
**haniad** *nm* derivation, descent
**haniaeth** *nf* abstraction
**haniaethol** *adj* abstract
**hanner** (hanerau, haneri) *nm, adj, adv* half
**hanu** *vb* proceed, be derived, be descended

**hapus** adj happy
**hapusrwydd** nm happiness
**hardd** adj beautiful, handsome
**harddu** vb beautify, embellish, adorn
**harddwch** nm beauty
**harnais** (-eisiau) nm harness
**harneisio** vb harness
**hatling** (-au, -od) nf mite, half a farthing
**hau** vb sow, disseminate
**haul** (heuliau) nm sun
**hawdd** adj easy
**hawddamor** nm, excl good luck, welcome
**hawddfyd** nm ease, prosperity
**hawddgar** adj amiable; comely
**hawddgarwch** nm amiability
**hawl** (-iau) nf claim; right; ~ **ac ateb** question and answer
**hawlio** vb claim, demand
**hawlydd** (-ion) nm claimant, plaintiff
**haws** adj easier
**heb** prep without
**heblaw** prep beside(s)
**hebog** (-au) nm hawk, falcon
**Hebraeg** nf, adj Hebrew (language)
**Hebreaidd, Hebreig** adj Hebrew, Hebraic
**Hebrees** (-au) nf Hebrew woman
**Hebreigydd** (-ion) nm Hebraist
**Hebrëwr** (-wyr) nm a Hebrew
**hebrwng** vb accompany, conduct, convey, escort
**hebryngydd** (-ion) nm conductor, guide
**hedeg** vb fly; run to seed
**hedegog** adj flying; high-flown
**hedfa** (-feydd) nf flight
**hedfan** vb fly, hover
**hedydd** (-ion) nm lark
**hedyn** (hadau) nm seed, germ
**hedd** nm peace, tranquillity
**heddgeidwad** (-waid) nm policeman
**heddiw** adv today

**heddlu** nm police force
**heddwas** (-weision) nm policeman
**heddwch** nm peace, quiet, tranquillity
**heddychiaeth** nf pacifism
**heddychlon** adj peaceful, peaceable
**heddychol** adj peaceable, pacific
**heddychu** vb pacify, appease
**heddychwr** (-wyr) nm pacifist, peace-maker
**heddyw** see **heddiw**
**hefelydd** adj similar
**hefyd** adv also, besides
**heffer** (heffrod) nf heifer
**hegl** (-au) nf leg, shank
**heglog** adj leggy, long-legged
**heglu** vb foot it, `hook it'
**heibio** adv past
**heidio** vb swarm, throng, flock
**heidden** nf grain of barley
**heigio** vb shoal, teem
**heini** adj active, lively, nimble, brisk
**heintio** vb infect
**heintus** adj infectious, contagious
**heislan** (-od) nf hackle, hatchel
**heislanu** vb hackle flax
**hel** vb gather, collect; drive, chase
**hela** vb hunt, spend (money, time); **cŵn ~** hounds
**helaeth** adj ample, abundant, extensive
**helaethrwydd** nm abundance
**helaethu** vb enlarge, extend, amplify
**helaethwych** adj sumptuous
**helbul** (-on) nm trouble
**helbulus** adj troubled, troublous
**helcyd** vb hunt ▷ nm worry, trouble
**helfa** (-fâu, -feydd) nf hunt, catch
**helfarch** (-feirch) nm hunter (horse)
**helgi** (-gwn) nm hound
**heli** nm salt water, brine
**heliwr** (-wyr) nm hunter, huntsman
**helm** (-au) nf helm, helmet, stack
**help** nm help, aid, assistance
**helpio, -u** vb help, aid, assist

**helwriaeth** *nf* game, hunting; chase
**helyg** *npl* (*nf*-**en**) willows
**helynt** (-**ion**) *nf* trouble, fuss, bother
**helltni** *nm* saltiness, saltness
**hem** *nm* rivet
**hem** (-**iau**) *nf* hem, border
**hen** *adj* old, aged, ancient, of old
**henadur** (-**iaid**) *nm* alderman
**henaduriad** (-**iaid**) *nm* Presbyterian, elder
**henaduriaeth** (-**au**) *nf* presbytery
**henafgwr, henafol** *see* **hy-**
**henaint** *nm* old age
**hendaid** (-**deidiau**) *nm* great-grandfather
**hender** *nm* oldness
**hendref** (-**i**, -**ydd**) *nf* winter dwelling, lowland farm
**heneb** (-**ion**) *nf* ancient monument
**heneiddio** *vb* grow old, age
**henfam** *nf* grandmother
**henffasiwn** *adj* old-fashioned
**hennain** (**heneiniau**) *nf* great-grandmother
**heno** *adv* tonight
**henoed** *coll n* elderly people, the aged
**henuriad** (-**iaid**) *nm* elder, presbyter
**heol** (-**ydd**) *nf* road
**hepgor** *vb* spare, dispense with
▷ (-**ion**) *nm* what may be dispensed with
**hepian** *vb* slumber, doze
**her** (-**iau**) *nf* challenge
**herc** (-**iau**) *nf* hop; limp
**hercian** *vb* hop, hobble, limp
**heresi** (-**ïau**) *nf* heresy
**heretic** (-**iaid**) *nm* heretic
**hereticaidd** *adj* heretical
**herfeiddio** *vb* dare, brave, defy
**herfeiddiol** *adj* daring, defiant
**hergwd** *nm* push, thrust, shove
**herio** *vb* challenge, dare, brave, defy
**herw** *nm* raid; outlawry
**herwa** *vb* scout, prowl, raid
**herwgipio** *vb* kidnap

**herwgipiwr** (-**wyr**) *nm* kidnapper
**herwhela** *vb* poach (*game*)
**herwr** (-**wyr**) *nm* scout, raider; outlaw
**herwydd** *see* **oherwydd**
**hesb** *adj f of* **hysb**
**hesben** (-**nau**) *nf* hasp
**hesbin** (-**od**) *nf* yearling ewe
**hesbio** *vb* dry up
**hesbwrn** (-**yrniaid**) *nm* young ram
**hesg** *npl* (*nf*-**en**) sedge, rushes
**het** (-**iau**) *nf* hat
**heulo** *vb* shine (*as the sun*); sun
**heulog** *adj* sunny
**heulwen** *nf* sunshine
**heuwr** (-**wyr**) *nm* sower
**hi** *pron* she, her; it
**hidio** *vb* heed
**hidl** *adj*: **wylo yn ~** weep abundantly
**hidl** (-**au**) *nf* strainer, sieve
**hidlen** (-**ni**) *nf* strainer, sieve
**hidlo** *vb* distil, run; strain, filter
**hil** *nf* race, lineage, posterity
**hilio** *vb* bring forth, teem, breed
**hiliogaeth** *nf* offspring, issue, posterity
**hilydd** (-**ion**) *nm* racist
**hilyddiaeth** *nf* racism
**hin** *nf* weather
**hinfynegydd** (-**ion**) *nm* barometer
**hiniog** (-**au**) *nf* threshold, door-frame
**hinon** *nf* fair weather
**hinsawdd** (-**soddau**) *nf* climate
**hinsoddol** *adj* climatic
**hir** (~**ion**) *adj, prefix* long
**hiraeth** *nm* longing, nostalgia, grief; homesickness
**hiraethu** *vb* long, yearn, sorrow
**hiraethus** *adj* longing; homesick
**hirbell** *adj*: **o ~** from afar
**hirben** *adj* long-headed, shrewd
**hirhoedledd** *nm* longevity
**hirhoedlog** *adj* long-lived
**hirymarhous** *adj* longsuffering
**hirymaros** *nm* longsuffering
**hithau** *pron conj* she (on her part),

she also
**hobaid** (-eidiau) nf peck
**hobi** (hobïau) nm hobby
**hoced** (-ion) nf deceit, fraud
**hocedu** vb cheat, deceive, defraud
**hocedwr** (-wyr) nm cheat, fraud
**hoci** nm hockey
**hocys** npl mallows
**hodi** vb shoot, ear, run to seed
**hoe** nf spell, rest
**hoeden** (-nau) nf hoyden
**hoedl** (-au) nf lifetime, life
**hoel, -en** (-ion) nf nail
**hoelio** vb nail
**hoeliwr** (-wyr) nm nailer
**hoen** nf joy, gladness; vigour
**hoenus** adj joyous, blithesome, gay
**hoenusrwydd** nm liveliness,
  sprightliness
**hoenyn** (-nau) nm snare
**hoew** see **hoyw**
**hofran** vb hover
**hoff** adj dear, fond; favourite
**hoffi** vb like, love
**hoffter** nm fondness; delight
**hoffus** adj lovable, amiable,
  affectionate
**hogen** (-nod) nf girl; **-naidd** adj
  girlish
**hogfaen** (-feini) nm whetstone,
  hone
**hogi** vb sharpen, whet
**hogyn** (hogiau) nm boy, lad
**hongiad** (-au) nm suspension
**hongian** vb hang, dangle
**holgar** adj inquisitive, curious
**holi** vb ask, question, inquire
**holiad** (-au) nm interrogation,
  question
**holiadur** (-on) nm questionnaire
**holwr** (-wyr) nm questioner,
  interrogator; catechist, question-
  master
**holwyddoreg** (-au) nf catechism
**holwyddori** vb catechize
**holl** adj all, whole
**hollalluog** adj almighty,

omnipotent
**hollalluowgrwydd** nm
  omnipotence
**hollbresennol** adj omnipresent
**hollbresenoldeb** nm
  omnipresence
**hollfyd** nm universe
**hollgyfoethog** adj almighty
**holliach** adj whole, sound
**hollol** adj quite
**hollt** (-au) nf split, slit, cleft
**hollti** vb split, cleave, slit
**hollwybodaeth** nf omniscience
**hollwybodol** adj omniscient
**homili** (-ïau) nf homily
**hon** pron f of **hwn**
**honcian** vb waggle; jolt; limp
**honedig** adj alleged
**honiad** (-au) nm claim, assertion,
  allegation
**honni** vb assert, allege, profess,
  pretend
**honno** pron f of **hwnnw**
**hopran** (-au) nf mill-hopper; mouth
**hosan** (-au) nf stocking
**hoyw** adj alert, sprightly, lively, gay
**hoywdeb, -der** nm sprightliness
**hoywi** vb brighten, smarten
**hual** (-au) nm fetter, shackle
**hualu** vb fetter, shackle
**huan** nf the sun
**huawdl** adj eloquent
**hud** nm magic, illusion, charm,
  enchantment
**hudlath** (-au) nf magic wand
**hudo** vb charm, allure, beguile
**hudol** adj enchanting ▷ (-ion) nm
  enchanter
**hudoles** (-au) nf enchantress,
  sorceress
**hudoliaeth** (-au) nf enchantment,
  allurement
**hudolus** adj enchanting, alluring
**hudwr** (-wyr) nm enticer, allurer
**huddygl** nm soot
**hufen** nm cream
**hugan** (-au) nf cloak, covering; rug

**hulio** vb cover, spread
**hun** (-au) nf sleep, slumber
**hun** pron self; **yn ei dŷ ei ~** his own house
**hunan** (-ain) pron self ▷ prefix self-
**hunan-dyb** nm self-conceit
**hunangar** adj self-loving, selfish
**hunaniaeth** nf identity
**hunanladdiad** nm self-murder, suicide
**hunanol** adj selfish, conceited
**hunanoldeb** nm selfishness; conceit
**hunanymwadiad** nm self-denial
**hunanymwadu** vb deny oneself
**hunell** (-au) nf wink (of sleep)
**hunllef** (-au) nf nightmare
**huno** vb sleep
**huodledd** nm eloquence
**hur** (-iau) nm hire, wage
**hurio** vb hire
**huriwr** (-wyr) nm hirer; hireling
**hurt** adj stunned, stupid
**hurtio** vb stun, stupefy
**hurtrwydd** nm stupidity
**hurtyn** (-nod) nm stupid, blockhead
**hwb** (hybiau) nm push; effort; lift
**hwde** (hwdiwch) vb imper take, accept
**Hwngari** nf Hungary
**hwn** (f hon) adj, pron this (one)
**hwnnw** (f honno) adj, pron that one (absent)
**hwnt** adv beyond, away, aside; **tu ~** beyond
**hwp** nm push; **-io, -o** vb push
**hwrdd** (hyrddod) nm ram
**hwrdd** (hyrddiau) nm impulse, stroke
**hwre** vb see **hwde**
**hwsmon** (-myn) nm farm-bailiff
**hwtio** vb hoot, hiss
**hwy** pron they, them
**hwyad, -en** (hwyaid) nf duck
**hwyhau** vb lengthen, elongate
**hwyl** (-iau) nf sail; humour;
religious fervour
**hwylbren** (-nau, -ni) nm mast
**hwylio** vb sail; prepare, order
**hwyliog** adj fervent, eloquent
**hwylus** adj easy, convenient, comfortable
**hwyluso** vb facilitate
**hwylustod** nm ease, facility, convenience
**hwynt** pron them, they
**hwynt-hwy** pron they, they themselves
**hwyr** adj late ▷ nm evening
**hwyrach** adv perhaps ▷ adj later
**hwyrdrwm** adj sluggish, drowsy, dull
**hwyrfrydig** adj slow, tardy, reluctant
**hwyrfrydigrwydd** nm tardiness, reluctance
**hwyrhau** vb get late
**hwyrol** adj evening
**hwythau** pron conj they (on their part), they also
**hy** adj bold
**hybarch** adj venerable
**hyblyg** adj flexible, pliant, pliable
**hyblygrwydd** nm flexibility, pliancy
**hybu** vb improve in health; promote
**hyd** (-au, -oedd) nm length ▷ prep to, till, as far as
**hyder** nm confidence, trust
**hyderu** vb confide, rely, trust
**hyderus** adj confident
**hydred** (-ion) nm longitude
**hydredol** adj longitudinal
**hydref** (-au) nm autumn; **H~** October
**hydrefol** adj autumnal
**hydrin** adj tractable, docile
**hydwyll** adj gullible
**hydwylledd** nm gullibility
**hydwyth** adj supple, elastic
**hydwythedd** nm elasticity
**hydyn** adj tractable, docile
**hydd** (-od) nm stag

**hyddysg** adj well versed, learned
**hyf** see **hy**
**hyfder, -dra** nm boldness
**hyfedr** adj expert, skilful, clever
**hyfryd** adj pleasant, delightful, agreeable
**hyfrydu** vb delight
**hyfrydwch** nm delight, pleasure
**hyfwyn** adj kindly, genial
**hyfforddi** vb direct, instruct, train
**hyfforddiadol** adj training
**hyfforddiant** nm instruction, training
**hyfforddwr (-wyr)** nm guide, instructor
**hygar** adj amiable
**hygarwch** nm amiability
**hyglod** adj celebrated, renowned, famous
**hyglyw** adj audible
**hygoel** adj credible
**hygoeledd** nm credibility; credulity
**hygoelus** adj credulous, gullible
**hygyrch** adj accessible
**hyhi** pron f emphat. of **hi**
**hylaw** adj handy, convenient; dexterous
**hylif (-au)** nm, adj fluid, liquid
**hylithr** adj slippery, fluent
**hylosg** adj combustible, inflammable
**hylwydd** adj prosperous
**hyll** adj ugly, hideous
**hylltra** nm ugliness
**hyllu** vb mar, disfigure
**hyn** adj, pron this; these; that
**hynafgwr (-gwyr)** nm old man, elder
**hynafiad (-iaid)** nm ancestor
**hynafiaeth (-au)** nf antiquity
**hynafiaethol** adj antiquarian
**hynafiaethwr, -ydd (-wyr)** nm antiquary
**hynafol** adj ancient
**hynaws** adj kind, genial
**hynawsedd** nm kindness, geniality
**hynny** adj, pron that; those

**hynod** adj noted, notable, remarkable
**hynodi** vb distinguish, characterize
**hynodion** npl peculiarities
**hynodrwydd** nm peculiarity
**hynt (-iau, -oedd)** nf way, course
**hyrddio, -u** vb hurl, impel
**hyrddwynt (-oedd)** nm hurricane
**hyrwyddo** vb facilitate, promote
**hyrwyddwr (-wyr)** nm sponsor, promoter
**hysb (fhesb)** adj dry, barren
**hysbio** vb dry
**hysbyddu** vb exhaust, drain
**hysbys** adj known, evident; **dyn hysbys** nm wise man, sorcerer
**hysbyseb (-ion)** nf advertisement
**hysbysebu** vb advertise
**hysbysebwr (-wyr)** nm advertiser
**hysbysiad (-au)** nm announcement, advertisement
**hysbysrwydd** nm information
**hysbysu** vb inform, announce
**hysbyswr (-wyr)** nm informant, informer
**hysian, -io** vb hiss; set on, incite
**hytrach** adv rather
**hywaith** adj industrious, dexterous
**hywedd** adj trained, tractable

aeth (-au), **lladdfa,**
wyr) *nm* killer, slayer
ng, loose; **Y treigliad ~**
utation
*nf* litter (*for animals*)
lacken, loosen, relax,

milk
yield milk
dai) *nm* milk-house,

dj rich in milk; milky
tterance, speech ▷ *adj*

iaid) *nf* vowel
m blade
ol (*nf* -en) bulrushes
*nm* labour; corn
*adj* elaborate; laborious
abour, toil; till
edd) *nm* manpower,
e, workforce
laborious, toilsome,
g
vyr) *nm* labourer
ler
d, mire
u) *nf* patch, piece,
o
) *nm* voice, vote
mp, moist
on other, another
stride, leap, jump,

(**llamidyddion**) *nm*

*adj* prancing, frisky
de, leap, bound
church; village
n confusion, mess
m young man,

-i) *nf* young woman,

ennyrch),
(-i, -ydd) *nf* spot,

**llanw** *nm* flow (*of tide*) ▷ *vb* flow, fill
**llaprwth** *nm* lout
**llariaidd** *adj* mild, meek, gentle
**llarieidd-dra** *nm* meekness, gentleness
**llarieiddio** *vb* soothe, mollify
**llarp** (**-iau**) *nm* shred, clout
**llarpio** *vb* rend, tear, mangle, maul
**llarpiog** *adj* tattered, ragged
**llaswyr** (**-au**) *nm* psalter
**llath** (**-au**) *nf* yard, wand
**llathen** (**-ni**) *nf* yard
**llathr** *adj* bright, glossy, smooth
**llathraidd** *adj* smooth; of fine growth
**llathru** *vb* polish
**llau** *npl* (*nf* **lleuen**) lice
**llaw** (**dwylaw, dwylo**) *nf* hand
**llawcio** *vb* gulp, gorge, gobble
**llawchwith** *adj* left-handed
**llawdde** *adj* dexterous
**llawddryll** (**-iau**) *nm* pistol, revolver
**llawen** *adj* merry, joyful, glad, cheerful
**llawenhau** *vb* rejoice, gladden
**llawenychu** *vb* rejoice
**llawenydd** *nm* joy, gladness, mirth
**llawer** (**-oedd**) *nm, adj, adv* many, much
**llawes** (**llewys**) *nf* sleeve
**llawfaeth** *adj* reared by hand
**llawfeddyg** (**-on**) *nm* surgeon
**llawfeddygaeth** *nf* surgery
**llawfeddygol** *adj* surgical
**llaw-fer** *nf* shorthand
**llawfom** (**-iau**) *nf* grenade
**llawn** *adj* full ▷ *adv* quite
**llawnder, -dra** *nm* fullness, abundance
**llawr** (**lloriau**) *nm* floor, ground, earth
**llawryf** (**-oedd**) *nm* laurel, bay
**llawryfog, -ol** *adj* laureate
**llawysgrif** (**-au**) *nf* manuscript
**llawysgrifen** *nf* handwriting
**lle** (**-oedd, ~fydd**) *nm* place
**llecyn** (**-nau**) *nm* place, spot



# i

**i** *prep* to, into
**i** *pron* I, me
**iâ** *nm* ice
**iach** *adj* healthy, well
**iachâd** *nm* healing
**iacháu** *vb* heal; save
**iachawdwr** (**-wyr**) *nm* saviour
**iachawdwriaeth** *nf* salvation
**iachawr** (**-wyr**) *nm* healer
**iachus, -ol** *adj* healthy, healthful, wholesome
**iad** (**-au**) *nf* pate, cranium
**iaith** (**ieithoedd**) *nf* language; **yr ~ fain** English
**iâr** (**ieir**) *nf* hen
**iard** (**ierdydd**) *nf* yard
**iarll** (**ieirll**) *nm* earl
**iarllaeth** (**-au**) *nf* earldom
**iarlles** (**-au**) *nf* countess
**ias** (**-au**) *nf* shiver; thrill
**Iau** *nm* Jupiter; **Dydd ~** Thursday
**iau** (**ieuau**) *nm* liver
**iau** (**ieuau, ieuoedd**) *nf* yoke
**iawn** *adj* right ▷ *nm* right; atonement ▷ *adv* very
**iawndal** *nm* compensation
**iawnder** (**-au**) *nm* right, equity
**iawnol** *adj* atoning, expiatory
**idealaeth** *nf* idealism
**ideoleg** (**-au**) *nf* ideology
**idiom** (**-au**) *nm* idiom
**Iddew** (**-on**) *nm* Jew
**Iddewiaeth** *nf* Judaism
**Iddewes** (**-au**) *nf* Jewess
**Iddewig** *adj* Jewish

**iddwf** *nm*: **tân ~** erysipelas
**ie** *adv* yes, yea
**iechyd** *nm* health
**iechydaeth** *nf* hygiene, sanitation
**iechydol** *adj* hygienic, sanitary
**iechydwriaeth** *nf* salvation
**ieitheg** *nf* philology
**ieithegydd** (**-ion, -wyr**) *nm* philologist
**ieithwedd** (**-au, -ion**) *nf* diction, (literary) style
**ieithydd** (**-ion**) *nm* linguist
**ieithyddiaeth** *nf* linguistics, philology
**ieithyddol** *adj* linguistic, philological
**iet** (**-au, -iau**) *nf* gate
**ieuanc** (**-ainc**) *adj* young
**ieuenctid** *nm* youth
**ieuo** *vb* yoke
**ifanc** (**-ainc**) *adj* young
**ifori** *nm* ivory
**ig** (**-ion**) *nm* hiccup
**igam-ogam** *adj* zigzag
**igian** *vb* hiccup
**ing** (**-oedd**) *nm* agony, anguish
**ingol** *adj* agonizing, agonized
**ill** *pron* they; **~ dau** they both
**impio** *vb* sprout, shoot; bud, graft
**impyn** *nm* graft; scion
**inc** *nm* ink
**incil** (**-iau**) *nm* tape
**incwm** *nm* income
**India** *nf* India
**India'r Gorllewin** *npl* West Indies
**iod** *nm* iota, jot
**Iôn** *nm* the Lord
**Ionawr** *nm* January
**Iôr** *nm* the Lord
**Iorddonen** *nf* Jordan
**iorwg** *nm* ivy
**ir** *adj* fresh, green, raw
**irai** *nm* ox-goad
**iraid** (**ireidiau**) *nm* grease
**iraidd** *adj* fresh, succulent, luxuriant
**Iran** *nf* Iran
**Iraq** *nf* Iraq

**irder** *nm* freshness, greenness
**ireidd-dra** *nm* freshness, vigour
**ireiddio** *vb* freshen
**iriad** (-au) *nm* lubrication, greasing
**iro** *vb* grease, smear, rub, anoint
**irwr** (-wyr) *nm* greaser
**is** *adj* inferior, lower ▷ *prep* below, under ▷ *prefix* under-, sub-, vice-
**isadran** (-nau) *nf* subsection
**Isalmaen** *nf* Holland
**isel** *adj* low; base; humble; depressed
**iselder** (-au) *nm* lowness, depth; depression
**iseldir** (-oedd) *nm* lowland
**Iseldiroedd; Yr** *npl* Netherlands
**iselfryd** *adj* humble-minded
**iselfrydedd** *nm* humility, condescension
**iselhau** *vb* lower, abase, degrade
**isetholiad** (-au) *nm* by-election
**is-gadeirydd** *nm* vice-chairman
**is-ganghellor** *nm* vice-chancellor
**is-gapten** (-iaid, -einiaid) *nm* lieutenant
**isgell** *nm* broth, stock
**isiarll** (-ieirll) *nm* viscount
**islaw** *prep* below, beneath
**isod** *adv* below, beneath
**isop** *nm* hyssop
**isosod** *vb* sublet
**isradd** (-iaid) *nm* inferior, subordinate
**israddol** *adj* inferior
**israddoldeb** *nm* inferiority
**Israel** *nf* Israel
**iswasanaethgar** *adj* subservient
**isymwybod** *nm* subconscious
**isymwybyddiaeth** *nf* subconsciousness
**ithfaen** *nm* granite
**Iwerddon** *nf* Ireland
**Iwerddon Rydd** *nf* Eire
**Iwerydd** *nm* the Atlantic
**Iwgoslavia** *nf* Yugoslavia
**iwrch** (iyrchod) *nm* roebuck

# j

**jac codi baw** *nm* JCB
**jac-y-do** *nm* jackdaw
**jam** *nm* jam
**jamio** *vb* preserve
**Jamaica** *nf* Jamaica
**jar** (-iau) *nf* jar, hot water bottle
**jersi** (-s) *nf* jersey
**jest** *adv* just, almost
**jeti** (-iau) *nm* jetty
**jetlif** *nm* jet stream
**ji-binc** (-od) *nf* chaffinch
**jîns** *npl* jeans
**job** (-sys) *nf* job
**jobyn** *nm* job
**jôc** *nf* joke
**jocan** *vb* joke
**joci** (-s) *nf* jockey
**jwg** (jygiau) *nf* jug
**jyngl** (-oedd) *nm* jungle

# l

**label** (-i) *nf* label
**labelu** *vb* label
**labordy** (-dai) *nm* laboratory
**labro** *vb* labour
**labrwr** (-wyr) *nm* labourer
**lafant** *nm* lavender
**lamp** (-au) *nf* lamp
**lamplen** (-ni) *nf* lampshade
**lapio** *vb* lap, wrap
**larwm** *nm* alarm
**lawnt** (-iau) *nf* lawn
**lefain** *nm* leaven
**lefeinio** *vb* leaven
**lefeinllyd** *adj* leavened
**lefel** (-au) *nf* level
**leicio** *vb* like
**lein** (-iau) *nf* clothes line, line-out (rugby)
**lesbiad** (-iaid) *nf* lesbian
**letys** *npl* (*nf*-en) lettuce
**Libanus** *nf* Lebanon
**libart** *nm* back-yard
**Libya** *nf* Libya
**lifft** (-iau) *nm* lift
**lifrai** *nm/f* livery
**lili** *nf* lily
**lindys** *npl* (*nm*-yn) caterpillars
**locust** (-iaid) *nm* locust
**lodes** *see* **herlodes**
**loetran** *vb* loiter
**lol** *nf* nonsense
**lolfa** (-feydd) *nf* lounge
**lolian** *vb* talk nonsense
**lôn** (lonydd) *nf* lane
**loncian** *vb* jog

**lonciv**
**lori** (-ï
**losin**
**lot** (-ia
**Luxe**
**lŵan**
**lwc** *n*
**lwcus**
**lwmp**

**lladdedi**
**lladdwr**
**llaes** *adj*
 spirant
**llaesod** (
**llaesu** *vb*
 droop, fla
**llaeth** *nm*
**llaetha** *v*
**llaethdy**
 dairy
**llaethog**
**llafar** *nm*
 vocal; lou
**llafariad**
**llafn** (-au)
**llafrwyn**
**llafur** (-iau
**llafurfaw**
**llafurio** *vb*
**llafurlu** (-
 labour for
**llafurus** *a*
 painstaki
**llafurwr** (-
**llai** *adj* sma
**llaid** *nm* m
**llain** (lleini
 narrow str
**llais** (lleisia
**llaith** *adj* d
**llall** (lleill) *p*
**llam** (-au) *n*
 bound
**llamhidyd**
 porpoise
**llamsachu**
**llamu** *vb* st
**llan** (-nau) *n*
**llanast(r)** *n*
**llanc** (-iau) *n*
 youth, lad
**llances** (-au
 lass
**llannerch** (
**llanercha**
 patch, glade

**llab**
**llab**
**llac**
**llac**
**llac**
**llac**
**lla**
**lla**
**Lla**
**lla**
**lla**
**lla**
**lla**
**lla**
**lla**
**lla**
**lla**
**lla**

**llech** (-au, -i) *nf* slab, flag, slate
**llechgi** (-gwn) *nm* sneak
**llechres** (-i) *nf* table, catalogue, list
**llechu** *vb* hide, shelter; lurk, skulk
**llechwedd** (-au, -i) *nf* slope, hillside
**llechwraidd** *adj* stealthy, underhand, insidious
**lled** (-au) *nm* breadth, width
**lled** *adv* partly, rather
**lledaenu** *vb* spread, disseminate, circulate
**lleden** (lledod) *nf* flat-fish
**llediaith** *nf/m* foreign accent
**llednais** *adj* modest, delicate; meek
**llednant** (-nentydd) *nf* tributary
**lledneisrwydd** *nm* modesty, delicacy
**lled-orwedd** *vb* recline, lounge, loll
**lledr** (-au) *nm* leather; **~ y gwefusau** gums
**lledred** (-ion) *nm* latitude
**lledrith** *nm* magic, illusion, phantasm
**lledrithio** *vb* appear, haunt
**lledrithiol** *adj* illusory, illusive
**lledryw** *adj* degenerate
**lledu** *vb* widen, broaden, expand, spread
**lleddf** *adj* slanting; flat, minor; plaintive
**lleddfolyn** (-olion) *nm* sedative
**lleddfu** *vb* flatten; soften, soothe, allay
**llef** (-au) *nf* voice, cry
**llefain** *vb* cry
**llefareg** *nf* speech training
**llefaru** *vb* speak, utter
**llefarwr** (-wyr), **-ydd** (-ion) *nm* speaker
**lleferydd** *nm/f* utterance, voice, speech
**llefn** *adj f of* **llyfn**
**llefrith** *nm* sweet milk, new milk, milk
**llegach** *adj* weak, feeble, infirm
**lleng** (-oedd) *nf* legion
**lleiaf** *adj* least, smallest

**lleiafrif** (-au) *nm* minority
**lleian** (-od) *nf* nun
**lleiandy** (-dai) *nm* nunnery, convent
**lleibio** *vb* lap, lick
**lleidiog** *adj* miry
**lleidr** (lladron) *nm* thief, robber
**lleiddiad** (-iaid) *nm* assassin
**lleihad** *nm* diminution, decrease
**lleihau** *vb* lessen, diminish, decrease
**lleill** *see* **llall**
**lleisio** *vb* sound, utter, voice
**lleisiol** *adj* vocal
**lleisiwr** (-wyr) *nm* vocalist
**lleithder, -dra** *nm* damp, moisture
**lleithig** *nf* couch; footstool
**lleitho** *vb* damp, moisten
**llem** *adj f of* **llym**
**llen** (-ni) *nf* sheet; veil, curtain
**llên** *nf* literature, lore, learning
**llencyn** *nm* stripling, lad
**llencyndod** *nm* adolescence
**llengar** *adj* literary, learned
**llengig** *nf* diaphragm, midriff; **tor ~** rupture
**llên-ladrad** (-au) *nm* plagiarism
**llenor** (-ion) *nm* literary man
**llenwi** *vb* fill; flow in
**llenydda** *vb* practise literature
**llenyddiaeth** (-au) *nf* literature
**llenyddol** *adj* literary
**lleol** *adj* local
**lleoli** *vb* locate; localize
**lleoliad** *nm* location; localization
**llercian** *vb* lurk, loiter
**lles** *nm* benefit, profit, good, advantage; **y wladwriaeth les** the welfare state
**llesâd** *nm* advantage, profit, benefit
**llesáu** *vb* benefit, advantage
**llesg** *adj* feeble, faint; languid, sluggish
**llesgáu** *vb* weaken, languish, faint
**llesgedd** *nm* weakness, languor, debility
**llesmair** (-meiriau) *nm* faint,

swoon
**llesmeirio** *vb* faint, swoon
**llesol** *adj* advantageous, profitable, beneficial
**llestair, llesteirio** *vb* hinder, impede, baulk
**llestr** (-i) *nm* vessel
**llesyddiaeth** *nf* utilitarianism
**lletbai** *adj* askew, awry; oblique
**lletchwith** *adj* awkward, clumsy
**lletem** (-au) *nf* wedge, stud, rivet
**lletraws** *adj* diagonal
**lletwad** (-au) *nf* ladle
**llety** (-au) *nm* lodging(s)
**lletya** *vb* lodge
**lletygar** *adj* hospitable
**lletygarwch** *nm* hospitality
**lletywr** (-wyr) *nm* lodger; host
**lletywraig** (-wragedd) *nf* landlady
**llethol** *adj* oppressive, overpowering
**llethr** (-au) *nf* slope, declivity
**llethrog** *adj* sloping, steep, declining
**llethu** *vb* overlie; smother; oppress, overpower, overwhelm
**lleuad** (-au) *nf* moon
**lleuog** *adj* lousy
**llew** (-od) *nm* lion; **dant y ~** dandelion
**llewes** (-au) *nf* lioness
**llewpart** (-pardiaid) *nm* leopard
**llewych** *nm* light, brightness
**llewyg** (-on) *nm* faint, swoon
**llewygu** *vb* faint, swoon
**llewyrch** *nm* brightness, radiance, gleam
**llewyrchu** *vb* shine
**llewyrchus** *adj* flourishing, prosperous
**lleyg** (-ion) *adj* lay
**lleygwr** (-wyr) *nm* layman
**lliain** (-einiau) *nm* linen; cloth; towel
**lliaws** *nm* host, multitude
**llibin** *adj* limp, feeble; awkward, clumsy

**llid** *nm* wrath; irritation, inflammation
**llidiart** (-ardau) *nm* gate
**llidio** *vb* be angry, chafe, inflame
**llidiog** *adj* angry, wrathful; inflamed
**llidiowgrwydd** *nm* wrath, indignation
**llidus** *adj* inflamed
**llif** (-iau) *nf* saw
**llif** (-ogydd) *nm* stream, flood, current
**llifbridd** *nm* alluvium
**llifddor** (-au) *nf* floodgate
**llifddwfr** (-ddyfroedd) *nm* flood, torrent
**llifeiriant** (-iaint) *nm* flood
**llifeirio** *vb* flow, stream
**llifeiriol** *adj* streaming, overflowing
**llifio** *vb* saw
**llifiwr** (-wyr) *nm* sawyer
**llifo** *vb* flow, stream
**llifo** *vb* grind (*tool*)
**llifo** *vb* dye
**llifolau** (-euadau) *nm* floodlight
**llifwr** (-wyr) *nm* dyer
**llifyn** (-nau, -ion) *nm* dye
**llilinio** *vb* streamline
**llin** *nm* flax; **had ~** linseed
**llinach** (-au) *nf* lineage, pedigree
**llindagu** *vb* strangle, throttle, choke
**llinell** (-au) *nf* line; **~ gais** try line; **~ gwsg** touch-in-goal
**llinelliad** (-au) *nm* lineation, drawing
**llinellog** *adj* lined, ruled
**llinellol** *adj* lineal
**llinglwm** *nm*: **cwlwm ~** tight knot
**lliniaru** *vb* ease, soothe, allay
**llinorog** *adj* eruptive; purulent, suppurating
**llinos** (-od) *nf* linnet
**llinyn** (-nau) *nm* line, string, twine
**llinynnu** *vb* string
**llipa** *adj* limp, weak
**llipryn** (-nod) *nm* weakling
**lliprynnaidd** *adj* limp, flabby

**llith** (-iau, -oedd) *nf* lesson, lecture; bait, mash
**llithio** *vb* entice, allure, seduce; feed
**llithriad** (-au) *nm* slip, glide
**llithren** (-nau) *nf* chute
**llithrig** *adj* slippery, glib, fluent
**llithrigrwydd** *nm* slipperiness, glibness
**llithro** *vb* slip, glide, slide
**lliw** (-iau) *nm* colour, hue, dye
**lliwio** *vb* colour, dye
**lliwiog** *adj* coloured
**llo** (~i) *nm* calf
**lloc** (-iau) *nm* fold, pen
**lloches** (-au) *nf* refuge, shelter, den
**llochesu** *vb* harbour, shelter
**llochi** *vb* stroke, caress, fondle
**llodig** *adj* in heat (*of a sow*)
**llodrau** *npl* trousers, breeches
**Lloegr** *nf* England
**lloer** (-au) *nf* moon
**lloeren** (-ni, -nau) *nf* satellite
**lloerig** *adj, nm* lunatic
**llofnod, -iad** (-au) *nm* signature
**llofnodi** *vb* sign
**llofrudd** (-ion) *nm* murderer
**llofruddiaeth** (-au) *nf* murder
**llofruddio** *vb* murder
**llofruddiog** *adj* guilty of murder
**lloffa** *vb* glean
**lloffion** *npl* gleanings
**llofft** (-ydd) *nf* loft, bedroom, gallery
**lloffwr** (-wyr) *nm* gleaner
**lloffyn** *nm* bundle of gleanings
**llog** (-au) *nm* interest
**llogi** *vb* hire
**llogwr** (-wyr) *nm* hirer
**llong** (-au) *nf* ship
**llongddrylliad** (-au) *nm* shipwreck
**llongwr** (-wyr) *nm* sailor
**llongwriaeth** *nf* seamanship
**llom** *adj f of* **llwm**
**llon** *adj* glad, merry
**llonaid, llond** *nm* full
**llonder** *nm* gladness, joy
**llongyfarch** *vb* congratulate
**llongyfarchiad** (-au, -archion) *nm* congratulation
**lloniant** *nm* joy, cheer
**llonni** *vb* cheer, gladden
**llonydd** *adj* quiet, still ▷ *nm* quiet, calm
**llonyddu** *vb* quiet, still, calm
**llonyddwch** *nm* quietness, quiet
**llorgynllun** (-iau) *nm* ground plan
**llorio** *vb* floor, ground (*rugby*)
**llorwedd** *adj* horizontal
**llosg** *nm, adj* burning
**llosgach** *nm* incest
**llosgadwy** *adj* combustible
**llosgfa** (-fâu, -feydd) *nf* burning, inflammation
**llosgfynydd** (-oedd) *nm* volcano
**llosgi** *vb* burn, scorch; smart
**llosgwrn** (-yrnau) *nm* tail
**llosgydd** (-ion) *nm* incinerator
**llu** (-oedd) *nm* host
**lluched** *npl* (-en-) lightning
**lluchfa** (-feydd) *nf* snowdrift
**lluchio** *vb* throw, fling, pelt
**lluchiwr** (-wyr) *nm* thrower
**lludlyd** *adj* ashy
**lludu, lludw** *nm* ashes, ash
**lludded** *nm* weariness, fatigue
**lluddedig** *adj* wearied, tired, fatigued
**lluddedu** *vb* tire, weary
**lluddias, -io** *vb* hinder; forbid
**lluest** (-au) *nm* tent, booth
**lluestfa** (-feydd) *nf* encampment
**lluestu** *vb* encamp
**lluesty** (-tai) *nm* tent, booth
**llugoer** *adj* lukewarm
**lluman** (-au) *nm* banner, standard, ensign
**llumanwr** (-wyr) *nm* linesman
**llumon** *nm* chimney stack, peak
**llun** (-iau) *nm* form, image, picture
**Llun, Dydd Llun** *nm* Monday
**Llundain** *nf* London
**lluniad** (-au) *nm* drawing
**lluniadaeth** (-au) *nf* draughtsmanship
**lluniaeth** *nm* food, nourishment

**lluniaethu** vb order, ordain, decree
**lluniedydd** nm draughtsman
**lluniaidd** adj shapely
**llunio** vb form, shape, fashion
**lluniwr** (-wyr) nm former, maker
**llun-recordydd** (-ion) nm video-tape recorder
**lluosflwydd** adj perennial
**lluosi** vb multiply
**lluosiad** nm multiplication
**lluosill, -afog** adj polysyllabic
**lluosog** adj numerous; plural
**lluosogi** vb multiply
**lluosogiad** nm multiplication
**lluoswm** nm product (maths)
**lluosydd** nm multiplier
**llurgunio** vb mangle, mutilate
**llurguniwr** (-wyr) nm mangler, mutilator
**llurig** (-au) nf coat of mail, cuirass
**llus** npl (nf-en) bilberries, whinberries
**llusern** (-au) nf lantern, lamp
**llusg** (-ion) nm draught; drag
**llusgfad** (-au) nm tugboat
**llusgo** vb drag; trail; crawl; drawl
**llusgwr** (-wyr) nm slowcoach
**llutrod** nm mire, ashes, debris
**lluwch** nm dust; spray; snowdrift
**lluydd** nm host, army
**lluyddu** vb mobilise
**llw** (-on) nm oath
**llwch** nm dust, powder
**llwdn** (llydnod) nm young of animals
**llwfr** adj timid, cowardly
**llwfrdra** nm cowardice
**llwfrddyn, -gi** nm coward
**llwfrhau** vb faint
**llwglyd** adj hungry, famished
**llwgr** nm corruption ▷ adj corrupt
**llwgrwobrwy** (-on) nm bribe
**llwgrwobrwyo** vb bribe
**llwgu** vb starve, famish
**llwm** (f llom) adj bare; destitute, poor
**llwnc** nm gulp, swallow; gullet

**llwncdestun** nm toast (health)
**llwr, llwrw** nm track; **l ei ben** headlong; **l ei gefn** backwards
**llwy** (-au) nf spoon, ladle
**llwyaid** (-eidiau) nf spoonful
**llwybr** (-au) nm path, track
**llwybreiddio** vb direct, forward
**llwybro** vb walk
**llwyd** adj brown; grey; pale; hoary
**llwydaidd** adj greyish, palish
**llwydi, llwydni** nm greyness; mould, mildew
**llwydnos** nf dusk, twilight
**llwydo** vb turn grey; become mouldy
**llwydrew** nm hoar-frost
**llwydrewi** vb cast hoar-frost
**llwydd, -iant** nm success, prosperity
**llwyddiannus** adj successful, prosperous
**llwyddo** vb succeed, prosper
**llwyfan** (-nau) nm/f platform, stage
**llwyfandir** (-oedd) nm plateau
**llwyfannu** vb stage
**llwyfen** (llwyf) nf elm
**llwyn** (-i) nm grove; bush
**llwyn** (-au) nf loin
**llwynog** (-od) nm fox
**llwynoges** (-au) nf vixen
**llwynwst** nf lumbago
**llwyo** vb use a spoon; ladle
**llwyr** adj entire, complete, total ▷ adv entirely, altogether ▷ prefix total
**llwyredd** nm entireness, completeness
**llwyrymatal, -ymwrthod** vb abstain totally
**llwyrymwrthodwr** (-wyr) nm teetotaller
**llwyth** (-au) nm tribe, clan
**llwyth** (-i) nm load, burden
**llwytho** vb load, burden
**llwythog** adj laden, burdened
**llychlyd** adj dusty
**Llychlyn** nf Scandinavia

**i**

**i** *prep* to, into
**i** *pron* I, me
**iâ** *nm* ice
**iach** *adj* healthy, well
**iachâd** *nm* healing
**iacháu** *vb* heal; save
**iachawdwr (-wyr)** *nm* saviour
**iachawdwriaeth** *nf* salvation
**iachawr (-wyr)** *nm* healer
**iachus, -ol** *adj* healthy, healthful, wholesome
**iad (-au)** *nf* pate, cranium
**iaith (ieithoedd)** *nf* language; **yr ~ fain** English
**iâr (ieir)** *nf* hen
**iard (ierdydd)** *nf* yard
**iarll (ieirll)** *nm* earl
**iarllaeth (-au)** *nf* earldom
**iarlles (-au)** *nf* countess
**ias (-au)** *nf* shiver; thrill
**Iau** *nm* Jupiter; **Dydd ~** Thursday
**iau (ieuau)** *nm* liver
**iau (ieuau, ieuoedd)** *nf* yoke
**iawn** *adj* right ▷ *nm* right; atonement ▷ *adv* very
**iawndal** *nm* compensation
**iawnder (-au)** *nm* right, equity
**iawnol** *adj* atoning, expiatory
**idealaeth** *nf* idealism
**ideoleg (-au)** *nf* ideology
**idiom (-au)** *nm* idiom
**Iddew (-on)** *nm* Jew
**Iddewiaeth** *nf* Judaism
**Iddewes (-au)** *nf* Jewess
**Iddewig** *adj* Jewish

**iddwf** *nm*: **tân ~** erysipelas
**ie** *adv* yes, yea
**iechyd** *nm* health
**iechydaeth** *nf* hygiene, sanitation
**iechydol** *adj* hygienic, sanitary
**iechydwriaeth** *nf* salvation
**ieitheg** *nf* philology
**ieithegydd (-ion, -wyr)** *nm* philologist
**ieithwedd (-au, -ion)** *nf* diction, (literary) style
**ieithydd (-ion)** *nm* linguist
**ieithyddiaeth** *nf* linguistics, philology
**ieithyddol** *adj* linguistic, philological
**iet (-au, -iau)** *nf* gate
**ieuanc (-ainc)** *adj* young
**ieuenctid** *nm* youth
**ieuo** *vb* yoke
**ifanc (-ainc)** *adj* young
**ifori** *nm* ivory
**ig (-ion)** *nm* hiccup
**igam-ogam** *adj* zigzag
**igian** *vb* hiccup
**ing (-oedd)** *nm* agony, anguish
**ingol** *adj* agonizing, agonized
**ill** *pron* they; **~ dau** they both
**impio** *vb* sprout, shoot; bud, graft
**impyn** *nm* graft; scion
**inc** *nm* ink
**incil (-iau)** *nm* tape
**incwm** *nm* income
**India** *nf* India
**India'r Gorllewin** *npl* West Indies
**iod** *nm* iota, jot
**Iôn** *nm* the Lord
**Ionawr** *nm* January
**Iôr** *nm* the Lord
**Iorddonen** *nf* Jordan
**iorwg** *nm* ivy
**ir** *adj* fresh, green, raw
**irai** *nm* ox-goad
**iraid (ireidiau)** *nm* grease
**iraidd** *adj* fresh, succulent, luxuriant
**Iran** *nf* Iran
**Iraq** *nf* Iraq

**irder** *nm* freshness, greenness
**ireidd-dra** *nm* freshness, vigour
**ireiddio** *vb* freshen
**iriad** (-au) *nm* lubrication, greasing
**iro** *vb* grease, smear, rub, anoint
**irwr** (-wyr) *nm* greaser
**is** *adj* inferior, lower ▷ *prep* below, under ▷ *prefix* under-, sub-, vice-
**isadran** (-nau) *nf* subsection
**Isalmaen** *nf* Holland
**isel** *adj* low; base; humble; depressed
**iselder** (-au) *nm* lowness, depth; depression
**iseldir** (-oedd) *nm* lowland
**Iseldiroedd; Yr** *npl* Netherlands
**iselfryd** *adj* humble-minded
**iselfrydedd** *nm* humility, condescension
**iselhau** *vb* lower, abase, degrade
**isetholiad** (-au) *nm* by-election
**is-gadeirydd** *nm* vice-chairman
**is-ganghellor** *nm* vice-chancellor
**is-gapten** (-iaid, -einiaid) *nm* lieutenant
**isgell** *nm* broth, stock
**isiarll** (-ieirll) *nm* viscount
**islaw** *prep* below, beneath
**isod** *adv* below, beneath
**isop** *nm* hyssop
**isosod** *vb* sublet
**isradd** (-iaid) *nm* inferior, subordinate
**israddol** *adj* inferior
**israddoldeb** *nm* inferiority
**Israel** *nf* Israel
**iswasanaethgar** *adj* subservient
**isymwybod** *nm* subconscious
**isymwybyddiaeth** *nf* subconsciousness
**ithfaen** *nm* granite
**Iwerddon** *nf* Ireland
**Iwerddon Rydd** *nf* Eire
**Iwerydd** *nm* the Atlantic
**Iwgoslavia** *nf* Yugoslavia
**iwrch** (iyrchod) *nm* roebuck

# J

**jac codi baw** *nm* JCB
**jac-y-do** *nm* jackdaw
**jam** *nm* jam
**jamio** *vb* preserve
**Jamaica** *nf* Jamaica
**jar** (-iau) *nf* jar, hot water bottle
**jersi** (-s) *nf* jersey
**jest** *adv* just, almost
**jeti** (-iau) *nm* jetty
**jetlif** *nm* jet stream
**ji-binc** (-od) *nf* chaffinch
**jîns** *npl* jeans
**job** (-sys) *nf* job
**jobyn** *nm* job
**jôc** *nf* joke
**jocan** *vb* joke
**joci** (-s) *nm* jockey
**jwg** (jygiau) *nf* jug
**jyngl** (-oedd) *nm* jungle

**lonciwr**(-wyr) *nm* jogger
**lori**(-ïau) *nf* lorry
**losin** *npl* (*nf*-en) sweets
**lot**(-iau) *nf* lot
**Luxembourg** *nf* Luxembourg
**lŵans, lwfans** *nm* allowance
**lwc** *nf* luck
**lwcus** *adj* lucky
**lwmp**(lympiau) *nm* lump

**label**(-i) *nf* label
**labelu** *vb* label
**labordy**(-dai) *nm* laboratory
**labro** *vb* labour
**labrwr**(-wyr) *nm* labourer
**lafant** *nm* lavender
**lamp**(-au) *nf* lamp
**lamplen**(-ni) *nf* lampshade
**lapio** *vb* lap, wrap
**larwm** *nm* alarm
**lawnt**(-iau) *nf* lawn
**lefain** *nm* leaven
**lefeinio** *vb* leaven
**lefeinllyd** *adj* leavened
**lefel**(-au) *nf* level
**leicio** *vb* like
**lein**(-iau) *nf* clothes line, line-out (rugby)
**lesbiad**(-iaid) *nf* lesbian
**letys** *npl* (*nf*-en) lettuce
**Libanus** *nf* Lebanon
**libart** *nm* back-yard
**Libya** *nf* Libya
**lifft**(-iau) *nm* lift
**lifrai** *nm/f* livery
**lili** *nf* lily
**lindys** *npl* (*nm*-yn) caterpillars
**locust**(-iaid) *nm* locust
**lodes** *see* **herlodes**
**loetran** *vb* loiter
**lol** *nf* nonsense
**lolfa**(-feydd) *nf* lounge
**lolian** *vb* talk nonsense
**lôn**(lonydd) *nf* lane
**loncian** *vb* jog

**llabed**(-au) *nf* lappet, lapel, flap
**llabwst**(-ystiau) *nm* lubber, lout
**llabyddio** *vb* stone
**llac** *adj* slack, loose, lax
**llacio** *vb* slacken, loosen, relax
**llacrwydd** *nm* slackness, laxity
**llacs** *nm* mud, dirt
**llacsog** *adj* muddy, dirty
**llach**(-iau) *nf* lash, slash
**llachar** *adj* bright, brilliant, flashing
**llachio** *vb* lash, slash
**Lladin** *nf* Latin
**lladmerydd**(-ion) *nm* interpreter
**lladrad**(-au) *nm* theft, robbery
**lladradaidd** *adj* stealthy, furtive
**lladrata** *vb* thieve, steal
**lladron** *see* **lleidr**
**lladrones**(-au) *nf* female thief
**lladronllyd** *adj* thievish, pilfering
**lladd** *vb* cut; kill, slay, slaughter
**lladd-dy**(-dai) *nm* slaughter-house
**lladdedig**(-ion) *adj* killed, slain

**lladdedigaeth** (-au), **lladdfa,**
**lladdwr** (-wyr) nm killer, slayer
**llaes** adj long, loose; **Y treiglad ~** spirant mutation
**llaesod(r)** nf litter (for animals)
**llaesu** vb slacken, loosen, relax, droop, flag
**llaeth** nm milk
**llaetha** vb yield milk
**llaethdy** (-dai) nm milk-house, dairy
**llaethog** adj rich in milk; milky
**llafar** nm utterance, speech ▷ adj vocal; loud
**llafariad** (-iaid) nf vowel
**llafn** (-au) nm blade
**llafrwyn** npl (nf-en) bulrushes
**llafur** (-iau) nm labour; corn
**llafurfawr** adj elaborate; laborious
**llafurio** vb labour, toil; till
**llafurlu** (-oedd) nm manpower, labour force, workforce
**llafurus** adj laborious, toilsome, painstaking
**llafurwr** (-wyr) nm labourer
**llai** adj smaller
**llaid** nm mud, mire
**llain** (lleiniau) nf patch, piece, narrow strip
**llais** (lleisiau) nm voice, vote
**llaith** adj damp, moist
**llall** (lleill) pron other, another
**llam** (-au) nm stride, leap, jump, bound
**llamhidydd** (llamidyddion) nm porpoise
**llamsachus** adj prancing, frisky
**llamu** vb stride, leap, bound
**llan** (-nau) nf church; village
**llanast(r)** nm confusion, mess
**llanc** (-iau) nm young man, youth, lad
**llances** (-au, -i) nf young woman, lass
**llannerch** (llennyrch), **llanerchau** (-i, -ydd) nf spot, patch, glade

**llanw** nm flow (of tide) ▷ vb flow, fill
**llaprwth** nm lout
**llariaidd** adj mild, meek, gentle
**llarieidd-dra** nm meekness, gentleness
**llarieiddio** vb soothe, mollify
**llarp** (-iau) nm shred, clout
**llarpio** vb rend, tear, mangle, maul
**llarpiog** adj tattered, ragged
**llaswyr** (-au) nm psalter
**llath** (-au) nf yard, wand
**llathen** (-ni) nf yard
**llathr** adj bright, glossy, smooth
**llathraidd** adj smooth; of fine growth
**llathru** vb polish
**llau** npl (nf lleuen) lice
**llaw** (dwylaw, dwylo) nf hand
**llawcio** vb gulp, gorge, gobble
**llawchwith** adj left-handed
**llawdde** adj dexterous
**llawddryll** (-iau) nm pistol, revolver
**llawen** adj merry, joyful, glad, cheerful
**llawenhau** vb rejoice, gladden
**llawenychu** vb rejoice
**llawenydd** nm joy, gladness, mirth
**llawer** (-oedd) nm, adj, adv many, much
**llawes** (llewys) nf sleeve
**llawfaeth** adj reared by hand
**llawfeddyg** (-on) nm surgeon
**llawfeddygaeth** nf surgery
**llawfeddygol** adj surgical
**llaw-fer** nf shorthand
**llawfom** (-iau) nf grenade
**llawn** adj full ▷ adv quite
**llawnder, -dra** nm fullness, abundance
**llawr** (lloriau) nm floor, ground, earth
**llawryf** (-oedd) nm laurel, bay
**llawryfog, -ol** adj laureate
**llawysgrif** (-au) nf manuscript
**llawysgrifen** nf handwriting
**lle** (-oedd, ~fydd) nm place
**llecyn** (-nau) nm place, spot

**llychwino** *vb* spot, tarnish, soil, sully

**llychyn** *nm* particle of dust, mote

**llydan** *adj* broad, wide

**Llydaw** *nf* Brittany

**llydnu** *vb* bring forth, foal

**llyfn** (**fllefn**) *adj* smooth, sleek

**llyfnder, -dra** *nm* smoothness, sleekness

**llyfndew** *adj* plump, sleek

**llyfnhau** *vb* smooth, level

**llyfnu** *vb* smooth, level; harrow

**llyfr** (**-au**) *nm* book

**llyfrbryf** (**-ed**) *nm* bookworm

**llyfrgell** (**-oedd**) *nf* library

**llyfrgellydd** (**-ion**) *nm* librarian

**llyfrifeg** *nm/f* book-keeping

**llyfrnod** (**-au**) *nm* bookmark

**llyfrwerthwr** (**-wyr**) *nm* bookseller

**llyfrydd** (**-ion**) *nm* bibliographer, transcriber of books

**llyfryddiaeth** *nf* bibliography

**llyfrfa** *nf* (**-feydd**) library; bookroom; official publishing house of religious denomination, government etc

**llyfryn** (**-nau**) *nm* booklet, pamphlet

**llyfu** *vb* lick

**llyffant** (**-od, llyffaint**) *nm* frog, toad

**llyffethair** (**-eiriau**) *nf* fetter, shackle

**llyffetheirio** *vb* fetter, shackle

**llyg** (**-od**) *nm/f* shrew(-mouse)

**llygad** (**llygaid**) *nm* eye; **~ y dydd** daisy

**llygad-dynnu** *vb* bewitch

**llygadog** *adj* eyed, sharp-eyed

**llygadrwth** *adj* wide-eyed, staring

**llygadrythu** *vb* stare

**llygadu** *vb* eye

**llygatgraff** *adj* keen-eyed, sharp-sighted

**llygedyn** *nm* ray of light

**llygeidiog** *adj* eyed

**llygoden** (**llygod**) *nf* mouse; **~ fawr,**

**~ ffrengig** rat

**llygota** *vb* catch mice

**llygotwr** (**-wyr,** *f* **~aig**) *nm* mouser, ratter

**llygradwy** *adj* corruptible

**llygredig** *adj* corrupt, depraved, degraded

**llygredigaeth** (**-au**) *nf* corruption

**llygredd** *nm* corruptness, depravity

**llygriad** (**-au**) *nm* corruption, adulteration

**llygru** *vb* corrupt, adulterate

**llygrwr** (**-wyr**) *nm* corrupter, adulterator

**llynges** (**-au**) *nf* fleet, navy

**llyngeswr** (**-wyr**) *nm* navy-man

**llyngesydd** (**-ion**) *nm* admiral

**llyngyr** *npl* (**nf -en**) (intestinal) worms

**llym** (**fllem**) *adj* sharp, keen, severe

**llymaid** (**-eidiau**) *nm* sip, drink

**llymarch** (**llymeirch**) *nm* oyster

**llymder** *nm* sharpness, keenness, severity

**llymder, -dra** *nm* bareness, poverty

**llymeitian, -io** *vb* sip, tipple

**llymeitiwr** (**-wyr**) *nm* tippler, sot

**llymhau** *vb* make bare (*from* **llwm**)

**llymhau** *vb* sharpen (*from* **llym**)

**llymrïaid** *npl* (**nf -ïen**) sand-eels

**llymru** *nm* flummery

**llymsur** *adj* acrid

**llymu** *vb* sharpen, whet

**llyn** (**-noedd**) *nm* lake, pond, pool

**llynciad** (**-au**) *nm* draught, gulp

**llyncu** *vb* swallow, gulp, absorb

**llyncwr** (**-wyr**) *nm* swallower, guzzler

**llynedd** *nf* last year

**llyo** *vb* lick

**llys** (**-oedd**) *nm* court, hall, palace

**llysaidd** *adj* courtly, polite

**llysblant** *npl* step-children

**llyschwaer** *nf* step-sister

**llysenw** (**-au**) *nm* nickname

**llysenwi** *vb* nickname

**llysfab** *nm* step-son
**llysfam** *nf* step-mother
**llysferch** *nf* step-daughter
**llysfrawd** *nm* step-brother
**llysgenhadaeth** *nf* embassy, legation
**llysgenhadol** *adj* ambassadorial
**llysgenhadwr, llysgennad**
**llysiau** *npl* (*nm* -ieuyn) herbs, vegetables
**llysieuol** *adj* herbal, vegetable
**llysieuydd** (-ion, -wyr) *nm* botanist; vegetarian
**llysnafedd** *nm* snivel, slime
**llystad** *nm* step-father
**llyswenwyn** *nm* herbicide
**llysysol** *adj* herbivorous
**llysywen** (llysywod) *nf* eel
**llysywenna** *vb* catch eels
**llythrennol** *adj* literal
**llythyr** (-au) *nm* letter, epistle
**llythyrdy** (-dai) *nm* post-office
**llythyren** (llythrennau) *nf* letter, type
**llythyrwr** (-wyr) *nm* letter-writer
**llyw** (-iau) *nm* ruler; rudder, helm
**llywaeth** *adj* hand-fed, tame, pet
**llywiawdwr** (-wyr) *nm* ruler, governor
**llywio** *vb* rule, govern, direct, steer
**llywiwr** (-wyr) *nm* steersman, helmsman
**llywodraeth** (-au) *nf* government
**llywodraethol** *adj* governing, dominant
**llywodraethu** *vb* govern, rule
**llywodraethwr** (-wyr) *nm* governor, ruler
**llywydd** (-ion) *nm* president
**llywyddiaeth** (-au) *nf* presidency
**llywyddol** *adj* presidential
**llywyddu** *vb* preside

**mab** (meibion) *nm* boy, son; man, male
**mabaidd** *adj* filial
**maban** (-od) *nm* babe, baby
**mabandod** *nm* childhood, infancy
**mabinogi** *nm* tale, story
**mablygad** *nm* eyeball
**mabmaeth** (-au, -od) *nm* foster-son
**maboed** *nm* childhood, infancy, youth
**mabolaeth** *nf* sonship; boyhood, youth
**mabolaidd** *adj* youthful, boyish
**mabolgamp** (-au) *nf* game, sport, feat
**mabsant** *nm* patron saint
**mabwysiad** *nm* adoption
**mabwysiadol** *adj* adoptive; adopted
**mabwysiadu** *vb* adopt
**macrell** (mecryll) *nf/m* mackerel
**macsu** *vb* to brew
**macwy** (-aid) *nm* youth, page
**machlud, -o** *vb* set, go down; - **haul** sunset
**machludiad** *nm* setting, going down
**machnïydd** *nm* mediator
**madarch** *npl* (*nf* -en) mushrooms
**madfall** (-od) *nm* lizard
**madrondod** *nm* giddiness, stupefaction
**madroni** *vb* make or become giddy
**madru** *vb* putrefy, fester, rot

**madruddyn** *nm* cartilage; **~ y cefn** spinal cord
**maddau** *vb* pardon, forgive, remit
**maddeuant** *nm* pardon, forgiveness
**maddeugar** *adj* of a forgiving disposition
**maddeuol** *adj* pardoning, forgiving
**maddeuwr** (-wyr) *nm* pardoner
**mae** *vb* is, are; there is, there are
**maeden** *nf* slut, jade
**maeddu** *see* **baeddu**
**maen** (meini) *nm* stone
**maenol, maenor** (-au) *nf* manor
**maentumio** *vb* maintain
**maer** (-od, meiri) *nm* mayor
**maeres** (-au) *nf* mayoress
**maerol** *adj* mayoral
**maeryddiaeth** *nf* mayoralty
**maes** (meysydd) *nm* field; **i ~** out; **~ glanio** airport
**maesglaf** (-gleifion) *nm* outpatient
**maeslywydd** (-ion) *nm* field-marshal
**maestir** (-oedd) *nm* open country, plain
**maestref** (-i, -ydd) *nf* suburb
**maeth** *nm* nourishment, nutriment
**maethlon** *adj* nourishing, nutritious
**maethu** *vb* nourish, nurture
**maethydd** (-ion) *nm* nourisher
**maethyn** (-nau) *nm* nutrient; suckling
**mafon** *npl* (nf-en) raspberries
**magl** (-au) *nf* snare; mesh
**maglu** *vb* snare, mesh, trip
**magnel** (-au) *nf* gun, cannon
**magnelaeth** *nf* artillery
**magnelwr** (-wyr) *nm* gunner
**magnesiwm** *nm* magnesium
**magnetedd** *nm/f* magnetism
**magneteiddio** *vb* magnetise
**magu** *vb* breed, rear, nurse; gain, acquire
**magwraeth** *nf* nourishment, nurture
**magwyr** (-ydd) *nf* wall
**maharen** (meheryn) *nm* ram; wether
**Mai** *nm* May
**mai** *conj* that it is
**maidd** *nm* whey
**main** (meinion) *adj* fine, slender, thin; **~ y cefn** small of the back
**mainc** (meinciau) *nf* bench, form, seat
**maint** *nm* size, quantity, number
**maintioli** *nm* size, stature
**maip** *npl* (nf meipen) turnips
**maith** (meithion) *adj* long, tedious
**mâl** *adj* ground
**malais** *nm* malice
**maldod** *nm* dalliance, affection
**maldodi** *vb* pet, pamper, indulge
**maleisus** *adj* malicious
**maleithiau** *npl* chilblains
**malio** *vb* care, mind, heed
**Malta** *nf* Malta
**malu** *vb* grind, mince, chop, smash
**malurio** *vb* pound; crumble, moulder
**malurion** *npl* fragments, debris
**malwod** *npl* (nf-en, malwen) snails
**malwr** (-wyr) *nm* grinder
**mall** *nf* blight; **y fall** Belial, perdition
**malltod** *nm* rot, blight, blast
**mallu** *vb* rot, blast
**mam** (-au) *nf* mother; **~-gu** grandmother
**mamaeth** (-od) *nf* nurse
**mamal** (-iaid) *nm* mammal
**mamiaith** (-ieithoedd) *nf* mother-tongue
**mamog** (-iaid) *nf* dam, sheep with young
**mamolaeth** (-au) *nf* maternity
**mamwlad** (-wledydd) *nf* motherland
**man** (-nau) *nm/f* place, spot; blemish
**mân** *adj* small, fine, petty
**mandyllog** *adj* porous
**maneg** (menig) *nf* glove, gauntlet

**mangre** nf place, spot
**manion** npl scraps, trifles, minutiæ
**mantais (-eision)** nf advantage
**manteisio** vb take advantage, profit
**manteisiol** adj advantageous
**mantell (-oedd, mentyll)** nf mantle
**mantellog** adj mantled
**mantol (-ion)** nf balance
**mantolen (-ni)** nf balance-sheet
**mantoli** vb turn scale, balance, weigh
**manwaidd** adj delicate, fine
**mân-werthu** vb retail
**manwl** adj exact, precise, strict, particular
**manwl-gywir** adj precise
**manylion** npl particulars, details
**manylrwydd** nm exactness, precision
**manylu** vb go into detail, particularize
**manylwch** nm exactness, precision
**map (-iau)** nm map
**mapio** vb map
**mapiwr (-wyr)** nm cartographer
**marblen (marblys)** nf marble
**marc (-iau)** nm mark
**marcio** vb mark
**march (meirch)** nm horse, stallion
**marchlu (-oedd)** nm cavalry
**marchnad (-oedd)** nf market
**marchnadfa (-oedd)** nf marketplace
**marchnata** vb market, trade
**marchnatwr (-wyr)** nm merchant
**marchnerth (-oedd)** nm horsepower
**marchocáu** vb ride a horse
**marchog (-ion)** nm horseman, rider; knight
**marchogaeth** vb ride
**marchogwr (-wyr)** nm rider, horseman
**marchredyn** npl (nf-en) polypody fern

**marchwellt** nm tall, coarse grass
**marian** nm holm, strand, moraine
**marlad** nm drake
**marmalêd (-au)** nm marmalade
**marmor** nm marble
**marsialydd (-ion)** nm marshal
**marsiandïaeth** nf merchandise
**marsiandïwr (-wyr)** nm merchant
**marsipan** nm marzipan
**marw** vb die
**marw (meirw, meirwon)** n, adj dead
**marwaidd** adj lifeless, sluggish, moribund
**marwdon** nf dandruff
**marweidd-dra** nm deadness, sluggishness
**marweiddio** vb deaden, mortify
**marwhad** nm mortification
**marwhau** vb deaden, mortify
**marwnad (-au)** nf lament, elegy
**marwol** adj deadly, mortal, fatal
**marwolaeth (-au)** nf death
**marwoldeb** nm mortality
**marwolion** npl mortals
**marwor** npl (nm -yn) embers; charcoal
**marwydos** npl embers
**masarnen (masarn)** nf sycamore
**masgl (-au)** nf shell, pod
**masglo, -u** vb shell; interlace
**masnach (-au)** nf trade, traffic, commerce
**masnachol** adj commercial, business
**masnachu** vb do business, trade, traffic
**masnachwr (-wyr)** nm dealer, merchant
**masw** adj wanton
**maswedd** nm wantoness, ribaldry
**masweddol** adj wanton, ribald
**maswr (-wyr)** nm outside half
**mat (-iau)** nm mat
**mater (-ion)** nm matter
**materol** adj material; materialistic
**materoliaeth** nf materialism

**matog** (-au) *nf* mattock
**matras** (-resi) *nm* mattress
**matrics** (-au) *nm* matrix
**matsien** (matsys) *nf* match
**math** (-au) *nm* sort, kind
**mathemateg** *nm* mathematics
**mathru** *vb* trample, tread
**mathrwr** (-wyr) *nm* trampler
**mawl** *nm* praise
**mawn** *coll n* (*nf*-en) peat
**mawnog** *adj* peaty ▷ *nf* peat-bog
**mawr** (-ion) *adj* big, great, large
**mawredd** *nm* greatness, grandeur, majesty
**mawreddog** *adj* grand, majestic; grandiose
**mawrfrydig** *adj* magnanimous
**mawrfrydigrwydd** *nm* magnanimity
**mawrhau** *vb* magnify, enlarge
**mawrhydi** *nm* majesty
**Mawrth** *nm* Mars; March; **Dydd ~** Tuesday
**mawrygu** *vb* magnify, extol
**mebyd** *nm* childhood, infancy, youth
**mecaneg** *nf* mechanics
**mecanwaith** (-weithiau) *nm* mechanism
**mecanyddol** *adj* mechanical
**mechniaeth** *nf* surety, bail
**mechnïo** *vb* go bail, become surety
**mechnïol** *adj* vicarious
**mechnïydd** (-ion) *nm* surety, bail
**medel** (-au) *nf* reaping; reaping party
**medelwr** (-wyr) *nm* reaper
**medi** *vb* reap
**Medi** *nm* September
**medr** *nm* skill, ability
**medru** *vb* know, be able
**medrus** *adj* clever, skilful
**medrusrwydd** *nm* cleverness, skilfulness, skill
**medrydd** (-ion) *nm* gauge
**medd** *nm* mead
**medd** *vb* says

**meddal** *adj* soft, tender
**meddalhau, meddalu** *vb* soften
**meddalwch** *nm* softness
**meddalwedd** *nm* softwear
**meddiannol** *adj* possessing, possessive
**meddiannu** *vb* possess, occupy
**meddiant** (-iannau) *nm* possession
**meddu** *vb* possess, own
**meddw** (-on) *adj* drunk, intoxicated
**meddwdod** *nm* drunkenness, intoxication
**meddwi** *vb* get drunk, intoxicate, inebriate
**meddwl** *vb* think; mean ▷ (-yliau) *nm* thought; meaning; opinion
**meddwol** *adj* intoxicating
**meddwyn** (-won) *nm* drunkard, inebriate
**meddyg** (-on) *nm* physician, doctor
**meddygaeth** *nf* medicine
**meddygfa** (-feydd) *nf* surgery
**meddyginiaeth** (-au) *nf* medicine, remedy
**meddyginiaethol** *adj* medicinal, remedial
**meddyginiaethu** *vb* cure, remedy, heal
**meddygol** *adj* medicinal; medical
**meddylfryd** *nm* mind, affection, bent
**meddylgar** *adj* thoughtful
**meddylgarwch** *nm* thoughtfulness
**meddyliol** *adj* mental, intellectual
**meddyliwr** (-wyr) *nm* thinker
**mefus** *npl* (*nf*-en) strawberries
**megin** (-au) *nf* bellows
**megino** *vb* work bellows, blow
**megis** *conj, prep* as, so as, like a
**Mehefin** *nm* June
**meicrobioleg** *nm/f* microbiology
**meicro-brosesydd** *nm* micro-processor
**meicroffon** (-au) *nm* microphone
**meicro-sglodyn** (-ion) *nm*

microchip
**meicrosgop** (-au) *nm* microscope
**meichiad** (-iaid) *nm* swineherd
**meichiau** (-iafon) *nm* surety, bail
**meidrol** *adj* finite
**meidroldeb** *nm* finiteness
**meiddio** *vb* dare, venture
**meiddion** *npl* curds and whey
**meiddlyd** *adj* wheyey, curdled
**meilart** *nm* drake
**meillion** *npl* (*nf*-en) clover
**meim** (-iau) *nm/f* mime
**meimio** *vb* mime
**meinder** *nm* fineness, slenderness
**meindio** *vb* mind, care
**meinedd** *nm* slender part, small
**meingefn** *nm* small of the back
**meinhau** *vb* grow slender, taper
**meini** *see* **maen**
**meinllais** *nm* shrill voice, treble
**meintoli** *vb* quantify
**meintoliad** *nm* quantification
**meinwe** (-bledd) *nf* tissue
**meipen** (maip) *nf* turnip
**meirch** *see* **march**
**meirioli** *vb* thaw
**meirw** *see* **marw**
**meistr** (-iaid, -i, -adoedd) *nm* master
**meistres** (-i) *nf* mistress
**meistrolaeth** *nf* mastery
**meistrolgar** *adj* masterful, masterly
**meistroli** *vb* master
**meitin** *nm*: **ers ~** some time since
**meitr** (-au) *nm* mitre
**meithder** *nm* length
**meithrin** *vb* nurture, rear, foster
**meithrinfa** (-oedd) *nf* nursery
**mêl** *nm* honey
**mela** *vb* gather honey
**melan** *nf* melancholy
**melen** *adj f of* **melyn**
**melfaréd** *nm* corduroy
**melfed** *nm* velvet
**melin** (-au) *nf* mill
**melinydd** (-ion) *nm* miller

**melodaidd** *adj* melodious
**melodi** *nm* melody
**melyn** (*f* melen) *adj* yellow ▷ *nm* yellow; **~ wy** yolk of egg; **Y clefyd ~** jaundice
**melynaidd** *adj* yellowish, tawny
**melynder, -dra** *nm* yellowness
**melynddu** *adj* tawny, swarthy
**melyngoch** *adj* yellowish red, orange
**melyni** *nm* yellowness; jaundice
**melynu** *vb* yellow
**melynwyn** *adj* yellowish white, cream
**melys** *adj* sweet ▷ (-ion) *npl* sweets
**melyster, -tra** *nm* sweetness
**melysu** *vb* sweeten
**mellt** *npl* (*nf*-en) lightning
**melltennu** *vb* flash lightning
**melltigaid, -edig** *adj* accursed, cursed
**melltith** (-ion) *nf* curse
**melltithio** *vb* curse
**memorandwm** (-anda) *nm* memorandum
**memrwn** (-rynau) *nm* parchment, vellum
**men** (-ni) *nf* wain, waggon, cart
**mên** *adj* mean
**mendio** *vb* mend, heal, recover
**menestr** *nm* cup-bearer
**menig** *see* **maneg**
**mentr** *nf* venture, hazard
**mentro** *vb* venture, hazard
**mentrus** *adj* adventurous
**mentrwr** (-wyr) *nm* entrepreneur
**menyw** (-od) *nf* woman
**mêr** (merion) *nm* marrow
**mercwri** *nm* mercury
**merch** (-ed) *nf* daughter, woman
**Mercher** *nm* Mercury; **Dydd ~** Wednesday
**mercheta** *vb* womanise
**merchetaidd** *adj* effeminate
**merddwr** (-ddyfroedd) *nm* stagnant water
**merf, -aidd** *adj* insipid, tasteless,

flat
**merfdra, merfeidd-dra** *nm* insipidity
**merlota** *vb* pony-trek
**merlyn (-nod, merlod,** *f* **merlen)** *nm* pony
**merllyd** *adj* insipid
**merthyr (-on, -i)** *nm* martyr
**merthyrdod** *nm* martyrdom
**merthyru** *vb* martyr
**merwindod** *nm* numbness, tingling
**merwino** *vb* benumb, tingle, smart
**meryw** *npl* (*nf*-en) juniper trees
**mes** *npl* (*nf*-en) acorns
**mesa** *vb* gather acorns
**mesur (-au)** *nm* measure; metre; tune; bill
**mesur, mesuro** *vb* measure, mete
**mesureg** *nf* mensuration
**mesuriad (-au)** *nm* measurement
**mesurwr (-wyr)** *nm* measurer; surveyor
**mesurydd (-ion)** *nm* measurer, meter
**metamorffedd** *nm* metamorphism
**metel (-oedd)** *nm* metal; mettle
**metelaidd** *adj* metallic
**metelydd (-ion)** *nm* metallurgist
**metelyddiaeth** *nf* metallurgy
**metr (-au)** *nm* metre
**metrig** *adj* metric
**metrigeiddio** *vb* metricate
**meth (-ion)** *nm* miss, failure
**methdaliad (-au)** *nm* bankruptcy
**methdalwr (-wyr)** *nm* bankrupt
**methedig (-ion)** *adj* decrepit, infirm, disabled
**methiannus** *adj* failing, decayed
**methiant** *nm* failure
**methodoleg** *nf* methodology
**methu** *vb* fail, miss
**meudwy (-aid, -od)** *nm* hermit, recluse
**meudwyaidd** *adj* hermit-like, retiring

**meudwyol** *adj* eremitic
**mewian** *vb* mew
**mewn** *prep* in, within
**mewnadlu** *vb* inhale
**mewnforio** *vb* import ▷ (**-ion**) *npl* imports
**mewnfudwr (-wyr)** *nm* immigrant
**mewnol** *adj* inward, internal; subjective
**mewnwr (-wyr)** *nm* scrum-half
**mewnyn (mewnion)** *nm* filling
**México** *nf* Mexico
**mi** *pron* I, me
**mieri** *npl* (*nf* miaren) brambles
**mig** *nf*: **chwarae ~** play bo-peep
**mign, -en** *nf* bog, quagmire
**migwrn (-yrnau)** *nm* knuckle; ankle
**mil (-od)** *nm* animal
**mil (-oedd)** *nf* thousand
**milain** *adj* angry, fierce, savage, cruel
**mileindra** *nm* savageness, ferocity
**mileinig** *adj* savage, ferocious, malignant
**milfed** *adj* thousandth
**milfeddyg (-on)** *nm* veterinary surgeon
**milfil** *nf* million, an indefinite number
**milflwyddiant** *nm* millennium
**milgi (-gwn)** *nm* greyhound
**miliast (-ieist)** *nf* greyhound bitch
**militariaeth** *nf* militarism
**militarydd** *nm* militarist
**miliwn (-iynau)** *nf* million
**miliynydd (-ion)** *nm* millionaire
**milodfa (-oedd, -feydd)** *nf* menagerie
**milwr (-wyr)** *nm* soldier
**milwraidd** *adj* soldierly
**milwriad (-iaid)** *nm* colonel
**milwriaeth** *nf* warfare
**milwriaethus** *adj* militant
**milwrio** *vb* militate
**milwrol** *adj* military
**milltir (-oedd)** *nf* mile
**min (-ion)** *nm* edge; brink; lip

**mindlws** adj simpering, affected, precious
**mingamu** vb grimace
**minio** vb edge, sharpen; make impression
**miniog** adj sharp, keen, cutting
**minlliw** (-iau) nm lipstick
**minnau** pron conj I (on my part), I also
**mintai** (-eioedd) nf band, troop
**mintys** nm mint
**mirain** adj fair, beautiful, comely
**mireinder** nm beauty, comeliness
**miri** nm merriment, fun, festivity
**mis** (-oedd) nm month
**misio** vb miss, fail
**misol** (-ion) adj monthly
**misolyn** (-olion) nm monthly (magazine)
**mitsio** vb mitch, play truant
**miwsig** nm music
**mo** contr. of **dim o**; **nid oes mo'i debyg** there is none like him
**moch** npl (nm -yn) swine, pigs, hogs
**mocha** nf pig, litter
**mochaidd** adj swinish, hoggish
**mochynnaidd** adj piggish, swinish
**modfedd** (-i) nf inch
**modrwy** (-au) nf ring
**modrwyo** vb ring
**modrwyog** adj ringed
**modryb** (-edd) nf aunt
**modur** (-on) nm motor
**modurdy** (-dai) nm garage
**modurwr** (-wyr) nm motorist
**modylu** vb modulate
**modylydd** (-ion) nm modulator
**modd** (-ion, -au) nm mode, manner; means; mood
**moddion** npl means; medicine
**moddol** adj modal
**moel** (-ion) adj bare, bald; hornless, polled
**moel** (-ydd) nf hill
**moeli** vb make or become bald; hang (ears)
**moelni** nm bareness, baldness

**moelyn** nm bald-head
**moes** vb imper give, bring hither
**moes** (-au) nf morality; (pl) manners, morals
**moeseg** nf ethics
**Moesenaidd** adj Mosaic
**moesgar** adj mannerly, polite
**moesgarwch** nm politeness
**moesol** adj moral, ethical
**moesoldeb** nm morality
**moesoli** vb moralize
**moesolwr** (-wyr) nm moralist
**moeswers** (-i) nf moral
**moesymgrymu** vb bow
**moeth** (-au) nm luxury, indulgence
**moethi** vb pamper, indulge
**moethlyd** adj pampered, spoilt
**moethus** adj luxurious, pampered
**moethusrwydd** nm luxuriousness, luxury
**molawd** nm/f eulogy, panegyric
**molecwl** (-cylau) nm molecule
**molecwlar** adj molecular
**moled** (-au) nf kerchief; muffler
**moli, molianu** vb praise, laud
**moliannus** adj praised, praiseworthy
**moliant** (-iannau) nm praise
**mollt** (myllt) nm wether
**molltgig** nm mutton
**moment** (-au) nf moment
**momentwm** (momenta) nm momentum
**monarchiaeth** nf monarchy
**monarchydd** (-ion) nm monarchist
**monni** vb sulk, pout
**monocsid** (-au) nm monoxide
**monópoli** (-ïau) nm monopoly
**môr** (moroedd) nm sea, ocean
**Môr: Y Môr Canoldir** nm Mediterranean Sea; **Y Môr Coch** nm Red Sea; **Y Môr Tawel** nm Pacific Ocean; **Môr Udd** nm English Channel; **Môr y Gogledd** nm North Sea
**mor** adv how, so, as

**moratoriwm** (-atoria) *nm* moratorium

**mordaith** (-deithiau) *nf* voyage

**mordeithiwr** (-wyr) *nm* voyager

**mordwyaeth** *nf* navigation

**mordwyo** *vb* go by sea, voyage, sail

**mordwywr** (-wyr) *nm* mariner, sailor

**morddwyd** (-ydd) *nf/m* thigh

**morfa** (-feydd) *nm* moor, fen, marsh

**morfil** (-od) *nm* whale

**môr-forwyn** (-forynion) *nf* mermaid

**morfran** (-frain) *nf* cormorant

**morffoleg** *nm/f* morphology

**morffolegol** *adj* morphological

**morgainc** (-geinciau) *nf* gulf

**morgais** (-geisiau) *nf* mortgage

**morgeisî** *nm* mortgagee

**morgeisio** *vb* mortgage

**môr-gerwyn** *nf* whirlpool, vortex, abyss

**morglawdd** (-gloddiau) *nm* embankment, mole

**morgrug** *npl* (*nm* -yn) ants

**morio** *vb* voyage, sail

**môr-ladrad** (-au) *nm* piracy

**môr-leidr** (-ladron) *nm* pirate

**morlen** (-ni) *nm* chart

**morlo** (-loi) *nm* sea-calf, seal

**morllyn** (-noedd) *nf/m* lagoon

**Moroco** *nf* Morocco

**morol** *adj* maritime

**moron** *npl* (*nf* -en) carrots

**mortais** (-eisiau) *nf* mortise

**morteisio** *vb* mortise

**morter** (-au) *nm* mortar

**morthwyl** (-ion) *nm* hammer

**morthwylio** *vb* hammer

**morthwyliwr** (-wyr) *nm* hammerer

**morwr** (-wyr) *nm* seaman, sailor, mariner

**morwriaeth** *nf* seamanship, navigation

**morwydd** *npl* (*nf* -en) mulberry-trees

**morwyn** (-ynion) *nf* maid, virgin

**morwyndod** *nm* virginity

**morwynol** *adj* virgin, maiden

**moryd** (-iau) *nf* estuary

**moryn** (-nau) *nm* billow, breaker

**mosaig** (-au) *nm*, *adj* mosaic

**Moscow** *nf* Moscow

**motif** (-au) *nm* motive

**motiff** (-au) *nm* motif

**muchudd** *nm* jet

**mud** *adj* dumb, mute; dull

**mudan** (-od) *nm* mute

**mudandod** *nm* muteness

**mudanes** (-au) *nf* dumb woman

**mudferwi** *vb* simmer

**mudiad** (-au) *nm* removal; movement

**mudo** *vb* move, remove

**mudol** *adj* mobile, moving, migratory

**mudwr** (-wyr) *nm* remover

**mul** (-od) *nm* mule; donkey

**mulaidd** *adj* mulish, asinine

**mules** (-au) *nf* she-mule, she-ass

**mulfran** (-frain) *nf* cormorant

**mun** *see* **bun**

**munud** (-au) *nm/f* minute, moment

**munud** (-iau) *nm* sign, gesture; nod

**munudio** *vb* make gestures, gesticulate

**mur** (-iau) *nm* wall

**murddun** (-od) *nm* ruin, ruins

**murio** *vb* wall

**murlun** (-iau) *nm* mural

**murmur** *vb* murmur ▷ (-on) *nm* murmur

**mursen** (-nod) *nf* coquette; prude

**mursendod** *nm* prudery, affectation

**mursennaidd** *adj* prudish, affected

**mursennu** *vb* coquette, mince

**musgrell** *adj* feeble, decrepit

**musgrellni** *nm* feebleness, debility

**mwd** *nm* mud

**mwdwl** (mydylau) *nm* cock (of hay)

**mwg** *nm* smoke

**mwgwd** (mygydau) *nm* blind mask

**mwng** (myngau) *nm* mane
**mwngial** *vb* mumble
**mwlsyn** *nm* nincompoop; mule
**mwlwg** *nm* refuse, sweepings, chaff
**mwll** *adj* close, warm, sultry
**mwmian** *vb* hum, mumble
**mŵn** *see* **mwyn**
**mwnci** (-ïod) *nm* monkey
**mwncïaidd** *adj* monkeyish, apish
**mwnglawdd** *see* **mwyn-**
**mwnwgl** (mynyglau) *nm* neck
**mwnws** *coll n* small particles, dust, debris
**mwrdro** *vb* murder
**mwrllwch** *nm* fog, mist, vapour
**mwrn** *adj* sultry, close, warm
**mwrndra** *nm* sultriness
**mwrthwl** (myrthylau) *nm* hammer
**mws** *adj* stale, rank, stinking
**mwsg** *nm* musk
**mwsged** (-i) *nm/f* musket
**mwsogl, -wgl** *nm* moss
**mwstard, -tart** *nm* mustard
**mwstro** *vb* fidget, hurry
**mwstwr** *nm* muster; bustle, commotion
**mwy** *adj* more, bigger ▷ *adv* more, again
**mwyach** *adv* any more, henceforth
**mwyafrif** (-au) *nm* majority
**mwyalch, -en** (-od) *nf* blackbird
**mwyar** *npl* (nf-en) blackberries
**mwyara** *vb* gather blackberries
**mwydion** *npl* crumb; pith, pulp
**mwydo** *vb* moisten, soak, steep
**mwydro** *vb* moider, bewilder
**mwydyn** (mwydod) *nm* worm
**mwyfwy** *adv* more and more
**mwyhau** *vb* increase, enlarge, magnify
**mwyn** *nm* sake
**mwyn, mŵn** (-au) *nm* ore, mineral
**mwyn** *adj* kind, gentle, mild; dear
**mwynder** (-au) *nm* gentleness; (*pl*) delights
**mwyndoddi** *vb* refine

**mwyneidd-dra** *nm* kindness, gentleness
**mwynglawdd** (-gloddiau) *nm* mine
**mwyngloddio** *vb* mine
**mwynhad** *nm* enjoyment, pleasure
**mwynhau** *vb* enjoy
**mwyniant** (-iannau) *nm* pleasure
**mwynofydd** (-ion) *nm* mineralogist
**mwynoleg** *nf* mineralogy
**mwynwr** (-wyr) *nm* miner
**mwys** *adj* ambiguous, equivocal
**mwythau** *npl* indulgence, caresses
**mwytho** *vb* pet, fondle, pamper
**mwythus** *adj* pampered
**myctod** *nm* asphyxia
**mydr** (-au) *nm* metre, verse
**mydryddiaeth** *nf* versification
**mydryddol** *adj* metrical
**mydryddu, mydru** *vb* versify
**mydylu** *vb* cock
**myfi** *pron* I, me, myself
**myfïaeth** *nf* egotism
**myfïol** *adj* egotistic
**myfyrdod** (-au) *nm* meditation
**myfyrgar** *adj* studious, contemplative
**myfyrgell** (-oedd) *nf* study
**myfyrio** *vb* meditate, study
**myfyriol** *adj* meditative
**myfyriwr** (-wyr) *nm* student
**mygedol** *adj* honorary
**mygfa** (-feydd) *nf* suffocation
**myglyd** *adj* smoky; close; asthmatic
**myglys** *nm* tobacco
**mygu** *vb* smoke; suffocate, stifle, smother
**mygydu** *vb* blindfold
**mygyn** *nm* a smoke
**myngial** *vb* mumble, mutter
**myngog** *adj* maned
**myngus** *adj* indistinct, mumbling
**myllni** *nm* sultriness
**mympwy** (-on) *nm* whim, caprice, fad
**mympwyol** *adj* arbitrary,

capricious

**mymryn (-nau)** nm particle, bit, mite

**myn** prep by (in swearing)

**myn (-nod)** nm kid

**mynach (-aich, -od)** nm monk

**mynachaeth** nf monasticism

**mynachdy (-dai)** nm monastery, convent

**mynachlog (-ydd)** nf monastery, abbey

**mynawyd (-au)** nm awl

**mynci (-ïau)** nm hame(s)

**myned, mynd** vb go, proceed

**mynedfa (-oedd, -feydd)** nf entrance, passage

**mynediad** nm going; access, admission

**mynegai (-eion)** nm index, exponent

**mynegair (-eiriau)** nm concordance

**mynegfys (-edd)** nm forefinger, index

**mynegi** vb tell, express, relate, declare

**mynegiad (-au)** nm statement, declaration

**mynegiant** nm expression

**mynnu** vb will, wish; insist; get, obtain

**mynor (-ion)** nm marble

**mynwent (-au, -ydd)** nf churchyard, graveyard

**mynwes (-au)** nf breast, bosom

**mynwesol** adj bosom

**mynwesu** vb cherish

**mynych** adj frequent, often

**mynychiad** nm frequenting; repetition

**mynychu** vb frequent, attend; repeat

**mynydd (-oedd)** nm mountain

**mynydda** vb mountaineer

**mynydd-dir** nm hill-country

**mynyddig** adj mountainous, hilly

**mynyddwr (-wyr)** nm

mountaineer

**myrdd, -iwn (-iynau)** nm myriad

**myrllyd** adj myrrhy

**myrndra** nm sultriness

**myrr** nm myrrh

**myrtwydd** npl (nf-en) myrtles

**mysg** nm middle, midst; **y~** among

**mysgu** vb loose, undo

**myswynog (-ydd)** nf barren cow

**mysyglog** adj mossy

**mytholeg** nf mythology

**mytholegol** adj mythological

**na** conj nor, neither; than ▷ adv no, not

**nac** adv no, not ▷ conj nor, neither

**nacâd** nm refusal, denial

**nacaol** adj negative

**nacáu** vb refuse, deny

**nad** adv not

**nâd (nadau)** nf cry, howl; clamour

**Nadolig** nm Christmas

**Nadoligaidd** adj Christmassy

**nadu** vb cry (out), howl

**nadu** vb stop, hinder

**nadd** adj hewn, wrought

**naddion** npl chips; shreds; lint

**naddo** adv no (to questions in preterite tense)

**naddu** vb hew, chip, whittle

**Naf** nm Lord

**nag** *conj* than
**nage** *adv* not so, no
**nai** (**neiaint**) *nm* nephew
**naid** (**neidiau**) *nf* jump, leap, bound
**naïf** *adj* naïve
**naïfder** *nm* naïveté
**naill** *dem pron* the one ▷ *conj* either
**nain** (**neiniau**) *nf* grandmother
**nam** (-**au**) *nm* mark, blemish, flaw
**namyn** *pron* except, but, save
**nant** (**nentydd**) *nf* brook; gorge, ravine
**napcyn** (-**au**) *nm* napkin
**narcotig** *nm, adj* narcotic
**natur** *nf* nature; temper
**naturiaeth** (-**au**) *nf* nature
**naturiaethwr** (-**wyr**) *nm* naturalist
**naturiol** *adj* natural
**naturioldeb** *nm* naturalness
**naturus** *adj* angry, quick-tempered
**naw** *adj, nm* nine
**nawdd** *nm* protection; patronage
**nawddogaeth** *nf* patronage, protection
**nawfed** *adj* ninth
**nawn** *nm* noon
**naws** *nf* nature, disposition; essence, tincture
**nawseiddio** *vb* temper, soften
**neb** *nm* any one (*with negative understood*); no one
**nedd** *npl* (*nf*-**en**) nits
**neddau, neddyf** (**neddyfau**) *nf* adze
**nef** (-**oedd**) *nf* heaven
**nefol, -aidd** *adj* heavenly, celestial
**nefoli** *vb* make or become heavenly
**nefrosis** *nm* neurosis
**neges** (-**au, -euau**) *nf* errand, message
**negesa, -eua** *vb* run errands; trade
**negeseuwr** (-**wyr**) *nm* messenger
**negodi** *vb* negotiate
**negyddiaeth** *nf* negativism
**negyddol** *adj* negative
**neidio** *vb* leap, jump; throb

**neidiwr** (-**wyr**) *nm* leaper, jumper
**neidr** (**nadroedd, nadredd**) *nf* snake
**neiedd** *nm* nepotism
**neillog** (-**ion**) *nm* alternative
**neilltu** *nm* one side; **o'r ~** aside, apart
**neilltuad** *nm* separation
**neilltuaeth** *nf* separation, privacy, seclusion
**neilltuedig** *adj* separated, secluded
**neilltuo** *vb* set apart, separate
**neilltuol** *adj* particular, peculiar, special
**neilltuolion** *npl* peculiarities
**neilltuolrwydd** *nm* peculiarity, distinction
**neis** *adj* nice
**neisied** (-**i**) *nf* kerchief
**neithdar** *nm* nectar
**neithior** (-**au**) *nf* marriage feast
**neithiwr** *adv* last night
**nemor** *adj* few; **nid ~** hardly any
**nen** (-**nau, -noedd**) *nf* ceiling; heaven; **~ tŷ** house-top
**nenbren** *nm* roof-tree
**nenfwd** (-**fydau**) *nm* ceiling
**nepell** *adv* far; **nid ~** not far
**nerf** (-**au**) *nf* nerve
**nerfwst** *nm* neurasthenia
**nerth** (-**oedd**) *nm* might, power, strength
**nerthol** *adj* strong, powerful, mighty
**nerthu** *vb* strengthen
**nes** *adj* nearer; **yn ~ ymlaen** further on
**nes** *adv* till, until
**nesaf** *adj* nearest, next
**nesáu** *vb* draw near, approach
**nesnes** *adv* nearer and nearer
**nesu** *vb* draw near; **n draw** move away
**neu** *conj* or
**neuadd** (-**au**) *nf* hall
**newid** *vb* change, alter ▷ *nm* change

**newidiant** *nm* variability
**newidiol** *adj* changeable, variable
**newidydd** (-ion) *nm* transformer
**newidyn** (-nau) *nm* variable
**newydd** *adj* new, novel; fresh
▷ (-ion) *nm* news
**newyddbeth** (-au) *nm* novelty
**newydd-deb, -der** *nm* newness, novelty
**newyddiadur** (-on) *nm* newspaper
**newyddiaduriaeth** *nf* journalism
**newyddiadurwr** (-wyr) *nm* journalist
**newyddian** (-od) *n coll* novice, neophyte
**newyn** *nm* hunger, famine
**newynog** *adj* hungry, starving
**newynu** *vb* starve, famish
**ni** *pron* we, us
**ni, nid** *adv* not
**nifer** (-oedd, -i) *nm/f* number
**nifwl** *nm* mist, fog; nebula
**Nigeria** *nf* Nigeria
**Nihon** *nf* Japan
**ninnau** *pron conj* we (on our part), we also
**nionyn** (nionod) *nm* onion
**nis** *adv* not ... it; **~ cafodd** he did not find it
**nitrad** (-au) *nm* nitrate
**nith** (-oedd) *nf* niece
**nithio** *vb* sift, winnow
**nithiwr** (-wyr) *nm* sifter, winnower
**nithlen** (-ni) *nf* winnowing-sheet
**niwed** (-eidiau) *nm* harm, injury
**niwclear** *adj* nuclear
**niweidio** *vb* harm, hurt, injure, damage
**niweidiol** *adj* harmful, injurious
**niwl** (-oedd) *nm*, **-en** *nf* mist, fog, haze
**niwliog, niwlog** *adj* misty, foggy, hazy
**niwmatig** *adj* pneumatic
**niwmonia** *nm* pneumonia
**niwtral** *adj* neutral
**niwtraleiddio** *vb* neutralise

**niwtraliaeth** *nf* neutrality
**nobyn** (nobiau) *nm* knob
**nod** (-au) *nm/f* note; mark, token
**nodachfa** (-feydd) *nf* bazaar
**nodedig** *adj* appointed, set; remarkable
**nodi** *vb* mark, note, appoint, state
**nodiad** (-au) *nm* note
**nodiadur** (-on) *nm* notebook
**nodiant** *nm* notation
**nodwedd** (-ion) *nf* character, characteristic, feature
**nodweddiadol** *adj* characteristic
**nodweddu** *vb* characterize
**nodwydd** (-au) *nf* needle
**nodyn** (-nau, nodau, nodion) *nm* note
**nodd** (-ion) *nm* moisture; juice, sap
**nodded** *nm* refuge, protection
**noddfa** (-fâu, -feydd) *nf* refuge
**noddi** *vb* protect
**noddlyd** *adj* juicy, sappy
**noddwr** (-wyr) *nm* protector; patron
**noe** (-au) *nf* dish; kneading-trough
**noeth** *adj* naked, bare, exposed, raw
**noethder** *nm* bareness, nakedness
**noethi** *vb* bare, denude
**noethlymun** *adj* nude
**noethlymunwr** (-wyr) *nm* streaker
**noethlymunwraig** *nf* stripper
**noethni** *nm* nakedness, nudity
**noethwr** (-wyr) *nm* nudist
**nofel** (-au) *nf* novel
**nofelwr, -ydd** (-wyr) *nm* novelist
**nofiadwy** *adj* swimmable
**nofiedydd** (-ion) *nm* swimmer
**nofio** *vb* swim; float
**nofiwr** (-wyr) *nm* swimmer
**nogio** *vb* jib
**noglyd** *adj* jibbing
**nôl** *vb* fetch, bring
**Norwy** *nf* Norway
**nos** (-au, ~weithiau) *nf* night
**nosi** *vb* become night
**noson, noswaith** (nosweithiau)

*nf* a night, an evening
**noswyl (-iau)** *nf* eve of festival, vigil
**noswylio** *vb* cease work at eve
**nudden** *nf* fog, mist, haze
**nwy (-on)** *nm* gas
**nwyd (-au)** *nm* passion; emotion
**nwydd (-au)** *nm* substance, article;
  (*pl*) goods
**nwyf** *nm* vivacity, energy, vigour
**nwyfiant** *nm* vivacity, vigour
**nwyfus** *adj* sprightly, spirited, lively
**nwyol** *adj* gaseous
**nychdod** *nm* feebleness, infirmity
**nychlyd** *adj* sickly, feeble
**nychu** *vb* sicken, pine, languish
**nydd-dro (-droeau, -droeon)**
  *nm* twist
**nydd-droi** *vb* twist, screw
**nyddu** *vb* spin, twist
**nyddwr (-wyr)** *nm* spinner
**nyf** *coll n* snow
**nyni** *pron* we, us
**nyrs (-ys)** *nm/f* nurse
**nyrsio** *adj* nurse
**nytmeg** *nm* nutmeg
**nyth (-od)** *nm/f* nest
**nythu** *vb* nest, nestle

# O

**o** *prep* from; of, out of; by
**o** *excl* oh!, O!
**oblegid** *conj, prep* because, for

**obry** *adv* beneath, below
**obstetreg** *nm* obstetrics
**obstetregydd (-wyr)** *nm*
  obstetrician
**ocsid (-iau)** *nm* oxide
**ocsidiad** *nm* oxidisation
**ocsidio** *vb* oxidise
**ocsidydd (-ion)** *nm* oxidising agent
**ocsigen** *nm* oxygen
**och** *excl* oh!, alas, woe
**ochenaid (-eidiau)** *nf* sigh
**ocheneidio, ochneidio** *vb* sigh
**ochr (-au)** *nf* side
**ochrgamu** *vb* sidestep
**ochri** *vb* side
**ôd** *nm* snow
**od** *adj* odd, remarkable
**odiaeth** *adj* excellent, exquisite
  ▷ *adv* very, most, extremely
**odid** *adv* perchance, peradventure
**odl (-au)** *nf* rhyme; ode, song
**odli** *vb* rhyme
**odrif (-au)** *nm* odd number
**odrwydd** *nm* oddity
**odyn (-au)** *nf* kiln
**oddeutu** *prep* about
**oddi** *prep* out of, from
**oddieithr, oddigerth** *prep*
  except, unless
**oed (-au)** *nm* age; time
**oed-dâl (-iadau)** *nm*
  superannuation
**oedfa (-on, -feuon)** *nf* meeting,
  service
**oedi** *vb* delay; postpone, defer
**oediad (-au)** *nm* delay
**oedran** *nm* age, full age
**oedrannus** *adj* aged
**oedd** *vb* was, were
**oen (ŵyn)** *nm* lamb
**oena** *vb* lamb, yean
**oenig** *nf* ewe-lamb
**oer** *adj* cold, chill, frigid; sad
**oeraidd** *adj* coldish, cool, chilly
**oerddrws (-ddrysau)** *nm* wind gap
**oerfel** *nm* cold
**oergell (-oedd)** *nf* refrigerator

**oeri** *vb* cool, chill
**oerllyd** *adj* chilly, frigid; cool
**oernad** (-au) *nf* howl, wail, lamentation
**oernadu** *vb* howl, wail, lament
**oerni** *nm* cold, coldness, chillness
**oes** (-oedd, -au) *nf* age, lifetime; **yn ~ oesoedd** for ever and ever
**oes** *vb* there is, there are; is there?
**oesoffagws** *nm* oesophagus
**oesol** *adj* age-long, perpetual
**ofer** *adj* vain, idle; prodigal, dissipated; waste
**ofera** *vb* waste, squander, idle
**oferedd** *nm* vanity, dissipation
**ofergoel** (-ion) *nf* superstition
**ofergoeledd, -iaeth** *nm* superstition
**ofergoelus** *adj* superstitious
**oferwr** (-wyr) *nm* idler, waster
**ofn** (-au) *nm* fear, dread
**ofnadwy** *adj* awful, terrible, dreadful
**ofnadwyaeth** *nf* awe, terror, dread
**ofni** *vb* fear, dread
**ofnog** *adj* fearful, timorous
**ofnus** *adj* timid, nervous
**ofnusrwydd** *nm* timidity, nervousness
**ofwl** (-au) *nm* ovule
**ofydd** (-ion) *nm* ovate
**offeiriad** (-iaid) *nm* priest, clergyman
**offeiriadaeth** *nf* priesthood
**offeiriades** (-au) *nf* priestess
**offeiriadol** *adj* priestly, sacerdotal
**offeiriadu** *vb* officiate, minister
**offer** *npl* implements, tools, gear
**offeren** (-nau) *nf* mass
**offeryn** (-nau, offer) *nm* instrument, tool
**offerynnol** *adj* instrumental
**offerynoliaeth** *nf* instrumentality
**offrwm** (-ymau) *nm* offering, oblation
**offrymu** *vb* offer, sacrifice
**offrymwr** (-wyr) *nm* offerer, sacrificer
**offthalmia** *nm* ophthalmia
**offthalmosgop** (-au) *nm* ophthalmoscope
**og** (-au), **oged** (-au, -i) *nf* harrow
**ogof** (-au, -fâu, -feydd) *nf* cave, cavern; den
**ogylch** *prep* about
**ongl** (-au) *nf* angle, corner
**onglog** *adj* angled, angular
**oherwydd** *conj, prep* because, for
**ôl** *adj* back, hind, hindmost; **(olion)** *nm* mark, print, trace, track; **Yn ôl** according to; ago
**ôl-dâl** (-oedd) *nm* back-pay
**ôl-ddodiad** (-iaid) *nm* suffix
**ôl-ddyddio** *vb* post-date
**ôl-ddyled** (-ion) *nf* arrears
**olew** (-au) *nm* oil
**olewydd** *npl* (*nf-en*) olive-trees
**olifaid** *npl* olive-berries
**olrhain** *vb* trace
**olwr** (-wyr) *nm* back (*rugby*)
**olwyn** (-ion) *nf* wheel
**olwyno** *vb* wheel, cycle
**olwynog** *adj* wheeled
**olyniaeth** *nf* succession, sequence
**olynol** *adj* successive, consecutive
**olynu** *vb* succeed (to)
**olynwr** (-wyr), **-ydd** (-ion) *nm* successor
**ôlysgrif** (-au) *nf* postscript
**oll** *adv* all, wholly; ever, at all
**ombwdsman** (-myn) *nm* ombudsman
**omlet** (-i) *nm* omelette
**ond** *conj* but, only ▷ *prep* except, save, but
**onest** *adj* honest
**onestrwydd** *nm* honesty
**oni, onid** *adv* not?, is it not? ▷ *conj* if not, unless ▷ *prep* except, save, but
**onid e** *adv* otherwise, else; is it not?
**onis** *conj* if it is not; **~ caiff** if he does not get it
**onnen** (onn, ynn) *nf* ash
**opiniwn** (-ynau) *nm* opinion

**opiniynllyd, -iynus** *adj*
opinionated
**optimistaeth** *nf* optimism
**optimistaidd** *adj* optimistic
**optimwm** (**-tima**) *nm* optimum
**oracl** (**-au**) *nm* oracle
**oraclaidd** *adj* oracular
**oraens** *nm* orange
**ordeiniad** (**-au**) *nm* ordination,
ordinance
**ordeinio** *vb* ordain
**ordinhad** (**-au**) *nf* ordinance,
sacrament
**oren** (**-nau**) *nm/f* orange
**organ** (**-au**) *nf/m* organ
**organaidd** *adj* organic
**organeb** (**-au**) *nf* organism
**organig** *adj* organic
**organydd** (**-ion**) *nm* organist
**orgraff** (**-au**) *nf* orthography
**orgraffyddol** *adj* orthographical
**oriawr** (**oriorau**) *nf* watch
**oriel** (**-au**) *nf* gallery
**orig** *nf* little while
**oriog** *adj* fickle, changeable,
inconstant
**os** *conj* if
**osgo** *nm* slant, slope, inclination
**osgoi** *vb* swerve, avoid, evade, shirk
**oslef** *nf* tone, voice
**ow** *excl* oh!, alas!

# p

**pa** *adj* what, which
**pab** (**-au**) *nm* pope
**pabaeth** *nf* papacy
**pabaidd** *adj* papal, popish
**pabell** (**pebyll**) *nf* tent, tabernacle
**pabellu** *vb* tent, tabernacle,
encamp
**pabi** *nm* poppy
**pabwyr** *npl* (**nf-en**, *nm* **-yn**) rushes
**pabwyr** *nm* wick, candle-wick
**pabydd** (**-ion**) *nm* Roman Catholic
**pabyddiaeth** *nf* Roman
Catholicism
**pabyddol** *adj* Roman Catholic
**pac** (**-iau**) *nm* pack, bundle
**pacio** *vb* pack
**padell** (**-au, -i, pedyll**) *nf* pan, bowl
**padellaid** (**-eidiau**) *nf* panful
**pader** (**-au**) *nm* paternoster, Lord's
Prayer
**padera** *vb* repeat prayers, patter
**pae** *nm* pay, wage
**paediatreg** *nm* paediatrics
**paediatregydd** *nm* paediatrician
**paent** *nm* paint
**paentiad** (**-au**) *nm* painting
**pafiliwn** *nm* pavilion
**paffio** *vb* box, fight
**paffiwr** (**-wyr**) *nm* boxer
**pagan** (**-iaid**) *nm* pagan, heathen
**paganaidd** *adj* pagan, heathen
**paganiaeth** *nf* paganism,
heathenism
**pang** (**-au**) *nm*, **pangfa** (**-feydd**)
*nf* pang, fit

**paham** *adv* why, wherefore
**paill** *nm* flour; pollen
**pair** (peiriau) *nm* cauldron, furnace
**pais** (peisiau) *nf* coat, petticoat
**paith** (peithiau) *nm* prairie
**Pacistan** *nf* Pakistan
**pâl** (palau) *nf* spade
**paladr** (pelydr) *nm* ray, beam; staff; stem
**palaeolithig** *adj* palaeolithic
**palas** (-au) *nm* palace
**Palestina** *nf* Palestine
**palf** (-au) *nf* palm, hand; paw
**palfais** (-eisiau) *nf* shoulder
**palfalu** *vb* feel, grope
**palfod** (-au) *nf* smack, slap, buffet
**palff** *nm* fine, well-built man
**pali** *nm* silk brocade
**palis** (-au) *nm* pale, partition, wainscot
**palmant** (-mentydd) *nm* pavement
**palmantu** *vb* pave
**palmwydd** *npl* (nf-en) palm-trees
**palu** *vb* dig, delve
**palwr** (-wyr) *nm* digger
**pall** (-au) *nm* mantle; tent
**pall** *nm* fail, failing; lack; lapse
**pallu** *vb* fail, cease; neglect; refuse
**pam** *adv* why, wherefore (paham)
**pamffled** (-i, -au), -yn *nm* pamphlet
**pan** *conj* when
**pandy** (-dai) *nm* fulling-mill
**pannas** *npl* (nf panasen) parsnips
**pannu** *vb* full cloth
**pannwl** (panylau) *nm* dimple, hollow
**pannwr** (panwyr) *nm* fuller
**pant** (-iau) *nm* hollow, valley
**pantio** *vb* depress, dent, sink
**pantiog** *adj* hollow, sunken; dimpled
**papur** (-au) *nm* paper
**papuro** *vb* paper
**papurwr** (-wyr) *nm* paperer, paperhanger
**papuryn** *nm* scrap of paper

**pâr** (parau) *nm* pair; suit
**pâr** (peri) *nm* spear, lance
**para** *vb* last, endure, continue
**parabl** (-au) *nm* speech, discourse
**parablu** *vb* speak
**paradeim** (-au) *nm* paradigm
**paradwys** *nf* paradise
**paradwysaidd** *adj* paradisean
**paragraff** (-au) *nm* paragraph
**paratoad** (-au) *nm* preparation
**paratoawl** *adj* preparatory
**paratoi** *vb* prepare, get ready
**parc** (-iau) *nm* park, field
**parch** *nm* respect, reverence
**parchedig** (-ion) *adj* reverend; reverent
**parchedigaeth** *nf* reverence
**parchu** *vb* respect, revere, reverence
**parchus** *adj* respectful; respectable
**parchusrwydd** *nm* respectability
**pardwn** (-ynau) *nm* pardon
**pardynu** *vb* pardon
**parddu** *nm* fire-black, smut; soot
**pardduo** *vb* blacken, vilify, defame
**pared** (parwydydd) *nm* partition wall, wall
**paredd** *nm* parity
**parhad** *nm* continuance, continuation
**parhaol** *adj* lasting, perpetual
**parhau** *vb* last, continue; persevere
**parhaus** *adj* lasting; continual, perpetual
**Paris** *nf* Paris
**parlwr** (-yrau) *nm* parlour
**parlys** *nm* paralysis, palsy
**parlysu** *vb* paralyse
**parod** *adj* ready, prepared; prompt
**parodrwydd** *nm* readiness, willingness
**parôl** (-ion) *nm* parole
**parsel** (-i, -ydd) *nm* parcel
**parti** (-ïon) *nm* party
**partïaeth** *nf* partisanship
**partïol** *adj* partial, biassed, partisan
**parth** (-au) *nm* part, region; floor
**parthed** *prefix* about, concerning

**parthu** vb part, divide
**parwyden** (-nau) nf wall, side; breast
**pas** nm whooping-cough
**Pasg** nm Passover, Easter
**pasgedig** (-ion) adj fatted, fattened, fat
**pasiant** (-iannau) nm pageant
**pasio** vb pass
**past** nm paste
**pastai** (-eiod) nf pasty, pie
**pastio** vb paste
**pasturedig** adj pasteurised
**pasturo** vb pasteurise
**pastwn** (-ynau) nm baton, club, cudgel
**pastynu** vb club, cudgel, bludgeon
**patriarch** (-iaid, patrieirch) nm patriarch
**patriarchaeth** (-au) nf patriarchate
**patriarchaidd** adj patriarchal
**patrwm** (-ymau) nm pattern
**patrymlun** (-iau) nm template
**pathew** (-od) nm dormouse
**patholeg** nf pathology
**patholegol** adj pathological
**patholegydd** (-egwyr) nm pathologist
**pau** nf country
**paun** (peunod) nm peacock
**pawb** pron everybody, all
**pawen** (-nau) nf paw
**pawl** (polion) nm pole, stake
**pe** conj if
**pebyll** see **pabell**
**pecyn** (-nau) nm packet, package
**pech-aberth** (-au) nm sin-offering
**pechadur** (-iaid) nm sinner, offender
**pechadures** (-au) nf woman sinner
**pechadurus** adj sinful, wicked
**pechadurusrwydd** nm sinfulness
**pechod** (-au) nm sin, offence
**pechu** vb sin, offend
**Pecing** nf Peking
**ped** conj if

**pedair** adj f of **pedwar**
**pedeirongl** adj foursquare
**pedi** vb worry, grieve
**pedol** (-au) nf horseshoe
**pedoli** vb shoe
**pedrain** nf haunches, crupper
**pedrongl** adj square ▷ (-au) nf square
**pedronglog** adj quadrangular
**pedryfwrdd** (-fyrddau) nm quarter-deck
**pedwar** (f pedair) adj four
**pedwarawd** nm quartette
**pedwarcarnol** (-ion) adj four-footed, quadruped
**pedwaredd** adj f of **pedwerydd**
**pedwarplyg** adj fourfold, quarto
**pedwerydd** (f pedwaredd) adj fourth
**peddestr** nm pedestrian
**peddestrig** nm walking; pedestrian
**pefr** adj radiant, bright, beautiful
**pefrio** vb radiate, sparkle
**peg** (-iau) nm peg
**pegio** vb peg
**pegor** (-au) nm manikin; dwarf; imp
**pegwn** (-ynau) nm pivot, pole, axis
**Pegwn y Gogledd** nm North Pole
**pegynol** adj axial, polar
**peidio** vb cease, stop, desist
**peilon** (-au) nm pylon
**peilot** (-iaid) nm pilot
**peillio** vb bolt, sift
**peint** (-iau) nm pint
**peintiad** (-au) nm painting
**peintio** vb paint
**peintiwr** (-wyr) nm painter
**peipen** (peipiau) nf pipe
**peirianneg** nm engineering
**peiriannol** adj mechanical
**peiriannydd** (-ianyddion) nm engineer
**peiriant** (-iannau) nm machine, engine; ~ **golchi** washing machine
**peirianwaith** nm mechanism
**peiswyn** nm chaff

**peithyn** (-au) *nm* ridge-tile
**pêl** (pelau, peli) *nf* ball
**pelawd** (-au) *nf* over (*cricket*)
**pêl-droed** *nf* football
**pêl-fasged** *nf* basket-ball
**pelferyn** (-nau) *nm* ball-bearing
**pêl-foli** *nf* volley-ball
**pêl-rwyd** *nf* netball
**pelten** (pelts) *nf* blow
**pelydr** (-au) *nm* ray, beam
**pelydru** *vb* beam, gleam, radiate
**pelydryn** *nm* ray, beam
**pell** *adj* far, distant, remote, long
**pellen** (-nau, -ni) *nf* ball (of yarn)
**pellennig** *adj* far, distant, remote
**pellhau** *vb* put or remove far off
**pellter** (-au, -oedd) *nm* distance
**pen** (-nau) *nm* head; chief; end; top
**pen** *adj* head, chief, supreme
**penadur** (-iaid) *nm* sovereign
**penaduriaeth** *nf* sovereignty
**penagored** *adj* open, indefinite, undecided
**penarglwyddiaeth** *nf* sovereignty
**penbaladr** *adj* general, universal
**penben** *adv* at loggerheads
**penbleth** *nf* perplexity, quandary
**pen-blwydd** (-i) *nm* birthday
**penboeth** *adj* hot-headed, fanatical
**penboethni** *nm* fanaticism
**penboethyn** (-boethiaid) *nm* fanatic
**penbwl** (-byliaid) *nm* blockhead; tadpole
**pencadlys** *nm* head-quarters
**pencampwr** (-wyr) *nm* champion
**pencampwriaeth** (-au) *nf* championship
**pencerdd** (-ceirddiaid) *nm* chief musician
**penchwiban** *adj* giddy, flighty
**pendant** *adj* positive, emphatic
**pendantrwydd** *nm* positiveness
**pendefig** (-ion) *nm* prince, peer, noble

**pendefigaeth** *nf* aristocracy, peerage
**pendefigaidd** *adj* noble, aristocratic
**pendefiges** (-au) *nf* peeress
**penderfyniad** (-au) *nm* determination, resolution
**penderfynol** *adj* determined, resolute
**penderfynu** *vb* determine, resolve
**pendew** *adj* thick-headed, stupid
**pendifaddau** *adj*: **yn bendifaddau** especially
**pendil** (-iau) *nm* pendulum
**pendramwnwgl** *adj* topsyturvy; headlong
**pendraphen** *adj* helter-skelter, confused
**pendro** *nf* giddiness, vertigo; staggers
**pendroni** *vb* perplex oneself, worry over
**pendrwm** *adj* top-heavy; drowsy
**pendrymu** *vb* drowse, droop
**pendwmpian** *vb* nod, doze, slumber
**penddaredd** *nm* giddiness
**penddaru** *vb* make or become giddy
**pendduyn** (-nod) *nm* botch, boil
**penelin** (-oedd) *nm/f* elbow
**penelino** *vb* elbow
**penffest** (-au) *nm* headgear
**penffol** *adj* silly, idiotic
**penffrwyn** (-au) *nm/f* head-stall, halter
**pengaled** *adj* headstrong ▷ *nf* knapweed
**pengaledwch** *nm* stubbornness
**pengam** *adj* wrong-headed, perverse
**pen-glin** (-iau) *nf* knee
**penglog** (-au) *nf* skull
**pengryf** *adj* headstrong, stubborn
**pengryniad** (-iaid) *nm* roundhead
**peniad** (-au) *nm* header
**penigamp** *adj* excellent, splendid

**penisel** adj downcast, crestfallen
**penlinio** vb kneel
**penllwyd** adj grey-headed
**penllwydni** nm grey hair, white hair
**penllywydd** (-ion) nm sovereign
**penllywyddiaeth** nf sovereignty
**pennaeth** (penaethiaid) nm chief
**pennaf** adj chief, principal
**pennawd** (penawdau) nm heading; headline
**pennill** (penillion) nm verse, stanza
**pennod** (penodau) nf chapter
**pennoeth** adj bare-headed
**pennog** (penwaig) nm herring
**pennu** vb specify, appoint, determine
**penodi** vb appoint
**penodiad** (-au) nm appointment
**penodol** adj particular, specific
**penrhydd** adj unbridled, loose
**penrhyddid** nm licence, licentiousness
**penrhyn** (-noedd, -nau) nm cape, foreland
**pensaer** (-seiri) nm architect
**pensaernïaeth** nf architecture
**pensil** (-iau) nm pencil
**pensiwn** (-iynau) nm pension
**pen-swyddog** (-ion) nm chief officer
**pensyfrdan** adj stunned, dazed
**pensyfrdandod** nm giddiness, dizziness
**pensyfrdanu** vb stun, daze
**pensyth** adj perpendicular
**pentan** (-au) nm hob
**penteulu** (pennau teuluoedd) nm head of family
**pentewyn** (-ion) nm firebrand
**pentir** (-oedd) nm headland
**pentis** nm pentice, penthouse
**pentref** (-i, -ydd) nm village; homestead
**pentrefan** (-nau) nm hamlet
**pentrefol** adj village
**pentrefwr** (-wyr) nm villager

**pentwr** (-tyrrau) nm heap, pile
**penty** (-tai) nm cottage, shed
**pentyrru** vb heap, pile, accumulate
**penuchel** adj proud, haughty
**penwan** adj weak-minded
**penwyn** adj white-headed
**penwynni** nm white hair, grey hair
**penyd** (-iau) nm penance, punishment
**penyd-wasanaeth** nm penal servitude
**penysgafn** adj light-headed, giddy, dizzy
**penysgafnder** nm giddiness, dizziness
**pêr** adj sweet, delicious, luscious
**peraidd** adj sweet, mellow
**perarogl** (-au) nm perfume, fragrance
**perarogli** vb perfume; embalm
**peraroglus** adj fragrant, scented
**percoladur** (-on) nm percolator
**perchen, -nog** (~ogion) nm owner
**perchenogaeth** nf ownership
**perchenogi** vb possess, own
**perchentywr** (-wyr) nm householder
**pereidd-dra** nm sweetness
**pereiddio** vb sweeten
**pererin** (-ion) nm pilgrim
**pererindod** (-au) nm/f pilgrimage
**pererinol** adj pilgrim
**perfedd** (-ion) nm guts, bowels
**perfeddwlad** (-wledydd) nf interior, heartland
**perffaith** adj perfect
**perffeithio** vb perfect
**perffeithrwydd** nm perfection
**perffeithydd** (-ion) nm perfecter
**perfformiad** (-au) nm performance
**perfformio** vb perform
**perfformiwr** (-wyr) nm performer
**peri** vb cause, bid
**perl** (-au) nm pearl
**perlewyg** (-on) nm ecstasy, trance
**perlysiau** npl aromatic herbs;

spices
**perllan** (-nau) *nf* orchard
**perocsid** (-au) *nm* peroxide
**peroriaeth** *nf* melody, music
**persain** *adj* euphonious, melodious
▷ (-seiniau) *nf* euphony
**persawr** (-au) *nm* fragrance
**perseiniol** *adj* melodious
**persli** *nm* parsley
**person** (-au) *nm* person
**person** (-iaid) *nm* parson, clergyman
**personadu** *vb* impersonate
**personadwr** (-wyr) *nm* impersonator
**persondy** (-dai) *nm* parsonage
**personol** *adj* personal
**personoli** *vb* personify
**personoliad** (-au) *nm* personification
**personoliaeth** (-au) *nf* personality
**perswâd** *nm* persuasion
**perswadio** *vb* persuade
**pert** *adj* quaint, pretty; pert
**perth** (-i) *nf* bush, hedge
**perthnasedd** (-au) *nm* relativity, relevance
**perthnasiad** (-au) *nm* affiliation
**perthnasol** *adj* relevant
**perthyn** *vb* belong, pertain, be related
**perthynas** (-au) *nf* relation; relationship
**perthynol** *adj* relative
**perwyl** *nm* purpose, effect
**perygl** (-on) *nm* danger, peril, risk
**peryglu** *vb* endanger, imperil
**peryglus** *adj* dangerous, perilous
**pes** *conj* if ... it; ~ **adwaenasent** had they known him
**pesgi** *vb* feed, fatten
**pesimist** (-iaid) *nm* pessimist
**pesimistaidd** *adj* pessimistic
**pesimistiaeth** *nf* pessimism
**pestl** (-au) *nm* pestle
**peswch** *nm* cough
**pesychiad** (-au) *nm* cough

**pesychu** *vb* cough
**petris** *npl* (*nf*-en) partridges
**petrocemegolau** (*nm* petrocemogolyn) *npl* petrochemicals
**petrol** (-au) *nm* petrol
**petroleg** *nm/f* petrology
**petrus** *adj* hesitating; doubtful
**petruso** *vb* hesitate, doubt
**petruster** *nm* hesitation, doubt
**petryal** *nm, adj* square
**peth** (-au) *nm* thing; part, some
**petheuach** *npl* odds and ends, trifles
**peunes** (-od) *nf* peahen
**pianydd** (-ion) *nm* pianist
**piau** *vb* own, possess
**pib** (-au) *nf* pipe, tube; diarrhœa
**pibell** (-au, -i) *nf* pipe, tube
**pibgorn** (-gyrn) *nm* recorder (music)
**pibo** *vb* pipe; squirt
**pibonwy** (*nf*-en) *npl* icicles
**pibydd** (-ion) *nm* piper
**picell** (-au) *nf* dart, javelin, spear
**picellu** *vb* spear, stab
**picfforch** (-ffyrch) *nf* pitchfork
**picil** *nm* pickle, trouble
**picio** *vb* dart, hie
**piclo** *vb* pickle
**pictiwr** (-tiyrau) *nm* picture
**picwns** (*nf*-nen) *npl* wasps
**piff** (-iau) *nm* puff, sudden blast
**piffian** *vb* snigger, giggle
**pig** (-au) *nf* point, spike; beak; spout
**pigan** *vb* drizzle
**pigdwr** (-dyrau) *nm* spire, steeple
**pigiad** (-au) *nm* prick, sting; injection
**pigion** *npl* pickings, selections
**pigo** *vb* pick; peck; prick; sting
**pigog** *adj* prickly
**pigyn** *nm* thorn, prickle
**pilcod** *npl* (*nm*-yn) minnows
**pilen** (-nau) *nf* membrane, film; cataract
**piler** (-au, -i) *nm* pillar

**pilio** vb peel, pare
**pili-pala** nm butterfly
**Pilipinas** npl the Philippines
**pilsen** (pils) nf pill
**pilyn** nm garment, rag, clout
**pîn** nm pine, fir
**pin** (-nau) nm/f pin ▷ nm pen
**pinacl** (-au) nm pinnacle
**pinaclog** adj pinnacled
**pinafal** (-au) nf pineapple
**pinbwyntio** vb pinpoint
**pinc** (-od) nm finch, chaffinch
**pincio** vb pink; **parlwr ~** beauty parlour
**pincws** (-cysau) nm pincushion
**pindwll** (-dyllau) nm pinhole
**pinsiad** (-au) nm pinch
**pinsio** vb pinch
**pioden** (piod) nf magpie
**piser** (-au, -i) nm pitcher, jug, can
**pistyll** (-oedd) nm spout; cataract
**pistyllio** vb spout, gush
**pisyn** (-nau, pisiau) nm piece
**piti** nm pity
**pitw** adj petty, puny, paltry
**piw** (-od) nm dug, udder
**Piwritan** (-iaid) nm Puritan
**piwritanaidd** adj puritan, puritanical
**piwritaniaeth** nf puritanism
**pla** (plâu) nm/f plague, pestilence; nuisance
**pladur** (-iau) nf scythe
**pladurwr** (-wyr) nm mower
**plaen** adj plain, clear
**plaen** (-au) nm plane
**plaenio** vb plane
**plagio** vb plague, tease, torment
**plagus** adj annoying, troublesome
**plaid** (pleidiau) nf side, party; **P~ Cymru** The Welsh National Party
**planced** (-i) nf blanket
**planed** (-au) nf planet
**planhigfa** (-feydd) nf plantation
**planhigyn** (-higion) nm plant
**plannu** vb plant; dive
**plannwr** (planwyr) nm planter

**plant** npl (nm plentyn) children
**planta** vb beget or bear children
**plantos** npl (little) children
**plas** (-au) nm hall, mansion, palace
**plasaidd** adj palatial
**plastr** (-au) nm plaster
**plastro** vb plaster
**plastrwr** (-wyr) nm plasterer
**plât, plat** (-iau) nm plate
**platŵn** (-tynau) nm platoon
**platwydr** nm plate-glass
**ple** nm plea
**pledio** vb plead, argue
**pledren** (-nau, -ni) nf bladder
**pleidgarwch** nm partisanship
**pleidio** vb side with, support
**pleidiol** adj favourable, partial
**pleidiwr** (-wyr) nm partisan, supporter
**pleidlais** (-leisiau) nf vote, suffrage
**pleidleisio** vb vote
**pleidleisiwr** (-wyr) nm voter
**plencyn** (planciau) nm plank
**plentyn** (plant) nm child, infant
**plentyndod** nm childhood, infancy
**plentyneiddiwch** nm childishness
**plentynnaidd** adj childish, puerile
**plentynrwydd** nm childishness
**pleser** (-au) nm pleasure
**pleserdaith** (-deithiau) nf trip, excursion
**pleserus** adj pleasurable, pleasant
**plesio** vb please
**plet, pleten** (~iau) nf pleat
**pletio** vb pleat
**pletiog** adj pleated
**pleth** (-au) nf plait
**plethdorch** (-au) nf wreath
**plethu** vb plait, weave, fold
**plewra** (-e) nm pleura
**plicio** vb pluck, peel, strip
**plisg** coll n (nm -yn) shells, husks, pods
**plisgo** vb shell, husk
**plisman, -mon** (-myn) nm policeman

**plismones (-au)** *nf* policewoman
**plith** *nm* midst
**pliwrisi** *nm* pleurisy
**plocyn (plociau)** *nm* block
**plod** *adj, nm* plaid, tartan
**ploryn (-nod)** *nm* pimple
**plu** *npl* (**nf-en**), **pluf** *npl* (**nm-yn**) feathers; **~ eira** snow-flakes
**pluo, plufio** *vb* pluck, deplume; plume
**pluog** *adj* feathered, fledged
**plwc (plyciau)** *nm* pluck; space, while
**plwg (plygiau)** *nm* plug
**plwm** *nm* lead
**plws** *nm* plus
**plwtonium** *nm* plutonium
**plwyf (-i, -ydd)** *nm* parish
**plwyfol** *adj* parochial
**plwyfolion** *npl* parishioners
**plycio** *vb* pluck
**plyg (-ion)** *nm* fold, double; hollow
**plygain** *nm* cock-crow, dawn; matins
**plygeiniol** *adj* dawning; very early
**plygell (-au)** *nm* folder
**plygiad (-au)** *nm* folding, fold
**plygu** *vb* fold; bend, stoop; bow
**plymen** *nf* plummet
**plymio** *vb* plumb, sound
**plymwr (-wyr)** *nm* plumber
**po** *particle used before superlative:* **gorau po gyntaf** the sooner the better
**pob** *adj* each, every; all
**pobi** *vb* bake; roast; toast
**pobiad (-au)** *nm* baking, batch
**pobl (-oedd)** *nf* people
**poblog** *adj* populous
**poblogaeth (-au)** *nf* population
**poblogaidd** *adj* popular
**poblogeiddio** *vb* popularize
**poblogi** *vb* people, populate
**poblogrwydd** *nm* popularity
**pobwr (-wyr), -ydd (-ion)** *nm* baker
**poced (-i)** *nf* pocket

**pocedu** *vb* pocket
**pocer (-i, -au)** *nm* poker
**poen (-au)** *nm/f* pain, torment
**poenedigaeth** *nf* torment
**poeni** *vb* pain, torment; worry, grieve
**poenus** *adj* painful
**poenwr (-wyr)** *nm* tormentor, torturer
**poenydio** *vb* torment, torture; fret, vex
**poenydiwr (-wyr)** *nm* tormentor
**poer (-ion)** *nm* spittle, saliva
**poeri** *vb* spit, expectorate
**poeryn** *nm* spittle
**poeth** *adj* hot; burning; **dŵr ~** heart-burn
**poethder, -ni** *nm* hotness, heat
**poethdon (-nau)** *nf* heatwave
**poethi** *vb* heat
**pôl (polau)** *nm* poll
**polaredd** *nm* polarity
**polareiddiad** *nm* polarisation
**polareiddio** *vb* polarise
**polymorff** *nm* polymorph
**polymorffedd** *nm* polymorphism
**polyn (polion)** *nm* pole
**pomgranad (-au)** *nm* pomegranate
**pompiwn (-iynau)** *nm* pumpkin, gourd
**pompren** *nf* plank bridge, footbridge
**ponc (-iau), -en** *nf*, **-yn** *nm* hillock, tump; bank
**pont (-ydd)** *nf* bridge, arch
**pontffordd (-ffyrdd)** *nf* fly-over, viaduct
**pontio** *vb* bridge
**popeth** *nm* everything
**poplys** *npl* (**nf-en**) poplar-trees
**popty (-tai)** *nm* bakehouse; oven
**porc** *nm* pork
**porchell (perchyll)** *nm* little pig
**porfa (-feydd)** *nf* pasture, grass
**porffor** *adj, nm* purple
**pori** *vb* graze, browse; eat

**pornograffiaeth** *nf* pornography
**Portiwgal** *nf* Portugal
**portread** (-au) *nm* portrayal, pattern
**portreadu** *vb* portray
**porth** *nm* aid, help, succour
**porth** (pyrth) *nm* gate, gateway; porch door; **~ awyr** airport
**porthfa** (-feydd) *nf* port, harbour; ferry
**porthi** *vb* feed
**porthiannus** *adj* well-fed, high-spirited
**porthiant** *nm* food, sustenance, support
**porthladd** (-oedd) *nm* port, harbour, haven
**porthmon** (-myn) *nm* cattle-dealer
**porthor** (-ion) *nm* porter, door-keeper, commissionaire
**pôs** (-au) *nm* riddle, conundrum, puzzle
**posibilrwydd** *nm* possibility
**posib(l)** *adj* possible
**positif** *adj* positive
**positifiaeth** *nf* positivism
**post** (pyst) *nm* post; pillar
**poster** (-i) *nm* poster
**postfarc** (-iau) *nm* postmark
**postio** *vb* post
**postman, -mon** (-myn) *nm* postman
**postyn** (pyst) *nm* post
**pot** (-iau) *nm* pot
**potel** (-i) *nf* bottle
**potelaid** (-eidiau) *nf* bottleful
**potelu** *vb* bottle
**poten** (-ni) *nf* paunch; pudding
**potensial** (-au) *nm, adj* potential
**potes** *nm* pottage, broth, soup
**potio** *vb* pot; tipple
**potsiar** (-s) *nm* poacher
**potsio** *vb* poach
**pothell** (-au, -i) *nf* blister
**powdr** (-au) *nm* powder
**powl, -en** (-iau) *nf* bowl, basin
**powlio** *vb* roll; wheel, trundle

**powltis** (-au) *nm* poultice
**practis** *nm* practice
**praff** *adj* thick, stout
**praffter** *nm* thickness, stoutness, girth
**pragmatiaeth** *nf* pragmatism
**praidd** (preiddiau) *nm* flock
**pranc** (-iau) *nm* frolic, prank
**prancio** *vb* caper, prance
**pratio** *vb* pat, stroke, caress
**praw, prawf** (profion) *nm* test, trial, proof
**preblan** *vb* chatter, babble
**pregeth** (-au) *nf* sermon, discourse
**pregethu** *vb* preach
**pregethwr** (-wyr) *nm* preacher
**pregethwrol** *adj* preacher-like
**pregowtha** *vb* jabber, rant
**preifat** *adj* private
**preifatrwydd** *nm* privacy
**preimin** *nm* ploughing match
**prelad** (-iaid) *nm* prelate
**preladiaeth** *nf* prelacy
**preliwd** (-au) *nm* prelude
**premiwm** (-iymau) *nm* premium
**pren** (-nau) *nm* tree, timber; wood
**prentis** (-iaid) *nm* apprentice
**prentisiaeth** *nf* apprenticeship
**prentisio** *vb* apprentice
**prepian** *vb* babble, blab
**pres** *nm* brass; bronze; copper; money
**preseb** (-au) *nm* crib, stall
**presennol** *adj, nm* present
**presenoldeb** *nm* presence; attendance
**presenoli** *vb* be present (*reflexive*)
**presgripsiwn** (-iynau) *nm* prescription
**preswyl** *nm*, **-fa** (-feydd) *nf*, **-fod** *nm* abode, dwelling
**preswylio** *vb* dwell, reside, inhabit
**preswylydd** (-ion, -wyr) *nm* dweller, inhabitant
**pric** (-iau) *nm* stick, chip
**prid** *adj* dear, costly ▷ *nm* price, value

**pridwerth** *nm* ransom
**pridd** *nm* mould, earth, soil, ground
**priddell** (-au, -i) *nf* clod
**priddglai** *nm* loam
**priddlech** (-au, -i) *nf* tile
**priddlestr** (-i) *nm* earthenware vessel
**priddlyd** *adj* earthy
**pridd(i)o** *vb* earth
**priddyn** *nm* earth, soil, mould
**prif** *adj* prime, principal, chief
**prifardd** (-feirdd) *nm* chief bard
**prifathro** (-athrawon) *nm* headmaster, principal
**prifddinas** (-oedd) *nf* metropolis, capital
**prifiant** *nm* growth
**prifio** *vb* grow
**prifodl** (-au) *nf* chief rhyme
**prifysgol** (-ion) *nf* university
**priffordd** (-ffyrdd) *nf* highway
**prin** *adj* scarce, rare ▷ *adv* scarcely
**prinder, -dra** *nm* scarceness, scarcity
**prinhau** *vb* make or grow scarce, diminish
**print** (-iau) *nm* print
**printiedig** *adj* printed
**printio** *vb* print
**printiwr** (-wyr) *nm* printer
**priod** *adj* own; proper; married ▷ *n coll* husband or wife
**priodas** (-au) *nf* marriage, wedding
**priodasfab** (-feibion) *nm* bridegroom
**priodasferch** (-ed) *nf* bride
**priodasol** *adj* matrimonial
**priod-ddull** (-iau) *nm* idiom
**priodfab** (-feibion) *nm* bridegroom
**priodferch** (-ed) *nf* bride
**priodi** *vb* marry
**priodol** *adj* proper, appropriate
**priodoldeb** (-au) *nm* propriety
**priodoledd** (-au) *nf* attribute
**priodoli** *vb* attribute
**prior** (-iaid) *nm* prior
**priordy** (-dai) *nm* priory

**pris** (-iau) *nm* price, value
**prisiad, -iant** *nm* valuation
**prisio** *vb* price, value; prize
**prisiwr** (-wyr) *nm* valuer
**problem** (-au) *nm/f* problem
**proc** (-iau) *nm* poke
**procer** (-au, -i) *nm* poker
**procio** *vb* poke; throb
**procsi** *nm* proxy
**prodin** (-au) *nm* protein
**profedig** *adj* approved, tried
**profedigaeth** (-au) *nf* trouble, tribulation
**profedigaethus** *adj* beset with trials
**profi** *vb* prove; taste; try; experience
**profiad** (-au) *nm* experience
**profiadol** *adj* experienced
**profiannaeth** (-au) *nf* probation
**proflen** (-ni) *nf* proof-sheet
**profocio** *vb* provoke, tease
**profoclyd** *adj* provoking, provocative
**profwr** (-wyr) *nm* taster, tester
**proffes** (-au) *nf* profession
**proffesiwn** (-iynau) *nm* profession
**proffesu** *vb* profess
**proffid** *nf* profit
**proffidio** *vb* profit, benefit
**proffidiol** *adj* profitable
**proffwyd** (-i) *nm* prophet
**proffwydes** (-au) *nf* prophetess
**proffwydo** *vb* prophesy
**proffwydol** *adj* prophetic
**proffwydoliaeth** (-au) *nf* prophecy
**project** (-au) *nm* project
**proses** (-au) *nm/f* process
**prosesu** *vb* process
**prosesydd** *nm* processor; **~ geiriau** word processor
**protest** (-au) *nf* protest
**Protestannaidd** *adj* Protestant
**Protestant** (-aniaid) *nm* Protestant
**protestio** *vb* protest
**protestiwr** (-wyr) *nm* protestor

**prudd** *adj* grave, serious, sad; wise
**pruddaidd** *adj* sad, gloomy, mournful
**prudd-der** *nm* sadness, gloom
**pruddglwyf** *nm* depression, melancholy
**pruddglwyfus** *adj* depressed, melancholy
**pruddhau** *vb* sadden, depress
**Prwsia** *nf* Prussia
**pryd** (-iau) *nm* time; season ▷ (-au) *nm* meal
**pryd** *adv* while, when, since
**pryd** *nm* form, aspect; complexion
**Prydain** *nf* Britain
**Prydeindod** *nm* Britishness
**Prydeinig** *adj* British
**Prydeiniwr** (-wyr) *nm* Britisher
**pryder** (-on) *nm* anxiety, solicitude
**pryderu** *vb* be anxious
**pryderus** *adj* anxious, solicitous
**prydferth** *adj* beautiful, handsome
**prydferthu** *vb* beautify
**prydferthwch** *nm* beauty
**prydles** (-au, -i) *nf* lease
**prydlon** *adj* timely, punctual
**prydlondeb** *nm* punctuality
**prydydd** (-ion) *nm* poet
**prydyddu** *vb* compose poetry, poetize
**pryddest** (-au) *nf* poem in free metre
**pryf** (-ed) *nm* insect; worm; vermin
**pryfedog** *adj* verminous
**pryfleiddiad** (-au) *nm* insecticide
**pryfyn** *nm* worm
**prŷn** *adj* bought, purchased
**prynedigaeth** *nf/m* redemption
**prynhawn** (-au) *nm* afternoon
**prynhawnol** *adj* afternoon, evening
**pryniad** *nm* purchase
**prynu** *vb* buy, purchase; redeem
**prynwr** (-wyr) *nm* buyer; redeemer
**prysg** *nm* bush, wood
**prysgwydd** *npl* brushwood
**prysur** *adj* busy, hasty; diligent; serious

**prysurdeb** *nm* haste, hurry; busyness
**prysuro** *vb* hurry, hasten
**publican** (-od) *nm* publican (New Test.)
**pulpud** (-au) *nm* pulpit
**pulsau** *npl* pulses
**pum, pump** *adj* five
**pumawd** *nm* quintet
**pumed** *adj* fifth
**pumongl** (-au) *nm* pentagon
**punt** (punnoedd, punnau) *nf* pound (money)
**pupur** *nm* pepper
**pur** *adj* pure, sincere ▷ *adv* very, fairly
**purdan** *nm* purgatory
**purdeb** *nm* purity, sincerity
**puredigaeth** *nf* purification
**puredd** *nm* purity, innocence
**purfa** (-feydd) *nf* refinery
**purion** *adj* very well; right enough
**puro** *vb* purify, cleanse
**puror** *nm* harpist
**purwr** (-wyr) *nm* purifier, refiner
**purydd** (-ion) *nm* purist
**putain** (-einiaid) *nf* prostitute
**puteindra** *nm* prostitution
**puteinio** *vb* commit fornication
**puteiniwr** (-wyr) *nm* fornicator
**pw** *excl* pooh
**pwbig** *adj* pubic
**pwdin** *nm* pudding, dessert
**pwdlyd** *adj* sulking
**pwdr** *adj* rotten, corrupt, putrid
**pwdu** *vb* pout, sulk
**pŵer** (-au) *nm* power
**pwerus** *adj* powerful
**pwff** (pyffiau) *nm* puff, blast
**pwffian** *vb* puff
**pŵl** *adj* blunt, obtuse; dull, dim
**pwl** (pyliau) *nm* fit, attack, paroxysm
**pwll** (pyllau) *nm* pit, pool, pond; ~ glo coal pit; ~ tro whirlpool
**pwmp** (pympiau) *nm* pump

**pwn** (pynnau) *nm* pack, burden
**pwnc** (pynciau) *nm* point, subject, question
**pwniad** (-au) *nm* nudge, dig
**pwnio** *vb* nudge; beat, thump, wallop
**pwrcas** (-au) *nm* purchase
**pwrcasu** *vb* purchase
**pwrffil** *nm* purfle, train
**pwrpas** (-au) *nm* purpose
**pwrpasol** *adj* suitable
**pwrpasu** *vb* purpose, intend
**pwrs** (pyrsau) *nm* purse, bag; udder; scrotum
**pwt** (pytiau) *nm* anything short; stump
**pwt, -ian** *vb* prod, poke
**pwti** *nm* putty
**pwy** *pron* who
**Pŵyl** *nf* Poland
**pwyll** *nm* sense, discretion
**pwyllgor** (-au) *nm* committee
**pwyllgorwr** (-wyr) *nm* committee-man
**pwyllo** *vb* pause, consider, reflect
**pwyllog** *adj* discreet, prudent, deliberate
**pwynt** (-iau) *nm* point
**pwyntil** *nm* tab, tag; pencil
**pwyntio** *vb* point; fatten
**pwyo** *vb* beat, batter, pound
**pwys** (-au, -i) *nm* weight, burden, pressure; pound (lb.); importance
**pwysau** *nm* weight
**pwysedd** *nm* pressure
**pwysi** (-ïau) *nm* posy
**pwysig** *adj* important
**pwysigrwydd** *nm* importance
**pwyslais** (-leisiau) *nm* emphasis
**pwysleisio** *vb* emphasize
**pwyso** *vb* weigh, press; lean, rest; rely
**pwyswr** (-wyr) *nm* weigher
**pwyth** (-au) *nm* stitch; **talu'r ~** requite
**pwytho** *vb* stitch
**pwythwr** (-wyr) *nm* stitcher

**pybyr** *adj* strong, stout, staunch, valiant
**pybyrwch** *nm* stoutness, vigour, valour
**pydew** (-au) *nm* well, pit
**pydredig** *adj* rotten, putrid
**pydredd** *nm* rottenness, putridity, rot
**pydru** *vb* rot, putrefy
**pyg** *nm* pitch, bitumen
**pygddu** *adj* pitch-black
**pygu** *vb* pitch
**pyngad, pyngu** *vb* cluster
**pylni** *nm* bluntness, dullness
**pylor** *nm* dust, powder
**pylu** *vb* blunt, dull
**pyllog** *adj* full of pits
**pyllu** *vb* pit
**pymtheg** *adj, nm* fifteen
**pymthegfed** *adj* fifteenth
**pyncio** *vb* sing, play, make melody
**pynfarch** (-feirch) *nm* pack-horse; mill-race
**pynio** *vb* burden, load
**pys** *npl* (*nf*-en) peas
**pysgod** *npl* (*nm*-yn) fishes, fish; **~ a sglodion** fish and chips
**pysgodfa** (-feydd) *nf* fishery
**pysgota** *vb* fish
**pysgotwr** (-wyr) *nm* fisherman
**pystylad** *vb* stamp with the feet
**pytaten** (-tws) *nf* potato
**pythefnos** (-au) *nm/f* fortnight

# ph

**Pharisead** (-aid) *nm* Pharisee
**Phariseaeth** *nf* Pharisaism
**Phariseaidd** *adj* Pharisaic(al)
**Philistiad** (-iaid) *nm* Philistine
**Philistiaeth** *nf* Philistinism

**ridens** *nf* fringe, nap
**riwl** *nf* ruler
**robin goch** *nm* robin
**robin y gyrrwr** *nm* gadfly
**roced** (-i) *nf* rocket
**Românìa** *nf* Romania
**ruban** (-au) *nm* ribbon
**rŵan** *adv* now
**rwbel** *nm* rubble, rubbish
**rwber** *nm* rubber
**rwdins** *npl* (*nf* rwden) swedes
**Rwsia** *nf* Russia
**Rwsiad** (Rwsiaid) *nm* Russian (citizen)
**Rwsieg** *nm* Russian (language)

# r

# rh

**rabi** (-niaid) *nm* rabbi
**rabinaidd** *adj* rabbinical
**radio** *nm* radio
**radioleg** *nf* radiology
**radiws** *nm* radius
**ras** (-ys) *nf* race
**rasal, raser** (-elydd, -erydd) *nf* razor
**record** (-iau) *nf/m* record
**recordiad** (-au) *nm* recording
**reiat** *nf* row, riot
**reis** *nm* rice
**reit** *adv* right, very, quite

**rhaca** (-nau) *nf*, **-nu** *vb* rake
**rhacs** (*nm* rhecsyn) *npl* rags
**rhad** *adj* free; cheap
**rhad** (-au) *nm* grace, favour, blessing
**rhadlon** *adj* gracious, kind; genial
**rhadlondeb, -rwydd** *nm* graciousness, cheapness
**rhadus** *adj* economical
**rhaeadr** (-au) *nf* cataract, waterfall
**rhaeadru** *vb* pour, gush
**rhaff** (-au) *nf* rope, cord
**rhaffo, -u** *vb* rope
**rhag** *prep* before, against; from; lest
  ▷ *prefix* pre-, fore-, ante-
**rhagafon** (-ydd) *nf* tributary

**rhagair** (-au) *nm* preface
**rhagarfaethiad** *nm* predestination
**rhagarfaethu** *vb* predestine
**rhagarweiniad** *nm* introduction
**rhagarweiniol** *adj* introductory, preliminary
**rhagarwyddo** *vb* foretoken, portend
**rhagbaratoawl** *adj* preparatory
**rhagbrawf** (-brofion) *nm* foretaste; preliminary test
**rhagdraeth** (-au) *nm* preface, introduction
**rhag-dyb** (-ion) *nm* presupposition
**rhagdybied, -io** *vb* presuppose
**rhagddodiad** (-iaid) *nm* prefix
**rhagddywedyd, rhagddweud** *vb* foretell
**rhagenw** (-au) *nm* pronoun
**rhagenwol** *adj* pronominal
**rhagfarn** (-au) *nf* prejudice
**rhagfarnllyd** *adj* prejudiced
**rhagferf** (-au) *nf* adverb
**rhagflaenor** (-iaid) *nm* forerunner
**rhagflaenu** *vb* precede, anticipate, forestall
**rhagflaenydd** (-ion, -wyr) *nm* predecessor, precursor
**rhagflas** *nm* foretaste
**rhagfur** (-iau) *nm* bulwark
**rhagfyfyrio** *vb* premeditate
**rhagfynegi** *vb* foretell
**Rhagfyr** *nm* December
**rhaglaw** (-iaid, -lofiaid) *nm* prefect, viceroy, governor
**rhaglawiaeth** *nf* prefecture, governorship
**rhaglen** (-ni) *nf* programme
**rhagluniaeth** (-au) *nf* providence
**rhagluniaethol** *adj* providential
**rhaglunio** *vb* predestine, predestinate
**rhagod** *vb* ambush, hinder, waylay
**rhagofnau** *npl* forebodings
**rhagolwg** (-ygon) *nm* prospect, outlook

**rhagor** (-au, -ion) *nm* difference; more
**rhagorfraint** (-freintiau) *nf* privilege
**rhagori** *vb* exceed, excel, surpass
**rhagoriaeth** (-au) *nf* superiority; excellence
**rhagorol** *adj* excellent, splendid
**rhagoroldeb** *nm* excellence
**rhagorsaf** (-oedd) *nf* out-station; outpost
**rhagredegydd** (-ion) *nm* forerunner
**rhagrith** (-ion) *nm* hypocrisy
**rhagrithio** *vb* practise hypocrisy
**rhagrithiol** *adj* hypocritical
**rhagrithiwr** (-wyr) *nm* hypocrite
**rhagrybuddio** *vb* forewarn
**rhagweld** *vb* foresee
**rhagwelediad** *nm* foresight, prescience
**rhagwybod** *vb* foreknow
**rhagwybodaeth** *nf* foreknowledge
**rhagymadrodd** (-ion) *nm* introduction
**rhai** *pron* ones ▷ *adj* some
**rhaib** *nm* rapacity, greed; spell
**rhaid** (rheidiau) *nm* need, necessity
**rhaidd** (rheiddiau) *nf* antler
**rhain** *pron* these
**rhamant** (-au) *nf* romance
**rhamantus** *adj* romantic
**rhan** (-nau) *nf* part, portion; fate
**rhanbarth** (-au) *nm* division, district
**rhandir** (-oedd) *nm/f* division, district
**rhangymeriad** (-iaid) *nm* participle
**rhaniad** (-au) *nm* division
**rhannu** *vb* divide, share, distribute
**rhannwr** (rhanwyr) *nm* divider, sharer
**rhanrif** *nm* fraction
**rhathell** (-au) *nf* rasp
**rhathiad** *nm* friction, chafing

**rhathu** vb rub, rasp, file
**rhaw** (-iau, rhofiau) nf spade, shovel
**rhawd** nf course, career
**rhawg** adv for a long time (to come)
**rhawio, rhofio** vb shovel
**rhawn** coll n coarse long hair, horse-hair
**rhech** nf fart
**rhechain** vb fart
**rhedeg** vb run; flow
**rhedegfa** (-feydd) nf racecourse, race
**rhedegog** adj running, flowing
**rhedegydd** (-ion, -wyr) nm runner
**rhedfa** nf running, course, race
**rhediad** nm running, trend; slope
**rhedweli** (-ïau) nf artery
**rhedyn** npl (nf-en) fern
**rheffyn** (-nau) nm cord; string, rigmarole
**rheg** (-au, -feydd) nf curse
**rhegen yr ŷd, rhegen ryg** nf corncrake
**rhegi** vb curse
**rheglyd** adj given to cursing, profane
**rheng** (-au, -oedd) nf row, rank
**rheibio** vb raven, ravage, ravish
**rheibus** adj rapacious, of prey
**rheidiol** adj necessary, needful
**rheidrwydd** nm necessity, need
**rheidus** adj necessitous, needy
**rheilffordd** (-ffyrdd) nf railway
**rheini** pron those
**rheitheg** nf rhetoric
**rheithfarn** (-au) nf verdict
**rheithgor** (rheithwyr) nm jury
**rheithiwr** (-wyr) nm juryman, juror
**rheithor** (-ion, -iad) nm rector
**rhelyw** nm residue, rest, remainder
**rhemp** nf excess; defect
**rhent** (-i) nm rent
**rhentu** vb rent
**rheol** (-au) nf rule, regulation
**rheolaeth** nf rule, management, control

**rheolaidd** adj regular
**rheoleiddio** vb regulate; regularize
**rheoli** vb rule, govern, control
**rheolwr** (-wyr) nm ruler, controller
**rhes** (-i) nf line, stripe; row, rank
**rhesen** (rhesi) nf line, parting, streak, stripe
**rhesin** (-au, -ingau) nm raisin
**rhesog** adj striped; ribbed
**rhestl** (-au) nf rack
**rhestr** (-au, -i) nf list; row
**rhestru** vb list
**rheswm** (-ymau) nm reason
**rhesymeg** nf logic
**rhesymegol** adj logical
**rhesymol** adj reasonable, rational
**rhesymoldeb** nm reasonableness
**rhesymolwr** (-wyr) nm rationalist
**rhesymu** vb reason
**rhetoreg, rhethreg** nf rhetoric
**rhew** (-oedd, -ogydd) nm frost, ice
**rhewfryn** (-iau) nm iceberg
**rhewgell** (-oedd) nf freezer
**rhewi** vb freeze
**rhewllyd** adj icy, frosty, frigid
**rhewyn** (-au) nm ditch, stream
**rhewynt** (-oedd) nm freezing wind
**rhi** nm king, lord
**rhiain** (rhianedd) nf maiden
**rhialtwch** nm pomp; festivity, jollity
**rhibidirês** nf rigmarole
**rhibin** nm streak
**rhic** (-iau) nm notch, nick; groove
**rhiciog** adj notched; grooved; ribbed
**rhidyll** (-iau) nm riddle, sieve
**rhidyllio, -u** vb riddle, sift
**rhieingerdd** (-i) nf love-poem
**rhieni** npl parents
**rhif** (-au) nm, **rhifedi** nm number
**rhifo** vb number, count, reckon
**rhifol** (-ion) nm numeral
**rhifyddeg, -yddiaeth** nf arithmetic
**rhifyddwr** (-wyr) nm arithmetician
**rhifyn** (-nau) nm number

**rhigol** (-au, -ydd) *nf* rut, groove
**rhigwm** (-ymau) *nm* rigmarole; rhyme
**rhigymu** *vb* rhyme, versify
**rhigymwr** (-wyr) *nm* rhymester
**rhingyll** (-iaid) *nm* sergeant, bailiff
**rhimyn** (-nau) *nm* strip, string
**rhin** (-iau) *nf* virtue, essence
**rhincian** *vb* creak; gnash
**rhiniog** (-au) *nm* threshold
**rhinwedd** (-au) *nm/f* virtue
**rhinweddol** *adj* virtuous
**rhip** *nm* strickle
**rhisgl** *nm* bark
**rhith** (-iau) *nm* form, guise, appearance, image; foetus
**rhithio** *vb* appear
**rhithyn** *nm* atom, particle, scintilla
**rhiw** (-iau) *nf* hill, acclivity
**rhoch** *nf* grunt, groan; deathrattle
**rhochain, -ian** *nf* grunt
**rhod** (-au) *nf* wheel, orb; ecliptic
**rhodfa** (-feydd) *nf* walk, promenade, avenue
**rhodiad** *nm* walk
**rhodianna** *vb* stroll
**rhodio** *vb* walk, stroll
**rhodres** *nm* ostentation, affectation
**rhodresa** *vb* behave ostentatiously
**rhodresgar** *adj* ostentatious, affected
**rhodreswr** (-wyr) *nm* swaggerer
**rhodd** (-ion) *nf* gift, present
**rhoddi** *vb* give, bestow, yield; put
**rhoddwr** (-wyr) *nm* giver, donor
**rhoi** *vb* give, bestow, yield; put
**rhôl** (-iau) *nf*, **rholyn** *nm* roll
**rholbren** (-ni) *nm* rolling-pin
**rholio** *vb* roll
**rhombws** (rhombi) *nm* rhombus
**rhonc** *adj* rank, stark, out-and-out
**rhos** (-ydd) *nf* moor, heath; plain
**rhos** *npl* (*nm* -yn) roses
**rhost** *adj* roast, roasted
**rhostio** *vb* roast
**rhosyn** (-nau) *nm* rose

**rhuad** (-au) *nm* roaring, roar
**rhuadwy** *adj* roaring
**rhuchen** (rhuchion) *nf* husk; film, pellicle
**rhudd** *adj* red, crimson
**rhuddell** *nf* rubric
**rhuddem** (-au) *nf* ruby
**rhuddin** *nm* heart of timber
**rhuddion** *npl* bran
**rhuddygl** *nm* radish
**Rhufain** *nf* Rome
**Rhufeinaidd** *adj* Roman
**Rhufeiniad** (-iaid), **-iwr** (-wyr) *nm* Roman
**Rhufeinig** *adj* Roman
**rhugl** *adj* free, fluent, glib
**rhuglen** (-ni) *nf* rattle
**rhuglo** *vb* rattle
**rhuo** *vb* roar, bellow, bluster
**rhusio** *vb* start, scare, take fright
**rhuthr** (-au) *nm* rush; attack; sally
**rhuthro** *vb* rush; attack, assault
**rhwbio** *vb* rub, chafe
**rhwd** *nm* rust
**rhwng** *prep* between, among
**rhwnc** *nm* snort, snore; death-rattle
**rhwth** *adj* gaping, distended
**rhwyd** (-au, -i) *nf* net, snare
**rhwydo** *vb* net, ensnare
**rhwydog** *adj* reticulated, netted
**rhwydwaith** (-weithiau) *nm* network
**rhwydd** *adj* easy, expeditious, prosperous
**rhwyddhau** *vb* facilitate
**rhwyddineb** *nm* ease, facility
**rhwyf** (-au) *nf* oar
**rhwyflong** (-au) *nf* galley
**rhwyfo** *vb* row; sway; toss about
**rhwyfus** *adj* restless
**rhwyfwr** (-wyr) *nm* rower, oarsman
**rhwyg** (-iadau) *nf* rent, rupture; schism
**rhwygo** *vb* rend, tear
**rhwyll** (-au) *nf*, **-yn** *nm* buttonhole, aperture; lattice
**rhwyllwaith** *nm* fretwork,

lattice-work

**rhwym** adj bound ▷ (-au) nm bond, tie; obligation

**rhwymedig** adj bound, obliged

**rhwymedigaeth** (-au) nf bond, obligation

**rhwymedd** nm constipation

**rhwymiad** (-au) nm binding

**rhwymo** vb bind, tie; constipate

**rhwymwr** (-wyr) nm binder

**rhwymyn** (-nau) nm band, bond, bandage

**rhwysg** (-au) nm sway; pomp

**rhwysgfawr** adj pompous, ostentatious

**rhwystr** (-au) nm hindrance, obstacle

**rhwystro** vb hinder, prevent, obstruct

**rhwystrus** adj embarrassed, confused

**rhy** adv too

**rhybedio** vb rivet

**rhybudd** (-ion) nm notice, warning

**rhybuddio** vb warn, admonish, caution

**rhybuddiwr** (-wyr) nm warner

**rhych** (-au) nm/f furrow, rut, groove

**rhychog** adj furrowed, seamed

**rhychwant** (-au) nm span

**rhychwantu** vb span

**rhyd** (-au, -iau) nf ford

**rhydio** vb ford

**rhydlyd** adj rusty

**rhydu** vb rust

**rhydd** adj free; loose; liberal

**Rhyddfrydiaeth** nf Liberalism

**rhyddfrydig** adj liberal, generous

**Rhyddfrydol** adj liberal (in politics)

**Rhyddfrydwr** (-wyr) nm Liberal, Radical

**rhyddhad** nm liberation, emancipation

**rhyddhau** vb free, release, liberate

**rhyddhawr** (-wyr) nm liberator

**rhyddiaith** nf prose

**rhyddid** nm freedom, liberty

**rhyddieithol** adj prose, prosaic

**rhyddni** nm looseness, diarrhœa

**rhyfedd** adj strange, queer, wonderful

**rhyfeddnod** (-au) nm note of exclamation

**rhyfeddod** (-au) nm/f wonder, marvel

**rhyfeddol** adj wonderful, marvellous

**rhyfeddu** vb wonder, marvel

**rhyfel** (-oedd) nm/f war, warfare

**rhyfela** vb wage war, war

**rhyfelgar** adj warlike, bellicose

**rhyfelgri** nm war-cry, battle-cry

**rhyfelgyrch** (-oedd) nm campaign

**rhyfelwr** (-wyr) nm warrior

**rhyferthwy** nm torrent, inundation

**rhyfon** npl currants

**rhyfyg** nm presumption, foolhardiness

**rhyfygu** vb presume, dare

**rhyfygus** adj presumptuous; foolhardy

**rhyg** nm rye

**rhyglyddu** vb deserve, merit

**rhygnu** vb rub, grate, jar; harp

**rhygyngu** vb amble; caper, mince

**rhyngu** vb: **rhyngu bodd** please

**rhyngwladol** adj international

**rhyndod** nm shivering, chill

**rhynion** npl grits, groats

**rhynllyd** adj shivering, chilly

**rhynnu** vb starve with cold

**rhysedd** nm abundance, excess

**rhython** npl cockles

**rhythu** vb gape; stare

**rhyw** adj some, certain ▷ (-iau) nf/m sort; sex

**rhywbeth** nm something

**rhywfaint** nm some amount

**rhywfodd, rhywsut** adv somehow

**rhywiog** adj kindly, genial; fine; tender

**rhywiol** adj sexual

**rhywle** *adv* somewhere, anywhere
**rhywogaeth** (**-au**) *nf* species,
   sort, kind
**rhywun** (**rhywrai**) *nm* someone,
   anyone

# S

**Sabath, -oth** (**-au**) *nm* Sabbath
**Sabothol** *adj* Sabbath, sabbatic(al)
**sacrament** (**-au**) *nm/f* sacrament
**sacramentaidd** *adj* sacramental
**sach** (**-au**) *nf/m* sack
**sachaid** (**-eidiau**) *nf* sackful
**sachlen** *nf,* **sachliain** *nm* sackcloth
**sachu** *vb* sack, bag
**sad** *adj* firm, steady, solid; sober
**sadio** *vb* firm, steady
**sadistiaeth** *nf* sadism
**sadrwydd** *nm* firmness, steadiness
**Sadwrn** (**-yrnau**) *nm* Saturn;
   Saturday
**saer** (**seiri**) *nm* wright, mason,
   carpenter
**saernïaeth** *nf* workmanship,
   construction
**saernïo** *vb* fashion, construct
**Saesneg** *nf, adj* English
**Saesnes** (**-au**) *nf* Englishwoman
**saets** *nm* sage
**saeth** (**-au**) *nf* arrow, dart
**saethiad** (**-au**) *nm* shooting

**saethu** *vb* shoot, dart; blast
**saethwr** (**-wyr**) *nm* shooter, shot
**saethydd** (**-ion**) *nm* shooter, archer
**saethyddiaeth** *nf* archery
**saethyn** (**-nau**) *nm* projectile
**safadwy** *adj* stable
**safanna** *nm* savannah
**safbwynt** (**-iau**) *nm* standpoint
**safiad** *nm* standing; stature; stand
**safio** *vb* save
**safle** (**-oedd**) *nm* position, station,
   situation
**safn** (**-au**) *nf* mouth, jaws
**safnrhwth** *adj* open-mouthed,
   gaping
**safnrhythu** *vb* gape, stare
**safon** (**-au**) *nf* standard, criterion
**safoni** *vb* standardise
**safonol** *adj* standard
**saffir** *nm* sapphire
**saffrwm, saffron** *nm* crocus
**sagrafen** (**-nau**) *nf* sacrament
**sang** (**-au**) *nf* pressure, tread
**sangu, sengi** *vb* tread, trample
**saib** (**seibiau**) *nm* leisure; pause, rest
**saig** (**seigiau**) *nf* meal, dish
**sail** (**seiliau**) *nf* base, foundation
**saim** (**seimiau**) *nm* grease
**sain** (**seiniau**) *nf* sound, tone
**Sais** (**Saeson**) *nm* Saxon,
   Englishman
**saith** *adj, nm* seven
**sâl** *adj* poor; poorly, ill
**saldra** *nm* poorness; illness
**salm** (**-au**) *nf* psalm
**salmydd** (**-ion**) *nm* psalmist
**salw** *adj* poor, mean, vile; ugly
**salwch** *nm* illness
**Sallwyr** *nm* Psalter
**sampl** (**-au**) *nf* sample
**samplu** *vb* sample
**Sanct** *nm* the Holy One
**sanctaidd** *adj* holy
**sancteiddio** *vb* sanctify, hallow
**sancteiddrwydd** *nm* holiness,
   sanctity
**sandal** (**-au**) *nm* sandal

**sant** (**saint, seintiau**) nm saint

**santes** (**-au**) nf female saint

**sarff** (**seirff**) nf serpent

**sarhad** (**-au**) nm insult, disgrace, injury

**sarhau** vb insult, affront, injure

**sarhaus** adj insulting, offensive, insolent

**sarn** (**-au**) nf causeway ▷ nm litter, ruin, destruction

**sarnu** vb trample; litter; spoil, ruin

**sarrug** adj gruff, surly, morose

**sarugrwydd** nm gruffness, surliness

**sasiwn** (**-iynau**) nm C.M. Association

**satan** (**-iaid**) nm satan

**sathredig** adj common, vulgar

**sathru** vb tread, trample

**Saudi Arabia** nf Saudi Arabia

**sawdl** (**sodlau**) nm/f heel

**sawl** pron whoso, he that; **Pa ~** how many

**sawr, sawyr** nm savour

**sawrio, -u** vb savour

**sawrus** adj savoury

**saws** nm sauce

**sba** (**-on**) nm spa

**Sbaen** nf Spain

**sbageti** nm spaghetti

**sbaner** (**-i**) nm spanner

**sbâr** (**sbarion**) nm spare; (pl) leavings

**sbario** vb spare, save

**sbectol** nf spectacle(s)

**sbeit** nf spite

**sbeitio** vb spite

**sbeitlyd** adj spiteful

**sbel** (**-iau**) nf spell

**sbon** adv: **newydd ~** brand-new

**sbonc** (**-iau**) nm leap, jerk

**sboncen** nf squash

**sbort** nf sport, fun, game

**sbri** nm spree, fun

**sbring** nm spring

**sbwylio** vb spoil

**sebon** (**-au**) nm soap

**seboni** vb soap, lather; soft-soap, flatter

**sebonwr** (**-wyr**) nm flatterer

**sect** (**-au**) nf sect

**sectyddiaeth** nf sectarianism

**sectyddol** adj sectarian

**sech** adj f of **sych**

**sedd** (**-au**) nf seat, pew

**sef** conj that is to say, namely, to wit

**sefnig** nm pharynx

**sefydledig** adj established

**sefydliad** (**-au**) nm establishment, institution

**sefydlog** adj fixed, settled, stationary, stable

**sefydlo(w)grwydd** nm stability

**sefydlu** vb establish, found, settle

**sefyll** vb stand; stop; stay

**sefyllfa** (**-oedd**) nf situation, position

**sefyllian** vb stand about, loiter

**sefyllwyr** npl bystanders

**segur** adj idle

**segura** vb idle

**segurdod** nm idleness

**segurwr** (**-wyr**) nm idler

**seguryd** nm idleness

**seguryn, segurwr** (**-wyr**) nm idler

**sengi** vb tread, trample

**sengl** adj single

**seiat** (**-adau**) nf fellowship meeting, 'society'

**seibiant** nm leisure, respite

**seibio** vb pause

**seiciatreg** nm psychiatry

**seiciatrydd** nm psychiatrist

**seicoleg** nf psychology

**seidin** nm sidings

**seilio** vb ground, found

**seimio** vb grease

**seimllyd** adj greasy

**seinber** adj melodious, euphonious

**seindorf** (**-dyrf**) nf band

**seineg** nf phonetics

**seinfawr** adj loud

**seinfforch** (**-ffyrch**) nf tuning-fork

**seinio** vb sound, resound;

pronounce
**seintio** vb saint, canonize
**seintwar** nf sanctuary
**seinyddol** adj phonetic
**Seisnig** adj English
**Seisnigaidd** adj English, Anglicized
**Seisnigeiddio, -igo** vb Anglicize
**seithblyg** adj sevenfold
**seithfed** adj seventh
**seithongl (-au)** nf septangle, heptagon
**seithug** adj futile, fruitless, bootless
**sêl** nf zeal
**sêl (seliau)** nf seal
**Seland Newydd** nf New Zealand
**seld (-au)** nf dresser, sideboard, bookcase
**seler (-au, -i, -ydd)** nf cellar
**selio** vb seal
**selni** nm illness
**selog** adj zealous, ardent
**selsig (-od)** nf black-pudding, sausage
**semanteg** nf semantics
**seml** adj f of **syml**
**sen (-nau)** nf reproof, rebuke, censure, snub
**senedd (-au)** nf senate; parliament
**seneddol** adj senatorial, parliamentary
**seneddwr (-wyr)** nm senator
**sennu** vb rebuke, censure
**sentimentaleiddiwch** nm sentimentality
**sêr** see **seren**
**seraff (-iaid)** nm seraph
**serch** conj, prep although, notwithstanding
**serch (-iadau)** nm affection, love
**serchog** adj affectionate, loving
**serchowgrwydd** nm affectionateness, love
**serchu** vb love
**serchus** adj loving, affectionate, pleasant
**sêr-ddewin (-iaid)** nm astrologer

**sêr-ddewiniaeth** nf astrology
**seremoni (-ïau)** nf ceremony
**seremonïol** adj ceremonial
**seren (sêr)** nf star; asterisk
**serennog** adj starry
**serennu** vb sparkle, scintillate
**serfyll** adj unsteady
**seri** nm causeway, pavement
**serio** vb sear
**sero (-au)** nm zero
**serth** adj steep, precipitous; obscene
**serthedd** nm ribaldry, obscenity
**serwm** nm serum
**seryddiaeth** nf astronomy
**seryddol** adj astronomical
**seryddwr (-wyr)** nm astronomer
**sesbin** nm shoehorn
**set (-iau)** nf set
**sêt (seti)** nf seat, pew; **~ fawr** deacons' pew
**setl (-au)** nf settle
**setlo** vb settle
**sethrydd (-ion)** nm treader, trampler
**sew (-ion)** nm juice; pottage; delicacy
**sffêr** nf sphere
**sg-** see also **ysg-**
**sgâm (sgamiau)** nf scheme, dodge
**sgamio** vb scheme, dodge
**sgarff (-iau)** nf scarf
**sgaprwth** adj uncouth, rough
**sgil** nm pillion; **~ effaith** side effect
**sgiw** nf settle; **ar y ~** askew
**sglefren** nf slide
**sglefrio** vb skate, slide
**sgolor (-ion)** nm scholar
**sgôr** nm score
**sgrafell (-i)** nf scraper
**sgrech y coed** nf jay
**sgrechian** vb shriek
**sgrîn (-au)** nf screen
**sgriw (-iau)** nf screw
**sgwâr (-iau)** nm square
**sgwd (sgydiau)** nf cataract, waterfall

**sgwrs** (sgyrsiau) *nf* talk, chat, conversation

**sgwrsio** *vb* talk, chat

**si** *nm* whiz, buzz; rumour, murmur

**siaced** (-i) *nf* jacket, coat

**siâd** (sidau) *nf* pate

**sialc** *nm* chalk

**sialens** *nf* challenge

**sialensio** *vb* challenge

**siambr** *nf* chamber

**sianel** (-i, -ydd) *nf* channel

**siant** (-au) *nf* chant

**siâr** *nf* share

**siarad** *vb* talk, speak ▷ *nm* talk

**siaradus** *adj* talkative, garrulous

**siaradwr** (-wyr) *nm* talker, speaker

**siario** *vb* share

**siars** *nf* charge, command

**siarsio** *vb* charge, enjoin, warn

**siart** (-iau) *nm* chart

**siartr** (-au) *nf* charter

**siasbi** *nm* shoehorn

**siawns** *nf* chance

**siawnsio** *vb* chance

**sibrwd** *vb* whisper, murmur ▷ (-ydion) *nm* whisper, murmur

**sicr** *adj* sure, certain; secure

**sicrhau** *vb* assure, affirm, confirm; secure

**sicrwydd** *nm* certainty, assurance

**sidan** (-au) *nm* silk

**sidanaidd** *adj* silky

**sidanbryf** (-ed) *nm* silkworm

**siêd** *nm* escheat, forfeit

**sied** (-au) *nf* shed

**siesbin** *nm* shoehorn

**siew** *nf* show

**siffrwd** *vb* rustle, shuffle

**sigâr** *nf* cigar

**sigaret** (~au) *nf* cigarette

**sigledig** *adj* shaky, rickety, unstable

**siglen** (-nydd) *nf* swing; bog, swamp

**siglo** *vb* shake, quake, rock, swing, wag

**sil** (-od) *nm* spawn, fry

**silff** (-oedd) *nf* shelf

**silwair** *nm* silage

**sill** (-iau), **-af** (-au) *nf* syllable

**sillafiaeth** *nf* spelling

**sillafu** *vb* spell

**sillgoll** (-au) *nf* apostrophe

**simnai** (-neiau) *nf* chimney

**simsan** *adj* unsteady, tottering, rickety

**simsanu** *vb* totter

**sinach** (-od) *nf* balk, waste ground; skinflint

**sinc** *nm* zinc

**sinema** (sinemâu) *nf* cinema

**sinig** *nm* cynic

**sinigaidd** *adj* cynical

**sinsir** *nm* ginger

**sïo** *vb* hiss, whiz; murmur, purl

**sioe** (-au) *nf* show

**siôl** (-au) *nf* skull, pate

**siôl** (siolau) *nf* shawl

**siom** (-au) *nm* disappointment

**siomedig** *adj* disappointed, disappointing

**siomedigaeth** (-au) *nf* disappointment

**siomi** *vb* disappoint; balk, thwart; deceive

**siomiant** *nm* disappointment

**sionc** *adj* brisk, nimble, agile, active

**sioncio** *vb* brisk

**sioncrwydd** *nm* briskness, agility

**sioncyn y gwair** *nm* grasshopper

**siop** (-au) *nf* shop

**siopwr** (-wyr) *nm* shopman, shopkeeper

**sipian** *vb* sip, sup, suck

**siprys** *nm* mixed corn (oats and barley)

**sipsiwn** *npl* gipsies

**sir** (-oedd) *nf* shire, county

**siriol** *adj* cheerful, bright, pleasant

**sirioldeb** *nm* cheerfulness

**sirioli** *vb* cheer, brighten

**sirydd, -yf** (-ion) *nm* sheriff

**siryddiaeth** *nf* shrievalty

**sisial** *vb* whisper

**siswrn** (-yrnau) *nm* scissors

**siwgr** nm sugar
**siwmper** (-i) nf jumper
**siwr, siŵr** adj sure, certain
**siwrnai** (-eiau) nf journey ▷ adv once
**siwt** (-iau) nf suit
**slaf** (~iaid) nm slave, drudge
**slei** adj sly
**sleifio** vb slink
**sleisen** nf slice
**slic** adj slick
**slotian** vb paddle, dabble; tipple
**slumyn** see **ystlum**
**slwt** nf slut
**smala** adj droll
**smalio** vb joke
**sment** nm cement
**smocio** vb smoke (tobacco)
**smociwr** (-wyr) nm smoker
**smotyn** (smotiau) nm spot
**smygu** see **smocio**
**snisin** nm snuff
**snwffian** vb snuff, sniff; snuffle; whimper
**sobr** adj sober, serious
**sobreiddio, sobri** vb sober
**sobrwydd** nm sobriety, soberness
**socas** (-au) nf gaiter, legging
**sodomiaeth** nf sodomy
**sodr** nm solder
**soddi** vb submerge
**soeg** nm brewers' grains, draff
**sofl** npl (nm -yn) stubble
**sofliar** (-ieir) nf quail
**sofraniaeth** nf sovereignty
**sofren** (sofrod) nf sovereign (coin)
**solas** nm solace, joy
**sol-ffa** nm, **solffaeo** vb sol-fa
**sôn** vb, nm talk, mention, rumour
**soned** (-au) nf sonnet
**sonedwr** (-wyr) nm composer of sonnets
**soniarus** adj melodious, tuneful; loud
**soriant** nm indignation, displeasure
**sorod** npl dross, dregs, refuse

**sorri** vb chafe, sulk, be displeased
**sosban** (-nau, -benni) nf saucepan
**sosej** (-ys) nf sausage
**soser** (-i) nf saucer
**sosialaeth** nf socialism
**sothach** coll n refuse, rubbish, trash
**st-** see also **yst-**
**stac** (-iau) nf stack
**staen** (-au) nm, **-io** vb stain
**stâl** (-au) nf stall
**stamp** (-iau) nm/f stamp
**stampio** vb stamp
**starts** nm starch
**stên** (stenau) nf pitcher
**stesion** (-au) nf station
**sticil, -ill** nf stile
**stilio** vb question
**stiward** (-iaid) nm steward
**stiwdio** nf studio
**stoc** (-au) nf stock
**stomp** nf bungle, mess, muddle
**stompio** vb beat, pound; bungle, mess
**stompiwr** (-wyr) nm bungler
**stori** (-ïau, -ïâu, straeon) nf story, tale
**stormus** adj stormy
**stor(o)m** (stormydd) nf storm
**straegar** adj gossiping, gossipy
**strancio** vb play tricks
**strategaeth** nf strategy
**strategol** adj strategic
**strategydd** (-ion) nm strategist
**streic** (-iau) nf strike
**strwythur** nm structure
**stryd** (-oedd) nf street
**stwc** (stycau) nm pail, bucket
**stwff** (styffiau) nm stuff
**stwffio** vb stuff, thrust
**stwffwl** (styffylau) nm post; staple
**styffylydd** (-ion) nm stapler
**su** nm buzz, murmur, hum
**suad** nm buzzing, lulling; hum
**sucan** nm gruel
**sudd** (-ion) nm juice, sap
**suddgloch** (-glychau) nf diving-bell

**suddlong** (-au) *nf* submarine
**suddo** *vb* sink, dive; invest (money)
**sug** (-ion) *nm* juice, sap
**sugn** *nm* suck; suction; sap
**sugno** *vb* suck, imbibe, absorb
**Sul** (-iau) *nm* Sunday
**Sulgwyn** *nm* Whitsunday
**suo** *vb* buzz, hum; lull, hush
**sur** (-ion) *adj* sour, acid
**surdoes** *nm* leaven
**surni** *nm* sourness, staleness, tartness
**suro** *vb* sour
**suryn** *nm* acid
**sut** *nm* manner; plight; **pa ~? ~?** how? what sort of?
**swalpio** *vb* flounder, jump, bounce
**swci** *adj* tame, pet
**swcro** *vb* succour
**swcwr** *nm* succour
**swch** (sychau) *nf* ploughshare; tip, grimble; lips
**Sweden** *nf* Sweden
**swil** *adj* shy, bashful
**swilder** *nm* shyness, bashfulness
**swllt** (sylltau) *nm* shilling
**Swistir: y S-** *nf* Switzerland
**swm** (symiau) *nm* sum, bulk
**swmbwl** (symbylau) *nm* goad
**swmer** (-au) *nm* beam; pack
**swmp** *nm* bulk
**swmpus** *adj* bulky
**swn** *nm* noise, sound
**swnian** *vb* murmur, grumble, nag
**swnio** *vb* sound, pronounce
**swnllyd** *adj* peevish, querulous
**swnt** *nm* sound, strait
**swoleg** *nf* zoology
**swp** (sypiau) *nm* mass, heap; cluster
**swper** (-au) *nm/f* supper
**swpera, -u** *vb* give or take supper
**swrn** (syrnau) *nf* fetlock, ankle ▷ *nm* good number
**swrth** *adj* heavy, sluggish; sullen
**sws** (-ys) *nf* kiss
**swta** *adj* abrupt, curt
**swydd** (-au, -i) *nf* office; county

**swyddfa** (-feydd) *nf* office
**swyddog** (-ion) *nm* officer, official
**swyddogaeth** *nf* office, function
**swyddogol** *adj* official
**swyn** (-ion) *nm* charm, fascination, spell, magic
**swyngyfaredd** (-ion) *nf* sorcery, witchcraft
**swyngyfareddwr** (-wyr) *nm* sorcerer
**swyno** *vb* charm, enchant, bewitch
**swynol** *adj* charming, fascinating
**swynwr** (-wyr) *nm* magician, wizard
**swynwraig** (-wragedd) *nf* sorceress
**sy** *see* **sydd**
**syber** *adj* sober, decent; clean, tidy
**sych** (fsech) *adj* dry
**sychder** *nm* dryness, drought
**sychdir** (-oedd) *nm* dry land
**syched** *nm* thirst
**sychedig** *adj* thirsty, parched, dry
**sychedu** *vb* thirst
**sychin** *nm* drought
**sychlyd** *adj* dry
**sychu** *vb* dry, dry up; wipe dry, wipe
**sychydd** *nm* dryer
**sydyn** *adj* sudden, abrupt
**sydynrwydd** *nm* suddenness
**sydd** *vb* is, are
**syfi** *npl* (nfsyfïen) strawberries
**syflyd** *vb* stir, move, budge
**syfrdan** *adj* giddy, dazed, stunned
**syfrdandod** *nm* giddiness, stupor
**syfrdanol** *adj* stunning
**syfrdanu** *vb* daze, bewilder, stupefy, stun
**sylfaen** (-feini) *nf* foundation
**sylfaenol** *adj* basic
**sylfaenu** *vb* found
**sylfaenwr** (-wyr), **-ydd** (-ion) *nm* founder
**sylw** (-adau) *nm* notice, attention, remark
**sylwadaeth** *nf* observation
**sylwebaeth** *nf* commentary

**sylwedydd (-ion)** nm observer
**sylwedd (-au)** nm substance, reality
**sylweddol** adj substantial, real
**sylweddoli** vb realize
**sylweddoliad** nm realization
**sylwi** vb observe, regard, notice
**syllu** vb gaze
**symbal (-au)** nm cymbal
**symbol** nm symbol
**symboliaeth** nf symbolism
**symbyliad** nm stimulus, encouragement
**symbylu** vb goad, spur, stimulate
**symbylydd (-ion)** nm stimulant
**symio** vb sum
**syml (fseml)** adj simple
**symledd** nm simplicity
**symleiddiad** nm simplification
**symleiddio** vb simplify
**symlrwydd** nm simplicity
**symol** adj middling, fair
**symud** vb move, remove
**symudiad (-au)** nm movement, removal
**symudol** adj moving, movable, mobile
**syn** adj amazed; astonishing, surprising
**synagog (-au)** nm synagogue
**synamon** nm cinnamon
**syndod** nm marvel, amazement, surprise
**synfyfyrdod** nm reverie
**synfyfyrio** vb muse
**synhwyro** vb sense
**synhwyrol** adj sensible
**syniad (-au)** nm notion, idea, view
**syniadaeth** nf conception
**synied, -io** vb think, believe, feel
**synnu** vb marvel, be amazed, surprise, be surprised
**synnwyr (synhwyrau)** nm sense
**synwyroldeb** nm sensibleness
**synwyrusrwydd** nm sensuousness
**sypio** vb pack, heap, bundle

**sypyn (-nau)** nm package, packet
**syr** nm sir
**syrcas** nf circus
**syrffed** nm surfeit
**syrffedu** vb surfeit
**Syria** nf Syria
**syrthiedig** adj fallen
**syrthio** vb fall, tumble
**syrthni** nm listlessness, sloth; inertia
**system** nm/f system
**systematig** adj systematic
**syth** adj stiff; straight
**sythu** vb stiffen, straighten; starve with cold
**sythwelediad** nm intuition

**tabernacl (-au)** nm tabernacle
**tabl (-au)** nm table
**tablen** nf ale, beer
**tabŵ** nm taboo
**tabwrdd (-yrddau)** nm drum
**tabyrddu** vb drum, thrum
**taclau** npl (nm teclyn) tackle, gear
**taclo** vb tackle
**taclu** vb put in order, trim
**taclus** adj neat, trim, tidy
**tacluso** vb trim, tidy
**taclusrwydd** nm tidiness
**Tachwedd** nm November
**tacteg (-au)** nf tactic

**tad** (-au) *nm* father; **~-cu** grandfather

**tadmaeth** (-au, -od) *nm* fosterfather

**tadogaeth** *nf* paternity; derivation

**tadogi** *vb* father

**tadol** *adj* fatherly, paternal

**taenelliad** *nm* sprinkling, affusion

**taenellu** *vb* sprinkle

**taenellwr** (-wyr) *nm* sprinkler

**taenu** *vb* spread, expand, stretch

**taenwr** (-wyr) *nm* spreader, disseminator

**taeog** *adj* churlish, blunt ▷ (-au, -ion) *nm* churl

**taeogaidd** *adj* churlish, rude

**taer** *adj* earnest, importunate, urgent

**taerineb, taerni** *nm* earnestness, importunity

**taeru** *vb* insist, maintain; contend, wrangle

**tafarn** (-au) *nf/m* tavern, inn, public-house

**tafarndy** (-dai) *nm* public-house

**tafarnwr** (-wyr) *nm* inn-keeper, publican

**tafell** (-au, -i, tefyll) *nf* slice

**tafl** (-au) *nf* cast; scale; **ffon dafl** sling

**tafledigion** *npl* projectiles

**taflegryn** (taflegrau) *nm* missile

**tafleisiaeth** *nf* ventriloquism

**tafleisydd** (-ion, -wyr) *nm* ventriloquist

**taflen** (-nau, -ni) *nf* table, list, leaflet

**taflennu** *vb* tabulate

**tafliad** (-au) *nm* throw; set-back

**taflod** (-ydd) *nf* loft; **~ y genau** palate

**taflodol** *adj* palatal

**taflu** *vb* throw, fling, cast, hurl

**tafluniad** *nm* projection

**taflunio** *vb* project

**taflunydd** *nm* projector

**tafod** (-au) *nm* tongue

**tafodi** *vb* berate, scold

**tafodiaith** (-ieithoedd) *nf* speech, language, dialect

**tafod-leferydd** *nm* speech, utterance; **ar dafod-leferydd** by rote

**tafol** *nf* scales, balance

**tafol** *coll n* dock

**tafoli** *vb* weigh up, assess

**tafotrwg** *adj* foul-mouthed, abusive

**tafotrydd** *adj* garrulous, flippant

**tagell** (-au, tegyll) *nf* gill; wattle; dewlap; double chin

**tagellog** *adj* wattled; doublechinned

**tagfa** (-feydd) *nf* choking, strangling

**tagu** *vb* choke, stifle; strangle

**tangnefedd** *nm/f* peace

**tangnefeddu** *vb* make peace; appease

**tangnefeddus** *adj* peaceable, peaceful

**tangnefeddwr** (-wyr) *nm* peacemaker

**tai** *see* **tŷ**

**taid** (teidiau) *nm* grandfather

**tail** *nm* dung, manure

**tair** *adj f of* **tri**

**taith** (teithiau) *nf* journey, voyage, progress

**tal** *adj* tall, high, lofty

**tâl** (talau, taloedd) *nm* end, forehead

**tâl** (taliadau) *nm* pay, payment; **taloedd** rates

**talaith** (-eithiau) *nf* diadem; province, state

**talar** (-au) *nf* headland in field

**talcen** (-nau, -ni) *nm* forehead; gable

**taldra** *nm* tallness, loftiness, stature

**taleb** (-au, -ion) *nf* receipt, voucher

**taledigaeth** *nf* payment, recompense

**taleithiol** *adj* provincial

**talent** (-au) *nf* talent
**talentog** *adj* talented
**talfyriad** (-au) *nm* abbreviation, abridgement
**talfyrru** *vb* abbreviate, abridge
**talgryf** *adj* sturdy, robust; impudent
**taliad** (-au) *nm* payment
**talm** *nm* space, while; quantity, number; **er ys ~** long ago
**talog** *adj* jaunty
**talp** (-au, -iau) *nm* mass, lump
**talpiog** *adj* lumpy
**talu** *vb* pay, render; answer, suit; be worth
**talwr** (-wyr) *nm* payer
**talwrn** *nm* threshing floor; poetic contest
**tamaid** (-eidiau) *nm* morsel, bit, bite
**tan** *prep* to, till, until, as far; under
**tân** (tanau) *nm* fire
**tanbaid** *adj* fiery, hot, fervent; brilliant
**tanbeidrwydd** *nm* fierce heat, ardour
**tanchwa** (-oedd) *nf* fire-damp; explosion
**tanddaearol** *adj* underground, subterranean
**tanforol** *adj* submarine
**taniad** *nm* ignition, firing
**tanio** *vb* fire, stoke
**taniwr** (-wyr) *nm* firer, fireman, stoker
**tanlinellu** *vb* underline
**tanlwybr** *nm* subway
**tanlli** *adj*: **newydd sbon danlli** brand new
**tanllwyth** (-i) *nm* blazing fire
**tanllyd** *adj* fiery
**tannu** *vb* adjust, spread, make (bed)
**tanodd** *adv* below, beneath
**tant** (tannau) *nm* chord, string
**tanwent** *nm* fuel
**tanwydd** *coll n* firewood, fuel
**tanysgrifiad** (-au) *nm* subscription

**tanysgrifio** *vb* subscribe
**tanysgrifiwr** (-wyr) *nm* subscriber
**taradr** (terydr) *nm* auger; **~ y coed** woodpecker
**taran** (-au) *nf* (peal of) thunder
**taranfollt** (-au) *nf* thunderbolt
**taranu** *vb* thunder
**tarddell** *nf* source, spring
**tarddiad** (-au) *nm* source, derivation
**tarddle** (-oedd) *nm* source
**tarddu** *vb* sprout, spring; derive, be derived
**tarfu** *vb* scare, scatter
**targed** (-au) *nm* target
**tarian** (-au) *nf* shield
**tario** *vb* tarry
**taro** *vb* strike, smite, hit, knock; tap; stick; hot; suit
**tarren** (tarenni, -ydd) *nf* knoll, rock
**tarth** (-oedd) *nm* mist, vapour
**tarw** (teirw) *nm* bull
**tarwden** *nf* ringworm
**tas** (teisi) *nf* rick, stack
**tasel** *nm* tassel
**tasg** (-au) *nf* task
**tasgu** *vb* task; start, jump; splash, spirt
**tato, tatws** *npl* (*nf* taten, tatysen) potatoes
**taw** *nm* silence; **rhoi ~ ar** silence
**taw** *conj* that
**tawch** *nm* vapour, haze, mist, fog
**tawdd** *adj* melted, molten, dissolved
**tawedog** *adj* silent, taciturn
**tawedogrwydd** *nm* taciturnity
**tawel** *adj* calm, quiet, still, tranquil
**tawelu** *vb* calm; grow calm
**tawelwch** *nm* calm, quiet, tranquillity
**tawelydd** *nm* silencer
**tawlbwrdd** *nm* draughtboard, backgammon
**tawtologiaeth** *nf* tautology
**te** *nm* tea
**tebot** (-au) *nm* teapot

**tebyg** *adj* similar, like, likely
**tebygol** *adj* likely, probable
**tebygolrwydd** *nm* likelihood, probability
**tebygrwydd** *nm* likeness, resemblance
**tebygu** *vb* liken, resemble; suppose
**tecáu** *vb* beautify, adorn, embellish
**teclyn (taclau)** *nm* tool, instrument
**techneg** *nf* technique; **-ol** *adj* technical
**teg** *adj* fair, beautiful, fine
**tegan (-au)** *nm* plaything, toy, bauble
**tegell (-au, -i)** *nm* kettle, teakettle
**tegwch** *nm* fairness, beauty
**tei** *nm/f* tie
**teiar** *nm* tyre
**teigr (-od)** *nm* tiger
**teilchion** *npl* fragments, atoms, shivers
**teiliwr (-eilwriaid)** *nm* tailor
**teilo** *vb* dung, manure
**teilwng** *adj* worthy; deserved
**teilwra** *vb* tailor
**teilwres (-au)** *nf* tailoress
**teilwriaeth** *nf* tailoring
**teilyngdod** *nm* worthiness, merit
**teilyngu** *vb* deserve, merit; deign
**teim** *nm* thyme
**teimlad (-au)** *nm* feel, feeling, sensation, emotion; **-ol** *adj* emotional
**teimladrwydd** *nm* feelingness, sensibility
**teimladwy** *adj* feeling; sensitive
**teimlo** *vb* feel, touch, handle, manipulate
**teimlydd (-ion)** *nm* feeler, antenna, tentacle
**teios** *npl* cottages
**teip (-iau)** *nm* type
**teipiadur (-ion)** *nm* typewriter
**teipio** *vb* type
**teipydd (-ion)** *nm* typist
**teisen (-nau)** *nf* cake
**teitl (-au)** *nm* title

**teithi** *coll n* traits, characteristics, qualities
**teithio** *vb* travel, journey
**teithiol** *adj* travelling, itinerant
**teithiwr (-wyr)** *nm* traveller, passenger
**telathrebiaeth** *nf* telecommunication
**teledu** *nm* television ▷ *vb* televise
**teleffon (-au)** *nm* telephone
**teler (-au)** *nm* term, condition
**teligraff** *nm* telegraph
**telm (-au)** *nf* snare
**telori** *vb* warble; quaver
**telyn (-au)** *nf* harp
**telyneg (-ion)** *nf* lyric
**telynegol** *adj* lyrical
**telynegwr** *nm* lyric poet
**telynor (-ion)** *nm* harpist
**telynores** *nf* female harpist
**teml (-au)** *nf* temple
**tempro** *vb* temper
**temtasiwn (-iynau)** *nm/f* temptation
**temtio** *vb* tempt
**temtiwr (-wyr)** *nm* tempter
**tenant (-iaid)** *nm* tenant
**tenantiaeth** *nf* tenancy
**tenau** *adj* thin, lean; slender; rarified; sensitive
**tendio** *vb* tend, mind
**teneuad** *nm* dilution
**teneuo** *vb* thin, become thin, dilute
**teneuwch** *nm* thinness, leanness; tenuity
**tenewyn (-nau)** *nm* flank
**tenis** *nm* tennis
**tenlli(f)** *nm* lining
**tennyn (tenynnau)** *nm* cord, rope, halter
**têr** *adj* clear, refined, pure, fine
**teras (-au)** *nm* terrace
**terfyn (-au)** *nm* end, extremity, bound
**terfyniad (-au)** *nm* ending, termination
**terfynol** *adj* final; conclusive

**terfynu** vb end, terminate, determine
**terfysg** (-oedd) nm tumult, riot
**terfysgaeth** nf terrorism
**terfysgaidd, -lyd** adj riotous, turbulent
**terfysgu** vb riot, rage, surge
**terfysgwr** (-wyr) nm rioter, insurgent
**term** (-au) nm term
**terminoleg** nf terminology
**tes** nm sunshine, warmth, heat; haze
**tesog** adj sunny, hot, close, sultry
**testament** (-au) nm testament
**testamentwr** (-wyr) nm testator
**testun** (-au) nm text, theme, subject
**testunio** vb taunt, deride
**tetanws** nm tetanus
**teth** (-au) nf teat
**teulu** (-oedd) nm family
**teuluaidd** adj family, domestic
**tew** adj thick, fat, plump
**tewdra, -dwr** nm thickness, fatness
**tewhau** vb thicken, fatten
**tewi** vb keep silence, be silent
**tewychu** vb thicken, fatten; condense
**tewychydd** nm condenser
**tewyn** (-ion) nm ember, brand
**teyrn** (-edd, -oedd) nm monarch, sovereign
**teyrnas** (-oedd) nf kingdom, realm;
  **y Deyrnas Gyfunol** the United Kingdom
**teyrnasiad** (-au) nm reign
**teyrnasu** vb reign
**teyrnfradwr** (-wyr) nm traitor
**teyrnfradwriaeth** nf (high) treason
**teyrngar** adj loyal
**teyrngarwch** nm loyalty
**teyrnged** (-au) nf tribute
**teyrnwialen** (-wiail) nf sceptre
**ti** pron you; (fam)

**ticed** (-i) nm/f ticket
**tician** vb tick
**tid** (-au) nf chain
**tila** adj feeble, puny, insignificant
**tîm** (timau) nm team
**tin** (-au) nf bottom; rump; tail
**tinc** (-iadau) nm clang, tinkle
**tincian** vb tinkle, chink, clink, clank
**tip** (-iadau) nm tick (of clock)
**tipian** vb tick
**tipyn** (-nau, tipiau) nm bit
**tir** (-oedd) nm land, ground, territory
**tirio** vb land, ground
**tiriog** adj landed
**tiriogaeth** (-au) nf territory
**tiriogaethol** adj territorial
**tirion** adj kind, tender, gentle, gracious
**tiriondeb** nm kindness, tenderness
**tirlun** (-iau) nm landscape
**tirol** adj relating to land
**tirwedd** nf (Geog) relief
**tisian** vb sneeze
**titw** nf puss, pussy
**tithau** pron conj thou (on thy part), thou also
**tiwmor** nm tumour
**tiwn** (-iau) nf tune
**tiwnio** vb tune
**tlawd** (tlodion) adj poor
**tlodaidd** adj poorish, mean, dowdy
**tlodi** vb impoverish ▷ nm poverty
**tlos** adj f of **tlws**
**tloty** (-ai) nm poorhouse, workhouse
**tlotyn** (tlodion) nm pauper
**tlws** (f tlos) adj pretty
**tlws** (tlysau) nm jewel, gem; medal
**tlysni** nm prettiness
**to** (toeau) nm roof; generation
**toc** adv shortly, presently, soon
**tocio** vb clip, dock, prune
**tocyn** (tociau) nm pack, heap, hillock; slice of bread
**tocyn** (-nau) nm ticket
**tocynnwr** (-ynwyr) nm bus conductor

**toddedig** adj molten; melting
**toddi** vb melt, dissolve, thaw
**toddiant** (-nnau) nm solution
**toddion** npl dripping
**toddwr** (-wyr), **-ydd** (-ion) nm melter
**toes** nm dough
**toi** vb cover; roof; thatch
**toili** nm spectral funeral
**tolach** vb fondle
**tolc** (-iau) nm dent, dinge
**tolchen** (-au) nf clot
**tolchennu** vb clot
**tolcio** vb dent, dinge
**tolciog** adj dented, dinged
**toll** (-au) nf toll, custom
**tolli** vb take toll
**tom** nf dirt, mire, dung
**tomen** (-nydd) nf heap; dunghill
**tomlyd** adj dirty, miry
**ton** (-nau) nf wave, billow, breaker
**ton** (-nau) nm lay-land
**tôn** (tonau) nf tone; tune
**tonc** (-iau) nf tinkle, ring, clash
**toncio, -ian** vb tinkle, ring
**tonfedd** (-i) nf wavelength
**tonig** (-iau) adj tonic; (Med: Music) tonic
**tonnen** (tonennydd, -au) nf skin; sward; bog
**tonni** vb wave, undulate
**tonnog** adj wavy, billowy
**tonyddiaeth** nf tone, intonation
**topio** vb plug, stop up
**topyn** nm plug, stopper
**tor** (-ion) nm break, interruption
**tor** (-rau) nf belly; palm (of hand)
**torcalonnus** adj heartbreaking
**torch** (-au) nf wreath; coil
**torchi** vb wreathe; coil; roll, tuck
**torchog** adj wreathed; coiled
**tordyn** adj tight-bellied; hectoring
**toreithiog** adj abundant, teeming
**toreth** nf abundance
**torf** (-eydd) nf crowd, multitude
**torfynyglu** vb break neck of; behead

**torgoch** (-ion) nm roach
**torgwmwl** nm cloudburst
**torheulo** vb bask, sunbathe
**tori** (-ïaid) nm tory
**toriad** (-au) nm cut, break; fraction
**torïaeth** nf toryism
**torïaidd** adj tory, conservative
**torlan** (-nau, -lennydd) nf river bank
**torllengig** nm rupture
**torllwyth** (-i), **torraid** nf litter
**torogen** (-ogod) nf tick (in cattle)
**torri** vb break, cut; dig; write, trace
**torrwr** (torwyr) nm breaker, cutter
**tors** nm/f torch
**torsyth** adj swaggering
**torsythu** vb strut, swagger
**torth** (-au) nf loaf
**tost** adj severe, sharp, sore; ill
**tost** nm toast
**tosturi** (-aethau) nm compassion, pity
**tosturio** vb be compassionate, pity
**tosturiol** adj compassionate
**tosyn** (tosau) nm pimple
**töwr** (towyr) nm tiler
**tra** adv over; very ▷ conj while, whilst
**tra-arglwyddiaeth** (-au) nf tyranny
**tra-arglwyddiaethu** vb tyrannize
**tra-awdurdodi** vb lord it over, domineer
**trabludd** nm trouble, tumult, turmoil
**trac** (-iau) nm track
**trachefn** adv again
**trachwant** (-au) nm lust, covetousness
**trachwanta, -tu** vb lust, covet
**trachwantus** adj covetous
**tradwy** adv three days hence
**traddodi** vb deliver; commit
**traddodiad** (-au) nm tradition; delivery
**traddodiadol** adj traditional

**traddodwr** (-wyr) *nm* deliverer

**traean** *nm* one third, the third part

**traed** *see* **troed**

**traeth** (-au) *nm* strand, shore, beach

**traethawd** (-odau) *nm* treatise, essay; tract

**traethell** (-au) *nf* strand, sandbank

**traethiad** (-au) *nm* predicate

**traethodydd** (-ion) *nm* essayist

**traethu** *vb* utter, declare; treat

**trafael** (-ion) *nf* travail, trouble

**trafaelio** *vb* travel

**trafaeliwr** (-wyr) *nm* traveller

**trafaelu** *vb* travel; travail

**traflyncu** *vb* guzzle, gulp, devour

**trafnidiaeth** *nf* traffic

**trafod** *vb* handle; discuss; transact

**trafodaeth** (-au) *nf* discussion, transaction

**trafodion** *npl* transactions

**trafferth** (-ion) *nf/m* trouble

**trafferthu** *vb* trouble

**trafferthus** *adj* troublesome; troubled

**tragwyddol** *adj* everlasting, eternal

**tragwyddoldeb** *nm* eternity

**tragywydd** *adj* everlasting, eternal

**traha** *nm* arrogance, presumption

**trahaus** *adj* arrogant, haughty

**trahauster** *nm* arrogance, presumption

**trai** *nm* ebb

**trais** *nm* oppression, force, violence

**trallod** (-ion, -au) *nm* trouble, tribulation

**tralludi** *vb* afflict, vex, trouble

**trallodus** *adj* troubled; troublous

**trallodwr** (-wyr) *nm* troubler, afflicter

**tramgwydd** (-iadau) *nm* stumbling; offence

**tramgwyddo** *vb* stumble; offend; take offence

**tramgwyddus** *adj* scandalous; offensive

**tramor** *adj* foreign

**tramorwr** (-wyr) *nm* foreigner

**tramwy, -o** *vb* pass, traverse

**tramwyfa** (-feydd) *nf* passage, thoroughfare

**tranc** *nm* end, dissolution, death

**trancedig** *adj* deceased

**trancedigaeth** *nf* death, decease

**trannoeth** *adv* next day ▷ *nm* the morrow

**trapio** *vb* trap

**traphlith** *adv*: **blith draphlith** higgledy-piggledy

**tras** *nf* kindred, affinity

**traserch** *nm* great love, infatuation

**trasiedi** (trasiedïau) *nf* tragedy

**traul** (treuliau) *nf* wear; cost, expense; digestion

**trawiad** (-au) *nm* stroke, beat, flash

**trawiadol** *adj* striking

**traws** *adj* cross; froward, perverse

**trawsblannu** *vb* transplant

**trawsdoriad** *nm* cross-section

**trawsenwad** *nm* metonymy

**trawsfeddiannu** *vb* usurp

**trawsfudo** *vb* transmigrate

**trawsffurfio** *vb* transform

**trawsgludo** *vb* transport, conduct

**trawsgyweiriad** *nm* transposition, modulation

**trawsgyweirio** *vb* transpose, change key

**trawslif** *nm* cross-saw

**trawslythrennu** *vb* transliterate

**traws-sylweddiad** *nm* transubstantiation

**trawst** (-iau) *nm* beam

**trebl** *nm, adj* treble

**treblu** *vb* treble

**trech** *adj* superior, stronger, mightier

**trechu** *vb* overpower, overcome, conquer

**tref** (-i, -ydd) *nf* home; town

**trefedigaeth** (-au) *nf* settlement, colony

**trefgordd** (-au) *nf* township

**treflan** (-nau) *nf* small town, townlet

**trefn** (-au) *nf* order, method, system

**trefniad** (-au) *nm* arrangement, ordering

**trefniant** *nm* arrangement, organization

**trefnlen** (-ni) *nf* schedule

**trefnu** *vb* order, arrange, dispose

**trefnus** *adj* orderly, methodical

**trefnusrwydd** *nm* orderliness

**trefnydd** (-ion) *nm* arranger; Methodist

**trefol** *adj* town, urban

**treftadaeth** *nf* patrimony, inheritance

**trengi** *vb* die, perish, expire

**treial** (-on) *nm* trial

**treiddgar** *adj* penetrating, keen

**treiddgarwch** *nm* penetration, acumen

**treiddio** *vb* pass, penetrate

**treiddiol** *adj* penetrating

**treigl** (-au) *nm* turn, revolution, course

**treigl(i)ad** (-au) *nm* mutation; inflection

**treiglo** *vb* roll; mutate; inflect; decline

**treio** *vb* ebb

**treio** *vb* try

**treisiad** (-iedi) *nf* heifer

**treisio** *vb* force, ravish, violate, oppress, rape

**treisiwr** (-wyr) *nm* violator, oppressor; rapist

**trem** (-iau) *nf* sight, look, aspect

**tremio** *vb* look, gaze

**trên** (trenau) *nm* train

**trennydd** *adv* day after tomorrow

**tres** (-i) *nf* trace, chain; tress

**tresbasu, tresmasu** *vb* trespass

**tresglen** *nf* thrush

**treth** (-i) *nf* rate, tax, tribute; **~ y pen** community charge, poll tax

**trethadwy** *adj* rateable, taxable

**trethdalwr** (-wyr) *nm* ratepayer

**trethu** *vb* tax, rate, assess

**trethwr** (-wyr) *nm* taxer

**treuliad** *nm* digestion

**treulio** *vb* wear, consume; spend; digest

**tri** (ftair) *adj, nm* three

**triagl** *nm* treacle, balsam, balm

**triawd** (-au) *nm* trio

**triban** (-nau) *nm* triplet (*metre*); Plaid Cymru badge

**tribiwnlys** (-oedd) *nm* tribunal

**tric** (-iau) *nm* trick

**tridiau** *npl* three days

**trigain** *adj, nm* sixty

**trigfa** (-feydd), **-fan** (-nau) *nf* dwelling-place, abode

**trigiannol** *adj* residentiary

**trigiannu** *vb* reside, dwell

**trigiannydd** (-ianwyr) *nm* resident

**trigo** *vb* stay, abide; dwell; die (*animals*)

**trigolion** *npl* inhabitants, dwellers

**trimio** *vb* trim

**trin** (-oedd) *nf* battle

**trin** *vb* handle; treat; dress; till; transact

**trindod** (-au) *nf* trinity

**tringar** *adj* skilful, tender

**triniaeth** (-au) *nf* treatment

**trioedd** *npl* triads

**triongl** (-au) *nm/f* triangle

**trionglog** *adj* triangular

**trist** *adj* sad, sorrowful

**tristáu** *vb* sadden, grieve

**tristwch** *nm* sadness, sorrow

**triw** *adj* loyal, faithful

**tro** (~eau, -eon) *nm* turn, twist; conversion

**troad** (-au) *nm* bend, turning; figure of speech

**trobwll** (-byllau) *nm* whirlpool

**trobwynt** (-iau) *nm* turning-point

**trochfa** (-feydd) *nf* plunge, immersion

**trochi** *vb* dip, plunge, immerse; soil

**trochion** *npl* lather, suds, foam

**trochioni** *vb* lather, foam

**trochwr** (-wyr) nm immerser, immersionist
**troed** (traed) nm/f foot, base; leg; handle
**troedfainc** (-feinciau) nf footstool
**troedfedd** (-i) nf foot (=12 inches)
**troëdig** adj turned, converted, perverse
**tröedigaeth** (-au) nf turning, conversion
**troedio** vb foot, tread, trudge
**troednodyn** nm footnote
**troednoeth** adj barefoot, barefooted
**troedwst** nf gout
**troell** (-au) nf wheel, spinning-wheel
**troelli** vb spin; twist, wind
**troellog** adj winding, tortuous
**troellwr** (-wyr) nm disc-jockey
**troetffordd** (-ffyrdd) nf footway, footpath
**trofa** (-feydd) nf turn; bend, turning
**trofan** (-nau) nf tropic
**trofannol** adj tropical
**trofaus** adj perverse
**trofwrdd** (-fyrddau) nm turntable
**trogen** see **torogen**
**trogylch** (-au) nm orbit
**troi** vb turn, revolve; convert; plough
**trol** (-iau) nf cart
**trolian, -io** vb roll
**troliwr** (-wyr) nm carter
**trom** adj f of **trwm**
**tros** prep over, for, instead of, on behalf of
**trosedd** (-au) nm transgression, offence, crime
**troseddol** adj criminal
**troseddu** vb transgress, trespass, offend
**troseddwr** (-wyr) nm transgressor, trespasser, offender; criminal
**trosgais** (trosgeisiau) nm converted try
**trosglwyddiad** nm transference, transfer

**trosglwyddo** vb hand over, transfer
**trosgynnol** adj transcendental
**trosi** vb turn; translate; convert (a try)
**trosiad** (-au) nm translation; metaphor; conversion (rugby)
**trosodd** adv over, beyond
**trosol** (-ion) nm lever, crow-bar, bar; staff
**trostan** (-au) nf pole
**trotian** vb trot
**trothwy** (-au) nm threshold
**trowr** (-wyr) nm ploughman
**trowsus** (-au) nm trousers
**trowynt** (-oedd) nm whirlwind, tornado
**truan** (truain, f~es) adj poor, wretched, miserable ▷ (trueiniaid) nm wretch
**trueni** nm wretchedness; misery; pity
**truenus** adj wretched, miserable
**trugaredd** (-au) nf/m mercy, compassion
**trugarhau** vb have mercy, take pity
**trugarog** adj merciful, compassionate
**trugarowgrwydd** nm mercifulness
**trulliad** (-iaid) nm butler, cupbearer
**trum** (-au, -iau) nm ridge
**truth** nm flattery; rigmarole
**trwbl** nm, **-o** vb trouble
**trwch** nm thickness; **~ y blewyn** hair's breadth
**trwch** adj broken; unfortunate; wicked
**trwchus** adj thick
**trwm** (trymion), f (trom) adj heavy
**trwnc** (trynciau) nm trunk
**trwodd** adv through
**trwsgl** adj awkward, clumsy, bungling
**trwsiad** nm dress, attire
**trwsiadus** adj well-dressed, smart
**trwsio** vb dress, trim; mend, repair

**trwsiwr**(-**wyr**) *nm* mender, repairer
**trwst** *nm* noise, din, tumult
**trwstan** *adj* awkward, clumsy, untoward
**trwstaneiddiwch** *nm* awkwardness
**trwy** *prep* through, by, by means of
**trwyadl** *adj* thorough
**trwydded**(-**au**) *nf* leave, licence
**trwyddedu** *vb* license
**trwyn**(-**au**) *nm* nose, snout; point, cape
**trwyno** *vb* nose, nuzzle, sniff
**trwynol** *adj* nasal
**trwynsur** *adj* sour, morose
**trwyth**(-**i**) *nm* decoction, infusion, urine
**trwytho** *vb* steep, saturate, imbue
**trybedd, trybed** *nf* tripod, trivet
**trybelid** *adj* bright, brilliant
**trybestod** *nm* commotion, bustle, fuss
**trybini** *nm* trouble, misfortune, misery
**tryblith** *nm* muddle, chaos
**trychfil**(-**od**) *nm* insect, animalcule
**trychiad**(-**au**) *nm* cutting, fracture, section
**trychineb**(-**au**) *nm/f* disaster, calamity
**trychinebus** *adj* disastrous, calamitous
**trychu** *vb* cut, hew, pierce, lop
**trydan** *nm* electric fluid, electricity
**trydaneg** *nm/f* electrical engineering
**trydaniaeth** *nf* electricity; thrill
**trydanol** *adj* electric, electrical
**trydanu** *vb* electrify
**trydar** *nm, vb* chirp, chatter
**trydydd** (*f* **trydedd**) *adj* third
**tryfer**(-**i**) *nf* harpoon, trident
**tryferu** *vb* spear, harpoon
**tryfesur** *nm* diameter
**tryfrith** *adj* speckled; swarming, teeming
**trylediad**(-**au**) *nm* diffusion

**tryledu** *vb* diffuse
**tryloyw** *adj* pellucid, transparent
**tryloywder** *nm* transparency
**trylwyr** *adj* thorough
**trylwyredd** *nm* thoroughness
**trymaidd** *adj* heavy, close, oppressive
**trymder** *nm* heaviness, drowsiness
**trymfryd** *nm* sadness, sorrow
**trymhau** *vb* make or grow heavy
**trymllyd** *adj* heavy, close, oppressive
**tryryw** *adj* thoroughbred
**trysor**(-**au**) *nm* treasure
**trysordy**(-**dai**) *nm* treasurehouse
**trysorfa**(-**feydd**) *nf* treasury, fund
**trysori** *vb* treasure
**trysorlys** *nm* treasury, exchequer
**trysorydd**(-**ion**) *nm* treasurer
**trystio** *vb* make a noise; trust
**trystiog** *adj* noisy, rowdy
**trythyll** *adj* wanton, lascivious
**trythyllwch** *nm* lasciviousness
**trywanu** *vb* transfix, stab, pierce
**trywel** *nm* trowel
**trywydd** *nm* scent, trail
**Tseina** *nf* China
**tu** *nm* side, part, direction
**tua, tuag** *prep* towards; about
**tuchan** *vb* grumble, groan, murmur
**tudalen**(-**nau**) *nm/f* page
**tudded**(-**i**) *nf* covering; pillowcase
**tuedd**(-**iadau**) *nf* tendency, inclination
**tuedd**(-**au**) *nm* district, region
**tueddfryd** *nm* inclination, bent
**tueddol** *adj* inclined, apt
**tueddu** *vb* incline, tend, trend
**tufewnol** *adj* inward, internal
**tulath**(-**au**) *nf* beam, rafter
**Tunisia** *nf* Tunisia
**tunnell**(**tunelli**) *nf* ton; tun
**turio** *vb* root up, burrow, delve
**turn** *nm* lathe
**turniwr**(-**wyr**) *nm* turner
**turtur**(-**od**) *nf* turtle-dove
**tusw**(-**au**) *nm* wisp, bunch

**tuth** (-iau) *nm* trot
**tuthio** *vb* trot
**twb** (tybiau) *nm* tub
**twca** *nm* tuck-knife
**twffyn** (twffiau) *nm* tuft
**twlc** (tylciau) *nm* sty
**twlcio** *vb* horn, butt, gore
**twlciog** *adj* given to horning
**twll** (tyllau) *nm* hole
**twmpath** (-au) *nm* tump, hillock; bush; folk-dance
**twndis** (-au) *nm* funnel
**twndra** (-âu) *nm* tundra
**twnffed** (-i) *nm* funnel
**twnnel** (twnelau) *nm* tunnel
**twp** *adj* stupid, dull, obtuse
**twpdra** *nm* stupidity
**twpsyn** *nm* stupid person
**tŵr** (tyrau) *nm* tower
**twr** (tyrrau) *nm* heap; group, crowd
**Twrc** (Tyrciaid) *nm* Turk
**Twrci** *nf* Turkey
**twrci** (-ïod) *nm* turkey
**twrch** (tyrchod) *nm* hog; **~ daear** mole
**twrf** (tyrfau) *nm* noise; (*pl*) thunder
**twrnai** (-eiod) *nm* attorney, lawyer
**twrw** *nm* noise (**twrf**)
**twt** *excl* tut!
**twt** *adj* tidy, neat, smart
**twtio** *vb* tidy
**twyll** *nm* deceit, deception, fraud
**twyllo** *vb* deceive, cheat, swindle
**twyllodrus** *adj* deceitful, false
**twyllresymeg** *nf* sophism
**twyllresymiad** (-au) *nm* sophistry
**twyllwr** (-wyr) *nm* deceiver
**twym** *adj* warm, hot, sultry
**twymder, twymdra** *nm* warmness, warmth
**twymgalon** *adj* warm-hearted
**twymo, twymno** *vb* warm, heat
**twymyn** (-au) *nf* fever; **y dwymyn goch** scarlet fever; **y dwymyn doben** mumps
**twyn** (-i) *nm* hill, hillock, knoll; bush
**twysged** *nf* lot, quantity

**tŷ** (tai, teiau) *nm* house
**tyaid** (-eidiau) *nm* houseful
**tyb** (-iau) *nm/f* opinion, notion, surmise
**tybaco** *nm* tobacco
**tybed** *adv* I wonder; is that so?
**tybiaeth** (-au) *nf* supposition
**tybied, tybio** *vb* suppose, think, imagine
**tybiedig** *adj* supposed, putative
**tycio** *vb* prosper, succeed, avail
**tydi** *pron* thou, thyself
**tyddyn** (-nod) *nm* (small) farm, holding
**tyddynnwr** (-ynwyr) *nm* smallholder
**tyfadwy** *adj* growing
**tyfiant** *nm* growth
**tyfu** *vb* grow
**tyfwr** (-wyr) *nm* grower
**tynged** *nf* destiny, fate
**tyngedfennol** *adj* fateful, fatal
**tynghedu** *vb* destine, fate; adjure
**tyngu** *vb* swear, vow
**tyngwr** (-wyr) *nm* swearer
**tylath** *see* **tulath**
**tyle** *nm* slope, hill
**tylino** *vb* knead; **~ y corff** massage
**tylinwr** (-wyr) *nm* kneader, masseur
**tylwyth** (-au) *nm* household, family; **~ teg** fairies
**tyllog** *adj* holey
**tyllu** *vb* hole, bore, perforate, pierce
**tylluan** (-od) *nf* owl
**tyllwr** (-wyr) *nm* borer
**tymer** (-herau) *nf* temper
**tymestl** (-hestloedd) *nf* tempest, storm
**tymheredd** *nm* temperature
**tymherus** *adj* temperate
**tymhestlog** *adj* tempestuous, stormy
**tymhoraidd** *adj* seasonable
**tymhorol** *adj* temporal
**tymor** (-horau) *nm* season
**tymp** *nm* (appointed) time, season

**tympan** (-au) nf drum; timbrel
**tyn** adj tight
**tynder, -dra** nm tightness, tension
**tyndro** (~eon) nm wrench
**tyner** adj tender, gentle
**tyneru** vb make tender, soften
**tynerwch** nm tenderness, gentleness
**tynfa** (-feydd) nf draw, attraction
**tynfaen** (-feini) nm loadstone, magnet
**tynhau** vb tighten, strain
**tynnu** vb draw, pull; take off, remove
**tyno** nm hollow; tenon
**tyrchu** vb root up, burrow
**tyrchwr** (-wyr) nm mole-catcher
**tyrfa** (-oedd) nf multitude, host, crowd
**tyrfau** npl thunder
**tyrfedd** (-au) nm turbulence, thunder
**tyrfo, tyrfu** vb make a noise or commotion
**tyrpant** nm turpentine
**tyrpeg** nm turnpike
**tyrru** vb heap, amass; crowd together
**tyst** (-ion) nm witness
**tysteb** (-au) nf testimonial
**tystio** vb testify, witness
**tystiolaeth** (-au) nf testimony, evidence
**tystiolaethu** vb bear witness, testify
**tystlythyr** (-au) nm testimonial
**tystysgrif** (-au) nf certificate
**tywallt** vb pour, shed, spill
**tywalltiad** (-au) nm outpouring
**tywarchen** (tywyrch) nf sod, turf
**tywel** (-ion) nm towel
**tywod** nm sand
**tywodfaen** nm sandstone
**tywodlyd, -odog** adj sandy
**tywodyn** nm grain of sand
**tywydd** nm weather
**tywyll** adj dark, obscure; blind

**tywyllu** vb darken, obscure
**tywyllwch** nm darkness
**tywyn** (-au) nm sea-shore, strand
**tywynnu** vb shine
**tywys** vb lead, guide
**tywysen** (-nau, tywys) nf ear of corn
**tywysog** (-ion) nm prince
**tywysogaeth** (-au) nf principality
**tywysogaidd** adj princely
**tywysoges** (-au) nf princess
**tywysydd** (-ion) nm leader, guide

**theatr** (-au) nf theatre
**thema** (themâu) nf theme
**theorem** (-au) nf theorem
**theori** (-ïau) nf theory
**thermomedr** nm thermometer
**thesis** (-au) nm thesis
**thus** nm frankincense

# u

**ubain** *vb* howl, wail, moan; sob
**uchaf** *adj* uppermost, highest
**uchafbwynt** (-iau) *nm* climax;
zenith
**uchafiaeth** *nf* supremacy;
ascendancy
**uchafion** *npl* heights
**uchafrif** (-au) *nm* maximum
**uchder** *nm* height; top
**uchel** *adj* high, lofty; uppish; loud
**uchelder** (-au) *nm* highness, height
**ucheldir** (-oedd) *nm* highland
**uchelfryd** *adj* high-minded
**uchelgais** *nm/f* ambition
**uchelgeisiol** *adj* ambitious
**uchelion** *npl* heights
**uchelradd** *adj* of high degree,
superior
**uchelseinydd** (-ion) *nm*
loudspeaker
**uchelwr** (-wyr) *nm* gentleman,
nobleman
**uchelwydd** *coll n* mistletoe
**uchgapten** (-teiniaid) *nm* major
**uchod** *adv* above
**udo** *vb* howl
**udd** *nm* lord
**ufudd** *adj* obedient, humble
**ufudd-dod** *nm* obedience, humility
**ufuddhau** *vb* obey
**uffern** *nf* hell
**uffernol** *adj* infernal, hellish
**ugain** (ugeiniau) *adj, nm* twenty,
score
**Ulster** *nf* Ulster

**ulw** *coll n* ashes, powder ▷ *adv*
utterly
**un** *adj* one, only; same ▷ (-au) *coll*
*n* one, unit
**unawd** (-au) *nm/f* solo
**unawdydd** (-wyr) *nm* soloist
**unben** (-iaid, unbyn) *nm* sovereign
lord, despot
**unbenaethol** *adj* despotic
**unbennaeth** *nf* sovereignty,
despotism
**undeb** (-au) *nm* unity, union; **yr U~
Sofietaidd** the Soviet Union
**undebaeth** *nf* unionism
**undebol** *adj* united, union
**undebwr** (-wyr) *nm* unionist
**undod** (-au) *nm* unity; unit
**Undodaidd** *adj* Unitarian
**Undodiaeth** *nf* Unitarianism
**Undodwr** (-wyr, -iaid) *nm*
Unitarian
**undonedd** *nm* monotony
**undonog** *adj* monotonous
**uned** (-au) *nf* unit
**unfan** *nm* same place
**unfarn** *adj* unanimous
**unfryd, -ol** *adj* unanimous
**unfrydedd** *nm* unanimity
**unffurf** *adj* uniform
**unffurfiaeth** *nf* uniformity
**ungell** *adj* monocellular
**uniaith** *adj* monoglot
**uniawn** *adj* straight; right, upright;
just
**unig** *adj* sole, only; alone, lonely
**unigedd** *nm* loneliness, solitude
**unigol** *adj* singular; individual
▷ (-ion) *nm* individual
**unigoliaeth** *nf*, **-rwydd** *nm*
individuality
**unigrwydd** *nm* loneliness, solitude
**union** *adj* straight, direct; just,
exact
**uniondeb** *nm* straightness;
rectitude
**uniongred** *adj* orthodox
**uniongrededd** *nm/f* orthodoxy

**uniongyrch, -ol** *adj* immediate, direct
**unioni** *vb* straighten; rectify; make for
**unionsgwar** *adj* perpendicular
**unionsyth** *adj* straight, direct; erect
**unllygeidiog** *adj* one-eyed
**unman** *adv* anywhere
**unnos** *adj* of one night
**uno** *vb* join, unit, amalgamate
**unochrog** *adj* unilateral, biased
**unodl** *adj* of the same rhyme
**unol** *adj* united; **yr Unol Daleithiau** *npl* the United States
**unoli** *vb* unify
**unoliaeth** *nf* unity, oneness, identity
**unplyg** *adj* of one fold; folio; simple, ingenuous
**unplygrwydd** *nm* sincerity
**unrhyw** *adj* same; any
**unrhywiol** *adj* unisexual
**unsain** *adj* unison; **yn ~** in unison
**unsill** *adj* monosyllabic
**unswydd** *adj* of one purpose
**unwaith** *adv* once
**unwedd** *adj* like ▷ *adv* likewise
**urdd (-au)** *nf* order; rank
**urddas (-au)** *nm* dignity, honour
**urddasol** *adj* dignified, noble
**urddo** *vb* ordain, confer degree or rank
**us** *coll n* chaff
**ust** *excl, nm* hush
**ustus (-iaid)** *nm* justice, magistrate
**usuriaeth** *nf* usury
**utganu** *vb* sound a trumpet
**utganwr (-wyr)** *nm* trumpeter
**utgorn (-gyrn)** *nm* trumpet
**uwch** *adj* higher ▷ *prep* above, over
**uwchbridd (-oedd)** *nm* topsoil
**uwchgapten (-iaid)** *nm* major
**uwchradd** *nm, adj* superior
**uwchsonig** *adj* ultrasonic, supersonic
**uwd** *nm* porridge

**wadi (-iau)** *nm* wadi
**wagen (-ni)** *nf* truck, waggon
**waldio** *vb* wallop, beat
**warws (warysau)** *nm* warehouse
**wats (-iau)** *nm* watch
**wedi** *prep* after ▷ *adv* afterwards
**wedyn** *adv* afterwards, then
**weiren** *nf* wire
**weir(i)o** *vb* wire
**weithian, -ion** *adv* now, now at length
**weithiau** *adv* sometimes
**wel** *excl* well
**wele** *excl* behold, lo
**wermod** *nf* wormwood
**wfft** *excl* fie, for shame
**wfftio** *vb* cry fie, flout, scout
**whado** *vb* beat, thrash
**wiced (-i)** *nf* wicket
**wicedwr (-wyr)** *nm* wicket-keeper
**widw** *nf* widow
**Wien** *nf* Vienna
**wlser (-au)** *nm* ulcer
**wmbredd** *nm* abundance
**wraniwm** *nm* uranium
**wrth** *prep* by; with; to; because, since
**wy (-au)** *nm* egg
**wybr (-au), wybren (-nau, -nydd)** *nf* sky; cloud
**wybrol** *adj* ethereal
**wyf** *vb* I am
**wygell (-oedd)** *nf* ovary
**wylo** *vb* weep, cry
**wylofain** *vb* wail, weep ▷ *nm*

wailing
**wylofus** *adj* wailing, doleful, tearful
**ŵyn** *see* **oen**
**ŵyna** *vb* lamb
**wyneb**(-au) *nm* face, surface; front
**wyneb-ddalen** *nf* title-page
**wynebgaled** *adj* barefaced, impudent
**wyneblun**(-iau) *nm* frontispiece
**wynebu** *vb* face, front
**wynepryd** *nm* countenance
**wynwyn** *npl* onions
**ŵyr**(wyrion) *n coll* grandchild, grandson
**wysg** *nm* track; **yn ~ ei gefn** backwards
**wystrys** *npl, coll n* oysters
**wyth**(-au) *nf* eight
**wythawd**(-au, -odau) *nf* octave
**wythblyg** *adj* octavo
**wythfed** *adj* eighth
**wythnos**(-au) *nf* week
**wythnosol**(-ion) *adj* weekly
**wythnosolyn**(-olion) *nm* weekly paper
**wythongl**(-au) *nf* octagon
**wythwr**(-wyr) *nm* number eight (*rugby*)

# y

**y, yr, 'r** *adj* the
**y, yr** *preverbal and relative particle*

**ych**(-en) *nm* ox
**ychwaith** *adv* (nor) either, neither
**ychwaneg** *nm* more
**ychwanegiad**(-au) *nm* addition
**ychwanegol** *adj* additional
**ychwanegu** *vb* add, augment, increase
**ychydig** *adj, adv, nm* little, few
**ŷd**(ydau) *nm* corn
**ydlan**(-nau) *nf* stack-yard, rickyard
**ydwyf** *vb* I am
**ydys** *vb*: **yr ~ yn disgwyl** it is expected
**ydyw** *vb* is, are
**yfed** *vb* drink; absorb
**yfory** *adv* tomorrow
**yfwr**(-wyr) *nm* drinker
**yfflon** *npl* (*nm* yfflyn) shivers, pieces, bits ▷ *adj* highly annoyed
**yng** *prep* in (*mutation*); *of* **yn**
**yngan, -u** *vb* utter, speak
**ynghyd** *adv* together
**ynghylch** *prep* about, concerning
**ynglŷn â** *prep* in connection with
**ym** *prep* in (*mutation*); *of* **yn**
**ym-** *prefix* (*usu. reflexive or reciprocal*)
**yma** *adv* here, in this place; this
**ymadael, ymadaw** *vb* depart
**ymadawedig** *adj* departed, deceased
**ymadawiad** *nm* departure; decease
**ymadawol** *adj* farewell, valedictory
**ymado** *vb* depart
**ymadrodd**(-ion) *nm* speech, saying, expression
**ymadroddus** *adj* eloquent
**ymaddasu** *vb* adjust, adapt
**ymaelodi** *vb* become a member, join
**ymaelyd, ymafael, ymaflyd** *vb* take hold
**ymageru** *vb* evaporate
**ymagor** *vb* open, unfold, expand
**ymagweddiad**(-au) *nm* demeanour, attitude
**ymaith** *adv* away, hence

**ymarfer** vb practise, exercise
▷ (-**ion**) nf practice, exercise
**ymarferiad** (-**au**) nm exercise
**ymarhous** adj dilatory; long-suffering, patient
**ymaros** vb bear with, endure ▷ nm long-suffering, patience
**ymarweddiad** nm conduct, behaviour
**ymatal** vb forbear, refrain, abstain
**ymateb** vb answer, respond, correspond
**ymbalfalu** vb grope
**ymbaratoi** vb get oneself ready
**ymbarél** nm umbrella
**ymbelydredd** nm radiation
**ymbelydrol** adj radioactive
**ymbellhau** vb go further away
**ymbil** (-**iau**) nm supplication, entreaty
**ymbil, -io** vb implore, beseech, entreat
**ymboeni** vb take pains
**ymborth** nm food, sustenance
**ymbortheg** nf/m dietetics
**ymborthi** vb feed
**ymbriodi** vb marry; intermarry
**ymbwyllo** vb pause, reflect
**ymchwelyd** vb turn, return; overturn
**ymchwil** nf search, research, quest
**ymchwiliad** (-**au**) nm investigation
**ymchwydd** (-**iadau**) nm swelling, surge
**ymchwyddo** vb swell; surge
**ymdaith** vb journey, march
▷ (-**deithiau**) nf journey, march
**ymdebygu** vb grow like; resemble
**ymdeimlad** nm feeling, sense
**ymdeimlo** vb feel; be conscious of
**ymdeithio** vb travel, journey; sojourn
**ymdoddi** vb melt, become dissolved
**ymdopi** vb manage
**ymdrech** (-**ion**) nm/f effort, endeavour, struggle
**ymdrechgar** adj striving, energetic
**ymdrechu** vb wrestle; strive, endeavour
**ymdrin** vb treat, deal with
**ymdriniaeth** nf treatment; discussion
**ymdrochi** vb bathe
**ymdrochwr** (-**wyr**) nm bather
**ymdroi** vb linger, loiter, dawdle
**ymdrybaeddu** vb wallow
**ymdynghedu** vb vow
**ymddangos** vb appear, seem
**ymddangosiad** (-**au**) nm appearance
**ymddangosiadol** adj seeming, apparent
**ymddarostwng** vb submit
**ymddarostyngiad** nm humiliation, submission
**ymddatod** vb dissolve
**ymddeol** vb resign, retire
**ymddeoliad** (-**au**) nm retirement
**ymddiddan** vb talk, converse
▷ (-**ion**) nm talk, conversation
**ymddihatru** vb divest, undress
**ymddiheuriad** (-**au**) nm apology
**ymddiheuro** vb apologize
**ymddiosg** vb strip, undress
**ymddiried** vb trust ▷ nm trust, confidence
**ymddiriedaeth** nf trust, confidence
**ymddiriedolwr** (-**wyr**) nm trustee
**ymddiswyddo** vb resign
**ymddwyn** vb behave, act
**ymddygiad** (-**au**) nm behaviour, conduct; (pl) actions
**ymddyrchafu** vb exalt oneself; rise, ascend
**ymegnïo** vb exert oneself
**ymehangu** vb become enlarged, expand
**ymennydd** (**ymenyddiau**) nm brain
**ymenyn** nm butter

**ymerawdwr** (-wyr) *nm* emperor
**ymerodraeth** (-au) *nf* empire
**ymerodres** (-au) *nf* empress
**ymerodrol** *adj* imperial
**ymesgusodi** *vb* excuse oneself, apologize
**ymestyn** *vb* stretch, extend, reach
**ymestyniad** (-au) *nm* extension
**ymfalchïo** *vb* pride oneself
**ymfodloni** *vb* acquiesce
**ymfudo** *vb* emigrate
**ymfudwr** (-wyr) *nm* emigrant
**ymffrost** *nm* boast
**ymffrostio** *vb* boast, vaunt
**ymffrostiwr** (-wyr) *nm* boaster
**ymgadw** *vb* keep oneself (from), forbear
**ymgais** *nm/f* effort, attempt
**ymgasglu** *vb* gather together
**ymgecru** *vb* quarrel, wrangle
**ymgeisio** *vb* try, apply; aim at
**ymgeisydd** (-wyr) *nm* applicant, candidate
**ymgeledd** *nm* succour, care
**ymgeleddu** *vb* cherish, succour
**ymgeleddwr** (-wyr) *nm* succourer; tutor, guardian
**ymgilio** *vb* retreat, recede
**ymgiprys** *vb, nm* scramble
**ymglymu** *vb* involve, bind together
**ymglywed** *vb* feel (oneself), be inclined
**ymgnawdoliad** *nm* incarnation
**ymgodymu** *vb* wrestle, fight
**ymgofleidio** *vb* mutually embrace
**ymgom** (-ion) *nf* chat, conversation
**ymgomio** *vb* chat, converse
**ymgorfforiad** *nm* embodiment
**ymgreinio** *vb* prostrate oneself; grovel
**ymgroesi** *vb* cross oneself; beware
**ymgryfhau** *vb* strengthen oneself, be strong
**ymgrymu** *vb* bow down, stoop
**ymguddfa** *nf* shelter, hiding-place
**ymguddio** *vb* hide (oneself)
**ymgydio** *vb* copulate

**ymgydnabod** *vb* acquaint oneself
**ymgyfathrachu** *vb* have dealings with
**ymgyfeillachu** *vb* associate
**ymgyfoethogi** *vb* get rich
**ymgynghori** *vb* consult, confer
**ymgynghoriad** *nm* consultation
**ymgymeriad** (-au) *nm* undertaking
**ymgymryd** *vb* undertake
**ymgynefino** *vb* become familiar, get used to
**ymgynnal** *vb* bear up; support oneself; control oneself
**ymgynnull** *vb* assemble, congregate
**ymgyrch** (-oedd) *nm/f* campaign, expedition
**ymgyrraedd** *vb* stretch, strive after
**ymgysegriad** *nm* devotion, consecration
**ymgysegru** *vb* devote oneself
**ymhél** *vb* meddle
**ymhelaethu** *vb* abound; enlarge
**ymhell** *adv* far, afar
**ymhellach** *adv* further, furthermore
**ymherodr** *etc see* **ymerawdwr**
**ymhlith** *prep* among
**ymhlyg** *adj* implicit
**ymhoelyd** *vb* overturn, topple
**ymhoffi** *vb* take delight; boast
**ymholi** *vb* inquire
**ymholiad** (-au) *nm* inquiry
**ymhonni** *vb* lay claim to, pretend
**ymhonnwr** (-honwyr) *nm* pretender
**ymhŵedd** *vb* beseech, implore, crave
**ymhyfrydu** *vb* delight (oneself)
**ymiacháu** *vb* become healed, get well
**ymlacio** *vb* relax
**ymladd** *vb* fight ▷ (-au) *nm* fighting
**ymlâdd** *vb* kill oneself (with exertion), tire oneself out; **wedi ~**

dead beat

**ymladdfa** (-feydd) *nf* fight

**ymladdgar** *adj* pugnacious, warlike

**ymladdwr** (-wyr) *nm* fighter, combatant

**ymlaen** *adv* on, onward

**ymlafnio** *vb* toil, strive, struggle

**ymlawenhau** *vb* rejoice

**ymledu** *vb* spread, expand

**ymlenwi** *vb* fill oneself

**ymlid** *vb* pursue, chase

**ymlidiwr** (-wyr) *nm* pursuer

**ymlonyddu** *vb* grow calm or still

**ymlosgiad** *nm* combustion

**ymlusgiad** (-iaid) *nm* reptile

**ymlusgo** *vb* creep, crawl

**ymlwybro** *vb* make one's way

**ymlyniad** *nm* attachment

**ymlynu** *vb* attach, adhere, cleave (to)

**ymlynwr** (-wyr) *nm* adherent

**Ymneilltuaeth** *nf* Nonconformity

**ymneilltuo** *vb* retire

**Ymneilltuol** *adj* Nonconformist

**Ymneilltuwr** (-wyr) *nm* Nonconformist

**ymnesáu** *vb* approach, draw near

**ymochel, -yd** *vb* shelter; beware

**ymod, -i** *vb* move, stir

**ymofyn** *vb* ask, inquire, seek ▷ (-ion) *nm* inquiry

**ymofynnydd** (-ofynwyr) *nm* inquirer

**ymolchfa** (-feydd) *nf* wash; lavatory

**ymolchi** *vb* wash oneself, bathe

**ymollwng** *vb* sink, drop, give way, collapse

**ymorchestu** *vb* strive, labour

**ymorffwys** *vb* rest, repose

**ymorol** *vb* seek; take care, attend to, see to it

**ymosod** *vb* attack, assail, assault

**ymosodiad** (-au) *nm* attack, assault

**ymosodol** *adj* aggressive, offensive, forward

**ymosodwr** (-wyr) *nm* attacker, assailant

**ymostwng** *vb* stoop; humble oneself; submit

**ymostyngar** *adj* submissive

**ymostyngiad** *nm* submission

**ympryd** (-ion) *nm* fast

**ymprydio** *vb* fast

**ymprydiwr** (-wyr) *nm* faster

**ymrafael** (-ion) *nm* quarrel, contention

**ymrafaelgar** *adj* quarrelsome, contentious

**ymraniad** (-au) *nm* division, schism

**ymrannu** *vb* part, divide, separate

**ymrannwr** (-ranwyr) *nm* separatist

**ymreolaeth** *nf* self-government, Home Rule

**ymrestru** *vb* enlist

**ymresymiad** (-au) *nm* reasoning, argument

**ymresymu** *vb* reason, argue

**ymresymwr** (-wyr) *nm* reasoner

**ymrithio** *vb* appear

**ymroad** *nm* application, devotion

**ymroddedig** *adj* devoted

**ymroddgar** *adj* of great application

**ymroddi, ymroi** *vb* apply or devote oneself; yield or resign oneself, surrender, do one's best

**ymroddiad** *nm* application, devotion

**ymron** *adv* nearly, almost

**ymrous** *adj* assiduous

**ymrwyfo** *vb* struggle, toss about

**ymrwygo** *vb* tear, burst

**ymrwymiad** (-au) *nm* engagement

**ymrwymo** *vb* bind or engage oneself

**ymryson** *vb* contend, strive ▷ (-au) *nm* contention, strife, rivalry

**ymrysongar** *adj* contentious

**ymsefydlu** *vb* establish oneself,

settle

**ymsefydlwr** (-wyr) nm settler
**ymserchu** vb cherish, dote
**ymson** vb soliloquize ▷ (-au) nm soliloquy
**ymsuddiant** nm subsidence
**ymswyno** vb cross oneself; beware
**ymsymud** vb move
**ymuno** vb join, unite
**ymwacâd** nm kenosis
**ymwacáu** vb empty oneself
**ymwadiad** nm denial, abnegation
**ymwadu** vb deny (oneself); renounce
**ymwahanu** vb part, divide, separate
**ymwahanwr** (-wyr) nm separatist
**ymwared** nm deliverance
**ymwasgu** vb embrace, hug
**ymweithydd** (-ion) nm reactor
**ymweld** vb visit
**ymweliad** (-au) nm visit, visitation
**ymwelwr, -ydd** (-wyr) nm visitor, visitant
**ymwrando** vb hearken
**ymwroli** vb take heart, be of good courage
**ymwrthod** vb abstain; renounce
**ymwrthodiad** nm abstinence
**ymwthgar** adj pushing, obtrusive
**ymwthio** vb push oneself, obtrude
**ymwthiol** adj obtrusive, intrusive
**ymwybodol** adj conscious
**ymwybyddiaeth** nf consciousness
**ymwylltio** vb fly into a passion
**ymyl** (-au, -on) nm/f edge, border, margin
**ymylu** vb border
**ymylwe** nf selvedge
**ymyrgar** adj meddlesome, officious
**ymyrraeth, ymyrru, -yd** vb meddle, interfere ▷ nf interference
**ymyrrwr** (-yrwyr) nm meddler
**ymysg** prep among, amid
**ymysgaroedd** npl bowels

**ymysgwyd** vb bestir oneself
**yn** prep in, at, into; for also introduces verb-nouns
**yn** adj particle
**yna** adv there; then; thereupon; that
**ynad** (-on) nm judge, justice, magistrate
**yn awr** adv now, at present
**yndeintiad** (-au) nm indentation
**ynfyd** (-ion) adj foolish, rash
**ynfydrwydd** nm foolishness, folly
**ynfydu** vb rave, be mad
**ynfytyn** (-fydion) nm fool, madman
**ynni** nm energy, vigour
**yno** adv there
**yntau** pron conj he (on his part), he also
**ynteu, ynte** conj or, or else, otherwise; then
**Ynyd** nm Shrovetide
**ynys** (-oedd) nf island, river meadow
**ynysfor** (-oedd) nm archipelago
**Ynysoedd, Dedwydd; yr Ynysoedd** npl the Canary Islands
**ynysol** adj island, insular
**ynyswr** (-wyr) nm islander
**ynysydd** (-ion) nm insulator
**yr** see **y**
**yrhawg** adv for a long time (to come)
**yrŵan** adv now (N.W.)
**ys** vb it is ▷ conj as
**ysbaddu** vb castrate
**ysbaid** (-beidiau) nm/f space (of time)
**ysbail** (-beiliau) nf spoil, plunder
**ysbardun** nm/f spur
**ysbarduno** vb spur
**ysbeidiol** adj occasional, intermittent
**ysbeilio** vb spoil, plunder
**ysbeiliwr** (-wyr) nm spoiler, robber
**ysbienddrych** (-au) nm spying-glass
**ysbïo** vb spy, look

**ysbïwr** (-**wyr**) nm spy
**ysblander** nm splendour
**ysblennydd** adj splendid
**ysbonc** (-**iau**) nf jump, bound; spurt
**ysboncio** vb jump, bounce; spurt, splash
**ysborion** npl cast-offs
**ysbrigyn** nm sprig, twig
**ysbryd** (-**ion**, -**oedd**) nm spirit, ghost
**ysbrydegaeth** nf spiritualism
**ysbrydegol** adj spiritualistic
**ysbrydegydd** (-**ion**) nm spiritualist
**ysbrydiaeth** nf encouragement, inspiration
**ysbrydol** adj spiritual; high-spirited
**ysbrydoli** vb spiritualize; inspire; inspirit
**ysbrydoliaeth** nf inspiration
**ysbwng** nm sponge
**ysbwrial**, -**iel** nm rubbish, refuse
**ysbwylio** vb spoil
**ysbyty** (-**tai**) nm hospital; hospice
**ysfa** (-**feydd**) nf itching; hankering
**ysg-** see **sg-**
**ysgadan** npl (nm -**enyn**) herrings
**ysgafala** adj secure, careless, free
**ysgafn** adj light ▷ nm stack
**ysgafnder** nm lightness, levity
**ysgafnhau**, **ysgafnu** vb lighten
**ysgafnu** vb heap, pile
**ysgall** npl (nf -**en**) thistles
**ysgariad** nm, -**iaeth** nf separation, divorce
**ysgarlad** nm scarlet
**ysgarmes** (-**oedd**, -**au**) nf skirmish
**ysgaru** vb part, separate, divorce
**ysgatfydd** adv perhaps, peradventure
**ysgathru** vb spread, scatter
**ysgaw** coll n (nf -**en**) elder
**ysgeler** adj wicked, villainous, infamous
**ysgerbwd** (-**bydau**) nm skeleton, carcase

**ysgithr** (-**edd**) nm tusk, fang
**ysgithrog** adj fanged, tusked; craggy, rugged
**ysgiw** (-**ion**) nf settle
**ysglefrio** vb slide (on ice); skate
**ysglyfaeth** (-**au**) nf prey, spoil; carrion, filth
**ysglyfaethus** adj of prey; rapacious
**ysgogi** vb move, stir
**ysgogiad** (-**au**) nm movement, motion
**ysgol** (-**ion**) nf school; schooling
**ysgol** (-**ion**) nf ladder
**ysgoldy** (-**dai**) nm schoolhouse, schoolroom
**ysgolfeistr** (-**i**, -**iaid**) nm schoolmaster
**ysgolfeistres** (-**i**) nf schoolmistress
**ysgolhaig** (-**heigion**) nm scholar
**ysgolheictod** nm scholarship
**ysgolheigaidd** adj scholarly
**ysgolor** (-**ion**) nm scholar
**ysgoloriaeth** (-**au**) nf scholarship
**ysgorpion** (-**au**) nm scorpion
**Ysgotyn** (-**gotiaid**) nm Scot, Scotsman
**ysgrafell** (-**od**, -**i**) nf scraper; curry-comb
**ysgrafellu** vb scrape, curry
**ysgraff** (-**au**) nf boat, barge, ferry-boat
**ysgraffinio** vb scarify, graze, abrade
**ysgrech** (-**feydd**) nf scream, shriek
**ysgrechian**, -**in** vb scream, shriek
**ysgrepan** (-**au**) nf wallet, scrip
**ysgrif** (-**au**) nf writing, article, essay
**ysgrifbin** (-**nau**) nm, -**grifell** (-**au**) nf pen
**ysgrifen**, -**eniad** (-**iadau**) nf writing
**ysgrifennu** vb write
**ysgrifennwyr** (-**enwyr**) nm writer
**ysgrifennydd** (-**enyddion**) nm scribe, secretary
**ysgrifenyddiaeth** nf

secretaryship
**ysgriw** (-iau) *nf* screw
**ysgriwio** *vb* screw
**ysgrwbio** *vb* scrub
**ysgryd** *nm* shiver
**ysgrythur** (-au) *nf* scripture
**ysgrythurol** *adj* scriptural
**ysgrythurwr** (-wyr) *nm* scripturist
**ysgub** (-au) *nf* sheaf; broom
**ysgubo** *vb* sweep
**ysgubol** *adj* sweeping
**ysgubor** (-iau) *nf* barn, granary
**ysgubwr** (-wyr) *nm* sweeper, sweep
**ysgutor** (-ion) *nm* executor
**ysguthan** (-od) *nf* wood-pigeon; jade
**ysgwâr** *adj, nf* square
**ysgwario** *vb* square
**ysgŵd** *nm* jerk, toss, fling, shove
**ysgwïer** (-iaid) *nm* squire
**ysgwrfa** *nf* scouring, lathering
**ysgwrio** *vb* scour, scrub; lather
**ysgwyd** *vb* shake; flutter; wag
**ysgwydd** (-au) *nf* shoulder
**ysgwyddo** *vb* shoulder, jostle
**ysgydwad** *nm* shaking, shake
**ysgyfaint** *npl* lungs, lights
**ysgyfarnog** (-od) *nf* hare
**ysgymun** *adj* excommunicate, accursed
**ysgymundod** *nm* excommunication, ban
**ysgymuno** *vb* excommunicate
**ysgyrion** *npl* staves, splinters, shivers
**ysgyrnygu** *vb* grind the teeth, snarl
**ysgytiad** (-au) *nm* shock
**ysgytio** *vb* shake violently, shock
**ysgythru** *vb* cut, carve; prune
**ysictod** *nm* contusion; sprain
**ysig** *adj* bruised, sore, sprained
**ysigo** *vb* bruise, crush; sprain
**yslotian** *vb* dabble, tipple
**ysmala** *adj* droll, funny, amusing
**ysmaldod** *nm* fun, drollery
**ysmalio** *vb* joke, jest

**ysmaliwr** (-wyr) *nm* joker, wit
**ysmotyn** (ysmotiau) *nm* spot
**ysmwddio** *vb* iron
**ysmygu** *vb* smoke (tobacco)
**ysmygwr** (-wyr) *nm* smoker
**ysol** *adj* consuming, devouring; corrosive
**yst-** *see also* **st-**
**ystabl** (-au) *nf* stable
**ystad** (-au) *nf* state; estate; furlong
**ystadegau** *npl* statistics
**ystadegol** *adj* statistical
**ystadegydd** (-ion) *nm* statistician
**ystafell** (-oedd) *nf* chamber, room
**ystalwyn** (-i) *nm* stallion
**ystanc** (-iau) *nm* stake, bracket
**ystarn** (-au) *nf* stern
**ystelcian** *vb* skulk, loaf, loiter
**ystelciwr** (-wyr) *nm* loafer, loiterer
**ystên** (-enau) *nf* pitcher, ewer, milk-can
**ystinos** *nm* asbestos
**ystiwart** (-wardiaid) *nm* steward
**ystlum** (-od) *nm* bat
**ystlys** (-au) *nf* side, flank
**ystlyswr** (-wyr) *nm* linesman
**ystod** (-ion) *nf* course; swath; **Yn ~** during
**ystof** *nm/f* warp
**ystofi** *vb* warp; weave, plan
**ystôl** (-olion) *nf* stool, chair
**ystôr** (-orau) *nm* store, abundance
**ystordy** (-dai) *nm* storehouse, warehouse
**ystorfa** (-feydd) *nf* store, storehouse
**ystorio** *vb* store
**ystorïwr** (-ïwyr) *nm* storyteller
**ystorm** (-ydd) *nf* storm
**ystormus** *adj* stormy
**ystrad** (-au) *nm/f* vale, flat
**ystranc** (-iau) *nf* trick
**ystrancio** *vb* play tricks; jib
**ystrodur** (-iau) *nf* cart-saddle
**ystryd** (-oedd) *nf* street
**ystrydebol** *adj* stereotyped
**ystryw** (-iau) *nf* wile, craft, ruse

**ystrywgar** *adj* wily, crafty
**ystum** (-iau) *nm/f* bend; form; posture; (*pl*) grimaces
**ystumio** *vb* bend, distort; pose
**ystumog** (-au) *nf* stomach
**ystŵr** *nm* stir, noise, bustle, fuss
**Ystwyll** *nm* Epiphany
**ystwyrian** *vb* stretch and yawn, stir
**ystwyth** *adj* flexible, pliant, supple
**ystwythder** *nm* flexibility, pliancy
**ystwytho** *vb* make flexible; bend, soften
**ystyfnig** *adj* obstinate, stubborn
**ystyfnigo** *vb* behave obstinately
**ystyfnigrwydd** *nm* obstinacy

**ystyr** (-on) *nf/m* sense, meaning
**ystyrgar** *adj* thoughtful, meditative
**ystyriaeth** (-au) *nf* consideration, heed
**ystyried** *vb* consider, regard, heed
**ystyriol** *adj* mindful, heedful
**ysu** *vb* eat, consume; hanker; itch
**yswain** (-weiniaid) *nm* esquire
**yswil** *adj* shy, bashful, timid
**yswildod** *nm* shyness, bashfulness
**yswiriant** *nm* insurance
**yswirio** *vb* insure
**ysywaeth** *adv* more's the pity
**yw** *vb* is, are
**yw** *npl*, *coll n* (*nf-en*) yew

## ENWAU PERSONAU

## PERSONAL NAMES

**Adda** Adam
**Anghrist** Antichrist
**Andreas** Andrew
**Awstin** Augustine
**Bartholomeus** Bartholomew
**Beda** Bede
**Bedwyr** Bedivere
**Beti, Betsan, Betsi** Betty, Betsy
**Buddug** Boadicea; Victoria
**Bwda** Buddha
**Cadi** Catherine, Kate
**Cadog, Catwg** Cadoc
**Cai** Kay
**Caradog** Caratacos, Caractacus
**Caswallon** Cassivellaunus
**Catrin** Catherine
**Cesar** Caesar
**Crist** Christ
**Cystennin** Constantine
**Dafydd, Dewi** David
**Edmwnt, Emwnt** Edmund
**Efa** Eve
**Elen** Helen, Ellen
**Eleias** Elijah, Elias
**Eliseus** Elisha, Eliseus
**Emrys** Ambrose
**Ercwlff** Hercules
**Eseia, Esay** Isaiah
**Esyllt** Iseult
**Fychan** Vaughan
**Fyrsil, Fferyll** Virgil
**Ffowc** Foulkes
**Ffraid** Bride, Bridget
**Garmon** Germanus
**Geraint** Gerontius
**Gerallt** Gerald
**Glyndŵr** Glendower
**Gruffudd, Gruffydd** Griffith
**Gwallter** Walter
**Gwener** Venus
**Gwenfrewi, Gwenfrewi**
  Winifred
**Gwenhwyfar** Guinevere
**Gwilym** William
**Gwladus** Gladys

**Gwrtheyrn** Vortigern
**Harri** Harry, Henry
**Horas** Horace
**Hors** Horsa
**Hu, Huw** Hugh
**Iago** James
**Iau** Jove, Jupiter
**Iesu Grist** Jesus Christ
**Ieuan** Evan
**Ioan** John
**Iorwerth** Edward
**Iwan** John
**Lowri** Laura
**Luc** Luke
**Lleucu** Lucy
**Llwyd** Lloyd
**Llŷr** Lear
**Mabli** Mabel
**Mair** Mary
**Mali** Molly
**Mallt** Maud, Matilda
**Marc** Mark
**Marged, Margred** Margaret
**Mari** Mary
**Mawrth** Mars
**Mercher** Mercury
**Mererid** Margaret
**Meurig** Morris
**Mihangel** Michael
**Modlen, Magdalen** Magdalene
**Myrddin** Merlin
**Neifion** Neptune
**Ofydd** Ovid
**Oswallt** Oswald
**Owain** Owen
**Padrig** Patrick
**Pedr** Peter
**Peredur** Perceval
**Prys** Price, Preece
**Puw** Pugh
**Pyrs** Pierce
**Rheinallt** Reginald
**Rhisiart** Richard
**Rhobert** Robert
**Rhonwen** Rowena

## ENWAU PERSONAU

**Rhydderch** Roderick
**Rhys** Rees, Rice
**Sadwrn** Saturn
**Sebedeus** Zebedee
**Selyf** Solomon
**Siân** Jane
**Siarl** Charles
**Siarlymaen** Charlemagne
**Sieffre** Geoffrey
**Siencyn** Jenkin

## PERSONAL NAMES

**Siôn** John
**Sioned** Janet
**Siôr, Siors** George
**Steffan** Stephen
**Timotheus** Timothy
**Tomos** Thomas
**Tudur** Tudor
**Twm** Tom
**Wmffre** Humphrey

## ENWAU LLEOEDD

## PLACE NAMES

Aberdâr Aberdare
Aberdaugleddyf Milford Haven
Aberddawan Aberthaw
Abergwaun Fishguard
Aberhonddu Brecon
Abermo, Bermo Barmouth
Aberpennar Mountain Ash
Abertawe Swansea
Aberteifi Cardigan
Afon Menai Menai Straits
Amwythig Shrewsbury
Arberth Narberth
Babilon Babylon
Breudeth Brawdy
Brycheiniog Brecknock
Brynbuga Usk
Bryste, Caerodor Bristol
Caer Chester
Caerdroea Troy
Caerdydd Cardiff
Caerefrog York
Caerfaddon Bath
Caerfyrddin Carmarthen
Caergaint Canterbury
Caergrawnt Cambridge
Caergybi Holyhead
Caergystennin Constantinople
Caerhirfryn Lancaster,
   Lancashire
Caerliwelydd Carlisle
Caerloyw Gloucester
Caerlŷr Leicester(shire)
Caerllion Caerleon
Caernarfon Caernarvon
Caersallog Salisbury
Caerwrangon Worcester
Caer-wynt Winchester
Caer-Wysg Exeter
Caint Kent
Calfaria Calvary
Casllwchwr Loughor
Cas-mael Puncheston
Casnewydd Newport, Mon.
Castell-Nedd Neath
Castellnewydd Newcastle

Ceinewydd New Quay
Ceredigion Cardiganshire
Cernyw Cornwall
Clawdd Offa Offa's Dyke
Clwyd North East Wales
Coed-duon Blackwood
Conwy Conway
Côr y Cewri Stonehenge
Croesoswallt Oswestry
Crucywel Crickhowell
Cydweli Kidwelly
Dinas Basing Basingwerk
Dinbych Denbigh
Dinbych-y-pysgod Tenby
Donaw Danube
Drenewydd Newtown
Dyfed Demetia, South West Wales
Dyfnaint Devon
Dyfrdwy Dee
Efrog York
Eryri Snowdonia
Fflandrys Flanders
Fflint Flint
Gâl Gaul
Glynebwy Ebbw Vale
Gwent South East Wales
Gwlad-yr-haf Somerset
Gwy Wye
Gwynedd North West Wales
Gŵyr Gower
Hafren Severn
Hendy-gwyn Whitland
Henffordd Hereford
Hwlffordd Haverfordwest
Iâl Yale
Lacharn, Talacharn Laugharne
Lerpwl Liverpool
Llanandras Presteigne
Llanbedr Pont Steffan
   Lampeter
Llandaf Landaff
Llandudoch St Dogmaels
Llaneirwg St Mellons
Llanelwy St Asaph
Llaneurgain Northop

## ENWAU LLEOEDD

## PLACE NAMES

**Llanfair-ym-Muallt** Builth
**Llangatwg** Cadoxton
**Llangrallo** Coychurch
**Llanilltud Fawr** Llantwit Major
**Llanllieni** Leominster
**Llansawel** Briton Ferry
**Llanymddyfri** Llandovery
**Llwydlo** Ludlow
**Llyn Tegid** Bala Lake
**Maesyfed** Radnor
**Manaw** Isle of Man
**Manceinion** Manchester
**Meirionnydd** Merioneth
**Môn** Anglesey
**Morgannwg** Glamorgan
**Mynwy** Monmouth
**Mynyw** St David's
**Nanhyfer, Nyfer** Nevern
**Pennarlâg** Hawarden
**Pen-y-Fantach** Mumbles Head
**Penbedw** Birkenhead
**Pen-bre** Pembrey
**Penfro** Pembroke
**Penrhyn Gobaith Da** Cape of
  Good Hope
**Pen-y-bont ar Ogwr** Bridgend
**Pontarfynach** Devil's Bridge
**Pont-y-pŵl** Pontypool
**Porthaethwy** Menai Bridge
**Porthmadog** Portmadoc
**Powys** Mid Wales
**Rhuthun** Ruthin
**Rhydychen** Oxford
**Sain Ffagan** St Fagans
**Sili** Sully
**Solfach** Solva
**Tafwys** Thames
**Treamlod** Ambleston

**Trecelyn** Newbridge
**Trefaldwyn** Montgomery
**Trefdraeth** Newport, Pem
**Treforus** Morriston
**Trefyclo** Knighton
**Trefynwy** Monmouth
**Treffynnon** Holywell
**Tyddewi** St David's
**Tywi** Towy
**Wdig** Goodwick
**Wrecsam** Wrexham
**Wysg** the Usk
**Y Bont-faen** Cowbridge
**Y Fenni** Abergavenny
**Y Gelli (Gandryll)** Hay
**Y Gogarth** Great Orme
**Y Mot** New Moat
**Y Rhws** Rhoose
**Y Waun** Chirk
**Ynys Bŷr** Caldey Island
**Ynys Dewi** Ramsey Island
**Ynys Echni** Flat Holm
**Ynys Enlli** Bardsey Island
**Ynys Gybi** Holy Island
**Ynys Lawd** South Stack
**Ynys Seiriol** Puffin Island
**Ynysoedd Erch** Orkney Islands
**Ynysoedd Heledd** The Hebrides
**Ynysoedd y Moelrhoniaid** The
  Skerries
**Ynys y Garn** Guernsey
**Ynys Wyth** Isle of Wight
**Yr Wyddfa** Snowdon
**Yr Wyddgrug** Mold
**Ystrad-fflur** Strata Florida
**Ystrad Marchell** Strata Marcella
**Ystumllwynarth** Oystermouth
**Y Trallwng** Welshpool

# ENGLISH - WELSH
# SAESNEG - CYMRAEG

# a

**a, an** *adj*: **a man** dyn; **an ass** asyn
**aback** *adv* yn ôl; **taken ~** wedi synnu
**abandon** *vt* rhoi'r gorau i, gadael
**abandoned** *adj* wedi ei adael, ofer, afradlon
**abase** *vt* darostwng, iselhau, gostwng
**abash** *vt* cywilyddio
**abate** *vb* gostwng, lleihau; gostegu
**abattoir** *n* lladd-dy
**abbess** *n* abades
**abbey** *n* abaty, mynachlog
**abbot** *n* abad
**abbreviate** *vt* byrhau, talfyrru
**abbreviation** *n* byrfodd
**abdicate** *vb* ymddeol, ymddiswyddo
**abdomen** *n* bol
**abdominal** *adj* perthynol i'r bol
**abduct** *vt* dwyn ymaith drwy drais, cipio
**aberration** *n* cyfeiliorn, gwyriad
**abet** *vt* cefnogi, cynorthwyo, ategu
**abeyance** *n* dirymedd dros dro, oediad
**abhor** *vt* ffieiddio, casáu
**abhorrence** *n* ffieidd-dod, atgasrwydd, atgasedd
**abide** *vb* aros, trigo; goddef
**abiding** *adj* arhosol, gwastadol

**ability** *n* gallu, medr
**abject** *adj* distadl, dirmygedig
**ablative** *n* abladol
**ablaze** *adv* ar dân, yn wenfflam
**able** *adj* abl, galluog
**ablution** *n* golchiad; puredigaeth
**abnormal** *adj* anghyffredin, annormal
**aboard** *adv* ar fwrdd (llong)
**abode** *n* annedd, trigfa, cartrefle
**abolish** *vt* diddymu, dileu
**abominable** *adj* ffiaidd
**abomination** *n* ffieidd-dra
**aborigines** *npl* cyn-drigolion
**abort** *vb* erthylu, atal
**abortion** *n* erthyliad; erthyl
**abortive** *adj* seithug, ofer
**abound** *vi* amlhau, heigio; ymhelaethu
**about** *prep* am, oddeutu, tua ▷ *adv* oddeutu, o gwmpas
**above** *prep* uwch, uwchlaw ▷ *adv* fry
**abrasive** *adj* yn peri traul; annymunol
**abreast** *adj* ochr yn ochr, cyfystlys
**abridge** *vt* talfyrru, cwtogi
**abroad** *adv* allan, ar led, ar daen, dros y dŵr
**abrogate** *vt* diddymu, dileu

**abrupt** adj disymwth, sydyn, swta; serth

**abscess** n cornwyd, casgliad, crynhofa

**abscond** vi rhedeg i ffwrdd, dianc

**absence** n absenoldeb

**absent** adj absennol ▷ vt absenoli; **absent-minded** adj anghofus

**absenteeism** n absenoliaeth

**absolute** adj cwbl, hollol; diamodol ▷ n diamod, absolwt

**absolutely** adv yn hollol

**absolution** n gollyngdod; maddeuant

**absolve** vt rhyddhau, gollwng; maddau

**absorb** vt yfed, llyncu, sugno, sychu

**absorbent** adj amsugnol ▷ n amsugnydd

**absorption** n llynciad, sychiad

**abstain** vb ymatal, ymgadw

**abstemious** adj cymedrol, sobr

**abstention** n ymataliad

**abstinence** n dirwest, ymataliad

**abstinent** adj cymedrol, sobr

**abstract** vt tynnu, haniaethu, crynhoi ▷ adj haniaethol ▷ n crynodeb

**abstraction** n haniaeth; synfyfyrdod

**abstruse** adj tywyll, dyrys, astrus

**absurd** adj gwrthun, afresymol

**abundance** n digonedd, helaethrwydd

**abundant** adj aml, helaeth, digonol

**abuse** vt camddefnyddio, camdrin; difrïo

**abuse** n camddefnydd; difrïaeth

**abusive** adj sarhaus, gwatwarus

**abysmal** adj diwaelod, dwys, enbyd

**abyss** n y dyfnder, agendor

**academic, -al** adj athrofaol, academig

**academy** n ysgol, athrofa, academi

**accede** vi cytuno, cydsynio

**accelerate** vt cyflymu, chwimio

**accelerator** n ysbardun, chwimiadur

**accent** n acen; llediaith ▷ vt acennu

**accentuate** vt acennu; pwysleisio

**accept** vt derbyn (yn gymeradwy)

**acceptable** adj derbyniol, cymeradwy

**acceptance** n derbyniad

**access** n dyfodfa, dyfodiad, mynedfa, mynediad

**accessary** n cynorthwywr, cefnogydd

**accessible** adj hygyrch; hawdd dod ato

**accession** n esgyniad (i'r orsedd)

**accessory** adj cynorthwyol, cyfranogol; atodol

**accidence** n ffurfiant

**accident** n damwain, anap

**accidental** adj damweiniol

**accidentally** adv yn ddamweiniol

**acclaim** vt datgan cymeradwyaeth

**acclamation** n bloddest, cymeradwyaeth

**accommodate** vt cymhwyso; lletya

**accommodating** adj cyfaddasol

**accommodation** n lle, llety

**accompaniment** n cyfeiliant

**accompanist** n cyfeilydd

**accompany** vb hebrwng; cyfeilio

**accomplice** n cynorthwywr mewn trosedd

**accomplish** vt cyflawni, cwblhau

**accomplished** adj medrus

**accomplishment** n medr, dawn, camp

**accord** vb cytuno; cyflwyno ▷ n cydfod

**accordance** n: **in ~ with** yn unol â

**according** adv: **~ to** yn ôl

**accordingly** adv felly, gan hynny

**accordion** n acordion

**accost** vt cyfarch

**account** vb cyfrif ▷ n cyfrif; hanes

**accountable** adj cyfrifol, atebol

**accountant** n cyfrifydd

**accountancy** n cyfrifyddiaeth

account number n rhif cyfrif

accredit vt coelio, credu; awdurdodi

accrue vt deillio, codi, digwydd

accumulate vb casglu, pentyrru, cronni

accumulator n cronadur

accuracy n cywirdeb

accurate adj cywir

accurately adv yn gywir

accursed adj melltigedig, melltigaid

accusation n cyhuddiad

accusative adj gwrthrychol (gram), cyhuddol

accuse vt cyhuddo

accustom vt arfer, ymarfer, cynefino

accustomed adj cyfarwydd, cyffredin

ace n as; mymryn

ache vi poeni, gwynio ▷ n poen, cur

achieve vt cyflawni, gorffen, cwpláu, cwblhau

achievement n cyflawniad, camp

acid adj siarp, sur ▷ n suryn, asid

acidic adj asidig

acknowledge vt cydnabod, cyfaddef

acknowledgment n cydnabyddiaeth

acorn n mesen

acoustic adj clybodig

acoustics npl acwsteg

acquaint vt hysbysu, ymgydnabod

acquaintance n cydnabod, cydnabyddiaeth, adnabyddiaeth

acquainted adj cydnabyddus, cynefin, cyfarwydd

acquiesce vi dygymod, cydsynio

acquire vt cael, ennill

acquisition n caffaeliad

acquit vt rhyddhau

acre n erw, cyfair, acer

acrid adj chwerw, llymsur

acrimonious adj chwerw, sarrug, cecrus

acrobat n acrobat

across adv, prep yn groes, ar draws; trosodd

acrylic adj acrylig

act vb gweithredu, actio ▷ n act, gweithred, deddf

action n gweithred, gweithrediad

activate vb gweithredoli

active adj bywiog; gweithredol

activity n gweithgarwch, gweithgaredd

actor n actor, actiwr

actress n actores

actual adj gwir, gwirioneddol

actually adv mewn gwirionedd

actuary n ystadegydd, cyfrifydd

actuate vt ysgogi, cymell, cyffroi

acumen n treiddgarwch, craffter

acute adj llym, tost; craff

A.D. abbr O.C.

adage n dihareb, dywediad

adamant n adamant, diemwnt

adapt vt cyfaddasu

adapter n adaptydd

add vb chwanegu, atodi; adio

adder n neidr, gwiber

addict vt ymroddi, gorddibynnu

addiction n ymroddiad, gorddibyniaeth, tueddiad

addition n ychwanegiad

additional adj ychwanegol

additive n adiolyn

address vb annerch; cyfeirio ▷ n anerchiad; cyfeiriad

adduce vt dwyn ymlaen; nodi

adept n un cyfarwydd; campwr

adequate adj digonol

adhere vi ymlynu, glynu wrth

adhesion n glyniad, ymlyniad

adhesive adj glynol, ymlynol ▷ n adlyn, glud

adieu excl bydd wych! ffarwel!

adjacent adj cyfagos, gerllaw

adjective n ansoddair

adjoin vt cydio, cyffwrdd â

adjourn vt gohirio, oedi

adjudge vt dyfarnu, barnu

**adjudicate** vt beirniadu, barnu
**adjudicator** n beirniad
**adjunct** n atodiad, ychwanegiad
**adjure** vt tynghedu, tyngu
**adjust** vt cymhwyso, addasu, unioni
**ad-lib** adv yn rhydd, difyfyr
**administer** vt gweinyddu
**administration** n gweinyddiaeth
**administrative** adj gweinyddol
**admirable** adj rhagorol, campus
**admiral** n llyngesydd
**admiralty** n morlys
**admiration** n edmygedd
**admire** vt edmygu
**admission** n derbyniad; addefiad
**admit** vt derbyn; addef, cyfaddef
**admittance** n derbyniad; trwydded
**admixture** n cymysgiad, cymysgedd
**admonish** vt rhybuddio, ceryddu
**admonition** n rhybudd, cerydd
**ad nauseam** adv hyd syrffed
**ado** n helynt, heldrin, ffwdan
**adolescence** n llencyndod, adolesens
**adolescent** n adolesent, llencyn, llances
**adopt** vb mabwysiadu
**adoption** n mabwysiad
**adore** vt addoli
**adorn** vt addurno
**adrift** adv yn rhydd, diangor
**adroit** adj medrus, deheuig, hyfedr
**adulation** n gweniaith, truth
**adult** n (un) mewn oed, oedolyn
**adulterate** vt llygru
**adulterer** n godinebwr
**adulteress** n godinebwraig
**adultery** n godineb
**advance** vb symud ymlaen; dyrchafu; rhoi benthyg ▷ n benthyg, echwyn
**advanced** adj ar y blaen
**advancement** n dyrchafiad; lles, budd

**advancing** adj cynyddol, ar gynnydd
**advantage** n mantais
**advantageous** adj manteisiol
**advent** n dyfodiad; yr Adfent
**adventure** n antur, anturiaeth
**adverb** n adferf
**adversary** n gwrthwynebydd
**adverse** adj adfydus, gwrthwynebus, croes
**adversity** n adfyd, drygfyd
**advert** n hysbyseb
**advertise** vt hysbysu, hysbysebu
**advertisement** n hysbysiad, hysbyseb
**advertiser** n hysbysydd
**advertising** adj hysbysebol
**advice** n cyngor, cyfarwyddyd
**advisable** adj doeth, buddiol
**advise** vt cynghori, annog; hysbysu
**advisedly** adv ar ôl ystyried, yn bwyllog
**advisory** adj ymgynghorol
**advocate** n eiriolwr, bargyfreithiwr ▷ vt eiriol, dadlau, cefnogi, pleidio
**adze** n neddau, neddyf
**aerial** adj awyrol, wybrol
**aeroplane** n awyren
**aerosol** n erosol
**aesthetic** adj esthetig
**aesthetics** n estheteg
**afar** adv pell, hirbell
**affable** adj hynaws, caruaidd, clên
**affair** n achos; mater; helynt
**affect** vt effeithio; cymryd arno, ffugio
**affectation** n mursendod, rhodres, ffug
**affection** n serch, cariad; clefyd, haint; affeithiad (gram)
**affectionate** adj serchog, caruaidd
**affiliate** vt mabwysiadu, tadogi; uno
**affinity** n cyfathrach; tebygrwydd
**affirm** vb haeru, taeru; sicrhau, gwirio

**affirmation** n cadarnhad
**affirmative** adj cadarnhaol
**affix** vt sicrhau, gosod
**afflict** vt cystuddio
**affliction** n cystudd, adfyd
**affluence** n cyfoeth, digonedd
**affluent** adj goludog, cyfoethog, cefnog
**afford** vt rhoddi; fforddio
**afforestation** n coedwigaeth
**affray** n ymryson, ffrwgwd, ysgarmes
**affront** vt sarhau, tramgwyddo ▷ n sarhad
**afield** adv: **far ~** ymhell i ffwrdd
**aflame** adv ar dân
**afloat** adv yn nofio; ar daen, ar led
**afoot** adv ar droed
**afraid** adj ag ofn arno, ofnus
**afresh** adv o'r newydd, eilwaith
**Africa** n Affrica
**after** prep, conj wedi, ar ôl, yn ôl ▷ adv wedyn
**after-care** n gofal wedyn, ôl-ofal
**after-effects** n ôl-effeithiau
**afterlife** n y byd a ddaw
**aftermath** n adladd, adlodd
**afternoon** n prynhawn
**afters** n y cwrs terfynol
**afterthought** n syniad diweddar
**afterwards** adv wedi hynny, wedyn
**again** adv eilwaith, drachefn, eto
**against** prep erbyn, yn erbyn
**age** n oed, oedran; oes; henaint ▷ vb heneiddio
**aged** adj hen, oedrannus
**agency** n goruchwyliaeth, cyfrwng, asiantaeth
**agenda** n agenda
**agent** n goruchwyliwr; gweithredydd, cynrychiolydd
**aggravate** vt gwneuthur yn waeth
**aggregate** n cyfanswm, crynswth
**aggression** n ymosodiad, gormes
**aggressive** adj ymosodol, ymwthiol, gormesol
**aggrieve** vt blino, tramgwyddo

**aghast** adj syn, brawychedig
**agile** adj heini, sionc, gwisgi
**agitate** vt cynhyrfu, aflonyddu, cyffroi
**agnostic** n agnostig, anffyddiwr
**ago** adv yn ôl; **long ~** ers talm
**agog** adv yn awchus
**agonizing** adj mewn gwewyr meddwl
**agony** n ing, poen
**agrarian** adj tirol, gwledig
**agree** vi cytuno; dygymod; cyfateb
**agreeable** adj clên, dymunol, hyfryd
**agreement** n cytundeb
**agricultural** adj amaethyddol
**agriculture** n amaethyddiaeth
**aground** adv ar lawr, ar dir, i dir
**ahead** adv ymlaen, o flaen
**aid** vt cynorthwyo, helpu ▷ n cymorth, cynhorthwy
**ail** vb clafychu; blino, poeni
**ailment** n dolur, afiechyd, anhwyldeb
**aim** vb anelu, amcanu ▷ n amcan, nod
**air** n awyr; osgo; cainc, alaw ▷ vt awyru
**aircraft** n awyren
**airforce** n llu awyr
**airline** n cwmni hedfan
**airlock** n aerglo
**airport** n maes glanio
**air mail** n post awyr
**airtight** adj aerglos, aerdyn
**aisle** n ystlys eglwys; llwybr; eil
**ajar** adv cilagored
**akin** adv, adj perthynol, perthnasol
**alack** excl och fi!
**alacrity** n bywiogrwydd, parodrwydd
**alarm** vt dychrynu ▷ n braw, dychryn; rhybudd; larwm
**alarm-clock** n cloc larwm
**alas** excl och!
**albeit** conj er, er hynny, eto
**album** n albwm; record hir

**alcohol** n alcohol
**alcoholic** adj, n alcoholig, meddwyn
**alcove** n cilfach wely; hafdy, deildy, alcof
**alder** n gwernen
**ale** n cwrw
**alert** adj esgud, effro, gwyliadwrus
**algebra** n algebra
**Algeria** n Algeria
**alias** adv mewn modd, dan enw arall
**alibi** n dadlau bod mewn man arall
**alien** adj estronol ▷ n estron
**alight** vi disgyn
**align** vb cyfunioni
**alike** adj yr un fath ▷ adv yn gyffelyb
**aliment** n maeth, ymborth
**alimony** n alimoni
**alive** adv, adj yn fyw, byw
**alkali** n alcali
**alkaline** adj alcalïaidd
**all** adj holl; oll, i gyd ▷ adv yn hollol ▷ n y cwbl, y cyfan; pawb
**allay** vt lleddfu, lliniaru; tawelu
**all clear** adv yn glir
**allege** vt honni, haeru
**allegedly** adv yn honedig
**allegiance** n teyrngarwch, gwrogaeth
**allegory** n alegori
**allergic** adj alergig
**allergy** n alergedd
**alleviate** vt ysgafnhau, esmwytho
**alley** n llwybr, ale
**alliance** n cyfathrach, cynghrair
**allied** adj cynghreiriol
**alliteration** n cyflythreniad, cyseinedd
**all-night** adv drwy'r nos
**allocate** vt cyfleu, rhannu, dosbarthu
**allot** vb gosod, penodi
**allotment** n cyfran; rhandir
**all-out** adv yn llwyr, a'i holl egni
**allow** vt caniatáu, goddef
**allowance** n goddefiad; dogn; lwfans

**alloy** n aloi
**allude** vi cyfeirio, sôn
**allure** vb hudo, denu, llithio
**allusion** n crybwylliad, cyfeiriad (at)
**alluvium** n llifbridd, dolbridd
**ally** vt cynghreirio ▷ n cynghreiriad
**almighty** adj hollalluog, hollgyfoethog
**almond** n almon
**almoner** n elusennwr
**almost** adv bron, agos, braidd
**alms** n elusen, cardod
**aloft** adv yn uchel, fry, i fyny
**alone** adv, adj unig, ar ei ben ei hun
**along** adv ymlaen; ar hyd; **all ~** o'r cychwyn
**aloof** adv, adj yn cadw draw; pell
**aloud** adv yn uchel, yn groch
**alphabet** n egwyddor, abiéc
**alphabetical** adj yn nhrefn yr wyddor
**Alps** npl: **the ~** yr Alpau
**already** adv eisoes, yn barod
**also** adv hefyd
**altar** n allor
**alter** vb newid, altro
**alteration** n newid, cyfnewidiad
**altercation** n ymryson, ffrae
**alternate** adj bob yn ail ▷ vb digwydd bob yn ail; eilio
**alternating** adj bob yn ail
**alternative** n dewis arall
**alternatively** adv o ddewis arall
**although** conj er
**altitude** n uchder
**alto** n alto
**altogether** adv oll, i gyd, yn gyfan gwbl
**aluminium** n alwminiwm
**always** adv yn wastad(ol), bob amser
**a.m.** abbr a.m.
**amalgamate** vb cymysgu, cyfuno, uno
**amanuensis** n ysgrifennydd dros arall

**amass** vt casglu, cronni, pentyrru
**amateur** n amatur
**amateurish** adj trwsgl, anfedrus, amaturaidd
**amatory** adj carwriaethol
**amaze** vt synnu, rhyfeddu, aruthro
**amazement** n syndod
**amazing** adj rhyfeddol
**ambassador** n llysgennad
**amber** n ambr
**ambidextrous** adj deheuig â'i ddwy law
**ambiguity** n amwysedd
**ambiguous** adj amwys
**ambition** n uchelgais
**ambitious** adj uchelgeisiol
**amble** vi rhygyngu ▷ n rhygyng
**ambulance** n ambiwlans
**ambush** n, vb cynllwyn, rhagod
**ameliorate** vt gwella, diwygio
**amenable** adj hydrin; atebol; cyfrifol
**amend** vb gwella, diwygio, cywiro
**amendment** n gwelliant
**amends** n iawn
**amenity** n hyfrydwch; hynawsedd
**America** n yr Amerig
**American** adj Americanaidd ▷ n Americanwr
**amiable** adj hawddgar, serchus
**amicable** adj cyfeillgar
**amid, -st** prep ynghanol, ymhlith, ymysg
**amiss** adv ar fai, o'i le
**amity** n cyfeillgarwch
**ammonia** n amonia
**ammunition** n arlwy rhyfel; pylor etc
**amnesty** n maddeuant
**amok** adv yn wyllt, dilywodraeth
**among, -st** prep ymhlith, ymysg, rhwng
**amorous** adj hoff o garu, carwriaethus
**amorphous** adj di-ffurf, amorffus
**amount** vi cyrraedd; codi ▷ n swm
**amour** n carwriaeth

**ample** adj helaeth, eang; cyflawn, digon
**amplify** vt helaethu, ehangu
**amputate** vt torri aelod, trychu
**amulet** n peth a wisgir fel swyn
**amuse** vt difyrru, diddanu
**amusement** n difyrrwch, digrifwch
**an** see **a**
**anachronism** n camamseriad
**anaemia** n diffyg gwaed
**anaemic** adj di-waed, diwryg
**anaesthesia** n dideimladrwydd
**anaesthetic** adj, n anesthetig
**analogy** n cyfatebiaeth, cydweddiad
**analyse** vt dadansoddi, dadelfennu
**analysis (-yses)** n dadansoddiad
**analyst** n dadansoddwr
**analytical** adj dadansoddol
**anarchic, -al** adj anarchol
**anarchist** n anarchydd, terfysgwr
**anarchy** n anhrefn, aflywodraeth, anarchaeth
**anathema** n anathema
**anatomy** n anatomeg
**ancestor** n cyndad; (pl) hynafiaid
**ancestry** n ach, achau; hynafiaid
**anchor** n angor ▷ vb angori
**anchoress, -ite** n meudwy, ancr
**ancient** adj hen, hynafol; oesol
**ancillary** adj ategol, cynorthwyol
**and** conj a, ac
**anecdote** n hanesyn, chwedl
**anew** adv o'r newydd
**angel** n angel
**anger** n dicter, llid ▷ vt digio, llidio
**angle** n ongl ▷ vi genweirio, pysgota
**Anglican** adj perthynol i Eglwys Loegr, Anglicanaidd
**angling** n pysgota
**angry** adj dig, llidiog
**anguish** n ing
**angular** adj onglog
**animadvert** vi beirniadu, ceryddu, sennu

**animal** *n* anifail, mil ▷ *adj* anifeilaidd

**animate** *adj* byw ▷ *vt* bywhau; ysgogi

**animation** *n* bywiogrwydd

**animosity** *n* gelyniaeth, digasedd

**animus** *n* drwgdeimlad, gelyniaeth

**ankle** *n* migwrn, ffêr, swrn

**annals** *npl* cofnodion blynyddol

**annex** *vt* cysylltu, cydio; meddiannu

**annihilate** *vt* diddymu, difodi

**annihilation** *n* diddymiant, difodiant

**anniversary** *n* pen blwydd; cylchwyl flynyddol

**annotate** *vb* gwneud nodiadau

**announce** *vt* datgan, cyhoeddi

**announcement** *n* cyhoeddiad, hysbysiad

**announcer** *n* cyhoeddwr

**annoy** *vt* poeni, blino, cythruddo

**annoyance** *n* blinder, poendod

**annoying** *adj* trafferthus, blinderus

**annual** *adj* blynyddol

**annuity** *n* blwydd-dal

**annul** *vt* diddymu, dileu, dirymu

**anoint** *vt* eneinio, iro

**anomaly** *n* peth croes i reol, afreoleidd-dra

**anon** *adv* yn union, toc, yn y man

**anonymity** *n* cyflwr dienw

**anonymous** *adj* dienw, anhysbys

**anorak** *n* anorac

**another** *pron*, *n* arall

**answer** *vb* ateb ▷ *n* ateb, atebiad

**answerable** *adj* atebol, cyfrifol

**ant** *n* morgrugyn

**antagonism** *n* gelyniaeth, gwrthwynebiaeth

**antagonist** *n* gwrthwynebydd

**Antarctic** *n*: **the ~** Antartica

**antarctic** *adj* o gylch y pegwn deheuol

**ante-** *prefix* cyn, o flaen, rhag- ▷ *n* rhagflaenydd

**antecedent** *adj* blaenorol

**antediluvian** *adj* cynddilywaidd

**antelope** *n* gafrewig, antelop

**antenatal** *adj* cyn-geni

**anterior** *adj* blaen, blaenorol, cyn-

**anthem** *n* anthem

**anthology** *n* blodeugerdd

**anthracite** *n* glo caled, glo carreg

**anthropology** *n* anthropoleg

**anti-, ant-** *prefix* gwrth-, yn erbyn

**antibiotic** *n*, *adj* gwrthfiotig

**antichrist** *n* anghrist

**anticipate** *vt* achub y blaen, disgwyl

**anticlimax** *n* disgynneb

**antics** *npl* munudiau, ystumiau, maldod, stranciau

**antidote** *n* gwrthwenwyn

**antifreeze** *n*, *adj* gwrthrew, direwyn

**antipathy** *n* gwrthnaws; casineb

**antipodes** *npl* pellafoedd byd, eithafoedd

**antiquarian** *adj* hynafiaethol ▷ *n* hynafiaethydd

**antiquated** *adj* hen a di-les

**antique** *adj* hen, hynafol, henffasiwn

**antique** *n* hen beth

**antique-shop** *n* siop hen bethau

**antiquity** *n* hynafiaeth; y cynoesoedd

**anti-Semitism** *n* gwrth-Iddewiaeth

**antiseptic** *adj*, *n* antiseptig

**antisocial** *adj* gwrthgymdeithasol

**antithesis (-es)** *n* gwrthgyferbyniad

**antler** *n* cainc o gorn carw, rhaidd

**anvil** *n* eingion, einion

**anxiety** *n* pryder

**anxious** *adj* pryderus, awyddus

**any** *adj* un, unrhyw, rhyw, peth, dim

**anybody** *pron* unrhyw un, rhywun

**anyone** *pron* rhywun

**anything** *pron* dim, rhywbeth, rhywfaint

**anywhere** *adv* rhywle

**apace** *adv* ar garlam, ar ffrwst, ar frys

**apart** *adv* o'r neilltu, ar wahân
**apartheid** *n* aparteid
**apartment** *n* rhandy, lletty
**apathetic** *adj* difraw, difater, didaro
**apathy** *n* difrawder, difaterwch
**ape** *n* epa ▷ *vt* dynwared
**aperture** *n* bwlch, twll, agorfa
**apex** *n* blaen, brig, pen, copa
**aphis** (**aphides**) *n* pryf gwyrdd
**aphorism** *n* gwireb, dihareb
**apiece** *adv* yr un, ar wahân, un bob un
**apocalypse** *n* datguddiad
**apocryphal** *adj* anghanonaidd, apocryffaidd
**apologize** *vi* ymddiheuro, ymesgusodi
**apology** *n* ymddiheuriad, esgusawd
**apoplexy** *n* parlys mud, strôc
**apostasy** *n* gwrthgiliad
**apostate** *n* gwrthgiliwr
**apostle** *n* apostol
**apostolic, -al** *adj* apostolaidd
**apostrophe** *n* sillgoll, collnod (')
**apothecary** *n* apothecari, fferyllydd
**appal** *vt* brawychu, digalonni
**appalling** *adj* arswydus, gwarthus
**apparatus** *n* offer, aparatws
**apparel** *n* dillad, gwisg
**apparent** *adj* amlwg, eglur
**apparently** *adv* mae'n debyg
**apparition** *n* drychiolaeth, ysbryd
**appeal** *vi* apelio, erfyn ▷ *n* apêl
**appear** *vi* ymddangos, ymrithio
**appearance** *n* ymddangosiad
**appease** *vt* llonyddu, tawelu, dofi
**appellation** *n* enw, teitl
**append** *vt* atodi, ychwanegu
**appendicitis** *n* enyniad y coluddyn crog, apendiseitis
**appendix** *n* atodiad, ychwanegiad
**appertain** *vi* perthyn
**appetite** *n* archwaeth, chwant, awydd

**appetizer** *n* lluniaeth i greu blas, blasyn
**applaud** *vt* cymeradwyo, curo dwylo
**applause** *n* cymeradwyaeth
**apple** *n* afal; **~ of the eye** cannwyll llygad
**appliance** *n* offeryn, dyfais
**applicant** *n* ymgeisydd
**application** *n* cymhwysiad; cais; ymroddiad
**applied** *adj* cymwysedig
**apply** *vb* cymhwyso; ymroi; cynnig (am), ymgeisio
**appoint** *vb* gosod, penodi, pennu
**appointment** *n* cyhoeddiad; penodiad
**apportion** *vt* rhannu, dosbarthu
**apposite** *adj* addas, priodol
**appraise** *vt* prisio
**appreciate** *vt* prisio, gwerthfawrogi
**appreciation** *n* gwerthfawrogiad
**appreciative** *adj* gwerthfawrogol
**apprehend** *vt* ymaflyd mewn; dirnad; ofni
**apprehension** *n* dirnadaeth; ofn
**apprehensive** *adj* ofnus, pryderus
**apprentice** *n* prentis, dysgwr ▷ *vt* prentisio
**apprise** *vb* hysbysu; tafoli
**approach** *vb* nesáu, dynesu ▷ *n* dyfodfa
**approachable** *adj* hawdd mynd ato
**approbation** *n* cymeradwyaeth
**appropriate** *vt* meddiannu ▷ *adj* priodol, addas
**approval** *n* cymeradwyaeth
**approve** *vt* cymeradwyo; profi
**approximate** *vi* agosáu ▷ *adj* agos
**approximately** *adv* oddeutu, tua, yn agos i
**appurtenance** *n* peth perthynol
**apricot** *n* bricyllen
**April** *n* Ebrill
**apron** *n* (ar)ffedog, barclod

**apt** adj tueddol; cymwys, parod
**aquarium** n pysgodlyn, pysgoty
**aquatic** adj dyfrol, dyfriog
**aqueduct** n dyfrffos
**arable** adj: **~ land** tir âr
**arbiter** n dyddiwr, brawdwr, beirniad
**arbitrament** n rhaith, dedfryd
**arbitrary** adj gormesol, mympwyol
**arbitrate** vb cyflafareddu, athrywyn
**arbour** n deildy
**arc** n bwa, arc
**arcade** n arcêd
**arch** n bwa, pont; nen ▷ vt pontio
**arch-** prefix arch-, carn-, prif-
**archaeology** n archaeoleg
**archaic** adj hynafol, henaidd
**archangel** n archangel
**archbishop** n archesgob
**archdeacon** n archddiacon, archddiagon
**archdruid** n archdderwydd
**archer** n saethydd, saethwr
**archery** n saethyddiaeth
**archipelago** n twr ynysoedd, ynysfor
**architect** n pensaer
**architecture** n pensaernïaeth
**archive** n archif
**archway** n ffordd fwaol
**Arctic** n: **the ~** yr Artig
**arctic** adj gogleddol
**ardent** adj gwresog, poeth, angerddol
**ardour** n angerdd, aidd
**arduous** adj llafurus, blin, caled
**area** n arwynebedd, wyneb
**Argentina** n Ariannin
**argue** vb dadlau, ymresymu
**argument** n dadl, ymresymiad
**arid** adj sych, crin, cras, gwyw
**aright** adv yn iawn, yn briodol
**arise** vi cyfodi, codi
**aristocracy** n pendefigaeth
**aristocrat** n pendefig, gŵr mawr
**aristocratic** adj pendefigaidd, bonheddig
**arithmetic** n rhifyddeg
**arithmetician** n rhifyddgwr
**ark** n arch
**arm** n braich; cainc
**arm** n arf ▷ vb arfogi
**armament** n offer rhyfel; arfogaeth
**armchair** n cadair freichiau
**armed** adj arfog
**armful** adj coflaid, ceseiliaid
**armistice** n cadoediad
**armour** n arfogaeth, arfwisg
**armoured** adj wedi ei amddiffyn
**armoury** n arfdy
**armpit** n cesail
**armrest** n man i orffwys braich
**army** n byddin
**aroma** n perarogl(au)
**aromatic** adj peraroglaidd, pêr, persawrus
**around** adv, prep am, o amgylch
**arouse** vt deffro(i), dihuno; cyffroi
**arraign** vt cyhuddo o flaen brawdle
**arrange** vb trefnu
**arrangement** n trefn, trefniad, trefniant
**arrant** adj dybryd, cywilyddus
**array** vt trefnu, cyfleu; gwisgo ▷ n trefn; gwisg
**arrears** npl ôl-ddyled
**arrest** vt atal; dal, dala, restio
**arrival** n dyfodiad, cyrhaeddiad
**arrive** vi cyrraedd, dyfod
**arrogance** n balchder, traha
**arrogant** adj balch, trahaus
**arrogate** vt hawlio, trawshawlio
**arrow** n saeth
**arsenal** n arfdy, ystordy neu ffatri arfau
**arson** n llosgiad, llosg
**art** n celfyddyd; ystryw
**artefact** n celflun
**artery** n rhedweli
**artful** adj ystrywgar, dichellgar, cyfrwys
**art gallery** n oriel gelf
**arthritis** n gwynegon, crydcymalau

**article** n erthygl; nwydd; bannod
**articulate** vb cymalu; cynanu ▷ adj â meddwl clir, trefnus
**artifice** n dyfais; ystryw, dichell
**artificer** n saer, crefftwr, celfyddydwr
**artificial** adj celfyddydol; gosod, dodi, ffug
**artillery** n offer rhyfel, magnelau
**artisan** n crefftwr
**artist** n celfyddydwr, arlunydd, artist
**artistic** adj celfydd, celfyddgar, artistig
**as** conj, adv megis, fel; cyn, mor; â, ag
**asbestos** n ystinos, asbestos
**ascend** vb esgyn, dringo, dyrchafu
**ascendancy** n goruchafiaeth, uchafiaeth
**ascension** n esgyniad, dyrchafael
**ascent** n esgynfa, rhiw, gorifyny
**ascertain** vt cael gwybod, mynnu gwybod
**ascetic** n meudwy ▷ adj meudwyaidd, ymgosbol, asgetig
**ascribe** vt cyfrif i, priodoli, rhoddi
**ash** n onnen, onn
**ash (-es)** n lludw, ulw
**ashamed** adj ag arno gywilydd
**ashore** adv i'r lan, ar y lan
**ashtray** n plat lludw
**aside** adv o'r neilltu
**ask** vb gofyn, holi; ceisio
**askance** adv yn llygatraws, yn gam
**askew** adv ar osgo, ar letraws
**aslant** adv ar ei ogwydd, ar oledd
**asleep** adv yng nghwsg, yn cysgu
**asparagus** n merllys, asbaragws
**aspect** n golwg, golygwedd, wyneb, agwedd
**aspen** n aethnen
**asperity** n gerwindeb, llymder
**asperse** vt taenellu; gwaradwyddo
**aspersion** n difrïad, enllib
**asphyxiate** vt mygu, tagu
**aspirate** vt seinio ag anadl ▷ n yr (h)

**aspiration** n dyhead
**aspire** vi dyheu
**aspirin** n asbrin
**ass** n asyn; asen
**assail** vt ymosod ar, rhuthro ar
**assailant** n ymosodwr
**assassin** n bradlofrudd, llofrudd
**assassinate** vt bradlofruddio
**assault** n ymosodiad ▷ vt ymosod
**assay** n praw(f) ▷ vb profi; cynnig, ceisio
**assemble** vb cynnull, ymgynnull
**assembly** n cynulliad, cymanfa
**assent** vi cydsynio ▷ n cydsyniad
**assert** vt haeru, honni, mynnu
**assess** vt trethu, prisio, asesu
**assessment** n asesiad
**assessor** n aseswr, cyfeisteddwr
**asset** n ased
**assets** npl eiddo, meddiannau
**assiduous** adj dyfal, diwyd
**assign** vt gosod, penodi; trosglwyddo
**assimilate** vb cymathu; tebygu
**assist** vb cynorthwyo, cymorth, helpu
**assistance** n cymorth
**assistant** n cynorthwyydd
**assize** n brawdlys
**associate** vb cymdeithasu, cyfeillachu, cysylltu ▷ n cydymaith
**association** n cymdeithas, cymdeithasfa
**assort** vb trefnu, dosbarthu
**assorted** adj amryfath
**assortment** n dosbarthiad, pigion
**assuage** vt llonyddu, lliniaru, lleddfu
**assume** vt cymryd ar; tybied; honni
**assumption** n tyb(iaeth), bwriant, honiad, dyrchafiad (Mair i'r nefoedd)
**assurance** n sicrwydd; hyder, hyfder
**assure** vt sicrhau; yswirio
**asterisk** n serennig, seren (*)
**asthma** n caethder, diffyg anadl,

y fogfa
**asthmatic** adj byr ei wynt, caeth ei frest
**astonish** vt synnu
**astound** vt synnu, syfrdanu
**astral** adj serol
**astray** adv ar gyfeiliorn, ar grwydr
**astride** adv â'r traed ar led
**astrologer** n sêr-ddewin
**astrology** n sêr-ddewiniaeth
**astronaut** n gofodwr
**astronomer** n serydd, seryddwr
**astronomy** n seryddiaeth
**astute** adj craff, cyfrwys, call
**asunder** adv ar wahân, yn ddrylliau
**asylum** n noddfa; **lunatic ~** gwallgofdy
**at** prep yn, wrth, ger, ar
**atheist** n anffyddiwr
**Athens** n Athen
**athlete** n mabolgampwr
**athletics** npl mabolgampau
**atlantic** adj atlantaidd ▷ n: **the A~ (Ocean)** Môr Iwerydd
**atlas** n llyfr mapiau, atlas
**atmosphere** n awyrgylch
**atom** n mymryn, gronyn, atom
**atomic** adj atomig
**atone** vi gwneuthur iawn
**atonement** n iawn, cymod
**atrocious** adj erchyll, anfad, ysgeler
**attach** vb gosod, glynu; atafaelu
**attachment** n ymlyniad, serch
**attack** vt ymosod ar ▷ n ymosodiad
**attain** vt ennill; cyrraedd; cael gafael
**attainment** n cyrhaeddiad
**attempt** vt ceisio, cynnig ▷ n cynnig, ymgais
**attend** vb gweini; ystyried; dilyn, mynychu
**attendance** n gwasanaeth; presenoldeb
**attendant** n gweinydd ▷ adj yn dilyn, ynghlwm wrth
**attention** n sylw, ystyriaeth
**attentive** adj astud, ystyriol

**attenuate** vt teneuo, lleihau
**attest** vb tystio, gwirio; ardystio
**attic** n nenlofft, nenlawr
**attire** vt gwisgo ▷ n gwisg, dillad
**attitude** n ystum, agwedd, osgo
**attorney** n twrnai
**attract** vt tynnu, atynnu, denu, hudo
**attraction** n atyniad
**attractive** adj atyniadol
**attribute** n priodoledd
**attribute** vt priodoli, cyfrif i
**attrition** n rhathiad, treuliad, traul
**attune** vt hwylio, cyweirio
**auburn** adj gwinau, browngoch
**auction** n arwerthiant, ocsiwn
**auctioneer** n arwerthwr
**audacious** adj hy, digywilydd, haerllug
**audacity** n hyfdra, ehofndra, beiddgarwch
**audible** adj hyglyw, clywadwy
**audience** n gwrandawyr, cynulleidfa
**audio-visual** adj clyweledol
**audit** vt archwilio cyfrifon ▷ n archwiliad
**audition** n clywelediad
**auditor** n gwrandawr; archwilydd
**auger** n taradr, ebill
**augment** vt ychwanegu, atodi
**augur** n dewin ▷ vb darogan; argoeli
**August** n Awst
**august** adj urddasol, mawreddog
**aunt** n modryb
**aura** n naws, awyrgylch
**aural** adj clywedol
**auspices** npl nawdd
**auspicious** adj yn argoeli'n dda, ffafriol
**austere** adj gerwin, llym, tost, caled
**austerity** n gerwindeb, llymder
**Australia** n Awstralia
**Australian** n Awstraliad ▷ adj Awstralaidd
**Austria** n Awstria

**Austrian** *n* Awstriad ▷ *adj*
  Awstriaidd
**authentic** *adj* dilys, gwir
**author** *n* awdur, awdwr
**authoritarian** *adj* awdurdodus
**authoritative** *adj* awdurdodol
**authority** *n* awdurdod
**authorize** *vt* awdurdodi
**auto-** *prefix* hunan-, ym-
**autobiography** *n* hunangofiant
**autocracy** *n* unbennaeth
**autocrat** *n* unben; dyn awdurdodol
**autograph** *n* llofnod
**automatic** *adj* hunanysgogol,
  awtomatig
**automation** *n* awtomasiwn
**automobile** *n* cerbyd, modur
**autonomy** *n* ymreolaeth
**autumn** *n* hydref
**auxiliary** *adj* cynorthwyol, ategol
  ▷ *n* cynorthwywr
**avail** *vb* llesáu, tycio ▷ *n* lles, budd
**available** *adj* ar gael
**avalanche** *n* syrthfa, cwymp
  (eira *etc*)
**avarice** *n* cybydd-dod, trachwant
**avaricious** *adj* cybyddlyd, ariangar
**avenge** *vt* dial cam
**avenue** *n* mynedfa, rhodfa
**aver** *vt* gwirio, haeru
**average** *n* canolbris; cyfartaledd;
  cyffredin
**averse** *adj* gwrthwynebol, gelynol;
  croesi
**aversion** *n* gwrthwynebiad;
  casbeth
**avert** *vt* troi heibio, gochel, osgoi
**aviary** *n* adardy
**avidity** *n* awydd, awch, gwanc
**avocation** *n* gorchwyl,
  galwedigaeth
**avoid** *vt* gochel, osgoi, arbed
**avouch** *vt* gwirio, haeru; arddelwi
**avow** *vt* addef; cydnabod
**await** *vt* disgwyl, aros
**awake** *vb* deffro, dihuno ▷ *adj* effro
**award** *vt* dyfarnu ▷ *n* dyfarniad

**aware** *adj* hysbys, ymwybodol
**awareness** *n* arwybod,
  ymwybyddiaeth
**awash** *adj* llawn, cyforiog
**away** *adv* ymaith, i ffwrdd
**awe** *n* (parchedig) ofn ▷ *vt* rhoi
  arswyd
**awful** *adj* ofnadwy, arswydus
**awhile** *adv* am ennyd, am dro
**awkward** *adj* trwsgl, lletchwith,
  anghyfleus
**awl** *n* mynawyd
**awning** *n* cysgodlen, adlen
**axe** *n* bwyall, bwyell
**axiom** *n* gwireb
**axis** (**axes**) *n* echel, pegwn
**axle** *n* echel
**ay** *adv* ie
**aye** *adv* yn wastad(ol), byth
**azure** *n* glas y ffurfafen, asur
  ▷ *adj* asur

# b

**babble** *vb* baldordd, clebran ▷ *n*
  baldordd
**babe** *n* baban, plentyn bach
**baby** *n* baban, maban, babi
**babysitter** *n* gwarchodwr
  babanod
**bachelor** *n* dyn dibriod, hen lanc;
  baglor
**back** *n* cefn ▷ *vb* cefnogi; bacio

▷ *adv* yn ôl
**background** *n* cefndir
**backhander** *n* tâl dirgel; ergyd â chefn y llaw
**backpack** *n* cefnbwn
**backslide** *vi* gwrthgilio
**backward** *adv* yn ôl, ar ôl ▷ *adj* hwyrfrydig; digynnydd; araf
**backwater** *n* dŵr disymud ar ymyl afon, lle o'r neilltu, dibwys, cwter gwsg
**bacon** *n* cig moch, bacwn
**bad** *adj* drwg, drygionus; gwael, sâl
**badge** *n* bathodyn
**badger** *n* mochyn daear, broch ▷ *vt* profocio, poeni
**badminton** *n* badminton
**bad-tempered** *adj* â thymer ddrwg
**baffle** *vt* drysu, siomi, trechu
**bag** *n* cwd, cod, bag
**baggage** *n* clud, celfi, pac
**bagpipe** *n* pibgod
**bah** *excl* pw!
**bail** *n* meichiau, gwystl ▷ *vt* mechnïo
**bail, bale** *vt* hysbyddu cwch
**bailiff** *n* beili; hwsmon, goruchwyliwr
**bait** *vt* abwydo; baeddu, eirthio ▷ *n* abwyd
**bake** *vb* pobi, crasu
**baker** *n* pobydd
**bakery** *n* popty
**balance** *n* clorian, mantol; gweddill ▷ *vt* mantoli; cydbwyso
**balanced** *adj* cytbwys, cymesur
**balcony** *n* oriel, balcon
**bald** *adj* moel, penfoel
**bale** *n* pwn, sypyn, bwrn
**baleful** *adj* alaethus, gresynol, galarus
**baler** *n* byrnwr
**balk, baulk** *n* balc; siom ▷ *vt* balcio; siomi
**ball** *n* pêl, pellen
**ball** *n* dawns, dawnsfa

**ballad** *n* baled
**ballast** *n* balast
**ball bearings** *npl* berynnau pêl, pelferynnau
**ballerina** *n* balerina
**ballet** *n* bale
**balloon** *n* balŵn
**ballot** *n* balot, tugel
**balm** *n* balm, triagl
**bamboozle** *vb* twyllo, llygad-dynnu
**ban** *vt* gwahardd, ysgymuno
**banal** *adj* cyffredin, sathredig
**banana** *n* banana
**band** *n* band, rhwymyn; mintai; seindorf
**bandage** *n* rhwymyn ▷ *vb* rhwymo, rhwymynnu
**bandbox** *n* bocs hetiau
**bandit** *n* herwr, ysbeiliwr
**bandy** *vt* taflu (pêl *etc*) yn ôl a blaen
**bandy-legged** *adj* coesgam
**bane** *n* dinistr, melltith
**baneful** *adj* dinistriol, andwyol
**bang** *vb* curo, dulio, clepian ▷ *n* ergyd, twrf
**bangle** *n* breichled
**banish** *vt* alltudio, deol
**bank** *n* mainc; rhes
**bank** *n* glan, torlan; traethell
**bank** *n* banc, ariandy ▷ *vb* bancio
**banker** *n* bancwr
**bankrupt** *n* methdalwr
**bankruptcy** *n* methdaliad
**bank statement** *n* datganiad banc, adroddiad banc
**banner** *n* baner, lluman
**banns** *npl* gostegion
**banquet** *n* gwledd ▷ *vb* gwledda
**bantam** *n* coriar, dandi
**banter** *n* ysmaldod, cellwair ▷ *vb* cellwair, profocio
**baptism** *n* bedydd
**Baptist** *n* Bedyddiwr
**baptize** *vt* bedyddio
**bar** *n* bar, bollt; rhwystr; traethell ▷ *vt* bario; eithrio

**barb** n barf; adfach

**barbarian** n barbariad, anwariad

**barbaric** adj barbaraidd

**barbecue** n rhostfa

**barbed wire** n weiar bigog

**barber** n barbwr

**bard** n bardd, prydydd

**bare** adj noeth, llwm, moel, prin ▷ vt dinoethi

**barefooted** adj troednoeth

**barely** adv prin, o'r braidd

**bargain** n bargen ▷ vb bargeinio

**barge** n bad mawr

**bark** n barc, llong, llestr

**bark** vi cyfarth, coethi ▷ n cyfarthiad

**bark** n rhisgl ▷ vt dirisglo, digroeni

**barley** n haidd, barlys

**barm** n burum, berem, berman

**barmaid** n barferch

**barman** n barmon

**barn** n ysgubor

**barometer** n hinfynegydd, baromedr

**baron** n barwn, arglwydd

**baronet** n barwnig

**barrack** n lluest, lluesty, gwersyllty

**barrage** n argae, clawdd

**barrel** n baril, casgen

**barren** adj diffrwyth; amhlantadwy

**barricade** n atalglawdd ▷ vt cau

**barrier** n atalfa, rhwystr, terfyn, ffin

**barrister** n bargyfreithiwr

**barrow** n berfa, whilber; crug

**barter** vb cyfnewid, ffeirio ▷ n cyfnewid

**base** adj isel, gwael, distadl, gau

**base** n sylfaen; bôn ▷ vt sylfaenu, seilio

**baseball** n pel-fâs

**basement** n islawr

**bashful** adj swil, gwylaidd

**basic** adj gwaelodol, sylfaenol

**basin** n basn, cawg, dysgl

**basis** (bases) n sail, sylfaen

**bask** vi ymheulo, torheulo

**basket** n basged, cawell

**basketful** n basgedaid

**bass** n bas, isalaw; bâs, draenogiad y môr

**bastard** n bastard, plentyn gordderch/siawns

**baste** vt iro, brasteru; ffusto, ffonodio

**bastinado** n, vt ffonodio gwadnau'r traed

**bat** n ystlum

**bat** n bat ▷ vi batio

**batch** n pobiad, ffyrnaid; swp, sypyn

**bath** n ymolchfa, badd, baddon; bath

**bathe** vb ymdrochi, ymolchi, golchi

**bathroom** n ystafell ymolchi

**baton** n llawffon, baton, arweinffon

**battalion** n byddin, mintai, bataliwn

**batter** vt curo, pwyo ▷ n defnydd crempog, cytew

**battery** n magnelfa; batri

**battle** n brwydr, cad ▷ vi brwydro

**battlefield** n maes y gad

**battlement** n canllaw, murganllaw.

**battleship** n llongryfel

**bauble** n ffril, tegan

**baulk** see **balk**

**bawdy** adj anllad, anweddus

**bawl** vi gweiddi, crochlefain, bloeddio

**bay** n bae

**bay** vb, n cyfarth; **to hold at ~** rhoi cyfarth

**bay** n llawryf

**bay** adj gwinau, gwineugoch

**bayonet** n bidog ▷ vt bidogi

**bazaar** n basâr

**be** vi bod

**beach** n traeth, traethell ▷ vt gyrru ar y traeth

**beacon** n gwylfa, goleudy; coelcerth

**bead** n glain; **~s** paderau

**beadle** n rhingyll

**beak** n pig, gylfin, duryn

**beaker** *n* cwpan, diodlestr â phig, bicer

**beam** *n* trawst, paladr; pelydryn ▷ *vi* pelydru

**bean** *n* ffäen, ffeuen

**bear** *n* arth; arthes

**bear** *vt* dwyn, cludo; geni; dioddef, goddef

**beard** *n* barf; col ŷd

**bearing** *n* ymddygiad; traul

**beast** *n* bwystfil, anifail

**beat** *vt* curo ▷ *n* cur, curiad

**beatitude** *n* gwynfyd

**beautiful** *adj* prydferth, hardd, teg

**beauty** *n* prydferthwch, harddwch, tegwch; **~ parlour** parlwr pincio

**beaver** *n* afanc, llostlydan

**becalm** *vt* tawelu, llonyddu

**because** *adv, conj* oherwydd, oblegid, o achos; gan, am

**beck** *n* amnaid, awgrym

**beckon** *vb* amneidio

**become** *vb* dyfod; gweddu

**becoming** *adj* gweddus

**bed** *n* gwely; cefn, pâm

**bedding** *n* dillad gwely

**bedeck** *vt* addurno, trwsio

**bedew** *vt* gwlitho, gwlychu

**bedfellow** *n* cywely

**bedlam** *n* bedlam

**bedraggled** *adj* wedi caglo, dwyno; aflêr

**bedrid(den)** *adj* gorweiddiog

**bedroom** *n* ystafell wely, llofft

**bedsitter** *n* ystafell un gwely, ceginlofft

**bedstead** *n* pren neu haearn gwely

**bee** *n* gwenynen

**beech** *n* ffawydden

**beef** (beeves) *n* eidion; cig eidion, biff

**beehive** *n* cwch gwenyn

**beeline** *n* llinell unionsyth, ddiwyro

**beer** *n* cwrw

**beestings** *npl* llaeth newydd, llaeth toro

**beet** *n* betys

**beetle** *n* chwilen

**beetroot** *n* betys

**befall** *vb* digwydd

**befit** *vb* gweddu

**before** *prep* o flaen, gerbron, cyn ▷ *adv* o'r blaen

**beforehand** *adv* ymlaen llaw

**befriend** *vt* ymgeleddu, bod yn gefn

**beg** *vb* erfyn, deisyf, ymbil; cardota

**beget** *vb* cenhedlu, creu, peri

**beggar** *n* cardotyn ▷ *vt* tlodi, llymhau

**begin** *vb* dechrau

**beginning** *n* dechreuad

**beguile** *vt* hudo, twyllo; swyno, difyrru

**behalf** *n* plaid, rhan, achos, tu

**behave** *vb* ymddwyn

**behaviour** *n* ymddygiad

**behead** *vt* torri pen

**behest** *n* arch, archiad

**behind** *adv, prep* ar ôl, yn ôl, tu ôl, tu cefn

**behold** *vt* edrych, gweld ▷ *vb imper* wele

**behove** *vt* bod yn rhwymedig ar

**beige** *adj* beis

**being** *n* bod

**belated** *adj* diweddar; wedi ei ddal gan y nos

**belch** *vb* bytheirio

**belfry** *n* clochdy

**Belgium** *n* Gwlad Belg

**belie** *vt* anwireddu, siomi

**belief** *n* cred, crediniaeth, coel

**believe** *vb* credu, coelio

**believer** *n* credwr, credadun

**belittle** *vt* bychanu

**bell** *n* cloch

**belle** *n* merch brydweddol, meinwen

**bellicose** *adj* rhyfelgar, ymladdgar

**belligerent** *adj* rhyfelog ▷ *n* rhyfelblaid

**bellow** *vb* rhuo, bugunad

**bellows** *npl* megin

**belly** *n* bol, bola; cest, tor ▷ *vb* bolio

**belong** vi perthyn
**belongings** n meddiannau, eiddo
**beloved** adj annwyl, cu ▷ n
anwylyd
**below** adv, prep is, islaw, isod, obry,
oddi tanodd
**belt** n gwregys
**bemoan** vt galaru am, arwylo
**bemused** adj syfrdan
**bench** n mainc
**bend** vb plygu, camu ▷ n tro,
camedd
**beneath** adv, prep is, tan, oddi
tanodd
**benediction** n bendith
**benefactor** n cymwynaswr,
noddwr
**benefice** n bywoliaeth eglwysig
**beneficent** adj daionus, llesfawr
**beneficial** adj buddiol, llesol
**benefit** n budd, lles, elw ▷ vb
llesáu, elwa
**benevolent** adj daionus, haelionus
**benighted** adj a ddaliwyd gan y
nos; tywyll
**benign** adj tirion, mwyn
**bent** n tuedd, gogwydd
**benumb** vt merwino, fferru,
diffrwytho
**bequeath** vt cymynnu, cymynroddi
**bequest** n cymynrodd
**bereave** vt difuddio, amddifadu
**beret** n bere
**Berlin** n Berlin
**berry** n aeronen, mwyaren
**berserk** adj gwyllt, aflywodraethus
**berth** n lle llong; gwely llongwr;
swydd
**beseech** vt atolygu, deisyf, erfyn
**beseem** vt gweddu
**beset** vt cynllwyn; amgylchynu
**beside** prep gerllaw, wrth, yn ymyl;
**to be ~ oneself** o'i bwyll
**besides** adv, prep heblaw, gyda
**besiege** vt gwarchae ar
**besmirch** vt llychwino, pardduo
**bespeak** vt ymofyn ymlaen llaw

**best** adj, adv gorau
**bestial** adj bwystfilaidd
**bestir** vt cyffroi, ymysgwyd
**bestow** vt rhoddi, cyflwyno,
anrhegu
**bestride** vt eistedd neu gamu
yn groes i
**bet** n bet, cyngwystl ▷ vb betio,
dal am
**betoken** vt arwyddo, argoeli
**betray** vt bradychu
**betrayal** n brad
**betroth** vt dyweddïo
**better** adj gwell, rhagorach ▷ adv
yn well ▷ vt gwella
**between, betwixt** prep rhwng,
cydrhwng
**beverage** n diod
**bewail** vt cwyno, cwynfan,
galaru am
**beware** vi gochel, ymogelyd
**bewilder** vt drysu, mwydro,
pensyfrdanu
**bewitch** vt rheibio
**beyond** adv, prep tu hwnt
**bi-** prefix dau-, deu-
**bias** n tuedd, gogwydd, rhagfarn
▷ vt tueddu
**Bible** n Beibl
**bibliography** n llyfryddiaeth
**bibulous** adj yfgar, llymeitgar
**bicker** vi ffraeo, ymrafaelio,
ymgecru
**bicycle** n ceffyl haearn, deurod, beic
**bid** vb erchi; gwahodd; cynnig
**bide** vb aros, disgwyl
**biennial** adj dwyflynyddol
**bier** n elor
**bifocals** npl gwydrau deuffocal
**big** adj mawr; braisg
**bigamy** n dwywreigiaeth
**bigheaded** adj bras, mawreddog
**bigot** n penboethyn
**bikini** n bicini
**bilberries** npl llus
**bile** n bustl, geri
**bilingual** adj dwyieithog

**bilingualism** n dwyieithedd; dwyieitheg

**bill** n bil; mesur; rhaglen; hysbyslen

**bill** n pig, gylfin, duryn

**billet** n llety (milwr) ▷ vt lletya

**billiards** n biliards

**billion** n biliwn

**billow** n ton, gwaneg, moryn ▷ vi tonni

**billy-goat** n bwch gafr

**bin** n cist

**bind** vt rhwymo, caethiwo

**binge** n gloddest, sbri

**bingo** n bingo

**binoculars** n deulygadur

**biography** n bywgraffiad, cofiant

**biological** adj biolegol

**biology** n bywydeg, bioleg

**birch** n bedw, bedwen; gwialen fedw ▷ vt chwipio

**bird** n aderyn

**Biro** n biro

**birth** n genedigaeth

**birthday** n pen-blwydd; **birthday card** n carden pen-blwydd

**birthmark** n man geni

**biscuit** n bisgeden

**bisect** vt dwyrannu, rhannu

**bisector** n dwyrannydd

**bisexual** adj deurywiol

**bishop** n esgob

**bishopric** n esgobaeth

**bison** n ych gwyllt, bual

**bit** n tamaid; tipyn, dernyn; genfa, bit

**bitch** n gast

**bite** vb cnoi, brathu ▷ n cnoad, brath; tamaid

**bitter** adj chwerw, bustlaidd, tost

**bittern** n aderyn y bwn, bwmp y gors

**bitterness** n chwerwedd, chwerwder

**bitumen** n pyg

**bituminous** adj pyglyd

**bizarre** adj rhyfedd, od, chwithig

**blab** vb prepian, clepian ▷ n clepgi

**black** adj du ▷ n du, dyn du ▷ vt duo; **black ice** n iâ du

**blackberries** npl mwyar duon

**blackbird** n aderyn du, mwyalchen

**blackboard** n bwrdd du

**blackcurrant** n cyrensen ddu ▷ adj cwrens du

**blacken** vt duo, pardduo; tywyllu

**blackguard** n dihiryn ▷ vt difrïo

**blackleg** n bradwr

**blackmail** n arian bygwth, blacmel

**blacksmith** n gof

**bladder** n pledren, chwysigen

**blade** n llafn; eginyn, blewyn

**blame** vt beio ▷ n bai

**blameless** adj di-fai

**blanch** vt gwynnu, cannu

**bland** adj mwyn, tyner, tirion

**blandish** vt gwenieithio, truthio

**blank** adj gwag, syn; **~ verse** mesur di-odl; **blank cheque** n siec wag

**blanket** n blanced, gwrthban

**blare** vb canu utgorn ▷ n sain utgorn

**blarney** n gweniaith, truth

**blaspheme** vb cablu, difenwi

**blasphemy** n cabledd, cabl

**blast** n chwa, chwythiad, deifiad ▷ vt deifio; saethu; **~ furnace** ffwrnais chwythu

**blatant** adj stwrllyd, digywilydd, haerllug

**blaze** n fflam, ffagl ▷ vi fflamio, ffaglu

**bleach** vb cannu, gwynnu

**bleak** adj oer, digysgod, noeth, noethlwm

**blear** adj pŵl, dolurus, dyfriog

**bleat** vb brefu ▷ n bref

**bleed** vb gwaedu

**blemish** vt anafu, anurddo ▷ n anaf, bai, mefl

**blend** vb cymysgu ▷ n cymysgedd

**bless** vt bendithio

**blessed** adj bendigedig, gwyn ei fyd

**blessing** n bendith

**blight** n malltod ▷ vt mallu, deifio

**blind** adj dall, tywyll ▷ vt dallu ▷ n llen, bleind

**blindness** n dallineb

**blink** vb cau'r llygaid, ysmicio, amrantu

**bliss** n gwynfyd, dedwyddyd

**blister** n chwysigen, pothell ▷ vb pothellu

**blithe** adj llawen, llon, hoenus

**blitz** n blits

**blizzard** n ystorm erwin o wynt ac eira

**bloat** vb chwyddo, chwythu

**blob** n ysmotyn, bwrlwm

**block** n plocyn, cyff ▷ vt cau, rhwystro

**blockade** n gwarchae ▷ vb gwarchae ar

**blockhead** n penbwl, hurtyn

**blonde** adj o bryd golau

**blood** n gwaed; gwaedoliaeth; **blood pressure** n pwysedd gwaed

**bloody** adj gwaedlyd

**bloom** n blodeuyn; gwawr, gwrid ▷ vi blodeuo

**blossom** n blodeuyn ▷ vi blodeuo

**blot** n ysmotyn du, blot, mefl ▷ vb blotio

**blotch** n ysmotyn, blotyn, ystremp

**blouse** n blows

**blow** n dyrnod, ergyd

**blow** vb chwythu

**blow-dry** vb chwythu'n sych

**bludgeon** n pastwn

**blue** adj, n glas ▷ vt glasu

**bluff** adj garw, brochus

**blunder** n amryfusedd ▷ vb amryfuso

**blunt** adj pŵl, di-fin; plaen ▷ vt pylu

**blur** n ysmotyn, ystaen

**blurb** n broliant

**blurt** vt rhuthro dywedyd

**blush** vi cochi, gwrido ▷ n gwrid

**bluster** vi trystio, brochi ▷ n brawl, broch

**blustery** adj stormus, rhuadus

**boar** n baedd

**board** n bwrdd, bord; ymborth ▷ vb byrddio

**boarding house** n llety

**boast** n ymffrost ▷ vb ymffrostio

**boat** n bad, cwch

**bobbin** n gwerthyd

**bobby** n plismon

**bode** vt darogan, argoeli

**body** n corff

**bog** n cors, mignen, siglen

**boggle** vi petruso; rhusio, ffwndro

**bogus** adj ffug, gau, ffuantus

**bogy, -ey** n bwbach, bwci, bwgan

**boil** n cornwyd, casgliad

**boil** vb berwi

**boiler** n pair, crochan

**boisterous** adj terfysglyd, trystiog, brochus

**bold** adj hy, eofn; hyderus; eglur

**bollard** n bolard

**bolster** n gobennydd ▷ vt ategu

**bolt** n bollt ▷ vb bolltio; dianc; traflyncu

**bomb** n bom

**bombast** n chwyddiaith

**bombastic** n chwyddedig

**bona fide** adj o'r iawn ryw, dilys, didwyll

**bond** n rhwymyn; ysgrifrwym ▷ adj caeth

**bondage** n caethiwed

**bone** n asgwrn

**bonfire** n coelcerth, banffagl

**Bonn** n Bonn

**bonnet** n bonet

**bonny** adj braf, nobl

**bonus** n bonws, ychwanegiad

**booby** n hurtyn, penbwl

**book** n llyfr

**boom** n bŵm

**boom** vb trystio, utganu ▷ n trwst, swae

**boon** n ffafr, bendith, caffaeliad

**boor** n taeog

**boost** vb gwthio, hybu

**boot** n botasen, esgid

**booth** n bwth, lluest, lluesty, caban

**booty** n ysglyfaeth, anrhaith, ysbail

**booze** vi diota, meddwi ▷ n diod feddwol

**border** n ffin, goror, ymyl ▷ vb ymylu

**bore** vb tyllu, ebillio ▷ n twll

**bore** n pla, dyn diflas ▷ vt blino, diflasu, llethu

**bored** adj wedi syrffedu ar beth, wedi alaru

**boring** adj diflas, annifyr, llethol

**born** adj wedi ei eni

**borough** n bwrdeistref

**borrow** vt benthyca

**bosom** n mynwes, côl

**boss** n meistr

**botany** n llysieueg

**botch** n ystomp ▷ vb ystompio, bwnglera

**both** adj, pron, adv y ddau, ill dau

**bother** vb blino, trafferthu ▷ n helynt, trafferth

**bottle** n potel, costrel ▷ vt potelu, costrelu; **bottle opener** n agorwr poteli

**bottom** n gwaelod, godre, tin

**bough** n cainc, cangen

**boulder** n carreg fawr, clogfaen

**bounce** vb neidio, adlamu; bostio, ymffrostio

**bound** n terfyn, ffin, cyffin ▷ vt ffinio

**bound** vi llamu, neidio

**boundary** n ffin, terfyn

**bounty** n daioni, haelioni, ced

**bouquet** n blodeuglwm, pwysi

**bout** n sbel, term; ornest, ffrwgwd

**bow** n bwa; dolen

**bow** vb plygu, crymu, ymgrymu ▷ n moesymgrymiad

**bow** n pen blaen llong, bow

**bowels** npl ymysgaroedd, perfedd

**bower** n deildy

**bowl** n cawg, basn

**bowler** n het galed; bowliwr

**box** n bocs, pren bocs

**box** n bocs, blwch, cist; sedd, côr; bwth

**box** n bonclust ▷ vb taro bonclust; paffio; **box office** n swyddfa docynnau

**boy** n bachgen, hogyn, mab, gwas

**boycott** n, vb ymwrthod â pherthynas a chydweithrediad, boicot(io)

**boyfriend** n cariadfab, anwylyd

**boyhood** n bachgendod, mebyd

**brace** n rhwymyn; pâr ▷ vt tynhau, cryfhau

**bracelet** n breichled

**bracket** n braced, cromfach

**bracken** n rhedyn ungoes

**brag** n brol, ymffrost, bocsach ▷ vb brolio, ymffrostio

**braid** n pleth, brwyd ▷ vt plethu, brwydo

**brain** n ymennydd

**brake** n dryslwyn, prysglwyn

**brake** n brêc ▷ vt brecio

**bramble** n miaren

**bran** n eisin, bran, rhuddion

**branch** n cangen, cainc ▷ vi canghennu

**brand** n pentewyn; nod ▷ vt gwarthnodi

**brandish** vb ysgwyd, chwifio

**brandy** n brandi

**brash** adj byrbwyll, ehud

**brass** n pres, efydd

**brassière** n bronglwm

**brat** n crwt, crwtyn; croten

**bravado** n gwag-ymffrost, bocsach, gorchest

**brave** adj dewr, gwrol, glew ▷ vt herio

**bravo** excl da iawn! campus!

**brawl** vi ffraeo, terfysgu ▷ n ffrae, ffrwgwd

**brawn** n cnawd

**bray** vt pwyo, briwio, malurio

**bray** vi brefu (megis asyn), nadu

**brazen** adj haerllug, hy

**Brazil** n Brasil

**breach** n adwy, rhwyg, tor; trosedd

**bread** *n* bara
**breadth** *n* lled
**break** *vb* torri ▷ *n* toriad, tor
**breakdown** *n* salwch, colli iechyd;
(*car*) torri lawr
**breakfast** *n* brecwast ▷ *vb*
brecwasta
**breakwater** *n* morglawdd
**breast** *n* bron, dwyfron, mynwes
▷ *vt* wynebu, ymladd â
**breath** *n* anadl, gwynt
**breathalyser** *n* anadlydd,
anadliadur
**breathe** *vb* anadlu, chwythu
**breathing** *n* anadliad; anadlu
**breech** *n* tin, bôn
**breeches** *npl* llodrau, clos
**breed** *vb* magu; epilio; bridio ▷ *n*
rhywogaeth, brid
**breeze** *n* awel, awelan (chwa
**brethren** *npl* brodyr (ffigurol yn
bennaf)
**brevity** *n* byrder, byrdra
**brew** *vt* darllaw, bragu
**brewer** *n* darllawydd, bragwr
**bribe** *n* llwgrwobrwy ▷ *vt*
llwgrwobrwyo
**brick** *n* bricsen, priddfaen ▷ *vt*
bricio
**bride** *n* priodferch, priodasferch
**bridegroom** *n* priodfab
**bridesmaid** *n* morwyn briodas
**bridge** *n* pont ▷ *vt* pontio
**bridle** *n* ffrwyn ▷ *vt* ffrwyno
**brief** *adj* byr
**brier, briar** *n* miaren, drysïen
**brigade** *n* brigâd, mintai, torf
**brigand** *n* ysbeiliwr, carnleidr,
herwr
**bright** *adj* disglair, claer, gloyw,
hoyw
**brilliance** *n* disgleirdeb
**brilliant** *adj* disglair, llachar ▷ *n*
gem
**brim** *n* ymyl, min, cyfor; cantel
**brimstone** *n* brwmstan
**brindled** *adj* brith, brych

**brine** *n* heli
**bring** *vt* dwyn, cyrchu, dyfod â, dod â
**brink** *n* min, ymyl, glan
**brisk** *adj* bywiog, heini, sionc
**bristle** *n* gwrychyn, gwrych ▷ *vi*
codi gwrychyn
**Britain** *n* Prydain
**British** *adj* Prydeinig, Brytanaidd
**Briton** *n* Brython, Prydeiniwr
**Brittany** *n* Llydaw
**brittle** *adj* brau, bregus
**broach** *vt* agor baril, gollwng; agor
ymddiddan
**broad** *adj* llydan; eang; bras
**broaden** *vb* lledu, ehangu
**broccoli** *n* brocoli, math o fresych
**brochure** *n* llyfryn
**brogue** *n* llediaith (Gwyddelod)
**broil** *vt* briwlio
**broken** *adj* toredig, briw, drylliedig
**broker** *n* brocer, dyn canol
**broll** *n* terfysg, ymrafael, ymryson
**bronchitis** *n* bronceitis
**bronze** *n* pres, efydd
**brooch** *n* tlws
**brood** *n* nythaid; hil, epil ▷ *vi* deor;
synfyfyrio
**brook** *n* nant, cornant, afonig
**broom** *n* banadl; ysgub, ysgubell
**broth** *n* potes, cawl
**brothel** *n* puteindy
**brother** (-s, **brethren**) *n* brawd
**brotherly** *adj* brawdol; ~ **love**
brawdgarwch
**brow** *n* ael, talcen; crib
**brown** *adj* brown, llwyd, gwinau;
**brown paper** *n* papur llwyd; **brown
sugar** *n* siwgr coch
**browse** *vi* brigbori, pori, blewynna
**bruise** *vb* cleisio, ysigo ▷ *n* clais
**brunette** *n* gwineuferch
**brunt** *n* pwys a gwres, ergyd
**brush** *n* brws ▷ *vt* brwsio, ysgubo
**brushwood** *n* manwydd,
prysgwydd
**brusque** *adj* cwta, anfoesgar, taeog
**Brussels sprouts** *npl* ysgewyll

Brwsel
**brutal** *adj* creulon, bwysfilaidd
**brute** *n* anifail, creadur (direswm)
**bubble** *n* bwrlwm ▷ *vb* byrlymu
**buccaneer** *n* môr-leidr, môr-herwr
**buck** *n* bwch; coegyn ▷ *vb*
  llamsachu
**bucket** *n* bwced, ystwc
**buckle** *n* bwcl, gwäeg ▷ *vb* byclu,
  gwaegu
**bud** *n* blaguryn, eginyn ▷ *vb*
  blaguro, egino
**budge** *vb* syflyd, chwimio
**budget** *n* cwd, coden; cyllideb
**buff** *adj* llwydfelyn
**buffalo** *n* bual
**buffet** *n* cernod ▷ *vt* cernodio,
  baeddu
**buffoon** *n* digrifwas, croesan,
  ysgentyn
**bug** *n* drewbryf, bwg
**bugbear** *n* bwgan, bwbach, bwci
**bugle** *n* corn, utgorn
**build** *vt* adeiladu ▷ *n* corffolaeth
**building** *n* adail, adeilad,
  adeiladaeth
**bulb** *n* bwlb
**bulge** *n* chwydd ▷ *vt* chwyddo
**bulk** *n* swm, crynswth
**bull** *n* tarw
**bulldozer** *n* peiriant clirio ffordd,
  tarw dur
**bullet** *n* bwled, bwleden
**bulletin** *n* bwletin
**bullfight** *n* ymladd teirw
**bullfinch** *n* coch y berllan
**bullion** *n* aur neu arian clamp,
  bwliwn
**bullock** *n* bustach, eidion, ych
**bull's eye** *n* trawiad union
**bully** *n* gormeswr, bwli ▷ *vt*
  gormesu, erlid
**bulrushes** *npl* llafrwyn, hesg
**bulwark** *n* gwrthglawdd; canllaw
**bumbailiff** *n* bwmbeili
**bumble-bee** *n* cacynen
**bump** *vb* bwmpio, hergydio ▷ *n*
  bwmp, hergwd
**bumper** *adj* llawn, helaeth
**bumpkin** *n* lleban, llabwst, llelo
**bumptious** *adj* hunandybus,
  rhodresgar
**bumpy** *adj* aflonydd, anwadal, garw
**bun** *n* bynsen, bynnen, teisen
**bunch** *n* swp; cwlwm, pwysi ▷ *vb*
  sypio
**bundle** *n* bwndel, coflaid ▷ *vt*
  bwndelu
**bungalow** *n* tŷ unllawr, byngalo
**bungle** *vb* bwnglera, ystompio ▷ *n*
  bwnglerwaith
**bunion** *n* corn ar fys troed
**bunker** *n* bwncer
**bunkum** *n* lol, ffiloreg, truth
**bunting** *n* (defnydd) banerau
**buoy** *n* bwi ▷ *vt* cynnal, cadw rhag
  suddo
**buoyant** *adj* hynawf; calonnog
**burden** *n* baich ▷ *vt* beichio,
  llwytho
**bureau** *n* ysgrifgist; swyddfa
**bureaucracy** *n* biwrocratiaeth
**burgess, burgher** *n* dinesydd,
  bwrdais
**burglar** *n* torrwr tŷ, bwrgler
**burial** *n* claddedigaeth, angladd
**burlesque** *n* digrifwawd,
  gwatwargerdd
**burly** *adj* corffol, praff, mawr
**burn** *vb* llosgi, ysu ▷ *n* llosg, llosgiad
**burnish** *vt* caboli, llathru, gloywi
**burrow** *n* twll cwningen ▷ *vb* tyllu,
  tyrchu
**bursar** *n* bwrser, swyddog ariannol
**bursary** *n* amneriaeth,
  ysgoloriaeth
**burst** *vb* byrstio, ymrwygo,
  ymddryllio, torri ▷ *n* rhwyg
**bury** *vt* claddu
**bus** *n* bws
**bush** *n* perth, llwyn; prysgwydd,
  drysi
**bushel** *n* bwysel, mesur wyth
  galwyn

# C

**business** n busnes, masnach, gwaith; **business trip** n taith fusnes

**businessman/woman** n gŵr busnes/gwraig fusnes

**bus-stop** n atalfa bws, arosfan

**bust** n penddelw; mynwes

**bustle** vi trafferthu, ffwdanu ▷ n ffwdan

**busy** adj prysur

**busybody** n ymyrrwr, dyn busneslyd, trwyn

**but** conj, prep ond, eithr

**butcher** n cigydd ▷ vt cigyddio, lladd

**butler** n trulliad, bwtler

**butt** n nod, targed; cyff clêr

**butt** vt cornio, hyrddu, twlcio, hwylio

**butt** n casgen, baril

**butter** n ymenyn ▷ vt rhoi ymenyn ar

**buttercup** n blodyn yr ymenyn

**butterfly** n glöyn byw, iâr fach yr haf, pili-pala

**buttermilk** n llaeth enwyn

**buttery** n bwtri

**buttock** n ffolen

**button** n botwm ▷ vt botymu

**buttress** n ateg, gwanas ▷ vt ategu

**buxom** adj glandeg, gweddgar, nwyfus

**buy** vt prynu

**buzz** vb suo, sisial, mwmian ▷ n su, sŵn gwenyn

**by** prep gan, wrth, trwy, ger, gerllaw ▷ adv heibio, yn agos ▷ prefix rhag-, is-

**by-election** n isetholiad

**by(e)-law** n is-ddeddf

**by-gone** n yr hyn a fu

**bypass** n ffordd osgoi

**by-product** n isgynnyrch

**bystander** n un yn sefyll gerllaw

**byword** n ymadrodd cynefin, cyffredin

**cab** n cab

**cabal** n clymblaid, cabal ▷ vi clymbleidio

**cabaret** n cabare

**cabbage** n bresychen, bresych

**cabin** n caban ▷ vt cabanu, caethiwo

**cabinet** n cell, cist; cabinet

**cable** n rhaff fferf; cebl tanfor

**cackle** vi clegar

**cactus** n mwl ysgallen, cactws

**cad** n taeog, bryntyn, cenau

**caddie** n gwas golffwr

**cadence** n goslef, diweddeb

**cadet** n mab ieuengaf; cadlanc

**café** n tŷ bwyta, caffe

**cage** n cawell, caets ▷ vt cau, carcharu

**cairn** n carn, carnedd, crug

**cajole** vt twyllo drwy weniaith

**cake** n teisen, cacen ▷ vb torthi; caglu

**calamity** n adfyd, trallod, trychineb

**calcine** vb llosgi'n galch

**calculate** vb cyfrif, bwrw cyfrif, clandro

**calculation** n cyfrif

**calculator** n cyfrifiannell

**calendar** n calendr, almanac

**calf** (**calves**) n llo

**calf** n (of the leg) croth (coes)

**calibre** n calibr

**call** vb galw ▷ n galwad, galw; ymweliad

**calling** n galwedigaeth

**callous** adj croendew, dideimlad, caled

**calm** adj tawel ▷ n tawelwch ▷ vb tawelu

**calorie** n calori, uned gwres

**calumny** n anair, enllib, athrod, cabl

**calve** vi bwrw llo

**Calvinism** n Calfiniaeth

**camber** n camber

**Cambodia** n Cambodia

**Cambrian** adj Cymreig

**camel** n camel

**cameo** n cameo

**camera** n ystafell; teclyn tynnu lluniau, camera

**camouflage** n cuddliw, dull o ddieithrio ▷ vb dieithrio, cuddio

**camp** n gwersyll ▷ vi gwersyllu

**campaign** n ymgyrch, rhyfelgyrch

**campbed** n gwely plyg

**campsite** n maes gwersylla

**campus** n campws

**can** n tyn, piser, stên ▷ vb gallu; **can opener** n agorwr caniau

**Canada** n Canada

**Canadian** adj Canadaidd ▷ n Canadiad

**canal** n camlas; pibell

**canary** n caneri

**Canary Islands** npl: **the ~** yr Ynysoedd Dedwydd

**cancel** vt dileu, dirymu, diddymu

**cancer** n dafad wyllt, cancr, cranc

**candid** adj teg, onest, plaen

**candidate** n ymgeisydd

**candle** n cannwyll

**candlestick** n canhwyllbren

**candour** n onestrwydd, didwylledd

**candy** n candi

**cane** n corsen, cansen ▷ vt curo â chansen

**canine** adj perthynol i'r ci

**canister** n tun cadw te, bocs (te)

**canker** n cancr ▷ vb cancro

**canned** adj ar gadw mewn can tun

**cannibal** n canibal

**cannon** n magnel

**canny** adj call, cyfrwys, ffel

**canoe** n ceufad, canŵ

**canon** n canon, rheol

**canopy** n gortho, nenlen

**cant** n ffugsancteiddrwydd, rhagrith ▷ vi rhagrithio

**cantankerous** adj cwerylgar, cynhennus

**cantata** n cantata, cantawd

**canteen** n cantîn

**canter** vi rhygyngu ▷ n rhygyng

**canticle** n cantigl, canig, cân, emyn

**canto** n cân, adran o gân

**canton** n rhandir, talaith

**canvas** n cynfas, lliain bras

**canvass** vb trafod; ymofyn pleidleisiau, canfasio

**canyon** n ceunant, canion

**cap** n cap, capan ▷ vt capio

**capable** adj galluog, cymwys, cyfaddas

**capacity** n gallu, cymhwyster; cynnwys

**cape** n penrhyn, pentir, trwyn

**cape** n mantell, cêp

**caper** n pranc ▷ vi prancio

**capital** adj prif, pen ▷ n priflythyren; prifddinas; cyfalaf

**capitalism** n cyfalafiaeth

**capital punishment** n y gosb eithaf

**capitulate** vi ymostwng ar amodau

**caprice** n mympwy, chwilen

**capsize** vb dymchwelyd, troi

**capsule** n capswl

**captain** n capten

**caption** n pennawd, teitl

**captivate** vt swyno, hudo, denu

**captive** adj caeth ▷ n carcharor

**captivity** n caethiwed; caethglud

**captor** n daliwr, deiliad

**capture** n daliad ▷ vt dal

**car** n car, cerbyd; **~ wash** golfcha geir

**caravan** n carafán; men; **caravan site** n maes carafanau

carbine n dryll byr, byrddryll
carbohydrate(s) n carbohydrad(au)
carbon n carbon
carbuncle n carbwncl
carburettor n carburadur
carcass, -ase n celain, ysgerbwd
card n cerdyn, carden
card vt cribo gwlân
cardiac adj perthynol i'r galon
Cardiff n Caerdydd
cardigan n cardigan
cardinal adj prif, arbennig ▷ n cardinal
care n gofal, pryder ▷ vi gofalu, malio
career n gyrfa, hynt ▷ vi carlamu
careful adj gofalus, gwyliadwrus
careless adj diofal, esgeulus
caress n anwes, mwythau ▷ vt anwesu
caret n gwallnod, diffygnod (^)
caretaker n gofalwr
cargo n llwyth (llong), cargo
caricature n gwawdlun, digriflun
caring adj gofalus
carnage n galanastra, lladdfa
carnal adj cnawdol
carnation n blodyn cigliw
carnival n carnifal
carnivorous adj cigysol, rheibus
carol n carol ▷ vi caroli, canu
carouse vi gloddesta, cyfeddach
carp vi pigo beiau, cecru, cadw sŵn
car park n maes parcio
carpenter n saer coed
carpet n carped ▷ vt carpedu
carriage n cerbyd; cludiad; ymarweddiad
carrier n cariwr, cludydd; carrier bag n cludfag
carrion n burgyn, celain, ysgerbwd
carrot n moronen
carry vb cario, cludo, cywain
cart vb men, trol, cert, cart, car
cartilage n madruddyn
carton n carton

cartoon n digriflun, cartŵn
cartridge n cetrisen
carve vt cerfio, naddu; torri cig
cascade n rhaeadr
case n achos, cyflwr; dadl
case n cas, gwain; cist wydr
casement n ffenestr adeiniog, casment
cash n arian parod; cash desk n safle talu
cashier n ariannwr, trysorydd
cashier vt diswyddo
casing n plisgyn; casin
casino n casino
cask n casgen, baril
casket n cistan, prenfol, blwch
casserole n llestr coginio a dal bwyd
cassette n casét
cassock n llaeswisg ddu offeiriad, casog
cast vb bwrw, taflu ▷ n tafliad; ~ iron haearn bwrw
caste n llwyth; gradd, braint; cast
castigate vt cystwyo
casting-vote n pleidlais y cadeirydd
castle n castell ▷ vi castellu
castrate vt disbaddu
casual adj damweiniol, achlysurol
casualty n un wedi ei anafu
casuistry n achosionaeth
cat n cath
cataclysm n dilyw, dylif, rhyferthwy
catacomb n claddgell, claddogof
catalogue n catalog
catapult n blif, catapwlt
cataract n rhaeadr, sgwd; pilen
catarrh n llif annwyd, gormwyth
catastrophe n trychineb
catch vt dal ▷ n bach, clicied; dalfa
catching adj heintus
catchment area n dalgylch
catechism n holwyddoreg, catecism
category n trefn, dosbarth

**cater** vi arlwyo, darmerth, darparu
**caterpillar** n lindys
**cathartic** n carthlyn
**cathedral** n eglwys gadeiriol
**catholic** adj catholig; pabyddol ▷ n catholigydd; pabydd
**catkins** npl cenawon cyll, cywion gwyddau
**cattle** npl gwartheg, da
**caucus** n clymblaid
**caudle** n sucan
**cauldron** n crochan, pair, callor
**cauliflower** n blodfresychen
**causality** n achosiaeth
**cause** n achos ▷ vt achosi, peri
**causeway** n sarn, cawsai
**caustic** adj ysol, llosg, deifiol
**cauterize** vt serio
**caution** n pwyll, gwyliadwriaeth; rhybudd ▷ vt rhybuddio
**cautious** adj gwyliadwrus
**cavalcade** n mintai o farchogion
**cavalier** n marchog, marchfilwr
**cavalry** n gŵyr meirch
**cave** n ogof
**cavern** n ceudwll, ogof
**caviar(e)** n grawn pysgod, cafiâr
**cavil** vi cecru
**cavity** n ceudod, gwagle
**caw** vi crawcian
**cease** vb peidio, darfod
**cedar** n cedrwydden
**cede** vt rhoi i fyny, gildio, trosglwyddo
**ceiling** n nen, nenfwd
**celebrate** vt clodfori; dathlu; gweinyddu
**celebrated** adj clodfawr, enwog, hyglod
**celebrity** n bri, enwogrwydd; gŵr o fri
**celery** n seleri
**celestial** adj nefol, nefolaidd
**celibate** adj dibriod
**cell** n cell
**cellar** n seler
**cement** n sment ▷ vt smentio; cadarnhau

**cemetery** n mynwent, claddfa
**censer** n thuser
**censor** n beirniad; sensor
**censure** n cerydd, sen ▷ vt ceryddu
**census** n cyfrifiad
**cent** n y ganfed ran o ddoler
**centenarian** n canmlwyddiad
**centenary** n canmlwyddiant
**centigrade** adj canradd, sentigred
**central** adj canol, canolog; **central heating** n gwres canolog
**centre** n canol, canolfan, canolbwynt ▷ vb canolbwyntio
**centre-forward** n canolwr blaen
**centre-threequarter** n canolwr
**centrifugal** adj allgyrchol
**centripetal** adj mewngyrchol
**centurion** n canwriad
**century** n canrif
**ceramic** adj perthynol i grefft y crochenydd, ceramig
**cereal** n grawn, ŷd
**cerebral** adj ymenyddol
**ceremony** n seremoni, defod
**certain** adj sicr; neilltuol; rhyw, rhai
**certainly** adv yn sicr, yn siwr
**certainty** n sicrwydd
**certificate** n tystysgrif
**certify** vt hysbysu, tystio
**cesspool** n carthbwll
**chafe** vb rhwbio; llidio ▷ n llid, cythrudd
**chaff** n us, manus, mân us
**chaffer** vi edwica, bargeinio, bargenna
**chaffinch** n pinc, asgell fraith
**chagrin** n cythrudd, siom
**chain** n cadwyn ▷ vt cadwyno
**chair** n cadair ▷ vt cadeirio
**chairman** n cadeirydd
**chalet** n bwthyn (haf)
**chalice** n cwpan cymun, caregl
**chalk** n sialc ▷ vt sialcio
**challenge** n her, sialens ▷ vt herio, sialensio
**chamber** n ystafell, siambr

**chamberlain** n gwas ystafell, siambrlen

**champ** vt cnoi, dygnoi

**champagne** n gwin Champagne

**champion** n pencampwr; pleidiwr ▷ vt cymryd plaid

**chance** n damwain, siawns ▷ vt digwydd

**chancel** n cangell

**chancellor** n canghellor

**chandelier** n canhwyllyr

**chandler** n canhwyllydd, masnachydd

**change** vb newid, cyfnewid ▷ n newid

**changing-room** n ystafell newid

**channel** n sianel, gwely; rhigol

**chant** vt corganu ▷ n corgan, salmdon

**chaos** n tryblith, anhrefn

**chap** vt agennu, torri (am ddwylo)

**chapel** n capel

**chaplain** n caplan

**chapter** n pennod; cabidwl

**char** vb golosgi, deifio

**character** n cymeriad; nod, arwydd

**characteristic** adj nodweddiadol ▷ n nodwedd

**charcoal** n marwor, golosg, sercol

**charge** vb siarsio; cyhuddo; rhuthro; codi; llwytho ▷ n siars; gofal; cyhuddiad; rhuthr; pris; ergyd

**charger** n march rhyfel, cadfarch

**chariot** n cerbyd

**charity** n cariad; cardod, elusen

**charlatan** n un yn honni gwybodaeth; cwac

**charm** n swyn, cyfaredd ▷ vt swyno

**charming** adj cyfareddol, swynol, cwrtais

**chart** n siart

**charter** n siarter, breinlen ▷ vt breinio; llogi; **charter flight** n hediad siartr

**charwoman** n morwyn wrth y dydd

**chary** adj gwagelog, gochelgar, gofalus

**chase** vt ymlid, erlid, hel ▷ n helwriaeth

**chasm** n hafn, ceunant, agendor

**chaste** adj diwair, pur, dillyn

**chasten** vt puro, coethi; ceryddu

**chastise** vb ceryddu, cosbi, cystwyo

**chastity** n diweirdeb, purdeb

**chat** vi sgwrsio, ymgomio ▷ n sgwrs, ymgom

**chattel** n catel

**chatter** vi trydar, cogor; clebran; rhincian

**chatterbox** n clebryn, clebren

**chatty** adj siaradus, parod am sgwrs

**chauffeur** n gyrrwr

**cheap** adj rhad, salw

**cheat** n twyll; twyllwr ▷ vt twyllo

**check** n rhwystr, atalfa ▷ vt atal, ffrwyno

**cheek** n grudd, boch; digywilydd-dra

**cheeky** adj digywilydd, haerllug, eg(e)r

**cheer** n calondid, cysur; arlwy ▷ vb llonni, sirioli, sirio

**cheerful** adj llon, siriol

**cheers!** excl iechyd da!

**cheese** n caws

**chef** n prif gogydd

**chemical** adj cemegol ▷ n cyffur

**chemise** n crys merch

**chemist** n fferyllydd; cemegwr

**chemistry** n cemeg

**cheque** n archeb (ar fanc), siec; **cheque book** n llyfr siec; (col) llyfr main; **cheque card** n carden siec

**chequer** vt amryliwio, britho

**chequered** adj brith, anwadal

**cherish** vt meithrin, coleddu, mynwesu

**cherry** n ceiriosen

**cherub** n ceriwb

**chess** n gwyddbwyll

**chest** n cist, coffr; brest

**chestnut** n castan

**chevalier** n marchog
**chew** vb cnoi; **~ the cud** cnoi cil
**chewing gum** n gwm cnoi
**chick, chicken** n cyw (iâr)
**chicken-pox** n brech yr ieir
**chide** vt ceryddu, dwrdio
**chief** adj pen, pennaf, prif ▷ n
  pennaeth
**chieftain** n blaenor, pennaeth
**chilblain** n llosg eira, cibwst,
  malaith
**child (-ren)** n plentyn
**childhood** n plentyndod, mebyd
**Chile** n Chile
**chill** n oerni, annwyd ▷ adj oer,
  anwydog ▷ vb oeri, fferru, rhynnu
**chime** n sain cloch neu gloc ▷ vb
  canu (clychau)
**chimera** n anghenfil; bwgan,
  bwbach
**chimney** n corn mwg, simnai
**chin** n gên
**China** n China, Tseina
**china** n llestri te (tsieni)
**chink** n agen, hollt
**chip** vb hacio, naddu ▷ n asglodyn,
  pric
**chips** npl sglodion
**chiropodist** n troedfeddyg
**chirp** vi yswitian, grillian, trydar
**chisel** n cŷn, gaing
**chit** n nodyn byr
**chivalry** n urddas marchog; sifalri
**chives** n cennin sifi
**chocolate** n siocled
**choice** n dewis, dewisiad ▷ adj
  dewisol, dethol
**choir** n côr; cafell
**choke** vb tagu; mygu; topio, cau
**choler** n geri, bustl; dicter, llid
**cholera** n y geri marwol, colera
**choose** vb dewis, dethol, ethol
**chop** vt torri ▷ n golwyth
**choral** adj corawl
**chord** n tant; cord
**chore** n y dwt
**chorus** n côr, cytgan, byrdwn, corws

**Christ** n Crist
**christen** vt bedyddio, enwi
**Christendom** n (gwledydd) Cred
**Christian** adj Cristnogol ▷ n
  Cristion
**Christianity** n Cristnogaeth
**Christmas** n Nadolig
**Christmassy** adj Nadoligaidd
**chrome** n crôm
**chronic** adj parhaol (am
  anhwyldeb)
**chronicle** n cronicl ▷ vt croniclo
**chronology** n amseryddiaeth
**chrysanthemum** n ffarwel haf
**chubby** adj wynepgrwn, tew
**chuck** vt taro dan yr ên; taflu, lluchio
**chuckle** vi chwerthin yn nwrn dyn
**chum** n cyfaill mebyd ▷ vi
  cyfrinachu
**chunk** n tafell dew, toc
**church** n eglwys, llan ▷ vt eglwysa
**churchyard** n mynwent
**churl** n taeog, costog, cerlyn
**churlish** adj afrywiog, taeogaidd
**churn** n buddai ▷ vb corddi
**chutney** n picl cymysg
**cider** n seidr
**cigar** n sigâr
**cigarette** n sigarét
**cincture** n gwregys, rhwymyn
**cinder** n marworyn, colsyn
**cine-camera** n camera sine
**cinema** n sinema
**cinnamon** n sinamon
**cipher** n gwagnod (O); ysgrifen
  ddirgel ▷ vi cyfrif
**circle** n cylch ▷ vb cylchu
**circuit** n cylch; cylchdaith
**circular** adj crwn ▷ n cylchlythyr
**circulate** vb cylchredeg, lledaenu
**circum-** prefix cylch-, am-
**circumcise** vt enwaedu
**circumference** n cylchyn;
  cylchedd
**circumflex** n acen grom, to (^)
**circumlocution** n cylchymadrodd
**circumscribe** vt cyfyngu

circumspect adj gwyliadwrus, gofalus
circumstance n amgylchiad
circumstantial adj amgylchus
circumvent vb twyllo
circus n syrcas
cistern n dyfrgist, pydew, sistern
citadel n castell, amddiffynfa, caer
cite vt gwysio; dyfynnu
citizen n dinesydd
city n dinas
civic adj dinesig
civil adj gwladol; moesgar
civilian n dinesydd (anfilwrol)
civilization n gwareiddiad
civilize vt gwareiddio
civil service n gwasanaeth sifil, gwasanaeth gwladol
civil war n rhyfel cartref
clack vi clecian, clepian, clegar
claim vt hawlio ▷ n hawl
clamber vi dringo, cribo
clammy adj gludiog, cleiog, toeslyd
clamour n gwaedd, dadwrdd ▷ vi crochlefain
clamp n ystyffwl, craff
clan n tylwyth, llwyth
clandestine adj lladradaidd
clang, clank vb cloncio ▷ n clonc
clap n twrf, trwst ▷ vb curo; taro; clepian
claret n claret
clarify vt gloywi, puro; egluro
clarinet n clarinet
clarion n utgorn
clash vb taro, gwrthdaro ▷ n gwrthdrawiad
clasp n gwaeg, bach, clesbyn ▷ vt gwaegu; cofleidio
class n dosbarth ▷ vt dosbarthu
classic n clasur, campwaith, llên goeth ▷ adj clasurol
classical adj clasurol
classics npl clasuron
classify vb dosbarthu
classroom n ystafell ddosbarth
clatter vb clewtian, clepian, trystio

▷ n trwst
clause n adran, cymal
claw n crafanc, ewin ▷ vt crafangu, cripio
clay n clai
clean adj glân, glanwaith ▷ vt glanhau
cleaner n glanhawr, glanheydd
cleaning n glanhad, glanheuad
cleanly adv yn lân
cleanse vt glanhau
cleanser n glanhawr
clear adj clir, eglur, gloyw; croyw ▷ vt clirio
cleave vi glynu (wrth)
cleave vt hollti; fforchogi
clef n allwedd, cleff
cleft n hollt, agen
clement adj tyner, tirion, trugarog
clench vt cau yn dynn, clensio
clergy n offeiriaid
clergyman n clerigwr, offeiriad
clerical adj clerigol; perthynol i glerc
clerk n clerc
clever adj medrus, deheuig, clyfar
cleverness n medr, deheurwydd, clyfrwch
click vi clician, clepian ▷ n clic
client n cyflogydd cyfreithiwr, cwsmer
cliff n clogwyn, allt
climate n hinsawdd
climax n uchafbwynt
climb vb dringo
climbing adj dringol
clinch vt clensio; cau, cloi
cling vi glynu, cydio
clinic n meddygfa, clinig
clinical adj clinigol
clink vi tincian
clip vt cneifio, tocio, clipio
clique n clic, clymblaid
cloak n mantell, clogyn, clog ▷ vt cuddio, celu
cloakroom n ystafell ddillad
clock n cloc

**clod** n tywarchen

**clog** n clocsen ▷ vt llesteirio; tagu; clocsio

**cloister** n clwysty

**close** vb cau; terfynu ▷ n diwedd, diweddglo

**close** adj agos, clòs; caeth, tyn

**close** n clas, clos, buarth, clwt, cae

**closed shop** n gwaith cyfyngedig, gwaith i rai yn unig

**closet** n cell, ystafell; geudy

**close-up** n llun agos

**closure** n cau, gorffen, darfod

**clot** n tolchen ▷ vb tolchi, ceulo

**cloth** n brethyn, lliain

**clothe** vt dilladu, gwisgo

**clothes** npl dillad, gwisgoedd

**clothes peg** n bachyn dillad

**clothier** n brethynnwr, dilledydd

**clothing** n dillad

**cloud** n cwmwl ▷ vt cymylu

**clout** n cernod, clewt; clwt ▷ vt clewtian; clytio

**clover** n meillion, clofer

**clown** n lleban; croesan, clown

**club** n pastwn; clwb ▷ vb pastynu; clybio

**clue** n pen llinyn, arwydd

**clump** n clwmp, clamp, cyff

**clumsy** adj trwsgl, anfedrus, lletchwith

**cluster** n clwstwr, swp ▷ vb casglu, tyrru

**clutch** n crafanc; gafael; (pl) hafflau ▷ vb crafangu

**clutter** n dadwrdd, helynt

**co-** prefix cyd-

**coach** n cerbyd; hyfforddwr ▷ vb hyfforddi

**coagulate** vb ceulo

**coal** n glöyn, glo

**coalesce** vi cyfuno, cyd-doddi

**coalition** n cyfuniad; cynghrair, clymblaid

**coarse** adj garw, aflednais; bras

**coast** n arfordir, glan ▷ vi hwylio gyda'r lan

**coastal** adj arfordirol

**coastguard** n gwyliwr y glannau

**coastline** n morlin

**coat** n cot; **coat hanger** n cambren (dillad); **coat of arms** n arfbais

**coating** n caen, golchiad

**coax** vb hudo, denu, perswadio

**cobble, -stone** n carreg balmant

**cobbler** n crydd, cobler

**cobweb** n gwe pryf cop, gwe'r cor

**cock** n ceiliog; mwdwl; cliced (dryll) ▷ vb mydylu; codi cliced

**cockerel** n cyw ceiliog, ceiliogyn

**cock-eyed** adj â llygad tro

**cockles** npl cocos, cocs, rhython

**cockpit** n sedd peilot; ymladdfan ceiliogod

**cockroach** n chwilen ddu

**cock-sure** adj gorbendant, gorhyderus

**cocktail** n coctêl

**cocoa** n coco

**coconut** n cneuen goco, coconyt

**cod** n y penfras; cod

**code** n côd

**coerce** vb gorfodi, gorthrechu

**coercion** n gorfodaeth, gorthrech

**coffee** n coffi

**coffin** n arch, ysgrîn

**cog** n dant olwyn, còg

**cogent** adj cryf, grymus, argyhoeddiadol

**cohabit** vi cyd-fyw

**cohere** vb cydlynu

**cohesion** n cydlyniad

**coil** vb torchi ▷ n torch

**coin** n arian bath ▷ vb bathu

**coincide** vi cyd-ddigwydd, cyd-daro

**coincidence** n cyd-ddigwyddiad

**coke** n golosg, côc

**colander** n hidl

**cold** adj oer ▷ n oerfel, oerni, annwyd; **to catch a –** dal annwyd

**colic** n bolwst, colig

**collapse** vb disgyn, cwympo ▷ n cwymp, methiant

**collapsible** adj plygadwy

**collar** n coler ▷ vb coleru; **~ bone** pont yr ysgwydd
**collateral** adj cyfochrog, cyfystlys
**colleague** n cydweithiwr
**collect** n colect ▷ vb crynhoi, hel, ymgynnull, casglu
**collection** n casgliad
**collector** n casglwr
**college** n coleg
**collide** vb gwrthdaro
**collie** n ci defaid
**collier** n glöwr; llong lo
**colliery** n gwaith glo, pwll glo, glofa
**collision** n gwrthdrawiad
**colloquial** adj llafar, tafodieithol
**colon** n gorwahannod, colon (:); coluddyn mawr
**colonel** n cyrnol
**colonial** adj trefedigaethol
**colony** n trefedigaeth, gwladfa
**colossal** adj cawraidd, anferth
**colour** n lliw, baner ▷ vb lliwio; cochi; **~ bar** gwahanfur lliw; **~ blind** lliwddall
**coloured** adj lliw
**colourful** adj lliwgar
**colouring** n lliwiad
**colourless** adj di-liw
**colt** n ebol
**column** n colofn
**columnist** n newyddiadurwr, colofnydd
**coma** n hunglwyf, côma
**comb** n crib ▷ vb cribo
**combat** n brwydr, gornest ▷ vb brwydro
**combination** n cyfuniad
**combine** vb cyfuno; **~ harvester** cynaeafydd, combein
**come** vi dod, dyfod; **to ~ across** dod ar draws; **to ~ to light** dod i'r golwg; **to ~ to an end** dod i ben; **to ~ by** meddiannu; **to ~ to pass** digwydd
**comedian** n comedïwr
**comedy** n comedi
**comfort** n cysur, diddanwch ▷ vt cysuro, diddanu

**comfortable** adj cysurus, cyffyrddus
**comfortably** adv yn gysurus, yn gyffyrddus
**comic** adj comic, digrif, ysmala
**comma** n rhagwahannod, atalnod, coma
**command** vb gorchymyn ▷ n gorchymyn, awdurdod
**commandeer** vb meddiannu
**commander** n cadlywydd, comander
**commandment** n gorchymyn
**commando** n mintai (o filwyr), un o'r fintai
**commemorate** vt coffáu, dathlu
**commence** vb dechrau
**commend** vt cymeradwyo, canmol
**commensurate** adj cymesur
**comment** vi sylwi, esbonio ▷ n sylw
**commentary** n sylwebaeth
**commentator** n esboniwr, sylwebydd
**commerce** n masnach
**commercial** adj masnachol
**commiserate** vt cydymdeimlo â, cyd-dosturio â
**commission** n comisiwn, dirprwyaeth ▷ vb comisiynu
**commissionaire** n porthor
**commissioner** n comisiynydd
**commit** vt cyflawni; traddodi; cyflwyno
**commitment** n ymrwymiad; traddodiad
**committee** n pwyllgor
**commodity** n nwydd (masnachol)
**common** adj cyffredin ▷ n tir cyffredin, cytir, comin; **the C~ Market** y Farchnad Gyffredin
**commoner** n cominwr, gwerinwr
**commonplace** adj dibwys, cyffredin
**commons** npl y cyffredin; **House of C~** Tŷ'r Cyffredin
**common sense** n synnwyr

cyffredin

**commonwealth** n cymanwlad

**commotion** n cyffro, terfysg

**communal** adj cymunol, cymunedol

**commune** vi ymddiddan; cymuno ▷ n cymundod; comun

**communicate** vb cyfathrebu; cymuno

**communication** n cyfathrebiad, cysylltiad, neges

**communion** n cymun, cymundeb

**communism** n comiwnyddiaeth

**communist** n comiwnydd

**community** n cymdeithas, cymuned; ~ **centre** canolfan gymuned

**commute** vt cymudo, pendilio

**commuter** n cymudwr, pendiliwr

**compact** n cytundeb, cyfamod; bag lan, compact ▷ adj cryno ▷ vt crynhoi; ~ **disc** cryno ddisg

**companion** n cydymaith

**companionship** n cwmnïaeth, cyfeillach

**company** n cymdeithas, cwmni; **keep ~ with** cadw cwmni â

**comparative** adj cymharol

**comparatively** adv yn gymharol

**compare** vt cymharu, cyffelybu

**comparison** n cymhariaeth

**compartment** n adran, cerbydran

**compass** n cwmpawd; cwmpas ▷ vt amgylchu

**compassion** n tosturi

**compatible** adj cydweddol, cyson

**compatriot** n cydwladwr

**compel** vt cymell, gorfodi

**compendium** n crynodeb, talfyriad

**compensate** vt talu iawn, digolledu

**compensation** n iawndal

**compete** vi cystadlu

**competence** n cymhwysedd

**competent** adj cymwys, digonol

**competition** n cystadleuaeth

**competitive** adj cystadleuol

**competitor** n cystadleuydd

**complacency** n ymfoddhad

**complacent** adj hunan-foddhaus, digonol

**complain** vi cwyno, achwyn, grwgnach

**complaint** n cwyn, achwyniad; anhwyldeb

**complement** n cyflawnder, cyflenwad

**complementary** adj cyflenwol

**complete** adj cyflawn ▷ vt cyflawni

**completely** adv yn llwyr

**completion** n cwblhad

**complex** adj cymhleth, dyrys

**complexion** n gwedd, pryd, gwawr

**compliance** n cydsyniad

**complicate** vt cymhlethu; drysu

**complicated** adj cymhleth, dyrys

**complication** n cymhlethdod

**compliment** n cyfarchiad; canmoliaeth

**comply** vi cydsynio, ufuddhau

**component** n cydran, cyfansoddyn

**compose** vt cyfansoddi; cysodi; tawelu

**composed** adj hunanfeddiannol

**composer** n cyfansoddwr

**composition** n cyfansoddiad, traethawd

**composure** n tawelwch, hunan-feddiant

**compound** adj cyfansawdd ▷ n cymysg ▷ vb cymysgu

**comprehend** vt amgyffred, dirnad

**comprehension** n amgyffred, dirnadaeth

**comprehensive** adj cynhwysfawr; ~ **school** Ysgol Gyfun

**compress** vt gwasgu, crynhoi ▷ n plastr

**comprise** vt amgyffred, cynnwys

**compromise** n cymrodedd, cyfaddawd ▷ vb cymrodeddu, cyfaddawdu

**compulsion** n gorfodaeth

**compulsive** adj trwy orfod, o
anfodd
**compulsory** adj gorfodol
**computer** n cyfrifiadur; **~**
**operator** cyfrifiadurwr; **~ science**
cyfrifanneg, cyfrifiadureg
**comrade** n cydymaith
**concave** adj ceugrwm
**conceal** vb cuddio, celu, dirgelu
**concede** vt caniatáu, addef
**conceit** n tyb, mympwy; hunandyb,
hunanoldeb, cysêt
**conceited** adj hunandybus,
hunanol, balch
**conceive** vb dirnad; tybied, synied;
beichiogi
**concentrate** vt crynodi,
canolbwyntio
**concentration** n crynodiad,
ymroddiad
**concept** n cysyniad
**conception** n syniad; beichiogiad
**concern** vt perthyn, ymwneud (â),
gofalu (am), pryderu, bod a wnelo â
▷ n busnes, diddordeb; gofal, pryder
**concerned** adj yn teimlo pryder,
pryderus, gofalus, yn ymboeni
**concerning** prep ynglŷn â,
ynghylch
**concert** n cyngerdd ▷ vt cyd-drefnu
**concerted** adj cydunol, wedi ei
gyd-drefnu
**concertina** n consertina
**conclude** vb diweddu; casglu,
barnu
**conclusion** n diwedd; casgliad
**conclusive** adj terfynol
**concoct** vt llunio, dyfeisio
**concoction** n cymysgedd
**concourse** n tyrfa, torf
**concrete** adj diriaethol ▷ n concrit
**concur** vi cydredeg; cydgroesi;
cytuno
**concurrently** adv yn gyfredol
**concussion** n cyd-drawiad,
ysgytiad
**condemn** vb condemnio, collfarnu

**condensation** n cywasgiad,
cyddwysedd
**condense** vb cywasgu, cyddwyso,
cwtogi
**condensed** adj cyddwys
**condition** n cyflwr, ansawdd; amod
▷ vb cyflyru; amodi
**conditional** adj amodol
**conditionally** adv ar amod
**conditioner** n cyflyrydd
**condole** vt cydofidio, cydymdeimlo
**condolence** n cydymdeimlad
**condom** n condom; **condoms** npl
(col) sachau dyrnu
**condominium** n cydlywodraeth,
condominiwm
**condone** vt maddau, esgusodi,
cymeradwyo
**conduce** vi arwain, tueddu
**conducive** adj tueddol i, â thuedd i
**conduct** n ymddygiad,
ymarweddiad, tywys
**conduct** vt arwain
**conductor** n arweinydd; tocynnwr
**cone** n pigwrn, côn
**confection** n cyffaith
**confectioner** n cyffeithiwr
**confer** vb ymgynghori, cyflwyno
**conference** n cynhadledd
**confess** vb cyffesu, cyfaddef
**confession** n cyffesiad, cyffes
**confetti** n conffeti
**confide** vb ymddiried
**confidence** n ymddiried, hyder;
**self-~** hunanhyder
**confident** adj hyderus
**confidential** adj cyfrinachol
**confine** vt cyfyngu, carcharu,
caethiwo
**confined** adj caeth, cyfyng
**confinement** n caethiwed,
adeg geni
**confirm** vt cadarnhau; conffirmio
**confirmation** n cadarnhad;
bedydd esgob, conffirmasiwn
**confirmed** adj cyson, arferol,
gwastadol, wedi ei gadarnhau

**confiscate** vt atafaelu
**conflict** n gwrthdrawiad, ymryson
**conflict** vi anghytuno, gwrthdaro
**conflicting** adj anghyson
**conform** vb cydymffurfio;
cydffurfio
**confound** vt cymysgu, drysu
**confront** vt wynebu
**confrontation** n gwrthdaro
**confuse** vt cymysgu, drysu
**confused** adj cymysg; didrefn;
dyrys; tywyll
**confusion** n anhrefn
**confute** vt gwrthbrofi,
dymchwelyd
**congeal** vb rhewi, fferru, tewychu,
ceulo
**congenial** adj cydnaws, hynaws
**congest** vb cronni, gorlanw
**congested** adj gorlawn
**congestion** n gorlenwad, tagfa,
crynhoad
**congratulate** vt llongyfarch
**congratulations** n
llongyfarchiadau
**congregate** vb ymgynnull
**congregation** n cynulleidfa
**congress** n cyngres, cymanfa
**conjunction** n cysylltiad
**conjunctivitis** n llid yr amrant
**conjure** vb consurio
**conjurer** n consurwr
**connect** vb cysylltu, cydio
**connected** adj cysylltiedig,
cysylltiol
**connection** n cysylltiad,
perthynas; **in ~ with** ynglŷn â
**connive** vi goddef, cau llygaid rhag
**conquer** vt gorchfygu, trechu
**conqueror** n gorchfygwr,
concwerwr
**conquest** n buddugoliaeth,
concwest
**conscience** n cydwybod
**conscientious** adj cydwybodol
**conscious** adj ymwybodol
**consciousness** n ymwybyddiaeth

**conscript** n gorfodog, gŵr rhif
▷ vb gorfodi
**conscription** n gorfodaeth filwrol
**consecrate** vt cysegru
**consecutive** adj olynol
**consent** vi cydsynio ▷ n cydsyniad,
caniatâd
**consequence** n canlyniad
**consequently** adv o ganlyniad
**conservation** n cadwraeth,
gwarchodaeth
**conservative** adj ceidwadol ▷ n
ceidwadwr
**conservatory** n tŷ gwydr
**conserve** vt cadw, diogelu,
amddiffyn
**consider** vb ystyried
**considerable** adj cryn
**considerate** adj ystyriol, tosturiol
**consideration** n ystyriaeth
**considering** prep ag ystyried
**consign** vt traddodi, trosglwyddo
**consist** vt cynnwys
**consistency** n cysondeb
**consistent** n cyson
**consolation** n cysur, diddanwch
**console** vt cysuro, diddanu
**consonant** adj cysain; cyson ▷ n
cytsain
**conspicuous** adj amlwg
**conspiracy** n bradwriaeth, brad,
cynllwyn
**conspire** vb bradfwriadu,
cynllwynio
**constable** n cwnstabl,
heddgeidwad
**constant** adj cyson
**constantly** adv yn gyson
**constipate** vt rhwymo
**constipated** adj rhwym
**constipation** n rhwymedd
**constituency** n etholaeth
**constituent** adj cyfansoddol ▷ n
etholwr; cyfansoddyn
**constitution** n cyfansoddiad
**constitutional** adj cyfansoddiadol
**constraint** n cyfyngydd, cyfyngiad

**construct** vt ffurfio, llunio, adeiladu, saernïo
**construction** n adeiladwaith, lluniad; cystrawen
**constructive** adj ymarferol, adeiladol
**construe** vt cyfieithu; dehongli
**consul** n ynad, conswl; consul
**consulate** n consuliaeth
**consult** vb ymgynghori
**consultant** n ymgynghorwr
**consume** vb treulio, difa, ysu; nychu
**consumer** n prynwr, treuliwr, defnyddiwr
**consummate** adj perffaith, cyflawn
**consummate** vt perffeithio, cyflawni
**consumption** n traul; darfodedigaeth
**contact** n cyffyrddiad, cyswllt; **contact lenses** npl gwydrau cyffwrdd
**contagious** adj heintus
**contain** vt cynnwys, dal
**container** n cynhwysydd
**contaminate** vt halogi, llygru, heintio
**contemplate** vb ystyried, myfyrio; bwriadu
**contemporary** adj cyfoes(ol) ▷ n cyfoeswr
**contempt** n dirmyg, diystyrwch; **~ of court** dirmyg llys
**contemptuous** adj dirmygus
**contend** vb ymryson, cystadlu
**contender** n cystadleuydd
**content** adj bodlon ▷ vt bodloni
**content** n cynnwys
**contented** adj bodlon
**contention** n cynnen, ymryson
**contentment** n bodlonrwydd
**contents** npl cynnwys, cynhwysiad
**contest** n cystadleuaeth, ymryson
**contest** vb amau, ymryson, ymladd
**contestant** n cystadleuydd

**context** n cyd-destun
**continent** adj cymedrol; diwair
**continent** n cyfandir
**continental** adj cyfandirol
**contingency** n damwain, digwyddiad
**continual** adj parhaus, gwastadol
**continuation** n parhad
**continue** vb parhau, para, dal (i)
**continuous** adj parhaol, di-fwlch, di-dor
**contort** vt gwyrdroi, dirdynnu
**contour** n amlinell, cyfuchlinedd
**contra-** prefix gwrth-, croes-
**contraband** adj, n (nwyddau) gwaharddedig
**contraceptive** n cyfarpar gwrth-genhedlu
**contract** n cytundeb, cyfamod
**contract** vb byrhau; cytuno, cyfamodi
**contraction** n talfyriad, cywasgiad
**contractor** n contractwr, adeiladydd
**contradict** vt gwrth-ddweud
**contraption** n dyfais
**contrary** adj gwrthwyneb, croes; **on the ~** i'r gwrthwyneb
**contrast** n gwrthgyferbyniad ▷ vb gwrthgyferbynnu
**contribute** vb cyfrannu
**contribution** n cyfraniad
**contributor** n cyfrannwr
**contrive** vb dyfeisio, llwyddo, trefnu
**control** vt llywodraethu, rheoli ▷ n rheolaeth, awdurdod; **self ~** hunan-reolaeth
**controversial** adj dadleuol
**controversy** n dadl
**convalesce** vi ymadfer, gwella
**convene** vt galw, gwysio, cynnull
**convenience** n cyfleustra, hwylustod
**convenient** adj cyfleus, gweddus, hwylus
**convent** n cwfaint, lleiandy

**convention** n confensiwn, cynhadledd
**conventional** adj confensiynol
**conversant** adj cyfarwydd, cynefin
**conversation** n ymddiddan, sgwrs
**converse** vi ymddiddan, ymgomio
**converse** adj, n gwrthwyneb, cyferbyniol
**conversion** n tröedigaeth, tro
**convert** vt troi, newid, trosi; **~ed try** trosgais
**convertible** adj trosadwy
**convex** adj crwm
**convey** vt cludo; trosi, trosglwyddo; cyfleu
**conveyor belt** n cludfelt
**convict** vt barnu'n euog, euogfarnu; argyhoeddi
**convict** n troseddwr
**conviction** n euogfarn; argyhoeddiad
**convince** vt argyhoeddi
**convincing** adj argyhoeddiadol
**convulse** vt dirgrynu, dirdynnu
**cook** n cogydd, cogyddes ▷ vb coginio, gwneud bwyd
**cooker** n cwcer; **pressure ~** gwascogydd, sosban wyllt
**cookery** n coginiaeth
**cooking** n coginiaeth
**cool** adj oeri, oeraidd; hunanfeddiannol ▷ vb oeri, claearu
**coop** n cawell, cut ieir ▷ vt cutio
**co-operate** vi cydweithio, cydweithredu
**co-operation** n cydweithrediad
**co-operative** n cydweithfa ▷ adj cydweithredol
**co-opt** vt cyfethol
**co-ordinate** n cyfesuryn ▷ vb cyfesur, cyd-drefnu
**cop** n plismon ▷ vt dal
**cope** n copa, crib
**cope** vi ymdaro â, ymdopi â
**copious** adj helaeth, dibrin
**copper** n copr, copor
**copse** n prysgwydd, prysglwyn

**copy** n copi ▷ vt copïo
**copyright** n hawlfraint
**coracle** n cwrwgl
**coral** n cwrel
**cord** n cortyn, rheffyn, tennyn ▷ vt rheffynnu
**cordial** adj o galon, calonnog ▷ n cordial, gwirod
**cordon** n rhes, cadwyn
**corduroy** n melfaréd, rib
**core** n calon, perfedd, craidd
**cork** n corc, corcyn ▷ vt corcio
**corkscrew** n corcsgriw
**cormorant** n mulfran, bilidowcar
**corn** n ŷd, llafur
**corn** n corn (ar droed)
**corned beef** n corn-bîff
**corner** n congl, cornel, cil ▷ vt cornelu; **~ kick** cic gornel
**cornet** n corned
**cornflakes** npl creision ŷd
**cornflour** n blawd corn
**coronation** n coroniad
**coroner** n crwner
**coronet** n coronig
**corporal** adj corfforol
**corporate** adj yn un corff, corfforedig
**corporation** n corfforaeth; cest
**corporeal** adj corfforol; materol
**corps** n corfflu
**corpse** n corff (marw), celain
**corpuscle** n corffilyn
**correct** adj cywir ▷ vt cywiro, ceryddu
**correction** n cywiriad; cerydd
**correspond** vi cyfateb; gohebu
**correspondence** n cyfatebiaeth; gohebiaeth
**correspondent** n gohebydd
**corridor** n coridor
**corrode** vb cyrydu, ysu, rhydu, treulio
**corrugated** adj rhychiog, gwrymiog
**corrupt** adj llygredig, pwdr ▷ vb llygru

**corruption** n llygredigaeth
**corset** n staes
**cosmetic** n cosmetig
**cost** vi costio ▷ n cost, traul
**costly** adj drudfawr, drud, prid
**costume** n gwisg, costiwm
**cosy** adj cysurus, clyd
**cot** n gwely bychan, cot
**cottage** n bwthyn
**cotton** n cotwm; edau; **~ wool**
gwlân cotwm
**couch** n glwth, soffa ▷ vb gorwedd
**cough** n peswch ▷ vb pesychu
**council** n cyngor; **~ house** tŷ cyngor
**councillor** n cynghorwr
**counsel** n cyngor ▷ vt cynghori
**counsellor** n cynghorwr,
cyfarwyddwr
**count** n cyfrif ▷ vb rhifo, cyfrif; **~ the
cost** bwrw'r draul
**count** n iarll
**countenance** n wynepryd;
cefnogaeth ▷ vt cefnogi
**counter** n cownter
**counter-** prefix gwrth- ▷ adj croes
▷ adv yn erbyn, yn groes
**counteract** vt gwrthweithio
**counterfeit** n ffug, twyll ▷ adj gau,
ffug ▷ vt ffugio
**counterfoil** n gwrthddalen
**countermand** vt gwrthorchymyn
**counterpane** n cwrlid, cwilt gwely
**counterpart** n rhan gyfatebol,
cymar
**countess** n iarlles
**countless** adj aneirif, di-rif
**country** n gwlad, bro ▷ adj
gwladaidd, gwledig; **~ music** canu
gwlad
**countryman** n gwladwr
**countryside** n cefn gwlad
**county** n sir, swydd
**coup** n ergyd, trawiad, dymchwel,
llwyddiannus
**couple** n cwpl ▷ vt cyplu, cyplysu
**couplet** n cwpled
**coupon** n cwpon

**courage** n gwroldeb, dewrder
**courier** n cennad; tywyswr
**course** n cwrs, hynt ▷ vt hela,
ymlid; **of ~** wrth gwrs; **in the ~ of** yn
ystod; **in due ~** yn ei bryd; **crash ~**
cwrs carlam
**court** n llys; cwrt; cyntedd ▷ vt caru
**courteous** adj cwrtais
**courtesy** n cwrteisrwydd, cwrteisi
**courtier** n gŵr llys, llyswr
**courtly** adj llysaidd, boneddigaidd
**court-martial** n cwrt-marsial ▷ vb
dodi ar brawf
**courtship** n carwriaeth
**courtyard** n buarth, cwrt, clos, iard
**cousin** n cefnder; cyfnither
**cove** n cil, cilfach
**covenant** n cyfamod ▷ vb
cyfamodi
**cover** vt gorchuddio, toi; amddiffyn
▷ n gorchudd, clawr; **cover charge**
n tâl am wasanaeth; **book ~** clawr
llyfr; **to take ~** cuddio, cysgodi
**covert** adj cêl, cudd, dirgel
**covert** n lloches; prysglwyn
**covet** vt chwennych, chwenychu
**cow** n buwch; **barren ~** myswynog;
**milking ~** buwch odro; **~ in calf**
buwch gyflo
**coward** n llwfrddyn, llwfryn, llwfrgi
**cowardice** n llwfrdra
**cowardly** adj llwfr
**cowboy** n cowboi
**cower** vi swatio, cyrcydu
**cowl** n cwcwll, cwfl
**cowpox** n brech y fuwch
**cowslip** n briallu Mair
**coxwain** n llywydd cwch, cocs
**coy** adj swil, gwylaidd
**crab** n cranc
**crab (apple)** n afal sur, afal crabas
**crack** vb cracio, hollti ▷ n crac
**cracker** n cracer; bisgeden
**crackle** vi clindarddach
**cradle** n crud, cawell; cadair fagu
**craft** n crefft; cyfrwystra, dichell;
llong, bad

**craftsman** *n* crefftwr
**craftsmanship** *n* crefftwriaeth
**crafty** *adj* cyfrwys, dichellgar
**crag** *n* craig, clegr, clogwyn
**cram** *vb* gorlenwi, stwffio, saco
**cramp** *n* cwlwm gwythi, cramp;
  creffyn ▷ *vt* caethiwo, gwasgu
**cramped** *adj* clòs
**cranberries** *npl* llugaeron
**crane** *n* garan, crëyr, crychydd,
  craen ▷ *vt* estyn (gwddf)
**cranium** (-ia) *n* penglog
**crank** *n* cranc; mympwywr ▷ *vi*
  cam-droi; troi
**crankshaft** *n* camwerthyd,
  cranciafft
**cranny** *n* agen, hollt, agennig
**crape** *n* crêp
**crash** *vb* gwrthdaro, cwympo ▷ *n*
  gwrthdrawiad, cwymp; **crash
  helmet** *n* helmed ddiogelwch
**crate** *n* cawell
**crater** *n* safn llosgfynydd; ceudod,
  cawg
**cravat** *n* cadach gwddf, crafat
**crave** *vb* crefu, deisyf, chwennych,
  dyheu
**craving** *n* blys, chwant
**crawl** *vi* ymlusgo, cropian; crafu
**crayon** *n* creon
**craze** *n* ysfa
**crazy** *adj* penwan, gorffwyll, o'i gof
**creak** *vi* gwichian
**cream** *n* hufen
**creamery** *n* hufenfa
**creamy** *adj* hufennog
**crease** *n* ôl plygiad, plyg ▷ *vt* crychu
**create** *vt* creu
**creation** *n* cread, creadigaeth
**creative** *adj* creadigol
**creator** *n* crëwr, creawdwr
**creature** *n* creadur
**crêche** *n* meithrinfa
**credence** *n* cred, coel, ffydd
**credentials** *npl* credlythyrau
**credible** *adj* credadwy, hygoel,
  hygred

**credit** *n* coel, cred; clod, credyd ▷ *vt*
  coelio; **~ card** cerdyn credyd
**creditor** *n* credydwr
**credulous** *adj* hygoelus
**creed** *n* credo
**creek** *n* cilfach
**creep** *vi* ymlusgo, cropian
**creeper** *n* dringiedydd
**creepy** *adj* iasol
**cremate** *vt* amlosgi
**crematorium** *n* amlosgfa
**crêpe** *n* crêp
**crescent** *n* hanner lleuad; cilgant
  ▷ *adj* cynyddol
**cress** *n* berwr
**crest** *n* crib; mwng; arwydd ar
  arfbais
**Crete** *n* Creta
**crevice** *n* agen, hollt, rhigol
**crew** *n* criw, gwerin llong; haid
**crib** *n* preseb; caban; gwely plentyn
  ▷ *vt* copïo
**cricket** *n* criced; cricsyn
**crime** *n* trosedd
**criminal** *adj* troseddol ▷ *n*
  troseddwr
**crimson** *adj, n* rhuddgoch
**cringe** *vi* cynffonna, ymgreinio
**crinkle** *vb* crychu ▷ *n* crych, plyg
**cripple** *n* cloff, efrydd ▷ *vt* cloffi,
  efryddu
**crisis** (**crises**) *n* argyfwng
**crisp** *adj* cras, crych
**crisps** *npl* creision tatws
**criterion** (-ia) *n* maen prawf, safon
**critic** *n* beirniad
**critical** *adj* beirniadol; pryderus;
  peryglus
**criticism** *n* beirniadaeth
**criticize** *vt* beirniadu
**croak** *vi* crawcian ▷ *n* crawc
**crochet** *vb* crosio ▷ *n* crosiet,
  gwaith crosio
**crockery** *n* llestri
**crocodile** *n* crocodil
**crocus** *n* saffrwn, crocus
**croft** *n* tyddyn, crofft

**crony** n cyfaill agos, cydymaith
**crook** n crwca, bagl, ffon fugail; troseddwr
**crooked** adj crwca, cam
**crop** n cnwd, cynnyrch; crombil ▷ vt tocio, torri
**cross** n, adj croes ▷ vb croesi
**cross-cut** vb trawsdorri
**cross-examine** vb croesholi
**crossing** n croesfan
**cross-road** n croesffordd
**cross-section** n trawsdoriad
**crosswise** adv ar groes
**crossword** n croesair
**crotchet** n crosied
**crouch** vi cyrcydu ▷ n cwrcwd
**crow** n brân
**crow** vi canu fel ceiliog; ymffrostio
**crow-bar** n trosol, bar haearn
**crowd** n torf, tyrfa ▷ vb tyrru, heidio
**crowded** adj llawn o bobl
**crown** n coron; corun ▷ vt coroni
**crucial** adj hanfodol, terfynol
**crucifix** n croeslun
**crucifixion** n croeshoeliad
**crucify** vt croeshoelio
**crude** adj cri, crai; llymrig, amrwd
**cruel** adj creulon
**cruelty** n creulondeb
**cruet** n criwed
**cruise** vi morio ▷ n mordaith
**cruiser** n gwiblong
**crumb** n briwsionyn
**crumble** vb briwsioni, malurio ▷ n briwsiongrwst
**crumbly** adj briwsionllyd
**crumpet** n crymped; lefren
**crumple** vb crychu, gwasgu
**crunch** vb creinsio
**crupper** n pedrain, crwper, pen ôl
**crusade** n rhyfel y groes, croesgad
**crush** vb gwasgu, llethu ▷ n gwasgiad, torf
**crust** n crawen, crofen, crystyn
**crutch** n bagl, ffon fagl
**crux** n craidd
**cry** vb llefain, wylo, crio ▷ n llef, sgrech, cri

**cryptic** adj dirgel, cyfrin
**crystal** n grisial ▷ adj grisialaidd
**crystallisation** n crisialiad
**cub** n cenau
**cube** n ciwb ▷ vb ciwbio
**cubic** adj ciwbig; **~ root** gwreiddyn ciwb
**cubicle** n cuddygl
**cuckoo** n cog, cwcw; gwirionyn
**cucumber** n cucumer
**cud** n cil
**cuddle** vb anwylo, anwesu, tolach
**cue** n awgrym; ciw
**cuff** n torch llawes
**cuff** vt cernodio ▷ n cernod, dyrnod
**cul-de-sac** n pen ffordd, heol hosan
**cull** vt dewis, pigo
**culminate** vi cyrraedd ei anterth, diweddu
**culmination** n anterth
**culpable** adj beius, camweddus
**culprit** n troseddwr, drwgweithredwr
**cult** n addoliad, cwlt
**cultivate** vt diwyllio, trin, meithrin
**cultural** adj diwylliannol
**culture** n diwylliant; gwrtaith
**cultured** adj diwylliedig, coeth
**cumbersome** adj afrosgo, beichus
**cunning** adj dichellgar, cyfrwys ▷ n cyfrwystra
**cup** n cwpan
**cupboard** n cwpwrdd
**cup-tie** n gornest gwpan
**curate** n curad
**curator** n curadur
**curb** n genfa, atalfa; cwrbyn ▷ vt ffrwyno
**curd** n caul, ceuled; caws
**curdle** vb ceulo, cawsio, cawsu
**cure** n iachâd, gwellhad; meddyginiaeth ▷ vb iacháu, gwella; halltu
**curfew** n hwyrgloch
**curiosity** n cywreinrwydd, chwilfrydedd

**curious** adj cywrain; chwilfrydig; hynod
**curl** n cwrl, cudyn ▷ vb cyrlio
**curlew** n gylfinir
**curly** adj cyrliog, crych
**currants** npl grawn Corinth, cwrens; **currant bread** bara brith
**currency** n arian breiniol
**current** adj rhedegol, cyfredol, cyfoes ▷ n ffrwd, llif; **~ account** cyfrif cyfredol; **~ affairs** materion cyfoes
**currently** adv ar hyn o bryd
**curriculum** n cwricwlwm; **National C~** Cwricwlwm Cenedlaethol
**curry** vt trin lledr ▷ n cyrri; **to ~ favour** cynffonna, ceisio ffafr
**curse** n melltith, rheg ▷ vb melltithio, rhegi
**cursory** adj brysiog, diofal
**curt** adj cwta, byr, cryno
**curtail** vt cwtogi, talfyrru; prinhau
**curtain** n llen
**curtsy** n cyrtsi
**curve** vb camu, gwyro, troi ▷ n tro; cromlin
**cushion** n clustog
**custard** n cwstard
**custodian** n ceidwad
**custody** n dalfa, cadwraeth
**custom** n defod; cwsmeriaeth; toll
**customary** adj arferol
**customer** n cwsmer
**customs** npl y tollau; **customs officer** n swyddog tollau
**cut** vb torri ▷ n toriad, archoll, briw; **~ back** torri yn ôl; **~ in** torri ar draws; **~ out** torri allan; **~ through** torri trwodd
**cute** adj ciwt, cyfrwys
**cuticle** n croen, pilen, cwticl
**cutlery** n cwtleri
**cutlet** n golwyth, cydled
**cycle** n cylch; cyfres; beic ▷ vb seiclo
**cycling** n beicio
**cyclist** n beiciwr

**cyclone** n trowynt
**cygnet** n cyw alarch, alarchen
**cylinder** n rhol; silindr
**cymbal** n symbal
**cynic** n gwawdiwr, sinig
**cynical** adj gwawdlyd, dirmygus
**cynicism** n coegni, gwawd
**cyst** n coden
**cystitis** n llid y bledren
**Czechoslovakia** n Tsiecoslofacia

# d

**dab** vt dabio ▷ n dab
**dabble** vb dablo
**dad, dada, daddy** n tad, tada, tyta, dada
**daffodil** n cenhinen Bedr
**daft** adj hurt, gwirion
**dagger** n dagr, bidog
**daily** adj dyddiol, beunyddiol ▷ adv beunydd, bob dydd
**dainty** n danteithfwyd, amheuthun ▷ adj danteithiol, dillyn, del
**dairy** n llaethdy; **~ products** cynhyrchion llaeth
**dais** n esgynlawr, llwyfan
**daisy** n llygad y dydd
**dale** n dyffryn, glyn, dôl, cwm, bro
**dam** n argae, cronfa ▷ vt argáu, cronni
**dam** n mamog, mam (anifail)
**damage** n niwed, difrod ▷ vt

niweidio, difrodi; **damages** npl
iawn
**damn** vb damnio, rhegi, melltithio
**damnation** n damnedigaeth
**damned** adj colledig
**damp** adj llaith ▷ n lleithder ▷ vb
lleitho
**damson** n eirinen ddu
**dance** vb dawnsio ▷ n dawns;
**folk ~** dawns werin; **public folk ~**
twmpath dawns
**dancer** n dawnsiwr
**dandelion** n dant y llew
**dandruff** n marwdon, cen
**Dane** n brodor o Ddenmarc, Daniad
**danger** n perygl, enbydrwydd
**dangerous** adj peryglus, enbyd
**dangle** vb hongian; siglo
**dapper** adj del, twt, sionc, heini
**dare** vb beiddio, mentro
**dare-devil** n un byrbwyll, un
mentrus
**daring** adj beiddgar, mentrus ▷ n
beiddgarwch
**dark** adj tywyll ▷ n tywyllwch, nos
**darken** vb tywyllu
**darkness** n tywyllwch
**darling** n anwylyd, cariad ▷ adj
annwyl
**darn** vt cyweirio, trwsio ▷ n
cyweiriad, trwsiad
**dart** n dart, picell, saeth ▷ vb dartio,
rhuthro
**dash** vb rhuthro, chwalu,
chwilfriwio ▷ n rhuthr; llinell (-)
**dashboard** n dashfwrdd
**data** npl data
**date** n dyddiad, amseriad; datysen
(ffrwyth) ▷ vb dyddio; **out of ~**
henffasiwn, wedi dyddio; **up to ~**
hyd yn hyn, cyfoes
**dated** adj dyddiedig
**daub** vb dwbio, iro
**daughter** n merch; **~-in-law** merch
yng nghyfraith
**dawdle** vi ymdroi, swmera
**dawn** vi gwawrio, dyddio ▷ n

gwawr
**day** n diwrnod, dydd; **by ~** liw dydd;
**to~** heddiw; **next ~** trannoeth; **the
~ before yesterday** echdoe
**day-break** n gwawr, toriad dydd
**day-dream** vb pensynnu,
synfyfyrio
**daylight** n golau dydd
**day-time** n y dydd
**daze** vt synnu, syfrdanu; dallu
**dazzle** vb disgleirio, pelydru; dallu
**dazzling** adj disglair, llachar
**deacon** n diacon, blaenor
**dead** adj marw; difywyd ▷ adv
hollol; **the ~** y meirw; **~ centre** yn
ei ganol; **~ tired** wedi blino 'n lân; **~
heat** cwbl gyfartal
**deaden** vb lleddfu, marweiddio
**deadlock** n methu symud mlaen
na nôl
**deadly** adj marwol, angheuol
**Dead Sea** n: **the ~** y Môr Marw
**deaf** adj byddar
**deafen** vb byddaru
**deafness** n byddardod
**deal** vb delio; trin ▷ n trafodaeth,
dêl; **a great ~** llawer iawn; **to ~ with**
ymwneud â
**dealer** n masnachwr
**dean** n deon
**dear** adj annwyl, cu, hoff; drud ▷ n
anwylyd, cariad; **~ me** o'r annwyl!
**death** n angau, marwolaeth, tranc;
**Black D~** y Pla Du
**deathly** adj, adv fel angau,
angheuol, marwol
**death rate** n cyfradd marw
**debar** vt atal, lluddias, cau allan
**debase** vt iselu, darostwng, llygru
**debate** vb dadlau, ymryson ▷ n dadl
**debit** n debyd
**debt** n dyled
**debtor** n dyledwr
**decade** n degawd
**decadence** n dirywiad, adfeiliad
**decapitate** vt torri pen
**decay** vi dadfeilio, pydru ▷ n

dadfeiliad
**decease** n tranc, marwolaeth ▷ vi
marw, trengi
**deceased** n ymadawedig,
trancedig
**deceit** n twyll, dichell, hoced
**deceive** vt twyllo, hocedu, siomi
**December** n Rhagfyr
**decent** adj gweddus, gweddaidd
**deception** n twyll, ffug, dichell
**deceptive** adj twyllodrus,
dichellgar
**decide** vb penderfynu
**decided** adj pendant, penderfynol
**decidedly** adv yn siŵr, yn ddiau
**deciduous** adj collddail
**decimal** adj degol ▷ n degolyn; ~
**system** system ddegol; ~ **point**
pwynt degol; **recurring** ~ degolyn
cylchol
**decipher** vt datrys, dehongli
**decision** n penderfyniad
**decisive** adj penderfynol, pendant
**deck** n bwrdd llong, dec; **deck chair**
n cadair haul
**deck** vt trwsio, addurno
**declaration** n datganiad; cau
batiad
**declare** vb mynegi, datgan,
cyhoeddi
**decline** vb dadfeilio; gwrthod ▷ n
dadfeiliad; darfodedigaeth
**decompose** vb pydru, braenu;
dadelfennu
**decorate** vt addurno, arwisgo
**decoration** n addurn, tlws
**decorator** n addurnwr, peintiwr
tai
**decoy** n hud, magl ▷ vt hudo, llithio
**decrease** vb lleihau, gostwng
▷ n lleihad
**decree** n gorchymyn, dyfarniad ▷ vb
gorchymyn, dyfarnu
**dedicate** vt cysegru, cyflwyno
**dedication** n cysegriad, cyflwyniad
**deduce** vt tynnu, casglu,
diddwytho

**deduct** vt tynnu ymaith, didynnu
**deduction** n diddwythiad,
didyniad
**deed** n gweithred
**deem** vt meddwl, ystyried, barnu
**deep** adj dwfn; dwys ▷ n dwfn,
dyfnder; **deep freeze** n rhewgell; ~
**litter** gwasarn
**deepen** vb dyfnhau, trymhau,
dwysáu
**deeply** adv yn ddwys
**deer** (deer) n carw, hydd
**deface** vt difwyno, anurddo, hagru
**default** n diffyg, gwall, pall, meth
▷ vb methu, torri
**defeat** vt gorchfygu, trechu ▷ n
gorchfygiad
**defect** n diffyg, nam
**defective** adj diffygiol
**defence** n amddiffyn, amddiffyniad
**defenceless** adj diamddiffyn
**defend** vt amddiffyn
**defendant** n diffynnydd
**defender** n amddiffynnwr
**defer** vb oedi, gohirio
**defiance** n her, herfeiddiad
**defiant** adj herfeiddiol
**deficient** adj diffygiol, prin, yn
eisiau
**deficit** n diffyg
**defile** vi symud yn rhes ▷ n
culffordd, bwlch, ceunant
**defile** vt halogi, difwyno
**define** vt diffinio
**definite** adj penodol, pendant
**definitely** adv yn bendant, heb os
**definition** n diffiniad
**deflate** vb dadchwythu
**deflect** vb gwyro, osgoi
**deform** vt anffurfio, hagru,
aflunieiddio
**deformed** adj afluniaidd, anffurf
**deformity** n anffurfiad
**defraud** vt twyllo, hocedu; ysbeilio
**defray** vt talu (treuliau)
**defrost** vt (fridge) dadrewi
**defroster** n dadrewydd

**deft** *adj* medrus, hylaw, deheuig
**defunct** *adj* marw, trancedig
**defy** *vt* beiddio, herfeiddio, herio
**degenerate** *vi* dirywio ▷ *adj* dirywiedig
**degrade** *vt* diraddio, difreinio
**degree** *n* gradd
**dehydrate** *vb* dihydradu
**dehydration** *n* dihydrad
**de-ice** *vb* toddi
**deign** *vb* ymostwng, teilyngu
**deity** *n* duwdod; duw
**deject** *vt* digalonni
**dejected** *adj* digalon
**delay** *vb* oedi, gohirio ▷ *n* oediad
**delectable** *adj* hyfryd, hyfrydlon
**delegate** *vt* dirprwyo ▷ *n* dirprwy, cynrychiolydd
**delete** *vt* dileu
**deliberate** *vb* ystyried yn bwyllog ▷ *adj* pwyllog, bwriadol
**deliberately** *adv* yn fwriadol
**delicacy** *n* amheuthun, danteithfwyd; **delicacies** danteithion
**delicate** *adj* tyner; cain; gwanllyd
**delicious** *adj* danteithiol, blasus
**delight** *vb* difyrru; ymhyfrydu ▷ *n* hyfrydwch
**delightful** *adj* hyfryd, braf
**delinquency** *n* bai, trosedd
**delinquent** *n* troseddwr, tramgwyddwr ▷ *adj* troseddol, tramgwyddus
**delirious** *adj* wedi drysu, yn drysu, gwallgof
**deliver** *vt* traddodi; gwaredu, danfon; cludo
**deliverance** *n* gwaredigaeth
**delivery** *n* traddodiad; danfoniad
**dell** *n* glyn, pant, ceunant, cwm
**delude** *vt* twyllo, hudo
**deluge** *n* dilyw, dylif ▷ *vt* gorlifo
**delusion** *n* twyll, cyfeiliornad; lledrith
**delve** *vb* cloddio, palu, ymchwilio
**demand** *vt* gofyn, hawlio, mynnu
▷ *n* gofyn, hawl
**demean** *vt* ymddwyn
**demeanour** *n* ymddygiad
**demented** *adj* gwallgof, gorffwyll
**demesne** *n* treftadaeth, tiriogaeth; bro
**demi-** *prefix* hanner
**demise** *n* marwolaeth
**democracy** *n* gweriniaeth, democrat, democratiaeth
**democrat** *n* gwerinydd, gweriniaethwr
**democratic** *adj* gwerinol, democratig
**demolish** *vt* dymchwelyd, distrywio
**demonstrate** *vb* arddangos, profi; gwrthdystio
**demonstration** *n* arddangosiad; gwrthdystiad
**demonstrator** *n* arddangoswr; gwrthdystiwr
**demote** *vb* darostwng
**demur** *vi* codi gwrthwynebiad, petruso
**demure** *adj* swil, gwylaidd
**den** *n* ffau, gwâl, lloches
**denial** *n* gwadiad; nacâd, gwrthodiad; **self-~** hunanymwadiad
**Denmark** *n* Denmarc
**denomination** *n* enw, enwad
**denote** *vt* arwyddo, dynodi, hynodi
**denounce** *vt* lladd ar, cyhuddo, condemnio
**dense** *adj* tew, dwys; pendew, hurt
**density** *n* dwysedd, trwch
**dent** *n* tolc ▷ *vt* tolcio
**dental** *adj* deintiol
**dentist** *n* deintydd
**dentistry** *n* deintyddiaeth
**dentures** *npl* danedd gosod/dodi
**deny** *vt* gwadu, gomedd, gwrthod
**deodorant** *n* diaroglydd
**depart** *vi* ymadael; cychwyn
**department** *n* adran, dosbarth; **department store** *n* siop adrannol

**departure** n ymadawiad; cychwyniad
**depend** vi dibynnu
**dependable** adj dibynadwy
**dependant** n dibynnydd
**dependent** adj dibynnol
**depict** vt darlunio
**deplete** vt gwacáu, gwagu, hysbyddu
**depopulate** vt diboblogi
**deport** vt alltudio
**deportation** n alltudiaeth
**deportment** n ymddygiad, ymarweddiad
**deposit** vt dodi i lawr; adneuo; gwaddodi ▷ n adnau, blaendal; gwaddod; ~ **account** cyfrif cadw
**depot** n storfa; gorsaf
**depreciate** vb dibrisio
**depredation** n anrheithiad
**depress** vt gostwng, iselu; digalonni
**depressed** adj digalon, iselfryd
**depression** n iselder (ysbryd); dibwysiant (tywydd); pant; dirwasgiad (diwydiant)
**deprivation** n enbydrwydd, amddifadedd, colled
**deprive** vt amddifadu
**deprived** adj amddifadus
**depth** n dyfnder
**deputation** n dirprwyaeth
**deputise** vt dirprwyo
**deputy** n dirprwy
**derail** vb taflu oddi ar gledrau
**derelict** adj wedi ei adael, diberchen, diffaith
**deride** vt gwatwar, gwawdio
**derision** n gwatwar, gwawd, dirmyg
**derive** vb derbyn, cael; tarddu, deillio
**derogatory** adj amharchus, difrïol, dilornus, gwawdus
**descant** vi desgant, cyfalaw
**descend** vi disgyn
**descent** n disgyniad, disgynfa; hil, ach

**describe** vt disgrifio, darlunio
**description** n disgrifiad, darluniad
**desecrate** vt digysegru, halogi
**desert** n haeddiant
**desert** adj diffaith, anial ▷ n diffeithwch
**desert** vb gadael, cefnu ar; encilio
**deserter** n enciliwr, ffoadur
**deserve** vb haeddu, teilyngu
**deserving** adj haeddiannol, teilwng
**design** n arfaeth; cynllun ▷ vb arfaethu; cynllunio
**designer** n cynllunydd, dylunydd
**desirable** adj dymunol, dewisol
**desire** vb dymuno ▷ n dymuniad, chwant
**desk** n desg
**desolate** adj anghyfannedd, diffaith ▷ vt anghyfanheddu
**despair** n anobaith ▷ vi anobeithio
**desperate** adj diobaith, anobeithiol; gorffwyll
**desperation** n anobaith, enbydrwydd, gorffwylltra
**despicable** adj dirmygedig, ffiaidd
**despise** vt dirmygu, diystyru
**despite** prep er, er gwaethaf
**despoil** vt anrheithio, ysbeilio
**despondent** adj digalon, isel-ysbryd
**despot** n unben, gormeswr
**dessert** n pwdin, melysfwyd
**destination** n cyrchfan, pen y daith
**destiny** n tynged, tynghedfen
**destitute** adj anghenus, amddifad
**destroy** vt distrywio, difetha, dinistrio
**destroyer** n dinistrydd; distrywlong
**destruction** n distryw, dinistr
**detach** vt datod, gwahanu, dadgysylltu
**detached** adj ar wahân
**detachment** n adran; didoliad;

mintai (o filwyr)

**detail** n manylyn; (pl) manylion ▷ vb manylu, neilltuo; **in ~** yn fanwl

**detain** vt cadw, atal, caethiwo

**detect** vt canfod, darganfod, datgelu

**detection** n darganfyddiad, datgeliad

**detective** n cuddswyddog, ditectif; **~ story** stori dditectif

**detention** n carchariad, ataliad

**deter** vt cadw rhag, atal, rhwystro

**detergent** n golchydd

**deteriorate** vb dirywio, gwaethygu

**determination** n penderfyniad

**determine** vb penderfynu, pennu

**determined** adj penderfynol

**deterrent** n atalrym, ataliad

**detest** vt ffieiddio, casáu, atgasu

**detour** n cylch

**detract** vt tynnu oddi wrth, bychanu

**detriment** n colled, niwed, anfantais

**detrimental** adj niweidiol, colledus, o anfantais

**devaluation** n gwerthostyngiad, datbrisiad

**devastate** vt diffeithio, difrodi

**devastating** adj difrodus

**develop** vb datblygu

**developing** adj datblygol, ar ei brifiant

**development** n datblygiad

**device** n dyfais

**devil** n diafol, diawl, cythraul

**devilish** adj dieflig

**devious** adj diarffordd, troellog; cyfeiliornus

**devise** vt dyfeisio

**devoid** adj amddifad

**devolution** n datganoli

**devote** vt cysegru, cyflwyno, ymroddi

**devoted** adj ffyddlon, ymroddgar

**devotion** n defosiwn, ymroddiad

**devour** vt ysu, difa, traflyncu

**devout** adj duwiol, crefyddol, defosiynol

**dew** n gwlith ▷ vb gwlitho

**diabetes** n clefyd melys/siwgr

**diabetic** adj, n diabetig

**diabolical** adj dieflig

**diagnosis** n diagnosis

**diagonal** n croeslin ▷ adj croeslinol

**diagram** n darlun eglurhaol, diagram

**dial** n deial ▷ vb deialu

**dialect** n tafodiaith

**dialogue** n ymddiddan, deialog, sgwrs

**diameter** n tryfesur, diamedr

**diamond** n diemwnt

**diaphragm** n llengig; diaffram

**diarrhoea** n rhyddni, dolur rhydd

**diary** n dyddiadur, dyddlyfr

**dice** n dîs

**dictate** vb arddywedyd, gorchymyn

**dictate** n arch, galwad, gorchymyn

**dictation** n arddywediad

**dictatorship** n unbennaeth

**dictionary** n geiriadur

**diddle** vt twyllo, hocedu

**die** vi marw, trengi, trigo, darfod

**diehard** n un di-ildio

**diesel** n disel

**diet** n ymborth, lluniaeth, deiet

**dietetics** n deieteg

**differ** vi gwahaniaethu

**difference** n gwahaniaeth

**different** adj gwahanol

**differentiate** vb gwahaniaethu

**difficult** adj anodd, caled

**difficulty** n anhawster

**diffident** adj petrusgar, anhyderus

**dig** vb palu, cloddio, ceibio

**digest** vb treulio, toddi; cymathu

**digest** n crynhoad

**digestion** n treuliad, traul

**digit** n digid, bys

**digital** adj digidol

**dignified** adj urddasol

**dignify** vt anrhydeddu, urddasu

**dignity** n urddas, teilyngdod
**digress** vi gwyro, crwydro
**dike, dyke** n clawdd, ffos; argae
**dilapidate** vb adfeilio, malurio
**dilapidated** adj adfeiliedig
**dilemma** n dilema
**diligence** n diwydrwydd, dyfalwch
**diligent** adj diwyd, dyfal
**dilute** vt cymysgu â dwfr, teneuo,
gwanhau
**dim** adj pŵl, aneglur ▷ vb tywyllu,
cymylu
**dimension** n mesur, maintioli,
dimensiwn
**diminish** vb lleihau, prinhau
**diminutive** adj bychan; bachigol
▷ n bachigyn
**dimmer** n pylydd
**dimple** n pannwl, pant ▷ vb panylu
**din** n twrf, dadwrdd, mwstwr
**dine** vi ciniawa
**diner** n ciniawr
**dinghy** n dingi
**dingle** n cwm, glyn, pant
**dingy** adj tywyll, dilewyrch;
tlodaidd
**dining room** n ystafell fwyta
**dinner** n cinio; **dinner jacket** n cot
ginio, cot giniawa
**dint** n tolc; grym ▷ vt tolcio
**diocesan** adj esgobaethol ▷ n
esgob
**diocese** n esgobaeth
**dioxide** n deuocsid
**dip** vb trochi, gwlychu; gostwng
▷ n trochfa
**diphthong** n deusain, dipton
**diploma** n tystysgrif, diploma
**diplomacy** n diplomyddiaeth
**diplomat** n diplomydd
**diplomatic** adj diplomyddol
**dire** adj dygn, arswydus, echryslon
**direct** adj union, uniongyrchol ▷ vt
cyfarwyddo, cyfeirio
**direction** n cyfarwyddyd; cyfeiriad
**directly** adv yn union, yn ddi-oed
**director** n cyfarwyddwr

**directory** n cyfarwyddiadur
**dirge** n galarnad, marwnad
**dirt** n baw, llaid, llaca
**dirty** adj budr, brwnt ▷ vt budro,
diwyno, maeddu
**disability** n anabledd
**disable** vt analluogi
**disabled** adj anabl
**disadvantage** n anfantais
**disagree** vi anghytuno
**disagreeable** adj annymunol, cas
**disappear** vi diflannu
**disappearance** n diflaniad
**disappoint** vt siomi
**disappointed** adj siomedig
**disappointment** n siomedigaeth
**disapprove** vb anghymeradwyo
**disarm** vb diarfogi
**disarmament** n diarfogiad
**disarray** n anhrefn ▷ vb anrhefnu
**disaster** n trychineb, aflwydd
**disband** vb dadfyddino; gwasgaru
**disbelief** n anghrediniaeth, angoel
**disc** n disg(en)
**discard** vt rhoi heibio, gwrthod
**discern** vt canfod, dirnad
**discerning** adj deallus, craff
**discharge** vb dadlwytho, rhyddhau
▷ n gollyngdod, rhyddhad, gollwng
**discipline** n disgyblaeth ▷ vt
disgyblu
**disclaim** vt diarddel, gwadu
**disclose** vt dadlennu, datguddio
**disclosure** n datguddiad,
dadleniad
**disco** n disgo
**discomfit** vt gorchfygu,
dymchwelyd
**discomfort** vt anghysuro ▷ n
anghysur
**discompose** vt aflonyddu, cyffroi
**disconcert** vt aflonyddu, cyffroi,
tarfu
**disconnect** vb datgysylltu
**disconsolate** adj digysur,
anniddan, galarus
**discontent** n anfodlonrwydd

**discontented** *adj* anfodlon
**discontinue** *vb* torri, atal
**discord** *n* anghytgord
**discount** *n* disgownt
**discourage** *vt* digalonni
**discourteous** *adj* anghwrtais
**discover** *vt* darganfod, canfod
**discovery** *n* darganfyddiad
**discredit** *n* anfri, anghlod, amarch ▷ *vt* anghoelio; amau, difrïo
**discreet** *adj* call, synhwyrol, pwyllog
**discrepancy** *n* anghysondeb
**discretion** *n* barn, pwyll, synnwyr
**discriminate** *vb* gwahaniaethu
**discrimination** *n* gwahaniaethu, rhagfarn, anffafriaeth
**discursive** *adj* crwydrol, anghysylltiol
**discuss** *vt* trin, trafod
**discussion** *n* trafodaeth, sgwrs
**disdain** *vb* diystyru, dirmygu, diystyrwch ▷ *n* dirmyg
**disease** *n* afiechyd, clefyd, clwyf
**disembark** *vb* glanio
**disengage** *vb* datgyweddu, rhyddhau
**disentangle** *vb* datod, datrys
**disestablish** *vt* datgysylltu
**disfigure** *vt* anffurfio, anharddu, hagru
**disgrace** *vt* gwaradwyddo ▷ *n* gwaradwydd, gwarth
**disgraceful** *adj* gwaradwyddus, gwarthus
**disguise** *vt* dieithrio, ffugio, lledrithio ▷ *n* rhith, dieithrwch
**disgust** *n* diflastod, ffieidd-dod ▷ *vt* diflasu, ffieiddio
**disgusting** *adj* ffiaidd, brwnt, gwrthun
**dish** *n* dysgl; dysglaid
**dishcloth** *n* cadach llestri
**dishearten** *vt* digalonni
**dishevelled** *adj* anhrefnus, aflêr, anniben
**dishonest** *adj* anonest

**dishonour** *n* amarch, gwarth ▷ *vb* amharchu
**dishwasher** *n* peiriant golchi llestri
**disillusion** *vb* dadrithio
**disincentive** *n* gwrthgymhelliant
**disinfect** *vb* diheintio
**disinfectant** *n* diheintydd
**disintegrate** *vb* datod, chwalu
**disinterested** *adj* heb ddiddordeb, diduedd
**disjointed** *adj* datgymalog
**disk** *n* disg(en)
**dislike** *vt* casáu ▷ *n* casineb
**dislocate** *vt* rhoi o'i le, datgymalu
**dislodge** *vt* symud, syflyd, gwared
**dismal** *adj* tywyll, dilewyrch, digalon
**dismay** *vt* brawychu, siomi, digalonni ▷ *n* braw, siom, chwithdod
**dismiss** *vt* gollwng; diswyddo
**dismount** *vb* disgyn, dymchwelyd
**disobedience** *n* anufudd-dod
**disobedient** *adj* anufudd
**disobey** *vb* anufuddhau
**disorder** *n* anhrefn; anhwyldeb ▷ *vt* anhrefnu
**disorderly** *adj* afreolus, anniben
**disown** *vt* gwadu, diarddel
**disparage** *vt* amharchu, bychanu, difrïo
**disparaging** *adj* amharchus, gwaradwyddus
**disparity** *n* anghyfartaledd, rhagor
**dispatch** *vb* anfon; diweddu ▷ *n* neges
**dispel** *vt* chwalu, gwasgaru
**dispensary** *n* fferyllfa
**dispense** *vb* rhannu; gweinyddu; hepgor
**disperse** *vb* gwasgaru, chwalu, taenu
**dispirit** *vt* digalonni, llwfrhau
**dispirited** *adj* digalon, gwangalon
**display** *vt* arddangos ▷ *n* arddangosiad

**displease** vt anfodloni, anfoddio, digio

**displeasure** n anfodlonrwydd, dicter

**disposable nappies** npl clytiau untro

**dispose** vt hepgor, gwaredu

**disposition** n anianawd

**disprove** vt gwrthbrofi

**dispute** vb dadlau, ymryson ▷ n dadl

**disqualify** vb difreinio, atal

**disquiet** vt anesmwytho

**disregard** vt diystyru, esgeuluso ▷ n diystyrwch, esgeulustra

**disreputable** adj gwarthus, amharchus

**disrespect** n amarch

**disrupt** vb rhwygo, amharu ar

**dissatisfaction** n anfodlonrwydd

**dissatisfy** vt anfodloni

**dissect** vb difynio, trychu; dadansoddi

**disseminate** vt hau, taenu, lledaenu

**dissent** vi anghytuno ▷ n anghytundeb; ymneilltuaeth

**dissertation** n traethawd

**dissimilar** adj annhebyg, gwahanol

**dissipate** vt chwalu, gwasgaru, afradloni

**dissociate** vt anghysylltu, gwahanu, diaelodi

**dissolute** adj afradlon, ofer

**dissolution** n ymddatodiad, datodiad, diddymiad

**dissolve** vb toddi, datod; datgorffori, diddymu

**distance** n pellter

**distant** adj pell, pellennig, oeraidd

**distaste** n difiastod, cas

**distend** vt estyn, lledu, chwyddo

**distil** vb distyllu, dihidlo

**distillery** n distyllty

**distinct** adj gwahanol; eglur

**distinction** n arbenigrwydd, rhagoriaeth, gwahaniaeth

**distinctive** adj gwahanredol, arbennig

**distinguish** vb gwahaniaethu; hynodi

**distinguished** adj enwog, amlwg

**distort** vt ystumio, anffurfio, gwyrdroi

**distract** vb tynnu ymaith, drysu, mwydro

**distraction** n dryswch, diffyg sylw

**distress** n cyfyngder, ing, trallod

**distressing** adj trallodus, blin, poenus

**distribute** vt rhannu, dosbarthu

**distribution** n dosbarthiad, rhaniad

**distributor** n dosbarthydd, dosbarthwr

**district** n dosbarth, ardal, rhandir; ~ **council** cyngor dosbarth

**distrust** n drwgdybiaeth ▷ vb drwgdybio

**disturb** vt aflonyddu, cyffroi

**disturbance** n aflonyddwch, cyffro, terfysg

**disturbed** adj blinderus, cynhyrfus

**ditch** n ffos

**ditto** adv eto, yr un, yr un peth

**dive** vi ymsuddo, deifio

**diverse** adj gwahanol; annhebyg

**diversion** n difyrrwch, adloniant; dargyfeiriad

**divert** vt dargyfeirio, difyrru

**divide** vb rhannu, dosbarthu, gwahanu ▷ n gwahanfa

**divided** adj rhanedig

**dividend** n buddran; difidend

**divine** adj dwyfol ▷ n diwinydd ▷ vb dewinio, dyfalu

**divinity** n duwdod; diwinyddiaeth

**division** n rhan, rhaniad; cyfraniaeth; **long division** n rhannu hir

**divorce** vt ysgar(u) ▷ n ysgariad

**divorced** adj wedi ysgaru

**divulge** vt datguddio, dadlennu

**dizzy** adj penysgafn, pensyfrdan

**DJ** n troellwr

**do** vb gwneud, gwneuthur

**docile** adj dof, hywedd, hydrin

**dock** n (dail) tafol

**dock** vt tocio, cwtogi

**dock** n doc, porthladd ▷ vt docio; cwtogi

**dockyard** n iard longau

**doctor** n doctor, meddyg; doethor, doethur

**doctrine** n athrawiaeth

**document** n ysgrif, gweithred, dogfen

**documentary** adj dogfennol

**dodge** vb osgoi, twyllo ▷ n cast, ystryw

**doe** n ewig

**dog** n ci ▷ vb dal i ddilyn

**dogged** adj cyndyn, ystyfnig

**dogmatic** adj athrawiaethol; awdurdodol, pendant

**dole** n dôl, dogn; **on the ~** yn ddi-waith, ar y clwt ▷ vt dogni, rhannu

**doleful** adj trist, prudd, galarus

**doll** n dol, doli

**dollar** n doler

**dolphin** n dolffin

**domain** n tiriogaeth, maes

**dome** n cromen, cryndo

**domestic** adj teuluaidd, cartrefol; gwâr, dof

**dominant** adj trech

**dominate** vb dominyddu

**dominion** n rheolaeth; dominiwn, tiriogaeth

**don** vt gwisgo (dilledyn) ▷ n athro (coleg)

**donate** vb rhoddi

**donation** n rhodd

**donkey** n asyn, mul

**donor** n rhoddwr

**doodle** vb dwdlan

**doom** n dedfryd, barn, tynged ▷ vt dedfrydu, tynghedu, collfarnu

**doomsday** n dydd barn

**door** n drws, dôr, porth

**doorkeeper** n porthor

**door-step** n rhiniog, trothwy

**doorway** n porth, drws

**dope** n cyffur ▷ vb rhoi cyffur

**dormant** adj ynghwsg; di-rym

**dormitory** n ystafell gysgu, hundy

**dose** n dogn ▷ vt dogni

**dot** n dot ▷ vb dotio

**dote** vi dotio, gwirioni, ffoli, dylu

**double** adj, n dwbl ▷ vb dyblu, plygu; **~ glazing** gwydro dwbl, ffenestri dwbl; **~ flat** meddalnod dwbl

**double-bass** n bas dwbl

**double-dealing** n twyll

**doubt** vb amau, petruso ▷ n amheuaeth; (pl) amheuon

**doubtful** adj amheus, petrus

**doubtless** adv yn ddiamau, diau

**dough** n toes

**doughnut** n toesen

**douse** vb trochi; diffodd

**dove** n colomen

**dowdy** adj aflêr, anniben

**down** n manblu

**down** n gwaun, rhos, mynydd-dir

**down** adv i lawr, i waered; **~ and out** digalon, truenus

**downcast** adj digalon, prudd

**downfall** n cwymp, codwm, dinistr

**downpour** n tywalltiad, pistylliad ▷ vb tywallt, pistyllio

**downright** adj diamheuol

**downstairs** n y llawr ▷ adv ar y llawr

**downwards** adv i lawr, i waered

**dowry** n gwaddol

**doze** vi hepian ▷ n cyntun

**dozen** n deuddeg, dwsin

**drab** adj llwydaidd, salw

**draft** n drafft, braslun ▷ vb drafftio braslunio

**drag** vb llusgo ▷ n car llusg

**dragon** n draig

**dragon-fly** n gwas y neidr

**drain** n traen, carthffos

**drain** vb draenio, diferu, yfed; **~ing board** bwrdd diferu

**drainage** n draeniad; **~ basin** dalgylch afon

**drake** n ceiliog hwyad, meilart

**drama** n drama

**dramatic** adj dramatig

**dramatise** vb dramadeiddio, dramodi

**dramatist** n dramodydd

**drape** vt gwisgo, gorchuddio

**draper** n dilledydd

**drastic** adj cryf, llym, trwyadl

**draught** n dracht, llymaid, drafft(en); tynfa (llong)

**draughts** npl drafftiau

**draughtsman** n drafftsmon, lluniedydd

**draw** n atyniad, tynfa ▷ vb tynnu, llusgo; lluniadu, darlunio; **~ to scale** graddlunaidu; **~n game** gêm gyfartal

**drawback** n anfantais

**drawer** n drâr, drôr

**drawing** n lluniad, llun

**drawing room** n ystafell groeso

**drawl** vb llusgo (geiriau)

**dread** vb ofni, arswydo ▷ n ofn, arswyd

**dreadful** adj ofnadwy

**dream** vb breuddwydio ▷ n breuddwyd

**dreamy** adj breuddwydiol

**dreary** adj llwm, diflas, digysur

**dredge** vb glanhau

**dregs** npl gwaddod, gwaelodion, gwehilion

**drench** vt gwlychu; drensio

**dress** vb gwisgo, dilladu ▷ n gwisg

**dresser** n dreser, gwisgwr

**dressing** n dresin; **salad ~** dresin salad; **~ gown** gŵn gwisgo

**dressmaker** n gwniadwraig

**dressmaking** n gwniadwaith ▷ vb gwneud dillad

**dribble** vb dribl(ad), drefl ▷ vb driblo, dreflu, glafoerio

**drier** n peiriant sychu

**drift** n drifft, lluwch; tuedd ▷ vb drifftio, lluwchio

**drill** vb drilio ▷ n dril

**drink** vb yfed ▷ n diod, llymaid

**drinker** n yfwr, diotwr

**drinking water** n dŵr yfed

**drip** vb diferu, defnynnu ▷ n diferiad

**dripping** adj diferol ▷ n toddion, saim

**drive** n dreif, gyriant, cymhelliad ▷ vb dreifio, gyrru

**drivel** vi glafoerio, driflan, dreflu ▷ n glafoerion

**driver** n gyrrwr

**driving** adj trwm, â grym y tu ôl iddo, grymus ▷ n gyrru

**driving licence** n trwydded yrru

**drizzle** vb briwlan ▷ n glaw mân

**droll** adj digrif, ysmala

**drone** n gwenynen ormes; diogyn

**droop** vi llaesu, ymollwng; nychu

**drop** n diferyn, dafn, cwympiad ▷ vb diferu, cwympo, gollwng; **~ goal** gôl adlam

**drought** n tywydd sych, sychder, sychdwr

**drover** n porthmon, gyrrwr

**drown** vb boddi

**drowsy** adj cysglyd, marwaidd, swrth

**drudgery** n caledwaith, slafdod

**drug** n cyffur

**druid** n derwydd

**drum** n tabwrdd, drwm ▷ vb tabyrddu

**drunk** adj meddw, brwysg

**drunkard** n meddwyn

**dry** adj sych, hysb, cras ▷ vb sychu; **dry cleaners** n sych lanhawyr

**dryness** n sychder, craster

**dry rot** n sych-bydredd, tyllau pryfed

**dual** adj deuol; **~ carriageway** ffordd ddeuol

**dub** vt urddo, galw, llysenwi; dwbio, lleisio (ffilm)

**dubious** adj amheus, petrus

**Dublin** n Dulyn

**duchess** n duges
**duchy** n dugiaeth
**duck** n hwyad, hwyaden
**duck** vb trochi; gostwng pen, gwyro
**duckling** n cyw hwyaden
**dud** n ffugbeth
**due** adj dyledus, dyladwy ▷ n dyled, haeddiant
**duel** n gornest
**duet** n deuawd
**duke** n dug
**dull** adj dwl, hurt; marwaidd; diflas; cymylog; pŵl ▷ vb pylu, lleddfu
**dumb** adj mud
**dumbfound** vt syfrdanu, drysu
**dummy** n dymi; delw; ffug-bas (rygbi) ▷ vb ffug-basio
**dump** n dymp, storfa ▷ vb dympio
**dumpling** n tymplen, poten
**dunce** n hurtyn, twpsyn, penbwl
**dune** n twyn
**dung** n tom, tail
**dungarees** npl dyngarîs
**dungeon** n daeardy, daeargell, dwnsiwn
**dupe** n gwirionyn ▷ vt twyllo
**duplex** adj dwplecs
**duplicate** adj dyblyg ▷ n copi ▷ vt dyblygu
**duplicity** n dichell, rhagrith
**durable** adj parhaol, parhaus, cryf
**duration** n parhad
**duress** n gorfodaeth
**during** prep yn ystod
**dusk** n cyfnos, gwyll
**dust** n llwch ▷ vt taenu neu sychu llwch, dwstio
**dustbin** n bin sbwriel
**duster** n cadach, dwster
**dustman** n dyn lludw
**dusty** adj llychlyd
**Dutch** n Iseldireg; **Dutchman** n Iseldirwr
**dutiful** adj ufudd, ufuddgar
**duty** n dyletswydd; toll; **customs ~** tolldal; **import ~** toll fewnforio; **export ~** toll allforio

**dwarf** n cor, corrach ▷ adj corachaidd
**dwell** vi trigo, preswylio
**dwelling** n annedd, preswyl
**dwindle** vi darfod, lleihau, dirywio
**dye** vb lliwio, llifo ▷ n lliw, lliwur
**dyke** n morglawdd, cob
**dynamic** adj dynamig
**dynamics** n dynameg

# e

**each** adj, pron pob, pob un; **~ other** ei gilydd
**eager** adj awyddus, awchus
**eagle** n eryr
**ear** n clust, dolen; tywysen; **~ache** clust dost
**earl** n iarll
**early** adj cynnar, bore, boreol ▷ adv yn fore
**earmark** n clustnod, nod clust ▷ vb clustnodi, neilltuo
**earn** vt ennill, elwa
**earnest** adj difrif, difrifol, taer
**earnest** n ern, ernes ▷ vb gwystl
**earnings** npl enillion
**earphone** n ffôn clust
**earring** n clustlws
**earshot** n clyw
**earth** n daear, pridd ▷ vt priddo
**earthenware** npl llestri pridd
**earthly** adj daearol, ar wyneb daear

**earthquake** n daeargryn

**ease** n esmwythdra, esmwythyd; rhwyddineb ▷ vb esmwytho

**easel** n isl

**east** n dwyrain ▷ adj dwyreiniol; **E~ Germany** Dwyrain yr Almaen

**Easter** n y Pasg

**eastern** adj dwyreiniol

**eastwards** adj, adv tua'r dwyrain

**easy** adj hawdd, rhwydd

**easy-chair** n cadair esmwyth

**easy-going** adj didaro, di-hid

**eat** vt bwyta, ysu

**eaves** npl bargod, bondo

**eavesdrop** vb clustfeinio

**ebb** n trai ▷ vi treio

**eccentric** adj od, hynod; echreiddig

**ecclesiastic** adj eglwysig ▷ n clerigwr

**echo** n atsain, carreg ateb ▷ vb atseinio

**eclipse** n eclips, diffyg, clip ▷ vb tywyllu

**ecology** n ecoleg

**economic** adj economaidd

**economical** adj cynnil, darbodus

**economics** n economeg

**economize** vb cynilo

**economy** n cynildeb, darbodaeth, economi

**ecstasy** n gorfoledd, gorawen, hwyl

**edge** n min, ymyl ▷ vb minio, hogi; symud; **to be on** ▷ bod ar bigau'r drain

**edible** adj bwytadwy

**edict** n cyhoeddiad, gorchymyn

**Edinburgh** n Caeredin

**edit** vt golygu, paratoi i'r wasg

**edition** n argraffiad

**editor** n golygydd

**editorial** adj golygyddol

**educate** vt addysgu

**education** n addysg

**educational** adj addysgol

**eel** n llysywen

**eerie** adj iasol, annaearol

**effect** n effaith; canlyniad ▷ vt effeithio; **after-~s** sgil-effeithiau

**effective** adj effeithiol

**effectiveness** n effeithiolrwydd

**effeminate** adj merchetaidd

**efficiency** n effeithlonrwydd

**efficient** adj effeithiol, cymwys

**effort** n ymdrech, ymgais

**effusive** adj teimladol, arddangosiadol

**e.g.** adv abbr er enghraifft, e.e.

**egg** n wy; **scrambled ~** cymysgwy

**egg** vt annog, annos

**egg cup** n cwpan wy

**egg shell** n masgl/plisgyn wy

**ego** n ego, yr hunan

**egoism** n myfïaeth, egoistiaeth

**egotism** n hunanoldeb

**egotist** n un hunanol

**Egypt** n yr Aifft

**eiderdown** n cwrlid plu

**eight** adj, n wyth

**eighteen** adj, n deunaw, un deg wyth

**eighth** adj wythfed

**eighty** adj, n pedwar ugain, wyth deg

**Éire** n Iwerddon Rydd, Gweriniaeth Iwerddon

**either** adj un o'r ddau ▷ conj naill ai ▷ adv, conj na, nac, ychwaith

**ejaculate** vb saethu; gweiddi; ebychu

**eject** vt bwrw allan; diarddel

**eke** vt estyn allan; hel neu grafu

**elaborate** adj llafurfawr, manwl

**elaborate** vb manylu

**elapse** vi mynd heibio, treiglo

**elastic** adj hydwyth, ystwyth; **elastic band** n cylch lastig

**elated** adj gorawenus, calonnog

**elation** n gorawen

**elbow** n elin, penelin

**elder** n henuriad, hynafgwr ▷ adj hŷn

**elderly** adj oedrannus

**eldest** adj hynaf

**elect** vt ethol, dewis ▷ adj etholedig

**election** n etholiad; etholedigaeth
**elector** n etholwr
**electorate** n etholaeth
**electric** adj trydanol, electrig;
   **electric blanket** n blanced drydan;
   **electric fire** n tân trydan
**electrician** n trydanwr
**electricity** n trydan
**electrify** vt gwefreiddio, trydanu
**electronic** adj electronig
**elegant** adj cain, dillyn, lluniaidd
**elegy** n marwnad, galarnad
**element** n elfen
**elementary** adj elfennol
**elephant** n cawrfil, eliffant
**elevate** vt dyrchafu, codi
**eleven** adj, n un ar ddeg
**eleventh** adj unfed ar ddeg
**elf** (**elves**) n ellyll, coblyn
**elicit** vb mynnu gan
**eligible** adj cymwys, etholadwy,
   dewisol
**eliminate** vt dileu, deol
**elm** n llwyf, llwyfen
**elongate** vt hwyhau, estyn
**elongated** adj hirgul
**eloquent** adj huawdl
**else** adv arall, amgen, pe amgen
**elsewhere** adv mewn lle arall
**elude** vt osgoi
**elusive** adj di-ddal, gwibiog,
   ansafadwy
**emaciate** vt teneuo, culhau, curio
**emaciated** adj tenau, curiedig
**emanate** vi deillio, tarddu, llifo
**emancipate** vt rhyddfreinio,
   rhyddhau
**embankment** n clawdd, cob
**embargo** n gwaharddiad
**embark** vb mynd neu osod ar
   long; hwylio; **to ~ on** ymgymryd
   â, dechrau
**embarrass** vt rhwystro, drysu
**embarrassed** adj mewn penbleth,
   trafferthus
**embarrassing** adj dyrys, anffodus
**embarrassment** n chwithedd,

embaras
**embassy** n llysgenhadaeth
**embed** vb mewnosod
**embers** npl marwor, marwydos
**embezzle** vt celcio, darnguddio,
   lladrata
**embitter** vt chwerwi
**emblem** n arwyddlun
**embody** vt corffori
**emboss** vt boglynnu
**embrace** vt cofleidio; cynnwys ▷ n
   cofleidiad
**embroider** vt brodio
**embroidery** n brodwaith
**embryo** n cynelwad, embryo
**emend** vt cywiro, diwygio
**emerald** n emrallt
**emerge** vi dyfod allan, dyfod i'r
   golwg, ymddangos
**emergence** n ymddangosiad
**emergency** n cyfyngder, taro,
   argyfwng; **in an ~** mewn taro
**emigrate** vi allfudo, ymfudo
**eminent** adj enwog, amlwg, o fri
**emit** vt rhoddi neu fwrw allan
**emotion** n cyffro, teimlad,
   emosiwn
**emotional** adj emosiynol
**empathy** n empathi
**emperor** n ymerawdwr, ymherodr
**emphasis** n pwys, pwyslais
**emphasize** vt pwysleisio
**emphatic** adj pwysleisiol, pendant
**empire** n ymerodraeth
**empirical** adj empeiraidd
**employ** vt cyflogi; arfer, defnyddio
   ▷ n gwasanaeth
**employee** n gŵr cyflog
**employer** n cyflogwr
**employment** n cyflogaeth, gwaith
**empower** vt awdurdodi, galluogi
**empress** n ymerodres
**empty** adj gwag, coeg ▷ vb gwagu,
   arllwys, gwacáu, dihysbyddu
**empty-handed** adj gwaglaw
**emulate** vt ymgystadlu â; efelychu
**emulsion** n emwlsiwn

**enable** vt galluogi
**enact** vt deddfu, ordeinio; cyflawni
**enchant** vt swyno, cyfareddu, hudo
**enclose** vt amgáu
**enclosed** adj amgaeëdig
**enclosure** n lle caeëdig, lloc
**encompass** vt amgylchu, cylchynu
**encore** n encôr ▷ adv eto
**encounter** vt cyfarfod, taro ar ▷ n
   ymgyfarfod, brwydr
**encourage** vt cefnogi, calonogi,
   annog
**encouragement** n cefnogaeth,
   calondid, anogaeth
**encroach** vi llechfeddiannu
**encyclopaedia** n gwyddoniadur
**end** n diwedd; diben ▷ vb diweddu,
   dibennu, terfynu; **~ point** pwynt
   terfyn; **from ~ to ~** o ben bwy gilydd
**endanger** vt peryglu
**endear** vt anwylo
**endeavour** vi ymdrechu ▷ n
   ymdrech
**ending** n diwedd, dibeniad,
   terfyniad
**endless** adj diddiwedd
**endorse** vt cefnogi, arnodi,
   ardystio
**endorsement** n arnodiad,
   ardystiad
**endow** vt gwaddoli, cynysgaeddu,
   donio
**endowment** n gwaddol,
   cynhysgaeth
**endurance** n dygnwch
**endure** vb parhau; dioddef, goddef
**enemy** n gelyn
**energetic** adj grymus, egnïol
**energy** n ynni, egni
**enforce** vt gorfodi
**enforcement** n gorfodaeth
**engage** vb ymrwymo, dyweddïo;
   cyflogi; ymladd
**engaged** adj ymrwymedig, wedi
   dyweddïo; prysur
**engagement** n ymrwymiad,
   dyweddïad; brwydr

**engaging** adj deniadol
**engender** vt achosi, peri
**engine** n peiriant, injan
**engineer** n peiriannydd
**engineering** n peirianneg
**England** n Lloegr
**English** adj Saesneg, Seisnig ▷ n
   Saesneg; **~ Channel** Môr Udd
**Englishman (-men)** n Sais; (pl)
   Saeson
**engrave** vt ysgythru
**engraving** n ysgythrad
**engulf** vt llyncu
**enhance** vb chwanegu, mwyhau,
   chwyddo, hyrwyddo
**enjoy** vt mwynhau; meddu
**enjoyable** adj pleserus
**enjoyment** n mwynhad
**enkindle** vt ennyn
**enlarge** vt ehangu, helaethu
**enlighten** vt goleuo; hysbysu
**enlightened** adj goleuedig; golau
**enlist** vb ymrestru, listio; ennill
**enmity** n gelyniaeth
**enormity** n anfadrwydd,
   ysgelerder
**enormous** adj dirfawr, anferth,
   enfawr
**enough** adj, n, adv digon
**enquire** vb ymofyn, ymholi,
   gofyn, holi
**enquiry** n ymholiad
**enrage** vt ffyrnigo, cynddeiriogi
**enrich** vt cyfoethogi
**enrol** vt cofrestru
**enrolment** n cofrestrad
**ensign** n lluman, baner; llumanwr
**enslave** vt caethiwo
**ensue** vi dilyn, canlyn
**ensure** vt diogelu, sicrhau
**entail** vt gorfodi, gofyn
**entangle** vt drysu, maglu, rhwydo
**enter** vb mynd i mewn, treiddio;
   cofnodi
**enterprise** n anturiaeth, menter
**enterprising** adj anturiaethus,
   mentrus

**entertain** vt difyrru, adlonni; croesawu
**entertainer** n difyrrwr, diddanwr
**entertaining** adj difyrrus, diddan
**entertainment** n difyrrwch, adloniant
**enthrall** vb swyno
**enthrone** vt gorseddu
**enthusiasm** n brwdfrydedd
**enthusiastic** adj brwdfrydig, eiddgar
**entice** vb hudo, denu, llithio
**entire** adj cyfan, hollol, llwyr
**entirely** adv yn gyfan gwbl, yn llwyr
**entirety** n cyfanrwydd
**entrails** npl perfedd, ymysgaroedd
**entrance** n mynediad, mynedfa; ~ **fee** tâl mynediad
**entrance** vt swyno
**entreat** vt erfyn, ymbil, deisyf
**entrust** vt ymddiried
**entry** n mynediad, mynedfa; cofnodiad
**envelop** vt amgáu
**envelope** n amlen
**envious** adj cenfigennus
**environment** n amgylchedd, amgylchfyd
**environmental** adj amgylchol
**envisage** vb rhagweld
**envoy** n cennad, negesydd
**envy** n cenfigen, eiddigedd ▷ vt cenfigennu, eiddigeddu
**epic** adj arwrol, arwraidd ▷ n arwrgerdd, epig
**epidemic** adj heintus ▷ n haint
**epiglottis** n epiglotis
**epilepsy** n epilepsi
**Epiphany** n Yr Ystwyll
**episcopate** n esgobaeth
**episode** n digwyddiad, gogyfran, episôd
**epistle** n epistol, llythyr
**epitaph** n beddargraff
**epitome** n crynodeb, talfyriad
**equable** adj gwastad, cyson, tawel
**equal** adj cyfartal ▷ n cydradd ▷ vt

bod yn gyfartal; **without ~** heb ei ail
**equality** n cydraddoldeb, cyfartaledd
**equalize** vb cydraddoli, cyfartalu
**equally** adv yn ogystal â, yn llawn, yn gyfartal
**equanimity** n tawelwch, anghyffro
**equate** vt cyfartalu, cymharu
**equation** n hafaliad; **simple equation** n hafaliad syml; **quadratic equation** n hafaliad dwyradd; **simultaneous equation** n hafaliad cydamserol
**equator** n y cyhydedd
**equatorial** adj cyhydeddol
**equestrian** adj marchogol ▷ n marchog
**equilateral** adj hafalochrog
**equilibrium** n cydbwysedd, cymantoledd
**equip** vt taclu, paratoi, cymhwyso, cyfarparu
**equipment** n cyfarpar, offer
**equipoise** n cydbwysedd
**equivalent** adj cyfwerth, cyfartal
**equivocal** adj amwys
**era** n cyfnod
**eradicate** vt difodi, difa
**erase** vt dileu, rhwbio allan
**eraser** n dilëydd, rwber
**erect** adj syth, unionsyth ▷ vt codi, adeiladu
**ermine** n carlwm
**erode** vb ysu, treulio, erydu
**erosion** n erydiad
**erotic** adj serchol, nwydol, erotig
**err** vi cyfeiliorni
**errand** n neges, cenadwri
**erratic** adj ansefydlog, crwydraidd
**error** n cyfeiliornad, camgymeriad; bai, gwall; **in ~** ar gam
**erupt** vb echdorri, torri allan
**eruption** n echdoriad, tarddiad
**escalator** n escaladur
**escapade** n pranc, direidi
**escape** vb dianc, osgoi ▷ n

dihangfa

**escort** vt hebrwng ▷ n gosgordd
**especial** adj arbennig, neilltuol
**especially** adv yn arbennig, yn enwedig
**espionage** n ysbïaeth
**esquire** n yswain, ysgwier
**essay** n ymgais; traethawd, ysgrif
**essay** vt profi, ymgeisio
**essence** n hanfod; rhinflas
**essential** adj hanfodol, anhepgor ▷ n hanfod, anghenraid
**essentially** adv yn hanfodol
**essentials** npl hanfodion, anhepgorion
**establish** vt sefydlu
**establishment** n sefydliad
**estate** n stad, ystad, eiddo;
  **industrial ~** stad ddiwydiannol
**esteem** vt parchu, edmygu, cyfrif ▷ n parch, bri
**estimate** vt, n amcangyfrif
**estimation** n amcangyfrif, parch, bri
**estrange** vt dieithrio
**estuary** n aber
**et cetera** adv ac yn y blaen
**eternal** adj tragwyddol, bythol
**eternally** adv yn dragwyddol, yn oes oesoedd, byth bythoedd
**eternity** n tragwyddoldeb
**ethical** adj moesegol
**ethics** npl moeseg
**Ethiopia** n Ethiopia
**ethnic** adj ethnig, cenhedlig
**ethos** n ethos, naws, natur
**etiquette** n moesau, arfer
**etymology** n geirdarddiad
**eucharist** n cymun, cymundeb
**Europe** n Ewrob, Ewrop
**European** adj Ewropeaidd ▷ n Ewropead
**evacuate** vt ymgilio, ymadael (â)
**evade** vt gochelyd, osgoi
**evangelical** adj efengylaidd
**evangelist** n efengylydd
**evangelize** vt efengylu

**evaporate** vb ymageru, anweddu
**evaporated milk** n llaeth anwedd(og)
**evasion** n osgoad, gocheliad
**eve** n min nos, noswyl
**even** adj gwastad, llyfn; cyfartal ▷ adv hyd yn oed; **~ number** eilrif
**evening** n noswaith, yr hwyr, min nos; **evening class** n dosbarth nos; **evening dress** n gwisg ffurfiol
**evensong** n prynhawnol weddi, gosber
**event** n digwyddiad; **in the ~ of** os bydd
**eventful** adj llawn digwyddiadau
**eventuality** n achlysur, digwyddiad posibl
**eventually** adv o'r diwedd
**ever** adv bob amser, erioed, byth; **~ and anon** byth a hefyd
**evergreen** n, adj bythwyrdd, anwyw
**everlasting** adj tragwyddol, bythol
**evermore** adv byth, byth bythoedd
**every** adj pob
**everybody** pron pawb, pob un
**everyday** adj bob dydd, beunyddiol
**everyone** pron pawb, pob un
**everything** pron popeth
**everywhere** adv ym mhobman
**evict** vt troi allan, dadfeddiannu
**evidence** n tystiolaeth, prawf
**evident** adj amlwg, eglur
**evil** adj drwg, drygionus ▷ n drwg, drygioni
**evoke** vt galw neu dynnu allan; gwysio
**evolution** n esblygiad
**evolve** vb datblygu; esblygu
**ewe** n dafad, mamog
**ex-** prefix allan o; cyn-
**exact** adj manwl, cywir, union
**exact** vt hawlio, mynnu
**exacting** adj manwl, gorthrymus
**exactly** adv yn union, i'r dim
**exaggerate** vt chwyddo, gorliwio
**exaggeration** n gormodiaith,

gorliwiad
**exalt** vt dyrchafu, mawrygu
**examine** vt arholi, archwilio
**examination** n arholiad,
archwiliad
**examiner** n arholwr, archwiliwr
**example** n esiampl, enghraifft
**exasperate** vt llidio, cythruddo
**exasperation** n llid, cythrudd
**excavate** vt cloddio
**exceed** vt rhagori ar, bod yn fwy na
**exceedingly** adv tros ben, tra
**excel** vb rhagori
**excellent** adj rhagorol, ardderchog,
godidog, campus
**except** prep ac eithrio, eithr,
namyn, oddieithr, heblaw
**exception** n eithriad
**exceptional** adj eithriadol
**excerpt** n dyfyniad, detholiad
**excess** n gormod, gormodedd
**excessive** adj gormodol, eithafol
**exchange** vt cyfnewid, ffeirio
▷ n cyfnewid, cyfnewidfa; ~ **rate**
cyfradd cyfnewid
**exchequer** n trysorlys
**excise** n toll ▷ vt gosod toll
**excite** vt cynhyrfu, cyffroi
**excited** adj cynhyrfus
**excitement** n cynnwrf
**exciting** adj cyffrous
**exclaim** vt llefain, gweiddi,
bloeddio, ebychu
**exclamation** n llef, gwaedd,
ebychiad; ~ **mark** ebychnod
**exclude** vt cau allan, bwrw allan
**exclusion** n gwaharddiad,
gwrthodiad
**exclusive** adj cyfyngedig
**excommunicate** vt esgymuno
**excrement** n carth, tom, baw
**excrete** vt ysgarthu
**excruciating** adj dirdynnol
**excursion** n gwibdaith,
pleserdaith
**excuse** vt esgusodi ▷ n esgus
**execute** vt cyflawni, gweithredu;

dienyddio
**execution** n cyflawniad,
dienyddiad
**executioner** n dienyddiwr
**executive** adj gweithiol,
gweithredol ▷ n gweithredwr; ~
**committee** pwyllgor gwaith
**executor** n ysgutor
**exemplify** vt egluro, dangos,
enghreifftio
**exempt** adj rhydd, esgusodol ▷ vt
rhyddhau, esgusodi
**exercise** n ymarfer, ymarferiad ▷ vb
ymarfer; ~ **book** llyfr ysgrifennu,
ymarfer
**exert** vt ymegnïo, ymdrechu
**exertion** n ymdrech, ymroddiad
**exhale** vb anadlu allan
**exhaust** vt disbyddu, diffygio,
gwacáu ▷ n disbyddwr, gwacäwr;
exhaust (pipe) n pibell nwyon
**exhausted** adj lluddedig, blin,
disbyddedig, wedi ymlâdd
**exhaustion** n gorluddedd
**exhaustive** adj trwyadl
**exhibit** vt dangos, arddangos
**exhibition** n arddangosfa;
ysgoloriaeth
**exhilarate** vt llonni, sirioli,
bywiogi
**exile** n alltud; alltudiaeth ▷ vt
alltudio
**exist** vi bod, bodoli
**existence** n bod(olaeth), hanfod; **in**
~ mewn bod, ar glawr
**exit** n allanfa ▷ vb mynd allan,
ymadael
**exodus** n ymadawiad
**exonerate** vt esgusodi
**exorbitant** adj afresymol,
gormodol
**exotic** adj estron, egsotig
**expand** vb lledu, ehangu, datblygu
**expanse** n ehangder
**expansion** n ehangiad, ymlediad
**expect** vb disgwyl
**expectancy** n disgwyliad

**expectation** n disgwyliad
**expediency** n hwylustod
**expedient** adj hwylus, cyfleus
▷ n ystryw
**expedite** vt hyrwyddo, hwyluso
**expedition** n ymgyrch, alldaith
**expel** vt bwrw allan, diarddel
**expend** vt gwario, treulio
**expenditure** n gwariant
**expense** n traul, cost
**expenses** npl treuliau
**expensive** adj drud, costus
**experience** n profiad ▷ vt profi
**experienced** adj profiadol
**experiment** n arbrawf ▷ vi arbrofi
**expert** n arbenigwr ▷ adj medrus,
deheuig
**expertise** n medr, dawn,
arbenigaeth
**expire** vb anadlu allan; darfod,
marw
**expiry** n diwedd, terfyn
**explain** vt egluro, esbonio
**explanation** n eglurhad, esboniad
**explanatory** adj eglurhaol,
esboniadol
**explicit** adj eglur, manwl, echblyg
**explode** vb ffrwydro, chwalu
**exploit** n camp, gorchest ▷ vt
gweithio, gwneud elw o, ymelwa ar
**exploitation** n ymelwad
**explore** vt fforio, chwilio
**explorer** n fforiwr
**explosion** n ffrwydriad; tanchwa
**explosive** n ffrwydrydd/yn ▷ adj
ffrwydrol
**exponent** n esboniwr, dehonglwr
**export** vt allforio ▷ n allforyn
**exporter** n allforiwr
**expose** vt amlygu, dinoethi
**expound** vt esbonio
**express** vt mynegi, datgan ▷ adj
cyflym, clir ▷ n trên cyflym
**expression** n mynegiant
**expressly** adv yn unig swydd, yn
benodol
**expulsion** n diarddeliad

**exquisite** adj odiaeth, rhagorol;
coeth
**extempore** adv, adj byrfyfyr,
o'r frest
**extend** vb estyn, ymestyn; ehangu
**extension** n helaethiad, ehangiad,
(ym)estyniad
**extensive** adj ymestynnol, helaeth
**extent** n ehangder, maint, hyd,
mesur; **to some ~** i raddau
**extenuate** vt lleihau, lleddfu;
esgusodi
**exterior** adj allanol ▷ n tu allan
**exterminate** vt difodi, dileu
**external** adj allanol
**extinct** adj wedi diffodd, wedi
darfod, diflanedig
**extinguish** vt diffodd; diddymu,
dileu
**extinguisher** n diffoddwr
**extol** vt moli, moliannu, clodfori
**extort** vt cribddeilio, gwasgu
**extortionate** adj gormodol
**extra** adj ychwanegol ▷ adv tu
hwnt, dros ben ▷ n peth dros ben,
ychwanegiad
**extract** vt echdynnu, tynnu;
dyfynnu, rhinio ▷ n echdyniad;
dyfyniad; rhin, darn
**extracurricular** adj allgyrsiol
**extramural** adj allanol
**extraordinary** adj hynod,
anghyffredin
**extravagant** adj gwastraffus,
afradlon
**extreme** adj i'r eithaf, eithafol
▷ n eithaf
**extremely** adv dros ben, gor-
**extremity** n pen, eithaf; cyfyngder
**extrovert** adj allblyg, alltro ▷ n
alltroedydd, person allblyg
**eye** n llygad; crau; dolen ▷ vt
llygadu, sylwi ar, gwylio
**eyeball** n cannwyll y llygad
**eyebrow** n ael
**eyelashes** npl blew yr amrant
**eye-level** n llinell orwel

**eyelid** n amrant
**eye-opener** n agoriad llygad
**eyesight** n golwg
**eyesore** n hyllbeth
**eyewitness** n llygad-dyst

# f

**fable** n chwedl, dameg; anwiredd
**fabric** n adail, adeilad, defnydd
**fabricate** vt llunio, dyfeisio, ffugio
**fabrication** n ffug, anwiredd
**fabulous** adj chwedlonol, diarhebol
**face** n wyneb, wynepryd ▷ vb
wynebu; **face cloth** n clwtyn
ymolchi; **~ value** arwynebwerth
**facilitate** vt hwyluso, hyrwyddo
**facility** n hwylustod, cyfleustra,
rhwyddineb
**fact** n ffaith, gwirionedd; **as a
matter of ~** mewn gwirionedd
**factor** n ffactor, elfen, nodwedd;
**prime ~** ffactor cysefin
**factory** n ffatri
**factual** adj ffeithiol
**faculty** n cynneddf; cyfadran
**fad** n mympwy, chwilen
**fade** vb diflannu, gwywo; colli ei liw
**fag** vb slafio, ymlâdd, blino ▷ n
caledwaith; lludded; gwas bach
**fail** vi ffaelu, methu, pallu, diffygio;
**without ~** yn ddi-ffael
**failure** n methiant, pall,

aflwyddiant
**faint** adj llesmeiriol, gwan, llesg ▷ vi
llewygu ▷ n llesmair, llewyg
**fair** n ffair
**fair** adj teg, glân; gweddol; golau
**fairly** adv yn deg/lân, yn weddol
**fairness** n glendid, tegwch
**fairy** n un o'r tylwyth teg
**fairy-tale** n stori hud, chwedl
werin
**faith** n ffydd, cred, coel
**faithful** adj ffyddlon, cywir
**faithfully** adv yn fyddlon, yn gywir;
**yours ~** yr eiddoch yn gywir
**fake** n ffug ▷ vb ffugio
**falcon** n hebog, curyll
**fall** vi cwympo, syrthio ▷ n cwymp;
**~ out** cweryla; **~ through** methu
**fallacy** n cyfeiliornad, gwall
**fallow** n braenar ▷ vt braenaru
**false** adj gau, ffug, ffals, twyllodrus;
**~ teeth** dannedd gosod/dodi
**falter** vb petruso, methu, pallu
**fame** n enwogrwydd, clod, bri
**familiar** adj cynefin, cyfarwydd
**familiarity** n cynefindra
**family** n teulu, tylwyth
**famine** n newyn
**famish** vb newynu, llwgu
**famous** adj enwog
**fan** n gwyntyll; ffan ▷ vt gwyntyllio,
chwythu
**fanatic** n penboethyn, ffanatig
**fanaticism** n penboethni,
ffanatigiaeth
**fanciful** adj ffansïol
**fancy** n dychymyg, ffansi, serch ▷ vt
dychmygu, ffansïo, serchu; **~ dress**
gwisg ffansi
**fang** n ysgithr, dant, pig, blaen
**fantastic** adj ffantastig, rhyfeddol
**fantasy** n ffantasi
**far** adj pell(ennig) ▷ adv ymhell; **as
~ as** hyd at
**farce** n ffars
**fare** n cost, pris; ymborth ▷ vi bod,
dod ymlaen, byw

**farewell** *excl* yn iach, ffarwel ▷ *n* ffarwel; **to bid ~** canu'n iach
**farm** *n* fferm ▷ *vt* amaethu, ffarmio
**farmer** *n* ffarmwr, ffermwr, amaethwr; **Young F~s' Club** Clwb y Ffermwyr Ifainc
**farmhouse** *n* ffermdy
**farming** *n* ffermio; **intensive ~** ffermio dwys
**farmyard** *n* buarth, clos
**fascinate** *vt* hudo, swyno
**fascinating** *adj* hudol, swynol
**fascism** *n* ffasgaeth
**fashion** *n* ffasiwn, arfer, dull ▷ *vt* llunio, gwneud
**fashionable** *adj* ffasiynol
**fast** *vi* ymprydio ▷ *n* ympryd
**fast** *adj* tyn, sownd; buan, cyflym, clau
**fasten** *vb* sicrhau, cau, clymu, ffasno
**fastener** *n* ffasnydd
**fastening** *n* ffasnin
**fastidious** *adj* cysetlyd
**fat** *adj* tew, bras ▷ *n* braster, bloneg, saim
**fatal** *adj* angheuol, marwol; andwyol
**fatality** *n* trychineb, marwolaeth
**fate** *n* tynged, ffawd ▷ *vt* tynghedu
**fateful** *adj* tyngedfennol
**father** *n* tad ▷ *vt* tadogi
**father-in-law** *n* tad-yng-nghyfraith
**fatherly** *adj* tadol
**fathom** *n* gwryd ▷ *vt* plymio
**fatigue** *n* lludded, blinder ▷ *vt* lluddedu, blino
**fatten** *vb* tewhau, pesgi
**fatty** *adj* seimlyd, brasterog
**fatuous** *adj* ynfyd, ffôl
**fault** *n* bai, diffyg, nam, anaf; **at ~** ar fai
**faultless** *adj* di-fai, perffaith
**faulty** *adj* gwallus, diffygiol
**favour** *n* ffafr, cymwynas ▷ *vt* ffafrio; **in ~ of** o blaid

**favourable** *adj* ffafriol
**favourite** *adj*, *n* ffefryn ▷ *adj* hoff
**fawn** *n* elain ▷ *adj* llwyd
**fawn** *vi* cynffonna, gwenieithio
**fear** *n* ofn, braw, arswyd ▷ *vb* ofni, arswydo
**fearful** *adj* ofnus, brawychus, arswydus
**feasible** *adj* dichonadwy
**feast** *n* gwledd, gŵyl ▷ *vb* gwledda
**feat** *n* camp, gorchest
**feather** *n* pluen, plufyn ▷ *vt* pluo, plufio
**feature** *n* arwedd, nodwedd
**February** *n* Chwefror, Mis Bach
**federal** *adj* cynghreiriol, ffederal
**fee** *n* ffi, tâl, cyflog
**feeble** *adj* gwan, eiddil
**feed** *vb* porthi, ymborthi, bwydo ▷ *n* porthiant, ffîd, ymborth, gwledd
**feedback** *n* adborth, ymateb ▷ *vb* adborthi
**feel** *vb* teimlo, clywed, profi
**feeler** *n* teimlydd; ymchwiliad
**feeling** *n* teimlad, synhwyriad
**feign** *vb* cymryd arno, ffugio
**fell** *vb* cwympo, cymynu ▷ *n* croen; ffridd, rhos
**fellow** *n* cymar; cymrawd ▷ *prefix* cyd-
**fellowship** *n* cymdeithas, cyfeillach; cymrodoriaeth
**felt** *n* ffelt ▷ *vb* ffeltio
**female** *adj*, *n* benyw
**feminine** *adj* benywaidd, benywol
**feminist** *n* ffeminist
**femur** *n* ffemwr
**fence** *n* clawdd, ffens ▷ *vb* cau, amgáu
**fencing** *n* ffensio, cleddyfaeth
**fend** *vb* cadw draw; ymdaro, ymdopi
**ferment** *n* eples, cynnwrf ▷ *vb* eplesu, cynhyrfu
**fermentation** *n* eplesiad
**fern** *n* rhedynen, rhedyn
**ferocious** *adj* ffyrnig, gwyllt, milain
**ferret** *n* ffured ▷ *vt* ffuredu,

chwilota

**ferry** n porth, fferi ▷ vb cludo dros

**ferry-boat** n ysgraff

**fertile** adj ffrwythlon, toreithiog

**fertilisation** n ffrwythloniad

**fertility** n ffrwythlonder

**fertilize** vb ffrwythloni; gwrteithio

**fertilizer** n gwrtaith

**fervent** adj brwd, gwresog, tanbaid, taer

**fester** vi crawni, gori, crynhoi

**festival** n gŵyl, dydd gŵyl; **singing ~** cymanfa ganu

**festive** adj llawen, llon

**festivity** n rhialtwch, miri, ysbleddach

**fetch** vt cyrchu, hôl, ymofyn, nôl

**fête** n gŵyl, miri ▷ vi gwledda

**feud** n cynnen, ffiwd

**feudal** adj ffiwdal

**feudalism** n ffiwdaliaeth

**fever** n twymyn, clefyd, gwres

**feverish** adj â thwymyn

**few** adj ychydig, prin, anaml

**fiancé(e)** n darpar-ŵr/wraig

**fib** n anwiredd, celwydd

**fibre** n edefyn, ffibr

**fibreglass** n ffibr gwydrog

**fickle** adj anwadal, oriog, gwamal

**fiction** n ffuglen

**fictitious** adj ffug, ffugiol

**fiddle** n ffidil, crwth ▷ vi canu'r ffidl; ffidlan

**fidelity** n ffyddlondeb, cywirdeb

**fidget** vt ffwdanu, aflonyddu ▷ n un ffwdanus, un aflonydd

**field** n cae, maes ▷ vb maesu

**field marshal** n maeslywydd

**field work** n gwaith maes

**fiend** n cythraul, ellyll, ysbryd drwg

**fierce** adj ffyrnig, milain; tanbaid

**fiery** adj tanllyd, tanbaid

**fifteen** adj, n pymtheg

**fifth** adj, n pumed

**fifty** adj, n hanner cant, deg a deugain

**fig** n ffigysen

**fight** vb ymladd, cwffio, brwydro, rhyfela ▷ n ymladdfa, brwydr

**fighter** n ymladdwr, brwydrwr

**fighting** n ymladd

**figment** n creadigaeth (y dychymyg)

**figurative** adj ffigurol, cyffelybiaethol

**figure** n ffigur; llun, ffurf ▷ vb cyfrif; llunio; ymddangos; **~ of speech** troad ymadrodd

**figurehead** n arweinydd (mewn enw)

**file** n ffeil, rhathell; rhes ▷ vb ffeilio, rhathu

**fill** vb llenwi ▷ n llenwad, llonaid, gwala

**fillet** n llain, ffiled; **fillet steak** n stêc ffiled

**filling** n llenwad, mewnyn

**filly** n eboles

**film** n pilen, caenen; ffilm ▷ vb ffilmio, gwneud ffilm; **~ strip** stribed ffilm

**filter** n hidl, hidlydd ▷ vb hidlo, ffiltro; **filter tip** n hidl difaco

**filth** n brynti, budreddi, baw

**filthy** adj brwnt, budr, aflan

**filtrate** n hidlif ▷ vb hidlo

**fin** n adain, asgell, ffin

**final** adj terfynol, olaf; **semi-~** cynderfynol

**finale** n ffinale, diweddglo

**finally** adv o'r diwedd, yn olaf

**finance** n cyllid ▷ vb cyllido, codi arian

**financial** adj cyllidol, ariannol

**find** vt darganfod ▷ n darganfyddiad

**finding** n darganfyddiad, dedfryd

**fine** adj main; mân; gwych; braf

**fine** n dirwy ▷ vt dirwyo

**finery** n gwychder

**finger** n bys ▷ vt bysio, bodio; **little ~** bys bach; **third ~** bys y fodrwy; **middle ~** y bys canol

**fingerprint** n bysbrint, ôl bys

**finicky** adj cysetlyd, gorfanwl

**finish** vb diweddu, gorffen, cwblhau
▷ n diwedd; gorffeniad
**finished** adj gorffenedig
**finite** adj meidrol
**Finland** n y Ffindir
**fir** n ffynidwydden
**fire** n tân ▷ vb tanio, ennyn; **wild
~** tân gwyllt; **~ precautions**
rhagodion tân
**firearm** n arf-tân
**firebrigade** n brigâd dân
**fire engine** n peiriant tân
**fire escape** n grisiau tân
**fire-extinguisher** n diffoddydd
tân
**fireguard** n sgrin dân
**fireman** n taniwr, diffoddwr tân
**fireplace** n lle tân
**fireside** n aelwyd
**firewood** n coed tân, cynnud
**fireworks** npl tân gwyllt
**firm** n cwmni, ffyrm ▷ adj cadarn,
diysgog
**firmly** adv yn gadarn, yn ddiysgog
**first** adj cyntaf, blaenaf, prif ▷ adv yn
gyntaf; **first aid** n cymorth cyntaf;
**first class** adj dosbarth cyntaf;
**first floor** n llawr cyntaf; **first-hand**
adj o lygad y ffynnon; **first-rate** adj
campus, ardderchog, rhagorol
**fish** n pysgodyn, pysgod ▷ vb
pysgota; **~ and chips** pysgodyn a
sglodion
**fisherman** n pysgotwr
**fishing** n pysgota
**fishing rod** n genwair, gwialen
bysgota
**fishmonger** n gwerthwr pysgod
**fishy** adj amheus; pysgodol
**fist** n dwrn
**fit** n llewyg, ffit, mesur
**fit** adj ffit, addas, cymwys, gweddus;
abl, iach ▷ vb ffitio, gweddu, taro
**fitful** adj anwadal, gwamal
**fitment** n cynhalydd
**fitness** n ffitrwydd, addasrwydd
**fitter** n ffitiwr

**fitting** n ffitiad ▷ vb ffitio ▷ adj
priodol, gweddus, addas; **~s** mân
daclau, ffitiadau
**five** adj pum ▷ n pump
**fix** vb sicrhau, sefydlu, gosod ▷ n
cyfyngder, cyfyng-gyngor
**fixation** n sefydlogiad, sefydledd
**fixed** n sefydlog
**fixture** n gosodyn, peniant (byd
chwarae)
**fizz** vi sïo
**fizzle** vb hisian, sïo
**fizzy** adj byrlymog
**flabbergast** vt synnu, syfrdanu
**flabby** adj llipa, llac, llaes
**flag** n baner, lluman; fflagen ▷ vb
llumanu; llaesu
**flake** n fflaw, caenen; pluen (eira)
**flamboyant** adj coegwych
**flame** n fflam ▷ vi fflamio, ffaglu
**flame-resistant** adj gwrthfflam
**flan** n fflan
**flank** n ystlys, ochr ▷ vb ymylu,
ystlysu
**flannel** n gwlanen
**flap** n llabed, fflap ▷ vb fflapio
**flare** vb fflêr, fflach; fflerio, fflachio
**flash** vb fflachio ▷ n fflach
**flashback** n ôl-fflach
**flashlight** n fflachlamp
**flashy** adj gorwych
**flask** n costrel, fflasg
**flat** n fflat, gwastad; meddalnod
▷ adj fflat, gwastad, lleddf ▷ vb
fflatio
**flatten** vb gwastatáu
**flatter** vt gwenieithio
**flattery** n gweniaith
**flatulence** n gwynt (yn y cylla)
**flaunt** vb fflawntio, rhodresa
**flavour** n blas, cyflas ▷ vt blasu,
cyflasu
**flavouring** n cyflasyn
**flaw** n bai, diffyg, nam
**flax** n llin
**flaxen** adj golau, o lin
**flay** vt blingo

**flea** n chwannen

**flee** vb ffoi, cilio, dianc, diflannu

**fleece** n cnu ▷ vt cneifio; ysbeilio

**fleet** n llynges, fflyd ▷ adj cyflym, buan

**fleeting** adj diflanedig

**flesh** n cig, cnawd; **~ and blood** cig a gwaed; **~ and bones** cnawd ac esgyrn

**flex** n fflecs

**flexible** adj hyblyg, ystwyth

**flick** vt cyffwrdd â blaen chwip, cnithio

**flier** n ehedwr

**flight** n hediad, ffo, rhes

**flighty** adj gwamal, penchwiban

**flimsy** adj tenau, simsan, bregus

**flinch** vi cilio yn ôl, gwingo, llwfrhau

**fling** vt taflu, bwrw, lluchio ▷ n rhwysg, tafliad

**flint** n callestr, carreg dân, fflint

**flip** vb cnithio ▷ n cnith

**flippant** adj tafodrydd, gwamal

**flipper** n asgell

**flirt** vb cellwair caru, fflyrtan ▷ n fflyrten, fflyrtyn

**flit** vi gwibio

**float** n arnofyn, fflôt, trol ▷ vb arnofio

**flock** n diadell, praidd ▷ vi heidio

**flog** vt fflangellu, chwipio

**flood** n llif, dilyw, cenllif ▷ vt llifo, gorlifo

**floodlight** n llifolau ▷ vb llifoleuo

**floor** n llawr ▷ vt llorio; methu; **ground ~** daearlawr; **first ~** llawr cyntaf

**flop** n methiant, ymollwng

**flora** n fflora, planhigion

**floral** adj fflurol

**florid** adj blodeuog

**florist** n tyfwr neu werthwr blodau

**flounce** vi swalpio, ysboncio ▷ n llam, ysbonc

**flounder** n lleden fach ▷ vb ymdrybaeddu, ffwndro

**flour** n blawd, can

**flourish** vb blodeuo; ffynnu; ysgwyd ▷ n rhwysg; cân cyrn

**flout** vb gwawdio, wfftio, diystyru

**flow** vi llifo, llifeirio ▷ n llif, llanw

**flow chart** n siart rhediad

**flower** n blodeuyn, blodyn ▷ vi blodeuo; **~pot** pot blodau

**flowery** adj blodeuog

**flu** n ffliw, anwydwst

**fluctuate** vi codi a gostwng, amrywio, anwadalu

**flue** n pibell simnai, ffliw

**fluency** n huodledd, llithrigrwydd

**fluent** adj llithrig, rhugl

**fluff** n fflwcs, fflwff ▷ vb bwnglera, methu

**fluid** adj hylif, llifol ▷ n hylif, llifydd

**fluke** n pry'r afu; ffliwc, lwc

**fluoride** n ffliworid

**flurry** n cyffro, ffwdan

**flush** n gwrid; rhuthr dŵr ▷ adj cyfwyneb, gorlawn ▷ vb gwrido, cochi; gorlifo

**fluster** vb ffwdanu, cyffroi ▷ n ffwdan, cyffro

**flute** n ffliwt

**flutter** vb dychlamu, siffrwd ▷ n dychlamiad, siffrwd

**fly** n gwybedyn, cleren, pryf

**fly** vb ehedeg, ehedfan; ffoi ▷ n pryf, cleren, copis; **~ into a passion** ymwylltio, gwylltu

**flying** adj hedegog, cyflym

**flyover** n pontffordd, trosffordd

**foal** n ebol, eboles ▷ vb bwrw ebol; **in ~** cyfebol

**foam** n ewyn ▷ vi ewynnu, glafoerio

**focus** n canolbwynt, ffocws ▷ vb canolbwyntio

**fodder** n porthiant, ebran

**foe** n gelyn

**fog** n niwl

**foggy** adj niwlog

**foil** vt rhwystro, trechu ▷ n ffoil, ffwyl, dalen

**fold** n plyg; corlan ▷ vb plygu, corlannu

**folder** n plygell
**folding** n plygiant
**foliage** n dail, deiliant
**folio** n ffolio
**folk** npl pobl, gwerin
**folklore** n llên gwerin
**folk song** n cân werin
**follow** vb canlyn, dilyn
**follower** n dilynwr, canlynwr
**following** adj dilynol, canlynol ▷ n dilyniad, canlynwyr
**folly** n ffolineb, ynfydrwydd
**fond** adj hoff, annwyl
**fondle** vt anwylo, anwesu
**font** n bedyddfaen
**food** n bwyd, ymborth, lluniaeth; **tinned ~** bwyd tun; **food poisoning** n gwenwyn bwyd
**fool** n ffŵl, ynfytyn ▷ vb ynfydu, twyllo
**foolhardy** adj rhyfygus
**foolish** adj ffôl, ynfyd, annoeth
**foot (feet)** n troed; troedfedd ▷ vb troedio; **foot and mouth disease** n clwyf y traed a'r genau; **~ rot** clwy'r traed
**football** n pêl-droed
**footballer** n peldroediwr
**footbrake** n brêc troed
**footbridge** n pont gerdded, pompren
**foothold** n gafael troed, troedle
**footing** n sylfaen, safle
**footlights** npl golau'r godre
**footman** n gwas (â lifrai)
**footmark** n ôl troed
**footnote** n troednodiad
**footpath** n llwybr troed
**footprint** n ôl troed
**footstep** n cam, ôl troed
**footway** n troedffordd
**footwear** n troedwisg
**for** prep i, at, am, dros, er ▷ conj canys, oblegid, oherwydd, gan, achos
**forage** n bwyd (anifail), porthiant ▷ vb chwilio am fwyd

**forasmuch** conj yn gymaint ag, am, gan, oherwydd
**foray** n cyrch, rhuthr ▷ vb gwneud cyrch, rhuthro
**forbid** vt gwahardd, gwarafun, gomedd
**forbidden** adj gwaharddedig
**force** n grym; trais ▷ vt gorfodi; **centrifugal ~** grym allgyrchol; **centripetal ~** grym mewngyrchol; **the ~s** y lluoedd arfog
**forceful** adj grymus, egnïol
**forceps** n gefel fain
**forcible** adj nerthol, effeithiol
**ford** n rhyd ▷ vt rhydio
**fore** adj blaen, blaenaf ▷ adv ymlaen ▷ prefix cyn-, rhag-, blaen-; **to the ~** amlwg, blaenllaw
**forearm** n elin ▷ vb rhagarfogi
**forebode** vt rhagargoeli, rhagarwyddo, darogan
**foreboding** n rhagargoel
**forecast** n rhagolygon, rhagolwg ▷ vb rhagddweud, darogan
**forefather** n cyndad
**forefinger** n mynegfys
**forefront** n lle blaen ▷ adj blaen
**forego** vb hepgor; **foregone conclusion** penderfyniad ymlaen llaw
**foreground** n blaendir
**forehead** n talcen
**foreign** adj estron, tramor; **~ affairs** materion tramor
**foreigner** n estron, tramorwr
**foreman** n fforman
**foremost** adj blaenaf ▷ adv ym mlaenaf
**forensic** adj fforensig
**forerunner** n rhagredegydd
**foresee** vt rhagweld, rhagwybod
**foreseeable** adj rhagweladwy
**foreshadow** vb rhagarwyddo, rhagargoeli
**foresight** n rhagwelediad
**forest** n coedwig, fforest ▷ vt coedwigo, fforestu

**forestry** n coedwigaeth; **~ commission** Comiswn Coedwigo
**foretaste** n rhagflas ▷ vb rhagbrofi
**foretell** vt rhagfynegi, darogan
**forever** adv am byth
**foreword** n rhagair, rhagymadrodd
**forfeit** n fforffed ▷ vt fforffedu, colli
**forge** n gefail, ffwrn ▷ vb gofannu; ffugio
**forget** vt anghofio
**forgetful** adj anghofus
**forgive** vt maddau
**forgiveness** n maddeuant
**forgo** vt gadael, hepgor, mynd heb
**fork** n fforch, fforc ▷ vb fforchio
**forlorn** adj amddifad, truan, anobeithiol
**form** n ffurf; mainc; ffurflen ▷ vb ffurfio; **application ~** ffurflen gais
**formal** adj ffurfiol, defodol
**former** adj blaenaf, blaenorol
**formerly** adv gynt, yn flaenorol
**formidable** adj arswydus, ofnadwy, grymus
**formula** n rheol, fformwla
**forsake** vt gadael, ymadael â, gwrthod, cefnu ar
**fort** n caer, castell, amddiffynfa
**forte** n cryfder ▷ adj uchel, cryf
**forth** adv allan, ymlaen; **and so ~** ac felly yn y blaen
**forthcoming** adj ar ddod, gerllaw
**forthright** adj union, plaen
**forthwith** adv yn ddioed, ar unwaith
**fortify** vt cadarnhau, cryfhau
**fortitude** n gwroldeb, dewrder
**fortnight** n pythefnos
**fortnightly** adj, adv bob pythefnos
**fortress** n amddiffynfa, caer, castell
**fortunate** adj ffodus, ffortunus
**fortunately** adv yn ffodus, yn lwcus
**fortune** n ffawd; ffortun
**fortune teller** n un sy'n dweud ffortun
**forty** adj, n deugain

**forum** n fforwm
**forward** n blaenwr ▷ adj eofn, hy; blaen ▷ adv ymlaen ▷ vb anfon ymlaen; hwyluso, hyrwyddo; **inside ~** mewnwr; **wing ~** blaenasgellwr
**fossil** n ffosil ▷ adj ffosilaidd
**fossilise** vb ffosileiddio
**foster** vt magu, meithrin, coleddu
**foster-child** n plentyn maeth
**foster-mother** n mamfaeth
**foul** adj aflan; annheg; afiach ▷ n ffowl(en) ▷ vb ffowlio, llychwino; **~ play** anfadwaith; **~ throw** camdaflu
**found** vt dechrau, sylfaenu, sefydlu
**foundation** n sail, sylfaen
**founder** vb ymddryllio, suddo ▷ n sylfaenydd
**foundry** n ffowndri, efail
**fountain** n ffynnon, ffynhonnell
**four** adj, n pedwar; (f) pedair
**foursome** n pedwarawd
**fourteen** adj, n pedwar (pedair) ar ddeg
**fourth** adj pedwerydd; (f) pedwaredd
**fowl** n dofedn, ffowlyn, ffowl
**fox** n cadno, llwynog
**foyer** n cyntedd
**fraction** n ffracsiwn; **improper ~** ffracsiwn pendrwm; **vulgar ~** ffracsiwn cyffredin; **proper ~** ffracsiwn bondrwm
**fracture** n toriad, drylliad ▷ vt torri, dryllio
**fragile** adj brau, bregus
**fragment** n dryll, darn, briwsionyn
**fragrance** n perarogl, persawr
**frail** adj brau, bregus, gwan, eiddil
**frame** n ffrâm; agwedd ▷ vt fframio, llunio; **~ of mind** agwedd meddwl
**framework** n fframwaith
**franchise** n etholfraint ▷ vb etholfreinio
**frank** adj didwyll, agored
**frankincense** n thus
**frantic** adj cyffrous, gwallgof

**fraternal** *adj* brawdol
**fraternity** *n* brawdoliaeth
**fraud** *n* twyll, hoced
**fraudulent** *adj* twyllodrus
**fraught** *adj* llwythog, llawn
**fray** *n* ymryson, ymgiprys, ffrae, rhaflad ▷ *vb* treulio, rhaflo
**freak** *n* mympwy, peth od
**freckle** *n* brych, brychni
**free** *adj* rhydd; hael; di-dâl, rhad ▷ *vb* rhyddhau
**freedom** *n* rhyddid, rhyddfraint
**free expression** *n* rhyddfynegiant
**freehold** *adj* rhydd-ddaliadol
**free kick** *n* cic rydd
**freely** *adv* yn rhydd, yn hael
**freemason** *n* saer rhydd
**free trade** *n* masnach rydd
**free verse** *n* mesur rhydd, y wers rydd
**free will** *n* ewyllys rydd, o'i fodd
**freeze** *vb* rhewi, fferru
**freeze-dry** *vb* sychrewi
**freezer** *n* rhewgist, rhewgell
**freezing point** *n* rhewbwynt
**freight** *n* llwyth llong ▷ *vt* llwytho llong
**French** *adj* Ffrengig ▷ *n* Ffrangeg; **French beans** *npl* ffa Ffrengig
**Frenchman** *n* Ffrancwr
**Frenchwoman** *n* Ffrances
**frenzy** *n* gorffwylltra, cynddaredd
**frequency** *n* amlder, mynychder
**frequent** *adj* mynych, aml ▷ *vt* mynychu
**frequently** *adv* yn fynych, yn aml
**fresh** *adj* ffres, crai, cri, croyw, newydd
**freshen** *vb* ffresáu, ireiddio
**freshness** *n* ffresni, creider, irder
**fret** *vb* sorri, poeni ▷ *n* soriant, trallod, ffret
**friar** *n* brawd, mynach
**friction** *n* ffrithiant, ymrafael
**Friday** *n* dydd Gwener
**fridge** *n* oergell, rhewadur
**friend** *n* cyfaill, ffrind

**friendly** *adj* cyfeillgar
**friendship** *n* cyfeillgarwch
**frieze** *n* ffrîs
**fright** *n* dychryn, ofn, braw
**frighten** *vb* dychrynu, brawychu, codi ofn ar
**frightful** *adj* dychrynllyd, brawychus
**frigid** *adj* oer, rhewllyd; oeraidd, oerllyd; **frigid zone** *n* cylchfa rew
**frill** *n* ffril
**fringe** *n* ymyl, ymylwe, rhidens ▷ *vb* ymylu, rhidennu; **~ benefits** cilfanteision
**frisk** *vt* prancio
**fritter** *vt* afradu, ofera, gwastraffu
**frivolous** *adj* gwamal; diystyr, disylwedd
**frizzy** *adj* crychlyd
**fro** *adv*: **to and ~** yn ôl ac ymlaen
**frock** *n* ffrog
**frog** *n* llyffant (melyn), broga; bywyn, ffroga
**frolic** *vi* prancio, campio ▷ *n* pranc
**from** *prep* o, oddi, oddi wrth, gan
**front** *n* wyneb, blaen, ffrynt, talcen ▷ *vb* wynebu ▷ *adj* blaen; **~ door** drws ffrynt; **~ page** tudalen flaen; **~ room** ystafell (ffrynt)
**frontier** *n* ffin, terfyn, goror
**frost** *n* rhew
**frostbite** *n* ewinrhew
**frosty** *adj* rhewllyd
**froth** *n* ewyn ▷ *vi* ewynnu
**frown** *vi* cuchio, gwgu ▷ *n* cuwch, gwg
**frozen** *adj* wedi rhewi
**frugal** *adj* cynnil, darbodus
**fruit** *n* ffrwyth, ffrwythau; **~ juice** sudd ffrwyth; **~ salad** salad ffrwythau
**fruiterer** *n* gwerthwr ffrwythau
**fruitful** *adj* ffrwythlon, toreithiog
**fruition** *n* ffrwythloniad
**frustrate** *vt* rhwystro, llesteirio
**frustration** *n* llesteiriant
**fry** *vb* ffrio ▷ *n* afu, sil, silod; **small**

**fry** *n* pobl ddibwys
**frying-pan** *n* ffrimpan, padell ffrio
**fudge** *n* cyffug
**fuel** *n* tanwydd; cynnud; **~ cell** cynudydd
**fugitive** *adj* ar ffo, diflanedig ▷ *n* ffoadur
**fulfil** *vt* cyflawni
**fulfilment** *n* cyflawniad
**full** *adj* llawn, cyflawn ▷ *n* llonaid
**full-back** *n* cefnwr
**fuller** *n* pannwr
**full stop** *n* atalnod
**fulltime** *adj* llawn amser
**fully** *adv* yn gyfan gwbl, yn gyflawn, yn hollol
**fulsome** *adj* ffiaidd, diflas (am weniaith *etc*)
**fumble** *vb* palfalu, bwnglera
**fume** *n* tarth, mwg; llid ▷ *vb* mygu; llidio, sorri
**fun** *n* difyrrwch, digrifwch, hwyl
**function** *n* swydd, swyddogaeth; ffwythiant (mathemateg)
**functional** *adj* swyddogaethol, ffwythiannol, defnyddiol
**fund** *n* cronfa, trysorfa
**fundamental** *adj* sylfaenol
**funeral** *n* angladd, cynhebrwng, claddedigaeth
**fungus** *n* ffwng
**funnel** *n* twmffat, twndis, corn
**funny** *adj* digrif, ysmala; rhyfedd, hynod
**fur** *n* blew, ffwr; cen; **fur coat** *n* cot ffwr
**furious** *adj* cynddeiriog, ffyrnig, gwyllt
**furlong** *n* ystad, wythfed ran milltir
**furnace** *n* ffwrn, ffwrnais
**furnish** *vt* dodrefnu, rhoddi
**furnishings** *npl* dodrefn
**furniture** *n* dodrefn, celfi
**furrow** *n* cwys, rhych ▷ *vt* cwyso, rhychu
**furry** *adj* blewog
**further** *adj* pellach ▷ *adv* ymhellach

▷ *vt* hyrwyddo; **~ education** addysg bellach
**fury** *n* cynddaredd, ffyrnigrwydd
**fuse** *n* ffiws, toddyn, diogelydd ▷ *vb* ffiwsio
**fuss** *n* ffwdan, helynt, stŵr ▷ *vb* ffwdanu
**fussy** *adj* ffwdanus
**futile** *adj* ofer, di-les
**future** *adj*, *n* dyfodol
**fuzzy** *adj* blewog, aneglur

# g

**gabble** *vb* bregliach, clebran ▷ *n* cleber
**gable** *n* piniwn, talcen tŷ
**gadget** *n* dyfais
**Gaelic** *n* Gaeleg ▷ *adj* Gaelaidd
**gaff** *n* bach pysgota
**gag** *n* smaldod; safnglo ▷ *vb* smalio; safngloi, cau ceg
**gaiety** *n* llonder, difyrrwch, miri
**gaily** *adv* yn llawen
**gain** *vb* ennill, elwa ▷ *n* ennill, elw, budd
**gait** *n* cerddediad, osgo
**gale** *n* awel, gwynt cryf; tymestl
**gall** *n* bustl, chwydd ▷ *vb* dolurio, blino; **gall bladder** *n* coden y bustl; **~ stones** cerrig y bustl
**gallant** *adj* gwrol, dewr ▷ *n* carwr
**gallery** *n* oriel, llofft

**galley** *n* rhwyflong; gali
**gallon** *n* galwyn
**gallop** *n* carlam ▷ *vb* carlamu
**gallows** *n* crocbren
**galore** *n, adv* digonedd
**galvanize** *vt* galfaneiddio, galfanu; symbylu
**gamble** *vb* hapchwarae, gamblo ▷ *n* gambl
**game** *n* chwarae, camp; helwriaeth ▷ *adj* calonnog, dewr, glew
**game-keeper** *n* cipar
**gammon** *n* palfais (mochyn); ffwlbri, lol
**gander** *n* ceiliagwydd, clacwydd
**gang** *n* mintai, torf, haid, gang
**gangster** *n* troseddwr
**gangway** *n* tramwyfa, eil, ale; pont
**gaol** *n* carchar ▷ *vt* carcharu
**gap** *n* bwlch, adwy
**gape** *vi* rhythu, syllu ▷ *n* rhythiad
**garage** *n* modurdy, garej
**garbage** *n* ysgarthion, ysbwriel, sothach
**garble** *vt* darnio, llurgunio
**garden** *n* gardd ▷ *vi* garddio
**gardener** *n* garddwr
**gardening** *n* garddwriaeth
**gargle** *n* golch gwddf ▷ *vb* golchi gwddf
**garish** *adj* coegwych
**garland** *n* coronbleth, garlant, talaith
**garlic** *n* garlleg
**garment** *n* dilledyn, gwisg
**garnish** *vt* addurno, harddu
**garrison** *n* gwarchodlu, garsiwn
**garrulous** *adj* tafodrydd, siaradus
**garter** *n* gardas, gardys ▷ *vb* gardysu
**gas** *n* nwy ▷ *vb* gwenwyno â nwy; **~ cooker** ffwrn nwy; **~ fire** tân nwy; **~ ring** cylch nwy
**gash** *n* archoll, hollt, hac ▷ *vt* archolli, hacio
**gasket** *n* gasged
**gas-mask** *n* mwgwd nwy

**gasometer** *n* tanc nwy
**gasp** *vb* ebychu, anadlu'n drwm
**gate** *n* porth, llidiart, clwyd, gât, iet ▷ *vb* porthio, porthellu
**gate-crasher** *n* ymyrrwr
**gatehouse** *n* porthordy
**gateway** *n* mynedfa
**gather** *vb* casglu, cynnull, crynhoi, hel
**gathering** *n* casgliad, cynulliad
**gaudy** *adj* coegwych, gorwych
**gauge** *n* mesur; lled; meidrydd ▷ *vt* mesur, meidryddu
**Gaul** *n* Gâl
**Gaulish** *n* Galeg
**gaunt** *adj* llwm, tenau
**gauntlet** *n* dyrnfol, maneg ddur; **to throw down the ~** herio
**gauze** *n* rhwyllen, gaws, meinwe
**gay** *adj* llon, bywiog, ofer, hoyw
**gaze** *vi* edrych, syllu, tremio ▷ *n* golwg, trem
**gazette** *n* newyddiadur (swyddogol)
**gazetteer** *n* geiriadur daearyddol
**GCSE** *n abbr* TGAU = Tystysgrif Gyffredin Addysg Uwchradd
**gear** *n* gêr, offer, taclau ▷ *vb* taclu, harneisio
**gearbox** *n* gergist, blwch gêr, gerbocs
**gelignite** *n* geligneit
**gem** *n* glain, gem, tlws
**gender** *n* cenedl
**genealogy** *n* achau; achyddiaeth
**general** *adj* cyffredin, cyffredinol ▷ *n* cadfridog; **general election** *n* etholiad cyffredinol
**generalize** *vb* cyffredinoli
**generally** *adv* yn gyffredinol
**generate** *vt* cenhedlu, cynhyrchu, generadu
**generation** *n* cenhedliad; cenhedlaeth, to
**generator** *n* cynhyrchydd; generadur
**generosity** *n* haelioni**

**generous** adj hael, haelionus, haelfrydig
**genetic** adj genetig
**genetics** n geneteg
**Geneva** n Genefa
**genial** adj hynaws, rhadlon, tyner, tirion
**genital** adj cenhedlol; **genitals** npl organau cenhedlu
**genius** n athrylith
**genteel** adj bonheddig, boneddigaidd
**gentle** adj bonheddig; mwyn, tyner
**gentleman** n gŵr bonheddig
**gently** adv yn dyner, addfwyn; gan bwyll
**gentry** npl bonedd
**gents** npl toiledau dynion
**genuine** adj dilys, diffuant, pur
**geography** n daearyddiaeth
**geology** n daeareg
**geometry** n geometreg
**geriatrics** n geriatreg
**germ** n hedyn, eginyn, germ
**German** adj Almaenaidd ▷ n Almaenwr; Almaeneg; **~ measles** y frech Almeinig
**Germany** n yr Almaen
**germinate** vi egino, atyfu
**germination** n eginiad, atyfiant
**gesture** n ystum, arwydd, mosiwn
**get** vb cael, caffael, ennill; **to ~ on with it** bwrw arni, bwrw iddi
**geyser** n geyser
**Ghana** n Ghana
**ghastly** adj erchyll, gwelw
**gherkin** n gercin
**ghost** n ysbryd, drychiolaeth, bwgan
**giant** n cawr ▷ adj cawraidd
**gibberish** n cleber, baldordd
**gibe** vb gwawdio ▷ n gwawd
**giblets** npl giblets, syrth gŵydd
**Gibraltar** n Gibralter
**giddiness** n pendro
**giddy** adj penfeddw, penchwiban
**gift** n rhodd, dawn, anrheg, gwobr

**gifted** adj dawnus, talentog
**gigantic** adj cawraidd, dirfawr, anferth
**giggle** vb lledchwerthin, giglan
**gill** n tagell; gil, chwarter peint
**gimmick** n gimig
**gin** n jin; hoenyn
**ginger** n sinsir
**gingerly** adj, adv gochelgar, gwyliadwrus
**gipsy, gy-** n sipsi
**giraffe** n siráff
**girder** n trawst
**girdle** n gwregys, rhwymyn ▷ vt gwregysu
**girl** n merch, geneth, hogen
**girlfriend** n cariadferch, anwylyd
**girth** n cengl; cylchfesur, cwmpas
**gist** n cnewyllyn pwnc, ergyd, sylwedd
**give** vb rhoddi, rhoi; **~ up** rhoi'r gorau i
**glacier** n rhewlif, iäen, glasier
**glad** adj llawen, llon, balch
**gladiator** n cleddyfwr, ymladdwr
**gladly** adv yn llawen, â phleser
**glamorous** adj swynol, cyfareddol, hudol
**glamour** n swyn, cyfaredd, hud
**glance** vb ciledrych, tremio ▷ n cipolwg, trem, cip
**gland** n chwarren, cilchwyrnen, gland
**glare** vb disgleirio; rhythu ▷ n disgleirdeb, tanbeidrwydd
**glass** n gwydr; gwydraid ▷ pl gwydrau, sbectol
**glassy** adj gloyw, pŵl
**glaze** vt gwydro; sgleinio ▷ n sglein, gwydredd
**glazier** n gwydrwr
**gleam** n pelydryn, llewyrch ▷ vi pelydru, llewyrchu
**glean** vb lloffa
**glebe** n clastir, tir eglwys
**glee** n llonder, hoen; rhangan
**glen** n glyn, cwm, dyffryn

**glib** adj llyfn, llithrig, rhugl, ffraeth

**glide** vi llithro, llifo ▷ n llithr, llithrad

**gliding** n, vb llithran

**glimmer** vi llewyrchu'n wan ▷ n llewyrchyn, llygedyn

**glimpse** n trem, cipolwg

**glint** vb fflachio ▷ n fflach, llewyrch

**glisten** vi disgleirio

**glitter** vi tywynnu, pelydru ▷ n pelydriad

**gloat** vb llawenhau

**global** adj hollfydol, cyffredinol

**globe** n pêl, pelen

**gloom** n caddug, prudd-der, tywyllwch

**gloomy** adj prudd, digalon, tywyll

**glorify** vt gogoneddu

**glorious** adj gogoneddus

**glory** n gogoniant ▷ vi ymffrostio, gorfoleddu

**gloss** n disgleirdeb arwynebol, sglein; glòs, esboniad

**glossary** n geirfa

**glossy** adj llathraidd

**glove** n maneg

**glow** vi twymo, gwrido ▷ n gwres, gwrid

**glower** vi cuchio, gwgu

**glue** n glud ▷ vt gludio, asio

**glum** adj prudd, digalon, trist

**glut** vt gorlenwi, glythu ▷ n gormodedd, gorlawnder

**glutton** n glwth

**gluttony** n glythineb

**gnarled** adj cnotiog, ceinciog, garw

**gnat** n gwybedyn, cylionen

**gnaw** vb cnoi, deintio, cnewian

**gnome** n gwireb; ysbryd, coblyn

**go** vi mynd, cerdded, rhodio ▷ n tro

**goad** n swmbwl ▷ vt symbylu

**goal** n gôl, nod, bwriad; **goal posts** npl pyst gôl; **~ shooter** saethwr

**goalkeeper** n golgeidwad, golwr

**goat** n gafr

**goblin** n ellyll, coblyn, bwgan

**god** n duw; **G~** Duw

**godchild** n mab bedydd, merch fedydd

**goddess** n duwies

**godfather** n tad bedydd

**godhead** n duwdod

**godly** adj duwiol

**godmother** adj mam fedydd

**godsend** n caffaeliad

**goggles** npl gwydrau

**gold** n aur ▷ adj aur, euraid

**golden** adj euraid

**goldfish** npl eurbysg, pysgod aur

**goldsmith** n gof aur, eurych

**golf** n golff; **~ links** maes golff; **golf course** n maes golffio

**golfer** n golffwr

**gong** n gong, cloch fwyd

**good** adj da, daionus; cryn ▷ n da, daioni, lles; **~ morning** bore da; **~ afternoon** prynhawn da; **~ evening** noswaith dda; **~ night** nos da; **~ enough** digon da; **no ~** dim gwerth, da i ddim; **G~ Friday** Dydd Gwener y Groglith; **~ humour** natur dda

**good-bye** excl, n da bo chi, yn iach! ffarwel

**good-looking** adj golygus

**goodly** adj hardd, teg

**good-natured** adj hynaws, rhadlon

**goodness** n daioni

**goods** npl nwyddau, eiddo

**goodwill** n ewyllys da; braint (masnachol)

**goose** (geese) n gŵydd

**gooseberry** n eirinen Fair, gwsbersen

**gooseflesh** n croen gŵydd

**gore** n gwaed, gôr ▷ vb cornio

**gorge** n hafn, ceunant ▷ vb safnio, traflyncu

**gorgeous** adj ysblennydd, gwych

**gorilla** n gorila

**gorse** n eithin

**gory** adj gwaedlyd

**gosling** n cyw gŵydd

**gospel** n efengyl

**gossip** n clec, clonc, clebryn, clebran

▷ *vb* clebran, clecian, hel straeon

**gout** *n* gowt, cymalwst

**govern** *vb* llywodraethu, rheoli, llywio

**governess** *n* athrawes

**government** *n* llywodraeth

**governor** *n* llywodraethwr

**gown** *n* gŵn

**grab** *vb* crafangu, cipio ▷ *n* gwanc, crap

**grace** *n* gras, rhad, graslonrwydd; gosgeiddrwydd ▷ *vt* harddu, prydferthu, addurno

**graceful** *adj* graslon, rhadlon; gosgeiddig, lluniaidd

**gracious** *adj* graslon, grasol, rhadlon, hynaws

**grade** *n* gradd, safon ▷ *vb* graddio

**gradient** *n* graddiant

**gradual** *adj* graddol

**gradually** *adv* yn raddol

**graduate** *vb* graddio, graddoli ▷ *n* gŵr gradd, graddedig

**graduation** *n* graddedigaeth, graddnod

**graffiti** *n* graffiti

**graft** *n* impyn, hunan-les ▷ *vt* impio, grafftio

**grain** *n* grawn, gronyn; mymryn; graen ▷ *vb* graenu, graenio

**gram** *n* gram

**grammar** *n* gramadeg; **grammar school** *n* ysgol ramadeg

**grammatical** *adj* gramadegol

**granary** *n* ysgubor

**grand** *adj* mawreddog, ardderchog, crand; prif, uchel

**grandchild** *n* ŵyr, wyres; **great grandchild** *n* gorwyr(es)

**granddaughter** *n* wyres

**grandfather** *n* taid, tad-cu; **great grandfather** *n* hen daid, hen-dad-cu

**grandmother** *n* nain, mam-gu

**grandson** *n* ŵyr

**granite** *n* gwenithfaen, ithfaen

**grant** *vt* rhoddi, caniatáu ▷ *n* rhodd, grant; **to take for ~ed** cymryd yn ganiataol

**granulated** *adj* gronynnog

**granule** *n* gronynnell

**grapefruit** *n* grawnffrwyth

**grapes** *n* grawnwin

**graph** *n* graff

**graphic** *adj* graffig; byw

**graphics** *npl* graffigwaith, graffeg

**grapple** *n* gafl, gafaelfach ▷ *vb* gafaelyd, mynd i'r afael â

**grasp** *vb* gafael; amgyffred ▷ *n* gafael, amgyffrediad

**grasping** *adj* trachwantus

**grass** *n* glaswellt, porfa

**grasshopper** *n* ceiliog y rhedyn, sioncyn y gwair

**grate** *n* grat ▷ *vb* rhygnu, crafellu; merwino

**grateful** *adj* diolchgar; dymunol

**grater** *n* grater, crafellydd

**gratify** *vt* boddio, boddhau

**grating** *adj* garw, cras ▷ *n* gratin

**gratitude** *n* diolchgarwch

**gratuity** *n* cildwrn, rhodd

**grave** *adj* difrifol, dwys

**grave** *n* bedd, beddrod

**gravel** *n* graean, gro, grafel

**gravestone** *n* beddfaen, carreg fedd

**graveyard** *n* mynwent

**gravitate** *vi* disgyrchu, treiglo

**gravity** *n* disgyrchiant; pwysigrwydd; **centre of ~** craidd disgyrchiant

**gravy** *n* grefi, isgell, sew

**graze** *vb* pori; crafu, rhwbio, ysgythru

**grease** *n* saim, iraid ▷ *vt* iro, seimio

**greaseproof** *adj* gwrthsaim

**greasy** *adj* seimllyd, ireidlyd

**great** *adj* mawr; **a ~ many** llawer iawn

**greatly** *adv* yn fawr

**Greece** *n* Groeg

**greed** *n* trachwant, gwanc

**greedy** *adj* barus, trachwantus,

gwancus

**Greek** n Groeg; Groegwr ▷ adj Groegaidd

**green** adj gwyrdd, glas, ir ▷ vb glasu

**greenery** n gwyrddlesni

**greengrocer** n grîngroser, gwerthwr llysiau

**greenhouse** n tŷ gwydr

**Greenland** n Grønland

**greet** vt annerch, cyfarch

**greeting** n cyfarchiad

**grenade** n grenâd

**grey** adj llwyd, llwydwyn, glas

**greyhound** n milgi

**grid** n grid, alch; **~ reference** cyfeirnod grid

**grief** n gofid, galar, hiraeth

**grievance** n cwyn

**grieve** vb gofidio, galaru, hiraethu

**grievous** adj gofidus, poenus, blin, difrifol

**grill** n gril, gridyll ▷ vb grilio, gridyllu; **mixed ~** gril cymysg

**grille** n gril, dellt

**grim** adj sarrug, milain, difrifol

**grimace** n ystum ▷ vi ystumio

**grimy** adj budr, brwnt, diraen

**grin** vb lledwenu ▷ n gwên

**grind** vb malu (ŷd etc), llifo (arf), llifanu

**grip** vb gafael, gwasgu ▷ n gafael, crap

**grisly** adj erch, erchyll, hyll, milain

**gristle** n madruddyn, gwythi

**grit** n grit, grud, graean; pybyrwch

**groan** vi, n griddfan

**grocer** n groser

**groceries** npl nwyddau

**groin** n cesail morddwyd, gwerddyr

**groom** n priodfab; gwastrawd ▷ vb trwsio

**groove** n rhigol, rhych ▷ vt rhigoli, rhychu

**grope** vi ymbalfalu

**gross** n gros; crynswth ▷ adj bras, aflednaîs; **~ profit** elw gros

**grotto** n groto

**ground** n llawr, daear, tir; sail; gwaelod ▷ vt daearu, llorio; **ground floor** n daearlawr

**groundless** adj di-sail

**groundwork** n sylfaen, sail

**group** n grŵp, twr, bagad ▷ vt grwpio; **discussion ~** cylch trafod

**grouse** n grugiar ▷ vb grwgnach

**grove** n llwyn, celli

**grovel** vi ymgreinio

**grow** vb tyfu, prifio, cynyddu, codi

**grower** n tyfwr

**growing** adj yn tyfu

**growl** vi chwyrnu

**growth** n twf, tyfiant, cynnydd

**grub** n pryf, cynrhonyn; bwyd ▷ vb dadwreiddio

**grubby** adj budr, brwnt

**grudge** vt gwarafun, grwgnach ▷ n dig, cenfigen, cas

**gruesome** adj erchyll, hyll, ffiaidd

**gruff** adj sarrug, garw, swta

**grumble** vi grwgnach, tuchan

**grumpy** adj sarrug, diserch

**grunt** vi rhochian ▷ n rhoch

**guarantee** n gwarant, ernes ▷ vt gwarantu, mechnïo

**guard** n gard, gwarchodydd; sgrin ▷ vb gwarchod

**guarded** adj gwyliadurus, gofalus

**guardian** n gwarcheidwad

**guerilla** n herfilwr

**guess** vb dyfalu, dyfeisio ▷ n amcan

**guesswork** n dyfaliad

**guest** n gwestai, gŵr/gwraig (g)wadd

**guffaw** n crechwen ▷ vb crechwenu

**guidance** n cyfarwyddyd

**guide** n arweinydd ▷ vt arwain, cyfarwyddo

**guide book** n teithlyfr

**guide-dog** n arweingi

**guide-lines** npl canllawiau

**guild** n cymdeithas, corfforaeth, urdd

**guile** n twyll, dichell, ystryw

**guillotine** n gilotîn

**guilt** n euogrwydd, bai
**guilty** adj euog
**guinea pig** n mochyn cwta
**guise** n dull, modd, rhith, diwyg
**guitar** n gitâr
**gulf** n gwlff, geneufor; gagendor
**gull** n gwylan; gwirionyn ▷ vt twyllo
**gullet** n corn gwddf, sefnig
**gullible** adj hygoelus
**gully** n rhigol, ffos
**gulp** vt llawcian, traflyncu ▷ n llawc, traflwnc
**gum** n gwm, glud ▷ vt gymio, gludio
**gumboots** npl esgidiau rwber
**gums** npl cig y dannedd, gorcharfanau, crib y dannedd, gorfant
**gun** n gwn, dryll
**gunner** n gynnwr
**gunpowder** n powdr gwn
**gunshot** n ergyd gwn
**gunsmith** n gof gynnau (bach)
**gurgle** vi byrlymu
**gush** vb ffrydio, llifeirio ▷ n ffrwd, hyrddwynt
**gust** n chwythwm
**gusto** n awch, blas, sêl
**gut** n perfeddyn, coluddyn ▷ vt diberfeddu; difrodi, ysbeilio
**gutter** n ffos, cwter, cafn
**guttural** adj gyddfol
**guzzle** vb llawcio, traflyncu
**gym** n campfa
**gymnasium** n gymnasiwm, campfa
**gymnast** n mabolgampwr
**gynaecologist** n gynaecolegydd
**gynaecology** n gynaecoleg
**gypsy** n sipsi
**gyrate** vi troi, chwyrlïo

# h

**ha** excl ha!
**haberdashery** n dilladach, siop ddillad
**habit** n arferiad; anian; gwisg ▷ vt gwisgo, dilladu
**habitable** adj cyfannedd, cyfanheddol
**habitat** n cartref, cynefin
**habitation** n trigfa, preswylfa
**habitual** adj arferol, cyson
**habituate** vt arfer, cynefino
**hack** vb hacio, torri ▷ n hac
**hack** n hurfarch; cystog, slâf
**hackneyed** adj ystrydebol, cyffredin
**hades** n annwfn
**haddock** n corbenfras, hadog
**haemorrhage** n gwaedlif
**haemorrhoids** npl clwyf y marchogion
**haft** n carn
**hag** n gwrach, gwiddon
**haggard** adj gwyllt, curiedig
**haggle** vi bargeinio'n daer
**hail** n cenllysg, cesair ▷ vb bwrw cesair
**hail** excl henffych well ▷ vb cyfarch, galw
**hair** n gwallt, blew, rhawn; **~'s breadth** trwch y blewyn; **~ splitting** hollti blew
**hairbrush** n brws gwallt
**haircut** n triniaeth gwallt, toriad, crop
**hairdresser** n triniwr gwallt

**hair dryer** *n* sychwr gwallt
**hair spray** *n* chwistrelliad gwallt; chwistrellydd gwallt
**hairy** *adj* blewog
**hake** *n* cegddu
**hale** *adj* iach, cryf, hoenus
**half** (**halves**) *n* hanner
**half-back** *n* hanerwr
**half-breed** *adj* cymysgryw
**half-dead** *adj* lledfyw
**half-hearted** *adj* diawydd, llugoer
**halfpenny** *n* dimai
**halibut** *n* halibwt
**hall** *n* llys, neuadd, plas; cyntedd
**hallmark** *n* dilysnod
**hallo** *excl* helô
**hallow** *vt* cysegru, sancteiddio
**Halloween** *n* nos Galangaeaf
**hallucination** *n* geuddrych, rhithwelediad
**halo** *n* corongylch, gogoniant, halo, lleugylch
**halt** *vb* sefyll ▷ *n* safiad; gorsaf, arosfa
**halter** *n* cebystr, tennyn
**halve** *vt* haneru
**ham** *n* morddwyd, ham
**hames** *npl* mynci
**hamlet** *n* pentref
**hammer** *n* morthwyl, mwrthwl, gordd ▷ *vb* morthwylio
**hammock** *n* hamog, gwely crog
**hamper** *vt* rhwystro, llesteirio
**hamstring** *n* llinyn y gar
**hand** *n* llaw; (*of clock*) bys ▷ *vt* estyn, trosglwyddo; **to be on ~** bod with law; **hand-off** *n* hwp llaw; **in-hand** *adj* ar waith
**handbag** *n* bag llaw
**handbook** *n* llawlyfr
**handbrake** *n* brec llaw
**handcuff** *n* gefyn llaw
**handful** *n* dyrnaid, llond llaw
**handicap** *n* rhwystr, llestair, anfantais; blaen; **~ped children** plant dan anfantais
**handicraft** *n* crefft

**handiwork** *n* gwaith llaw
**handkerchief** *n* cadach poced, hances, macyn, neisied
**handle** *n* carn, coes, troed, dolen, clust, dwrn ▷ *vt* trin, trafod; **to fly off the ~** colli tymer
**handlebars** *npl* cyrn
**handmade** *adj* wedi ei wneud â llaw
**handmaid, -en** *n* llawforwyn
**handrail** *n* canllaw
**handsome** *adj* golygus, hardd, prydferth; hael
**handwriting** *n* llawysgrifen
**handy** *adj* hylaw, deheuig, cyfleus
**hang** *vb* crogi, hongian, dibynnu
**hangar** *n* awyrendy
**hang-gliding** *vb* barcuta
**hangover** *n* blinder ddoe, pen mawr
**hank** *n* cengl
**hanker** *vi* blysio, crefu, dyheu, hiraethu
**hanky-panky** *n* twyll, dichell ▷ *adj* twyllodrus, dichellgar
**hap** *n* hap, damwain
**haphazard** *adj, adv* damweiniol, ar siawns
**happen** *vi* digwydd
**happily** *adv* yn hapus
**happiness** *n* dedwyddwch, hapusrwydd
**happy** *adj* dedwydd, hapus
**happy-go-lucky** *adj* didaro, di-hid
**harangue** *n* araith, arawd ▷ *vb* areithio
**harass** *vt* poeni, blino, gofidio
**harassment** *n* poen, blinder
**harbour** *n* porthladd, harbwr ▷ *vb* llochesu
**hard** *adj* caled, anodd; **~ of hearing** trwm ei glyw; **to be ~ done by** cael cam; **~ headed** hirben
**hardboard** *n* caledfwrdd
**harden** *vb* caledu
**hardener** *n* caledwr
**hardness** *n* caledwch

**hardship** n caledi
**hard shoulder** n llain galed
**hard-up** adj prin o arian
**hardware** n nwyddau metel
**hardwood** n pren caled
**hardy** adj caled, cryf, gwydn;
hy, eofn
**hare** n ysgyfarnog, ceinach
**harebrained** adj byrbwyll, gwyllt
**harelip** n bylchfin, gwefus fylchog
**hark** excl gwrando! clyw!; **~ back**
dychwelyd
**harlot** n putain
**harm** n niwed, drwg, cam ▷ vt
niweidio, drygu
**harmful** adj niweidiol
**harmless** adj diniwed, diddrwg
**harmonious** adj cytûn
**harmonise** vb cytgordio, cytuno
**harmony** n harmoni, cynghanedd
**harness** n harnais, gêr ▷ vt
harneisio
**harp** n telyn ▷ vi canu'r delyn
**harpoon** n tryfer ▷ vt tryferu
**harrow** n og ▷ vt llyfnu; rhwygo,
dryllio
**harrowing** adj dychrynllyd,
ofnadwy, deifiol
**harry** vt difrodi, blino
**harsh** adj garw, gerwin, aflafar
**harshness** n craster, gerwindeb
**hart** n hydd
**harvest** n cynhaeaf ▷ vt cynaeafu
**harvester** n cynaeafwr; **combine
harvester** n combein
**hash** n briwgig; cymysgfa, cybolfa
**hasp** n hesben
**haste** n brys, hast ▷ vi brysio,
prysuro
**hasten** vb brysio, prysuro, hastu
**hastily** adv yn frysiog
**hasty** adj brysiog, byrbwyll
**hat** n het
**hatch** vb deor, gori ▷ n deoriad
**hatch** n gorddrws, rhagddor, dôr
**hatchery** n deorfa
**hatchet** n bwyell (fach)

**hate** vt casáu ▷ n cas, casineb
**hateful** adj cas, atgas
**hatred** n cas, casineb, digasedd
**haughtiness** n balchder, traha,
ffroenucheledd
**haughty** adj balch, ffroenuchel,
trahaus
**haul** vb tynnu, llusgo, halio ▷ n dalfa
**haulage** n cludiad, cludiant
**haulier** n haliwr
**haunch** n morddwyd, pedrain
**haunt** vt cyniwair, mynychu;
trwblu, aflonyddu ▷ n cyniweirfa,
cynefin, cyrchfa
**have** vt cael, meddu; **I ~ blue eyes**
mae llygaid glas gennyf; **I ~ a cold**
mae annwyd arnaf
**haven** n hafan, porthladd
**haversack** n ysgrepan
**havoc** n hafog, difrod
**hawk** n hebog, cudyll, curyll ▷ vb
heboca
**hawk** vt gwerthu o dŷ i dŷ, pedlera
**haws** npl crawel y moch, criafol
y moch
**hawthorn** n draenen wen
**hay** n gwair
**hayfever** n clefyd y gwair
**hayrick** n tas wair
**hazard** n perygl, llestair, antur ▷ vt
anturio, peryglu
**hazardous** adj peryglus, enbydus
**haze** n niwl, tarth, tawch
**hazel** n collen ▷ adj gwinau golau
**haziness** n aneglurder
**hazy** adj aneglur, niwlog
**he** pron ef, efe; efo, fo, o
**head** n pen ▷ vb blaenori, penio
**headache** n dolur (cur) yn y pen,
pen tost
**header** n peniad
**headgear** n penffest, penwisg
**heading** n pennawd
**headlamp** n lamp fawr
**headland** n pentir, penrhyn; talar
**headline** n pennawd, teitl, hedin
**headlong** adv pendramwnwgl

**headmaster** n prifathro
**headmistress** n prifathrawes
**headphone** n ffôn pen
**headquarters** npl pencadlys
**headstrong** adj cyndyn
**headway** n cynnydd
**heal** vb iacháu, meddyginiaethu
**health** n iechyd; **health food shop** n siop bwyd iach; **Health Service** n y Gwasanaeth Iechyd
**healthy** adj iach, iachus
**heap** n crug, pentwr ▷ vt crugio, pentyrru
**hear** vb clywed
**hearing** n clyw
**hearing aid** n cymorth clywed
**hearken** vi gwrando, clustfeinio
**hearsay** n sôn, siarad ▷ adj o ben i ben, ail-law
**hearse** n hers
**heart** n calon
**heart-ache** n ing, dolur calon
**heart attack** n trawiad
**heartburn** n dŵr poeth
**hearten** vb calonogi
**hearth** n aelwyd
**heartland** n perfeddwlad
**hearty** adj calonnog, cynnes
**heat** n gwres, poethder; (Sport) rhagras ▷ vb twymo, poethi
**heater** n gwresogydd
**heath** n rhos, rhostir
**heathen** adj paganaidd ▷ n pagan
**heather** n grug
**heating** vb gwres
**heave** vb codi, dyrchafu; chwyddo; taflu ▷ n hwb
**heaven** n nef, nefoedd
**heavenly** adj nefol, nefolaidd
**heavily** adv yn drwm, yn drymaidd
**heavy** adj trwm, trymaidd, trymllyd
**heavyweight** n (Sport) pwysau trwm
**Hebrew** n Hebrëwr; Hebraeg ▷ adj Hebraeg; Hebreig
**heckle** vb ymyrryd
**hectare** n hectar

**hedge** n clawdd, gwrych, perth
**hedgehog** n draenog
**heed** vt ystyried, talu sylw ▷ n ystyriaeth
**heel** n sawdl ▷ vb sodli
**heifer** n anner, heffer, treisiad
**height** n uchder, uchelder, taldra
**heinous** adj dybryd, anfad, ysgeler
**heir** n etifedd, aer
**heiress** n etifeddes, aeres
**helicopter** n hofrennydd
**hell** n uffern
**hellish** adj uffernol
**hello** excl helô!, hylô!, clyw!, gwrando!
**helm** n llyw; llywyddiaeth
**helmet** n helm
**help** vt helpu, cymorth, cynorthwyo ▷ n help, cymorth, cynhorthwy
**helper** n cynorthwywr, helpwr
**helpful** adj defnyddiol, cymwynasgar, gwasanaethgar, buddiol
**helping** n dogn, cyfran (o fwyd)
**helpless** adj diymadferth
**helter-skelter** adv blith-draphlith
**hem** n hem, ymyl ▷ vt hemio
**hemi-** prefix hanner
**hemisphere** n hemisffer
**hemlock** n cegid
**hemp** n cywarch
**hen** n iâr
**hence** adv oddi yma ▷ excl ymaith!
**henceforth, -forward** adv rhag llaw, mwyach, o hyn ymlaen
**henchman** n gwas, canlynwr, cefnogydd
**hepatitis** n llif yr afu, hepatitis
**her** pron ei, hi, hithau
**herald** n herald ▷ vt cyhoeddi; rhagflaenu
**herb** n llysieuyn, sawr-lysieuyn
**herbal** adj llysieuol
**herbicide** n llysleiddiad
**herd** n gyr, cenfaint, gre ▷ vb heidio
**here** adv yma
**hereditary** adj etifeddol

**heredity** n etifeddeg
**heresy** n heresi, gau athrawiaeth
**heretic** n heretic, camgredwr
**heritage** n etifeddiaeth, treftadaeth
**hermit** n meudwy
**hernia** n bors, hernia, torllengig
**hero** n arwr, gwron
**heroic** adj arwrol
**heroine** n arwres
**heron** n crëyr, crychydd
**herring** n pennog, ysgadenyn
**hesitant** adj petrusgar
**hesitate** vi petruso
**hesitation** n petruster
**heterodox** adj anuniongred
**heterodoxy** n anuniongrededd
**heterogeneous** adj anghydryw, afryw, heterogenus
**heterosexual** n anghyfunryw
**hew** vt naddu, torri, cymynu
**hewer** n cymynwr, torrwr
**hexa-** prefix chwech
**heyday** n anterth
**hiatus** n hiatws
**hibernate** vi gaeafu
**hiccup** n yr ig ▷ vi igian
**hide** vb cuddio, celu, ymguddio
**hide** n croen
**hide-and-seek** n chwarae mig
**hideous** adj hyll, erchyll
**hiding place** n cuddfan, lloches
**hierarchy** n gradd, offeiriadaeth
**higgle** vi taeru, bargenna
**high** adj uchel; mawr; cryf; llawn
**highbrow** adj uchel-ael
**high chair** n cadair ar gyfer plentyn
**highland** n ucheldir
**highly** adv yn fawr, yn uchel
**highness** n uchelder
**high-priest** n archoffeiriad
**high-spirited** adj calonnog, nwyfus
**high water** n pen llanw
**highway** n priffordd, ffordd fawr
**highwayman** n lleidr penffordd
**hijack** vb cipio

**hike** vb crwydro ▷ n taith gerdded
**hilarious** adj llawen, llon, siriol, hoenus
**hill** n bryn, allt, gorifyny
**hillock** n bryncyn, ponc, twmpath
**hilly** adj bryniog, mynyddig
**hilt** n carn cleddyf
**him** pron ef, efe, yntau
**hind** adj ôl
**hind** n ewig
**hinder** vt rhwystro, atal, lluddias, llesteirio
**hindrance** n rhwystr, llestair, lludd
**hinge** n colyn drws ▷ vb troi, dibynnu
**hint** n awgrym ▷ vt awgrymu
**hinterland** n cefnwlad
**hip** n clun, pen uchaf y glun
**hippie** n hipi
**hips** npl egroes
**hire** vt cyflogi, hurio, llogi ▷ n cyflog, hur
**hiss** vb chwythu, sïo, hysio, hisian
**historian** n hanesydd
**historic** adj hanesyddol
**historical** adj hanesyddol
**hit** vb taro ▷ n ergyd, trawiad
**hitch** vb bachu ▷ n cwlwm; atalfa, rhwystr
**hitchhike** vb bodio
**hitchhiker** n bodiwr
**hither** adv yma, hyd yma, tuag yma
**hitherto** adv hyd yma, hyd yn hyn
**hive** n cwch gwenyn; **hive off** vb rhannu, trosglwyddo, newid
**hoar** adj llwyd, penllwyd ▷ n llwydrew, barrug
**hoard** n cronfa, cuddfa ▷ vt cronni
**hoarfrost** n barrug, llwydrew
**hoarse** adj cryg, cryglyd
**hoax** vt twyllo ▷ n cast, tric, twyll
**hob** n pentan
**hobble** vb hercian
**hobby** n difyrwaith, hobi
**hobby horse** n ceffyl pren; hoff beth
**hobgoblin** n bwbach, bwci, bwgan

**hoe** n hof ▷ vb hofio
**hog** n mochyn
**hoist** vt codi, dyrchafu
**hold** vb dal, credu; atal; cadw ▷ n gafael, dalfa
**hold** n ceudod llong, howld
**holdall** n celsach
**holding** n deiliadaeth; tyddyn
**hold up** n (robbery) lladrad arfog; (in traffic) rhwystr
**hole** n twll, ffau
**holiday** n gŵyl, dygwyl
**holiness** n sancteiddrwydd
**Holland** n Isalmaen
**hollow** adj cau, gwag ▷ n ceudod, pant ▷ vt tyllu, cafnio
**holly** n celyn, celynnen
**holocaust** n lladdfa
**holster** n gwain
**holy** adj sanctaidd, glân
**Holy Ghost/Spirit** n Ysbryd Glân
**homage** n gwrogaeth
**home** n, adj cartref ▷ adv adref; **at ~** gartref
**homeland** n mamwlad
**homeless** adj digartref
**homely** adj cartrefol
**home rule** n ymreolaeth, hunan-lywodraeth
**homesick** adj hiraethus
**homestead** n tyddyn
**homework** n gwaith cartref
**homicide** n dynleiddiad, llofruddiaeth
**homily** n pregeth, homili
**homogeneous** adj cydryw, homogenus
**homosexual** n gwrywgydiwr
**homosexuality** n gwrywgydiaeth
**hone** n carreg hogi, hôn ▷ vb hogi
**honest** adj (g)onest, didwyll
**honesty** n (g)onestrwydd
**honey** n mêl
**honeycomb** n dil mêl, crwybr ▷ vt tyllu, britho
**honeymoon** n mis mêl
**honeysuckle** n gwyddfid

**honorary** adj mygedol
**honour** n anrhydedd ▷ vt anrhydeddu
**honourable** adj anrhydeddus
**hood** n cwfl, cwcwll
**hoodwink** vt dallu, twyllo
**hoof** n carn
**hook** n bach; cryman ▷ vb bachu
**hooker** n bachwr
**hooligan** n adyn, dihiryn
**hoop** n cylch, cant ▷ vt cylchu, cantio
**hoot** vb hwtian, hwtio ▷ n hŵt
**hop** vb hercian ▷ n llam, herc
**hope** n gobaith ▷ vb gobeithio
**horde** n torf, haid, mintai
**horizon** n gorwel
**horizontal** adj llorwedd
**hormone** n hormon
**horn** n corn ▷ vt cornio, twlcio
**horned** adj corniog
**hornet** n gwenynen feirch, cacynen
**horoscope** n horosgôp
**horrible** adj erchyll, ofnadwy
**horrid** adj erchyll, echrydus, anferth
**horrify** vt brawychu
**horror** n arswyd, erchylltod
**horse** n march, ceffyl
**horsehair** n rhawn
**horseman** n marchog
**horsemanship** n marchogaeth
**horseplay** n direidi
**horseshoe** n pedol
**horticultural** adj garddwriaethol
**horticulture** n garddwriaeth
**horticulturist** n garddwriaethwr
**hose (hose)** n hosan; (hoses) n pibell ddŵr
**hospitable** adj lletygar, croesawus
**hospital** n ysbyty
**hospitality** n lletygarwch, croeso
**host** n llu, byddin
**host** n lletywr, gwesteiwr
**hostage** n gwystl
**hostel** n llety efrydwyr, neuadd breswyl
**hostess** n croesawferch
**hostile** adj gelyniaethus

hot adj poeth, twym, brwd, gwresog
hotbed n magwrfa
hotch-potch n cymysgfa, cybolfa
hotel n gwesty
hotelier n gwestywr
hot-headed adj penboeth, byrbwyll
hot-water bottle n jar/potel dŵr twym
hound n bytheiad, helgi ▷ vt hela, erlid, annos
hour n awr
house n tŷ, annedd ▷ vb lletya
household n teulu, tylwyth
householder n deiliad tŷ
housekeeper n gofalyddes
housewife n gwraig tŷ
housing n tai
hovel n penty, hofel
hover vi hofran
hovercraft n hofrenfad
how adv pa mor, pa fodd, pa sut, sut
howbeit adv er hynny
however adv pa fodd bynnag, sut bynnag
howl vi udo, oernadu ▷ n udiad, oernad
hoyden n rhampen, hoeden
hub n both olwyn; canolbwynt
hubbub n mwstwr
huddle vb tyrru, gwthio
hue n gwawr
huff vb sorri, tramgwyddo ▷ n soriant
hug vt cofleidio, gwasgu
huge adj anferth, enfawr, dirfawr
hulk n corff llong, llong foel, hwlc
hull n corff llong; cibyn, plisgyn
hullabaloo n dadwrdd, helynt, halibalŵ
hum vb mwmian ▷ n si, sibrwd
human adj dynol
humane adj tirion, tosturiol, trugarog
humanism n dyneiddiaeth
humanist n dyneiddiwr
humanistic adj dyneiddiol

humanitarian n dyngarwr
humanitarianism n dyngaroldeb
humanity n dynoliaeth, dynolryw
humble adj gostyngedig, ufudd ▷ vt darostwng
humble-bee n cacynen
humbug n twyll, ffug, hoced; twyllwr ▷ vt twyllo
humdrum adj diflas
humid adj llaith
humiliate vt bychanu, gwaradwyddo, darostwng, iselu
humiliation n darostyngiad
humility n gostyngeiddrwydd
humour n hwyl, donioldeb ▷ vt boddio
hump n crwmach, crwmp, crwb
hunch n syniad, tybiaeth
hunch backed adj cefngrwm
hundred adj cant, can ▷ n cant; cantref
Hungary n Hwngari
hunger n newyn, chwant bwyd ▷ vi newynu
hungry adj newynog
hunk n cwlff(yn)
hunt vb hela, erlid ▷ n helwriaeth, hela
hunter n heliwr; ceffyl hela
hunting n hela
hurdle n clwyd
hurl vt hyrddio
hurly-burly n hwrli-bwrli, dwndwr
hurricane n corwynt
hurried adj brysiog
hurry vb brysio ▷ n brys
hurt vb niweidio, dolurio, brifo ▷ n niwed, dolur
hurtful adj niweidiol
hurtle vb gwrthdaro, chwyrlïo
husband n gŵr, priod ▷ vt cynilo
husbandry n amaethyddiaeth, hwsmonaeth
hush excl ust ▷ vb distewi ▷ n distawrwydd
husk n plisgyn, cibyn ▷ vt plisgo
husky adj sych, cryglyd

**hussy** n maeden
**hustings** n hwstyng, llwyfan etholiad
**hustle** vb gwthio, prysuro
**hut** n bwth, caban, cwt
**hutch** n cwt cwningen, cwb
**hyacinth** n croeso haf
**hybrid** adj croesryw
**hydration** n hydradiad
**hydraulic** adj hydrolig
**hydraulics** n hydroleg
**hydro-** prefix dwfr
**hydroelectric** adj hydroelectrig
**hydrophobia** n hydroffobia
**hygiene** n iechydaeth, gwyddor glendid
**hymn** n emyn ▷ vb emynu
**hyper-** prefix gor-, tra-
**hyperbole** n gormodiaith
**hypermarket** n archfarchnad
**hyphen** n cyplysnod, cysylltnod (-)
**hypnotism** n swyngwsg, hypnotiaeth
**hypnotize** vt swyno, rheibio
**hypochondria** n pruddglwyf, y felan
**hypocrisy** n rhagrith
**hypocrite** n rhagrithiwr
**hypothesis** (-theses) n damcaniaeth
**hyssop** n isop
**hysteria** n y famwst, hysteria
**hysterical** adj hysterig

◆

**I** pron mi, myfi; fi, i; minnau, innau
**ice** n iâ, rhew ▷ vt taenu (megis) â rhew
**iceberg** n mynydd rhew
**ice cream** n hufen iâ
**Iceland** n Gwlad yr Iâ
**ice lolly** n loli iâ
**ice rink** n llain iâ
**icicle** n clöyn iâ, cloch iâ, pibonwy
**icing** n eising
**icy** adj rhewllyd
**idea** n drychfeddwl, syniad
**ideal** adj delfrydol, ideal ▷ n delfryd
**idealism** n delfrydiaeth
**idealist** n delfrydiwr
**idealistic** adj delfrydol
**idealize** vb delfrydu
**identical** adj yr un (yn union)
**identify** vt adnabod (fel yr un un); uniaethu
**identikit (picture)** n tebyglun
**identity** n unfathiant, hunaniaeth
**idiocy** n gwiriondeb, penwendid
**idiom** n priod-ddull, idiom
**idiosyncrasy** n tymer, anianawd
**idiot** n gwirionyn, hurtyn
**idle** adj segur, ofer ▷ vb segura, ofera
**idleness** n segurdod, diogi
**idol** n eilun
**idolater** n eilunaddolwr
**idolatry** n eilunaddoliaeth
**idolise** vb addoli, gwirioni
**idyll** n bugeilgerdd; canig
**if** conj os, pe
**igloo** n iglw

**ignite** *vb* ennyn, tanio, cynnau
**ignition** *n* taniad
**ignoble** *adj* anenwog, isel, gwael, salw
**ignominious** *adj* gwarthus, gwaradwyddus
**ignorance** *n* anwybodaeth
**ignorant** *adj* anwybodus
**ignore** *vt* anwybyddu, diystyru
**il-** *prefix* di-, an-
**ill** *adj* drwg; gwael, claf ▷ *adv* yn ddrwg ▷ *n* drwg, niwed
**ill-advised** *adj* annoeth, ffôl
**illegal** *adj* anghyfreithlon
**illegible** *adj* annarllenadwy, aneglur
**illegitimate, illicit** *adj* anghyfreithlon
**illiterate** *adj* anllythrennog
**illness** *n* afiechyd, anhwylder, anhwyldeb
**illogical** *adj* afresymegol
**ill-timed** *adj* anamserol
**ill-treat** *vb* camdrin
**illuminate** *vt* goleuo, addurno
**illumination** *n* golau, esboniad
**illusion** *n* rhith, lledrith, rhithganfyddiad
**illustrate** *vt* egluro; darlunio
**illustration** *n* eglureb; darlun
**illustrative** *adj* darluniol, eglurhaol
**illustrious** *adj* enwog, hyglod
**ill-will** *n* gelyniaeth, casineb
**im-** *prefix* di, an-
**image** *n* delw, llun; delwedd
**imagery** *n* delweddaeth
**imaginary** *adj* dychmygol
**imagination** *n* dychymyg, darfelydd
**imaginative** *adj* dychmygus
**imagine** *vt* dychmygu, tybio
**imbalance** *n* anghydbwysedd
**imbecile** *adj, n* (un) penwan
**imbue** *vt* trwytho
**imitate** *vt* dynwared, efelychu
**immaculate** *adj* difrycheulyd, pur, glân

**immaterial** *adj* dibwys
**immature** *adj* anaeddfed
**immediate** *adj* agos, presennol
**immediately** *adv* ar unwaith
**immemorial** *adj* er cyn cof
**immense** *adj* anferth, eang, dirfawr
**immerse** *vt* trochi, suddo
**immigrant** *n* mewnfudwr
**immigrate** *vi* mewnfudo
**imminent** *adj* gerllaw, agos, wrth y drws
**immobile** *adj* diymod, disymud
**immoral** *adj* anfoesol
**immortal** *adj* anfarwol
**immortality** *n* anfarwoldeb
**immortalize** *vb* anfarwoli
**immovable** *adj* diysgog, ansymudol
**immune** *adj* rhydd rhag
**immunization** *n* gwrth-heintiad
**immunize** *vb* gwrtheintio
**immure** *vt* caethiwo, carcharu
**immutable** *adj* anghyfnewidiol, digyfnewid
**imp** *n* dieflyn, cenau
**impact** *n* ardrawiad, gwrthdrawiad
**impair** *vt* amharu
**impale** *vt* trywanu
**impart** *vt* cyfrannu, rhoddi
**impartial** *adj* diduedd, amhleidiol, teg
**impassable** *adj* na ellir mynd heibio iddo
**impasse** *n* ataliad, pen draw
**impassioned** *adj* brwd, hwyliog, cyffrous
**impassive** *adj* digyffro, didaro
**impatient** *adj* diamynedd
**impeach** *vt* cyhuddo, cwyno yn erbyn, uchelgyhuddo
**impeccable** *adj* di-fai
**impede** *vt* atal, rhwystro, llesteirio
**impediment** *n* atalfa, rhwystr, nam
**impel** *vt* gyrru, hyrddio, cymell
**impending** *adj* agos, gerllaw
**imperative** *n* gorchymyn ▷ *adj*

gorchmynnol, gorfodol

**imperfect** adj amherffaith

**imperial** adj ymerodrol

**imperil** vt peryglu

**imperious** adj awdurdodol, trahaus

**impermeable** adj anathraidd

**impersonal** adj amhersonol

**impersonate** vt personoli, cynrychioli, portreadu (person)

**impertinent** adj amherthnasol; digywilydd

**imperturbable** adj tawel, digyffro

**impervious** adj na ellir ei dreiddio, anhydraidd

**impetuous** adj byrbwyll, nwydwyllt

**impetus** n cymhelliad, symbyliad

**impinge** vi taro yn erbyn, gwrthdaro, cyffwrdd â

**impious** adj annuwiol, diras

**implacable** adj anghymodlon

**implant** vt plannu, gwreiddio

**implement** n offeryn, arf ▷ vb gweithredu

**implication** n ymhlygiad, goblygiad

**implicit** adj dealledig; ymhlyg, goblygedig

**implore** vt atolygu, ymbil, erfyn, crefu

**imply** vt arwyddo, awgrymu

**impolite** adj anfoesgar

**import** vt mewnforio ▷ n (pl) mewnforion; arwyddocâd; pwys

**importance** n pwys, pwysigrwydd

**important** adj pwysig

**importer** n mewnforiwr

**importune** vt dyfal geisio, taer erfyn

**impose** vb gosod ar; twyllo

**imposing** adj llethol, mawreddog

**impossibility** n amhosibilrwydd

**impossible** adj amhosibl

**impostor** n twyllwr

**imposture** n twyll, hoced

**impotence** n anallu, analluedd

**impotent** adj di-rym, analluog

**impound** vi ffaldio; atafaelu

**impoverish** vt tlodi, llymhau

**impracticable** adj anymarferol

**imprecate** vt rhegi, melltithio

**impregnable** adj cadarn, di-syfl

**impregnate** vt ffrwythloni; trwytho

**impress** vt argraffu, pwyso, dylanwadu ▷ n argraffiad

**impression** n argraff

**impressionable** adj hawdd ei argyhoeddi

**impressive** adj trawiadol

**imprint** vt argraffu ▷ n argraff, delw

**imprison** vt carcharu

**improbable** adj annhebygol

**impromptu** adj, adv ar y pryd, byrfyfyr

**improper** adj anweddus

**improve** vb gwella, diwygio

**improvement** n gwelliant

**improvise** vb addasu ar y pryd

**impudent** adj digywilydd, haerllug

**impulse** n cymhelliad, ysgogiad

**impulsive** adj byrbwyll

**impunity** n bod heb gosb; **with ~** yn ddi-gosb

**impure** adj amhur, aflan

**impute** vt cyfrif i; priodoli; bwrw ar

**in** prep yn, mewn, i mewn, o fewn

**in-** prefix di-, an-

**inability** n anallu

**inaccessible** n anhygyrch

**inaccurate** adj anghywir, anfanwl

**inaction** n segurdod

**inadequate** adj annigonol

**inadmissible** adj annerbyniol

**inadvertent** adj anfwriadol, amryfus

**inane** adj gwag, gwageddus, ofer

**inanimate** adj difywyd, dienaid

**inappropriate** adj anaddas

**inasmuch** adv yn gymaint (â)

**inaudible** adj anhyglyw, na ellir ei glywed

**inaugurate** vt urddo, cysegru,

agor, dechrau

**inauguration** n agoriad, dechreuad

**inborn** adj cynhenid, greddfol

**inbreed** vb mewnfrido

**incandescent** adj gwynias

**incantation** n swyn, swyngyfaredd

**incapable** adj analluog

**incapability** n anallu

**incapacitate** vt anghymhwyso, analluogi

**incarcerate** vt carcharu

**incarnation** n ymgnawdoliad

**incendiary** adj llosg ▷ n bom tân

**incense** n arogldarth

**incense** vt llidio, cythruddo

**incentive** adj cymelliadol ▷ n cymhelliad

**inception** n dechreuad, agoriad

**incessant** adj di-baid, di-dor

**incest** n llosgach

**inch** n modfedd

**incident** n digwyddiad

**incidental** adj digwyddiadol, achlysurol

**incidentally** adv gyda llaw

**incinerate** vb llosgi'n ulw

**incineration** n llosgiad llwyr

**incinerator** n llosgydd, ffwrnais

**incipient** adj dechreuol

**incise** vt torri, trychu

**incisive** adj llym, miniog

**incite** vt annog, cyffroi, annos

**inclement** adj gerwin, garw, drycinog

**inclination** n tuedd, gogwydd

**incline** vb tueddu, gogwyddo ▷ n llethr

**include** vt cynnwys

**including** prep gan gynnwys

**inclusive** adj cynwysedig, gan gynnwys

**incognito** adj yn ddirgel, dan ffugenw

**incoherent** adj digyswllt, anghysylltus

**income** n incwm; ~ **tax** treth incwm

**incompatible** adj anghytûn

**incompetent** n anghymwys

**incomplete** adj anghyflawn

**incomprehensible** adj annealladwy

**incongruous** adj anghydweddol, anaddas

**inconsistency** n anghysondeb

**inconsistent** adj anghyson

**inconspicuous** adj anamlwg

**incontestable** adj diymwad, diamheuol

**inconvenience** n anghyfleustra

**inconvenient** adj anghyfleus

**incorporate** vb corffori, ymgorffori

**incorporated** adj corfforedig

**incorrect** adj anghywir

**incorrigible** adj anwelladwy

**increase** vb cynyddu ▷ n cynnydd

**incredible** adj anhygoel, anghredadwy

**incredulity** n anghrediniaeth

**incredulous** adj anghrediniol

**increment** n cynnydd, ychwanegiad

**incriminate** vt cyhuddo, euogi

**incubate** vb gori, deor

**incubator** n deorydd

**incumbent** adj rhwymedig ar ▷ n periglor, offeiriad, clerigwr

**incur** vt rhedeg i ddyled; achosi

**incursion** n cyrch

**indebted** adj dyledus

**indecent** adj anweddus

**indecision** n petruster

**indecisive** adj amhendant

**indeed** adv yn wir; iawn, dros ben

**indefatigable** adj diflin, dyfal

**indefinite** adj amhenodol, amhendant

**indelible** adj annileadwy

**indelicate** adj aflednais

**indemnify** vb digolledu

**indemnity** n iawn

**indented** adj bylchog, danheddus

**indenture** n cytundeb, cyfamod
**independence** n annibyniaeth
**independent** adj annibynnol ▷ n annibynnwr
**indescribable** adj annisgrifiadwy
**indeterminate** adj amhenodol, penagored
**index** n mynegai; mynegfys
**India** n India
**Indian** adj Indiaidd ▷ n Indiad
**indicate** vt dangos, arwyddo
**indicative** adj arwyddol, mynegol
**indicator** n dangosydd
**indict** vt cyhuddo
**indifference** n difaterwch, difrawder
**indifferent** adj difater; dibwys
**indigenous** adj cynhenid
**indigent** adj anghenus, tlawd, rheidus
**indigestion** n diffyg traul, camdreuliad
**indignant** adj dig, digofus, dicllon
**indignation** n dig, digofaint, llid
**indignity** n amarch, sarhad, anfri
**indirect** adj anuniongyrchol
**indiscreet** adj annoeth
**indiscriminate** adj diwahaniaeth
**indispensable** adj anhepgorol
**indisposed** adj anhwylus
**indisputable** adj diamheuol
**indissoluble** adj annatod
**indistinct** adj aneglur, anhyglyw, bloesg
**indite** vt cyfansoddi, traethu
**individual** adj unigol ▷ n un, unigolyn
**indoctrinate** vb trwytho (ag athrawiaeth), credorfodi
**indoctrination** n credorfodaeth
**indolence** n seguryd, syrthni
**indolent** adj segur, swrth, dioglyd
**indomitable** adj anorchfygol, di-ildio
**indoor** adj, adv dan do
**indubitable** adj diamheuol
**induce** vt darbwyllo, denu, cymell

**inducement** n anogiad
**induct** vt sefydlu; anwytho
**induction** n anwythiad
**indulge** vb boddio; maldodi
**indulgence** n ymfoddhad; maldod
**indulgent** adj ffafriol, maldodus
**industrial** adj diwydiannol, gweithfaol
**industrialize** vb diwydiannu
**industrious** adj diwyd, dyfal, gweithgar
**industry** n diwydrwydd; diwydiant
**inebriate** vt meddwi ▷ n meddwyn
**inedible** adj anfwytadwy
**ineffable** adj anhraethol, anhraethadwy
**ineffective** adj aneffeithiol
**inefficiency** n anallu
**inefficient** adj analluog
**ineligible** adj anghymwys
**inept** adj heb fod yn taro, gwrthun, gwirion
**inequality** n anghysondeb
**inert** adj swrth, diynni, diegni
**inertia** n anegni, inertia
**inestimable** adj amhrisiadwy
**inevitable** adj anochel, anesgorol
**inexhaustible** adj dihysbydd
**inexorable** adj di-ildio, anhyblyg
**inexpensive** adj rhad
**inexperience** n diffyg profiad
**inexperienced** adj amhrofiadol, dibrofiad
**infallible** adj anffaeledig
**infallibility** n anffaeledigrwydd
**infamous** adj gwaradwyddus, gwarthus
**infancy** n mabandod, mebyd, maboed
**infant** n maban, baban; un dan oed
**infantry** n gwŷr traed, milwyr traed
**infatuate** vt gwirioni, ffoli, dwlu
**infatuated** adj wedi ffoli, wedi gwirioni
**infect** vt heintio, llygru
**infection** n haint
**infectious** adj heintus

**infer** vt casglu
**inferior** adj is, israddol ▷ n isradd
**inferiority** n israddoldeb
**inferiority complex** n cymhleth y taeog
**infernal** adj uffernol, dieflig
**infertile** adj anffrwythlon
**infertility** n anffrwythlondeb
**infest** vt bod yn bla, heigiannu
**infidel** n anffyddiwr
**infidelity** n anffyddlondeb
**infield** adj mewnfaes
**infinite** adj anfeidrol
**infinitesimal** adj anfeidrol fach, gorfychan
**infinitive** adj annherfynol ▷ n berfenw
**infirm** adj egwan, gwan, gwanllyd
**infirmary** n ysbyty, clafdy
**infirmity** n gwendid, llesgedd
**inflame** vb ennyn, cyffroi, llidio
**inflamed** adj llidus
**inflammable** adj hylosg, hyfflam
**inflammation** n enyniad, enynfa, llid
**inflatable** adj y gellir ei chwyddo neu ei chwythu
**inflate** vt chwyddo
**inflation** n chwyddiant
**inflect** vt ffurfdroi; treiglo
**inflexible** adj anhyblyg
**inflexibility** n anhyblygrwydd
**inflict** vt peri, gweinyddu (cosb, poen etc)
**influence** n dylanwad ▷ vt dylanwadu
**influenza** n ffliw
**influx** n dylifiad
**inform** vb hysbysu
**informal** adj anffurfiol
**information** n gwybodaeth, hysbysrwydd
**infra-** prefix is-
**infra-red** adj is-goch
**infrastructure** n seilwaith
**infrequent** adj anaml
**infringe** vt torri, troseddu

**infuriate** vt ffyrnigo, cynddeiriogi
**infuse** vt tywallt, arllwys; trwytho
**infusion** n trwyth, hydreiddiad
**ingenious** adj medrus, cywrain, celfydd
**ingenuous** adj didwyll, diddichell
**ingenuousness** n didwylledd, diffuantrwydd
**ingrained** adj wedi greddfu; cynhenid
**ingratiate** vt ennill ffafr
**ingratitude** n anniolchgarwch
**ingredients** npl cynhwysion, defnyddiau
**inhabit** vt cyfaneddu, trigo, preswylio
**inhabitable** adj cyfannedd, trigadwy
**inhabitant** n preswyliwr
**inhale** vt anadlu
**inhere** vi glynu, ymlynu, bod
**inherent** adj cynhenid, greddfol
**inherit** vt etifeddu
**inheritance** n etifeddiaeth
**inheritor** n etifedd, etifeddwr
**inhibit** vt gwahardd, atal
**inhibition** n ataliad, atalnwyd
**inhibitor** n atalydd
**inhuman** adj annynol, creulon
**inimical** adj gelyniaethus
**inimitable** adj digyffelyb
**iniquitous** adj drwg, traws
**iniquity** n anwiredd, camwedd
**initial** adj dechreuol ▷ n llythyren gyntaf
**initiate** vt egwyddori; derbyn; dechrau
**initiative** n cynhoredd, menter
**inject** vt chwistrellu
**injection** n chwistrelliad, pigiad
**injunction** n gorchymyn, gwaharddiad
**injure** vt niweidio, anafu
**injury** n niwed, cam, anaf
**injustice** n anghyfiawnder, cam
**ink** n inc ▷ vt incio
**inkling** n awgrym, arwydd

**inland** adj canoldirol ▷ n canolwr;
   **Inland Revenue** n Cyllid y Wlad
**inlet** n cilfach, bae
**inmate** n trigiannydd, preswylydd
**inmost** adj nesaf i mewn, dyfnaf
**inn** n tafarn, tafarndy, gwesty
**innate** adj cynhenid, cynhwynol,
   greddfol
**inner** adj mewnol
**innings** npl batiad
**innkeeper** n tafarnwr
**innocence** n diniweidrwydd
**innocent** adj diniwed, gwirion,
   dieuog
**innocuous** adj diniwed, diberygl
**innovate** vi newid, cyflwyno
**innovation** n newyddbeth
**innuendo** n ensyniad
**innumerable** adj aneirif, afrifed,
   dirifedi, di-rif
**inoculate** vt brechu
**inoculation** n brechiad
**inoffensive** adj di-ddrwg
**inordinate** adj anghymedrol, di-rôl
**inorganic** adj anorganig
**input** n mewnbwn, cyfraniad
**inquest** n cwest; trengholiad
**inquire** vb ymofyn, ymholi, gofyn,
   holi
**inquiry** n ymholiad
**inquisition** n ymchwiliad;
   chwil-lys
**inquisitive** adj ymofyngar, holgar
**in-road** n cyrch
**insane** adj gwallgof, gorffwyll,
   ynfyd
**insanitary** adj afiachus, brwnt
**insatiable** adj anniwall
**inscribe** vt arysgrifio
**inscription** n arysgrif
**inscrutable** adj anolrheiniadwy,
   anchwiliadwy
**insect** n pryf, trychfil
**insensibility** n dideimladrwydd
**insensible** adj dideimlad
**insert** vb mewnosod
**in-service** adj mewn swydd

**inside** n tu mewn ▷ adj mewnol
   ▷ prep y tu mewn i ▷ adv i mewn,
   o fewn
**inside-forward** n mewnwr
**inside-half** n mewnwr
**inside-out** adv o chwith
**inside-right** n mewnwr de
**insidious** adj llechwraidd
**insight** n mewnwelediad
**insignificance** n dinodedd
**insignificant** adj di-nod, distadl,
   dibwys
**insincere** adj annidwyll, ffuantus,
   rhagrithiol
**insincerity** n annidwylledd
**insinuate** vb ensynio
**insipid** adj diflas, merfaidd
**insist** vi mynnu
**insolence** n haerllugrwydd
**insolent** adj haerllug
**insolvent** adj methdalus, wedi torri
**insomnia** n anhunedd
**inspect** vt arolygu, archwilio
**inspector** n arolygwr
**inspiration** n ysbrydoliaeth
**inspire** vb ysbrydoli
**instability** n ansadrwydd
**install** vt sefydlu, gorseddu
**instalment** n cyfran, rhandal
**instance** n enghraifft ▷ vt enwi,
   nodi
**instant** adj taer, ebrwydd ▷ n
   eiliad, moment; **instant coffee** n
   coffi powdr
**instantaneous** adj yn y fan;
   disymwth
**instantly** adv ar drawiad
**instead** adv yn lle
**instep** n mwnwgl troed, cefn troed
**instigate** vt annog, cymell
**instil** vt argymell
**instinct** n greddf
**institute** n athrofa
**institution** n sefydliad
**instruct** vt hyfforddi
**instruction** n hyfforddiant
**instructor** n hyfforddwr

**instrument** n offeryn
**insubordinate** adj anufudd, gwrthryfelgar
**insufferable** adj annioddefol
**insufficient** adj annigonol
**insular** adj ynysol, cul
**insulate** vt ynysu, inswleiddio
**insult** vt sarhau ▷ n sarhad
**insuperable** adj anorfod, anorchfygol
**insurance** n yswiriant; **insurance policy** n polisi yswiriant
**insure** vb yswirio
**insurgent** adj gwrthryfelgar ▷ n gwrthryfelwr
**insurrection** n terfysg, gwrthryfel
**intact** adj cyfan, dianaf
**integral** adj cyfan, cyflawn
**integrate** vb cyfannu
**integrity** n cywirdeb, gonestrwydd
**intellect** n deall
**intellectual** n deallusyn ▷ adj deallus, deallgar
**intelligence** n deallgarwch, deallusrwydd; hysbysrwydd
**intelligent** adj deallus
**intelligible** adj dealladwy
**intend** vt bwriadu, amcanu, golygu
**intense** adj angerddol, dwys
**intensive care unit** n uned ofal arbennig
**intent** adj dyfal, diwyd, astud
**intent** n bwriad, amcan; ystyr; diben
**intention** n bwriad
**intentional** adj bwriadol
**inter** vt claddu, daearu
**inter-** prefix rhwng, cyd
**interaction** n rhyngweithiad
**interbreed** vb rhyngfridio
**intercede** vi cyfryngu, eiriol
**intercept** vt rhyng-gipio, rhwystro, rhagod
**intercession** n cyfryngdod, eiriolaeth
**interchange** vt cyfnewid, ymgyfnewid

**intercourse** n cyfathrach
**interdict** vt gwahardd ▷ n gwaharddiad
**interest** n budd, buddiant; diddordeb; llog ▷ vt diddori
**interested** adj â chanddo ddidordeb
**interesting** adj diddorol
**interests** npl diddordebau
**interface** n cydwyneb
**interfere** vt cyfryngu, ymyrryd, ymhêl
**interference** n ymyrraeth
**interim** adj dros dro ▷ n cyfamser
**interior** adj mewnol ▷ n tu mewn, canol, perfeddwlad
**interject** vt ebychu
**interlock** vb cyd-gloi
**interloper** n ymwthiwr, ymyrrwr
**interlude** n egwyl; anterliwt
**intermediary** n canolwr, cyfryngwr
**intermediate** adj canol, canolradd
**intern** vt carcharu
**internal** adj mewnol
**international** adj cydwladol, rhyngwladol
**interpolate** vt dodi i mewn, rhyngosod
**interpolation** n rhyngosodiad
**interpose** vb gosod rhwng, cyfryngu, rhyngwthio
**interpret** vt dehongli; cyfieithu
**interpretation** n dehongliad; cyfieithiad
**interpreter** n lladmerydd, cyfieithydd
**interrelation** n cydberthynas
**interrogate** vt holi
**interrogative** adj gofynnol
**interrupt** vt torri ar, torri ar draws, ymyrryd
**intersect** vb croesi ei gilydd; croesdorri
**intersection** n croesdoriad
**intersperse** vb gwasgaru, britho
**interval** n egwyl, saib

**intervene** *vi* ymyrryd
**interview** *n* cyfweliad ▷ *vb* cyfweld
**intestines** *npl* perfedd, coluddion
**intimacy** *n* agosatrwydd
**intimate** *adj* cyfarwydd, agos ▷ *n* cydnabod
**intimate** *vt* arwyddo, hysbysu
**intimidate** *vt* dychrynu, brawychu
**into** *prep* i, i mewn i
**intolerable** *adj* annioddefol
**intonation** *n* tonyddiaeth, goslef
**intone** *vt* llafarganu
**intoxicate** *vt* meddwi
**intoxication** *n* meddwdod
**intractable** *adj* anhydrin, afreolus
**intransitive** *adj* cyflawn (gramadeg)
**intrepid** *adj* di-ofn, diarswyd, gwrol, dewr
**intricate** *adj* dyrys, cymhleth, astrus
**intrigue** *vi, n* cynllwyn
**intrinsic** *adj* priodol, hanfodol
**introduce** *vt* cyflwyno
**introduction** *n* cyflwyniad, rhagarweiniad
**introductory** *adj* dechreuol, agoriadol, rhagarweiniol
**introspection** *n* mewnsylliad
**introvert** *adj* mewnblyg
**intrude** *vb* ymyrryd
**intruder** *n* ymyrrwr, ymwthiwr
**intrusion** *n* ymwthiad, ymyrraeth
**intuition** *n* sythwelediad
**inundate** *vt* gorlifo, boddi
**inundation** *n* gorlifiad
**inure** *vt* cyfarwyddo, caledu
**invade** *vt* goresgyn
**invalid** *adj* di-rym, annilys
**invalid** *n* un afiach, un methedig
**invaluable** *adj* amhrisiadwy
**invariable** *adj* gwastad, dieithriad
**invariably** *adv* yn ddieithriad
**invasion** *n* goresgyniad
**invective** *n* difrïaeth, cabledd
**invent** *vt* dyfeisio, dychmygu
**inventory** *n* rhestr, stocrestr

**inverse** *adj* (yn y) gwrthwyneb, yn groes
**inversion** *n* gwrthdro
**invert** *vt* troi wyneb i waered, gwrthdroi
**inverted commas** *npl* dyfynodau
**invest** *vt* buddsoddi; arwisgo
**investigate** *vt* chwilio, archwilio, ymchwilio
**investigation** *n* ymchwiliad
**investigator** *n* ymchwiliwr
**investiture** *n* arwisgiad
**investment** *n* buddsoddiad
**investor** *n* buddsoddwr
**invidious** *adj* annymunol
**invigilate** *vb* arolygu
**invigilator** *n* arolygwr, gwyliwr
**invigorate** *vt* cryfhau, grymuso
**invincible** *adj* anorchfygol
**inviolable** *adj* dihalog, cysegredig
**invisible** *adj* anweledig, anweladwy
**invitation** *n* gwahoddiad
**invite** *vt* gwahodd
**invoice** *n* anfoneb
**involuntary** *adj* o anfodd, anfwriadol
**involve** *vt* drysu; cynnwys, ymneud
**involvement** *n* ymwneud, ymglymiad
**inward** *adj* mewnol
**iodine** *n* ïodin
**ion** *n* ïon
**ionisation** *n* ïoneiddiad
**ionise** *vb* ïoneiddio
**iota** *n* mymryn, iod, gronyn
**ir-** *prefix* di-, an-
**Iran** *n* Iran
**Iraq** *n* Iraq
**irate** *adj* dig, llidiog
**Ireland** *n* Iwerddon
**iris** *n* enfys; elestr
**Irish** *adj* Gwyddelig ▷ *n* Gwyddeleg
**irksome** *adj* blin, trafferthus, diflas
**iron** *n, adj* haearn ▷ *vt* smwddio
**ironic** *adj* eironig

**ironing board** n bwrdd smwddio
**ironmonger** n gwerthwr nwyddau haearn
**irony** n eironi
**irradiate** vt arbelydru
**irradiation** n arbelydredd
**irrational** adj direswm, afresymol
**irreconcilable** adj anghymodlon
**irrefutable** adj anatebadwy
**irregular** adj afreolaidd
**irregularity** n afreoleidd-dra
**irrelevant** adj amherthnasol
**irreparable** adj anadferadwy
**irreproachable** adj diargyhoedd, di-fai
**irresistible** adj anorchfygol
**irretrievable** adj anadferadwy
**irrevocable** adj di-alw-yn-ôl
**irrigate** vt dyfrhau
**irritable** n croendenau, anniddig, llidiog
**irritate** vt blino, poeni, cythruddo
**is** vi mae, sydd, yw, ydy(w), oes
**island, isle** n ynys
**islet** n ynysig
**isolate** vt neilltuo, gwahanu
**isolated** adj wedi ei neilltuo, wedi ei wahanu
**isolation** n neilltuaeth, arwahanrwydd
**Israel** n Israel
**Israelite** n Israeliad
**issue** n llif; agorfa, arllwysfa; hilogaeth, plant; canlyniad, pwnc mewn dadl ▷ vb tarddu, deillio; rhoi allan, cyhoeddi
**isthmus** n culdir
**it** pron efe, fe, ef, efo, fo, o; hi
**Italian** adj Eidalaidd ▷ n Eidalwr; (Ling) Eidaleg
**italic** adj italig
**italicize** vb italeiddio
**italics** npl llythrennau italaidd
**Italy** n Yr Eidal
**itch** vi ysu, cosi ▷ n y crafu, ysfa
**item** n peth, pwnc, darn, tamaid
**iterate** vt ailadrodd

**itinerant** adj teithiol
**itinerary** n taith, teithlyfr
**itinerate** vi teithio, cylchdeithio
**itself** pron ei hun, ei hunan
**ivory** n ifori
**ivy** n eiddew, iorwg

# j

**jab** n jab, pigiad ▷ vb procio, gwanu
**jabber** vi bragawthan, clebran ▷ n clebar
**jack** n jac
**jackass** n asyn gwryw; hurtyn
**jackdaw** n corfran, jac-y-do
**jacket** n siaced
**jade** vt blino, lluddedu
**jagged** adj danheddog, ysgithrog
**jail** n carchar
**jam** n jam; tagfa
**jam** vt jamio, tagu
**Jamaica** n Jamaica
**jangle** vi clochdar
**janitor** n porthor
**January** n Ionawr
**Japan** n Nihon, Japán, Siapán
**Japanese** adj Siapaneaidd ▷ n Siapanead; (Ling) Siapaneg
**jar** n anghytsain; anghydfod ▷ vb rhygnu
**jar** n jar
**jargon** n ffregod, bregiaith, jargon
**jaundice** n y clefyd melyn

**jaunt** vi gwibio, rhodio ▷ n gwibdaith
**jaunty** adj llon, bywiog, talog
**javelin** n picell, gwaywffon
**jaw** n gên, cern; (pl) safn
**jay** n sgrech y coed
**jazz** n jas
**jealous** adj eiddigus, cenfigennus, gwenwynllyd
**jealousy** n cenfigen, eiddigedd
**jeans** n jîns
**jeep** n jîp
**jeer** vb gwawdio, gwatwar
**jelly** n jeli
**jellyfish** n slefren fôr
**jeopardy** n perygl, enbydrwydd
**jerk** n plwc, ysgytiad ▷ vb plycio, ysgytio
**jerkin** n siercyn, siaced
**jersey** n siersi
**Jerusalem** n Caersalem, Jerwsalem
**jest** n cellwair, ysmaldod ▷ vi cellwair, ysmalio
**Jesus** n Iesu
**jet** n ffrwd, jet; muchudd ▷ vb ffrydio, pistyllio
**jettison** vt taflu (llwyth) dros y bwrdd
**jetty** n jeti, glanfa
**Jew** n Iddew
**jewel** n gem, tlws
**jeweller** n gemydd
**jewellery** n gemwaith, gemau
**Jewish** adj Iddewig
**jib** n hwyl flaen llong, jib
**jib** vi nogio, strancio
**jig** n dawns fywiog, jig
**jig-saw** n jig-so
**jilt** vt siomi cariad
**jingle** n rhigwm, tinc ▷ vb tincial
**job** n tasg, gorchwyl, gwaith
**Job Centre** n Canolfan Gwaith
**jobless** adj diwaith
**jockey** n joci
**jocose** adj cellweirus, direidus, ysmala
**jocular** adj ffraeth, ysmala

**jog** vb loncian
**jogger** n lonciwr
**join** vb cydio, cysylltu, uno, ymuno, asio
**joiner** n asiedydd, saer coed
**joint** n cyswllt, cymal ▷ adj cyd; ~ **of meat** darn o gig
**joist** n dist, trawst
**joke** n cellwair, maldod ▷ vb cellwair, ysmalio
**jolly** adj braf, difyr, llawen
**jolt** n ysgytiad ▷ vb ysgytio
**Jordan** n Iorddonen
**jostle** n hergwd ▷ vb gwthio
**jot** n iod, tipyn ▷ vt nodi
**jotter** n nodlyfr
**journal** n newyddiadur
**journalism** n newyddiaduraeth
**journalist** n newyddiadurwr
**journey** n taith, siwrnai ▷ vt teithio
**jovial** adj llon, llawen
**joy** n llawenydd, gorfoledd
**joyful** adj llon, llawen, gorfoleddus
**J.P.** see **justice of the peace**
**jubilant** adj gorfoleddus
**jubilee** n jiwbili
**Judaism** n Iddewaeth
**judge** n barnwr, beirniad ▷ vb barnu, beirniadu
**judg(e)ment** n barn, brawd, dyfarniad; dedfryd
**judicial** adj barnwrol, ynadol
**judiciary** n barnwyr gwlad, barnwriaeth
**judicious** adj call, synhwyrol, doeth
**jug** n jwg
**juggle** vb siwglo
**juggler** n siwglwr
**juice** n sug, sugn, sudd, nodd
**juicy** adj llawn sudd
**July** n Gorffennaf
**jumble** vb cymysgu, cyboli ▷ n cymysgfa, cybolfa
**jumble sale** n ffair sborion
**jump** vb neidio, llamu ▷ n naid, llam
**jumper** n neidiwr; siwmper

**jumpy** adj ofnus
**junction** n cydiad; uniad; cyffordd
**juncture** n cyfwng, cyswllt
**June** n Mehefin
**jungle** n jyngl, coedwig; drysi
**junior** adj iau, ieuengach; ieuaf;
  **junior school** n ysgol iau
**junk** n sothach
**jurisdiction** n awdurdod
**juror, juryman** n rheithiwr
**jury** n rheithgor
**just** adj cyfiawn, uniawn, teg ▷ adv
  yn union; prin, braidd; newydd; ~
  **now** gynnau (fach)
**justice** n cyfiawnder; ynad, ustus;
  **justice of the peace** n ynad
  heddwch
**justify** vt cyfiawnhau
**jut** vi taflu allan, ymwthio
**juvenile** adj ieuanc

# k

**kale** n cêl, celys
**kangaroo** n cangarŵ
**keel** n gwaelod llong, trumbren,
  cilbren
**keen** adj craff, llym, awchus, brwd
**keep** vb cadw, cynnal ▷ n cadw;
  amddiffynfa
**keeper** n ceidwad
**keepsake** n cofrodd
**kennel** n cenel, cwb ci, cwt ci

**kerb** n cwrbyn
**kerchief** n cadach, neisied, hances,
  macyn
**kernel** n cnewyllyn
**kestrel** n cudyll
**kettle** n tegell
**kettle-drum** n tympan
**key** n agoriad, allwedd; cywair; **key
  ring** n cylch allweddi; **key worker** n
  gweithiwr allweddol
**keyboard** n allweddell
**keyhole** n twll clo
**khaki** adj, n caci
**kick** vb cicio, gwingo ▷ n cic
**kid** n myn; hogyn, plentyn, crwt
**kidnap** vt herwgipio
**kidney** n aren; **kidney beans** npl ffa
  dringo, cidnebêns
**kill** vt lladd
**killer** n lladdwr
**killing** n lladd
**kiln** n odyn
**kilo** n cilo
**kilogram** n cilogram
**kilometre** n cilomedr
**kilowatt** n cilowat
**kin** n perthynas, tras, carennydd
**kind** n rhyw, rhywogaeth, math
**kind** adj caredig
**kindergarten** n ysgol feithrin
**kindle** vb ennyn, cynnau
**kindly** adj caredig, hynaws, tirion
**kindness** n caredigrwydd
**kindred** n perthynas; perthynasau
  ▷ adj perthynol
**king** n brenin
**kingdom** n teyrnas
**kingfisher** n glas y dorlan
**kink** n cinc
**kiosk** n ciosg, bwth
**kipper** n ciper, ysgadenyn hallt
  (neu sych)
**kirk** n eglwys (Albanaidd)
**kiss** vt cusanu ▷ n cusan
**kit** n cit, pac
**kitchen** n cegin; **kitchen garden** n
  gardd lysiau

**kitchenette** n cegin fach
**kite** n barcut
**kitten** n cath fach ▷ vb bwrw cathod
**kleptomania** n ysfa ladrata
**knack** n cnac, medr
**knacker** n prynwr hen geffylau, nacer
**knapsack** n ysgrepan
**knave** n cnaf, dihiryn
**knead** vt tylino
**knee** n glin, pen-lin, pen-glin
**kneel** vi penlinio
**knell** n cnul
**knickers** npl nicers
**knife (knives)** n cyllell
**knight** n marchog ▷ vt urddo yn farchog
**knighthood** n urdd marchog
**knit** vb gwau; clymu
**knitting needle** n gwaell
**knob** n cnap, cnwc; dwrn
**knock** vb cnocio, taro, curo ▷ n cnoc, ergyd
**knot** n cwlwm; cymal, cwgn, cainc ▷ vt clymu
**know** vb gwybod, adnabod
**knowing** adj gwybodus
**knowingly** adv yn fwriadol
**knowledge** n gwybodaeth
**knowledgeable** adj gwybodus
**knuckle** n cymal, migwrn, cwgn

**label** n llabed, label ▷ vt llabedu, enwi
**labial** adj gwefusol
**labialize** vb gwefusoli
**laboratory** n labordy
**laborious** adj llafurus
**labour** n llafur; gwewyr esgor ▷ vb llafurio; **the L~ Party** Y Blaid Lafur; **labour force** n llafurlu
**labourer** n gweithiwr, labrwr
**labyrinth** n drysfa
**lace** n las, les; carrai ▷ vb cau (esgidiau)
**lacerate** vt rhwygo, llarpio, dryllio darnio
**lack** n eisiau, diffyg, gwall ▷ vb bod mewn eisiau
**lackadaisical** adj diynni, llipa
**laconic** adj byreiriog, byr, cwta
**lacquer** n lacer ▷ vb lacro
**lad** n bachgen, hogyn, llanc
**ladder** n ysgol; rhwyg (mewn hosan)
**lade** vt llwytho
**ladies** npl toiledau merched
**ladle** n lletwad, llwy
**lady** n arglwyddes; boneddiges, bonesig
**ladybird** n buwch goch gota
**lag** vi llusgo ar ôl, ymdroi, llercian
**lagging** n ynysydd, lagin
**lagoon** n morlyn, lagŵn
**lair** n gwâl, lloches, ffau
**laity** n lleygwyr
**lake** n llyn

**lamb** n oen ▷ vb bwrw ŵyn, wyna
**lame** n cloff ▷ vt cloffi
**lament** vb galaru, cwynfan, cwyno
**lamentation** n galar, galarnad
**laminate** adj haenog ▷ vb haenogi, lamineiddio, laminadu
**lamp** n lamp, llusern
**lampoon** n dychangerdd, gogangerdd ▷ vb dychanu
**lamppost** n polyn lamp
**lampshade** n lamplen
**lance** n gwaywffon, picell ▷ vt lansio, agor dolur
**lance corporal** n is-gorpral
**land** n tir, gwlad ▷ vb tirio, glanio
**landing** n glaniad, glanio; glanfa; pen y grisiau
**landlady** n perchennog llety, gwraig llety
**landlord** n meistr tir; lletywr, tafarnwr
**landscape** n tirlun
**lane** n lôn, wtre, beidr
**language** n iaith; **language laboratory** n labordy iaith
**languid** adj egwan, llesg
**languish** vi nychu, dihoeni, llesgáu
**languor** n llesgedd, nychdod
**lank** adj cul, tenau, main, llipa
**lanky** adj meindal
**lantern** n llusern
**lap** n arffed, glin
**lap** vb plygu, lapio ▷ n plyg, tro, cylch
**lap** vb llepian, lleibio
**lapel** n llabed
**lapse** n cwymp, methiant, gwall ▷ vi llithro, cwympo, methu
**larceny** n lladrad
**larch** n llarwydden
**lard** n bloneg ▷ vt blonegu
**larder** n bwtri, pantri
**large** adj mawr, helaeth, eang, maith
**largely** adv gan mwyaf
**lark** n ehedydd
**lark** n sbort, difyrrwch, miri ▷ vi cellwair, prancio

**larva** (-ae) n cynrhonyn, larfa
**laryngitis** n gwddf tost, laringitis
**larynx** n afalfreuant, bocs llais
**lascivious** adj anllad, trythyll, anniwair
**lash** n llach, fflangell ▷ vb llachio, fflangellu; rhwymo
**lass** n llances
**lasso** n dolenraff, lasŵ ▷ vt dolenraffu
**last** adj olaf, diwethaf ▷ adv yn olaf, yn ddiwetha; **at ~** o'r diwedd; **~ night** neithiwr; **~ week** yr wythnos ddiwethaf
**last** vi parhau, para
**latch** n cliced ▷ vt clicedu
**late** adj hwyr, diweddar; **~ developers** plant hwyrgynnydd
**lately** adv yn ddiweddar
**latent** adj dirgel, cudd
**later** adv wedyn, eto, yn ddiweddarach
**lateral** adj ochrol
**latest** adj diweddaraf
**lath** n eisen, dellten
**lathe** n turn
**lather** n trochion ▷ vb seboni, trochioni; golchi
**Latin** adj, n Lladin
**Latin America** n America Ladin
**latitude** n lledred; penrhyddid
**latter** adj diwethaf
**lattice** n dellt, rhwyllwaith
**laud** vt canmol, clodfori, moli
**laudable** adj canmoladwy
**laugh** vb chwerthin ▷ n chwerthiniad
**laughable** adj chwerthinllyd, digrif
**laughing stock** n cyff gwawd
**laughter** n chwerthin
**launch** vb lansio
**launderette** n landret, golchdy
**laundry** n golchdy; dillad golch
**laureate** adj llawryfog
**laurel** n llawryf
**lavatory** n tŷ bach, ymolchfa, ystafell ymolchi

**lavender** n lafant
**lavish** adj hael, afradlon, gwastraffus ▷ vb afradu, gwastraffu
**lavishness** n haelioni, afradlonedd
**law** n cyfraith, deddf; **~ and order** cyfraith a threfn; **~ of the land** cyfraith gwlad
**lawful** adj cyfreithlon
**lawgiver** adj deddfroddwr
**lawless** adj digyfraith
**lawlessness** n anghyfraith
**lawn** n lawnt, llannerch; **lawn tennis** tenis (lawnt)
**lawnmower** n peiriant torri porfa
**lawsuit** n cyngaws, cyfraith
**lawyer** n cyfreithiwr, twrnai
**lax** adj llac, esgeulus, diofal
**laxative** n carthlyn
**lay** n cân, cerdd
**lay** vt gosod, dodi; dodwy
**lay** adj lleyg
**layby** n gorffwysfan
**layer** n haen
**laze** vb diogi, segura
**laziness** n diogi
**lazy** adj diog, dioglyd
**lea** n doldir, dôl
**lead** n plwm
**lead** vb arwain, tywys ▷ n blaenoriaeth
**leader** n arweinydd; erthygl flaen
**leadership** n arweinyddiaeth
**leaf** (leaves) n deilen, dalen
**leaflet** n taflen
**league** n cynghrair ▷ vi cynghreirio
**leak** n agen, coll ▷ vi gollwng, diferu, colli
**lean** adj main, tenau, cul ▷ n cig coch
**lean** vb pwyso, gogwyddo
**leap** vb neidio, llamu ▷ n naid, llam; **leap year** n blwyddyn naid
**leapfrog** n chwarae naid
**learn** vb dysgu
**learned** adj dysgedig, hyddysg
**learner** n dysgwr

**learning** n dysg, dysgeidiaeth
**lease** n prydles ▷ vt prydlesu
**leasehold** n prydles
**leash** n cynllyfan, tennyn ▷ vt cynllyfanu
**least** adj lleiaf; **at ~** o leiaf
**leather** n lledr
**leave** n cennad, caniatâd
**leave** vb gadael, ymadael
**leaven** n lefain ▷ vt lefeinio
**Lebanon** n Libanus
**lecherous** adj trythyll, anllad
**lechery** n trythyllwch, anlladrwydd
**lectern** n darllenfa
**lecture** n darlith ▷ vb darlithio
**lecturer** n darlithydd
**ledge** n silff, ysgafell; crib
**ledger** n llyfr cyfrifon
**lee** n ochr gysgodol, cysgod gwynt
**leech** n gelen
**leek** n cenhinen
**leer** vi cilwenu
**lees** npl gwaddod, gwaelodion
**left** adj aswy, chwith
**left-handed** adj llawchwith
**left-handedness** n llawchwithedd
**left luggage** n lle cadw bagiau
**leg** n coes
**legacy** n etîfeddiaeth, cymynrodd
**legal** adj cyfreithiol, cyfreithlon
**legalize** vb cyfreithloni
**legation** n llysgenhadaeth
**legend** n chwedl
**legible** adj darllenadwy, eglur
**legion** n lleng, llu
**legislate** vi deddfu
**legislation** n deddfwriaeth
**legislative** adj deddfwriaethol
**legitimate** adj cyfreithlon
**leisure** n hamdden
**leisurely** adj hamddenol
**lemon** n lemwn
**lemonade** n diod lemwn, lemonêd
**lend** vt benthyca, rhoi benthyg
**length** n hyd, meithder
**lengthen** vb estyn, hwyhau

**lengthy** adj hir, maith
**leniency** n tiriondeb, tynerwch
**lens** n lens; **concave ~ lens** ceugrwm; **convex ~ lens** amgrwm
**Lent** n y Grawys
**lentil** n corbysen, lentil
**leonine** adj llewaidd
**leopard** n llewpart
**leper** n dyn gwahanglwyfus, gwahanglaf
**leprosy** n gwahanglwyf
**less** adj, adv llai
**lessee** n prydlesai
**lessen** vb lleihau
**lesson** n gwers; llith
**lest** conj rhag, rhag ofn, fel na
**let** vt gadael, goddef; gollwng; gosod, rhentu
**lethal** adj marwol, angheuol
**lethargy** n cysgadrwydd, syrthni
**letter** n llythyren; llythyr
**letterbox** n bocs llythyrau
**lettering** n llythreniad
**lettuce** n letysen
**level** n, adj lefel, gwastad ▷ vt lefelu, gwastatáu; **spirit level** n lefelydd
**level crossing** n croesfan
**level-headed** adj pwyllog
**lever** n trosol
**leveret** n ysgyfarnog ieuanc, lefren
**Levite** n Lefiad
**levity** n ysgafnder, gwamalrwydd
**levy** vt codi, trethu ▷ n treth
**lewd** adj anllad, anweddus
**lexicographer** n geiriadurwr
**lexicon** n geiriadur
**liability** n cyfrifoldeb, rhwymedigaeth
**liable** adj atebol
**liaison** n cyswllt
**liar** n gŵr celwyddog, celwyddgi
**libel** n athrod, enllib ▷ vt athrodi, enllibio
**liberal** adj hael, rhyddfrydig, rhyddfrydol ▷ n rhyddfrydwr
**liberate** vt rhyddhau
**liberation** n rhyddhad

**liberty** n rhyddid
**librarian** n llyfrgellydd
**library** n llyfrgell
**Libya** n Libya
**licence** n trwydded; penrhyddid; **driving licence** n trwydded yrru
**license** vt trwyddedu
**licensed** adj trwyddedig
**licentious** adj penrhydd, ofer, anllad
**lick** vt llyfu, llyo; curo
**lid** n caead, clawr
**lie** n celwydd, anwiredd ▷ vi dweud celwydd
**lie** vi gorwedd
**liege** adj ffyddlon, ufudd
**lieutenant** n is-gapten; rhaglaw
**life** (lives) n bywyd, einioes, oes, buchedd, hoedl
**lifebelt** n nofdorch, gwregys achub
**lifeboat** n bad achub
**lifeguard** n achubwr
**life insurance** n yswiriant bywyd
**life jacket** n siaced achub
**lifeless** adj difywyd, marw(aidd)
**lifetime** n oes, einioes, hoedl
**lift** vt codi, dyrchafu ▷ n codiad; lifft
**ligament** n giewyn, gewyn
**light** n golau, goleuni ▷ adj golau ▷ vb goleuo, cynnau
**light** adj ysgafn
**light bulb** n bwlb golau
**lighter** n goleuydd, taniwr
**light-footed** adj ysgafndroed
**light-headed** adj penchwiban
**light-hearted** adj ysgafnfryd
**lighthouse** n goleudy
**lightning** n mellt, lluched
**lightning conductor** n cludydd mellt
**lightship** n goleulong
**like** adj tebyg, cyffelyb
**like** vb caru, hoffi
**likeable** adj hoffus; dymunol
**likelihood** n tebygolrwydd
**likely** adj, adv tebygol, tebyg
**liken** vt cyffelybu

**likeness** n tebygrwydd
**likewise** adv yn gyffelyb, yn yr un modd
**lilac** n lelog
**lily** n lili, alaw
**lily-of-the-valley** n lili'r dyffrynnoedd
**limb** n aelod, cainc
**lime** n calch
**limekiln** n odyn galch
**limelight** n amlygrwydd
**limestone** n carreg galch
**limit** n terfyn, ffin ▷ vt cyfyngu
**limited** adj cyfyngedig
**limp** adj llipa, ystwyth, hyblyg
**limp** vi hercian, cloffi
**limpet** n brenigen, llygad maharen
**line** n llin, llinell, lein, rhes; llinach ▷ vt llinellu, rhesu
**lineage** n ach, llinach
**linear** adj llinellog, llinellaidd, llinol, unionlin; **~ equation** hafaliad llinol
**linen** n lliain
**line-out** n lein, llinell
**liner** n leiner
**linesman** n llumanwr
**linger** vb ymdroi, aros
**lingo** n iaith ddieithr, cleber
**linguist** n ieithydd
**linguistics** n ieithyddiaeth
**liniment** n ennaint, eli
**lining** n leinin
**link** n dolen, cyswllt ▷ vb cydio, cysylltu
**linnet** n llinos
**lino** n leino
**linseed** n had llin, llinad
**lintel** n capan drws, lintel
**lion** n llew
**lip** n gwefus, min, gwefl
**lipstick** n minlliw
**liquid** n llyn, hylif ▷ adj gwlyb, hylif
**liquidate** vb talu, clirio (dyled), dirwyn i ben, diddymu, dileu
**liquidize** vb hylifo
**liquor** n diod, gwirod
**lisp** n bloesgni ▷ vb siarad yn floesg

**list** n rhestr, llechres ▷ vt rhestru
**list** n gogwydd, goledd ▷ vi pwyso, gwyro, gogwyddo
**listen** vi gwrando
**listener** n gwrandawr
**listless** adj llesg, diynni
**listlessness** n llesgedd
**litany** n litani
**literacy** n llythrennedd
**literal** adj llythrennol
**literary** adj llenyddol
**literature** n llenyddiaeth
**lithe, lithesome** adj ystwyth, hyblyg
**lithograph** n lithograff
**litigate** vb cyfreithio
**litmus** n litmws
**litre** n litr
**litter** n elorwely; ysbwriel, gwasarn; torllwyth, tor
**little** adj bach, bychan; mân, ychydig ▷ n ychydig, tipyn
**liturgy** n litwrgi
**live** adj byw, bywiol, bywiog
**live** vi byw
**livelihood** n bywoliaeth
**livelong** adj maith, hirfaith
**lively** adj bywiog, hoyw, heini, sionc
**liven** vb bywiogi
**liver** n iau, afu
**livery** n lifrai
**living** n bywoliaeth; personiaeth
**lizard** n madfall, modrchwilen
**load** n llwyth ▷ vb llwytho
**loaf** (loaves) n torth
**loaf** vb ystelcian, sefyllian, diogi
**loafer** n diogyn, segurwr
**loam** n tywotglai, marl, priddglai
**loan** n benthyg, benthyciad
**loath, loth** adj anewyllysgar, anfodlon
**loathe** vt ffieiddio, casáu
**loathsome** adj atgas, ffiaidd
**lobby** n cyntedd, porth, lobi
**lobster** n cimwch
**local** adj lleol; **local government** n llywodraeth leol

**locality** n lle, safle, ardal, cymdogaeth
**locate** vt lleoli, sefydlu, gosod
**location** n lleoliad
**loch** n llyn
**lock** n clo; llifddor ▷ vb cloi, cau
**lock** n cudyn; (pl) gwallt
**locked** adj ar glo, ynghlo, dan glo
**locker** n cwpwrdd clo
**locomotion** n ymsymudiad
**locomotive** adj ymsymudol ▷ n peiriant rheilffordd
**locust** n locust
**lodge** n lluest, llety; cyfrinfa ▷ vb lletya
**lodger** n lletywr
**lodging** n: **lodgings** npl llety
**loft** n taflod, llofft
**lofty** adj uchel, aruchel, dyrchafedig
**log** n cyff, boncyff, pren
**loggerheads** npl benben
**logic** n rhesymeg
**logical** adj rhesymegol
**loin** n llwyn, lwyn
**loiter** vi ymdroi, loetran, sefyllian
**loll** vi gorweddian, diogi
**lollipop** n lolipop
**London** n Llundain
**loneliness** n unigrwydd
**lonely** adj unig
**long** adj, adv hir, maith, llaes
**long** vi hiraethu, dyheu
**longevity** n hirhoedledd, hiroes
**long-headed** adj call, hirben
**longing** n hiraeth, dyhead
**longitude** n hydred
**longitudinal** adj hydredol
**long sight** n golwg hir
**long-suffering** adj hirymarhous ▷ n hirymaros
**long-term** adj yn y tymor hir
**long-winded** adj hirwyntog
**look** vb edrych, syllu ▷ n edrychiad, golwg
**looking-glass** n drych
**lookout** n gwyliwr
**loom** n gwŷdd

**loom** vi ymrithio, ymddangos
**loon** n gwirionyn, dihiryn
**loop** n dolen ▷ vb dolennu
**loophole** n dihangdwll
**loose** adj rhydd, llac ▷ vt gollwng
**loosen** vb rhyddhau, llacio
**loot** n anrhaith, ysbail ▷ vb ysbeilio, anrheithio
**looter** n ysbeiliwr, anrheithiwr
**lop** vt tocio
**lopsided** adj unochrog, anghymesur, anghyfartal
**lord** n arglwydd ▷ vb arglwyddiaethu
**lord mayor** n arglwydd faer
**lordship** n arglwyddiaeth
**lore** n dysg, llên, traddodiad
**lorry** n lori; **lorry driver** n gyrrwr lori
**lose** vb colli
**loss** n colled
**lost property office** n swyddfa eiddo coll
**lot** n coelbren, rhan, tynged; **a ~** llawer
**lotion** n golchdrwyth, eli
**lottery** n hapchwarae, raffl
**lotus** n alaw'r dŵr
**loud** adj uchel, croch; **loud speaker** n corn siarad
**lounge** n lolfa ▷ vi segura, gorweddian
**louse** (lice) n lleuen
**lousy** adj lleuog, brwnt
**lout** n lleban, llabwst, delff
**love** n cariad, serch ▷ vt caru
**loveliness** n prydferthwch
**lovely** adj hawddgar, teg, hyfryd
**lover** n cariad, carwr
**loving** adj cariadus, serchog
**loving-kindness** n trugaredd, cariad
**low** adj isel
**low** vi brefu ▷ n bref (buwch)
**lower** vb gostwng, darostwng, iselu
**lower** vi gwgu, duo, hel cymylau
**lowliness** n gostyngeiddrwydd

**lowly** adj isel, iselfrydig, gostyngedig
**low tide** n llanw isel; trai
**low water** n trai, distyll
**loyal** adj teyrngar
**loyalty** n teyrngarwch, ffyddlondeb
**lozenge** n losin
**lubricate** vt iro, llithrigo, seimio
**lucid** adj eglur, clir
**luck** n lwc, damwain, hap, ffawd
**lucky** adj ffodus, lwcus
**ludicrous** adj chwerthinllyd, gwrthun
**lug** vb llusgo, tynnu
**luggage** n clud, bagiau, celfi
**luggage rack** n silff eiddo
**lukewarm** adj claear, llugoer
**lull** vt suo, gostegu ▷ n gosteg
**lullaby** n hwiangerdd
**lumbago** n llwynwst
**lumber** n llanastr, anialwch
**lumber** vb pentyrru; llusgo
**luminous** adj golau, disglair, llachar
**lump** n lwmp, clamp, clap, talp; ~ **sum** cyfandaliad
**lunacy** n lloerigrwydd, gwallgofrwydd
**lunatic** n lloerig, gwallgofddyn
**lunch** vb ciniawa (ganol dydd)
**lunch, luncheon** n byrbryd, cinio canol dydd
**lung** n ysgyfaint
**lunge** n hergwd, gwth, rhuthr
**lurch** n cyfyngder, dryswch, trybini ▷ vi gwegian
**lure** n hud ▷ vt hudo, denu
**lurid** adj erchyll, erchliw, fflamgoch
**lurk** vi llercian, llechu
**luscious** adj melys
**lush** adj toreithiog, ffrwythlon
**lust** n chwant, trachwant ▷ vi trachwantu
**lustre** n gloywder, disgleirdeb, llewyrch
**lusty** adj heini, cryf, pybyr, grymus
**Luxembourg** n Luxembourg

**luxuriant** adj toreithiog, bras, ffrwythlon
**luxurious** adj moethus
**luxury** n moeth, moethusrwydd, amheuthun
**lying** adj celwyddog
**lyre** n telyn gron
**lyric** adj telynegol ▷ n telyneg

**mace** n brysgyll, byrllysg
**macerate** vb meddalu, mwydo; nychu, curio
**machine** n peiriant
**machinery** n peiriannau
**mackerel** n macrell
**mackintosh** n cot law
**mad** adj cynddeiriog, gwallgof, gwyllt, ynfyd
**madden** vb gwallgofi, ffyrnigo
**made-to-measure** adj wedi ei dorri gan deiliwr
**madman** n ynfytyn, gwallgofddyn
**madness** n ynfydrwydd, gwallgofrwydd
**madrigal** n madrigal
**magazine** n ystorfa, arfdy; cylchgrawn
**maggot** n cynrhonyn
**magic** adj cyfareddol ▷ n hud, dewiniaeth, swyngyfaredd
**magician** n swynwr, dewin

**magistrate** *n* ynad
**magnanimous** *adj* mawrfrydig
**magnet** *n* magned
**magnetic** *n* magnetig
**magnificent** *adj* gwych, ysblennydd
**magnify** *vt* mawrhau, mwyhau, chwyddo
**magnifying-glass** *n* chwyddwydr
**magnitude** *n* maint, maintioli
**magpie** *n* pi, pia, pioden, piogen
**maid** *n* merch, morwyn
**maiden name** *n* enw morwynol
**mail** *n* y post
**mail** *n* arfwisg
**maim** *vt* anafu, anffurfio, llurgunio
**main** *n* prif bibell; prif gebl; cefnfor;
  **in the ~** yn bennaf, gan mwyaf
**main** *adj* pennaf, prif, mwyaf; **main road** *n* priffordd, ffordd fawr
**mainland** *n* y tir mawr
**mainly** *adv* yn bennaf
**mainstay** *n* prif gynhaliaeth
**maintain** *vt* dal, cynnal, maentumio
**maintenance** *n* cynhaliaeth, gofalaeth
**maize** *n* indrawn, injan corn
**majesty** *n* mawrhydi, mawredd
**majestic** *adj* mawreddog, urddasol
**major** *adj* mwy, mwyaf, pennaf ▷ *n* uwchgapten
**majority** *n* mwyafrif; oedran llawn
**make** *vt* gwneud, gwneuthur, peri ▷ *n* gwneuthuriad
**maker** *n* gwneuthurwr, creawdwr
**making** *n* gwneuthuriad, ffurfiad
**make-up** *n* colur
**malady** *n* drwg, anhwyldeb, dolur
**male** *n, adj* gwryw
**malevolence** *n* malais
**malevolent** *adj* drygnaws, maleisus
**malformation** *n* camffurfiad
**malice** *n* malais
**malign** *vt* enllibio, difrïo, pardduo
**malignant** *adj* llidiog, adwythig, gwyllt

**mallet** *n* gordd
**malnutrition** *n* gwallfaethiad, camluniaeth
**malt** *n* brag ▷ *vb* bragu
**maltreat** *vb* cam-drin
**maltreatment** *n* camdriniaeth
**mammal** *n* mamal
**mammoth** *n* mamoth ▷ *adj* anferth
**man** (men) *n* dyn, gŵr
**manacle** *n* gefyn ▷ *vt* gefynnu
**manage** *vb* trin, llywodraethu, rheoli; ymdaro, ymdopi, llwyddo
**manageable** *adj* hydrin
**management** *n* rheolaeth, goruchwyliaeth
**manager** *n* goruchwyliwr, rheolwr
**mandate** *n* gorchymyn, arch
**mane** *n* mwng
**mange** *n* clafr, clefri, brech y cŵn
**manger** *n* mansier, preseb
**mangle** *vt* llurgunio
**mangle** *n* mangl
**manhood** *n* dyndod
**mania** *n* gwallgofrwydd, gorawydd
**maniac** *n* gwallgofddyn
**manifest** *adj* amlwg ▷ *vt* amlygu, dangos
**manifesto** *n* datganiad, maniffesto
**manifold** *adj* amryw, amrywiol
**manipulate** *vt* trin, trafod
**mankind** *n* dynolryw
**manly** *adj* dynol, gwrol
**manner** *n* modd; moes
**mannerism** *n* dullwedd
**mannerly** *adj* boneddigaidd, moesgar
**manners** *npl* moesau
**manor** *n* maenor, maenol
**manse** *n* tŷ gweinidog, mans
**manservant** *n* gwas
**mansion house** *n* trigfan y maer
**manslaughter** *n* dynladdiad
**mantelpiece** *n* silff ben tân
**mantle** *n* mantell ▷ *vt* mantellu

**manual** adj perthynol i'r llaw ▷ n llawlyfr

**manufacture** n gwaith, nwydd ▷ vt gwneuthur, gwneud

**manure** n tail, gwrtaith, achles ▷ vt teilo, gwrteithio, achlesu

**manuscript** n llawysgrif

**many** adj aml, sawl, llawer; **as ~** cymaint, cynifer; **how ~** sawl

**map** n map

**maple** n masarnen

**mar** vt difetha, andwyo, hagru

**maraud** vb ysbeilio, anrheithio

**marble** n marmor, mynor; marblen

**March** n (mis) Mawrth

**march** vb ymdeithio ▷ n ymdaith

**march** n mers, goror, cyffin

**marchionness** n ardalyddes

**mare** n caseg

**margarine** n margarîn

**margin** n ymyl, cwr, goror

**marigold** n gold Mair, gold

**marine** adj morol ▷ n môr-filwr; llynges

**mariner** n morwr, llongwr, mordwywr

**marital** n priodasol

**maritime** adj morol, arforol

**mark** n nod, marc ▷ vt nodi, marcio, craffu, sylwi

**market** n marchnad ▷ vb marchnata

**maroon** vb rhoi a gadael ar ynys anial

**marquis** n ardalydd

**marriage** n priodas

**married** adj priod

**marrow** n mêr; **vegetable marrow** n pwmpen

**marry** vb priodi

**Mars** n Mawrth

**marsh** n morfa, cors, mignen

**marshal** n cadlywydd, marsialydd ▷ vt byddino, trefnu

**mart** n mart

**martial** adj milwraidd, milwrol

**martinet** n disgyblwr llym

**martyr** n merthyr ▷ vt merthyru

**martyrdom** n merthyrdod

**marvel** n rhyfeddod ▷ vi rhyfeddu, synnu

**marvellous** adj rhyfeddol, gwych

**marxism** n marcsiaeth

**marxist** adj marcsaidd

**mascara** n masgara, colur llygaid

**masculine** adj gwryw, gwrywaidd

**mash** n cymysg, stwns ▷ vt stwnsio

**mask** n mwgwd ▷ vt mygydu, cuddio

**mason** n saer maen, masiwn, meiswn

**mass** n pentwr, talp, crynswth, mas; (pl) y werin

**mass** n offeren

**massacre** n cyflafan ▷ vt cyflafanu

**massive** adj anferth

**mast** n hwylbren

**master** n meistr, athro, capten (llong) ▷ vt meistroli

**masterpiece** n campwaith, gorchest

**mastery** n meistrolaeth, goruchafiaeth

**masticate** vt cnoi, malu

**mastiff** n gafaelgi, cystowci, catgi

**mat** n mat ▷ vt matio, plethu

**match** n matsen

**match** n cymar; priodas; ymrysonfa, gêm ▷ vb cystadlu; cyfateb

**matchless** n digymar, digyffelyb

**mate** n cymar, cydymaith; mêt ▷ vt cymharu

**material** adj materol; o bwys ▷ n defnydd

**materialism** n materoliaeth

**maternal** adj mamol; o du'r fam

**maternity** n mamolaeth

**mathematics** npl mathemateg

**matins** npl boreol weddi, plygain

**matriculate** vb ymaelodi mewn prifysgol, matricwleiddio

**matrimony** n priodas

**matron** n gwraig briod, meistres,

matron, modron
**matter** n mater; crawn ▷ vi bod o bwys
**mattock** n caib, matog
**mattress** n matras
**mature** adj aeddfed; mewn oed ▷ vb aeddfedu
**maturity** n aeddfedrwydd
**maul** vt baeddu, pwyo ▷ n sgarmes
**mauve** n lliw porffor, piws
**maxim** n dihareb, gwireb, rheol
**maximum** n uchafswm, uchafrif, uchafbwynt
**May** n Mai; **May Day** n Calan Mai
**may** n blodau drain gwynion
**maybe** adv efallai, hwyrach, dichon
**mayor** n maer
**mayoress** n maeres
**me** pron myfi, mi, fi, i; minnau
**mead** n medd
**meadow** n dôl, gwaun, gweirglodd
**meagre** adj cul, tenau, prin, tlodaidd, llwm
**meal** n blawd
**meal** n pryd o fwyd
**meals on wheels** npl pryd ar glud
**mean** n cyfrwng, modd; canol; cymedr
**mean** vt meddwl, golygu, bwriadu
**mean** adj gwael, isel, crintach, iselwael
**meander** n ystum (afon) ▷ vi dolennu, troelli, ymdroelli
**meaning** n ystyr, meddwl
**meanness** n cybydd-dod, crintachrwydd
**means** npl cyfrwng, modd(ion), cyfoeth; **by all ~** ar bob cyfrif, wrth gwrs
**meantime, -while** adv yn y cyfamser
**measles** npl y frech goch
**measure** vt, n mesur
**measurement** n mesur, mesuriad
**meat** n ymborth, bwyd; cig
**mechanic** n peiriannydd
**mechanical** adj peiriannol,

peirianyddol, mecanyddol
**mechanics** npl mecaneg
**mechanism** n peirianwaith
**medal** n bathodyn, medal
**meddle** vi ymyrryd, busnesa, ymhél
**media** npl cyfryngau
**mediaeval** adj canoloesol
**medial** adj canol, canolog
**mediate** vi canoli, cyfryngu
**medical** adj meddygol
**medicine** n meddyginiaeth; ffisig, moddion
**mediocre** adj canolig, cyffredin
**meditate** vb myfyrio
**meditation** n myfyrdod
**Mediterranean** n: **the ~** y Môr Canoldir
**medium** n canol; cyfrwng ▷ adj canol, canolig
**medley** n cymysgfa, cybolfa; cymysgedd, cadwyn o alawon
**meek** adj llariaidd, addfwyn
**meekness** n addfwynder
**meet** vb cyfarfod, cwrdd ▷ adj addas
**meeting** n cyfarfod, cyfarfyddiad
**melancholy** adj prudd, pruddglwyfus ▷ n pruddglwyf, y felan
**mêlée** n ymgiprys, ysgarmes
**mellifluous** adj melyslais, melysber
**mellow** adj aeddfed, meddal ▷ vb aeddfedu
**melody** n peroriaeth, melodi
**melt** vb toddi, ymdoddi
**member** n aelod; **Member of Parliament** n Aelod Seneddol
**membership** n aelodaeth
**membrane** n pilen, croenyn
**memento** n cofarwydd
**memoir** n cofiant
**memorable** adj cofiadwy, bythgofiadwy
**memorandum** n cofnod, cofnodiad
**memorial** adj coffadwriaethol ▷ n coffadwriaeth; cofeb; deiseb

**memorise** vt dysgu ar gof
**memory** n cof; coffadwriaeth
**menace** n bygythiad ▷ vt bygwth
**menagerie** n milodfa, sioe (siew) anifeiliaid
**mend** vb gwella, cyweirio, trwsio, helpu
**mendacity** n anwiredd, celwydd
**mendicant** adj cardotaidd, cardotlyd ▷ n cardotyn
**menial** adj gwasaidd, isel ▷ n gwas
**meningitis** n llid yr ymennydd
**menstruation** n y misglwyf
**mensuration** n mesureg
**mental** adj meddyliol
**mention** vt crybwyll, sôn ▷ n crybwylliad
**mentor** n cynghorwr, cyfarwyddwr
**menu** n bwydlen, arlwy
**mercantile** adj marchnadol, masnachol
**mercenary** adj ariangar, chwannog i elw ▷ n huriwr, milwr cyflog
**merchandise** n marsiandïaeth
**merchant** n masnachwr, marsiandwr
**merciful** adj trugarog, tosturiol
**mercifully** adv drwy drugaredd
**merciless** adj didrugaredd
**mercuric** adj mercurig
**mercury** n arian byw, mercwri
**mercy** n trugaredd
**mere** adj unig, pur, moel, noeth, hollol
**mere** n llyn, llwch
**merge** vb soddi, suddo, colli, ymgolli, uno
**merger** n ymsoddiad, cyfuniad, ymdoddiad, uniad
**meridian** n nawn; cyhydedd; anterth
**merit** n haeddiant, teilyngdod ▷ vt haeddu, teilyngu
**mermaid** n môr-forwyn
**merriment** n digrifwch, difyrrwch
**merry** adj llawen, llon

**merry-go-round** n ceffylau bach
**mesh** n masgl, magl, rhwydwaith
**mess** n saig; llanastr, annibendod ▷ vb bwyta; ymhél; maeddu
**message** n cenadwri, neges
**messenger** n cennad, negesydd
**messieurs (Messrs)** npl meistri
**metabolism** n metaboleg, metabolaeth
**metal** n metel ▷ adj metelaidd
**metamorphosis (-ses)** n trawsffurfiad, metamorffosis
**metaphor** n trosiad
**metaphysics** n metaffiseg
**mete** vb mesur
**meteor** n seren wib
**meter** n mesurydd; medr
**method** n trefn, method, dull
**meticulous** adj gorfanwl
**metonymy** n trawsenwad
**metre** n mesur, mydr
**metrical** adj mydryddol
**metric system** n system fedrig
**metropolis** n prifddinas
**mettle** n metel, anian, ysbryd
**mew** vi mewian
**Mexico** n México
**miasma** n tawch heintus
**Michaelmas** n gŵyl Fihangel
**microbe** n trychfilyn, meicrob
**micro-chip** n meicro-sglodyn
**microphone** n meicroffon, meic
**microscope** n chwyddwydr, meicrosgop
**microwave** n meicrodon; **~ oven** ffwrn meicrodon
**mid** adj canol
**midday** n canol dydd, hanner dydd
**middle** n, adj canol
**middle-aged** adj canol oed
**middling** adj canolig, gweddol, symol
**midge** n gwybedyn
**midget** n corrach
**midnight** n canol nos, hanner nos
**midriff** n llengig
**midst** n canol, plith

**midsummer** n canol haf;
  **Midsummer Day** n gŵyl Ifan
**midwife** (**-wives**) n bydwraig
**mien** n golwg, pryd, gwedd, agwedd
**might** n nerth, cadernid, gallu
**mighty** adj cadarn, galluog, nerthol
**migrant** n mudwr, ymfudwr,
  crwydrwr ▷ adj mudol, crwydrol
**migrate** vi symud, mudo
**migration** n mudiad, ymfudiad
**milch** adj blith, llaethog
**mild** adj tyner, tirion, mwyn; gwan,
  ysgafn
**mildew** n llwydi, llwydni
**mildness** n tynerwch, tiriondeb,
  mwynder
**mile** n milltir
**mileage** n milltiredd
**milestone** n carreg filltir
**militant** adj milwriaethus
**military** adj milwrol
**militate** vi milwrio
**milk** n llaeth, llefrith ▷ vt godro
**milkman** n dyn llaeth
**milkshake** n ysgytlaeth, llaeth
  'di guro
**Milky Way** n: **the ~** Y Llwybr
  Llaethog, Caer Wydion
**mill** n melin ▷ vt melino, malu
**millennium** n mil blynyddoedd
**miller** n melinydd
**millimetre** n milimedr
**milliner** n hetwraig
**million** n miliwn
**millionaire** n miliynydd
**millstone** n maen melin
**mime** n meim
**mimic** vt dynwared, gwatwar
**mimicry** n dynwarededd
**mince** vt malu ▷ n briwgig,
  briwfwyd
**mind** n meddwl, bryd, cof ▷ vb
  gofalu, cofio
**mine** n mwynglawdd, pwll
**miner** n mwynwr, glöwr
**mineral** adj mwynol ▷ n mwyn
**mineral water** n dŵr pistyll

**mingle** vb cymysgu, britho
**mingy** adj cybyddlyd, crintach
**miniature** n mân ddarlun ▷ adj
  bychan
**minimize** vt lleihau, bychanu
**minimum** n lleiafswm, isafrif
**mining** n mwyngloddiaeth;
  **opencast mining** n mwyngloddio
  brig
**minister** n gweinidog ▷ vb
  gwasanaethu, gweinidogaethu
**ministry** n gweinidogaeth,
  gweinyddiaeth, gwasanaeth
**minnow** n pilcodyn, pilcyn, sildyn,
  silcyn
**minor** adj llai, lleiaf, lleddf; un
  dan oed
**minority** n maboed, mebyd;
  lleiafrif
**minster** n mynachlog; eglwys
  gadeiriol
**minstrel** n clerwr, cerddor
**mint** n bathdy ▷ vt bathu
**mint** n mintys
**minus** adj, pron llai, heb, yn fyr o
  ▷ n minws
**minute** adj bach, bychan, mân;
  manwl
**minute** n munud; cofnod; **minute
  book** n llyfr cofnodion
**minx** n coegen, mursen, maeden
**miracle** n gwyrth
**miraculous** adj gwyrthiol
**mirage** n rhithlun, lleurith
**mire** n llaid, llaca, tom, baw
**mirror** n drych ▷ vt adlewyrchu
**mirth** n llawenydd, digrifwch,
  afiaith
**mis-** prefix cam-
**misadventure** n anffawd,
  damwain
**misanthropist** n dyngasäwr
**misapprehension** n
  camddeallltwriaeth
**misbehave** vi camymddwyn
**misbehaviour** n camymddygiad
**miscarriage** n erthyliad;

**miscarriage of justice** n aflwyddo cyfiawnder
**miscarry** vi erthylu; aflwyddo; colli
**miscellaneous** adj amrywiol
**mischance** n anffawd, damwain
**mischief** n drwg, drygioni, direidi
**mischievous** adj drygionus, direidus
**misconception** n camsyniad, cam-dyb
**misconduct** n camymddygiad ▷ vb camymddwyn
**misdeed** n drwgweithred, camwedd
**misdemeanour** n camwedd, trosedd
**miser** n cybydd
**miserable** adj truenus, gresynus, anhapus
**misery** n trueni, gresyni, adfyd
**misfortune** n anffawd, aflwydd
**misgivings** npl amheuon, ofnau
**misguide** vb camarwain
**mishandle** vb cam-drin
**mishap** n anap, anffawd, aflwydd
**misinterpret** vb camesbonio
**misjudge** vb camfarnu, camddeall
**mislead** vb camarwain, twyllo
**misnomer** n camenw
**misprint** n cambrint ▷ vb camargraffu
**misread** vb camddarllen
**misrepresent** vt camddarlunio, camliwio
**miss** vt methu, ffaelu, colli ▷ n meth
**missal** n llyfr offeren
**missile** n saethyn, taflegryn
**missing** adj yn eisiau, yngholl, ar goll
**mission** n cenhadaeth
**missionary** n cenhadwr ▷ adj cenhadol
**missive** n llythyr
**misspell** vb camsillafu
**mist** n niwl, nudden; tarth; caddug
**mistake** vt camgymryd, methu ▷ n camgymeriad, gwall

**mistletoe** n uchelwydd
**mistress** n meistres; athrawes; Mrs
**mistrust** vt drwgdybio, amau
**misty** adj niwlog
**misunderstanding** n camddealltwriaeth
**mite** n hatling; mymryn, tamaid
**mitigate** vt lleddfu, lliniaru, lleihau
**mitre** n meitr
**mix** vb cymysgu
**mixture** n cymysgedd, cymysgfa
**moan** n, vb ochain, griddfan, udo
**moat** n ffos (castell)
**mob** n torf, tyrfa, haid ▷ vt ymosod ar, baeddu
**mobile** adj symudol, symudadwy; mudol (cemeg)
**mobilize** vt dygyfor, byddino
**mock** vb gwatwar ▷ adj gau, ffug
**mockery** n gwatwar; ffug
**mode** n modd, dull
**model** n cynllun, patrwm ▷ vt llunio
**moderate** adj cymedrol ▷ vt cymedroli
**moderation** n cymedroldeb
**modern** adj modern, diweddar
**modernize** vb moderneiddio
**modest** adj gwylaidd; diymhongar
**modesty** n gwylder, gwyleidd-dra
**modify** vt newid, lleddfu
**modulate** vb cyweirio neu reoli llais
**moiety** n hanner, hanereg
**moist** adj llaith, gwlyb
**moisture** n lleithder, gwlybaniaeth, gwlybwr
**moisturizer** n lleithydd
**molar** n cilddant
**mole** n man geni
**mole** n gwadd, twrch daear
**mole** n morglawdd
**molecule** n molecwl ▷ adj molecylig
**molehill** n pridd y wadd
**molest** vt molestu, aflonyddu, blino
**mollify** vt meddalu, tyneru,

dyhuddo
**mollycoddle** *vb* maldodi
**molten** *adj* tawdd
**moment** *n* moment; pwys, pwysigrwydd
**momentum** *n* momentwm
**monarch** *n* brenin, teyrn, penadur
**monarchy** *n* brenhiniaeth
**monastery** *n* mynachlog, mynachdy
**monastic** *adj* mynachaidd
**Monday** *n* dydd Llun
**monetary** *adj* ariannol
**money** *n* arian, pres
**mongrel** *adj* cymysgryw ▷ *n* mwngrel
**monitor** *n* monitor
**monk** *n* mynach
**monkey** *n* mwnci
**mono-** *prefix* un-
**monogamy** *n* unwreigiaeth
**monoglot** *adj* uniaith ▷ *n* person uniaith
**monolith** *n* maen hir
**monologue** *n* ymson
**monopoly** *n* monopoli
**monosyllable** *n* gair unsill
**monotheism** *n* undduwiaeth
**monotone** *adj, n* unsain, un-dôn
**monotonous** *adj* undonog
**monotony** *n* undonedd, unrhywiaeth
**monsoon** *n* monswn
**monster** *n* anghenfil; clamp ▷ *adj* anferth
**monstrous** *adj* angenfilaidd, anferth, gwrthun
**month** *n* mis
**monthly** *adj* misol ▷ *n* misolyn
**monument** *n* cofadail, cofgolofn
**mood** *n* hwyl, tymer; modd
**moody** *adj* oriog, cyfnewidiol
**moon** *n* lleuad, lloer; **harvest moon** *n* lleuad fedi
**moonlight** *n* golau leuad
**moonshine** *n* ffiloreg, ffwlbri, lol
**moor** *n* morfa, rhos, gwaun

**moor** *vt* angori, bachu, sicrhau
**moorhen** *n* iâr fach y dŵr
**moorland** *n* rhostir, gweundir
**mop** *n* mop ▷ *vt* mopio, sychu
**mope** *vi* pendrymu, delwi
**moraine** *n* marian
**moral** *adj* moesol ▷ *n* moeswers, addysg
**morality** *n* moesoldeb
**morals** *npl* moesau
**morass** *n* cors, mignen
**morbid** *adj* afiach
**mordant** *adj* brathog, llym
**more** *adj* mwy, ychwaneg, rhagor ▷ *adv* mwy, mwyach
**moreover** *adv* heblaw hynny, hefyd
**moribund** *adj* ar farw, ar dranc
**morning** *n* bore ▷ *adj* bore, boreol
**Morocco** *n* Moroco
**morose** *adj* sur, sarrug, afrywiog, blwng
**morphology** *n* ffurfianneg, morffoleg
**morrow** *n* trannoeth
**morsel** *n* tamaid, tameidyn
**mortal** *adj* marwol, angheuol ▷ *n* dyn marwol
**mortar** *n* cymrwd, morter; breuan, morter
**mortgage** *n* morgais, arwystl ▷ *vt* morgeisio, arwystlo
**mortify** *vb* marwhau; blino, siomi
**mortise** *n* mortais ▷ *vt* morteisio
**mortuary** *n* marwdy
**mosaic** *adj* brith, amryliw ▷ *n* brithwaith, mosaig
**Moscow** *n* Moscow
**mosque** *n* mosg
**moss** *n* mwswgl, mwsogl
**most** *adj* mwyaf, amlaf
**mostly** *adv* gan mwyaf, fynychaf
**mote** *n* brycheuyn, llychyn
**moth** *n* gwyfyn
**mother** *n* mam; **mother-in-law** *n* mam yng nghyfraith, chwegr
**motion** *n* symudiad, ysgogiad; cynigiad

**motive** adj symudol, ysgogol ▷ n cymhelliad, amcan, motif
**motley** adj brith, cymysg
**motor** n modur
**motor cycle** n beic modur
**motorist** n modurwr
**motorway** n traffordd
**mottle** vt britho, brychu
**motto** n arwyddair
**mould** n pridd, daear, gweryd ▷ vt priddo
**mould** n mold; delw ▷ vt moldio, llunio, delweddu
**mould** n llwydni, llwydi
**moulder** vi malurio, adfeilio
**moult** vb bwrw plu, mudo
**mound** n twmpath, clawdd, crug
**mount** n mynydd, bryn
**mount** vb esgyn, dringo, codi, mynd ar gefn; gosod
**mountain** n mynydd
**mountaineer** n mynyddwr
**mourn** vb galaru
**mournful** adj galarus, dolefus, alaethus
**mourning** n galar; galarwisg
**mouse (mice)** n llygoden ▷ vb llygota
**moustache** n trawswch, mwstas
**mouth** n genau, safn, ceg ▷ vb cegu, safnu
**move** vb symud, syflyd; cymell; cynnig; cyffroi
**movement** n symudiad; ysgogiad
**mow** vt lladd (gwair) ▷ n mwdwl, medel
**MP** n abbr AS (aelod seneddol)
**much** adj llawer ▷ adv yn fawr
**mucilage** n glud, llys, llysnafedd
**muck** n tail, tom, baw ▷ vt tomi, baeddu
**mucus** n llys, llysnafedd
**mud** n mwd, llaid, llaca, baw
**muddle** vi drysu ▷ n dryswch
**mug** n cwpan, godart
**mulberry** n morwydden
**mule** n mul, bastart mul

**multi-** prefix aml, lluosog
**multifarious** n amryfath, lluosog
**multiple** adj amryfal ▷ n cynhwysrif, lluosrif
**multiplicand** n lluosrif, lluosyn
**multiplication** n amlhad, lluosogiad, lluosiad
**multiplicity** n lluosowgrwydd
**multiply** vb amlhau, lluosogi, lluosi
**multi-storey** adj aml-lawr
**multitude** n lliaws, tyrfa
**mumble** vb grymial, myngial
**mummy** n mwmi
**mumps** n clwy'r pennau, y dwymyn doben
**munch** vt cnoi
**mundane** adj bydol, daearol
**municipal** adj dinesig, bwrdeisiol
**munificent** adj hael, haelionus
**munitions** npl arfau neu offer rhyfel
**mural** adj murol ▷ n murlun
**murder** vt llofruddio ▷ n llofruddiaeth
**murderer** n llofrudd
**murky** adj tywyll, cymylog, dudew
**murmur** vb, n murmur, grwgnach
**muscle** n cyhyr, cyhyryn
**muscular** adj cyhyrog
**muse** n awen, awenydd
**muse** vi myfyrio, synfyfyrio
**museum** n amgueddfa
**mushroom** n madarch
**music** n miwsig, cerdd, cerddoriaeth, peroriaeth
**musical** adj cerddorol
**musician** n cerddor
**mussel** n misglen; **mussels** npl cregyn gleision
**must** vb def rhaid
**mustard** n mwstart
**muster** vb casglu, cynnull, byddino ▷ n cynulliad, mwstwr
**musty** adj wedi llwydo, hendrwm, mws
**mutable** adj anwadal, cyfnewidiol
**mutate** vb treiglo (llythrennau)

**mutation** n cyfnewidiad, treiglad
**mute** adj mud ▷ n mudan
**muteness** n mudandod
**mutilate** vt anafu, hagru, llurgunio
**mutiny** n terfysg, gwrthryfel
**mutter** vb myngial, grymial, mwmian
**mutton** n cig dafad, cig mollt, cig gwedder
**mutual** adj cyd, o boptu, y naill a'r llall
**muzzle** n genau, ffroen; pennor ▷ vt cau safn, rhoi taw ar
**my** pron fy
**myriad** n myrdd
**myrmidon** n anfadwas, dihiryn
**myrrh** n myrr
**myrtle** n myrtwydd
**myself** pron myfi fy hun
**mysterious** adj dirgel, rhyfedd, dirgelaidd
**mystery** n dirgelwch
**mystic** n cyfriniwr, cyfrinydd
**mystify** vt synnu, syfrdanu
**myth** n dameg, chwedl, myth
**mythology** n chwedloniaeth

# n

**nab** vb cipio, dal
**nadir** n isafbwynt, ory
**nag** vb cecru, ffraeo, cadw sŵn ▷ n ceffyl

**nail** n hoel, hoelen; ewin ▷ vt hoelio; nail file n ffeil/rhathell ewinedd
**naïve** adj diniwed, diddichell, gwirion
**naked** adj noeth
**namby-pamby** adj merf, merfaidd, llipa
**name** n enw ▷ vt enwi, galw
**namely** adv sef, nid amgen
**namesake** n cyfenw
**nanny** n nani
**nap** vi cysgu, pendwmpian ▷ n cyntun
**nape** n gwar, gwegil
**napkin** n napcyn, cadach, cewyn
**nappy** n cewyn, clwt
**narcotic** adj narcotig ▷ n moddion cwsg
**narrate** vt adrodd (hanes)
**narrative** n hanes, chwedl, stori
**narrow** adj cul, cyfyng ▷ vb culhau, cyfyngu
**nasal** adj trwynol
**nasty** adj cas, brwnt, budr, ffiaidd
**natal** adj genedigol
**nation** n cenedl
**national** adj cenedlaethol
**nationalism** n cenedlaetholdeb
**nationalist** n cenedlaetholwr
**nationality** n cenedl, cenedligrwydd
**nationalization** n gwladoliad
**nationalize** vb gwladoli, cenedlaetholi
**native** n brodor ▷ adj brodorol; cynhenid
**nativity** n genedigaeth
**natural** adj anianol, naturiol
**naturalist** n naturiaethwr
**naturalize** vb naturioli, breinio, cywladu, brodori
**nature** n anian, natur; naturiaeth
**naught** n dim
**naughtiness** n drygioni, direidi
**naughty** adj drwg, drygionus
**nausea** n clefyd y môr; cyfog; ffieidd-dod

**nauseous** adj cyfoglyd, ffiaidd, atgas
**nautical** adj morwrol, mordwyol
**naval** adj llyngesol, morol
**nave** n corff eglwys
**nave** n both, bŵl
**navel** n bogail
**navigate** vt morio, mordwyo, llywio
**navvy** n cloddiwr, ceibiwr
**navy** n llynges
**nay** adv na, nage; nid hynny yn unig
**naze** n trwyn, penrhyn, pentir
**neap** adj, n: **~ tide** nêp, llanw isel
**near** adj, adv, prep agos, ger, gerllaw ▷ vb agosáu, nesu
**nearby** adv gerllaw, yn ymyl
**nearly** adv bron
**nearness** n agosrwydd
**neat** adj del, destlus, twt, trefnus; pur
**nebula** (-ae) n niwlen; niwl sêr
**nebulous** adj niwlog
**necessarily** adv o angenrheidrwydd
**necessary** adj angenrheidiol
**necessitate** vt gorfodi, gwneud yn angenrheidiol
**necessitous** adj anghenus, rheidus
**necessity** n angen, anghenraid, rhaid
**neck** n gwddf, mwnwgl, gwar
**necklace** n mwclis
**necromancy** n dewiniaeth
**nectar** n neithdar
**need** n, vb (bod mewn) angen, eisiau
**needful** adj rheidiol, angenrheidiol
**needle** n nodwydd; gwaell
**needlework** n gwniadwaith
**needless** adj afreidiol, dianghenraid
**nefarious** adj anfad, drygionus, ysgeler
**negation** n nacâd, gwadiad, negyddiad
**negative** adj nacaol, negyddol

**neglect** vt esgeuluso ▷ n esgeulustra
**negligence** n esgeulustod
**negligent** adj esgeulus
**negotiate** vb trafod, trefnu, negodi
**negotiation** n trafodaeth, cyd-drafodaeth
**negro** n dyn du, negro
**neigh** vi gweryru ▷ n gweryriad
**neighbour** n cymydog
**neighbourhood** n cymdogaeth
**neither** conj na, nac, ychwaith ▷ adj, pron na'r naill na'r llall, nid yr un o'r ddau
**Nemesis** n dialedd
**neo-** prefix newydd, diweddar
**nephew** n nai
**nepotism** n neigaredd
**nerve** n giewyn, gewyn, nerf ▷ vt gwroli
**nervous** adj gieuol; nerfus, ofnus
**nest** n nyth ▷ vb nythu
**nestle** vb nythu, gwasgu'n glos at
**nestling** n aderyn bach, cyw
**net** n rhwyd, rhwyden
**net** adj union, cywir, net ▷ vt rhwydo
**netball** n pêl rwyd
**nether** adj isaf
**Netherlands** npl: **the ~** yr Iseldiroedd
**nettle** n danadl ▷ vt pigo; llidio
**network** n rhwydwaith
**neuralgia** n gieuwst
**neurasthenia** n nerfwst
**neuritis** n newritis
**neurosis** n newrosis
**neuter** adj diryw
**neutral** adj amhleidiol ▷ n amhleidydd
**neutrality** n newtraliaeth, amhleidiaeth
**neutralize** vt dieffeithio, dirymu
**never** adv ni ... erioed, ni ... byth
**nevertheless** adv, conj eto, er hynny
**new** adj newydd; **New Year** n Y

Calan, Y Flwyddyn Newydd;
New York n Efrog Newydd; New
Zealand n Seland Newydd
**newcomer** n newydd-ddyfodiad
**newness** n newydd-deb
**news** n newydd, newyddion, hanes
**newsagent** n gwerthwr papurau
newyddion
**newspaper** n papur newydd,
newyddiadur
**newt** n madfall, genau-goeg,
modrchwilen
**next** adj nesaf ▷ adv yn nesaf
**nib** n blaen, nib
**nibble** vb deintio, cnoi
**nice** adj neis, hardd, tlws; manwl,
cynnil
**niche** n cloer, cilfach
**nickname** n llysenw ▷ vt llysenwi
**niece** n nith
**niggard** n cybydd ▷ adj cybyddlyd,
crintach
**nigger** n dyn du (mewn dirmyg)
**nigh** adj, adv agos
**night** n nos; noson, noswaith; **by ~**
liw nos; **dead of ~** cefn nos; **night
club** n clwb nos
**nightdress** n gŵn nos, coban
**nightfall** n y cyfnos, yr hwyr
**nightingale** n eos
**nightmare** n hunllef
**nil** n dim
**nimble** adj gwisgi, heini, sionc
**nimbleness** n sioncrwydd
**nincompoop** n penbwl, gwirionyn
**nine** adj, n naw
**nineteen** adj, n pedwar (pedair) ar
bymtheg, un deg naw
**ninety** adj, n deg a phedwar ugain,
naw deg
**ninth** adj nawfed
**nip** vb brathu, cnoi; deifio
**nipple** n diden, teth, tethan
**nit** n nedden
**nitrate** n nitrad
**nitre** n neitr
**nitrogen** n nitrogen

**nitrous** n nitrus
**no** adj ni ... neb, dim ▷ adv ni etc,
dim; nac oes, nage, naddo
**nobility** n bonedd, urddas,
mawredd
**noble** adj ardderchog, urddasol,
pendefigaidd ▷ n pendefig
**nobleman** n pendefig
**nobody** n neb
**nocturnal** adj nosol, gyda'r nos
**nod** vb amneidio; pendrymu ▷ n
amnaid
**noise** n sŵn, twrf, trwst
**noisome** adj niweidiol, atgas,
ffiaidd
**noisy** adj swnllyd
**nomad** n nomad, crwydrwr ▷ adj
crwydrol
**nom de plume** n ffugenw
**nomenclature** n cyfundrefn
enwau
**nominal** adj enwol, mewn enw
**nominate** vt enwi, enwebu
**nomination** n enwebiad
**nominative** adj enwol
**non-** prefix an-, di-
**nonagenarian** n un deng mlwydd
a phedwar ugain
**non-alcoholic** adj dialcohol
**nonce** n: **for the ~** am y tro
**nonchalance** n difrawder,
difaterwch
**nonchalant** adj didaro, difater
**nonconformist** n anghydffurfiwr,
ymneilltuwr
**nonconformity** n
anghydffurfiaeth, ymneilltuaeth
**nondescript** adj anodd ei
ddarlunio, od
**none** pron neb, dim, dim un
**nonentity** n dyn dibwys, neb
**nonplus** vt drysu, dymchwelyd
**nonsense** n lol, dyli, gwiriondeb
**non-violence** n didreisedd
**non-violent** adj di-drais, didrais
**noodle** n gwirionyn, ffwlcyn; nwdl
**nook** n congl, cornel, cilfach

**noon** n nawn, hanner dydd, canol dydd
**noose** n cwlwm rhedeg, magl
**nor** conj na, nac
**normal** adj rheolaidd, cyffredin, safonol
**normality** n normalrwydd
**north** n gogledd ▷ adj gogleddol; **North Pole** n Pegwn y Gogledd; **North Sea** n Môr y Gogledd
**northern** adj gogleddol; **Northern Ireland** n Gogledd Iwerddon
**Norway** n Norwy
**nose** n trwyn ▷ vb trwyno, ffroeni, gwyntio
**nosebleed** n gwaedlif o'r trwyn
**nosegay** n blodeuglwm, pwysi
**nostalgia** n hiraeth
**nostril** n ffroen
**not** adv na, nac, nad, ni, nid
**notable** adj nodedig, hynod, enwog
**notary** n nodiadur, nodiedydd
**notation** n nodiant
**notch** n rhic, bwlch, hecyn, rhwgn, rhint
**note** n nod, nodyn ▷ vt nodi, sylwi
**noted** adj nodedig, hynod, enwog
**note pad** n pad ysgrifennu
**notepaper** n papur ysgrifennu
**noteworthy** adj nodedig
**nothing** n dim; **~ at all** dim byd, dim o gwbl
**notice** n sylw, rhybudd ▷ vt sylwi
**noticeboard** n hysbysfwrdd
**notify** vt hysbysu, rhoi rhybudd
**notion** n tyb, amcan, syniad
**notoriety** n enw gwael
**notorious** adj hynod, carn, rhemp
**notwithstanding** conj er ▷ prep er, er gwaethaf
**nought** n dim; gwagnod (o)
**noun** n enw
**nourish** vt maethu, meithrin
**nourishing** adj maethlon
**nourishment** n maeth
**novel** adj newydd ▷ n nofel
**novelist** n nofelydd

**November** n Tachwedd
**novice** n newyddian, nofis
**now** adv, conj, n yn awr, yr awron, yrŵan, weithian, bellach; **just ~** gynnau; **~ and then** yn awr ac yn y man
**nowadays** adv yn y dyddiau hyn
**nowhere** adv dim yn unlle
**noxious** adj niweidiol, afiach
**nozzle** n ffroenell
**nuclear** adj niwclear
**nucleus** n cnewyllyn, bywyn
**nude** adj noeth, noeth lymun
**nudge** vt pwnio, penelino
**nugatory** adj ofer, disylwedd, dirym
**nugget** n clap aur
**nuisance** n pla, poendod, budreddi
**null** adj diddim, dirym, ofer
**numb** adj diffrwyth, cwsg ▷ vt fferru, merwino
**number** n nifer, rhif, rhifedi; rhifyn ▷ vt rhifo, cyfrif; **number plate** n plat rhif car, plat cofrestru
**numeral** n rhifol, rhifnod
**numeration** n cyfrifiad
**numerator** n rhifiadur
**numerical** adj rhifiadol
**numerous** adj niferog, lluosog, aml
**nun** n lleian, mynaches
**nurse** n mamaeth, gweinyddes, nyrs ▷ vt magu, meithrin, nyrsio
**nursery** n magwrfa, meithrinfa
**nurture** n maeth, magwraeth, meithriniad ▷ vt maethu, meithrin
**nut** n cneuen; gwain, gweinell
**nutcracker** n gefel gnau
**nutriment** n maeth
**nutrition** n maeth, maethiad
**nutritious** adj maethlon
**nutshell** n plisgyn (masgl) cneuen
**nuzzle** vb trwyno, turio, ymwasgu
**nylon** n neilon

# O

oaf n delff, hurtyn, awff, llabwst
oak n derwen; derw
oakum n carth, breisgion
oar n rhwyf
oat n ceirchen; (pl) ceirch
oatcake n bara ceirch, teisen geirch
oath n llw
oatmeal n blawd ceirch
obdurate adj caled, cyndyn, ystyfnig, anhyblyg
obedience n ufudd-dod
obedient adj ufudd
obese adj tew, corffol
obey vb ufuddhau
obituary n marwgoffa
object n gwrthrych; amcan ▷ vb gwrthwynebu
objection n gwrthwynebiad
objectionable adj annymunol
objective adj gwrthrychol ▷ n amcan, nod
obligation n dyled, rhwymau
oblige vt rhwymo; boddio; gorfodi
obliging adj caredig, cymwynasgar
oblique adj lleddf, gŵyr, ar osgo
obliterate vt dileu
oblivion n angof, ebargofiant
oblong adj hirgul ▷ n oblong
obnoxious adj atgas, ffiaidd
obscene adj serth, anllad, anniwair, brwnt
obscure adj tywyll; anhysbys ▷ vt tywyllu
obsequious adj gwasaidd, cynffongar

observation n sylw; sylwadaeth
observatory n arsyllfa
observe vb sylwi, arsyllu; cadw
observer n sylwedydd, arsyllwr
obsolete adj anarferedig, ansathredig
obstacle n rhwystr, atalfa
obstinate adj cyndyn, ystyfnig, gwrthnysig
obstreperous adj trystiog, afreolus
obstruct vt cau, tagu; rhwystro, lluddio
obtain vt cael, caffael, ennill
obtrude vb gwthio ar, ymwthio
obtrusive adj ymwthgar
obtuse adj pŵl, di-fin, hurt; ~ angle ongl aflem
obvious adj eglur, amlwg
occasion n achlysur ▷ vt achlysuro
occasional adj achlysurol, anaml
occidental adj gorllewinol
occult adj cudd, dirgel, cêl, cyfrin
occupation n gwaith, galwedigaeth; meddiant
occupy vt meddu, meddiannu; llenwi; dal
occur vi digwydd; taro i'r meddwl
occurrence n digwyddiad
ocean n môr, cefnfor, cyfanfor, eigion
o'clock adv o'r gloch
octagon n wythongl
octave n wythawd, octef
octavo adj wythblyg ▷ n llyfr wythblyg
October n Hydref
octogenarian n gŵr pedwar ugain mlwydd oed
odd adj od, hynod; ~ number odrif
odds npl ots, gwahaniaeth; mantais
ode n awdl
odious adj atgas, cas, ffiaidd
odium n atgasrwydd; gwaradwydd; bai
odour n arogl, aroglau, sawr
of prep o; gan; am; ynghylch; of

**course** wrth gwrs

**off** adv ymaith, i ffwrdd ▷ prep oddi, oddi wrth, oddi ar; **~ and on** yn awr ac yn y man

**offal** n syrth, gwehilion, perfedd

**offence** n tramgwydd, trosedd, camwedd

**offend** vb tramgwyddo, troseddu, pechu; digio

**offender** n troseddwr

**offensive** adj tramgwyddus, atgas, ffiaidd; ymosodol

**offer** vb cynnig, cyflwyno; offrymu ▷ n cynnig

**offering** n offrwm, aberth

**office** n swydd; swyddfa

**officer** n swyddog, swyddwr

**official** adj swyddogol ▷ n swyddog

**officiate** vi gweinyddu

**officious** adj ymyrgar, busneslyd

**offside** n camochr, camsefyll ▷ vb camochri, camsefyll

**offspring** n hiliogaeth, epil, hil, plant

**oft, often** adv yn aml, yn fynych

**ogle** vb cilwenu, ciledrych

**ogre** n anghenfil, bwystfil, cawr

**oh** excl O!

**oil** n olew, oel ▷ vt iro, oelio

**oil rig** n llwyfan olew

**ointment** n ennaint, eli

**okay** excl popeth yn iawn

**old** adj hen, oedrannus; **of ~** gynt; **~ age** henaint, henoed; **~ and infirm** hen a methedig; **old-fashioned** adj henffasiwn, od; **old stager** n hen law

**olive** n olewydden

**omelette** n crempog wyau

**omen** n argoel, arwydd, rhagarwydd

**ominous** adj argoelus, bygythiol

**omission** n gwall

**omit** vt gadael allan, esgeuluso

**on** prep ar, ar warthaf ▷ adv ymlaen

**once** adv unwaith; gynt

**one** adj, n un; **one-way** adj (street, traffic) unffordd

**onion** n wynwynyn, wnionyn

**only** adj unig ▷ adv yn unig; ond

**onset** n ymosodiad, cyrch; cychwyn

**onslaught** n ymosodiad, rhuthr, cyrch

**onus** n baich, dyletswydd, cyfrifoldeb

**onward** adj, adv, **onwards** adv ymlaen

**ooze** n llaid, llysnafedd ▷ vi chwysu

**opaque** adj afloyw, tywyll

**open** adj agored ▷ vb agor, ymagor

**open-air** n, adj awyr agored

**opencast** n (coal) (glo) brig

**opening** n agoriad, agorfa

**operate** vb gweithredu, gweithio

**operation** n gweithrediad; gweithred, triniaeth lawfeddygol

**operator** n gweithredydd, trafodwr

**opiate** n cysglyn

**opinion** n tyb, meddwl, barn, opiniwn

**opponent** n gwrthwynebydd

**opportune** adj amserol, cyfleus

**opportunity** n cyfle, egwyl

**oppose** vt gwrthwynebu, cyferbynnu

**opposite** adj, adv, prep gwrthwyneb, cyferbyn

**opposition** n gwrthwynebiad, gwrthblaid

**oppress** vt gorthrymu, llethu

**optician** n optegydd

**optimism** n optimistiaeth

**optimist** n optimist

**option** n dewisiad, dewis

**or** conj neu, ai, ynteu, naill ai

**oracle** n oracl

**oral** adj geneuol, llafar, anysgrifenedig

**orally** adv ar lafar

**orange** n oren, oraens ▷ adj melyngoch

**oration** n araith, anerchiad

**orator** n areithiwr, areithydd

**orb** n pêl, pelen, pellen; y llygad
**orbit** n rhod, tro, cylchdro, chwyldro
**orchard** n perllan
**orchestra** n cerddorfa
**ordain** vt ordeinio, urddo
**ordeal** n prawf llym
**order** n trefn; gorchymyn, archeb;
  urdd ▷ vb ordeinio, trefnu,
  gorchymyn; archebu; urddo; **in ~
  that** er mwyn
**orderly** adj trefnus ▷ n gwas milwr
**ordinal** adj trefnol
**ordinarily** adv fel rheol
**ordinary** adj cyffredin, arferol
**ordination** n ordeiniad, urddiad
**ore** n mwyn
**organ** n organ, offeryn
**organist** n organydd
**organization** n trefn; cyfundrefn;
  trefniadaeth
**organize** vb trefnu
**organized** adj trefnus; **~ by**
  trefnwyd gan
**organizer** n trefnydd
**orgy** n gloddest, cyfeddach
**oriental** adj dwyreiniol ▷ n
  dwyreiniwr
**orientate** vb cyfeirio
**orifice** n genau, ceg, agorfa
**origin** n dechreuad, tarddiad
**original** adj, n gwreiddiol
**originality** n gwreiddioldeb
**originate** vb dechrau, tarddu
**ornament** n addurn ▷ vt addurno
**ornate** adj addurnedig, mawrwych
**ornithology** n adaryddiaeth,
  adareg
**orphan** n, adj amddifad
**orthodox** adj uniongred
**orthography** n orgraff
**oscillate** vb siglo, dirgrynu,
  osgiladu
**ostensible** adj ymddangosiadol,
  proffesedig
**ostentation** n rhodres
**ostentatious** adj rhodresgar
**ostracize** vt diarddel, alltudio

**ostrich** n estrys
**other** adj, pron arall, llall, amgen
**otherwise** adv amgen
**otter** n dyfrgi, dwrgi
**ounce** n owns
**our** pron ein, ein … ni
**oust** vt disodli
**out** adv allan, i maes
**outcast** n alltud, digartref,
  gwrthodedig
**outcome** n canlyniad, ffrwyth
**outcrop** n brig, cribell ▷ vb brigo
**outcry** n gwaedd; dadwrdd;
  gwrthdystiad
**outdo** vt rhagori ar, trechu
**outdoor** adj yn yr awyr agored
**outer** adj allanol, nesaf allan, cyrion
**outing** n pleserdaith, gwibdaith
**outlandish** adj dieithr, estronol,
  anghysbell, diarffordd
**outlast** vb goroesi
**outlaw** n herwr
**outlay** n traul, cost
**outlet** n allfa
**outline** n amlinelliad, braslun;
  amlinell ▷ vb amlinellu
**outlive** vb goroesi
**outlook** n rhagolwg, argoel;
  golygfa
**outset** n dechrau, dechreuad
**outside** n tu allan, tu faes ▷ adj, adv
  allan(ol), oddi allan ▷ prep tu allan
  i, tu faes i
**outside-forward** n blaenwr mas
**outside-half** n maswr
**outside-left** n asgellwr chwith
**outside-right** n asgellwr de
**outskirts** npl cyrrau, maestrefi
**outstanding** adj amlwg; dyledus
**outward** adj allanol
**outwards** adv tuag allan
**outweigh** vt gorbwyso
**oval** adj hirgrwn
**ovary** n wygell, wyfa, ofari
**ovation** n cymeradwyaeth
**oven** n ffwrn, popty
**over** prep uwch, tros ▷ adv gor,

rhy, tra
**overall** *adj* o ben i ben ▷ *n* troswisg
**overbearing** *adj* gormesol
**overcast** *adj* cymylog
**overcharge** *vt* gorbrisio, codi gormod
**overcoat** *n* cot fawr/uchaf
**overcome** *vt* gorchfygu, trechu, cael y gorau ar
**overdo** *vb* gorwneud
**overflow** *n* gorlif(iad) ▷ *vb* gorlifo
**overhead** *adj, adv* uwchben
**overheat** *vi* gorboethi
**overload** *vb* gorlwytho
**overlook** *vb* edrych dros; esgeuluso
**overnight** *adv* dros nos
**overpopulate** *vb* gorboblogi
**overpower** *vb* trechu
**overrun** *vb* goresgyn
**overseas** *adv* tramor, dros y môr
**overtake** *vt* goddiweddyd
**overthrow** *n* dymchweliad ▷ *vt* dymchwelyd
**overture** *n* cynnig; agorawd
**overturn** *vt* troi, dymchwelyd
**overwhelm** *vt* llethu, gorlethu
**overwork** *vb* gorweithio
**owe** *vt* bod mewn dyled
**owl** *n* tylluan, gwdihŵ
**own** *adj* eiddo dyn ei hun, priod ▷ *vt* meddu; arddel, addef
**owner** *n* perchen, perchennog
**ox (-en)** *n* ych, eidion
**oxide** *n* ocsid
**oxygen** *n* ocsigen
**oyster** *n* llymarch, wystrysen

# P

**pace** *n* cam, camre; cyflymdra ▷ *vb* camu, cerdded
**pacific** *adj* heddychol, tawel
**Pacific Ocean** *n* Môr Tawel
**pacifism** *n* heddychiaeth
**pacifist** *n* heddychwr
**pacify** *vt* heddychu, tawelu
**pack** *n* pac, swp, pwn ▷ *vb* pacio, pynio
**package** *n* pecyn, bwndel, sypyn
**packed lunch** *n* tocyn, pryd wedi ei bacio
**packet** *n* sypyn, paced
**pact** *n* cyfamod, cynghrair
**pad** *n* pad ▷ *vt* padio
**paddle** *n* padl, rhodl, rhwyf ▷ *vb* rhodli, padlo
**paddling pool** *n* pwll padlo
**paddock** *n* marchgae, cae bach
**padlock** *n* clo clap, clo clwt, clo egwyd
**pagan** *n* pagan ▷ *adj* paganaidd
**page** *n* tudalen
**pageant** *n* pasiant
**pail** *n* ystwc, crwc, bwced
**pain** *n* poen, gwayw, dolur ▷ *vt* poeni
**painful** *adj* poenus
**painkiller** *n* lleddfydd poen, lladdwr poen, dofydd poen
**painstaking** *adj* gofalus, trylwyr, diwyd
**paint** *n* paent, lliw ▷ *vt* peintio, lliwio
**painter** *n* peintiwr; arlunydd

**painting** n llun, darlun
**pair** n pâr, dau, cwpl ▷ vb paru
**Pakistan** n Pakistan
**palace** n plas, palas, palasty
**palaeo-, paleo-** prefix hen, hynafol
**palatable** adj archwaethus, blasus
**palate** n tafod y genau; blas, archwaeth
**palatial** adj palasaidd, gwych
**palaver** n cleber, baldordd ▷ vb clebran, baldorddi
**pale** adj gwelw, llwyd, glas, gwelwlas ▷ vb gwelwi
**pale** n pawl, cledr; clawdd, ffin
**Palestine** n Palestina
**palisade** n palis, gwalc
**pall** vb diflasu
**pallet** n gwely gwellt, matras
**pallid** adj gwelw, llwyd
**pallor** n gwelwedd
**palm** n palf, cledr llaw ▷ vt palfu
**palm** n palmwydden; **P~ Sunday** Sul y Blodau
**palpable** adj amlwg, dybryd, teimladwy
**palpitate** vi curo, dychlamu
**palsy** n parlys ▷ vt parlysu, diffrwytho
**paltry** adj distadl, gwael, pitw
**pamper** vt mwytho, maldodi
**pamphlet** n pamffled, llyfryn
**pan-** prefix oll-
**pan** n padell
**pancake** n crempog, cramwythen, ffroisen
**pandemonium** n dadwrdd, terfysg, mwstwr
**pander** vb porthi, gweini
**pane** n cwar, cwarel, paen
**panegyric** n molawd
**panel** n panel
**pang** n gloes, gwasgfa, brath, gwayw
**panic** n dychryn, panig
**pansy** n trilliw, llysiau'r Drindod
**pant** vi dyheu
**pantaloons** npl llodrau

**panties** npl pantos
**pantomime** n pantomeim
**pantry** n bwtri, pantri
**pants** npl pants
**papacy** n pabaeth
**papal** adj pabaidd
**paper** n papur ▷ vb papuro; **blotting paper** n papur sugno; **tissue paper** n papur sidan; **brown paper** n papur llwyd
**paperback** n llyfr clawr meddal
**paperclip** n clip papur
**papist** n pabydd
**papyrus (-i)** n papurfrwyn
**par** n cyfartaledd, llawn werth
**parable** n dameg
**parachute** n parasiwt
**parade** n rhodfa; rhodres, rhwysg
**paradise** n paradwys, gwynfa, gwynfyd
**paradox** n gwrthddywediad, paradocs
**paradoxical** adj paradocsaidd
**paradoxically** adv yn baradocsaidd
**paraffin** n paraffîn
**paragraph** n paragraff
**parallel** adj cyfochrog, cyflin, paralel
**paralyze** vt parlysu, diffrwytho
**paralysis** n parlys
**paralytic** adj, n claf o'r parlys
**paramount** adj pen, pennaf, prif
**paramour** n gordderch
**parapet** n canllaw, rhagfur
**paraphernalia** npl meddiannau, taclau, celfi, petheuach
**paraphrase** n aralleiriad ▷ vt aralleirio
**parasite** n un yn byw ar gefn un arall, cynffonnwr
**parcel** n parsel, swp, sypyn
**parch** vb crasu, deifio, golosgi, sychu
**parched** adj cras, crasboeth
**parchment** n memrwn
**pardon** n maddeuant, pardwn ▷ vt

maddau, pardynu
**parent** n tad neu fam; (pl) rhieni
**parenthesis** (-ses) n sangiad, ymadrodd rhwng cromfachau
**pariah** n dyn ysgymun
**parings** npl pilion, creifion
**Paris** n Paris
**parish** n plwyf ▷ adj plwyf, plwyfol
**parishioner** n plwyfolyn; (pl) plwyfolion
**parity** n cydraddoldeb, cyfartaledd
**park** n parc, cae, coetgae ▷ vb parcio
**parking meter** n amserydd parcio, rheolydd parcio
**parking ticket** n tocyn parcio
**parlance** n ymadrodd, iaith
**parliament** n senedd
**parliamentary** adj seneddol
**parlour** n parlwr
**parochial** adj plwyfol
**parody** n parodi ▷ vb gwatwar, dynwared
**parole** n gair, addewid, parôl
**parricide** n tadladdiad; tadleiddiad
**parrot** n parot, perot
**parry** vt osgoi, gochelyd, troi heibio
**parse** vt dosbarthu
**parsimonious** adj crintach, cybyddlyd
**parsimony** n crintachrwydd
**parsley** n persli
**parsnip** n panasen
**parson** n person, offeiriad
**part** n rhan; parth; plaid ▷ vb rhannu, parthu; gwahanu; ymadael
**partake** vb cyfrannu, cyfranogi
**partial** adj rhannol; pleidiol, tueddol
**participate** vb cyfranogi
**participle** n rhangymeriad
**particle** n mymryn, gronyn; geiryn
**particular** adj neilltuol, penodol; manwl ▷ n pwnc; (pl) manylion
**parting** n ymadael
**partisan** n pleidiwr
**partition** n canolfur, gwahanfur,

palis
**partly** adv mewn rhan, yn rhannol
**partner** n partner; cymar
**partridge** n petrisen
**part-time** adj rhan amser
**party** n plaid; parti, mintai
**pass** vb myned heibio, llwyddo, pasio; treulio, bwrw ▷ n cyflwr, sefyllfa; bwlch; trwydded; **to pass away** vb marw; **reverse pass** n pas wrthol
**passable** adj y gellir mynd heibio iddo; purion
**passage** n tramwyfa; mordaith; cyfran
**passenger** n teithiwr
**passing** n ymadawiad, tranc, pasio ▷ adj yn pasio, diflannol
**passion** n dioddefaint; gwŷn, nwyd
**passionate** adj angerddol, nwydwyllt
**passive** adj goddefol
**Passover** n y Pasg
**passport** n trwydded deithio, pasbort
**past** adj, n gorffennol ▷ prep wedi ▷ adv heibio
**paste** n past ▷ vt pastio, gludio
**pastern** n egwyd
**pasteurize** vb pasteureiddio
**pasteurized** adj wedi ei basteureiddio
**pastime** n difyrrwch, adloniant
**pastor** n bugail (eglwys), gweinidog
**pastoral** adj bugeiliol ▷ n bugeilgerdd
**pastry** n pasteiod, pasteiaeth, tarten; crwst
**pasture** n porfa ▷ vb porfelu, pori
**pasty** n pastai
**pat** vt patio, pratio, canmol ▷ adj parod, cymwys, priodol
**patch** n clwt, darn ▷ vt clytio
**patchwork** n clytwaith
**paten** n plat cymundeb
**patent** adj agored, cyhoedd,

amlwg; breintiedig ▷ n breintlythyr
**paternal** adj tadol
**paternoster** n pader
**path** n llwybr
**pathetic** adj gresynus, pathetig
**pathological** adj patholegol
**pathos** n teimlad, dwyster
**patience** n amynedd
**patient** adj amyneddgar, dioddefus
▷ n dioddefydd, claf
**patriarch** n patriarch
**patrimony** n treftadaeth; gwaddol
**patriot** n gwladgarwr
**patriotic** adj gwladgarol
**patrol** n gwyliadwriaeth, gwylfa,
patrôl
**patron** n noddwr
**patronage** n nawdd,
nawddogaeth
**patronize** vt noddi, nawddogi
**patronizing** adj nawddogol
**patronymic** n tadenw
**patter** vb curo (fel glaw ar ffenestr)
**patter** vb padera ▷ n clebar,
siaradach
**pattern** n patrwm, cynllun
**paucity** n prinder
**paunch** n bol, cest
**pauper** n dyn tlawd, tlotyn
**pause** n saib, seibiant, hoe ▷ vi
aros, sefyll, ymbwyllo
**pave** vt palmantu
**pavement** n palmant, pafin
**pavilion** n pabell, pafiliwn
**paw** n palf, pawen ▷ vb palfu,
pawennu
**pawky** adj direidus
**pawn** n gwystl; (Chess) gwerin ▷ vt
gwystlo
**pay** vb talu ▷ n tâl, cyflog, pae, hur;
**back ~** ôl-dâl
**payment** n taliad, tâl
**pea** n pysen
**peace** n heddwch, tangnefedd
▷ excl gosteg!, ust!
**peaceful** adj heddychol,
tangnefeddus, llonydd

**peach** n eirinen wlanog
**peacock** n paun
**peak** n pig; crib, copa; uchafbwynt
**peal** n sain clychau; twrf (taran)
▷ vb canu
**peanut** n cneuen ddaear
**pear** n gellygen
**pearl** n perl
**peasant** n gwladwr, gwerinwr
**peasantry** n gwerin
**peat** n mawn
**pebble** n carreg lefn, cerrigyn, gröyn
**peck** vb pigo, cnocellu ▷ n cnoc,
pigiad
**peculiar** adj priod, priodol; hynod
**peculiarity** n hynodrwydd
**pecuniary** adj ariannol
**pedagogue** n athro plant,
ysgolfeistr
**pedal** n pedal ▷ vb pedalu
**pedant** n pedant
**pedantic** adj pedantig
**peddle** vb pedlera
**pedestal** n troed, bôn, gwaelod
**pedestrian** adj ar draed, pedestrig
▷ n gŵr traed, cerddwr; **pedestrian
crossing** n croesfan
**pedigree** n ach, achau, bonedd
**pedlar** n pedler
**pee** n pisiad ▷ vb pisio
**peel** n pil, croen, rhisgl ▷ vb pilio,
plicio, crafu
**peep** vi cipedrych, sbïo ▷ n
cipolwg, cip
**peer** vi ciledrych, syllu
**peer** n gogyfurdd, cydradd; pendefig
**peevish** adj anniddig, blin, piwis
**peg** n hoel bren, peg ▷ vt pegio
**Peking** n Peking
**pelf** n golud
**pellet** n peled, pelen, haelsen
**pelt** vt lluchio, taflu, peledu, baeddu
**pelvis** n pelfis
**pen** n pin, ysgrifbin ▷ vt ysgrifennu
**pen** n lloc, ffald, cwt ▷ vt ffaldio,
llocio
**penal** adj penydiol

**penalize** vb cosbi

**penalty** n cosb, cosbedigaeth;
  **penalty (kick)** n cic gosb

**penance** n penyd

**pence** npl ceiniogau, pres

**pencil** n pwyntil, pensel, pensil;
  **pencil sharpener** n naddwr
  pensiliau

**pendant** n tlws

**pending** prep hyd, nes, yn ystod

**pendulous** adj yn hongian, yn siglo

**pendulum** n pendil

**penetrate** vb treiddio; dirnad

**penfriend** n cyfaill llythyru

**penguin** n pengwin

**penicillin** n penisilin

**peninsula** n gorynys

**penis** n cala, pidyn

**penitence** n edifeirwch

**penitent** adj edifar, edifarus,
  edifeiriol

**penitentiary** n carchar

**penknife (-knives)** n cyllell boced

**pen name** n ffug enw

**pennant, pennon** n penwn,
  banner

**penniless** adj heb geiniog

**penny (pence, pennies)** n ceiniog

**pension** n blwydd-dal, pensiwn

**pensioner** n pensiynwr

**pensive** adj synfyfyriol, meddylgar

**pent** adj wedi ei gau i mewn, caeth

**Pentateuch** n pumllyfr Moses

**penult** n goben

**people** n pobl, gwerin ▷ vt pobli,
  poblogi

**pepper** n pupur

**peppermint** n mintys poethion;
  botwm gwyn

**per** prep trwy, wrth, yn ôl

**peradventure** adv efallai

**perceive** vt canfod, gweld, dirnad,
  deall

**percentage** n hyn a hyn y cant,
  canran

**perceptible** adj canfyddadwy

**perception** n canfyddiad, canfod

**perceptive** adj yn gallu dirnad

**perch** n perc; clwyd ▷ vb clwydo

**perchance** adv efallai, hwyrach

**percolate** vb hidlo, diferu

**percussion** n trawiad,
  gwrthdrawiad; ~ **band** seindorf
  daro

**peremptory** adj pendant,
  awdurdodol

**perennial** adj drwy'r flwyddyn;
  bythol, lluosflwydd

**perfect** adj perffaith ▷ vt
  perffeithio

**perfection** n perffeithrwydd

**perfectly** adv yn berffaith

**perfervid** adj brwd, tanbaid

**perfidy** n brad, dichell, ffalster

**perforate** vt tyllu

**perforated** adj tyllog

**perforation** n twll

**perforce** adv o orfod, drwy drais

**perform** vb cyflawni; chwarae,
  perfformio

**performance** n perfformiad

**performer** n perfformiwr

**perfume** n perarogl, persawr ▷ vt
  perarogli

**perfunctory** adj o raid, diofal,
  esgeulus

**perhaps** adv efallai, hwyrach, ond
  odid, dichon

**peril** n perygl, enbydrwydd

**perimeter** n amfesur, perimedr

**period** n cyfnod; cyfadran (miwsig);
  diweddnod; misglwyf

**periodic** adj cyfnodol

**periodical** n cyfnodolyn

**peripatetic** adj crwydrol,
  cylchynol, peripatetig

**peripheral** adj ymylol

**periphery** n ymylon, cylchfesur

**periphrastic** adj cwmpasog

**perish** vi colli, trengi, marw, darfod;
  llygru

**periwinkle** n gwichiad

**perjure** vt: ~ **oneself** tyngu anudon

**perjury** n anudon, anudoniaeth

**perk** n mantais; **to ~ up** bywhau, adfywio

**perky** adj bywiog, eofn, hyf

**permanent** adj parhaol, arhosol, sefydlog

**permeate** vt treiddio, trwytho

**permissible** adj wedi ei ganiatáu

**permission** n caniatâd, cennad

**permissive** adj goddefol; **the ~ society** y gymdeithas oddefol

**permit** vb caniatáu ▷ n trwydded

**peroration** n diweddglo araith, perorasiwn

**perpendicular** adj syth, unionsyth

**perpetrate** vt cyflawni (rhyw ddrwg)

**perpetual** adj parhaol, parhaus, bythol

**perpetuate** vt parhau, anfarwoli

**perplex** vt drysu, cythryblu, trallodi

**persecute** vt erlid

**persevere** vi dyfalbarhau

**persist** vi dal ati; mynnu, taeru, dyfalbarhau

**persistent** adj dyfal, taer, cyndyn, parhaus

**person** n person

**personable** adj golygus, prydweddol, hawddgar

**personal** adj personol; **personal assistant** n cynorthwyydd personol

**personality** n personoliaeth

**personally** adv yn bersonol

**perspective** n persbectif, safbwynt

**perspiration** n chwys

**perspire** vb chwysu

**persuade** vt darbwyllo, perswadio

**pert** adj eofn, tafodrydd

**pertain** vi perthyn

**pertinent** adj perthynol, cymwys

**perturb** vt cyffroi, aflonyddu, cythruddo

**peruse** vt darllen, chwilio

**pervade** vt treiddio, trwytho

**perverse** adj gwrthnysig, trofaus, croes

**pervert** vt gwyrdroi, llygru, camdroi ▷ n cyfeiliornwr

**pessimism** n pesimistiaeth

**pessimist** n pesimist

**pest** n pla, haint, poendod

**pester** vt blino, aflonyddu, poeni

**pestilence** n haint, pla

**pet** n anwylyn, ffafryn ▷ adj llywaeth, swci ▷ vt anwesu, canmol

**petal** n petal

**petite** adj bychan

**petition** n deisyfiad; deiseb, petisiwn

**petitioner** n deisebwr

**petrel** n aderyn drycin

**petrified** adj stond

**petrify** vb parlysu

**petroleum** n petroliwm

**petrol pump** n pwmp petrol

**petrol station** n gorsaf betrol

**petticoat** n pais

**petty** adj bach, bychan, mân, gwael

**petulant** adj annidig, anfoddog, anynad

**pew** n eisteddle, côr, sedd

**pewit, peewit** n cornicyll, cornchwiglen

**pewter** n piwter

**phantom** n rhith, drychiolaeth

**Pharisee** n Pharisead

**pharmacy** n fferylliaeth; fferyllfa

**pharynx** n sefnig

**phase** n golwg, gwedd, agwedd; tro

**pheasant** n ceiliog coed, coediar, ffesant

**phenomenon** (-na) n ffenomen; rhyfeddod

**phial** n ffiol

**philander** vi gwamalio caru

**philanthropist** n dyngarwr

**philanthropy** n dyngarwch

**Philippines** n Pilipinas

**Philistine** n Philistiad

**philology** n ieitheg

**philosopher** n athronydd

**philosophical** adj athronyddol

**philosophy** n athroniaeth

phlegm n cornboer, llysnafedd,
fflem
phlegmatic adj difraw, digyffro,
difywyd
phobia n ffobia
phone n ffôn, teleffon ▷ vb ffonio;
phone book n cyfeiriadur ffôn;
phone box n caban ffôn; phone call
n galwad ffôn
phonetic adj seinegol
phonetician n seinegydd
phonetics n seineg
phoney adj ffug
phonology n ffonoleg
phosphorus n ffosfforws
photocopier n llungopïydd
photocopy n llungopi ▷ vb
llungopïo
photograph n llun, ffotograff
photographer n ffotograffydd
photography n ffotograffiaeth
phrase n ymadrodd; cymal ▷ vt
geirio
phraseology n geiriad,
geirweddiad
physical adj corfforol, materol;
ffisegol; physical education n
addysg gorfforol
physician n meddyg, ffisigwr
physicist n ffisegydd/wr
physics n ffiseg
physiology n ffisioleg
physiotherapy n ffisiotherapi
physique n corffolaeth,
cyfansoddiad
piano n piano
pick n caib ▷ vb ceibio
pick vb pigo, dewis, dethol ▷ n
dewis
pickaxe n caib
picket n polyn, cledren; gwyliwr,
gwyliadwriaeth, picedwr ▷ vb
picedu
pickle n picl, heli ▷ vt piclo, halltu
picnic n picnic
pickpocket n pigwr pocedi,
codleidr

pictorial adj darluniadol
picture n llun, darlun, pictiwr; ~
book llyfr lluniau
picturesque adj darluniaidd,
gwych, byw
pie n pastai; pie chart n siart olwyn
piebald adj brith; brithryw
piece n darn, dryll, rhan ▷ vt clytio,
asio, uno
piecemeal adv bob yn damaid
pied adj brith, brithliw
pier n piler; pier
pierce vb brathu, gwanu, trywanu
piety n duwioldeb
piffle n lol, oferedd, gwegi
pig n mochyn ▷ vb porchellu, bwrw
perchyll
pigeon n colomen
pigeonhole n cloer
pigeon-house n colomendy
piggy bank n cadw-mi-gei, blwch
cynilo
pig-headed adj pendew, ystyfnig
pigment n paent, lliw
pigsty n twlc mochyn
pigtail n pleth
pike n gwaywffon; penhwyad
pile n crug, pentwr ▷ vt pentyrru
pile n pawl, cledr
pile n blew, ceden
piles npl clwyf y marchogion
pilfer vb chwiwladrata
pilgrim n pererin
pilgrimage n pererindod
pill n pelen, pilsen
pillage n ysbail, anrhaith ▷ vt
ysbeilio, anrheithio
pillar n colofn, piler; pillar box n
bocs postio
pillion n sgil
pillory n rhigod, pilwri
pillow n gobennydd, clustog; pillow
case n cas gobennydd
pilot n cyfarwyddwr llongau, peilot
pimple n ploryn, tosyn
pin n pin ▷ vt pinio, hoelio
pinafore n brat, piner

**pincers** *npl* gefel, pinsiwrn
**pinch** *vb* pinsio, gwasgu; cynilo ▷ *n* pins, pinsiad; gwasgfa, cyfyngder
**pincushion** *n* pincas, pincws
**pine** *n* pinwydden
**pine** *vi* dihoeni, nychu, curio
**pineapple** *n* afal pîn
**pinion** *n* asgell, adain ▷ *vt* torri esgyll
**pink** *adj*, *n* pinc
**pinpoint** *vb* pinbwyntio
**pint** *n* peint
**pioneer** *n* arloeswr, arloesydd
**pious** *adj* duwiol, duwiolfrydig, crefyddol
**pip** *n* hedyn afal *etc*
**pipe** *n* pib, pibell ▷ *vb* canu pibell
**piping** *adj*: **~ hot** chwilboeth
**piquant** *adj* pigog, llym, tost
**pique** *vt* llidio, cyffroi; ymfalch'io ▷ *n* soriant
**pirate** *n* môr-leidr
**piss** *vb* pisio
**pissed** *adj* meddw
**pistol** *n* llawddryll, pistol
**pit** *n* pwll, pydew ▷ *vt* pyllu; **coal ~** pwll glo
**pitch** *n* pyg ▷ *vt* pygu
**pitch** *vb* bwrw; gosod; taro (tôn) ▷ *n* gradd, mesur, traw
**pitcher** *n* piser, ystên, cawg
**pitchfork** *n* picfforch, picwarch; seinfforch
**piteous** *adj* truenus, gresynus
**pitfall** *n* magl, perygl
**pith** *n* bywyn; mwydion; mêr; grym, sylwedd
**pithy** *adj* cryno, cynhwysfawr
**pitiful** *adj* truenus, tosturiol
**pitiless** *adj* didostur, didrugaredd
**pittance** *n* dogn, cyfran (annigonol)
**pity** *n* tosturi, trueni, gresyn ▷ *vt* tosturio, gresynu
**pivot** *n* colyn, pegwn
**placable** *adj* cymodlon, hynaws
**placard** *n* murlen, hysbyslen

**placate** *vt* cymodi, heddychu, dyhuddo
**place** *n* lle, man, mangre ▷ *vt* cyfleu, gosod; **to take ~** digwydd; **in the first ~** yn y lle cyntaf
**placid** *adj* araf, tawel, llonydd
**plagiary** *n* llên-ladrad; llên-leidr
**plague** *n* pla, haint ▷ *vt* poeni, blino
**plaice** *n* lleden
**plaid** *n* plod
**plain** *adj* plaen, eglur ▷ *n* gwastadedd
**plaintiff** *n* achwynwr, hawlydd
**plait** *n* pleth ▷ *vt* plethu
**plan** *n* cynllun, plan ▷ *vt* cynllunio, planio
**plane** *adj*, *n* gwastad, lefel
**plane** *n* plaen; awyren ▷ *vt* plaenio
**planet** *n* planed
**plank** *n* astell, estyllen, planc
**planning** *n* cynllunio; **planning permission** *n* caniatâd cynllunio
**plant** *n* planhigyn, llysieuyn; offer; ffatri ▷ *vt* plannu
**plaster** *n* plaster ▷ *vt* plastro
**plastic** *n*, *adj* plastig; **~ bag** cwdyn plastig
**plat** *n* darn o dir, clwt, lawnt
**plate** *n* plat; llestri aur *etc* ▷ *vt* golchi â metel
**plateau** *n* gwastatir uchel
**platform** *n* llwyfan, esgynlawr
**platitude** *n* sylw hen a diflas, gwireb
**platoon** *n* platŵn
**platter** *n* plat, dysgl, noe
**plaudit** *n* banllef o gymeradwyaeth
**plausible** *adj* teg neu resymol yr olwg, ffals
**play** *vb* chwarae; canu (offeryn) ▷ *n* chwarae
**player** *n* chwaraewr
**playful** *adj* chwareus
**playground** *n* chwaraele
**playgroup** *n* grŵp chwarae
**playing field** *n* maes chwarae
**plaything** *n* tegan

**playwright** n dramodydd

**plea** n ple, dadl, hawl; esgus

**plead** vb pledio, dadlau, eiriol, ymbil

**pleasant** adj hyfryd, pleserus, difyr, siriol

**please** vb boddhau, boddio, rhyngu bodd; **if you ~** os gwelwch yn dda

**pleased** adj boddhaus, bodlon, hapus; **~ to meet you** mae'n dda gen i gwrdd â chi

**pleasing** adj dymunol

**pleasure** n pleser, hyfrydwch

**pleat** n plet, pleten ▷ vt pletio

**plebeian** n gwerinwr, gwrêng

**plebiscite** n pleidlais y bobl

**pledge** n gwystl, ernes ▷ vt gwystlo

**plenary** adj llawn, cyflawn, diamodol

**plenty** n digon, helaethrwydd

**plethora** n gorgyflawnder

**pleurisy** n eisglwyf, plewrisi

**pliable, pliant** adj ystwyth, hyblyg

**pliers** npl gefel fechan

**plight** n cyflwr, drych, anghyflwr

**plight** vt addo, gwystlo

**plod** vb troedio, ymlafnio, llafurio, slafio

**plot** n darn o dir; brad, cynllwyn; cynllun, plot, ystofiad ▷ vb cynllwyn; cynllunio

**plotter** n cynllwynwr

**plough** n aradr, gwŷdd ▷ vb aredig, troi

**ploy** n cynllun, strategaeth

**pluck** vt tynnu; pluo ▷ n glewder

**plucky** adj dewr, gwrol, glew

**plug** n topyn, plwg ▷ vt topio, plygio

**plum** n eirinen

**plumage** n plu

**plumber** n plymwr

**plumbing** n gwaith plymwr

**plume** n pluen, plufyn ▷ vt pluo, plufio

**plummet** n plymen

**plump** adj tew, llyfndew, graenus ▷ vb pleidleisio i un (yn unig)

**plunder** n ysbail, anrhaith ▷ vt ysbeilio, anrheithio

**plunge** n plymiad ▷ vb plymio, trochi, bwrw

**pluperfect** adj gorberffaith

**plural** adj lluosog

**plus** n plws, ychwaneg ▷ prep, adj ychwanegol

**plush** n plwsh

**ply** vb arfer, defnyddio, gyrru; poeni

**plywood** n pren haenog (tair-haen, pum-haen)

**pneumatic** adj â'i lond o wynt, awyrog

**pneumonia** n llid yr ysgyfaint, niwmonia

**poach** vb herwhela, potsio

**poach** vt berwi (wy) heb ei blisg

**poacher** n herwheliwr, potsiwr

**pock** n brech, ôl brech

**pocket** n poced, llogell ▷ vt pocedu; **~ knife** cyllell boced; **~ money** arian poced

**pod** n coden, plisgyn, masgl, cibyn

**podgy** adj byrdew

**poem** n cerdd, cân

**poet** n bardd, prydydd

**poetry** n barddoniaeth, prydyddiaeth

**poignant** adj llym, tost, ingol, aethus, awchlym

**point** n pwynt; man; blaen ▷ vb pwyntio; blaenllymu; dangos; **point of view** n safbwynt; **to be on the ~ of doing sth** bod ar fin gwneud rhywbeth; **to get the ~** deall; **there's no ~ (in doing)** does dim diben gwneud; **to ~ out** nodi

**pointed** adj pigfain

**pointedly** adv yn llym

**pointer** n cyfeirydd; mynegfys

**pointless** adj dibwynt, diystyr, gwag

**poise** vb mantoli; hofran ▷ n ystum, osgo

**poison** n gwenwyn ▷ vt gwenwyno

**poisoning** n gwenwyno

**poisonous** adj gwenwynig

**poke** vb gwthio, pwnio, procio
**poker** n pocer
**poky** adj cyfyng, gwael
**polar** adj pegynol
**pole** n pawl, polyn; pegwn
**polemic** adj dadleuol ▷ n dadl
**police** n heddlu; **police car** n car heddlu; **police station** n gorsaf heddlu
**policeman** n heddwas, heddgeidwad, plismon
**policewoman** n heddferch, plismones
**policy** n polisi
**polish** vb cwyro, caboli, gloywi, llathru ▷ n cwyr
**polite** adj moesgar, boneddigaidd
**politic** adj call, cyfrwys, doeth, buddiol
**political** adj gwleidyddol
**politician** n gwleidydd, gwleidyddwr
**politics** n gwleidyddiaeth
**poll** n pen, copa; pôl ▷ vb cneifio; pleidleisio, polio; ~ **tax** treth y pen, treth gymunedol
**pollen** n paill
**polling booth** n bwth pleidleisio
**polling day** n dydd pleidleisio
**polling station** n gorsaf bleidleisio
**pollute** vt halogi, difwyno, llygru
**pollution** n llygredd
**polo neck** n jersi polo
**polygamy** n amlwreigiaeth
**polysyllable** n gair lluosill
**polytechnic** n polytechnig
**pomegranate** n pomgranad
**pomp** n rhwysg
**pompous** adj rhwysgfawr, balch
**pond** n llyn, pwll
**ponder** vb ystyried, myfyrio, pwyso
**ponderous** adj pwysfawr, trwm
**pong** n drewdod
**pontiff** n archoffeiriad; y Pab
**pontoon** n ysgraff
**pony** n merlyn, poni, merlen; ~

**trekking** merlota
**pooh** excl pw!
**pool** n pwll, llyn
**pool** n cronfa; pwll ▷ vt cydgyfrannu
**poor** adj tlawd, truan, gwael, sâl
**poorly** adj sâl, gwael, claf
**pop** vb ffrwydro, ysgortio; picio, plannu, taro
**pope** n pab
**popery** n pabyddiaeth
**pop-gun** n gwn clats
**poplar** n poplysen
**poppy** n pabi (coch), llygad y bwgan
**populace** n gwerin, gwerinos
**popular** adj poblogaidd
**population** n poblogaeth
**populous** adj poblog
**porcelain** n porslen
**porch** n porth, cyntedd
**porcine** adj mochaidd
**porcupine** n ballasg
**pore** n twll chwys
**pore** vi astudio, myfyrio, synfyfyrio
**pork** n cig moch, porc
**porker** n mochyn, porcyn
**porous** adj tyllog
**porpoise** n llamhidydd
**porridge** n uwd
**port** n porth, porthfa, porthladd
**port** n ochr aswy llong wrth edrych ymlaen
**port** n gwin Oporto, gwin coch
**portable** adj cludadwy
**portcullis** n porthcwlis
**portent** n argoel; rhyfeddod, gwyrth
**porter** n porthor
**portfolio** n cas papurau, portffolio; swydd
**porthole** n ffenestr llong; gyndwll
**portion** n rhan, cyfran, gwaddol
**portly** adj tew, corffol
**portrait** n llun, darlun
**portray** vt portreadu, darlunio
**Portugal** n Portiwgal
**pose** vb sefyll, ymddangos, cymryd ar ▷ n ystum, rhodres

**posh** adj hardd, coeth
**position** n safle, sefyllfa, swydd
**positive** adj cadarnhaol, pendant, posidiol
**posse** n mintai, torf
**possess** vt meddu, meddiannu
**possession** n meddiant
**possessor** n perchen, perchennog
**possibility** n posibilrwydd
**possible** adj posibl, dichonadwy
**possibly** adv dichon, efallai
**post** n post, cledr ▷ vt gosod, cyhoeddi
**post** n post, llythyrfa; safle, swydd ▷ vb postio
**post-** prefix wedi, ar ôl
**postage** n cludiad (llythyr, etc.)
**postal** adj post
**postal order** n archeb bost
**postbox** n bocs postio
**postcard** n cerdyn post
**postcode** n côd post
**poster** n hysbyslen, poster
**posterior** adj ar ôl, ôl
**posterity** n cenedlaethau'r dyfodol, hiliogaeth
**postgraduate** adj graddedig
**posthumous** adj ar ôl marw
**postman** n postmon
**postmark** n postfarc
**postmaster** n postfeistr
**post office** n llythyrdy, swyddfa'r post
**postpone** vt gohirio, oedi
**postscript** n ôl-ysgrif
**posture** n agwedd, ystum, osgo
**postwar** adj ar ôl y rhyfel
**posy** n blodeuglwm, pwysi
**pot** n pot, potyn; crochan ▷ vb potio
**potato** (-oes) n taten, pytaten
**potency** n nerth, grym
**potent** adj cryf, galluog, grymus, nerthol
**potential** adj dichonadwy, dichonol ▷ n potensial
**pothole** n ceubwll
**potion** n dogn, llymaid, llwnc

**pottage** n cawl, potes
**potter** n crochenydd
**potter** vb diogi, ymdroi, sefyllian, swmera
**pottery** n llestri pridd; gwaith llestri pridd; priddweithfa
**potty** n pot
**pouch** n cod, coden, cwd ▷ vb cydu
**poultice** n powltis
**poultry** n dofednod, ffowls
**pounce** vb disgyn ar, dyfod ar warthaf
**pound** n pwys; punt
**pound** n ffald ▷ vt ffaldio
**pound** vb pwyo, pwnio, malu, malurio
**pour** vb tywallt, arllwys; bwrw
**pout** vi pwdu, sorri, terru, monni
**poverty** n tlodi
**poverty-stricken** adj tlawd, llwm
**powder** n powdr, llwch, pylor ▷ vt powdro
**powdered milk** n llaeth powdr
**powder room** n ystafell bincio
**power** n gallu, nerth, grym, awdurdod; pŵer
**power cut** n toriad yn y cyflenwad
**power failure** n pall ar y cyflenwad
**powerful** adj nerthol, grymus
**powerless** adj dirym
**power station** n pŵerdy
**pox** n brech
**practicable** adj dichonadwy
**practical** adj ymarferol
**practice** n arfer, arferiad, ymarferiad
**practise** vb arfer, ymarfer
**practising** adj ymarferol; yn dilyn ei swydd
**practitioner** n meddyg; cyfreithiwr
**prairie** n gwastatir, gweundir, paith
**praise** vt canmol, moli ▷ n canmoliaeth, mawl
**pram** n coets, pram
**prance** vi prancio
**prank** n cast, ystranc, pranc

**prawn** n corgimwch
**pray** vb gweddïo; **I ~ thee** atolwg
**prayer** n gweddi
**pre-** prefix cyn-, rhag-, blaen-
**preach** vb pregethu
**preacher** n pregethwr
**preamble** n rhagymadrodd,
  rhaglith
**precarious** adj ansicr, peryglus,
  enbyd
**precaution** n rhagofal,
  rhagocheliad, gofal
**precede** vb blaenori, blaenu,
  rhagflaenu
**precedence** n blaenoriaeth
**precedent** n cynsail
**precentor** n arweinydd y gân,
  codwr canu
**preceptor** n athro, hyfforddwr
**precinct** n cyffin, rhodfa
**precious** adj gwerthfawr, prid, drud
**precipice** n dibyn, diffwys, clogwyn
**precipitate** vt bwrw, hyrddio
  ▷ vi gwaddodi, gwaelodi ▷ adj
  byrbwyll, anystyriol
**précis** n crynodeb
**precise** adj penodol, manwl
**preclude** vt cau allan, atal,
  rhwystro
**precocious** adj hen o'i oed,
  henaidd, henffel
**precondition** n rhagamod
**precursor** n rhagredegydd,
  rhagflaenydd
**predatory** adj anrheithgar,
  ysglyfaethus
**predecessor** n rhagflaenydd
**predestination** n rhagarfaethiad
**predicament** n cyflwr, helynt,
  sefyllfa
**predicate** vt haeru, honni ▷ n
  traethiad
**predict** vt rhagfynegi,
  rhagddywedyd, proffwydo
**predilection** n hoffter, tuedd,
  tueddfryd
**predominate** vi bod yn bennaf neu

yn fwyaf, arglwyddiaethu, rhagori
**pre-eminent** adj ar y blaen i bawb
**preen** vb pincio, harddu
**preface** n rhagymadrodd, rhaglith
**prefect** n rhaglaw; swyddog
**prefer** vt dewis yn hytrach, bod yn
  well gan
**preferable** adj gwell
**preference** n dewis, hoffter,
  ffafraeth, blaenoriaeth
**preferential** adj ffafriol
**preferment** n dyrchafiad, codiad
**prefix** vt rhagddodi ▷ n
  rhagddodiad
**pregnancy** n beichiogaeth
**pregnant** adj beichiog, llawn
**prehistoric** adj cynhanesiol
**prejudice** n rhagfarn; niwed ▷ vt
  rhagfarnu, niweidio
**prejudiced** adj rhagfarnllyd
**prelate** n esgob, prelad
**preliminary** adj arweiniol,
  rhagarweiniol
**prelude** n rhagarweiniad; preliwd
  (cerdd.)
**premarital** adj cyn priodi
**premature** adj anaeddfed,
  cynamserol
**premier** adj blaenaf, pennaf, prif ▷ n
  prifweinidog
**première** n blaenberfformiad
**premise** n rhagosodiad; (pl)
  adeiladau etc ▷ vt rhagosod
**premium** n gwobr, tâl, taliad
**preoccupied** adj wedi ymgolli
**preoccupy** vt rhagfeddiannu;
  llenwi, ymgolli
**prepaid** adj wedi ei dalu ymlaen
  llaw, rhagdalwyd
**preparation** n paratoad,
  darpariaeth
**preparatory** adj rhagbaratoawl
**prepare** vb paratoi, darparu,
  darbod, arlwyo
**prepared** adj parod; effro
**preposition** n arddodiad
**preposterous** adj afresymol,

gwrthun

**prerequisite** n rhaganghenraid

**prerogative** n braint, rhagorfraint

**presage** n argoel, rhagargoel ▷ vt
argoeli

**presbyter** n henuriad, offeiriad

**Presbyterian** adj Henadurol,
Presbyteraidd ▷ n Presbyteriad

**presbytery** n henaduriaeth; tŷ
offeiriad Pabyddol

**prescience** n rhagwybodaeth

**prescribe** vb gorchymyn,
cyfarwyddo

**prescription** n cyngor,
cyfarwyddyd, presgripsiwn

**presence** n gŵydd, presenoldeb

**present** adj, n presennol

**present** n anrheg ▷ vt anrhegu;
cyflwyno; dangos

**presentiment** n rhagargoel

**presently** adv yn fuan

**preserve** vt cadw, diogelu ▷ n jam

**preside** vi llywyddu

**president** n llywydd, arlywydd

**press** vb gwasgu ▷ n gwasg; gwrŷf;
cwpwrdd

**pressing** adj taer, dwys

**pressure** n gwasgiad, gwasgfa,
pwys

**prestige** n bri, dylanwad, braint

**presumable** adj y gellir ei dybio

**presumably** adv yn ôl pob tebyg,
gellid tybio

**presume** vb tybio, tebygu; beiddio,
rhyfygu

**presumption** n rhyfyg; tyb

**presumptuous** adj rhyfygus

**pretence** n rhith, esgus, ffug

**pretend** vb ffugio, cymryd ar, cogio;
proffesu; honni hawl

**pretension** n honiad, hawl

**preter-** prefix tu hwnt i, mwy na

**pretext** n esgus, cochl

**pretty** adj tlws, del, pert ▷ adv
cryn, go

**prevail** vi tycio, ffynnu; gorfod,
trechu

**prevalent** adj cyffredin; nerthol

**prevent** vt rhagflaenu; atal,
rhwystro

**preview** n rhagolwg

**previous** adj blaenorol, cynt

**prey** n ysglyfaeth, aberth ▷ vi
ysglyfaethu

**price** n pris, gwerth ▷ vt prisio;
**price list** n rhestr prisiau, taflen
brisiau; telerau npl

**prick** n pigyn, swmbwl ▷ vb pigo;
picio, codi

**prickle** n draen ▷ vb pigo, tymhigo

**pride** n balchder ▷ vt balchïo,
ymfalchïo

**priest** n offeiriad

**priesthood** n offeiriadaeth

**prig** n sychfoesolyn, mursennwr,
coethyn

**prim** adj cymen, cymhenllyd

**primary** adj prif, cyntaf, cysefin;
cynradd; **primary school** n ysgol
gynradd

**primate** n archesgob

**prime** adj prif, cyntaf; gorau ▷ n
anterth

**prime** vt llwytho, llenwi, cyflenwi

**primer** n llyfr cyntaf, cynlyfr

**primeval** adj cynoesol, cyntefig

**primitive** adj cyntefig; garw,
amrwd

**primordial** adj cyntefig, cysefin

**primrose** n briallen; (pl) briallu

**prince** n tywysog

**principal** adj prif ▷ n pen; prifathro;
corff

**principality** n tywysogaeth

**principle** n egwyddor, elfen

**print** n argraff, print, ôl ▷ vb
argraffu, printio

**printed** adj argraffedig, wedi ei
argraffu

**prior** adj cynt, blaenorol ▷ n prior,
priol

**priority** n blaenoriaeth

**priory** n priordy, mynachdy

**prise, prize** vt dryllio'n agored

â throsol

**prism** n prism

**prison** n carchar, carchardy

**prisoner** n carcharor

**pristine** adj hen, cyntefig, cysefin

**private** adj preifat, cyfrinachol, personol; **private enterprise** n ymroddiad unigol

**privation** n amddifadrwydd, diffyg

**privilege** adj braint, rhagorfraint

**privy** adj dirgel, cudd, cyfrin ▷ n geudy

**prize** n gwobr ▷ vt prisio, gwerthfawrogi

**prize** n ysbail, caffaeliad, gwobr

**pro-** prefix am, yn lle; o blaid

**probability** n tebygolrwydd

**probable** adj tebygol, tebyg

**probate** n prawf ewyllys

**probation** n prawf

**probe** n profiedydd ▷ vt profi, chwilio

**probity** n uniondeb, cywirdeb

**problem** n pwnc, drysbwnc, problem

**procedure** n trefn, arfer, defod, dull

**proceed** vi myned, deillio, tarddu; erlyn ▷ n (pl) enillion, elw

**process** n gweithrediad, goruchwyliaeth, dull

**procession** n gorymdaith; deilliad

**proclaim** vt cyhoeddi, datgan

**proclamation** n cyhoeddiad, proclamasiwn

**proclivity** n gogwydd, tuedd

**proconsul** n rhaglaw

**procrastinate** vi oedi, gohirio

**procreate** vt cenhedlu

**procure** vb ceisio, caffael, cael

**prod** vt procio, pwnio, symbylu

**prodigal** adj afradlon, hael

**prodigious** adj aruthrol, anferth

**prodigy** n rhyfeddod, gwyrth

**produce** vt cynhyrchu, epilio; dwyn ▷ n cynnyrch, ffrwyth

**product** n cynnyrch, ffrwyth

**production** n cynhyrchiad; (pl) cynhyrchion

**profane** adj anghysegredig, halogedig ▷ vt anghysegru, halogi

**profess** vb proffesu, arddel

**profession** n proffes, galwedigaeth

**professional** adj proffesiynol

**professor** n proffeswr; athro

**proffer** vt, n cynnig

**proficient** adj hyddysg, cyfarwydd

**profile** n ystlyslun, cernlun

**profit** n budd, lles, elw, proffid ▷ vb llesáu, proffidio

**profiteer** vi gwneud elw

**profligate** adj afradlon, ofer

**profound** adj dwfn, dwys, angerddol

**profundity** n dyfnder

**profuse** adj hael, helaeth, toreithiog

**progenitor** n cyndad

**progeny** n hil, epil, hiliogaeth

**prognostic** n argoel, rhagarwydd

**programme** n rhaglen

**progress** n cynnydd; taith ▷ vi cynyddu

**progressive** adj cynyddgar, progresif

**prohibit** vt gwahardd

**project** n bwriad, cynllun; project

**project** vb bwrw; bwriadu; ymestyn; taflunio (ffilm)

**projectile** n teflyn

**projector** n taflunydd

**proletariat** n gwerin, gwrêng

**prolific** adj epiliog, ffrwythlon, toreithiog

**prolix** adj maith, amleiriog

**prologue** n rhagair, prolog

**prolong** vt hwyhau, estyn

**promenade** n rhodfa ▷ vb rhodianna

**prominent** adj yn sefyll allan, amlwg

**promise** n addewid ▷ vb addo, argoeli

**promissory** adj addewidiol

**promontory** n pentir, penrhyn

**promote** vt hyrwyddo, meithrin, dyrchafu
**promoter** n hyrwyddwr
**prompt** adj parod, buan ▷ vt cofweini; cymell
**promptitude** n parodrwydd
**promulgate** vt cyhoeddi, lledaenu
**prone** adj â'i wyneb i waered; tueddol
**prong** n fforch, pig fforch
**pronominal** adj rhagenwol
**pronoun** n rhagenw
**pronounce** vb cynanu, yngan; cyhoeddi, datgan
**pronunciation** n cynaniad
**proof** n prawf; proflen
**prop** n ateg, post, prop ▷ vt ategu
**propaganda** n propaganda
**propagate** vt epilio, cenhedlu; lledaenu
**propel** vt gyrru ymlaen, gwthio
**propensity** n tuedd, tueddfryd, gogwydd
**proper** adj priod, priodol, gweddus
**property** n priodoledd; eiddo; priodwedd (cemeg)
**prophecy** n proffwydoliaeth
**prophesy** vb proffwydo
**prophet** n proffwyd
**propinquity** n agosrwydd, cyfnesafrwydd
**propitiate** vt cymodi, dyhuddo
**propitiation** n cymod, iawn
**propitious** adj tirion, ffafriol
**proportion** n cyfartaledd, cyfrannedd
**proportional** adj cyfrannol
**proportionate** adj cymesur
**proposal** n cynnig
**propose** vb cynnig, bwriadu
**proposition** n cynigiad; gosodiad
**propound** vt cynnig, gosod gerbron
**proprietor** n perchen, perchennog
**propriety** n priodoldeb, gwedduster
**propulsion** n gwthiad, gyriad

**prorogue** vt gohirio
**prosaic** adj rhyddieithol, cyffredin
**proscribe** vt deol, diarddel, gwahardd
**prose** n rhyddiaith
**prosecute** vt erlyn, dilyn, dwyn ymlaen
**prosecutor** n erlynydd
**proselyte** n proselyt
**prosody** n mydryddiaeth
**prospect** n rhagolwg, golwg, golygfa
**prospectus** n rhaglen, hysbyslen, prosbectws
**prosper** vb llwyddo, tycio, ffynnu
**prosperity** n llwyddiant, hawddfyd, ffyniant
**prostitute** n putain ▷ vt darostwng
**prostrate** adj yn gorwedd ar ei wyneb; ar lawr yn lân ▷ vt bwrw i lawr; ymgrymu
**protect** vt amddiffyn, noddi
**protection** n amddiffyn, nawdd, diogelwch
**protective** adj amddiffynnol
**protector** n amddiffynnydd
**protest** vb gwrthdystio ▷ n gwrthdystiad
**prototype** n cynddelw, cynllun
**protract** vt estyn, hwyhau
**protrude** vb gwthio allan
**protuberance** n chwydd
**proud** adj balch
**prove** vb profi
**provender** n ebran, gogor, porthiant
**proverb** n dihareb
**provide** vt darparu
**providence** n rhagluniaeth, darbodaeth
**provident** adj darbodus
**providential** adj rhagluniaethol
**province** n talaith, tiriogaeth; cylch, maes
**provision** n darpariaeth; **provisions** npl darbodion; ymborth

proviso n amod
provocation n anogaeth, cyffroad, cythrudd
provoke vt annog, cyffroi, cythruddo, profocio
provost n maer, profost
prow n pen blaen bad neu long
prowess n dewrder, glewder, grymuster
prowl vi ysglyfaetha, prowlan
proximate adj nesaf, agos at; agos
proximity n agosrwydd
proxy n dirprwy
prude n mursen, coegen
prudence n pwyll, synnwyr, callineb
prudent adj pwyllog, synhwyrol, call, doeth
prune n eirinen sech
Prussia n Prwsia
pry vi chwilota, chwilenna
psalm n salm
psalmody n caniadaeth y cysegr, salmyddiaeth
psalter n llyfr salmau, sallwyr
pseudo- prefix gau, ffug
pseudonym n ffugenw
pshaw excl wfft, pw, och, ffei
psychiatrist n seiciatrydd
psychological adj seicolegol, meddyliol
psychology n seicoleg
puberty n aeddfedrwydd oed, blaenlencyndod, puberdod
public adj cyhoeddus ▷ n y cyhoedd; public house n tŷ tafarn; public library n llyfrgell gyhoeddus
publican n publican; tafarnwr
publicity n cyhoeddusrwydd
publish vt cyhoeddi
pucker vb crychu, crybachu
pudding n pwdin
puddle n corbwll; pydew, llaca
puerile adj bachgennaidd, plentynnaidd
puff n pwff, chwa, chwyth ▷ vb pwffio, chwythu

pugilist n paffiwr, ymladdwr
pugnacious adj ymladdgar, cwerylgar
puissant adj galluog, grymus, nerthol
pull vt tynnu ▷ n tynfa, tyniad
pullet n cywen
pulley n chwerfan, troell, pwli
pullover n gwasgod wlân
pulmonary adj ysgyfeiniol
pulp n bywyn, mwydion
pulpit n pulpud
pulsate vb curo (megis y galon)
pulse n curiad y galon, curiad y gwaed
pulse n pys, ffa etc
pulverize vt malu yn llwch, chwilfriwio
pummel vt pwnio, dyrnodio, curo
pump n sugnedydd, pwmp ▷ vb pwmpio
pumpkin n pwmpen
pun n gair mwys, mwysair
punch n pwns; dyrnod ▷ vb pwnsio, dyrnodio
punctilious adj cysetlyd, gorfanwl
punctual adj prydlon
punctuate vt atalnodi
puncture n twll ▷ vt tyllu
pundit n ysgolhaig, doethwr
pungent adj llym, llymdost, siarp
punish vt cosbi, ceryddu; poeni
punishment n cosb, cosbedigaeth
punitive adj cosbol
puny adj eiddil, bychan, tila, pitw
pupil n ysgolhaig, ysgolor, disgybl; cannwyll llygad
puppet n delw, dol, pyped; gwas
puppy n ci bach
purblind adj cibddall, coegddall
purchase vt prynu, pwrcasu ▷ n pryniant, pwrcas
pure adj pur, noeth
purgative adj carthol ▷ n carthlyn
purgatory n purdan
purge vt puro, glanhau, carthu, coethi ▷ n carthlyn

**purification** n puredigaeth
**purify** vt puro, coethi, glanhau
**Puritan** n Piwritan
**purity** n purdeb
**purl** vi crychleisio, byrlymu
**purlieu** n cyffin, ffin, cymdogaeth
**purloin** vt lladrata, dwyn
**purple** adj, n porffor
**purport** n ystyr, rhediad, ergyd ▷ vt arwyddo, proffesu, honni
**purpose** n pwrpas, bwriad, arfaeth ▷ vt bwriadu, arfaethu
**purr** vb canu crwth, grwnan
**purse** n pwrs, cod ▷ vb crychu
**pursue** vb dilyn, erlyn, erlid, ymlid
**pursuit** n ymlidiad; ymchwil, gorchwyl
**purulent** adj crawnllyd, gorllyd
**purvey** vb darparu lluniaeth, darmerth
**purview** n amcan, maes, cylch
**pus** n crawn, gôr
**push** vb gwthio ▷ n gwth, ysgŵd; ymdrech
**pushchair** n coets
**puss** n titw, pws; ysgyfarnog
**pustule** n ploryn, llinoryn
**put** vb gosod, dodi, rhoddi, rhoi
**putative** adj tybiedig, cyfrifedig
**putrefaction** n pydredd, madredd
**putrefy** vb pydru, madru
**putrid** adj pwdr, mall
**putty** n pwti ▷ vt pwti̇o
**puzzle** n dryswch, penbleth, pos ▷ vb drysu, pyslo
**pygmy** n corrach
**pyjamas** npl gwisg nos, gŵn nos
**pyramid** n pyramid, bera
**pyre** n cynnau angladdol, coelcerth
**pyrotechnic** adj, n (o natur) tân gwyllt

# q

**quack** n crachfeddyg, cwac
**quack** vi cwacian
**quadrangle** n pedrongl
**quadrant** n cwadrant
**quadruped** n pedwarcarnol
**quadruple** adj pedwarplyg
**quadruplet** n pedrybled
**quaff** vb drachtio, cofftio, yfed
**quagmire** n siglen, cors, mignen, sybwll
**quail** n sofliar
**quaint** adj od, henffasiwn
**quake** vi crynu
**Quaker** n Crynwr
**qualification** n cymhwyster; cymhwysiad
**qualified** adj cymwys
**qualify** vt cymhwyso, cyfaddasu
**quality** n ansawdd, rhinwedd
**qualm** n petruster, amheuaeth
**quandary** n penbleth, cyfyng-gyngor
**quantity** n swm, maint, mesur
**quarantine** n cwarant, neilltuaeth
**quarrel** n ymrafael, ffrae, cweryl ▷ vi ffraeo
**quarry** n chwarel, cloddfa, cwar ▷ vb cloddio
**quarry** n ysglyfaeth
**quart** n chwart, cwart
**quarter** n chwarter, cwarter; cwr, man; trugaredd; (pl) llety; **a ~ of an hour** chwarter awr; **~ final** rownd gogynderfynol; **quarter-sessions** n llys chwarter

quartet, -te n pedwarawd
quarto adj, n (llyfr) pedwarplyg
quartz n creigrisial, cwarts
quash vt diddymu, dirymu
quaver vi cwafrio, crynu ▷ n cwafer
quay n cei
queen n brenhines
queer adj od, hynod, digrif, ysmala
quell vt llonyddu, gostegu, darostwng
quench vt diffodd, dofi, torri
quern n llawfelin, breuan
querulous adj cwynfanllyd, blin
query n holiad, gofyniad ▷ vb holi, amau
quest n ymchwil, ymchwiliad, cwest
question n gofyniad, cwestiwn ▷ vt holi, amau
questionable adj amheus
question mark n gofynnod
questionnaire n holiadur
queue n cynffon, cwt, ciw
quibble n geirddadl, mân-ddadl ▷ vi geirddadlau, mân-ddadlau, hollti blew
quick adj byw; buan, cyflym, clau; to the ~ i'r byw
quicken vb cyflymu
quicksilver n arian byw
quid n punt
quiescent adj distaw, llonydd, digyffro
quiet adj llonydd, tawel, distaw ▷ n llonyddwch, tawelwch ▷ vt llonyddu, tawelu
quill n pluen, plufyn, cwilsyn
quilt n cwilt, cwrlid ▷ vt cwiltio
quintet n pumawd
quintuplet n pumled
quip n gair ffraeth, ateb parod
quit vt gadael, symud ▷ adj rhydd
quits adj yn gyfartal
quite adv cwbl, llwyr, hollol
quiver n cawell saethau
quiver vi crynu, dirgrynu
quixotic adj mympwyol, gwyllt

quiz vt holi, pyslo, profocio
quoit n coeten, coetan
quondam adj wedi bod, gynt, hen
quorum n nifer gofynnol, corwm
quota n rhan, cyfran, dogn, cwota
quotation n dyfyniad; prisiant
quote vt dyfynnu; nodi (prisiau)
quoth vt meddai, ebe

r

rabbi n rabi
rabbit n cwningen
rabble n ciwed, tyrfa ddireol
rabid adj cynddeiriog
rabies n y gynddaredd
race n ras, gyrfa, rhedfa ▷ vi rasio
race n hil
racial adj hiliol
racism n hiliaeth
rack n rac, clwyd, rhestl; arteithglwyd ▷ vt arteithio, dirdynnu
racket n twrf, mwstwr; (Tennis etc) raced
racy adj blasus; arab, ffraeth
radiant adj disglair, llachar, tanbaid
radiate vb pelydru, rheiddio
radiation n ymbelydredd
radiator n rheiddiadur
radical adj gwreiddiol, cynhenid; trylwyr ▷ n rhyddfrydwr, radical
radio n radio

**radioactive** adj ymbelydrol
**radio station** n gorsaf radio
**radish** n rhuddygl, radis
**radius** (-ii) n cylch; radius
**raffle** n raffl
**raft** n cludair, ysgraff, rafft
**rafter** n tulath, ceibren, trawst
**rag** n carp, clwt
**rag doll** n doli glwt
**rage** n cynddaredd ▷ vi terfysgu, cynddeiriogi
**ragged** adj carpiog, bratiog
**raid** n rhuthr, cyrch ▷ vb anrheithio, ysbeilio
**rail** n canllaw, cledren, rheilen ▷ vb cledru
**rail** vi difrïo, difenwi, cablu
**raillery** n difyrrwch, cellwair
**railway** n rheilffordd; **railway station** n gorsaf reilffordd
**raiment** n dillad, gwisg
**rain** n glaw ▷ vb glawio, bwrw glaw
**rainbow** n enfys
**raincoat** n cot law
**rainy** adj glawog
**raise** vt codi, cyfodi, dyrchafu
**raisin** n rhesinen
**rake** n cribin, rhaca ▷ vb cribinio, crafu, rhacanu
**rally** vb atgynnull; adgyfnerthu, gwella ▷ n cynulliad
**ram** n hwrdd, maharen ▷ vt hyrddio, pwnio
**ramble** vi gwibio, crwydro ▷ n gwib
**rampant** adj uchel ei ben, rhonc
**rampart** n caer, rhagfur, gwrthglawdd
**ramshackle** adj bregus, candryll
**rancid** adj â blas cryf arno, drewllyd
**rancour** n digasedd, chwerwder
**random** n antur, siawns, damwain ▷ adj damweiniol
**range** n amrediad; cwmpas; ystod; lle tân â ffwrn ▷ vb rhestru, cyfleu; crwydro
**ranger** n coedwigwr, ceidwad parc
**rank** n rheng, gradd ▷ vb rhestru;

**the ~ and file** y bobl gyffredin
**rank** adj mws; gwyllt, bras; rhonc, noeth
**rankle** vi gori, madru; cnoi, llidio
**ransack** vt chwilio, chwilota, ysbeilio
**ransom** n pridwerth ▷ vt prynu, gwaredu
**rant** vi bragaldian, brygawthan
**rap** n cnoc, ergyd ▷ vt cnocio, curo
**rap** n gronyn, mymryn, blewyn
**rapacious** adj rheibus, ysglyfaethus
**rape** vt treisio ▷ n trais
**rapid** adj cyflym, buan, chwyrn, gwyllt
**rapist** n treisiwr
**rapture** n perlewyg, gorawen, afiaith
**rare** adj anaml, prin; godidog; tenau
**rascal** n dihiryn, cnaf, gwalch, cenau
**rash** adj byrbwyll, rhyfygus, anystyriol
**rash** n brech, tarddiant
**rasher** n ysglisen, sleisen, tafell, golwyth
**rasp** vb rhasglio, crafu, rhygnu
**raspberry** n afanen, mafonen
**rat** n llygoden fawr, llygoden ffrengig ▷ vi llygota
**rate** vt ffraeo, dwrdio, dweud y drefn
**rate** n cyflymder; treth; cyfradd (of interest)
**rateable value** n gwerth trethiannol
**ratepayer** n trethdalwr
**rather** adv braidd, hytrach, go, lled
**ratify** vt cadarnhau
**ratio** n cyfartaledd; cymhareb
**ration** n dogn, saig ▷ vt dogni
**rational** adj rhesymol
**rationale** n rhesymwaith
**rationalization** n rhesymoliad
**rationalize** vb rhesymoli
**rattle** vb rhuglo, trystio ▷ n rhugl, rhwnc

**raucous** adj cryg, garw, aflafar

**ravage** vt anrheithio, diffeithio, difrodi

**rave** vi gwallgofi, ynfydu, gwynfydu

**ravel** vb drysu; dad-weu, datod

**raven** n cigfran

**ravenous** adj rheibus, gwancus

**ravine** n hafn, ceunant

**raving** adj ynfyd, dwl, gwallgof

**ravish** vt treisio, cipio; swyno, hudo

**ravishing** adj deniadol iawn

**raw** adj amrwd; crai, cri; noeth, dolurus, garw; dibrofiad ▷ n cig noeth, dolur

**ray** n paladr, pelydryn

**ray** n cath fôr

**raze** vt llwyr ddymchwelyd, dileu

**razor** n ellyn, rasal ▷ vt eillio; **razor blade** n llafn ellyn

**re** prep ym mater, mewn perthynas â

**re-** prefix ad-, ail-

**reach** vb cyrraedd, estyn ▷ n cyrraedd

**react** vi adweithio

**reaction** n adwaith

**reactionary** adj adweithiol

**reactor** n adweithydd

**read** vb darllen

**readable** adj darllenadwy

**reader** n darllenydd

**readily** adv yn barod, yn ddiffwdan

**reading** n darllen

**readjustment** n atgywiriad, addasiad

**ready** adj parod, rhwydd

**reafforestation** n ailfforestiad

**real** adj gwir, real, go-iawn

**reality** n gwirionedd, sylwedd; dirwedd, realiti

**realize** vt sylweddoli; troi yn arian

**really** adv gwir, hollol, mewn difrif

**realm** n teyrnas, gwlad, bro

**reap** vb medi

**reappear** vb ailymddangos

**rear** n cefn, pen ôl, ôl

**rear** vb codi, magu; codi ar ei draed ôl

**reason** n rheswm ▷ vb rhesymu

**reasonable** adj rhesymol

**reassurance** n calondid

**reassure** vt calonogi, cysuro

**rebate** n ad-daliad

**rebel** vi gwrthryfela ▷ n gwrthryfelwr

**rebellion** n gwrthryfel

**rebound** vi adlamu ▷ n adlam

**rebuff** n nacâd, sen ▷ vt nacáu, sennu

**rebuke** vt ceryddu ▷ n cerydd, sen

**rebut** vt gwrthbrofi, gwrthddywedyd

**recall** vt galw yn ôl; galw i gof, cofio

**recant** vb datgyffesu

**recapitulate** vt ailadrodd (yn gryno)

**recede** vi encilio, cilio yn ôl

**receipt** n derbyniad; derbynneb

**receive** vt derbyn

**receiver** n derbynnydd

**recent** adj diweddar

**receptacle** n llestr; cynheiliad (llysieueg)

**reception** n derbyniad, croeso; **reception desk** n man croeso, man derbyn

**receptionist** n croesawferch, croesawydd

**recess** n cil, encil; cilfach; gwyliau

**recessional** adj, n (emyn) ymadawol

**recipe** n cyfarwyddyd; rysáit

**recipient** n derbyniwr, derbynnydd

**reciprocal** adj cilyddol

**reciprocate** vb talu'n ôl, cydgyfnewid; cilyddu

**recital** n adroddiad, datganiad

**recitation** n adroddiad

**recite** vb adrodd

**reck** vb gofalu, ystyried

**reckless** adj anystyriol, rhyfygus, dibris

**reckon** vb cyfrif, barnu, bwrw

**reclaim** vt adennill, diwygio

**recline** vb lledorwedd, gorwedd,

gorffwys

**recluse** n meudwy, ancr
**recognition** n adnabyddiaeth,
  cydnabyddiaeth
**recognize** vt adnabod, cydnabod
**recoil** vi adlamu, gwrthneidio, cilio
**recollect** vt galw i gof, atgofio,
  cofio
**recommend** vt cymeradwyo,
  argymell
**recompense** vt ad-dalu,
  gwobrwyo, talu
**reconcile** vt cymodi, cysoni
**recondite** adj dwfn, cudd, cêl,
  tywyll
**recondition** vt atgyflyru, ail-
  wneud
**reconnaissance** n rhagchwiliad
**reconnoitre** vt chwilio, archwilio
**record** vt cofnodi, recordio ▷ n
  cofnod, record
**recorder** n (Law) cofiadur; (Mus)
  recordydd
**recording** n recordiad
**recount** vt adrodd
**re-count** vb ailgyfrif
**recoup** vb digolledu
**recourse** n cyrchfa; **to have ~ to**
  mynd at, defnyddio
**recover** vb cael yn ôl, adennill;
  ymadfer; adferiad
**recreation** n difyrrwch, adloniant
**recruit** n recriwt; newyddian ▷ vt
  codi gwŷr; adennill
**rectangle** n petryal
**rectangular** adj petryalog
**rectify** vt unioni, cywiro; puro,
  coethi
**rectilinear** adj unionlin
**rector** n rheithor
**rectory** n rheithoriaeth; rheithordy
**recuperate** vb adfer, ymadfer,
  cryfhau, gwella
**recur** vi ailddigwydd, dychwelyd
**recurrence** n ail-ddigwyddiad,
  ail-ymddangosiad
**recurring** adj cylchol

**recusant** n anghydffurfiwr
**red** adj, n coch, rhudd
**redeem** vt prynu (yn ôl), gwaredu
**redemption** n prynedigaeth
**redeploy** vb adleoli
**redeployment** n adleoliad,
  trawsgyflogaeth
**red herring** n (met) ysgyfarnog
**redirect** vb ailgyfeirio
**redo** vb ail-wneud
**redolent** adj yn sawru o
**redoubtable** adj i'w ofni; pybyr
**redress** vt unioni ▷ n iawn (am
  gam)
**Red Sea: the ~** y Môr Coch
**reduce** vt lleihau, gostwng;
  rhydwytho
**reduced** adj gostyngol
**reduction** n lleihad, gostyngiad
**redundancy** n anghyflogaeth
**redundant** adj gormodol;
  anghyflog, digyflog
**reed** n cawnen, corsen, calaf; pibell
**reef** n plyg hwyl, rîff ▷ vt plygu hwyl
**reef** n creigle (yn y môr), creigfa, rîff
**reek** n mwg, tarth, drewdod ▷ vb
  mygu, drewi
**reel** n ril ▷ vb dirwyn
**reel** vi troi, chwyldroi ▷ n dawns
**refectory** n ffreutur
**refer** vb cyfeirio, cyfarwyddo
**reference** n cyfeiriad; geirda
**refill** n adlenwad ▷ vt adlenwi
**refine** vb puro, coethi
**reflect** vb adlewyrchu; myfyrio
**reflection** n adlewyrchiad,
  myfyrdod, ailfeddwl
**reflex** n adweithred, atgyrch
**reflexive** adj atblygol
**reform** vb diwygio, gwella ▷ n
  diwygiad
**reformation** n diwygiad
**reformatory** n ysgol ddiwygio
**refrain** vb ymatal
**refrain** n byrdwn
**refresh** vt adfywio, dadebru,
  adlonni

**refresher course** n cwrs adolygu
**refreshing** adj adfywiol
**refreshments** npl ymborth, lluniaeth
**refrigerate** vt rheweiddio, cadw'n oer
**refrigerator** n rhewgell, oergell
**refuge** n noddfa, lloches
**refugee** n ffoadur
**refund** n ad-daliad ▷ vb ad-dalu
**refurbish** vb adnewyddu
**refusal** n gwrthodiad, nacâd
**refuse** vb gwrthod
**refuse** n ysbwriel, gwehilion, sothach
**refute** vt gwrthbrofi, datbrofi
**regal** adj brenhinol
**regard** vt edrych ar, ystyried ▷ n sylw, parch, hoffter
**regarding** prep ynglŷn â, ynghylch
**regardless** adj heb ofal, diofal
**regenerate** vt aileni
**régime** n trefn, cyfundrefn
**regiment** n catrawd
**region** n ardal, bro, gwlad
**regional** adj rhanbarthol
**register** n cofrestr ▷ vt cofrestru
**registered** adj cofrestredig
**registrar** n cofrestrydd
**registration** n cofrestriad; **registration number** n rhif cofrestru, rhif trethiant
**registry** n cofrestrfa
**regret** vt gofidio, edifaru ▷ n gofid
**regular** adj rheolaidd, cyson
**regulate** vt rheoleiddio, llywio, rheoli
**regulation** n rheol, trefniant
**rehabilitate** vt adfer i fri neu fraint, ailsefydlu
**rehabilitation** n adferiad
**rehearsal** n rihyrsal, practis
**rehearse** vt adrodd; ymarfer ymlaen llaw
**reign** vi teyrnasu ▷ n teyrnasiad
**reimburse** vt talu yn ôl, ad-dalu
**rein** n afwyn, awen ▷ vt ffrwyno

**reindeer** n carw
**reinforce** vt atgyfnerthu
**reinstate** vt adfer i safle neu fraint
**reiterate** vt ailadrodd, mynychu
**reject** vt gwrthod, bwrw ymaith
**rejection** n gwrthodiad
**rejoice** vb llawenhau, gorfoleddu
**rejoin** vb ateb, gwrthateb
**rejoinder** n ateb, gwrthateb
**rejuvenate** vb adfywiogi, adnewyddu
**relapse** vi ailglafychu, ailymhoelyd, atglafychu
**relate** vb adrodd, mynegi; perthyn
**related** adj yn perthyn; wedi ei ddweud
**relating to** prep yn ymwneud â
**relation** n adroddiad; perthynas
**relationship** n perthynas
**relative** adj perthnasol ▷ n perthynas; **~ pronoun** rhagenw perthynol
**relax** vb llacio, llaesu, ymollwng
**relaxing** adj ymlaciol
**relay** n cyflenwad newydd, cyfnewid; darlledu ▷ vb ailosod; **relay race** n ras gyfnewid
**release** vt rhyddhau, gollwng ▷ n rhyddhad
**relegate** vt alltudio, deol, darostwng
**relent** vi tyneru, tirioni, llaesu
**relevant** adj perthnasol
**reliable** adj y gellir dibynnu arno, dibynadwy
**reliance** n ymddiried, dibyniaeth, hyder, pwys
**relic** n crair; (pl) gweddillion
**relief** n cynhorthwy; gollyngdod, ymwared; tirwedd
**relieve** vt cynorthwyo; esmwytho, ysgafnhau; rhyddhau, gollwng
**religion** n crefydd
**religious** adj crefyddol
**relinquish** vt gollwng, gildio, gwadu
**relish** n blas; enllyn, mwyniant ▷ vb

blasio, hoffi
**reluctance** n amharodrwydd,
anfodlonrwydd
**reluctant** adj anfodlon,
anewyllysgar
**rely** vi hyderu, ymddiried, dibynnu
**remain** vi aros, parhau, gorffwys
**remainder** n gweddill, rhelyw
**remains** npl olion, gweddillion
**remand** vt aildraddodi; **remand
home** n cartref i droseddwyr ifanc
**remark** vb sylwi ▷ n sylw
**remarkable** adj nodedig, hynod,
rhyfedd, syn
**remedial** n adferol;
meddyginiaethol
**remedy** n meddyginiaeth ▷ vt
meddyginiaethu, gwella
**remember** vt cofio
**remembrance** n cof, coffa,
coffadwriaeth
**remind** vt atgofio, atgoffa, cofio
**reminiscence** n atgof
**remiss** adj esgeulus, diofal, llac
**remission** n maddeuant
**remit** vb maddau; arafu, peidio;
anfon
**remittance** n taliad
**remnant** n gweddill, gwarged
**remonstrance** n cwyn,
gwrthdystiad
**remonstrate** vi ymliw,
gwrthdystio
**remorse** n edifeirwch, gofid, atgno
**remote** adj pell, pellennig,
anghysbell
**remotely** adv o bell
**removable** adj symudadwy, y gellir
ei symud
**removal** n symudiad, diswyddiad
**remove** vb symud, dileu; mudo
**remunerate** vt talu, gwobrwyo
**renaissance** n dadeni
**rend** vb rhwygo, dryllio, llarpio
**render** vt talu; datgan; gwneud;
troi, cyfieithu
**rendezvous** n cyrchfa, man

cyfarfod
**renegade** n gwrthgiliwr
**renew** vt adnewyddu
**renounce** vt ymwrthod, ymwadu,
gwadu
**renovate** vt adnewyddu
**renown** n clod, bri, enwogrwydd
**rent** n rhwyg
**rent** n ardreth, rhent ▷ vt ardrethu,
rhentu
**rental** n rent
**repair** vi cyrchu, mynd
**repair** vi atgyweirio, trwsio ▷ n
cywair
**reparation** n iawn, ad-daliad
**repartee** n ateb parod
**repatriate** vb adfer i'w wlad ei hun
**repeal** vt diddymu ▷ n diddymiad
**repeat** vb ailadrodd, ailgyflawni
**repel** vt bwrw yn ôl
**repent** vb edifarhau, edifaru
**repentance** n edifeirwch
**repetition** n ailadroddiad
**repetitive** adj ailadroddus
**replace** vt ailosod, dodi'n ôl;
cymryd lle (arall)
**replacement** n un sy'n cymryd
lle arall
**replay** vb ailchwarae
**replenish** vt ail-lenwi, diwallu
**replete** adj llawn, cyflawn, gorlawn
**replica** n copi cywir, cyflun
**reply** vi ateb ▷ n ateb, atebiad
**report** vt adrodd, hysbysu ▷ n
adroddiad; sŵn ergyd
**reporter** n gohebydd
**repose** vb gorffwys ▷ n gorffwys
**repository** n ystorfa, trysorfa
**reprehend** vt ceryddu, argyhoeddi
**represent** vt portreadu; cynrychioli
**representative** adj yn cynrychioli
▷ n cynrychiolydd
**repress** vt atal, gostegu, llethu
**repression** n ataliad,
darostyngiad, gwrthodiad
**reprimand** n cerydd ▷ vt ceryddu
**reprisal** n dial

**reproach** vt ceryddu, gwaradwyddo, edliw ▷ n gwaradwydd

**reproduce** vt atgynhyrchu, epilio

**reproduction** n atgynhyrchiad, copi; epiliad

**reproof** n cerydd

**reprove** vt ceryddu, argyhoeddi

**reptile** n ymlusgiad

**republic** n gweriniaeth, gwerinlywodraeth

**repudiate** vt diarddel, diarddelwi, gwadu

**repugnant** adj croes, atgas, gwrthun

**repulse** vt bwrw'n ôl; nacáu ▷ n gwrthergyd

**repulsion** n gwrthnysedd

**repulsive** adj atgas, ffiaidd

**reputable** adj parchus, cyfrifol

**reputation** n gair, cymeriad, enw da

**repute** vt cyfrif, tybied ▷ n parch, bri

**request** n cais ▷ vt ceisio, gofyn

**requiem** n offeren dros y meirw; galargerdd

**require** vt gofyn, mynnu

**requisite** adj gofynnol, angenrheidiol

**requisition** n archeb ▷ vb hawlio

**requite** vt talu, gwobrwyo, talu'r pwyth

**rescind** vt diddymu, dirymu

**rescue** vt achub ▷ n achubiad

**research** n ymchwil, ymchwiliad ▷ vb ymchwilio

**resemblance** n tebygrwydd

**resemble** vt tebygu i

**resent** vt tramgwyddo, digio, cymryd yn chwith

**resentful** adj digofus, llidiog

**resentment** n dig, dicter

**reservation** n cadw, cadfa

**reserve** vt cadw yn ôl, cadw wrth gefn ▷ n yr hyn a gedwir, cronfa; swildod

**reserved** adj swil; wedi ei gadw; ~ **seat** sedd gadw

**reservoir** n cronfa, llyn

**reshuffle** vb aildrefnu

**reside** vi preswylio

**residential** adj preswyl

**residue** n gweddill

**resign** vb rhoi i fyny, ymddiswyddo, ymddeol

**resignation** n ymddiswyddiad; ymostyngiad

**resilience** n hydwythder, ystwythder

**resilient** adj hydwyth, ystwyth

**resin** n ystor, rhwsin

**resist** vb gwrthsefyll, gwrthwynebu

**resistance** n gwrthwynebiad, gwrthsafiad

**resolute** adj penderfynol

**resolution** n penderfyniad

**resolve** vb penderfynu ▷ n penderfyniad

**resonant** adj atseiniol

**resort** vi cyrchu ▷ n cyrchfa; ymwared

**resound** vb atseinio, diasbedain

**resource** n sgil, dyfais; (pl) adnoddau

**respect** vt parch ▷ n golwg; parch

**respectable** adj parchus

**respectful** adj boneddigaidd, yn dangos parch

**respective** adj priodol, ar wahân

**respite** n oediad, saib, seibiant, hamdden

**resplendent** adj disglair, ysblennydd

**respond** vi ateb, ymateb; porthi

**response** n ateb, atebiad

**responsibility** n cyfrifoldeb

**responsible** adj atebol, cyfrifol

**responsive** adj ymatebol

**rest** n, vb gorffwys ▷ n (Music) tawnod

**rest** vi aros, parhau ▷ n gweddill

**restaurant** n tŷ bwyta, bwyty

**restful** adj tawel, llonydd, esmwyth

**restitution** n adferiad; iawn
**restive** adj ystyfnig, ystranclyd, noglyd, diamynedd
**restless** adj aflonydd, rhwyfus
**restore** vt adfer; atgyweirio
**restrain** vt atal, ffrwyno
**restrained** adj cynnil, gochelgar, cymhedrol
**restraint** n atalfa, ffrwyn, caethiwed
**restrict** vt cyfyngu, caethiwo
**restriction** n cyfyngiad
**result** vi deillio, canlyn ▷ n canlyniad
**resume** vt ailddechrau
**résumé** n crynodeb
**resumption** n ailddechreuad
**resurgent** adj yn ailgodi, yn ailfyw
**resurrection** n atgyfodiad
**resuscitate** vb adfywhau, dadebru
**retail** vt manwerthu, adwerthu ▷ n adwerth
**retailer** n mân-werthwr
**retain** vb cadw, dal; llogi
**retaliate** vb talu'n ôl, talu'r pwyth, dial
**retaliation** n dial
**retard** vb rhwystro, oedi
**retch** vi cyfogi, chwydu
**retentive** adj yn dal heb ollwng; gafaelgar
**reticent** adj tawedog, distaw
**retina** n rhwyden y llygad, retina
**retinue** n gosgordd, gosgorddlu
**retire** vi ymneilltuo, encilio, cilio, ymddeol
**retired** adj wedi ymddeol
**retirement** n ymddeoliad
**retiring** adj swil
**retort** vb gwrthateb ▷ n ateb parod; ritort (cemeg)
**retrace** vb mynd yn ôl dros yr un ffordd, dychwelyd
**retract** vb tynnu'n ôl
**retrain** vb ailhyfforddi
**retreat** vi cilio, encilio, ffoi ▷ n encil, ffo

**retrench** vb cwtogi, cynilo
**retribution** n ad-daledigaeth, cosb, dial
**retrieve** vt olrhain; adennill, adfer
**retrogress** vi mynd yn ôl, dirywio
**retrospect** n ad-drem, adolwg
**return** vb dychwelyd ▷ n dychweliad; elw, enillion; **return (ticket)** n tocyn dwyffordd
**reveal** vt datguddio, amlygu, dangos
**revel** vi gloddesta; ymhyfrydu ▷ n gloddest
**revelry** n miri
**revenge** vb, n dial
**revenue** n cyllid, enillion, incwm
**reverberate** vb taro'n ôl; atseinio
**revere** vt parchu, anrhydeddu
**reverence** n parch, parchedigaeth
**reverend** adj parchedig
**reverent** adj parchus, gŵyl, gwylaidd
**reversal** n dymchweliad, cwymp
**reverse** adj gwrthwyneb, chwith ▷ vb troi, gwrthdroi ▷ n gwrthdro, aflwydd; **reverse charge call** n galwad y telir amdani'r pen arall; **reverse (gear)** n gêr ôl
**revert** vb troi yn ôl, dychwelyd
**review** vt adolygu ▷ n adolygiad
**reviewer** n adolygydd
**revile** vt difenwi, cablu, gwaradwyddo
**revise** vt cywiro, diwygio
**revision** n cywiriad; adolygiad
**revival** n adfywiad, diwygiad
**revive** vb adfywio, adnewyddu
**revoke** vb galw yn ôl, diddymu, dirymu
**revolt** vb gwrthryfela ▷ n gwrthryfel
**revolting** adj gwrthnaws, atgas, ffiaidd
**revolution** n chwyldro, chwyldroad
**revolutionary** adj chwildroadol ▷ n chwildrowr

**revolve** vb troi, amdroi, cylchdroi
**revolver** n llawddryll
**revulsion** n atgasedd
**reward** n gwobr ▷ vt gwobrwyo
**reword** vb ailysgrifennu, ailddweud
**rhapsody** n hwyl, ymfflamychiad
**rhetoric** n rhetoreg, rhethreg
**rheumatism** n cryd cymalau, gwynegon
**rhinoceros** n rhinoseros
**rhombus** n rhombws
**rhubarb** n rhiwbob
**rhyme** n odl, rhigwm ▷ vb odli, rhigymu
**rhythm** n rhythm, rhediad
**rib** n asen, eisen
**ribald** n masweddwr ▷ adj masweddol
**ribbon** n rhuban, ysnoden
**rice** n reis
**rich** adj cyfoethog, goludog, bras
**riches** npl cyfoeth, golud
**richness** n cyfoethogrwydd, braster, ffrwythlonrwydd
**rick** n tas
**rickets** npl y llech(au)
**rickety** adj simsan, bregus
**rid** vt gwared
**riddle** n dychmyg, pos
**riddle** n rhidyll ▷ vt rhidyllio, gogrwn
**ride** vb marchogaeth, marchocáu
**rider** n marchogwr; atodiad
**ridge** n grwn, trum, cefn, crib
**ridicule** n gwawd ▷ vt gwawdio, chwerthin am ben
**ridiculous** adj chwerthinllyd
**riding** n marchogaeth
**riding school** n ysgol farchogaeth
**rife** adj aml, cyffredin, rhemp
**riff-raff** n gwehilion y bobl, dihirod
**rifle** vt anrheithio, ysbeilio
**rifle** n dryll, reiffl
**rift** n agen, hollt, rhwyg
**rig** vb rigio, taclu ▷ n rig
**right** adj iawn, uniawn; deau ▷ adv yn iawn ▷ vt unioni, cywiro ▷ n

iawnder, hawl; **right angle** n ongl sgwâr; **~s and customs** braint a defod; **~ wing** (Pol) asgell dde
**righteous** adj cyfiawn
**righteousness** n cyfiawnder
**rightful** adj cyfreithlon, iawn, teg
**rigid** adj anhyblyg, manwl, caeth
**rigmarole** n ffregod, rhibidirês
**rigour** n llymder
**rile** vt cythruddo, ffyrnigo, llidio
**rim** n ymyl, cylch, cant
**rind** n pil, croen, crawen, rhisgl
**ring** n modrwy, cylch ▷ vb modrwyo
**ring** vb canu cloch, atseinio; modrwyo ▷ n sŵn cloch, tinc; **wedding ring** n modrwy briodas; **ring road** n cylchffordd
**rinse** vt golchi, trochi
**riot** n terfysg, gloddest ▷ vi terfysgu
**rip** vb rhipio, rhwygo, datod ▷ n rhwyg; **rip-off** n lladrad amlwg
**ripe** adj aeddfed
**ripple** n crych ▷ vb crychu
**rise** vi codi, cyfodi ▷ n codiad
**risk** n perygl, enbydrwydd ▷ vt peryglu, anturio, mentro
**rite** n defod
**ritual** adj defodol ▷ n defod
**rival** n cydymgeisydd ▷ vb cystadlu
**river** n afon
**rivet** n rhybed, hem, rifet ▷ vb rhybedu, hemio, rifetio
**rivulet** n afonig, nant, cornant
**road** n ffordd, heol; angorfa; **road map** n map ffyrdd, map moduro; **road works** n gwaith cynnal y ffordd
**roam** vi crwydro, gwibio
**roar** vi rhuo ▷ n rhu, rhuad
**roast** vb rhostio, crasu, pobi, digoni
**rob** vt lladrata, ysbeilio
**robber** n lleidr, ysbeiliwr
**robbery** n lladrad
**robe** n gwisg, gŵn
**robin** n brongoch
**robust** adj cadarn, cryf, grymus
**rock** vb siglo

**rock** n craig
**rockery** n gardd gerrig
**rocket** n roced
**rocky** adj creigiog; sigledig
**rod** n gwialen, llath
**rodent** n cnofil
**roe** n iyrches, ewig
**roe** n grawn pysgod, gronell
**roebuck** n iwrch
**rogue** n gwalch, cnaf
**role** n rhan, tasg, cymeriad
**roll** vb rholio, treiglo ▷ n rhòl; **roll call** n galw enwau (ar restr)
**rolling** adj tonnog; **rolling pin** n rholbren; **rolling stock** n rholstoc
**Roman** n Rhufeiniwr ▷ adj Rhufeinaidd, Rhufeinig; **Roman Catholic** n Pabydd
**romance** n rhamant ▷ vi rhamantu
**Romania** n Românía
**romantic** adj rhamantus
**Rome** n Rhufain
**romp** vi rhampio ▷ n rhamp; rhampen
**rood** n rhwd; y grog, y groes
**roof** n to, nen ▷ vt toi
**rook** n ydfran, brân
**room** n lle; ystafell; **room service** n gwasanaeth ystafell
**roomy** adj helaeth, eang
**roost** n clwyd ▷ vi clwydo
**rooster** n ceiliog
**root** n gwraidd, gwreiddyn ▷ vb gwreiddio; diwreiddio
**rope** n rhaff ▷ vt rhaffu, rhwymo
**rosary** n paderau, llaswyr
**rose** n rhosyn; **rose hips** npl egroes
**rosette** n ysnoden
**rostrum** n llwyfan, areithfa
**rosy** adj rhosynnaidd, gwritgoch, disglair
**rot** vb pydru, braenu ▷ n pydredd; lol
**rota** n rhod, trefn
**rotate** vi troi, cylchdroi, chwyldroi
**rote** n tafod-leferydd
**rotten** adj pwdr, pydredig, sâl
**rouge** n lliw coch, gruddliw

**rough** adj garw, gerwin, bras
**round** adj crwn ▷ n crwn, cylch, tro, rownd ▷ adv, prep o glych, o amgylch ▷ vb crynio, rowndio
**roundabout** n cylchdro, cylchfan, cylch ogylch; ceffylau bach ▷ adj o amgylch, cwmpasog
**rouse** vb dihuno, deffroi, cyffroi
**rout** n rhawt; ffo, dymchweliad ▷ vb ymlid, dymchwelyd
**route** n ffordd, llwybr, hynt
**routine** n defod, arfer
**rove** vb crwydro, gwibio
**roving** adj crwydrol
**row** n rhes, rhestr
**row** vb rhwyfo
**row** n terfysg; ffo, cythrwfl, ffrae
**rowan** n criafol
**rowdy** adj trystiog, afreolus
**rowel** n troell ysbardun, rhywel
**rowing boat** n cwch rhwyfo
**royal** adj brenhinol
**royalty** n brenhiniaeth; toll, tâl, breindal
**rub** vb rhwbio, rhathu, iro, crafu
**rubber** n rwber
**rubbish** n ysbwriel, sothach; lol; **rubbish bin** n bin ysbwriel; **rubbish dump** n tomen ysbwriel
**rubble** n rhwbel
**ruby** n rhuddem ▷ adj coch, rhudd
**ruck** n pentwr, crynswth, haid, ysgarmes
**rucksack** n rhychsach
**ruction** n helynt, terfysg
**rudder** n llyw
**ruddy** adj coch, gwridog, gwritgoch
**rude** adj anfoesgar; anghelfydd, garw
**rudiment** n egwyddor, elfen
**rue** vt galaru, gofidio, edifaru
**rueful** adj trist, truenus, gresynus
**ruffian** n adyn, anfadyn, dihiryn
**ruffle** vb crychu, cyffroi, aflonyddu
**rug** n hugan
**rugby** n rygbi
**rugged** adj garw, gerwin, clogyrnog

# S

**ruin** *n* distryw, dinistr; adfail ▷ *vb* difetha, andwyo
**rule** *n* rheol, llywodraeth; riwl ▷ *vb* rheoli, llywodraethu; llinellu
**ruler** *n* llywodraethwr; pren mesur, rhiwl
**ruling** *n* dyfarniad, barn ▷ *adj* llywodraethol, mewn grym
**rum** *n* rym ▷ *adj* od, rhyfedd
**rumble** *vi* trystio, tyrfu, godyrfu
**rummage** *vb* chwalu a chwilio, chwilota
**rumour** *n* chwedl, gair, sôn, achlust
**rump** *n* tin, bôn, cwman, cloren
**rumple** *vt* crychu, sybachu
**rumpus** *n* helynt, terfysg
**run** *vb* rhedeg, llifo ▷ *n* rhediad, rhedfa; **in the long ~** yn y pen draw
**rung** *n* ffon ysgol
**rupture** *n* rhwyg; tor llengig ▷ *vb* rhwygo
**rural** *adj* gwledig, gwladaidd
**ruse** *n* ystryw, dichell
**rush** *n* brwynen, pabwyryn
**rush** *vb* rhuthro ▷ *n* rhuthr; **rush hour** *n* awr brysur
**russet** *adj* llwytgoch
**Russia** *n* Rwsia
**rust** *n* rhwd ▷ *vb* rhydu
**rustic** *adj* gwladaidd, gwledig ▷ *n* gwladwr
**rusticate** *vt* anfon adref am dymor
**rustle** *vi* siffrwd, chwithrwd, rhuglo
**rusty** *adj* rhydlyd
**rut** *n* rhych, rhigol
**ruthless** *adj* didostur, diarbed, creulon
**rye** *n* rhyg

**Sabbath** *n* Sabath, Saboth
**sabotage** *n* difrod bwriadol ▷ *vb* difrodi
**sacerdotal** *adj* offeiriadol
**sack** *n* sach, ffetan ▷ *vt* sachu; difrodi; diswyddo
**sackcloth** *n* sachlen, sachliain
**sacrament** *n* sacrament, ordinhad
**sacred** *adj* cysegredig, glân, sanctaidd
**sacrifice** *n* aberth, offrwm ▷ *vb* aberthu
**sacrilege** *n* halogiad, cysegr-ysbeiliad
**sad** *adj* trist, athrist, prudd, digalon
**saddle** *n* cyfrwy ▷ *vt* cyfrwyo; beichio
**saddler** *n* cyfrwywr
**sadness** *n* tristwch, prudd-der
**safe** *adj* diogel, dihangol, saff ▷ *n* cell, cist, cloer
**safety** *n* diogelwch; **~ belt** gwregys diogelwch; **~ pin** pin cau
**saffron** *n* saffrwm ▷ *adj* melyn
**sag** *vb* segio, segian, sagio, ymollwng
**sage** *adj* doeth ▷ *n* gŵr doeth
**sage** *n* saets
**Sahara** *n* Sahara
**sail** *n* hwyl ▷ *vb* hwylio, morio, mordwyo
**sailing** *n* hwylio; **sailing boat** *n* llong hwylio
**sailor** *n* morwr, llongwr
**saint** *n* sant

**sake** n mwyn; **for the ~ of** er mwyn
**salary** n cyflog
**sale** n gwerth, gwerthiant, arwerthiant
**salient** adj amlwg
**saline** adj helïaidd, hallt ▷ n heli
**saliva** n haliw, poer, dŵr anadl
**sallow** adj melyn afiach
**salmon** n eog, gleisiad, samwn
**saloon** n neuadd, salŵn
**salt** n halen, halwyn (cemeg) ▷ adj hallt ▷ vt halltu; **salt cellar** n llestr halen; **salt water** n dŵr hallt, dŵr y môr
**salty** adj hallt
**salute** vt cyfarch; saliwtio ▷ n cyfarchiad; saliwt
**salvation** n iachawdwriaeth; **S~ Army** Byddin yr Iachawdwriaeth
**salve** n eli, ennaint ▷ vt elïo, lleddfu; achub
**same** adj yr un, yr unrhyw, yr un fath
**sample** n sampl, enghraifft ▷ vt samplu, samplo
**sanctify** vt sancteiddio
**sanctimonious** adj ffug-sanctaidd, sych-dduwiol
**sanction** n caniatâd, cosb; sancsiwn (moeseg) ▷ vt caniatáu; cosbi
**sanctity** n sancteiddrwydd
**sanctuary** n cysegr; noddfa, nawdd
**sand** n tywod ▷ vt tywodi; **sand castle** n castell tywod
**sandpaper** n papur gwydrog
**sandpit** n pwll tywod
**sandwich** n brechdan
**sandy** adj tywodlyd; melyngoch
**sane** adj iach, call, synhwyrol
**sanitary** adj iechydol; **sanitary towel** n tywel misglwyf, tywel iechydol
**sanitation** n iechydaeth
**sanity** n iechyd meddwl, iawn bwyll
**Santa Claus** n Siôn Corn
**sap** n nodd, sudd, sugn ▷ vt sugno, hysbyddu
**sap** vb tangloddio, diseilio
**sapling** n pren ieuanc
**sapphire** n saffir ▷ adj glas
**sarcasm** n gwawdiaith, coegni, gair du
**sarcastic** adj gwawdlym, coeglyd, brathog
**sardine** n sardîn
**sash** n gwregys; ffrâm ffenestr
**satchel** n sachell, cod lyfrau
**sate** vt digoni, llenwi, diwallu
**satellite** n canlynwr, cynffonnwr; lleuad; lloeren
**satiate** vt digoni, diwallu, syrffedu
**satin** n satin, pali
**satire** n dychan, gogan
**satirize** vb dychan, goganu
**satisfaction** n bodlonrwydd; iawn
**satisfactory** adj boddhaol; iawnol
**satisfy** vt bodloni, diwallu, digoni
**saturate** vt trwytho, mwydo
**Saturday** n dydd Sadwrn
**sauce** n saws; haerllugrwydd
**saucepan** n sosban
**saucer** n soser
**saucy** adj digywilydd, haerllug
**Saudi Arabia** n Saudi Arabia
**saunter** vi rhodianna, ymdroi, swmera
**sausage** n selsig, selsigen
**savage** adj gwyllt, ffyrnig, milain, anwar ▷ n dyn gwyllt, anwariad, anwarddyn
**save** vb achub, arbed, gwaredu; cynilo ▷ prep oddieithr, ond
**saving** adj achubol, darbodus
**savings** npl cynilion
**saviour** n achubwr, gwaredwr, iachawdwr
**savour** n sawr, blas ▷ vb sawru
**savoury** n blasusfwyd ▷ adj sawrus
**saw** n llif ▷ vb llifio
**sawdust** n blawd llif
**sawmill** n melin lifio
**say** vb dywedyd, dweud
**saying** n dywediad, ymadrodd, gair

**scab** n crachen, cramen; clafr
**scabies** n y crafu
**scaffold** n ysgaffald; dienyddle
**scald** vt ysgaldio, sgaldan(u) ▷ n
ysgaldiad
**scale** n clorian, tafol, mantol
**scale** n graddfa ▷ vb dringo
**scale** n cen ▷ vb cennu; digennu,
pilio
**scallop** n gylfgragen; gwlf ▷ vt
gylfu, minfylchu
**scalp** n copa, croen y pen ▷ vt
penflingo
**scamp** n cnaf, gwalch, dihiryn
**scamper** vi ffoi, carlamu, brasgamu
**scan** vb corfannu; sganio, edrych,
chwilio
**scandal** n tramgwydd, gwarth,
enllib
**Scandinavia** n Llychlyn
**scanner** n sganydd
**scant, -y** adj prin
**scapegoat** n bwch dihangol
**scapegrace** n dyn diras, oferwr,
dihiryn
**scar** n craith ▷ vt creithio
**scarce** adj, adv prin
**scarcely** adv prin, braidd, odid,
nemor
**scare** vt brawychu, tarfu ▷ n
dychryn
**scared** adj wedi cael ofn, wedi
rhuso, wedi brawychu
**scarf** n crafat, sgarff
**scarlatina** n y dwymyn goch
**scarlet** adj ysgarlad
**scarp** n llethr
**scathe** vt deifio, anafu, niweidio
**scathing** adj deifiol, miniog
**scatter** vb gwasgaru, chwalu,
taenu
**scavenger** n carthwr, carthydd
**scene** n lle; golwg, golygfa
**scenery** n golygfa
**scenic** adj hardd, golygfaol
**scent** n arogl, aroglau, trywydd;
perarogl ▷ vt arogli

**sceptic** n amheuwr
**sceptical** adj amheugar
**sceptre** n teyrnwialen
**schedule** n atodlen, cofrestr, taflen
**scheme** n cynllun; cynllwyn ▷ vb
cynllunio
**schism** n rhwyg, ymraniad, sism
**scholar** n ysgolhaig, ysgolor
**scholarly** adj ysgolheigaidd
**scholarship** n ysgolheictod;
ysgoloriaeth
**scholastic** adj athrofaol
**school** n ysgol, ysgoldy ▷ vt
disgyblu
**schoolbook** n llyfr ysgol
**schoolboy** n bachgen ysgol
**schoolchildren** npl plant ysgol
**schooldays** npl dyddiau ysgol
**schoolgirl** n merch ysgol
**schoolmaster** n athro
**schoolmistress** n athrawes
**schooner** n ysgwner
**sciatica** n clunwst
**science** n gwyddor, gwyddoniaeth
**scientific** adj gwyddonol
**scientist** n gwyddonydd
**scissors** npl siswrn
**scoff** n gwawd ▷ vi gwawdio,
gwatwar
**scold** vb dwrdio, tafodi, ceryddu,
cymhennu ▷ n cecren
**scone** n sgon
**scoop** n lletwad ▷ vt cafnu, cafnio
**scope** n ergyd, bwriad; cylch,
cwmpas, lle
**scorch** vb deifio, llosgi, greidio,
rhuddo
**score** n hac, rhic; cyfrif, dyled;
sgôr; ugain
**score** vb rhicio, cyfrif, sgori(o)
**scorn** n dirmyg ▷ vb dirmygu,
gwatwar
**scorpion** n ysgorpion
**Scot** n Ysgotyn, Albanwr
**scotch** vt hacio, darnio, trychu
**Scotch** adj Ysgotaidd, Albanaidd
**scot-free** adj croeniach, dianaf

**Scotland** n Yr Alban
**Scottish** adj Albanaidd
**scoundrel** n cnaf, dihiryn
**scour** vt carthu, ysgwrio
**scour** vb rhedeg; chwilio
**scourge** n fflangell, pla ▷ vt fflangellu
**scout** n sgowt, ysbïwr ▷ vt sgowta, ysbïo
**scowl** vb cuchio, gwgu ▷ n cilwg, gwg
**scraggy** adj esgyrnog, tenau, cul, salw
**scramble** vi, n ciprys, ymgiprys; **scrambled egg** n cymysgwy
**scrap** n tamaid, tameidyn, dernyn
**scrapbook** n llyfr lloffion
**scrape** vb crafu ▷ n helynt, helbul, crafiad
**scratch** vb crafu, cripio
**scrawl** vb ysgriblo, ysgriblan
**scream** vi ysgrechain ▷ n ysgrech, gwawch
**screech** vi ysgrechain ▷ n ysgrech
**screen** n llen, cysgod; sgrin ▷ vt cysgodi
**screw** n sgriw, hoel dro ▷ vb ysgriwio
**screwdriver** n tyrnsgriw
**scribble** n ysgribl ▷ vb ysgriblo, ysgriblan
**script** n llawysgrif, ysgrif, sgript
**scripture** n ysgrythur
**scroll** n rhôl, plyg llyfr
**scrub** n prysgwydd; ysgwrfa ▷ vt ysgwrio
**scruff** n gwar, gwegil
**scrum(mage)** n sgrym, ysgarmes
**scruple** n petruster (moesol) ▷ vi petruso
**scrupulous** adj gwyliadwrus, manwl
**scrutinize** vt chwilio, archwilio
**scrutiny** n archwiliad
**scuffle** vi, n ymgiprys, ymryson
**scull** n rhwyf unllaw, rhodl ▷ vb rhodli

**scullery** n cegin fach, cegin gefn
**sculptor** n cerflunydd
**sculpture** n cerfluniaeth; cerflun ▷ vb cerfio, torri
**scum** n sgum; gwehilion, sorod
**scurf** n cen, mardon
**scurrilous** adj bustlaidd, brwnt, difrïol
**scurry** vi ffrystio ▷ n ffrwst, ffwdan
**scurvy** adj crachlyd, crach ▷ n llwg
**scutter** vi ffoi, diengyd
**scuttle** n llestr glo
**scuttle** vt tyllu llong i'w suddo
**scuttle** vi heglu ffoi, dianc
**scythe** n pladur
**sea** n môr, cefnfor; moryn; **sea water** n dŵr y môr
**seaboard** n morlan, glan y môr
**seafood** n bwyd môr
**seagull** n gwylan
**seal** n morlo
**seal** n sêl, insel ▷ vt selio
**sea level** n lefel y môr
**seam** n gwnïad, gwrym; haen, gwythïen; craith
**seaman** n morwr, llongwr
**seamstress** n gwniadwraig, gwniadyddes
**seamy** adj annymunol
**seance** n seawns
**seaplane** n awyren fôr
**sear** adj sych, crin, gwyw ▷ vt serio, deifio
**search** vb chwilio, profi ▷ n ymchwil
**seashore** n glan y môr
**seasickness** n salwch y môr
**seaside** n glan y môr
**season** n tymor, amser, pryd, adeg ▷ vb tymheru; halltu; **high/low season** n tymor prysur/llac
**seasonal** adj tymhorol
**season ticket** n tocyn tymor
**seat** n sedd, sêt, eisteddle ▷ vi eistedd
**seat belt** n gwregys diogelwch
**seaweed** n gwymon, gwmon

**seaworthy** adj addas i'r môr, diogel

**secede** vi ymneilltuo, encilio; torri'n rhydd, ymwahanu

**secession** n ymneilltuad, enciliad; ymwahaniad

**seclude** vt cau allan, neilltuo

**second** adj ail ▷ n ail; eiliad ▷ vt eilio; **second class** adj ail ddosbarth, isradd

**secondary** adj eilradd, uwchradd; **secondary school** n ysgol uwchradd

**second-hand** adj ail-law

**secret** adj dirgel, cyfrinachol ▷ n cyfrinach

**secretary** n ysgrifennydd; **Secretary of State** n Ysgrifennydd Gwladol

**secretive** adj yn celu, tawedog

**sect** n sect, enwad

**sectarian** adj enwadol, cul

**section** n toriad, trychiad; rhan, adran

**sector** n sector

**secular** adj bydol; lleygol; seciwlar

**secure** adj sicr, diogel ▷ vt sicrhau, diogelu

**security** n diogelwch, sicrwydd, gwystl

**sedate** adj tawel, digyffro ▷ vb rhoi i gysgu, tawelu

**sedative** adj lleddfol, lliniarol

**sedge** n hesg

**sediment** n gwaelodion, gwaddod

**sedition** n terfysg, brad, gwrthryfel

**seduce** vt llithio, hudo, twyllo

**seductive** adj llithiol, deniadol

**see** n esgobaeth

**see** vb gweld, canfod

**seed** n had, hedyn ▷ vb hadu, hedeg

**seedy** adj hadog; salw; sâl, anhwylus

**seek** vb ceisio, ymofyn, chwilio

**seem** vi ymddangos

**seemly** adj gweddus, gweddaidd, addas

**seep** vb diferu, gollwng

**seer** n gweledydd

**seesaw** n siglenydd

**seethe** vb berwi, byrlymu

**segment** n darn, rhan, segment

**segregate** vt didoli, neilltuo, gwahanu

**seize** vb gafael mewn, atafaelu, dal, achub

**seizure** n daliad; strôc

**seldom** adv anfynych, anaml

**select** vt dewis, dethol

**self** (selves) n hun, hunan ▷ prefix hunan-, ym-

**self-catering** adj hunan arlwy

**self-conscious** adj hunanymwybodol, swil

**self-contained** adj annibynnol, ar wahân

**self-control** n hunanlywodraeth

**self-employed** adj hunangyflogedig

**self-evident** adj amlwg, eglur

**self-government** n ymreolaeth

**self-interest** n hunan-les

**selfish** adj hunanol

**self-possessed** adj hunanfeddiannol

**self-respect** n hunan-barch

**self-sacrifice** n hunanaberth

**selfsame** adj yr un, yr unrhyw

**self-satisfied** adj hunanddigonol

**self-service** n hunanwasanaeth

**self-sufficient** adj hunanddigonol, hy

**sell** vb gwerthu; siomi ▷ n siom

**seller** n gwerthwr

**sellotape** n selotâp

**semblance** n tebygrwydd, rhith

**semi-** prefix hanner, lled, go

**semicolon** n gwahannod (;)

**seminary** n athrofa, ysgol

**sempiternal** adj bythol, tragwyddol

**senate** n senedd

**send** vt anfon, danfon, gyrru

**senile** adj hen a methedig, heneiddiol

**senior** adj hŷn ▷ n hynaf
**seniority** n blaenoriaeth
**sensation** n ymdeimlad, teimlad; cyffro, ias, syndod
**sensational** adj iasol, cyffrous
**sense** n synnwyr, pwyll, ystyr
**senseless** adj dienaid, disynnwyr, hurt
**sensible** adj synhwyrol; teimladwy
**sensitive** adj teimladwy, croendenau; hydeiml
**sensual** adj cnawdol; trythyll, chwantus
**sensuous** adj teimladol, synhwyrus
**sentence** n brawddeg; barn, dedfryd ▷ vt dedfrydu
**sententious** adj doetheiriog
**sentiment** n syniad, teimlad
**sentry** n gwyliwr, gwyliedydd
**separate** adj ar wahân ▷ vb gwahanu, neilltuo, ysgar; ymwahanu
**separation** n gwahaniad
**sept-** prefix saith, seith-
**September** n Medi
**septic** adj braenol, pydrol, madreddol
**sepulchre** n bedd, beddrod
**sequel** n canlyniad
**sequence** n trefn, dilyniad
**sequester** vt neilltuo; atafaelu
**serenade** n hwyrgan, nosgan ▷ vt hwyrganu
**serene** adj teg; tawel, digynnwrf
**sergeant** n rhingyll, sarsiant
**serial** adj cyfresol, bob yn rhifyn ▷ n stori gyfres
**series** n rhes, cyfres
**serious** adj difrifol
**seriously** adv yn ddifrifol
**sermon** n pregeth
**serpent** n sarff
**serrated** adj danheddog
**serum** n serwm
**servant** n gwas; morwyn
**serve** vb gwasanaethu, gweini
**service** n gwasanaeth, oedfa; llestri; **service charge** n tâl am wasanaeth

**serviceable** adj gwasanaethgar, defnyddiol
**serviette** n napcyn
**servile** adj gwasaidd
**session** n eisteddiad; sesiwn; tymor
**set** vb gosod, dodi; plannu; sadio; sefydlu; machlud ▷ n set; impyn, planhigyn
**settee, settle** n sgiw, setl
**setting** n lleoliad, safle; machludiad
**settle** vb sefydlu; penderfynu; cytuno, setlo; plwyfo; talu
**settlement** n cytundeb; gwladfa
**seven** adj, n saith
**seventeen** adj, n dau (dwy) ar bymtheg, un deg saith
**seventh** adj seithfed
**seventy** adj, n deg a thrigain, saith deg
**sever** vb gwahanu, datod, torri
**several** adj amryw; gwahanol
**severance** n gwahaniad, datgysylltiad
**severe** adj caled, tost, llym, gerwin
**severity** n llymder, gerwindeb
**sew** vb gwnïo, pwytho
**sewage** n carthffosiaeth, carthion
**sewer** n ceuffos, carthffos
**sewing machine** n peiriant gwnïo
**sex** n rhyw
**sex education** n addysg ryw
**sextet** n chwechawd
**sexton** n clochydd; torrwr beddau
**sexual** adj rhywiol
**shabby** adj carpiog, gwael, aflêr
**shack** n caban
**shackle** n hual, gefyn, llyffethair
**shade** n cysgod; ysbryd ▷ vt cysgodi
**shadow** n cysgod ▷ vt cysgodi
**shadowy** adj cysgodol, rhithiol
**shady** adj cysgodol; amheus
**shaft** n paladr, saeth; llorp, braich; pwll; gwerthyd
**shaggy** adj cedenog, blewog

**shake** vb ysgwyd, siglo, crynu
**shaky** adj ansad, crynedig
**shallow** adj bas ▷ n basle, beisle
**sham** vb ffugio ▷ adj ffug, gau, coeg ▷ n ffug, ffugbeth
**shambles** npl galanastra
**shame** n cywilydd, gwaradwydd, gwarth ▷ vb cywilyddio, gwaradwyddo
**shamefaced** n swil, gwylaidd
**shameful** adj cywilyddus, gwarthus
**shampoo** vt golchi pen ▷ n siampŵ
**shank** n coes, gar, esgair; paladr
**shanty** n caban, bwthyn, penty
**shape** n siâp, llun ▷ vt siapio, llunio
**shapeless** adj afluniaidd, di-lun
**shapely** adj siapus, lluniaidd, gosgeiddig
**share** n rhan, cyfran ▷ vb rhannu; cyfranogi
**share** n swch aradr
**shareholder** n cyfranddaliwr
**shark** n siarc, morgi; twyllwr
**sharp** adj siarp, llym, miniog ▷ n llonnod (cerdd)
**sharpen** vb hogi, minio, awchlymu
**sharpener** n naddwr
**sharper** n siarpwr
**sharply** adv yn sydyn
**shatter** vb dryllio, chwilfriwio; ysigo
**shave** vb eillio, torri barf; rhasglio
**shavings** npl naddion
**shawl** n siôl
**she** pron hi ▷ adj, prefix benyw
**sheaf** (sheaves) n ysgub
**shear** vt cneifio; siero
**shears** npl gwellau
**sheath** n gwain; (contraceptive) maneg atal cenhedlu
**sheathe** vt gweinio
**shed** n penty, sied
**shed** vt tywallt; gollwng; colli; dihidlo, bwrw
**sheen** n disgleirdeb, llewyrch, gwawr

**sheep** (sheep) n dafad
**sheer** vi gwyro o'r ffordd, cilio
**sheer** adj pur, glân, noeth, syth, serth
**sheet** n llen; cynfas; hwylraff; taflen
**shekel** n sicl
**shelf** (shelves) n silff, astell
**shell** n cragen; plisgyn, masgl; tân-belen
**shellfish** npl cregynbysg
**shelter** n cysgod, lloches ▷ vb cysgodi, llochesu; ymochel; llechu
**shelve** vi llechweddu, llethru
**shelve** vt gosod naill ochr, troi o'r neilltu
**shepherd** n bugail ▷ vt bugeilio
**sheriff** n sirydd, siryf
**sherry** n sieri
**Shetland** n Shetland
**shield** n tarian ▷ vt cysgodi, amddiffyn
**shift** vb newid, symud; ymdaro ▷ n newid; tro, stem, shifft
**shilling** n swllt
**shilly-shally** n anwadalwch
**shimmer** vi tywynnu, caneitio, rhithio
**shin** n crimog, crimp coes
**shindy** n helynt, ffrwgwd, terfysg
**shine** vb disgleirio, llewyrchu, tywynnu ▷ n disgleirdeb, sglein, llewyrch
**shingle** n graean, gro
**shingle** n peithynen; estyllen
**shingles** npl yr eryr, yr eryrod
**shiny** adj gloyw, disglair
**ship** n llong ▷ vt trosglwyddo
**shipping** n llongau (gwlad)
**shipshape** adj, adv taclus, trefnus, twt
**shipwreck** n llongddrylliad
**shire** n sir
**shirk** vt gochel, osgoi
**shirt** n crys
**shiver** vi crynu
**shiver** vb dryllio, chwilfriwio

**shoal** n haig ▷ vi heigio
**shoal** n basle, beisle
**shock** n sioc, ergyd, ysgytiad ▷ vt ysgytio; tramgwyddo
**shocking** adj arswydus, ysgytiol
**shoddy** n brethyn eilban ▷ adj ffug, gwael
**shoe** n esgid; pedol ▷ vt pedoli
**shoehorn** n seisbin, siasbi
**shoelace** n carrai/lasen esgid
**shoemaker** n crydd
**shoe shop** n siop esgidiau
**shoot** vb tarddu, blaguro; saethu ▷ n ysbrigyn, blaguryn
**shooting** n saethu
**shop** n masnachdy, siop ▷ vb siopa
**shopkeeper** n siopwr
**shopper** n prynwr
**shopping** n siopa
**shore** n glan, traeth
**short** adj byr, cwta, prin
**shortage** n prinder, diffyg
**short circuit** n cylchedd byr
**shortcoming** n diffyg, bai
**short cut** n llwybr tarw, llwybr llygad, ffordd fer
**shorthand** n llaw-fer
**shorts** npl trowsus cwta
**shot** n ergyd; saethwr
**shoulder** n ysgwydd, palfais ▷ vt ysgwyddo; **shoulder blade** n sgapwla, pont yr ysgwydd
**shout** vb llwybor, gweiddi ▷ n bloedd, gwaedd
**shove** vb gwthio
**shovel** n llwyarn ▷ vt rhofio
**show** vb dangos, arddangos ▷ n arddangosfa, sioe, siew
**shower** n cawod, cawad ▷ vb cawodi, bwrw
**shred** n llarp, cerpyn ▷ vb rhwygo, torri'n fân
**shrew** n cecren, gwraig anynad; llyg
**shrewd** adj ffel, craff, call, cyfrwys
**shriek** n ysgrechian ▷ n ysgrech
**shrill** adj llym, main, meinllais
**shrimp** n berdysen ▷ vi berdysa

**shrine** n ysgrîn; creirfa; cysegr, seintwar
**shrink** vb crebachu, tynnu ato, cilio
**shrivel** vb crychu, crebachu
**shroud** n amdo, amwisg; (pl) rhaffau hwylbren ▷ vt amdoi, cuddio, celu
**Shrove Tuesday** n Mawrth Ynyd
**shrub** n prysgwydden, llwyn
**shrug** vb codi'r ysgwyddau
**shudder** n crynfa, echryd, arswyd ▷ vi crynu, arswydo
**shuffle** vb siffrwd; llusgo; gwingo, gwamalu
**shun** vt gochelyd, osgoi
**shunt** vb troi o'r neilltu, symud o'r ffordd, siyntio
**shut** vb cau ▷ adj caeëdig
**shutter** n caead, clawr, gwerchyr
**shuttle** n gwennol (gwëydd)
**shuttlecock** n gwennol
**shy** adj swil ▷ vi osgoi, rhusio
**siblings** npl plant
**sick** adj claf; yn chwydu, â chyfog arno; wedi diflasu
**sickbay** n canolfan iechyd
**sickening** adj atgas, diflas, cyfoglyd
**sickle** n cryman
**sickly** adj afiach, nychlyd
**side** n ochr, ystlys; tu, plaid ▷ vi ochri
**sidestep** vb ochrgamu
**sidetrack** vb troi o'r neilltu
**sideways** adv tua'r ochr, yn wysg ei ochr
**sidle** vi cerdded yn wysg ei ochr, gwyro
**siege** n gwarchae
**sieve** n gogr, gwagr, rhidyll, sife
**sift** vt gogrwn, nithio, hidlo, rhidyllio
**sigh** vb ochneidio ▷ n ochenaid
**sight** n golwg, golygfa ▷ vt gweld
**sightseeing** n taith i weld y wlad
**sign** n arwydd, argoel ▷ vb arwyddo, llofnodi
**signal** adj hynod ▷ n arwydd

**signatory** adj arwyddol ▷ n arwyddwr
**signature** n llofnod
**significance** n arwyddocâd, ystyr
**significant** adj arwyddocaol; o bwys
**signify** vb arwyddo, arwyddocáu
**signpost** n mynegbost, arwyddbost
**silence** n taw, distawrwydd ▷ vt rhoi taw ar
**silent** adj distaw, tawedog, mud
**silhouette** n llun du, cysgodlun, silŵet
**silicon** n silicon; ~ **chip** sglodyn silicon
**silk** n sidan
**silky** adj sidanaidd
**sill** n sil
**silly** adj gwirion, ffôl, disynnwyr
**silt** n gwaelodion, llaid ▷ vb gwaelodi, tagu
**silver** n arian ▷ vt ariannu; **silver paper** n papur arian
**silversmith** n gof arian
**silvery** adj ariannaid(d)
**similar** adj tebyg, cyffelyb
**simile** n cyffelybiaeth, cymhariaeth
**simmer** vi lledferwi, goferwi
**simper** vi cilwenu, glaswenu
**simple** adj syml, unplyg; gwirion, diniwed
**simplicity** n symlrwydd, unplygrwydd
**simplify** vt symleiddio
**simulate** vt ffugio, dynwared
**simultaneous** adj cyfamserol, ar y pryd
**sin** n pechod ▷ vb pechu
**since** conj gan, yn gymaint ▷ prep er, er pan
**sincere** adj diffuant, didwyll, pur
**sinew** n gewyn, giewyn
**sing** vb canu
**singe** vt deifio
**singer** n canwr, cantwr, cantores
**singing** n canu

**single** adj sengl, dibriod, gweddw; **single bed** n gwely sengl; **single-minded** adj unplyg, cywir; **single room** n ystafell sengl
**singlet** n gwasgod wlanen, crys isaf
**singular** adj unigol; hynod
**sinister** adj ysgeler; chwithig
**sink** vb soddi, suddo ▷ n sinc
**sinner** n pechadur
**sinuous** adj dolennog, troellog
**sip** vt llymeitian ▷ n llymaid, llymeidyn
**siphon** n siffon
**sir** n syr
**siren** n corn, seiren
**sirloin** n llwyn eidion
**sissy** n cadi(ffan)
**sister** n chwaer
**sister-in-law** n chwaer yng nghyfraith
**sit** vb eistedd
**site** n safle, lle ▷ vb lleoli
**sitting** n eisteddiad
**situated** adj yn sefyll, wedi ei leoli
**situation** n lle, safle; sefyllfa
**six** adj, n chwech
**sixteen** adj, n un ar bymtheg, un deg chwech
**sixth** adj chweched
**sixty** adj, n trigain, chwe deg
**sizable** adj gweddol fawr
**size** n maint, maintioli
**sizzle** vb ffrio
**skate** n cath fôr
**skate** n sgêt ▷ vb ysglefrio
**skateboard** n bwrdd sglefrio
**skein** n cengl, sgain
**skeleton** n ysgerbwd; amlinelliad
**sketch** n llun, braslun ▷ vb braslunio, tynnu
**skewer** n gwaell, gwachell
**ski** n sgi ▷ vb sgïo
**skid** vb llithro (naill ochr)
**skier** n sgïwr
**skiff** n sgafnfad, ceubal, sgiff
**skill** n medr, medrusrwydd
**skilled** adj medrus, crefftus

**skim** vb tynnu, codi (hufen)

**skimmed milk** n llaeth glas, llaeth sgim

**skimp** vb crintachu, cybydda

**skimpy** adj crintach

**skin** n croen ▷ vb blingo

**skinny** adj tenau; prin, crintach

**skip** vi llamu, sgipio

**skipper** n capten llong

**skipping-rope** n rhaff sgipio

**skirmish** n ysgarmes

**skirt** n godre, sgyrt ▷ vt dilyn gyda godre

**skit** n gogan

**skittish** adj nwyfus, gwantan, anwadal

**skittles** npl ceilys

**skulk** vi llechu, techu

**skull** n penglog

**skunk** n drewgi

**sky** n wybren, wybr, awyr

**skylark** n ehedydd

**skylight** n ffenestr do

**slab** n llech

**slack** adj llac, diofal, esgeulus ▷ n glo mân

**slacken** vb llacio, llaesu

**slag** n sorod, slag

**slake** vt torri (syched), slecio

**slam** vb cau yn glats, clepian

**slander** n enllib ▷ vt enllibio

**slang** n iaith sathredig, slang ▷ vt difrïo

**slant** vb gwyro, gogwyddo ▷ n gogwydd

**slanting** adj ar oledd/osgo

**slap** vt clewtian ▷ n clewt(en), palfod

**slapdash** adj ffwrdd-â-hi, rhywsut-rywfodd

**slash** n slaes, hac ▷ vt slasio, chwipio

**slate** n llech, llechen

**slate** vt sennu, difrïo

**slattern** n slwt, slebog, sopen

**slaughter** n lladdedigaeth, lladdfa ▷ vt lladd

**slaughterhouse** n lladd-dy

**slave** n slaf, caethwas ▷ vi slafio

**slavery** n caethiwed, caethwasanaeth

**slay** vt lladd

**sled, sledge, sleigh** n car llusg, sled

**sledgehammer** n gordd

**sleek** adj llyfn, llyfndew, graenus

**sleep** vb cysgu, huno ▷ n cwsg

**sleeper** n (person) cysgwr; pren neu ddefnydd arall i ddal y cledrau

**sleeping bag** n sach gysgu

**sleeping pill** n pilsen gysgu

**sleepy** adj cysglyd

**sleet** n eirlaw

**sleeve** n llawes

**sleight** n deheurwydd, cyfrwystra, dichell

**slender** adj main, eiddil, prin

**slice** n tafell, ysglisen ▷ vt tafellu, ysglisio

**slick** adj llyfn, tafodrydd, slic

**slide** vb llithro, sglefrio ▷ n llithren, sleid

**slight** adj ysgafn, eiddil, prin ▷ vt diystyru ▷ n diystyrwch, sarhad

**slightly** adj yn fain; ychydig

**slim** adj main, eiddil

**slime** n llaid, llaca; llys, llysnafedd

**sling** vt taflu, lluchio ▷ n ffon dafl

**slip** vb llithro, dianc; gollwng ▷ n slip

**slipper** n llopan, sliper

**slippery** adj llithrig, diafael, di-ddal

**slipshod** adj anniben

**slipway** n llithrfa

**slit** vb hollti, agennu, rhwygo ▷ n hollt

**slither** vb ymlusgo, llithro

**slobber** vb glafoerio, slobran

**sloe** n eirinen ddu fach, draenen ddu

**slog** vb gweithio'n galed

**sloop** n slŵp

**slop** n (pl) golchion ▷ vb gwlychu, trochi

**slope** n llethr, gogwydd ▷ vb

gogwyddo
**sloppy** adj lleidiog, tomlyd; meddal, masw; aniben
**slot** n agen, twll
**sloth** n diogi, seguryd, syrthni
**slouch** vb llaesu, ymollwng; cerdded yn aflêr
**sloven** n dyn aflêr, slebog
**slovenly** adj aniben
**slow** adj araf, hwyrfrydig, hwyrdrwm ▷ vb arafu
**slowly** adj yn araf (deg)
**sludge** n llaid, llaca
**slug** n gwlithen, malwoden
**sluggish** adj diog, dioglyd, swrth
**sluice** n llifddor
**slum** n slym
**slumber** vb hepian, cysgu ▷ n cwsg
**slump** n cwymp, gostyngiad; dirwasgiad
**slur** vb difrïo ▷ n llithriad, cyflusg (cerdd.); anfri
**slush** n llaid, llaca, eira gwlyb
**slut** n slwt, slebog
**sly** adj cyfrwys, ffals, dichellgar, tan din
**smack** n blas ▷ vi blasu, blasio, archwaethu
**smack** n smac, palfod ▷ vb smacio, chwipio
**smack** n llongan, smac
**small** adj bach, bychan, mân, main
**smallholder** n tyddynnwr
**small-pox** n y frech wen
**smart** vi gwynio, dolurio, llosgi ▷ n gŵyn, dolur ▷ adj llym, bywiog; ffel, ffraeth; crand
**smash** vb torri, malu, chwilfriwio
**smattering** n gwybodaeth fas, crap
**smear** vt iro, dwbio
**smell** n arogl, aroglau ▷ vb arogli
**smile** vb gwenu ▷ n gwên
**smirch** vt llychwino, difwyno
**smirk** vi cilwenu, glaswenu ▷ n cilwen
**smith** n gof

**smithy** n gefail (gof)
**smog** n smog, mwgwl
**smoke** n mwg ▷ vb mygu, ysmygu, smocio
**smoked** adj wedi ei fygu
**smoky** adj myglyd
**smooth** adj llyfn, esmwyth ▷ vt llyfnhau
**smother** vb mygu, llethu
**smoulder** vi mudlosgi
**smudge** n baw, staen, smotyn ▷ vb difwyno, trochi
**smug** adj hunanol, cysetlyd
**smuggle** vt smyglio
**smut** n parddu, huddygl, smotyn; siarad aflan
**smutty** adj aflan, brwnt
**snack** n tamaid, byrbryd; **snack bar** n lle am damaid
**snag** n rhwystr, maen tramgwydd
**snail** n malwoden, malwen
**snake** n neidr
**snap** vb clecian, torri'n glats; tynnu llun ▷ n clec
**snare** n magl, croglath ▷ vt maglu, rhwydo
**snarl** vi ysgyrnygu, chwyrnu
**snatch** vb cipio ▷ n cip, crap; tamaid
**sneak** vi llechian ▷ n llechgi
**sneaking** adj llechwraidd, cachgïaidd
**sneer** vb gwawdio, glaswenu ▷ n gwawd, glaswen
**sneeze** vi tisian
**sniff** vb ffroeni, gwyntio
**snigger** vb glaschwerthin
**snip** vb torri, cynhinio ▷ n demyn, toriad
**snipe** n gïach
**snippet** n tamaid, cynhinyn
**snob** n crechyn; (pl) crachach, snob
**snobbish** adj crachaidd, snoblyd
**snooker** n snwcer
**snooze** vb hepian ▷ n cyntun
**snore** vi chwyrnu
**snort** vi ffroeni, ffroenochi

**snotty** adj cas

**snout** n trwyn anifail, duryn

**snow** n eira, ôd ▷ vb bwrw eira, odi

**snowball** n pelen eira

**snowdrift** n lluwch

**snowflake** n pluen eira

**snow plough** n aradr eira

**snub** vt sennu ▷ n sen

**snub** adj pwt, smwt

**snub-nosed** adj trwyn smwt

**snuff** vb ffroeni, snwffian ▷ n trwynlwch, snisyn

**snug** adj cryno, clyd, diddos

**snuggle** vb ymwasgu at; llochi, anwesu

**so** adv, conj fel, felly; mor, cyn

**soak** vb mwydo, sucio; slotian

**soap** n sebon ▷ vb seboni; **soap opera** n opera sebon; **soap powder** n powdr golchi

**soapy** adj sebonllyd

**soar** vi eheddeg, esgyn

**sob** vi igian, beichio ▷ n ig, ebwch

**sober** adj sobr, sad ▷ vb sobri

**sobriety** n sobrwydd

**so-called** adj dywededig

**soccer** n pêl-droed, y bêl gron

**sociable** adj cymdeithasgar

**social** adj cymdeithasol; **social club** n clwb cymdeithasol; **social security** n nawdd cymdeithasol; **social work** n gwaith cymdeithasol

**socialism** n sosialaeth

**socialist** n sosialydd

**society** n cymdeithas, cyfeillach

**sociology** n cymdeithaseg

**sock** n hosan

**socket** n twll, crau, soced

**sod** n tywarchen

**soda water** n dŵr soda

**sodden** adj wedi mwydo, soeglyd

**sofa** n glwth, esmwythfainc, soffa

**soft** adj meddal, tyner; distaw; gwiriion; **soft drink** n diod ysgafn

**software** n meddalwedd

**soggy** adj gwlyb, lleidiog

**soil** n pridd, daear, gweryd

**soil** vt difwyno, baeddu ▷ n baw, tom

**solace** n cysur, diddanwch ▷ vt cysuro, diddanu

**solar** adj heulog, solar

**solder** n sawdring, sawdur, sodr ▷ vt asio, sawdurio, sodro

**soldier** n milwr

**sole** adj unig, unigol, un

**sole** n gwadn ▷ vt gwadnu

**sole** n (fish) lleden chwithig

**solemn** adj difrifol, dwys

**sol-fa** n sol-ffa ▷ vb solffeuo

**solicit** vt erfyn, ymofyn; llithio

**solicitor** n cyfreithiwr

**solid** adj caled, sylweddol, solet, cadarn

**solid** n solid

**solidarity** n undod

**solitary** adj unig; anghyfannedd

**solitude** n unigedd

**solo** n unawd

**soloist** n unawdydd

**soluble** adj toddadwy, hydawdd

**solution** n dehongliad, esboniad; toddiant

**solve** vt datrys, dehongli

**solvent** adj yn gallu talu, di-ddyled ▷ n toddfa

**sombre** adj tywyll, prudd

**some** adj rhai, rhyw, peth, ychydig ▷ pron rhywrai, rhywfaint ▷ adv ynghylch, tua, rhyw

**somebody** pron = **someone**

**somehow** adv rywfodd, rhywsut

**someone** pron rhywun

**somersault** n trosben ▷ vb troi tin tros ben, pen dra mwnwgl

**something** n rhywbeth

**sometime** adv rywbryd, gynt

**sometimes** adv weithiau, ar brydiau, ambell waith

**somewhat** adv go, lled, braidd

**somewhere** adv (yn) rhywle

**son** n mab

**song** n cân, cathl, cerdd

**sonic** adj sonig

**son-in-law** n mab yng nghyfraith
**sonnet** n soned
**soon** adv buan, ebrwydd, clau
**sooner** adv (time) ynghynt, yn gynt;
(preference): **I would ~ do** byddai'n
well gennyf wneud; **~ or later** yn
hwyr neu'n hwyrach
**soot** n huddygl, parddu
**soothe** vt lliniaru, lleddfu, dofi,
tawelu
**sop** n tamaid (wedi ei wlychu)
**sophism** n soffyddiaeth
**sophist** n soffydd
**sophistical** adj soffyddol
**sophisticated** adj soffistigedig
**sopping** adj gwlyb diferu
**soppy** adj teimladol; mwydlyd
**soprano** n soprano
**sorcerer** n swynwr, dewin
**sorcery** n swyngyfaredd,
dewiniaeth
**sordid** adj brwnt, cybyddlyd, gwael
**sore** adj tost, blin, dolurus ▷ n dolur
**sorrow** n tristwch, gofid, galar ▷ vi
tristáu, gofidio
**sorry** adj drwg gan, edifar; salw
**sort** n modd; math, bath ▷ vt trefnu,
dosbarthu
**sortie** n cyrch
**sorting office** n swyddfa
ddosbarthu
**so-so** adv gweddol
**sot** n diotyn, meddwyn
**soul** n enaid
**soul-destroying** adj yn fwrn
llethol
**sound** n sain, sŵn, trwst ▷ vb seinio
**sound** vb plymio, chwilio
**sound** n culfor, swnt
**sound** adj iach, iachus, dianaf,
cyfan, dilys; **sound effects** npl
effeithiau sain
**soundboard** n seinfwrdd
**soundly** adv yn drwm, yn llwyr
**soundproof** adj yn gwrthsefyll sŵn
**soup** n potes, cawl
**sour** adj sur ▷ vb suro

**source** n ffynhonnell, tarddiad
**south** n deau, de; **South Africa** n
De Affrica
**southern** adj deheuol
**souvenir** n cofrodd
**sovereign** adj pen ▷ n penadur;
sofren
**Soviet** adj Sofietaidd
**Soviet Union** n: **the ~** yr Undeb
Sofietaidd
**sow** n hwch
**sow** vt hau
**soya** n soya; **soya beans** npl ffa soya
**space** n lle, gwagle, gofod, encyd,
ysbaid
**spaceman** n gofodwr
**spaceship** n llong ofod
**spacious** adj eang, helaeth
**spade** n rhaw, pâl
**Spain** n Hisbaen
**span** n rhychwant ▷ vt rhychwantu
**spaniel** n adargi, sbaniel
**Spanish** adj Sbaenaidd ▷ n
Sbaeneg
**spank** vt slapio, smacio, palfodi,
chwipio tin
**spanner** n sbaner
**spar** vi cwffio, paffio
**spar** n polyn, cledren, ceibren
**spare** adj prin; tenau; sbâr ▷ vt
arbed; hepgor
**sparerib** n sbarib, asen-frân
**sparing** adj cynnil, prin
**spark** n gwreichionen
**sparkle** vi gwreichioni, serennu,
pefrio
**sparkling** adj gloyw, llachar;
byrlymog
**sparrow** n aderyn y to
**sparse** adj tenau, prin, gwasgarog
**spasm** n pwl, gwayw, brath
**spate** n llifeiriant sydyn
**spatter** vb tasgu
**spawn** n grawn, gronell; grifft; sil
▷ vb silio, bwrw grawn
**speak** vb llefaru, siarad
**speaker** n llefarydd, siaradwr

**spear** n gwaywffon, picell ▷ vt trywanu

**special** adj neilltuol, arbennig

**specialist** n arbenigwr

**speciality** n arbenigrwydd

**species** (**species**) n rhywogaeth

**specific** adj priodol, penodol, pendant

**specify** vt enwi, penodi

**specimen** n enghraifft, cynllun

**specious** adj teg yr olwg, rhithiol

**speck** n brycheuyn, ysmotyn

**speckle** vt britho, brychu

**spectacle** n drych, golygfa; (pl) sbectol

**spectator** n edrychwr, gwyliwr

**spectre** n drychiolaeth

**spectrum** (-ra) n spectrwm

**speculate** vi dyfalu; anturio, mentro

**speculation** n dyfaliad; antur, menter

**speech** n llafar, lleferydd, parabl, ymadrodd; araith

**speed** n cyflymder, buander ▷ vb prysuro, cyflymu; **speed limit** n ataliad cyflymder

**speedometer** n mesurydd cyflymdra

**spell** n cyfaredd, swyn

**spell** n sbel, hoe, ysbaid

**spell** vt sillafu

**spend** vb treulio, gwario, bwrw

**spendthrift** n afradwr, oferwr, gwastraffwr

**sperm** n had

**spew** vb chwydu

**sphere** n cronnell, sffêr, pêl; cylch, maes

**spice** n perlysiau, peraroglau, sbeis

**spick-and-span** adj fel y pin

**spicy** adj blasus; ffraeth, diddorol; coch

**spider** n cor, corryn, pryf copyn

**spike** n pig, hoel, cethren

**spikenard** n ysbignard, nard

**spill** vb colli, tywallt

**spin** vb nyddu, troi, troelli

**spinach** n pigoglys, sbinais

**spindle** n gwerthyd; echel

**spin-dryer** n trowasgwr

**spine** n asgwrn cefn; draen, pigyn

**spinner** n nyddwr

**spinning top** n top tro

**spinning-wheel** n troell

**spin-off** n mantais

**spinster** n merch ddibriod, hen ferch

**spiral** adj fel cogwrn tro, troellog

**spirant** adj llaes ▷ npl llaesion

**spire** n meindwr, pigwrn, pigdwr

**spirit** n ysbryd; gwirod

**spirited** adj calonnog, nwyfus, ysbrydol

**spiritual** adj ysbrydol

**spiritualist** n ysbrydegydd

**spit** n bêr

**spit** vb poeri

**spite** n sbeit, malais ▷ vt sbeitio

**spiteful** adj maleisus, sbeitlyd

**spittle** n poer, poeryn

**spittoon** n llestr poeri

**splash** vb sblasio; tasgu

**spleen** n y ddueg; pruddglwyf; natur ddrwg, gwenwyn

**splendid** adj ysblennydd, gwych, campus

**splendour** n ysblander, gwychder

**splint** n dellten, ysgyren, sblint

**splinter** vb ysgyrioni ▷ n ysgyren, fflaw

**split** vb hollti, rhannu, gwahanu

**spoil** n ysbail, anrhaith ▷ vb ysbeilio, ysbwylio, difetha

**spoke** n adain olwyn, sbogen, braich

**spokesman** n llefarwr, llefarydd

**spoliation** n ysbeiliad, ysbwyliad

**sponge** n sbwng ▷ vb ysbyngu

**sponsor** n mach, hyrwyddwr, noddwr; tad bedydd, mam fedydd

**spontaneous** adj gwirfoddol, digymell

**spook** n ysbryd, bwgan, bwci

**spool** n gwerthyd
**spoon** n llwy ▷ vb llwyo; caru
**spoonful** n llwyaid
**spoor** n brisg, ôl
**sporadic** adj achlysurol, gwasgarog
**spore** n had (rhedyn etc)
**sport** n sbort, chwarae, difyrrwch, cellwair, hwyl
**sportive** adj chwareus, nwyfus
**sports** npl mabolgampau, chwaraeon
**spot** n man, lle, llecyn; brycheuyn, ysmotyn ▷ vt mannu, brychu, ysmotio ▷ adj ar y pryd
**spotless** adj difrycheulyd, glân
**spotted** adj brith, brych
**spouse** n priod
**spout** vt pistyllio, ffrydio ▷ n pistyll
**sprain** vt ysigo
**sprawl** vi ymdaenu, ymdreiglo, ymrwyfo
**spray** n gwlith, tawch, trochion ▷ vt taenellu; chwistrellu
**spray** n ysbrigyn, cainc; chwystrellydd
**spread** vb lledu, taenu, lledaenu, gwasgaru
**spree** n sbri
**sprig** n brigyn, ysbrigyn
**sprightly** adj bywiog, hoenus, nwyfus
**spring** vb tarddu, codi, deillio; llamu, neidio ▷ n ffynnon; llam; sbring; gwanwyn; **spring-clean** n glanhau'r gwanwyn
**springy** adj sbringar
**sprinkle** vb taenellu, ysgeintio
**sprint** vb gwibio
**sprinter** n gwibiwr
**sprit** n sbryd
**sprite** n brigyd, bwgan, bwci
**sprout** vb tarddu, egino, glasu
**sprouts** npl (Brussels) ysgewyll Brysel
**spruce** adj twt, taclus, smart, crand ▷ n pyrwydden
**spry** adj sionc, heini, hoyw

**spur** n ysbardun, swmbwl ▷ vb ysbarduno, symbylu
**spurious** adj ffug, gau, annilys
**spurn** vb cicio, dirmygu, tremygu
**spurt** n ysbonc
**sputter** vb poeri siarad, baldorddi
**spy** n ysbïwr ▷ vb ysbïo
**squabble** vi cweryla, ffraeo ▷ n ffrwgwd, ffrae
**squad** n carfan, mintai
**squadron** n sgwadron
**squalid** adj brwnt, bawlyd, budr
**squall** vi ysgrechain ▷ n gwawch; storm o wynt
**squalor** n brynti
**squander** vt gwastraffu, afradu
**square** adj, n sgwâr, petryal
**squash** vt gwasgu, llethu ▷ n sboncen; **orange ~** sudd oren
**squat** vi swatio, cyrcydu
**squawk** vi gwawchio ▷ n gwawch
**squeak** vi gwichian ▷ n gwich
**squeal** vi gwichian
**squeamish** adj dicra, misi
**squeeze** vb gwasgu
**squelch** vt llethu, gostegu, rhoi taw ar
**squib** n tanen wyllt, fflachen; gogan, dychan
**squint** vb ciledrych, cibedrych ▷ n llygaid croes
**squire** n ysgweier, yswain
**squirm** vb gwingo
**squirrel** n gwiwer
**squirt** vb chwistrellu, tasgu ▷ n chwistrell, gwn dŵr
**stab** vb brathu, gwanu, trywanu
**stable** n ystabl
**stable** adj diysgog, sefydlog, safadwy, sad
**stack** n tas, bera; corn simnai, stac
**staff** n ffon; erwydd; staff
**stag** n carw, hydd
**stage** n pwynt; gradd, lefel; llwyfan
**stage-coach** n y goets fawr
**stagger** vb honclan, gwegian; syfrdanu

**stagnant** adj llonydd, marw
**stagnate** vi cronni, sefyll
**staid** adj sad, sobr
**stain** vb ystaenio, llychwino ▷ n staen
**stained glass window** n ffenestr liw
**stainless** adj difrycheulyd, gloyw
**stair** n gris, staer
**stake** n polyn, pawl, ystanc; cyngwystl
**stale** adj hen, hendrwm; diflas, mws
**stalk** vb torsythu, rhodio'n benuchel, mynd ar drywydd
**stalk** n paladr, gwelltyn, coes
**stall** n côr; stondin; talcen glo ▷ vb stolio
**stalls** npl (in cinema, theatre) seddau; stondinau
**stallion** n march, stalwyn
**stalwart** adj cadarn, pybyr, dewr
**stamen** n brigeryn
**stamina** n saf, ynni
**stammer** vb bloesgi, siarad ag atal arno
**stamp** n stamp, delw, argraff ▷ vb stampio; curo traed
**stampede** n chwalfa, rhuthr
**stanch** vt atal, sychu (gwaed)
**stanchion** n annel, ateg, post, gwanas
**stand** vb sefyll, bod, aros ▷ n safiad; eisteddle; stondyn
**standard** n lluman, baner; post; safon
**stanza** n pennill
**staple** n prif nwydd; edefyn (gwlân etc)
**staple** n ystwffwl, stapal
**stapler** n styffylwr
**star** n seren ▷ vb serennu
**starch** n starts
**stare** vb llygadrythu, synnu
**stark** adj syth, moel, rhonc ▷ adv hollol
**starling** n aderyn drudwy, drudwen, aderyn yr eira

**starry** adj serennog
**start** vb dechrau, cychwyn, codi, rhusio, tasgu
**startle** vt brawychu, dychrynu, rhusio
**starvation** n newyn
**starve** vb newynu; fferru, rhynnu
**state** n ystad, cyflwr, ansawdd; rhwysg; gwladwriaeth; talaith
**state** vt mynegi, datgan; penodi
**stately** adj urddasol, mawreddog
**statement** n mynegiad, datganiad, haeriad
**statesman (-men)** n gwladweinydd
**station** n gorsaf, stesion; safle, sefyllfa
**stationary** adj sefydlog
**stationer** n gwerthwr papurau
**stationer's** n (shop) siop bapurau
**stationmaster** n gorsaf-feistr
**statistics** npl ystadegau
**statue** n delw, cerfddelw, cerflun
**stature** n uchder, taldra, corffolaeth
**status** n safle, braint, statws
**statute** n deddf, cyfraith, ystatud
**staunch** adj pybyr, cywir
**stave** n estyllen, erwydd ▷ vt astellu; dryllio; ~ off cadw draw
**stay** vb aros; ategu; atal ▷ n arhosiad; ateg; (pl) staes
**stead** n lle
**steadfast** adj diysgog
**steadily** adv yn bwyllog, yn gyson
**steady** adj sad, diysgog; cyson, gwastad
**steak** n golwyth, stec
**steal** vb dwyn, lladrata, cipio
**stealth** n lladrad; **by ~** yn ddistaw bach
**stealthy** adj lladradaidd
**steam** n ager, anwedd, stêm, tarth ▷ vb ageru
**steamer** n agerlong, stemar
**steed** n march, ceffyl
**steel** n dur ▷ vt caledu
**steelworks** n gwaith dur

**steep** adj serth ▷ n dibyn, clogwyn, llethr

**steep** vt rhoi yng ngwlych, mwydo, sucio

**steeple** n clochdy

**steer** n bustach

**steer** vb llywio; cyfeirio

**steering** n llywio

**steering wheel** n llyw

**stem** n paladr, corsen, coes, bôn; ach; pen blaen

**stem** vt gwrthsefyll, gwrthladd, atal

**stench** n drewdod, drycsawr

**stenography** n llaw-fer

**step** vi camu; cerdded ▷ n cam; gris

**step-** prefix llys-

**stepdaughter** n llysferch

**stepfather** n llystad

**stepmother** n llysfam, mam wen

**stepsister** n llyschwaer

**stepson** n llysfab

**stereotype** n ystrydeb ▷ vt ystrydebu

**sterile** adj diffrwyth, sych

**sterilize** vb diffrwythloni, diheintio

**sterling** adj ysterling; diledryw, diffuant

**stern** adj llym, penderfynol

**stern** n starn, pen ôl llong

**stethoscope** n corn meddyg

**stevedore** n llwythwr a dadlwythwr llongau

**stew** vb araf ferwi, stiwio ▷ n stiw

**steward** n stiward, goruchwyliwr, distain

**stick** n pren, ffon, pric, gwialen

**stick** vb glynu; gwanu, brathu

**sticky** adj gludiog, glynol; anodd

**stiff** adj syth, anystwyth, anhyblyg, ystyfnig

**stiffen** vb sythu, ystyfnigo

**stifle** vt mygu, tagu, diffodd

**stigma** n gwarthnod, stigma

**stile** n camfa, sticil, sticill

**still** n distyllfa, stil

**still** adj llonydd; marw ▷ vb llonyddu

**still** adv eto, er hynny; byth

**stilt** n ystudfach

**stilted** adj annaturiol; mawreddog

**stimulant** n symbylydd; gwirod

**stimulate** vt symbylu

**stimulus** (-li) n symbyliad, swmbwl

**sting** vb pigo, brathu, colynnu ▷ n colyn

**stingy** adj crintach, cybyddlyd

**stink** vi, n drewi

**stinking** adj drewllyd

**stint** vt cynilo, cybydda ▷ n prinder

**stipend** n cyflog, tâl

**stipulate** vb amodi, mynnu

**stir** vb cyffroi, cynhyrfu, symud ▷ n stŵr, cynnwrf

**stirrup** n gwarthol

**stitch** n pwyth; gwayw, pigyn ▷ vt pwytho, gwnïo

**stoat** n carlwm

**stock** n cyff; stoc, ystôr; **stocks** npl cyffion

**stock exchange** n cyfnewidfa stoc

**stocking** n hosan

**stocky** adj cadarn, cryf, cydnerth

**stodgy** adj toeslyd, trymllyd, diflas

**stoke** vb edrych ar ôl tân, tanio

**stole** n ystola

**stolid** adj swrth, digyffro

**stomach** n cylla, stumog

**stone** n carreg, maen ▷ vt llabyddio

**stool** n ystôl

**stoop** vb plygu, crymu, gwargrymu, ymostwng

**stop** vb atal, rhwystro; stopio, cau; aros, sefyll ▷ n atalfa; atalnod

**stoppage** n (pay) ataliad; (strike) streic

**stopper** n topyn, caead

**storage** n stôr, storfa

**store** n ystôr, ystorfa ▷ vt ystorio

**storey, story** n uchdwr, llofft, llawr

**stork** n ciconia, chwibon

**storm** n (y)storm, tymestl

**stormy** adj stormus, tymhestlog, garw

**story** n hanes, chwedl, stori; celwydd

**stout** adj tew, ffyrf; pybyr, gwrol, glew

**stove** n stof, ffwrn

**stow** vt pacio, dodi o'r neilltu

**stowaway** n teithiwr cudd

**straddle** vi bongamu, lledu'r traed

**straggle** vi crwydro, gwasgaru

**straggler** n crwydryn

**straight** adj union, syth

**straighten** vb unioni

**straightforward** adj syml; didwyll, gonest

**straightway** adv yn y fan, yn syth

**strain** vb straenio, streifio, ysigo; tynhau; hidlo ▷ n straen

**strainer** n hidl(en)

**strait** adj cyfyng, cul, caeth ▷ n cyfyngder; culfor

**strand** n traeth, traethell, tywyn

**strand** n cainc (rhaff), edau

**strange** adj dieithr, estronol, rhyfedd

**stranger** n dyn dieithr, estron

**strangle** vt tagu, llindagu

**strap** n strap, cengl

**strategic** adj strategol

**strategy** n strategaeth

**stratum (-ta)** n haen

**straw** n gwellt; gwelltyn, blewyn

**strawberry** n mefysen, syfïen

**stray** vi crwydro, cyfeiliorni

**streak** n llinell, rhes, rhesen; stremp ▷ vb gwibio

**stream** n ffrwd ▷ vb ffrydio, llifo

**streamer** n rhuban, baner

**street** n heol, ystryd

**strength** n cryfder, nerth, grym

**strengthen** vb cryfhau, nerthu

**strenuous** adj egnïol, ymdrechgar

**stress** n pwys, straen, caledi

**stretch** vb estyn, tynhau ▷ n estyniad

**stretcher** n trestl, stretsier

**strew** vt gwasgaru, sarnu, chwalu, taenu

**strict** adj cyfyng, caeth, llym

**stricture** n cyfyngiad; cerydd, sen

**stride** vb camu, brasgamu ▷ n cam

**strife** n cynnen, ymryson, ymrafael

**strike** vb taro; gostwng ▷ n taro, streic

**striker** n streiciwr

**striking** adj trawiadol, hynod

**string** n llinyn, tant, cortyn

**stringent** adj caeth, llym, tyn

**strip** n llain, llafn, llefnyn; **film ~** striplun, stribed ffilm

**strip** vb diosg, ymddiosg, ymddihatru

**stripe** n rhes, rhesen; gwialennod

**striped** adj rhengog, rhesenog; â llinellau amliw ar hyd-ddo

**stripling** n glaslanc, llanc, llencyn

**strive** vi ymdrechu; ymryson

**stroke** n dyrnod, ergyd, trawiad; llinell

**stroke** vt llochi, dylofi, pratio, canmol

**stroll** vi crwydro, rhodianna

**strong** adj cryf, grymus, cadarn

**stronghold** n amddiffynfa, cadarnle

**structure** n adail, adeilad, saernïaeth, adeiledd, strwythur

**struggle** vi gwingo; ymdrechu ▷ n ymdrech

**strut** vi torsythu

**stub** n bonyn

**stubble** n sofl

**stubborn** adj cyndyn, ystyfnig

**stuck-up** adj ffroenuchel

**stud** n boglwm, boglyn, styden

**stud** n gre

**student** n myfyriwr, efrydydd

**studio** n stiwdio

**study** n astudiaeth, efrydiaeth ▷ npl efrydiau; myfyrgell, stydi ▷ vb myfyrio, efrydu, astudio

**stuff** n defnydd, stwff ▷ vb stwffio, gwthio

**stuffing** adj (bed) fflocys; (Culin) stwffin

**stuffy** adj myglyd, trymllyd, trymaidd
**stumble** vb tramgwyddo, baglu, syrthio
**stump** n bonyn, boncyff
**stun** vt syfrdanu, byddaru, hurtio
**stunt** vt crabio
**stunted** adj crablyd
**stupefy** vt syfrdanu, hurtio
**stupendous** adj aruthrol
**stupid** adj hurt, pendew, dwl, twp
**stupor** n syfrdandod, syrthni
**sturdy** adj talgryf, pybyr, cadarn, cryf
**stutter** vi siarad ag atal arno, bloesgi
**sty** n cwt, cut, twlc
**style** n dull, arddull; cyfenw, teitl ▷ vt cyfenwi
**stylish** adj dillyn, trwsiadus
**stylus** n (of record player) nodwydd
**suave** adj mwyn, tirion, hynaws, rhadlon
**sub-** prefix tan-, is-, go-
**subconscious** n isymwybod ▷ adj isymwybodol
**subdue** vt darostwng; lleddfu
**subject** adj darostyngedig; caeth; ufudd ▷ n deiliad; pwnc, testun; goddrych
**subject** vt darostwng, dwyn dan
**subjective** adj goddrychol
**subjugate** vt darostwng
**subjunctive** adj dibynnol
**sublime** adj aruchel, arddunol
**submarine** adj tanforol ▷ n llong danfor
**submerge** vb soddi, suddo
**submission** n ymostyngiad; ufudd-dod; cyflwyniad
**submissive** adj gostyngedig, ufudd
**submit** vb ymostwng, ymddarostwng; datgan barn; cyflwyno
**subnormal** adj isnormal
**subordinate** adj israddol ▷ vt darostwng

**subpoena** n gwŷs
**subscribe** vb tanysgrifio, cyfrannu
**subscription** n tanysgrifiad, cyfraniad
**subsequent** adj canlynol, dilynol
**subsequently** adv wedyn, ar ôl hynny
**subside** vi soddi, ymollwng; darfod
**subsidiary** adj israddol; ychwanegol, atodol
**subsidy** n arian cymorth, cymhorthdal
**subsist** vb byw, bod, bodoli, ymgynnal
**subsistence** n cynhaliaeth
**subsoil** n isbridd
**substance** n sylwedd, defnydd; da
**substantial** adj sylweddol
**substantiate** vt profi, gwirio
**substitute** n eilydd, dirprwy, un yn lle arall ▷ vt rhoi yn lle
**subterfuge** n ystryw, cast
**subterranean** adj tanddaearol
**subtle** adj cyfrwys, craff
**subtract** vt tynnu ymaith
**suburb** n maestref
**subvert** vt dymchwelyd, gwyrdroi
**subway** n isffordd
**succeed** vb dilyn, canlyn, llwyddo, ffynnu
**success** n llwyddiant, llwydd, ffyniant
**successful** adj llwyddiannus
**successfully** adv yn llwyddiannus
**succession** n dilyniad, olyniaeth
**successive** adj dilynol, olynol
**succinct** adj byr, cryno
**succour** vt swcro, ymgeleddu ▷ n swcr, ymgeledd
**succulent** adj ir, iraidd, noddlyd
**succumb** vi ymollwng dan, ildio, marw
**such** adj cyfryw, y fath, cyffelyb
**suck** vb sugno, dyfnu, llyncu, yfed
**suckle** vt rhoi bron, sugno
**suction** n sugn, sugniad, sugndyniad

**sudden** *adj* sydyn, disymwth, disyfyd
**suds** *npl* trochion sebon, sucion
**sue** *vb* erlyn; erfyn, deisyf
**suede** *n* swêd
**suet** *n* gwêr, swyf, siwed
**suffer** *vb* goddef, dioddef, gadael
**sufferer** *n* dioddefydd
**suffering** *n* dioddef
**suffice** *vb* bod yn ddigon, digoni
**sufficient** *adj* digon, digonol
**suffix** *n* olddodiad
**suffocate** *vb* mygu, tagu
**suffrage** *n* pleidlais
**suffuse** *vt* taenu, gwasgaru, ymledu
**sugar** *n* siwgr ▷ *vt* siwgro
**suggest** *vt* awgrymu
**suggestion** *n* awgrym, awgrymiad
**suicide** *n* hunanladdiad
**suit** *n* cwyn, cyngaws, hawl; deisyfiad, cais; siwt, pâr ▷ *vb* ateb, siwtio, gweddu, taro
**suitable** *adj* addas, cyfaddas, cymwys
**suitably** *adv* yn addas
**suitcase** *n* bag dillad
**suite** *n* cyfres; gosgordd, nifer
**suitor** *n* cwynwr; cariadfab
**sulk** *vi* sorri, pwdu, mulo
**sullen** *adj* sarrug, cuchiog, blwng
**sully** *vt* difwyno, llychwino
**sulphur** *n* sylffwr
**sultan** *n* swltan
**sultry** *adj* mwrn, mwll, clòs
**sum** *n* swm ▷ *vt* crynhoi, symio
**summarize** *vb* crynhoi
**summary** *adj* byr, cryno ▷ *n* crynodeb
**summer** *n* haf
**summerhouse** *n* tŷ haf
**summit** *n* pen, copa, crib
**summon** *vt* gwysio, dyfynnu
**summons** *n* gwŷs, dyfyn
**sump** *n* swmp
**sumptuous** *adj* moethus
**sun** *n* haul ▷ *vt* heulo

**sunbathe** *vb* torheulo, bolaheulo
**sunbeam** *n* pelydryn
**sunburn** *n* llosg haul
**Sunday** *n* dydd Sul
**sunder** *vt* ysgaru, gwahanu
**sundry** *adj* armryw, amrywiol
**sunflower** *n* blodyn yr haul
**sunglasses** *npl* sbectol haul
**sunny** *adj* heulog
**sunshine** *n* heulwen
**sunstroke** *n* ergyd (yr) haul
**suntan** *n* lliw haul
**sup** *vb* llymeitian; swpera, swpero ▷ *n* llymaid
**super-** *prefix* uwch, goruwch, gor-, tra-, ar-
**superannuation** *n* ymddeolaeth, pensiwn
**superb** *adj* ysblennydd, godidog
**supercilious** *adj* balch, ffroenuchel
**superficial** *adj* arwynebol, bas
**superfine** *adj* coeth
**superfluous** *adj* gormodol, afreidiol
**superintend** *vt* arolygu
**superintendent** *n* arolygwr, arolygydd
**superior** *adj* uwch, gwell, rhagorach; uwchraddol ▷ *n* uchafiad, uwchradd
**superiority** *n* rhagoriaeth
**superlative** *adj* uchaf; eithaf
**supermarket** *n* archfarchnad
**supernatural** *adj* goruwchnaturiol
**supersede** *vt* disodli
**superstition** *n* coelgrefydd, ofergoeliaeth
**superstitious** *adj* coelgrefyddol, ofergoelus
**supervene** *vi* digwydd
**supervise** *vt* arolygu
**supervision** *n* arolygiaeth
**supine** *adj* diofal, didaro, swrth
**supper** *n* swper
**supplant** *vt* disodli
**supple** *adj* ystwyth, hyblyg

**supplement** n atodiad ▷ vt atodi
**supplementary** adj atodol, ychwanegol
**suppliant** n ymbiliwr, erfyniwr
**supplicate** vb erfyn, ymbil, deisyf
**supplier** n cyflenwr, cyflenwydd
**supply** vt cyflenwi, cyflawni ▷ n cyflenwad
**support** vt cynnal ▷ n cynhaliaeth
**supporter** n cefnogwr, cefnogydd
**suppose** vt tybio, tybied, bwrw
**suppository** n tawddgyffur
**suppress** vt llethu, gostegu; atal; celu
**suppurate** vi crawni, gori
**supreme** adj goruchaf, prif, pennaf
**sur-** prefix gor-
**surcharge** n gordal, gordoll ▷ vb codi gormod
**sure** adj, adv siwr, sicr; diamau, diau
**surely** adv yn sicr, yn ddiau
**surety** n mach, meichiau, gwystl
**surf** n traethon, beiston; gorewyn ▷ vb brigo, brigdonni
**surface** n wyneb, arwynebedd, caen
**surfeit** n syrffed ▷ vb alaru, syrffedu
**surge** vi ymchwyddo ▷ n ymchwydd
**surgeon** n llawfeddyg
**surgery** n llawfeddygaeth; meddygfa, llys meddyg
**surgical** adj llawfeddygol
**surly** adj sarrug, afrywiog
**surmise** n tyb ▷ vt tybied, amau
**surmount** vt mynd dros, gorchfygu, trechu
**surname** n cyfenw ▷ vt cyfenwi
**surpass** vt rhagori ar, trechu
**surplice** n gwenwisg
**surplus** n gweddill, gormod, gwarged
**surprise** n syndod ▷ vt synnu
**surprising** adj syn, rhyfedd
**surrender** vb traddodi, ildio
**surreptitious** adj lladradaidd, llechwraidd

**surrogate** n dirprwy, rhaglaw esgob
**surround** vt amgylchu, amgylchynu
**surroundings** npl amgylchoedd
**surveillance** n arolygiaeth, gwyliadwriaeth
**survey** vt edrych, arolygu; mesur ▷ n arolwg
**survival** n goroesiad
**survive** vb goroesi
**survivor** n goroeswr
**susceptible** adj parod i, tueddol i
**suspect** vt drwgdybio, amau ▷ n un a ddrwgdybir
**suspend** vt crogi; gohirio, atal
**suspended sentence** n dedfryd wedi'i gohirio
**suspense** n pryder, petruster, oediad
**suspension** n ataliad; **suspension bridge** n pont grog
**suspicion** n drwgdybiaeth, amheuaeth
**suspicious** adj drwgdybus, amheus
**sustain** vt cynnal; dioddef, goddef
**sustained** adj parhaus, cyson
**sustenance** n cynhaliaeth, ymborth, bwyd
**swagger** vb rhodresa, torsythu, swagro
**swallow** n gwennol
**swallow** vt llyncu ▷ n llwnc
**swamp** n cors ▷ vt gorlifo, boddi
**swan** n alarch
**swank** vi bocsachu, rhodresa ▷ n bocsach
**swap** vb ffeirio
**swarm** n haid ▷ vi heidio, heigio
**swarm** vb dringo
**swarthy** adj melynddu, croenddu, tywyll
**swat** vb taro
**swathe** vt rhwymo, rhwymynnu
**sway** vb siglo, gwegian; llywio ▷ n llywodraeth, swae
**swear** vb tyngu, rhegi

**sweat** n chwys ▷ vb chwysu
**sweater** n cot wlan, sweter
**sweaty** adj chwyslyd
**swede** n rwden, sweden
**Swede** n Swediad
**Sweden** n Sweden
**Swedish** adj Swedaidd
**sweep** vb ysgubo ▷ n ysgubiad; ysgubwr
**sweeping** adj ysgubol
**sweet** adj melys, pêr, peraidd ▷ n pwdin
**sweeten** vb melysu; pereiddio
**sweetheart** n cariad
**sweetmeat** n fferin, melysyn
**swell** vb chwyddo ▷ n chwydd, ymchwydd; gŵr mawr
**swelling** n chwydd(i)
**swelter** vi crasu; lluddedu, dyddfu
**sweltering** adj llethol, tesog
**swerve** vi gwyro, osgoi, cilio, troi
**swift** adj cyflym, buan, chwyrn, clau
**swift** n gwennol ddu
**swig** n llymaid, dracht ▷ vb drachtio
**swill** n golchion; bwyd sur ▷ vb golchi; slotian
**swim** vb nofio ▷ n nawf
**swimmer** n nofiwr
**swimming** n nofio
**swimmingly** adv yn braf, yn hwylus
**swimming pool** n pwll nofio
**swimsuit** n dillad nofio, gwisg nofio
**swindle** vb twyllo, hocedu ▷ n twyll
**swine** (swine) n mochyn
**swing** vb siglo ▷ n sigl, siglen, swing
**swinge** vt llachio, baeddu
**swirl** vb troi, chwyldroi, chwyrndroi
**swish** vb chwipio
**switch** n swits, botwm ▷ vb troi, newid
**swivel** n bwylltid ▷ vb troi
**swollen** adj chwyddedig, wedi chwyddo
**swoon** vt llewygu, llesmeirio ▷ n llewyg
**swoop** vb dyfod ar warthaf, disgyn
**swop** vt cyfnewid, ffeirio
**sword** n cleddyf, cleddau, cledd
**sycamore** n sycamorwydden
**syllable** n sillaf
**syllabus** n rhaglen, maes llafur
**syllogism** n cyfresymiad
**symbol** n arwyddlun, symbol, symlen (estheteg)
**symbolism** n symboliaeth
**symmetrical** adj cymesur
**symmetry** n cymesuredd
**sympathetic** adj cydymdeimladol
**sympathize** vi cydymdeimlo
**sympathy** n cydymdeimlad
**symphony** n symffoni
**symposium** (-ia) n trafodaeth, cynhadledd
**symptom** n arwydd
**synagogue** n synagog
**synchronize** vb cyfamseru, cydamseru
**syncopation** n trawsacen (cerdd)
**syncope** n marwlewyg; syncopé
**syndicate** n cwmni
**synod** n cymanfa, senedd, synod
**synonym** n (gair) cyfystyr
**synopsis** (-ses) n cyfolwg; crynodeb
**syntax** n cystrawen
**synthesis** (-ses) n cyfosodiad, synthesis
**Syria** n Syria
**syringe** n chwistrell ▷ vt chwistrellu
**syrup** n sudd; triagl (melyn)
**system** n cyfundrefn; trefn, system
**systematic** adj cyfundrefnol
**systematize** vb cyfundrefnu

# t

**tab** *n* tafod, llabed
**tabby** *n* cath frech, cath fenyw
**tabernacle** *n* tabernacl, pabell
**table** *n* bwrdd, bord; tabl, taflen
**tableau** *n* golygfa (ddramatig)
**table-cloth** *n* lliain bord (bwrdd)
**tableful** *n* bordaid, byrddaid
**tablespoon** *n* llwy fwrdd
**tablet** *n* llechen, llech; tabled
**table tennis** *n* tennis bwrdd,
  ping pong
**taboo** *n* ysgymunbeth;
  gwaharddiad, tabŵ
**tabular** *adj* taflennol
**tabulate** *vt* tablu, taflennu
**tacit** *adj* dealledig (ond heb ei
  grybwyll)
**taciturn** *adj* tawedog
**tack** *n* tac, pwyth, brasbwyth
  ▷ *vb* tacio
**tackle** *n* taclau, offer, tacl (mewn
  rygbi), taclad ▷ *vb* ymosod ar, taclo
**tackler** *n* taclwr
**tact** *n* tact, callineb, doethineb
**tactful** *adj* doeth, pwyllog,
  synhwyrol
**tactician** *n* tactegydd
**tactics** *npl* cynlluniau, tactegau
**tactile** *adj* cyffyrddol
**tactless** *adj* di-dact, annoeth
**tadpole** *n* penbwl, penbwla
**tag** *n* pwyntl; clust, dolen
**tail** *n* cynffon, llosgwrn, cwt
**tailback** *n* cwt, tagfa
**tailor** *n* teiliwr

**taint** *vb* llygru, heintio, difwyno ▷ *n*
  llwgr, ystaen, mefl
**take** *vb* cymryd, derbyn, cael
**talcum** *n* talcwm
**tale** *n* chwedl, hanes, stori, clec, clep
**talent** *n* talent
**talisman** *n* swynbeth, swyn,
  cyfaredd
**talk** *vb, n* siarad
**talkative** *adj* siaradus
**tall** *adj* tal, hir, uchel
**tallness** *n* taldra
**tallow** *n* gwêr
**tally** *n* cyfrif ▷ *vb* cyfateb, cytuno
**talon** *n* ewin, crafanc (aderyn)
**tambourine** *n* tambwrîn
**tame** *adj* dof, gwâr ▷ *vt* dofi
**tamper** *vi* ymhél(â), ymyrryd(â)
**tampon** *n* tampwn
**tan** *vb* trin lledr; llosgi, melynu
**tangent** *n* tangiad, llinell gyffwrdd
**tangible** *adj* cyffyrddadwy,
  sylweddol
**tangle** *vb* drysu, cymysgu ▷ *n*
  dryswch, cymhlethdod
**tank** *n* dyfrgist, tanc
**tankard** *n* diodlestr, tancr
**tanker** *n* tancer, llong olew
**tannery** *n* barcerdy, crwynfa,
  tanerdy
**tantalize** *vt* poeni, poenydio,
  pryfocio
**tantamount** *adj* cyfwerth, cyfystyr
**tantrums** *npl* stranciau, nwydau
**tap** *vb* taro yn ysgafn
**tap** *n* tap, feis ▷ *vt* tapio, gollwng
**tape** *n* tâp, incil
**tape measure** *n* tâp mesur
**tape-recorder** *n* recordydd tâp,
  peiriant recordio, arnodydd
**taper** *n* cannwyll gŵyr, tapr ▷ *vb*
  meinhau, tapro
**tapestry** *n* tapestri
**tape-worm** *n* llyngeren
**tapioca** *n* tapioca
**tar** *n* tar; llongwr, morwr
**tardy** *adj* hwyrfrydig, araf,

diweddar, ymarhous
**target** n nod, targed
**tariff** n toll; rhestr taliadau, rhestr prisiau
**tarmac** n tarmac
**tarnish** vb pylu, cymylu, llychwino
**tarpaulin** n tarpolin
**tarry** vb aros, oedi, tario; trigo, preswylio
**tart** n tarten, pastai
**tart** adj sur, surllyd
**tartan** n brithwe, plod
**task** n gorchwyl, tasg ▷ vt rhoi tasg, trethu, llethu
**tassel** n tusw, tasel
**taste** vb chwaethu, blasu, profi ▷ n blas; chwaeth
**tatter** n rhecsyn, cerpyn
**tattered** adj carpiog
**tattle** vb clebran, clegar ▷ n cleber, baldordd
**tattoo** n tatŵ ▷ vb torri llun (yn y croen)
**taunt** vt edliw, dannod, gwatwar ▷ n gwaradwydd, sen
**taut** adj tyn
**tautologous** adj ailadroddol, cyfystyrol
**tautology** n tawtologaeth, ailadrodd, cyfystyredd
**tavern** n tafarn, tafarndy, tŷ tafarn
**tawdry** adj coegwych
**tawny** n melynddu, melyn
**tax** n treth ▷ vt trethu; cyhuddo
**taxi** n tacsi; **taxi rank** n lloc dacsi
**taxidermist** n stwffiwr anifeiliaid
**tea** n te
**tea-bag** n bag te, cwdyn te
**teacup** n disgl de, cwpan te
**tea-leaves** n dail te
**tea-party** n teparti
**teach** vt dysgu, addysgu
**teacher** n athro
**teaching** n dysgeidiaeth; dysgu
**teak** n tîc
**team** n gwedd, pâr, tîm
**teapot** n tebot

**tear** n deigryn, deigr
**tear** vb rhwygo, llarpio ▷ n rhwyg
**tearful** adj dagreuol
**tease** vt pryfocio, plagio, poeni
**teaser** n poenwr, poenydiwr
**teaspoon** n llwy de
**teaspoonful** n llond llwy de
**teat** n teth, diden, bron
**technical** adj technegol
**technician** n technegydd
**technique** n techneg
**technological** adj technolegol
**technology** n technoleg
**teddy (bear)** n arth anwes, tedi
**tedious** adj blin, anniben, poenus
**tedium** n diflastod, blinder
**teem** vb epilio, hilio, heigio
**teenager** n un yn yr arddegau
**teens** n arddegau
**teethe** vi torri dannedd
**teetotaller** n llwyrymwrthodwr, titotal
**telecast** n telediad
**telecommunication** n cysylltiad trwy'r teliffon, telegyfathrebaeth
**telegram** n teligram
**telegraph** n teligraff ▷ vb teligraffio
**teleology** n dibenyddiaeth
**telepathy** n telepathi
**telephase** n olgyflwr
**telephone** n teliffon, ffôn; **telephone box** n bocs ffonio; **telephone call** n galwad ffôn; **~ directory** cyfeirlyfr ffôn
**telescope** n ysbienddrych, telisgob
**televise** vb teledu
**television** n teledu
**tell** vb dweud, traethu, adrodd, mynegi; cyfrif, rhifo
**telltale** n clepgi, clepiwr, clepwraig
**temerity** n rhyfyg, hyfdra
**temper** n tymer, naws ▷ vt tymheru
**temperament** n anianawd
**temperamental** adj gwamal, oriog, di-ddal
**temperance** n dirwest

**temperate** adj cymedrol; tymherus
**temperature** n tymheredd
**tempest** n tymestl
**tempestuous** adj tymhestlog
**temple** n teml
**temple** n arlais
**temporal** adj tymhorol
**temporary** adj dros amser, tymhoroi
**temporize** vi oedi, anwadalu
**tempt** vt temtio, profi
**tempter** n temtiwr
**temptation** n temtiad, temtasiwn
**ten** adj, n deg
**tenable** adj daliadwy, y gellir ei ddal; diffynadwy
**tenacious** adj tyn ei afael, gwydn, gludiog, cyndyn
**tenacity** n cyndynrwydd
**tenant** n deiliad, tenant
**tench** n tens
**tend** vb tendio, gweini
**tend** vi tueddu, cyfeirio, symud
**tendance** n sylw, gofal, tendans
**tendency** n tuedd, gogwydd
**tendentious** adj pleidiol, pleidgar
**tender** adj tyner, tirion, mwyn; meddal
**tender** vb cynnig, cyflwyno ▷ n cynnig
**tenderness** n tynerwch
**tendon** n gewyn
**tendril** n tendril
**tenement** n annedd, rhandy
**tenet** n daliad, barn, tyb
**tenfold** adj dengwaith
**tennis** n tennis; **tennis ball** n pêl dennis; **tennis court** n cwrt tennis; **tennis racket** n raced tennis
**tenon** n tyno
**tenor** n cyfeiriad, tuedd, rhediad; tenor
**tense** adj tyn, dirdynnol, dwys, angerddol
**tense** n amser (berf)
**tension** n tyndra, pwys, tyniant
**tent** n pabell

**tentacle** n tentacl, braich
**tentative** adj arbrofiadol, dros dro; ansicr
**tenter-hook** n bach deintur; **on ~s** ar bigau'r drain
**tenth** adj degfed
**tenuous** adj tenau, main, prin
**tenure** n deiliadaeth
**tepid** adj claear
**tercentenary** n trichanmlwyddiant
**term** n terfyn; term; teler, amod; tymor ▷ vt galw, enwi
**terminal** adj terfynol, termol
**terminate** vb terfynu
**termination** n terfyniad
**terminology** n termynoleg
**terminus** n terfyn
**termites** npl morgrug gwynion
**tern** n môr-wennol
**terrace** n rhes dai, teras
**terrain** n tir, bro, ardal
**terrestrial** adj daearol
**terrible** adj dychrynllyd, ofnadwy, arswydus
**terrier** n daeargi
**terrific** adj dychrynllyd, arswydus
**terrify** vt brawychu, dychrynu
**terrifying** adj brawychus, dychrynllyd
**territorial** adj tiriogaethol
**territory** n tir, tiriogaeth
**terror** n dychryn, braw, arswyd, ofn
**terrorise** vb dychrynu, brawychu
**terrorist** n terfysgwr, brawychwr
**terror-stricken** adj wedi ei ddychrynu
**terse** adj byr a chryno
**terseness** n byrdra
**test** n prawf ▷ vt profi
**testament** n testament, cyfamod, ewyllys
**testator** n cymynnwr
**tester** n profwr
**testicle** n caill, carreg
**testify** vb tystio
**testimonial** n tysteb, tystlythyr

**testimony** n tystiolaeth; profiad
**testy** adj afrywiog, ffrom, croes
**tetanus** n gên glo, tetanws
**tether** n rhaff, tennyn ▷ vt clymu
**text** n testun, adnod
**textbook** n gwerslyfr
**textile** adj gweol
**textual** adj testunol
**texture** n gwe, gwead, cyfansoddiad
**Thailand** n Gwlad Thai
**than** conj na, nag
**thank** vt, n diolch
**thankful** adj diolchgar
**thankless** adj diddiolch
**thanks** npl diolch, diolchiadau
**thanksgiving** n diolchgarwch
**that** pron dem hwn (hon) yna (acw), hwnnw, honno, hynny ▷ rel a, y(r) ▷ adj hwn, hon, yma, yna, acw ▷ conj mai, taw
**thatch** n to, to gwellt ▷ vt toi
**thatcher** n töwr (â gwellt, etc)
**thaw** vb dadlaith, dadmer, meirioli, toddi
**the** adj yr, y
**theatre** n theatr, chwaraedy; maes, golygfa
**theatrical** adj theatraidd
**thee** pron ti, tydi, tithau
**theft** n lladrad
**their** pron eu
**theirs** pron yr eiddynt, eiddynt hwy
**theism** n duwiaeth, theistiaeth
**theist** n un sy'n credu yn Nuw
**them** pron hwy, hwynt, hwythau
**theme** n testun, pwnc, thema
**themselves** pron eu hunain
**then** adv y pryd hwnnw, yna ▷ conj yna
**thence** adv oddi yno, o hynny
**thenceforth** adv o'r amser hwnnw ymlaen
**theocracy** n theocratiaeth
**theologian** n diwinydd
**theological** adj diwinyddol
**theology** n diwinyddiaeth

**theorem** n theorem
**theoretical** adj damcaniaethol, mewn theori
**theorise** vb damcaniaethu
**theory** n damcaniaeth, tyb
**therapeutic** adj iachaol, meddygol
**therapy** n therapi
**there** adv yna, yno, acw; dyna, dacw
**thereafter** adv wedyn
**thereat** adv ar hynny, yna
**thereby** adv trwy hynny
**therefore** conj gan hynny, am hynny
**therefrom** adv oddi yno
**therein** adv yno, ynddo
**thereupon** adv ar hynny
**therewith** adv gyda hynny
**thermal** adj thermol, gwresol, brwd
**thermometer** n thermomedr, mesurydd gwres
**these** adj pl y rhai hyn, y rhai yma
**thesis** (-ses) n gosodiad; traethawd, thesis
**they** pron hwy, hwynt, hwynt-hwy
**thick** adj tew, praff, trwchus
**thicken** vb tewhau, tewychu
**thicket** n prysglwyn, llwyn
**thick-headed** adj pendew, hurt, twp
**thickness** n trwch, tewder
**thick-skinned** adj croendew
**thief** (thieves) n lleidr
**thieve** vi lladrata, dwyn
**thigh** n clun, morddwyd
**thimble** n gwniadur
**thin** adj tenau, cul, main; anaml, prin ▷ vb teneuo
**thine** pron eiddot ti; dy
**thing** n peth, dim
**think** vb meddwl
**thinker** n meddyliwr
**third** adj trydydd, trydedd
**thirst** n syched ▷ vi sychedu
**thirteen** adj, n tri (tair) ar ddeg, un deg tri (tair)
**thirty** adj, n deg ar hugain, tri deg
**this** adj, pron hwn, hon, hyn

**thistle** n ysgallen
**thither** adv yno, tuag yno
**thong** n carrai
**thorax** n y ddwyfron, y frest, thoracs
**thorn** n draen, draenen; pigyn, swmbwl
**thorny** n dreiniog, pigog
**thorough** adj trwyadl, trylwyr
**thoroughbred** adj tryryw, o rywogaeth dda
**thoroughfare** n tramwyfa
**thorough-going** adj trwyadl
**thoroughness** n trylwyredd
**those** adj pl y rhai hynny, y rhai yna
**thou** pron ti, tydi, tithau
**though** conj er, pe, cyd
**thought** n meddwl
**thoughtful** adj meddylgar, ystyriol
**thoughtless** adj difeddwl, anystyriol
**thousand** adj, n mil
**thraldom** n caethiwed
**thrall** n caethwr, caethwas
**thrash** vt dyrnu, ffusto, curo
**thread** n edau, edefyn
**threadbare** adj llwm, treuliedig, wedi treulio
**threat** n bygwth, bygythiad
**threaten** vt bygwth
**threatening** adj bygythiol
**three** adj, n tri, tair
**three-cornered** adj trichornel
**threefold** adj triphlyg
**three-legged** adj teircoes
**threepence** n tair ceiniog, pisyn tair
**thresh** vt dyrnu, ffusto
**thresher** n dyrnwr, ffustwr
**threshold** n trothwy, rhiniog, hiniog
**thrice** adv teirgwaith
**thrift** n darbodaeth, cynildeb
**thriftless** adj gwastraffus
**thrifty** adj darbodus, cynnil, diwastraff
**thrill** vb gwefreiddio ▷ n ias, gwefr

**thriller** n stori iasoer
**thrilling** adj cyffrous, gwefreiddiol
**thrive** vi llwyddo, ffynnu; prifio
**throat** n gwddf
**throb** vi dychlamu, curo
**throe** n dolur, poen, gloes, gwewyr
**thrombosis** n clot mewn gwythïen, thrombosis
**throne** n gorsedd, gorseddfainc
**throng** n tyrfa, torf ▷ vb tyrru, heidio
**throstle** n bronfraith
**throttle** n corn gwynt, corn gwddf, sbardun ▷ vt llindagu
**through** prep trwy ▷ adv trwodd
**throughout** prep trwy, trwy gydol ▷ adv trwodd
**throw** n tafliad ▷ vb taflu, bwrw, lluchio
**thrower** n taflwr
**thrush** n bronfraith
**thrush** n llindag, gân
**thrust** vb gwthio, gwanu, brathu ▷ n gwth
**thud** n twrf, sŵn trwm
**thug** n llindagwr, dihiryn
**thumb** n bawd ▷ vt bodio
**thump** vb dyrnodio, pwnio, dulio
**thumping** adj aruthrol
**thunder** n taran(au), tyrfau, trystau ▷ vb taranu
**thunderbolt** n llucheden
**thunderstorm** n storm dyrfau
**Thursday** n dydd Iau
**thus** adv fel hyn, felly
**thwart** vt croesi, gwrthwynebu
**thwart** vb rhwystro
**thy** pron dy, 'th
**thyme** n teim
**thyroid** n thiroid
**tiara** n talaith, coron, coronig
**tibia** n asgwrn y grimog
**tick** vi tipian, ticio ▷ n tipian, tic
**tick** vt marcio, ticio ▷ n nod, marc, tic
**tick** n lliain gwely, tic
**ticket** n tocyn, ticed; **ticket**

**collector** n tocynnwr; **ticket office** n swyddfa docynnau
**tickle** vb goglais, gogleisio ▷ n goglais
**ticklish** n gogleisiol; anodd, dyrys
**tide** n llanw, teid; amser, pryd; **high/low tide** n penllanw, trai
**tidiness** n taclusrwydd
**tidings** npl newyddion, chwedlau
**tidy** adj taclus, twt, trefnus, destlus
**tie** vt clymu, rhwymo ▷ n cwlwm, cadach
**tier** n rhes, rheng
**tiff** n ffrae fach
**tiger** n teigr, dywalgi
**tight** adj tyn, cryno, twt; cyfyng
**tighten** vb tynhau
**tightness** n tyndra
**tights** npl teits
**tigress** n teigres
**tile** n priddlech, teilsen
**till** prep, conj hyd
**till** vt trin, amaethu, llafurio
**tiller** n coes llyw; llafurwr, triniwr
**tilt** vb gogwyddo; gosod (â gwayw)
**tilth** n triniaeth tir, âr
**timber** n coed, pren
**time** n amser ▷ vt amseru
**timely** adj amserol, prydlon
**timepiece** n cloc, wats
**timetable** n amserlen
**timid** adj ofnus, ofnog, llwfr
**timidity** n ansoriwydd
**timing** n amseriad
**timorous** adj ofnus, ofnog
**tin** n alcam, tun
**tincture** n lliw
**tinfoil** n ffoel alcam
**tinge** vt lliwio, arlliwio ▷ n arlliw, gwawr
**tingle** vi ysu, llosgi, merwino
**tinker** n tincer; eurych ▷ vb tincera
**tinkle** vb tincian
**tinned** adj mewn tun, tun
**tint** n lliw, arlliw, gwawr ▷ vt lliwio
**tinted** adj wedi ei liwio
**tinworker** n gweithiwr tun,

gweithiwr alcam
**tiny** adj bychan, bach, pitw
**tip** n blaen, pen ▷ vt blaenu
**tip** vb troi, dymchwelyd; gwobrwyo ▷ n tip, tomen; cyngor; gwobr, cil-dwrn
**tipple** vb llymeitian, diota
**tippler** n diotwr, meddwyn
**tipsy** adj meddw, penfeddw, brwysg
**tiptoe** n: **on ~** ar flaenau ei draed
**tip-top** adj campus, penigamp
**tirade** n araith lem
**tire** vb blino, lluddedu, diffygio
**tire, tyre** n cant, cylch, teiar
**tired** adj blinedig
**tiredness** n blinder
**tireless** adj diflino
**tiresome** adj blin, diflas, plagus
**tiro, tyro** n newyddian, dechreuwr
**tissue** n gwe, meinwe; defnydd cnawd
**tissue paper** n papur sidan
**titanic** adj cawraidd, anferth, aruthrol
**titbit** n tamaid blasus, amheuthun
**tithe** n degwm ▷ vt degymu
**titivate** vb pincio, ymbincio
**title** n teitl, hawl, hawlfraint
**titled** adj â theitl
**title-deed** n dogfen hawlfraint
**title-page** n wyneb-ddalen
**titmouse** n gwas y dryw, yswidw
**titter** vi cilchwerthin, chwerthinial
**tittle** n gronyn, mymryn, tipyn
**tittle-tattle** n cleber
**titular** adj yn rhinwedd teitl; mewn enw
**to** prep i, at, hyd, er mwyn, wrth, yn
**toad** n llyffant du dafadennog
**toadstool** n caws llyffant, bwyd y boda, madarch
**toady** n cynffonnwr ▷ vt cynffonna
**toast** n tost; llwncdestun ▷ vb tostio, crasu
**toaster** n tostiwr
**tobacco** n tybaco, baco
**tobacconist** n gwerthwr tybaco

**toboggan** n tybogan, sled fach, car llusg

**today** adv heddiw

**toddle** vi cropian

**toddler** n plentyn bach

**toe** n bys troed; blaen carn ceffyl

**toe-cap** n blaen esgid

**toffee** n taffi, cyflaith

**together** adv ynghyd, gyda'i gilydd

**toil** vi llafurio, poeni ▷ n llafur

**toilet** n trwsiad, gwisgiad; ystafell ymolchi, tŷ bach; **toilet paper** n papur tŷ bach; **toilet water** n dŵr Groeg

**token** n arwydd, argoel; tocyn

**tolerable** adj goddefol; gweddol, symol, cymhedrol

**tolerant** adj goddefgar

**tolerate** vt goddef

**toleration** n goddefgarwch

**toll** n toll, treth

**toll** vb canu (cloch, cnul)

**tollbooth** n tollfa

**tomato** n tomato

**tomb** n bedd, beddrod

**tomboy** n hoeden, rhampen

**tom-cat** n gwrcath, cwrcyn

**tome** n cyfrol (fawr)

**tomfool** n ynfytyn, pen-ffŵl

**tomfoolery** n ynfydrwydd, ffwlbri

**tomorrow** adv yfory

**tomtit** n gwas y dryw, yswidw

**ton** n tunnell

**tonality** n tonyddiaeth

**tone** n tôn, oslef ▷ vb tyneru, lleddfu

**tongs** npl gefel

**tongue** n tafod; tafodiaith, iaith

**tonic** n meddyginiaeth gryfhaol, tonic; **tonic water** n dŵr tonig

**tonnage** n pwysau llwyth (llong); toll

**tonsil** n tonsil

**tonsillitis** n llid y tonsil

**tonsure** n corun, tonsur

**tonight** adv heno

**too** adv rhy; hefyd; **~ much** gormod

**tool** n arf, erfyn

**toot** vb canu corn

**tooth** (teeth) n dant

**toothache** n dannoedd

**toothbrush** n brws dannedd

**toothed** adj danheddog

**toothless** adj diddanedd, mantach

**toothpaste** n sebon dannedd, past dannedd

**toothpick** n pic dannedd

**toothsome** adj danteithiol, blasus

**top** n pen, brig, copa ▷ vt tocio; rhagori ar

**top** n cogwrn, top

**top-heavy** adj pendrwm

**topic** n pwnc

**topical** adj amserol

**topography** n daearyddiaeth leol

**topple** vb syrthio, cwympo, dymchwel

**topsyturvy** adv wyneb i waered, yn bendramwnwgl

**torch** n fflach, tors, ffagl

**torch-light** n golau tors

**torment** n poen, poenedigaeth ▷ vt poeni, poenydio

**tormentor** n poenydiwr

**torn** adj wedi ei rwygo, rhwygedig

**tornado** n hyrddwynt, corwynt

**torpedo** n torpedo

**torpid** adj marwaidd, cysglyd, swrth

**torrent** n cenllif, llifeiriant, rhyferthwy

**torrential** adj llifeiriol, trwm

**torrid** adj poeth, crasboeth

**torso** n corff (heb y pen a'r aelodau), torso

**tortoise** n crwban

**tortoise-shell** n cragen crwban, trilliw (am gath)

**tortuous** adj troellog, trofaus

**torture** n dirboen, artaith ▷ vt arteithio

**torturer** n arteithiwr

**tory** n tori, ceidwadwr ▷ adj torïaidd

**toryism** n torïaeth

**toss** vb taflu, lluchio, bwrw
**total** adj hollol, cyflawn ▷ n cyfan, cyfanswm
**totalitarian** adj totalitaraidd
**totalitarianism** n totalitariaeth
**totality** n cyfanrwydd
**totally** adv yn llwyr, yn gyfan, yn ei grynswth
**totter** vi honcian, siglo, gwegian
**touch** vb teimlo, cyffwrdd ▷ n teimlad
**touched** adj dan deimlad
**touching** adj teimladwy
**touch-line** n yr ystlys
**touchstone** n maen prawf, safon
**touchy** adj croendenau
**tough** adj gwydn, caled, cyndyn
**toughen** vb gwneud yn wydn, cryfhau
**tour** n tro, taith
**tourism** n twristiaeth
**tourist** n teithiwr, ymwelydd, twrist; **tourist office** n swyddfa twristiaid
**tournament** n twrnamaint
**tourniquet** n offeryn i atal gwaed
**tousle** vt dragio, anhrefnu
**tousled** adj anniben
**tout** vi poeni pobl am archebion, gwasgu ar
**tow** n carth
**tow** vt llusgo, tynnu
**toward, -s** prep tua, tuag at
**towel** n lliain sychu, tywel
**tower** n twr ▷ vi esgyn, ymgodi, sefyll yn uchel
**town** n tref; **town centre** n canol(y) dref; **town clerk** n clerc y dref; **town council** n cyngor y dref; **town hall** n neuadd y dref
**township** n trefgordd
**toxic** adj gwenwynig
**toy** n tegan ▷ vi chwarae, maldodi
**trace** n tres; ôl, trywydd
**trace** vt olrhain, dilyn ▷ n ôl
**tracery** n rhwyllwaith (maen etc)
**trachea** n breuant, corn gwynt,

pibell wynt
**track** n ôl, brisg; llwybr ▷ vt olrhain
**tracksuit** n tracwisg
**tract** n ardal, rhandir
**tract** n traethodyn
**tractable** adj hydyn, hydrin, hywedd
**traction** n tyniad, tyniant, llusgiad
**trade** n masnach; crefft ▷ vb masnachu
**trade-mark** n nod masnach
**trader** n masnachwr
**trade-union** n undeb llafur
**trade-wind** n gwynt y dwyrain, cylchwynt
**tradition** n traddodiad
**traditional** adj traddodiadol
**traduce** vt cablu, difenwi, enllibio
**traffic** vb masnachu, trafnidio ▷ n masnach, trafnidiaeth; **traffic jam** n tagfa; **traffic warden** n warden traffig
**traffic-lights** npl goleuadau traffig
**tragedy** n trasiedi, trychineb
**tragic** adj trychinebus, alaethus
**trail** n llusg, brisg, ôl ▷ vb llusgo
**trailer** n ôl-gerbyd, ôl-gart, cart; rhaglun (ffilm)
**train** vb hyfforddi, ymarfer ▷ n gosgordd; godre; trên, cerbydres
**trained** adj hyfforddedig, cymwys, wedi ei hyfforddi
**trainer** n hyfforddwr
**training** n hyfforddiant, disgyblaeth; **training shoes** npl esgidiau ymarfer
**trait** n nodwedd; (pl) teithi
**traitor** n bradwr, teyrnfradwr
**trajectory** n taflwybr
**trammel** n rhwyd; hual ▷ vt llyffetheirio, hualu
**tramp** vb crwydro, trampio ▷ n crwydryn
**trample** vb sathru, sangu, mathru
**trance** n llewyg, llesmair, perlewyg
**tranquil** adj tawel, llonydd, digyffro
**tranquility** n tawelwch,

llonyddwch
**tranquillizer** n tawelyn, tawelydd
**trans-, tran-, tra-** prefix tros-, tra-
**transact** vt trafod, gwneud, trin
**transaction** n trafodaeth
**transactions** n trafodion
**transcend** vt rhagori ar, trarhagori
**transcendent** adj tra-rhagorol
**transcendental** adj trosgynnol
**transcribe** vt copïo
**transcriber** n adysgrifiwr, copïwr, copïydd
**transcript** n copi, adysgrifiad
**transept** n croes (eglwys)
**transfer** vt trosglwyddo ▷ n trosglwyddiad
**transference** n trosglwyddiad
**transfiguration** n gweddnewidiad
**transfigure** vt gweddnewid
**transfix** vt trywanu, gwanu
**transform** vt trawsffurfio
**transformation** n trawsffurfiad
**transformer** n newidydd
**transfusion** n trosglwyddiad (gwaed), trallwysiad (gwaed)
**transgress** vt troseddu
**transgression** n trosedd, camwedd
**transgressor** n troseddwr
**transient** adj diflanedig, darfodedig
**transit** n mynediad dros, trosiad
**transition** n trosiad, trawsgyweiriad
**transitional** adj ar newid, tros dro
**transitive** adj (Gram) anghyflawn
**transitory** adj diflanedig, darfodedig
**translate** vt cyfieithu
**translation** n cyfieithiad
**transliterate** vt trawslythrennu
**translucent** adj tryloyw
**transmigrate** vi trawsfudo
**transmission** n trosglwyddiad
**transmit** vt anfon, trosglwyddo
**transmitter** n trosglwyddydd

**transmitting-station** n gorsaf drosglwyddo
**transmute** vt trawsnewid
**transparency** n tryloywder
**transparent** adj tryloyw
**transpire** vb dyfod yn hysbys, digwydd
**transplant** vt trawsblannu
**transport** vt trosglwyddo; alltudio ▷ n trosglwyddiad; cludiant; perlewyg, gorawen
**transpose** vt trawsddodi, trawsgyweirio
**transubstantiation** n traws-sylweddiad
**transverse** adj croes, traws
**trap** n trap, magl; car bach ▷ vt dal, maglu
**trapeze** n trapîs
**trappings** npl harnais, gêr
**trash** n sothach, gwehilion, ffwlbri, ysbwriel
**travail** vi trafaelu ▷ n trafael, llafur
**travel** vb teithio, trafaelio ▷ n teithio; (pl) teithiau; **travel agent** n asiant teithio
**traveller** n teithiwr, trafaeliwr; **traveller's cheque** n siec deithio
**travelling** adj teithiol
**traverse** vb mynd ar draws, croesi
**travesty** n parodi
**trawl** vb llusgrwydo ▷ n llusgrwyd
**trawler** n llong bysgota
**tray** n hambwrdd
**treacherous** adj twyllodrus
**treachery** n brad, bradwriaeth
**treacle** n triagl
**tread** vb sathru, sengi, troedio ▷ n sang
**treadmill** n troell droed
**treason** n brad, bradwriaeth
**treasonable** adj bradwrus
**treasure** n trysor ▷ vt trysori
**treasurer** n trysorydd
**treasury** n trysorfa, trysordy, y Trysorlys
**treat** vb trin; tretio; traethu ▷ n

gwledd, amheuthun

**treatise** n traethawd

**treatment** n triniaeth, ymdriniaeth

**treaty** n cyfamod, cytundeb

**treble** adj triphlyg ▷ n trebl ▷ vb treblu

**tree** n pren, coeden

**trefoil** n meillionen, meillion

**trek** vi mudo ▷ n mud, mudo

**trellis** n delltwaith

**tremble** vi crynu, echrydu, arswydo

**tremendous** adj dychrynllyd, ofnadwy, anferth

**tremor** n crynfa, cryndod, ias

**tremulous** adj crynedig

**trench** n ffos, rhigol, rhych ▷ vb ffosi

**trenchant** adj llym, miniog

**trencher** n trensiwr, treinsiwr, plat

**trend** vi tueddu ▷ n tuedd, gogwydd

**trepidation** n cryndod, ofn, dychryn

**trespass** vi troseddu ▷ n trosedd

**trespasser** n tresmaswr

**tress** n cudyn gwallt, tres

**trestle** n trestl

**tri-** prefix tri

**triad** n tri; (pl) trioedd

**trial** n prawf, profedigaeth, treial

**triangle** n triongl

**triangular** adj trionglog

**tribal** adj llwythol

**tribe** n llwyth, tylwyth, gwehelyth

**tribulation** n trallod, cystudd

**tribunal** n brawdle, llys, tribiwnlys

**tributary** adj dan deyrnged ▷ n rhagafon, isafon, cainc

**tribute** n teyrnged, treth

**trice** n munudyn, chwinciad

**trick** n tric, cast, ystryw ▷ vt castio

**trickery** n dichell, twyll, ystryw

**trickle** vi diferu, diferynnu

**trickster** n twyllwr, castiwr

**tricky** adj ystrywgar; anodd

**tricycle** n treisigl

**trident** n tryfer

**triennial** adj bob tair blynedd

**trifle** n gronyn, mymryn; gwaelbeth ▷ vt ofera, cellwair

**trifling** adj diwerth, dibwys

**trigger** n cliced, triger

**trigonometry** n trigonomeg

**trill** vb crychleisio, cwafrio ▷ n crychlais

**trillion** n triliwn

**trilogy** n cyfres o dair (nofel, drama etc)

**trim** adj taclus, twt, del ▷ vb taclu, trwsio ▷ n diwyg, trefn

**trinity** n trindod

**trinket** n tegan, tlws

**trio** n triawd

**trioxide** n triocsid

**trip** vb tripio, maglu; disodli ▷ n trip, tro

**tripartite** adj teiran

**tripe** n tripa

**triple** adj triphlyg

**triplet** n tripled

**tripod** n trybedd

**trite** adj cyffredin, sathredig

**triumph** n gorfoledd, buddugoliaeth ▷ vi gorfoleddu; buddugoliaethu

**triumphal** adj buddugol

**triumphant** adj buddugoliaethus

**triumvirate** n llywodraeth tri (Rhufain)

**trivet** n trybedd

**trivial** adj distadl, dibwys, diwerth

**trolley, -y** n troli

**troop** n byddin, torf, mintai ▷ vb tyrru; **troops** npl lluoedd, minteioedd

**trooper** n milwr (ar farch)

**trophy** n gwobr, tlws

**tropic** n trofan

**tropical** adj trofannol

**trot** vb tuthio, trotian ▷ n tuth, trot

**troubadour** n trwbadŵr, bardd telynegol

**trouble** vt blino, trafferthu ▷ n

blinder, trallod, helbul, trafferth
**troubled** adj aflonydd, anesmwyth, pryderus, ofnus, dyrys
**troubles** npl trafferthion, helbulon, pryderon, ofnau
**troublesome** adj blinderus, trafferthus
**trough** n cafn
**trounce** vt ffonodio, cystwyo, baeddu
**troupe** n mintai o berfformwyr
**trousers** npl llodrau, trowsus, trwser
**trousseau** n dillad priodasferch
**trout** n brithyll
**trow** vb tybied, meddylied, credu
**trowel** n trywel
**truant** n triawnt, mitsiwr
**truce** n cadoediad
**truck** n trwc, gwagen
**truck** vb cyfnewid, ffeirio
**truckle** vi plygu, ymostwng, ymgreinio
**truculent** adj ffyrnig, milain
**trudge** vb cerdded yn ffwdanus, trwmgerdded
**true** adj gwir, cywir
**truism** n gwireb, gwiredd
**truly** adv yn wir, yn ddiau, yn gywir
**trump** vb utganu; twyllo, ffugio ▷ n trwmp
**trumpery** n sothach, ffwlbri ▷ adj coeg, gwacsaw
**trumpet** n utgorn, corn, trwmped
**truncheon** n pastwn, trensiwn
**trundle** vb treiglo, rholio
**trunk** n cyff, cist, corff; duryn, trwnc
**trunks** npl trons
**truss** vb gwneud bwndel; gwaellu (ffowlyn)
**trust** n ymddiried, ymddiriedaeth, coel; ymddiriedolaeth ▷ vb hyderu, ymddiried, coelio
**trustee** n ymddiriedolwr
**trusteeship** n ymddiriedolaeth
**trustworthy** adj y gellir dibynnu arno

**trusty** adj ffyddlon, cywir, teyrngar
**truth** n gwir, gwirionedd
**truthful** adj geirwir
**truthfulness** n geirwiredd
**try** vb profi, cynnig, ceisio, treio
**trying** adj poenus, anodd, blin
**tryst** n oed
**T-shirt** n crys-T
**tub** n twba, twb, baddon
**tuba** n tiwba
**tube** n pib, pibell, tiwb, corn
**tuber** n cloronen, taten
**tuberculosis** n darfodedigaeth, dicáu, dicléin
**tubular** adj tiwbaidd; **~ bridge** ceubont
**tuck** vt cwtogi, plygu ▷ n plyg, twc
**Tuesday** n dydd Mawrth
**tuft** n cogyn, tusw, cudyn
**tug** vb llusgo, tynnu
**tuition** n addysg, hyfforddiant
**tulip** n tiwlip
**tumble** vb cwympo ▷ n codwm, cwymp
**tumbler** n gwydryn
**tumid** adj chwyddedig
**tummy** n bola
**tumour** n chwydd, casgliad, cornwyd
**tumult** n terfysg, cynnwrf
**tumultuous** adj terfysglyd
**tuna** n tiwna
**tune** n tôn, tiwn, cywair ▷ vb cyweirio
**tuneful** adj soniarus
**tunic** n crysbais, siaced
**Tunisia** n Tunisia
**tunnel** n ceuffordd, twnnel
**turban** n twrban
**turbid** adj afloyw, cymysglyd, lleidiog
**turbine** n twrbin
**turbot** n twrbot
**turbulence** n terfysg, cynnwrf
**turbulent** adj terfysglyd, afreolus
**turf** n tywarchen
**turgid** adj chwyddedig

**Turk** n Twrc
**turkey** n twrci
**Turkey** n Twrci
**Turkish** adj Twrcaidd
**turmoil** n trafferth, ffwdan, berw
**turn** vb troi ▷ n tro, trofa
**turncoat** n gwrthgiliwr
**turner** n turniwr
**turning** n tro; tröedigaeth
**turning point** n trobwynt
**turnip** n erfinen, meipen
**turnout** n cynulliad
**turnover** n cyfanswm busnes
**turnpike** n tollborth, tyrpeg
**turnstyle** n camfa dro
**turntable** n trofwrdd
**turpentine** n twrpant, turpant
**turpitude** n gwarth, ysgelerder
**turquoise** n maen glas
  (gwerthfawr)
**turret** n twred, tyryn
**turtle** n crwban môr
**turtle, -dove** n turtur
**tusk** n ysgithrddant, ysgithr
**tussle** n ymgiprys, ysgarmes
**tut** excl twt!
**tutelage** n hyfforddiant, nawdd
**tutor** n athro, hyfforddwr ▷ vt
  hyfforddi
**tutorial** adj tiwtorial
**twaddle** n lol, ffiloreg
**twang** vb clecian, swnio ▷ n sŵn,
  llediaith
**tweed** n brethyn gwlân, twid
**tweezers** n gefel fach
**twelfth** adj deuddegfed
**twelve** adj, n deuddeg, un deg dau
**twentieth** adj ugeinfed
**twenty** adj, n ugain
**twice** adv dwywaith
**twiddle** vt chwarae bodiau,
  cellwair
**twig** n brigyn, ysbrigyn, impyn
**twilight** n cyfnos, cyfddydd
**twill** n brethyn caerog
**twin** n gefell
**twine** n llinyn ▷ vb cyfrodeddu,

cordeddu
**twinge** n cnofa, brath, gwayw
**twinkle** vi serennu, pefrio
**twinkling** n chwinciad, amrantiad
**twirl** vb chwyrndroi, chwyldroi,
  nydd-droi
**twist** vb nyddu, nydd-droi,
  cyfrodeddu; troi, gwyrdroi ▷ n tro;
  edau gyfrodedd
**twit** n dannod, edliw; un ffôl
**twitch** vb tymhigo, brathgnoi
  ▷ n tymig
**twitch** n gwayw, brath, plwc ▷ vb
  brathu, tynnu'n sydyn, plycio
**twitter** vi trydar
**two** adj, n dau, dwy
**two-faced** adj dauwynebog
**twofold** adv deublyg
**two piece** n deuddarn
**tympan** n tabwrdd, tympan
**type** n math, teip
**typescript** n teipysgrif
**typewriter** n teipiadur, peiriant
  teipio
**typhoid** n twymyn yr ymysgaroedd
**typhoon** n corwynt
**typhus** n twymyn heintus, teiffws
**typical** adj arwyddol,
  nodweddiadol
**typify** vt arwyddo, nodweddu
**typist** n teipydd
**typographical** adj argraffyddol
**typography** n argraffwaith
**tyranny** n tra-arglwyddiaeth,
  gormes
**tyrannize** vb gormesu, treisio
**tyrant** n gormesteyrn, gormeswr
**tyre** n teiar
**tyro** n newyddian, dechreuwr

# u

ubiquitous *adj* ym mhob man, hollbresennol
udder *n* pwrs, cadair, piw
ugh *excl* ach! ych y fi!
ugly *adj* hagr, hyll
ugliness *n* hagrwch, hylldra
ulcer *n* casgliad, cornwyd, wlser
Ulster *n* Ulster
ulterior *adj* tu draw i, tu hwnt i, pellach; cudd
ultimate *adj* diwethaf, olaf, eithaf
ultimately *adv* o'r diwedd
ultimatum *n* y gair olaf, y rhybudd olaf
ultra *adj* eithafol ▷ *prefix* tu hwnt i, gor-
ultramodern *adj* modern iawn
umbrage *n* tramgwydd
umbrella *n* ymbrelo, brela, ambarél, ymbarél
umpire *n* dyfarnwr, canolwr
un- *prefix* an-, am-, ang-, af-, di-, heb
unable *adj* analluog
unaccented *adj* diacen
unacceptable *adj* anghymeradwy, annerbyniol
unaccompanied *adj* heb gwmni; heb gyfeiliant
unaccountable *adj* anesboniadwy
unaccustomed *adj* anghyfarwydd, anghynefin
unacquainted *adj* anghyfarwydd
unadulterated *adj* pur, digymysg
unaffected *adj* naturiol; heb ei

effeithio gan
unanimity *n* unfrydedd
unanimous *adj* unfrydol
unanimously *adv* yn unfryd
unarmed *adj* diamddiffyn, heb arfau
unassailable *adj* diysgog
unassuming *adj* diymhongar
unattainable *adj* anghyraeddadwy
unavoidable *adj* anorfod
unaware *adj* anymwybodol
unawares *adv* yn ddiarwybod
unbearable *adj* annioddefol
unbecoming *adj* anweddus, anweddaidd
unbeliever *n* anghredadun, anffyddiwr
unbelieving *adj* anghrediniol
unbiassed *adj* diduedd
unblemished *adj* di-nam, dinam
unbounded *adj* diderfyn
unbridled *adj* heb ei ffrwyno
unbroken *adj* di-dor
unbutton *vb* datod, datfotymu
uncalled (for) *adj* di-alw-amdano
uncanny *adj* rhyfedd, dieithr, annaearol
uncle *n* ewythr
unclean *adj* brwnt, aflan
uncomfortable *adj* anghysurus
uncommon *adj* anghyffredin
uncompromising *adj* di-ildio, digyfaddawd, cyndyn
unconcerned *adj* difater, didaro
unconditional *adj* diamod
unconfirmed *adj* heb ei gadarnhau
unconquerable *adj* anorchfygol
unconscionable *adj* digydwybod, afresymol
unconscious *adj* anymwybodol
unconstitutional *adj* anghyfansoddiadol
uncontaminated *adj* di-lwgr, pur
uncontrollable *adj* aflywodraethus
unconventional *adj*

anghonfensiynol

**uncouth** adj trwsgl, lletchwith, garw, amrwd

**uncover** vb datguddio

**unction** n eli; eneiniad, arddeliad, hwyl

**unctuous** adj seimlyd; rhagrithiol

**uncultivated** adj heb ei feithrin

**undamaged** adj heb ei niweidio

**undecided** adj petrus, mewn penbleth

**undefended** adj diamddiffyn

**undefiled** adj dihalog, pur

**undefined** adj amhenodol, annelwig

**undeniable** adj anwadadwy

**under** prep tan, is, islaw ▷ adv tanodd, oddi tanodd ▷ prefix is-, tan-

**undercurrent** n islif

**underestimate** vb prisio'n rhy isel

**undergraduate** n myfyriwr israddedig

**underground** adj tanddaearol

**underhand** adj llechwraidd, tan din

**underline** vb tanlinellu, pwysleisio

**undermine** vb tanseilio

**underneath** adv oddi tanodd ▷ prep tan

**underpass** n ffordd danddaearol, tanffordd

**underrate** vb tanbrisio, iselbrisio

**understand** vt deall, dirnad

**understanding** n amgyffred, dealltwriaeth

**undertake** vb ymgymryd

**undertaker** n ymgymerydd; saer (coffinau)

**undertaking** adj ymrwymiad

**undertone** n islais

**underworld** n annwn

**undeserved** adj anhaeddiannol

**undesirable** adj annymunol

**undeveloped** adj heb ei ddatblygu

**undeviating** adj diwyro

**undignified** adj anurddasol, diurddas

**undisciplined** adj diddisgyblaeth

**undisputed** adj diamheuol

**undisturbed** adj llonydd, tawel, digyffro

**undo** vt dadwneud; datod; andwyo, difetha

**undoing** n distryw, dinistr

**undoubted** adj diamheuol

**undress** vb dadwisgo

**undue** adj amhriodol

**undulate** vi tonni

**unearned** adj heb ei ennill

**unearthly** adj annaearol

**uneasiness** n anesmwythder, pryder

**uneasy** adj anesmwyth, aflonydd, pryderus

**unedifying** adj di-fudd, anadeiladol

**uneducated** adj annysgedig

**unemployed** adj di-waith, segur

**unemployment** n diweithdra, anghyflogaeth

**unending** adj diddiwedd

**unendurable** adj annioddefol

**unequal** adj anghyfartal

**unequalled** adj digymar, dihafal

**unequivocal** adj diamwys

**unerring** adj sicr

**uneven** adj anwastad

**uneventful** adj diddigwyddiad

**unexpected** adj annisgwyliadwy

**unfailing** adj di-feth

**unfair** adj annheg

**unfairness** n annhegwch

**unfaithful** adj anffyddlon

**unfamiliar** adj anghyfarwydd

**unfasten** vb datod

**unfathomable** adj annealladwy

**unfavourable** adj anffafriol

**unfeeling** adj dideimlad

**unfettered** adj dilyffethair

**unfinished** adj anorffenedig

**unfit** adj anghymwys; afiach

**unfitting** adj amhriodol

**unflinching** adj diysgog, dewr

**unfold** vb datblygu
**unforseen** adj heb ei ragweld
**unforgiving** adj anfaddeugar
**unfortunate** adj anffodus
**unfortunately** adj yn anffodus
**unfounded** adj di-sail
**unfrequented** adj anhygyrch, unig
**unfriendly** adj anghyfeillgar
**unfrock** vb diarddel
**unfulfilled** adj heb ei gyflawni
**unfurnished** adj diddodrefn
**ungainly** adv afrosgo, trwsgl
**ungentlemanly** adj
  anfoneddigaidd
**ungodly** adj annuwiol, drwg
**ungrammatical** adj anramadegol
**ungrateful** adj anniolchgar
**unguarded** adj ar awr wan
**unguent** n ennaint, eli
**unhallowed** adj halogedig
**unhappiness** n anhapusrwydd
**unhappy** adj anhapus
**unharmed** adj dianaf
**unhealthy** adj afiach
**unheeding** adj diofal
**unhesitating** adj dibetrus
**unhorse** vb taflu oddi ar geffyl
**unicorn** n uncorn, unicorn
**unification** n uniad
**uniform** adj unffurf ▷ n gwisg
  swyddogol
**uniformity** n unffurfiaeth
**unify** vt unoli, uno
**unilateral** adj unochrog
**unimpaired** adj dianaf
**unimpeded** adj dirwystr
**unimportant** adj dibwys
**uninspired** adj diawen
**unintelligent** adj anneallus
**unintelligible** adj annealladwy
**unintentional** adj anfwriadol
**uninteresting** adj anniddorol
**union** n undeb; uniad
**unionism** n undebaeth
**unionist** n undebwr; unoliaethwr
  (Iwerddon)
**unique** adj dihafal, digymar

**unison** n unsain, unseinedd
**unit** n un, rhif un; uned; undod
**Unitarian** n Undodwr ▷ adj
  Undodaidd
**Unitarianism** n Undodiaeth
**unite** vb uno, cyfuno, cyduno, cydio
**united** adj unol, unedig; **United
  States (of America)** n yr Unol
  Daleithiau
**United Kingdom** n: **the ~** y
  Deyrnas Unedig
**unity** n undod
**universal** adj cyffredinol
**universe** n bydysawd
**university** n prifysgol
**unjust** adj anghyfiawn, annheg
**unjustly** adv ar gam
**unkempt** adj heb ei gribo, aflêr,
  anniben
**unkind** adj angharedig
**unknown** adj anadnabyddus,
  anenwog
**unlace** vb datod
**unlawful** adj anghyfreithlon
**unlearned** adj annysgedig
**unless** conj oni, onid
**unlettered** adj anllythrennog
**unlike** adj annhebyg
**unlikely** adj annhebygol
**unlimited** adj diderfyn
**unload** vb dadlwytho
**unlock** vb datgloi
**unlucky** adj anlwcus
**unmanageable** adj
  aflywodraethus
**unmannerly** adj anfoesgar
**unmarried** adj dibriod
**unmask** vb dinoethi
**unmatched** adj digymar
**unmerciful** adj didrugaredd
**unmistakable** adj digamsyniol
**unmixed** adj digymysg
**unnatural** adj annaturiol
**unnecessary** adj dianghenraid
**unobserved** adj heb ei weld
**unobtrusive** adj anymwthiol
**unoccupied** adj gwag

**unopened** adj heb ei agor
**unopposed** adj yn ddiwrthwynebiad
**unorthodox** adj anarferol, anuniongred
**unpack** vb dadbacio
**unpaid** adj di-dâl, didal
**unparalleled** adj digyffelyb
**unpardonable** adj anfaddeuol
**unpatriotic** adj anwlatgar
**unpleasant** adj annymunol
**unpolluted** adj dihalog, pur
**unpopular** adj amhoblogaidd
**unpopularity** n amhoblogrwydd
**unpractical** adj anymarferol
**unprejudiced** adj diragfarn
**unprepared** adj amharod
**unprincipled** adj diegwyddor
**unprofitable** adj amhroffidiol
**unprotected** adj diamddiffyn
**unpublished** adj anghyhoeddedig
**unqualified** adj heb gymhwyster
**unquestionable** adj diamheuol
**unready** adj amharod
**unreasonable** adj afresymol
**unrelated** adj amherthnasol; heb berthyn
**unremitting** adj dyfal
**unrestrained** adj dilywodraeth
**unripe** adj anaeddfed
**unrivalled** adj digymar
**unruffled** adj tawel
**unruly** adj afreolus
**unsafe** adj anniogel
**unsatisfactory** adj anfoddhaol
**unsatisfied** adj anfodlon
**unsatisfying** adj annigonol
**unscathed** adj dianaf
**unscrew** vt agor; llacio; datroi
**unscrupulous** adj diegwyddor
**unseasonable** adj annhymorol
**unseat** vb troi o'i swydd; taflu (ceffyl)
**unseemly** adj anweddaidd
**unseen** adj anweledig
**unsettled** adj ansefydlog
**unshaken** adj diysgog, cadarn

**unsighted** adj heb allu gweld
**unsightly** adj diolwg, blêr
**unskilful** adj anfedrus
**unskilled** adj anghelfydd
**unsociable** adj anghymdeithasgar
**unsolicited** adj heb ei ofyn
**unsound** adj diffygiol, cyfeiliornus
**unsparing** adj diarbed, hael
**unspeakable** adj anhraethol
**unstable** adj ansefydlog
**unstained** adj dilychwin
**unsteadiness** n ansadrwydd
**unsteady** adj ansefydlog
**unsubstantial** adj ansylweddol
**unsuccessful** adj aflwyddiannus
**unsuitable** adj anaddas
**unsullied** adj dilychwin
**unsurmountable** adj anorchfygol
**unsurpassed** adj diguro
**unsuspecting** adj heb amau dim
**untainted** adj di-lwgr, pur
**untangle** vb datrys
**unthankful** adj anniolchgar
**unthinking** adj difeddwl
**untidy** adj anniben
**untie** vb datod
**until** prep, conj hyd, hyd oni, nes, tan
**untimely** adj anamserol
**untiring** adj diflino
**unto** prep i, at, hyd at, wrth
**untold** adj di-ben-draw
**untoward** adj anffodus, cyndyn
**untrodden** adj disathr
**untrue** adj celwyddog
**unusual** adj anarferol, anghynefin; anghyffredin; newydd; dieithr
**unutterable** adj anhraethadwy
**unvarying** adj digyfnewid, cyson
**unveil** vb dadorchuddio
**unversed** adj anhyddysg
**unwarranted** adj heb ei warantu
**unwary** adj diofal
**unwell** adj anhwylus
**unwholesome** adj afiach
**unwieldy** adj afrosgo
**unwilling** adj anfodlon, amharod
**unwise** adj annoeth

**unwittingly** adv yn ddiarwybod
**unworthiness** n annheilyngdod
**unworthy** adj annheilwng
**unwounded** adj dianaf, cyfan
**unyielding** adj di-ildio
**up** adj, prep i fyny, i'r lan
**upbringing** n magwraeth
**upheaval** n cyffro, terfysg
**uphill** adj i fyny
**uphold** vb cynnal
**upholsterer** n dodrefnwr, clustogwr
**upkeep** n cynhaliaeth
**upland** n ucheldir, blaenau
**uplifting** adj dyrchafol
**upon** prep ar, ar warthaf, ar uchaf
**upper** adj uwch, uchaf
**uppermost** adj, adv uchaf
**upright** adj syth, union, unionsyth
**uprising** n terfysg, gwrthryfel
**uproar** n terfysg, cythrwfl, dadwrdd
**uproot** vt diwreiddio
**upset** vb troi, dymchwelyd, cyffroi, gofidio
**upshot** n swm, canlyniad, diwedd
**upside-down** adj, adv (â'i) wyneb i waered
**upstairs** n llofft
**upstart** n crach fonheddwr
**upward** adj, adv, **upwards** adv i fyny
**uranium** n wraniwm
**urban** adj dinasol, dinesig
**urbane** adj hynaws, mwyn, boneddigaidd
**urbanize** vb gwneud yn drefol
**urchin** n draenog; crwtyn
**urethra** n pibell ddŵr o'r bledren
**urge** vt cymell, annog
**urgency** n brys
**urgent** adj taer, pwysig, yn gofyn brys
**urine** n troeth, trwnc, piso
**urn** n wrn
**us** pron ni, nyni, ninnau; 'n
**usage** n arfer, defod, triniaeth
**use** n iws, arfer, defnydd,

gwasanaeth, diben ▷ vb iwsio, arfer, defnyddio
**used** adj arferedig, mewn arfer, cynefin; (car) ail-law
**useful** adj defnyddiol
**useless** adj diwerth
**user** n defnyddiwr
**usher** n rhingyll; isathro; tywysydd ▷ vt arwain i mewn, dwyn ymlaen
**usual** adj arferol, cynefin
**usurer** n usuriwr
**usurp** vt trawsfeddiannu
**usurper** n trawsfeddiannwr
**usury** n usuriaeth, ocraeth
**utensil** n offeryn, llestr
**uterus** n croth, bru
**utilitarian** adj defnyddiol
**utilitarianism** n llesyddiaeth
**utility** n defnyddioldeb, budd, lles
**utilization** n defnydd
**utilize** vt defnyddio
**utmost** adj eithaf, pellaf
**utopia** n gwlad ddelfrydol (ddychmygol)
**utopian** adj defrydol, anymarferol
**utter** adj eithaf, pellaf; hollol, llwyr
**utter** vt yngan, traethu, dywedyd
**utterance** n parabl, ymadrodd, lleferydd
**uttermost** adj eithaf, pellaf
**U-turn** n tro pedol
**uvula** n tafod bach, tafodig
**uvular** adj tafodigol

# V

**vacancy** n lle gwag, swydd wag, gwacter
**vacant** adj gwag; syn, synfyfyriol, hurt
**vacate** vt ymadael â, gadael yn wag
**vacation** n seibiant, gwyliau
**vaccinate** vt brechu, bufrechu, torri'r frech
**vaccination** n y frech, brechiad
**vaccine** n brech
**vacillate** vi anwadalu, bwhwman
**vacuous** adj gwg, syn, hurt
**vacuum** n gwag, gwagle, gwactod
**vacuum cleaner** n sugnydd llwch
**vacuum flask** n thermos, jac
**vagabond** n crwydryn, dihiryn
**vagary** n mympwy
**vagrancy** n crwydro
**vagrant** adj crwydrol ▷ n crwydryn
**vague** adj amwys, amhenodol
**vagueness** n amwysedd
**vain** adj balch, coegfalch; ofer
**vale** n dyffryn, glyn, bro, cwm, ystrad
**valediction** n ffarwel
**valentine** n falant, folant
**valet** n gwas
**valiant** adj dewr, dewrwych, gwrol, glew
**valid** adj digonol, dilys, cyfreithlon, iawn
**validate** vb cadarnhau, dilysu
**validity** n dilysrwydd
**valley** n dyffryn, cwm, glyn
**valour** n dewrder, gwroldeb, glewder

**valuable** adj gwerthfawr
**valuation** n prisiad
**value** n gwerth ▷ vt gwerthfawrogi, prisio
**valuer** n prisiwr
**valve** n falf
**vampire** n sugnwr gwaed
**van** n blaen cad, y rheng flaenaf
**van** n men, fan
**vandal** n fandal
**vandalism** n fandaliaeth
**vane** n ceiliog gwynt
**vanguard** n blaen cad, blaenfyddin
**vanilla** n fanila
**vanish** vi diflannu, darfod
**vanity** n gwagedd, gwegi, coegfalchder
**vanquish** vt gorchfygu, trechu
**vanquisher** n gorchfygwr
**vantage** n mantais
**vapid** adj diflas, merf, marwaidd, egr
**vaporize** vb anweddu
**vaporous** adj llawn tarth
**vapour** n tawch, tarth, ager, anwedd
**variable** adj cyfnewidiol, anwadal, oriog
**variable** n newidyn (rhifyddiaeth)
**variance** n anghytundeb, anghydfod, amrywioldeb
**variant** n amrywiad
**variation** n amrywiad
**varicose** adj chwyddedig (am wythiennau)
**varied** adj amrywiol
**variegated** adj brith, brithliw
**variety** n amrywiaeth
**various** adj gwahanol, amrywiol
**varnish** n barnais, farnais ▷ vt barneisio, farneisio
**varnisher** n farneisiwr
**vary** vb amrywio; newid
**vase** n cwpan, cawg
**vaseline** n faselin, eli
**vassal** n caethddeiliad, taeog,

aillt, deiliad
**vast** adj dirfawr, anferth
**vastness** n mawredd, ehangder
**vat** n cerwyn
**Vatican** n plas y Pab
**vaticinate** vb proffwydo, darogan
**vaticination** n proffwydoliaeth, darogan
**vault** n daeargell, claddgell; cromen ▷ vb neidio, llamu
**vaulted** adj bwaog
**vaunt** vb ymffrostio, bostio, brolio
**veal** n cig llo
**vector** n fector
**veer** vb troi, cylchdroi; trawshwylio
**vegetable** adj llysieuol ▷ n llysieuyn ymborth
**vegetarian** n llysieuwr
**vegetate** vi tarddu, tyfu; ofera
**vegetation** n tyfiant llysiau, llystyfiant
**vehemence** n angerdd
**vehement** adj angerddol, tanbaid
**vehicle** n cerbyd; cyfrwng, moddion
**veil** n gorchudd, llen ▷ vt gorchuddio
**vein** n gwythïen
**velar** adj felar
**veldt** n anialdir, maestir
**vellum** n memrwn
**velocity** n buander, cyflymder, buanedd (mathemateg)
**velvet** n melfed
**venal** adj llygredig, anonest
**vend** vt gwerthu
**vendor** n gwerthwr
**veneer** n argaen, wynebiad; rhith, ffug
**venerable** adj hybarch
**venerate** vt parchu, anrhydeddu
**venereal** adj gwenerol
**Venetian blind** n llen Fenis
**vengeance** n dial, dialedd
**vengeful** adj dialgar
**venial** adj maddeuadwy, esgusodol
**venison** n cig carw, fenswn
**venom** n gwenwyn

**venomous** adj gwenwynig
**venous** adj gwythennol
**vent** n agorfa, twll, arllwysfa ▷ vt arllwys, gollwng
**ventilate** vt awyru, gwyntyllu
**ventilation** n awyriad, gwyntylliad
**ventilator** n awyrydd, gwyntyllydd
**ventriloquism** n tafleisiaeth
**ventricle** n bolgell y galon, fentrigl
**venture** n anturiaeth, mentr ▷ vb anturio, mentro
**venturesome** adj mentrus, anturus
**venue** n man cyfarfod
**Venus** n Gwener, duwies serch
**veracious** adj cywir, geirwir, gwir
**veracity** adj geirwiredd
**verandah** n feranda
**verb** n berf
**verbal** adj berfol; geiriol
**verbally** adv mewn geiriau, gair am air
**verbatim** adv air am air, air yng ngair
**verbiage** n amleiriaeth, geiriogrwydd
**verb-noun** n berfenw
**verbose** adj amleiriog
**verbosity** n geiriogrwydd
**verdant** adj gwyrddlas, gwyrdd
**verdict** n dyfarniad, dedfryd, rheithfarn
**verdure** n gwyrddlesni
**verge** n min, ymyl ▷ vi ymylu
**verger** n byrllysgydd, eglwyswas
**verification** n gwireddiad
**verify** vt gwiro, gwireddu
**verily** adv yn wir, yn ddiau
**verisimilitude** n tebygolrwydd
**veritable** adj gwirioneddol
**verity** n gwir, gwirionedd
**vermilion** n fermiliwn, lliw cochlyd
**vermin** npl pryfed, pryfetach; llygod etc
**vernacular** adj cynhenid, brodorol ▷ n iaith y wlad
**vernal** adj gwanwynol

**veronica** n feronica, llysiau
Llywelyn
**versatile** adj amryddawn
**versatility** n amlochredd
**verse** n gwers, adnod, pennill;
prydyddiaeth
**versed** adj cyfarwydd, hyddysg
**versify** vb mydru, prydyddu, prydu
**version** n cyfieithiad, trosiad;
esboniad
**vers libre** n gwers rydd
**versus** prep yn erbyn
**vertebra (-brae)** n un o gymalau'r
asgwrn cefn
**vertebrate** n anifail ag asgwrn
cefn
**vertex (-tices)** n pen, crib, copa
**vertical** adj syth, unionsyth, plwm
**vertigo** n y bendro, y ddot
**vervain** n llysiau hudol, y ferfain
**verve** n bywyd, egni, asbri
**very** adj, adv iawn, pur, tra;
diamheuol
**vespers** npl gosber
**vessel** n llestr
**vest** n gwasgod, crys isaf ▷ vb
arwisgo, cynysgaeddu
**vestal** adj gwyryfol ▷ n lleian,
gwyry
**vested** adj yn ymwneud ag eiddo
**vestibule** n porth, cyntedd
**vestige** n ôl, ôl troed, brisg
**vestigial** adj gweddilliol, ôl
**vestment** n gwisg, defodwisg
**vestry** n festri
**vesture** n gwisg, dilledyn, dillad
**vet** vb arholi, archwilio ▷ n meddyg
anifeiliaid
**vetch** n pys llygod
**veteran** n un hen a chyfarwydd
**veterinary** adj milfeddygol; ~
**surgeon** meddyg anifeiliaid,
milfeddyg
**veto (-oes)** n gwaharddiad ▷ vt
gwahardd
**vex** vt blino, poeni, poenydio,
cythruddo

**vexation** n blinder, gofid
**vexed** adj blin, dig
**vexing** adj blin, plagus
**via** prep trwy, ar hyd
**viable** adj abl i fodoli, dichonadwy
**viaduct** n pontffordd, fforddbont
**vial** n ffiol
**viand** n bwyd, ymborth
**vibrant** adj dirgrynol
**vibrate** vb crynu, dirgrynu
**vibration** n dirgryniad
**vicar** n ficer
**vicarage** n ficeriaeth; ficerdy
**vicarious** adj dirprwyol, mechnïol
**vice** n drygioni, drygedd, bai, gwŷd
**vice** n gwasg, feis
**vice-** prefix rhag-, is-
**vice-admiral** n is-lyngesydd
**vice-chairman** n is-gadeirydd
**vice-chancellor** n is-ganghellor
**vice-president** n is-lywydd
**viceroy** n rhaglaw
**vice-versa** adv i'r gwrthwyneb
**vicinity** n cymdogaeth
**vicious** adj drygionus, gwydus
**viciousness** n drygioni, sbeit
**vicissitude** n cyfnewidiad, tro
**victim** n aberth, ysglyfaeth
**victimise** vb erlid, gormesu
**victor** n gorchfygwr
**victorious** adj buddugol,
buddugoliaethus
**victory** n buddugoliaeth
**victual** n (pl) bwyd, lluniaeth ▷ vt
bwydo
**victualler** n gwerthwr bwyd;
**licensed victualler** n tafarnwr
**vide** vb gwêl
**videlicet (viz)** adv sef, h.y.
**vie** vi cystadlu, cydymgais
**Vienna** n Wien
**Vietnam** n Fietnam
**view** n golygfa, barn ▷ vt edrych
**viewer** n gwyliwr (teledu)
**viewpoint** n safbwynt
**vigil** n noswyl, gwylnos
**vigilant** adj gwyliadwrus

**vignette** n addurn, llun

**vigorous** adj grymus, egnïol

**vigour** n grym, nerth, egni, ynni

**viking** n môr-leidr (o Lychlyn gynt)

**vile** adj gwael, brwnt

**vileness** n brynti

**vilify** vt pardduo, difrïo

**villa** n fila

**village** n pentref

**villager** n pentrefwr

**villain** n cnaf, adyn, dihiryn

**villainous** adj anfad, ysgeler

**villainy** n anfadwaith

**vim** n grym, ynni

**vindicate** vt amddiffyn, cyfiawnhau

**vindication** n cyfiawnhad

**vindictive** adj dialgar

**vindictiveness** n dialedd

**vine** n gwinwydden

**vinegar** n finegr

**vineyard** n gwinllan

**vintage** n cynhaeaf gwin

**vintner** n gwinwr, gwinydd

**viola** n fiola

**violate** vt torri, troseddu, treisio, trochi

**violation** n treisiad, trosedd

**violence** n ffyrnigrwydd, trais

**violent** adj gwyllt, tanbaid, angerddol

**violet** n fioled, crinllys

**violin** n ffidil

**violinist** n feiolinydd, ffidler

**violoncello** n basgrwth

**viper** n gwiber

**viper's bugloss** n tafod y bwch

**virago** n cecren

**virgin** n gwyry, morwyn

**virginal** n fyrginal ▷ adj gwyryfol, morwynol

**virile** adj gwrol, egnïol

**virility** n gwrolaeth, gwroldeb

**virtual** adj rhinweddol

**virtually** adv i bob pwrpas

**virtue** n rhinwedd

**virtuoso** n un celfydd, carwr celfyddyd

**virulence** n gwenwyn, casineb

**virulent** adj gwenwynig, ffyrnig

**virus** n gôr, crawn; gwenwyn, firws

**visa** n fisa

**visage** n wyneb, wynepryd

**vis-à-vis** adv wyneb yn wyneb, gyferbyn

**viscid** adj gwydn, gludiog

**viscount** n is-iarll

**visible** adj gweladwy, gweledig

**vision** n gweledigaeth; golwg, gweled

**visionary** n breuddwydiwr ▷ adj breuddwydiol

**visit** vt ymweld, gofwyo ▷ n ymweliad

**visitation** n ymweliad, archwiliad

**visitor** n ymwelwr, ymwelydd

**visor** n miswrn, mwgwd

**vista** n golygfa

**visual** adj gweledol, golygol; **~ aids** cyfarpar gweld

**visualise** vb gwneud yn weledig, disgrifio, dychmygu

**vital** adj bywiol, bywydol, hanfodol

**vitality** n bywyd, bywiogrwydd

**vitalize** vb bywiocáu, bywiogi

**vitamin** n fitamin

**vitiate** vt llygru, difetha, dirymu

**vitreous** adj gwydrol, gwydraidd

**vitriol** n fitriol, asid sylffurig

**vitriolic** adj fitriolaidd, atgas, chwerw

**vituperate** vt cablu, difenwi, difrïo

**vituperative** adj difrïol

**vivacious** adj bywiog, heini, nwyfus

**vivacity** n hoen, nwyf

**viva voce** adv ar lafar

**vivid** adj byw, clir, llachar, tanbaid

**vividness** n eglurder

**vivify** vt bywhau, bywiocáu

**vivisection** n bywdrychiad, bywddifyniad

**vixen** n cadnawes, llwynoges

**viz.** adv sef (talfyriad o *videlicet*)

**vizier** *n* swyddog gwlad
(Mohametanaidd)
**vocable** *n* gair
**vocabulary** *n* geirfa
**vocal** *adj* lleisiol, llafarol, llafar
**vocalist** *n* lleisiwr, cantor
**vocalize** *vt* llafarseinio; llafarogi
**vocally** *adv* â'r llais
**vocation** *n* galwad, galwedigaeth
**vocative** *adj* cyfarchol
**vociferate** *vb* crochlefain, gweiddi
**vodka** *n* fodca
**vogue** *n* arfer, ffasiwn, bri
**voice** *n* llais, lleferydd; (*Gram*) stad
**voiced** *adj* llafarog, lleisiol
**voiceless** *adj* dilais, mud
**void** *adj* gwag; ofer, di-rym ▷ *n*
gwagle ▷ *vt* gwagu, gollwng;
gwacau
**volatile** *adj* hedegog, anwadal,
gwamal, ysgafn, cyfnewidiol
**volcanic** *adj* folcanig
**volcano** *n* llosgfynydd, mynydd tân
**vole** *n* llygoden y maes
**volition** *n* ewyllysiad, ewyllys
**volley** *n* cawod o ergydion; taro pêl
yn yr awyr
**volt** *n* uned grym trydan, folt
**voltage** *n* grym trydan
**voluble** *adj* rhugl, ymadroddus
**volume** *n* cyfrol; swm, crynswth,
folum (cemeg), cyfaint
(mathemateg)
**voluminous** *adj* mawr, helaeth
**voluntary** *adj* gwirfoddol
**volunteer** *n* gwirfoddolwr ▷ *vb*
gwirfoddoli
**voluptuary** *n* pleserwr, glythwr
**voluptuous** *adj* glwth, trythyll
**voluptuousness** *n* trythyllwch
**vomit** *vb* chwydu, cyfogi
**voracious** *adj* gwancus, rheibus
**vortex** *n* trobwll, chwyldro
**votary** *n* addunwr, diofrydwr;
pleidiwr
**vote** *n* pleidlais ▷ *vb* pleidleisio
**voter** *n* pleidleisiwr

**votive** *adj* addunedol, addunol
**vouch** *vb* gwirio, gwarantu
**vouchsafe** *vt* caniatáu, rhoddi
**vow** *n* adduned, diofryd ▷ *vb*
addunedu
**vowel** *n* llafariad; **~ affection**
affeithiad; **~ mutation** gwyriad
**voyage** *n* mordaith ▷ *vb*
mordeithio, mordwyo
**voyager** *n* mordeithiwr
**vulcanize** *vb* caledu rwber
**vulgar** *adj* cyffredin; isel, di-foes,
aflednais
**vulgarism** *n* ymadrodd aflednais
**vulgarity** *n* diffyg moes
**Vulgate** *n* Y Fwlgat
**vulnerable** *adj* archolladwy,
hyglwyf, hawdd ei niweidio
**vulture** *n* fwltur

**wad** *n* sypyn, wad
**wadding** *n* wadin
**waddle** *vi* siglo, honcian
**wade** *vb* beisio, rhydio
**wader** *n* rhydiwr
**wadi** *n* gwely afon (sy'n dueddol
i sychu)
**wafer** *n* afrlladen
**waft** *vt* chwifio, cludo, dygludo
**wag** *vb* ysgwyd, siglo, honcian
**wag** *n* cellweiriwr, wag

**wage** vt gwneuthur, dwyn ymlaen
**wage** n cyflog, hur
**wager** n cyngwystl ▷ vt cyngwystlo
**waggish** adj cellweirus
**waggle** vb siglo
**wagon** n men, gwagen
**wagtail** n sigl-i-gwt
**waif** n plentyn digartref
**wail** vb cwynfan, wylofain, udo
**wainscot** n palis
**waist** n gwasg, canol
**waistcoat** n gwasgod
**wait** vb aros; gweini ▷ n arhosiad
**waiter** n gweinydd
**waiting** n aros, sefyll
**waiting room** n ystafell aros
**waitress** n gweinyddes
**wake** vb deffro ▷ n gwylmabsant;
  gwylnos
**wake** n ôl, brisg
**wakefulness** n anhunedd
**waken** vb deffro, dihuno
**Wales** n Cymru
**walk** vb cerdded, rhodio ▷ n
  rhodfa; tro
**walker** n cerddwr
**walkie-talkie** n set radio symud
  a siarad
**walking** n cerddediad; cerdded; **~
  stick** ffon gerdded
**walkover** n goruchafiaeth hawdd,
  digystadleuaeth
**wall** n mur, gwal, pared ▷ vt murio
**wallaby** n cangarŵ bach
**wall-cress** n berwr y fagwyr
**wallet** n ysgrepan, gwaled
**wallflower** n llysiau'r fagwyr,
  blodau'r fagwyr, blodau mamgu
**wallop** vt curo, llachio, wado
**wallow** vi ymdreiglo, ymdrybaeddu
**wallpaper** n papur wal
**walnut** n cneuen Ffrengig
**walrus** n morfarch
**waltz** n wols
**wan** adj gwelw, gwelwlas, llwyd
**wand** n gwialen, llath, hudlath
**wander** vb crwydro, gwibio,
  cyfeiliorni
**wanderer** n crwydryn
**wandering** adj ar grwydr
**wanderlust** n elfen grwydro
**wane** vi darfod, treio, cilio, lleihau
**wangle** vb dyfeisio
**want** n angen, eisiau, diffyg ▷ vb
  bod mewn angen
**wanting** adj yn eisiau
**wanton** adj anllad, trythyll; diachos
**wantonness** n anlladrwydd
**war** n rhyfel ▷ vb rhyfela
**warble** vb telori
**warbler** n telor
**ward** n gwart, gward;
  gwarchodaeth ▷ vt gwarchod,
  amddiffyn
**warden** n gwarden, gwarcheidwad
**wardenship** n gwardeniaeth
**warder** n gwarchodwr, gwyliwr
**wardrobe** n cwpwrdd dillad,
  gwardrob
**ware** n nwydd; llestri, wâr
**warehouse** n ystordy, ystorfa,
  warws
**warfare** n milwriaeth, rhyfel
**wariness** n pwyll, gwyliadwriaeth
**warlike** adj rhyfelgar, milwraidd,
  milwrol
**warm** adj cynnes ▷ vb cynhesu
**warmonger** n rhyfelgi
**warmth** n cynhesrwydd
**warn** vt rhybuddio
**warning** n rhybudd
**warp** n ystof, dylif ▷ vb gwyro,
  lleddfu
**warrant** n gwarant, awdurdod ▷ vt
  gwarantu, cyfreithloni
**warrantor** n gwarantydd
**warren** n cwningar, parc cwningod
**warrior** n rhyfelwr
**warship** n llong rhyfel
**wart** n dafad, dafaden
**wary** adj gwyliadwrus, gochelgar
**was** vi oedd, bu
**wash** vb golchi ▷ n golchiad,
  golchfa; golchion

**washable** _adj_ golchadwy
**washing** _n_ golch
**washing machine** _n_ peiriant golchi
**washing powder** _n_ powdr golchi
**washing-up liquid** _n_ sebon golchi llestri
**wasp** _n_ cacynen, gwenynen feirch
**wassail** _n_ gwasael
**waste** _vb_ difrodi, gwastraffu, treulio ▷ _n_ gwastraff, traul
**wasteful** _adj_ gwastraffus
**wastepaper basket** _n_ basged sbwriel
**wastrel** _n_ oferwr, oferddyn
**watch** _vb_ gwylio, gwylied, gwarchod ▷ _n_ gwyliadwriaeth; oriawr, oriadur, wats
**watchful** _adj_ gwyliadwrus
**watchmaker** _adj_ oriadurwr, trwsiwr watsys
**watchman** _n_ gwyliwr
**watch-night** _n_ gwylnos
**watchword** _n_ arwyddair, cyswynair
**water** _n_ dwfr, dŵr ▷ _vb_ dyfrhau
**water-cock** _n_ tap
**watercolour** _n_ paent (i'w gymysgu â dŵr); dyfrlliw
**watercress** _n_ berwr dŵr
**waterfall** _n_ rhaeadr, pistyll, cwymp dŵr, sgwd
**waterhen** _n_ iâr fach y dŵr
**watering place** _n_ lle i anifeiliaid gael dŵr; tref ffynhonnau
**waterlogged** _adj_ llawn dŵr
**watermark** _n_ dyfrnod
**waterproof** _adj_ diddos
**watershed** _n_ trum, gwahanfa ddŵr
**water skiing** _n_ sglefrio ar ddŵr
**watertight** _adj_ diddos, heb ollwng dŵr neu leithder
**water wagtail** _n_ sigwti fach y dŵr
**watt** _n_ wat, uned pŵer trydan
**wattle** _n_ clwyd, pleiden; tagell ceiliog

**wave** _vb_ chwifio; tonni ▷ _n_ ton
**waver** _vi_ anwadalu, petruso, gwamalu
**wax** _n_ cwyr ▷ _vt_ cwyro
**wax** _vi_ cynyddu, tyfu
**wax-candle** _n_ cannwyll gŵyr
**waxworks** _npl_ arddangosfa delwau cwyr
**way** _n_ ffordd, modd, arfer
**wayfarer** _n_ fforddolyn, teithiwr, tramwywr
**wayfaring tree** _n_ ysgawen y gors
**waylay** _vt_ cynllwyn, rhagod
**wayside** _n_ ymyl y ffordd
**wayward** _adj_ cyndyn, ystyfnig, gwrthnysig
**we** _pron_ ni, nyni, ninnau
**weak** _adj_ gwan, egwan
**weaken** _vb_ gwanhau, gwanychu
**weakling** _n_ un gwan, edlych, ewach
**weakly** _adj_ gwanllyd
**weak-minded** _adj_ diniwed, gwirion
**weakness** _n_ gwendid
**weal** _n_ llwydd, llwyddiant, lles
**weald** _n_ fforest; gwlad agored
**wealth** _n_ golud, cyfoeth, da
**wealthy** _adj_ cyfoethog
**wean** _vt_ diddyfnu
**weapon** _n_ arf
**wear** _vb_ gwisgo, treulio ▷ _n_ traul; gwisg
**weariness** _n_ blinder
**weary** _adj_ blin, blinedig ▷ _vb_ blino
**weasel** _n_ gwenci, bronwen
**weather** _n_ tywydd, hin ▷ _vt_ dal, dioddef
**weather-beaten** _adj_ ag ôl y tywydd arno
**weatherglass** _n_ baromedr
**weathervane** _n_ ceiliog gwynt
**weave** _vb_ gwau, gweu
**weaver** _n_ gwehydd
**web** _n_ gwe
**webbing** _n_ webin
**web-footed** _adj_ â thraed gweog

**wed** vb priodi, ymbriodi
**wedding** n priodas
**wedge** n cŷn, gaing, lletem ▷ vt cynio; gwthio i mewn
**wedlock** n ystad priodas, priodas
**Wednesday** n dydd Mercher
**wee** adj bach, bychan, pitw
**weed** n chwynnyn, chwyn ▷ vb chwynnu
**week** n wythnos
**weekday** n diwrnod gwaith
**weekend** n dros y Sul, penwythnos
**weekly** n wythnosolyn (cylchgrawn) ▷ adj wythnosol ▷ adv yn wythnosol
**weep** vb wylo, wylofain, llefain
**weevil** n gwyfyn yr ŷd
**weft** n anwe
**weigh** vb pwyso; codi (angor)
**weight** n pwys, pwysau
**weighty** adj pwysig, trwm
**weir** n cored
**weird** adj annaearol, iasol
**welcome** excl, n croeso ▷ vt croesawu ▷ adj derbyniol, dymunol
**weld** vt asio
**welfare** n llwydd, lles
**welfare state** n gwladwriaeth les
**well** adv yn dda ▷ adj da, iach ▷ excl wel
**well** n ffynnon, pydew
**well-balanced** adj cytbwys
**wellbeing** n lles, budd
**well-bred** adj boneddigaidd
**well-fed** adj mewn cas cadw da
**wellingtons** npl esgidiau glaw
**well-off** adj cefnog, da ei fyd
**Welsh** adj Cymreig (o ran teithi); Cymraeg (o ran iaith) ▷ n Cymraeg
**Welshman** n Cymro
**Welshwoman** n Cymraes
**welt** n gwald, gwaldas
**welter** vi ymdrybaeddu
**wen** n wen
**wench** n geneth, llances
**wend** vt mynd, cerdded
**werewolf** n bleidd-ddyn

**Wesleyan** adj Wesleaidd
**west** n gorllewin ▷ adj gorllewinol; **West Germany** n Gorllewin yr Almaen; **West Indies** npl: **the West Indies** India'r Gorllewin
**westerly** adj gorllewinol, o'r gorllewin
**western** adj gorllewinol
**westwards** adv tua'r gorllewin
**wet** adj gwlyb ▷ vt gwlychu ▷ n gwlybaniaeth
**wetness** n gwlybaniaeth
**wetting** n gwlychfa
**wether** n mollt, gwedder
**whack** vb llachio, baeddu, ffonodio
**whale** n morfil
**wharf** n porthfa, llwythfa
**what** adj, pron yr hyn; pa beth, pa faint
**whatever** pron beth bynnag
**whatsoever** pron pa beth bynnag
**wheat** n gwenith
**wheedle** vt denu, hudo, llithio, truthio
**wheel** n olwyn, rhod, troell ▷ vt olwyno, powlio
**wheelbarrow** n berfa (drol), whilber
**wheelchair** n cadair olwyn
**wheelwright** n saer troliau
**wheeze** vi gwichian ▷ n gwich
**wheezy** adj gwichlyd
**whelk** n chwalc, gwalc
**whelp** n cenau
**when** adv pan, pa bryd
**whence** adv o ba le, o ba un
**whenever** adv pa bryd bynnag
**where** adv ym mha le; yn y lle, lle
**whereabouts** adv ymhle
**whereas** conj gan, yn gymaint â
**whereby** adv trwy yr hyn
**wherefore** adv paham, am hynny
**wherein** adv yn yr hyn
**whereof** adv y … amdano
**whereon** adv ar yr hwn
**wheresoever, wherever** adv pa le bynnag

**whereto** adv y ... iddo
**whereupon** adv ar hynny
**wherewithal** n modd, arian
**wherry** n ysgraff, ceubal, porthfad
**whet** vt hogi, minio, awchlymu
**whether** conj ai, pa un ai
**whetstone** n carreg hogi, hogfaen, agalen
**whey** n maidd, gleision
**which** pron pa un, pa rai; a ▷ adj pa
**whichever** pron, adj pa un bynnag
**whiff** n chwiff, pwff, chwyth, chwa
**Whig** n Chwig, Rhyddfrydwr
**while** n ennyd, talm, amser ▷ vt treulio ▷ (hefyd **whilst**) adv cyhyd, tra
**whim** n mympwy, chwim
**whimper** vb swnian crio
**whimsical** adj ysmala, mympwyol
**whimsicality** n bod yn fympwyol
**whin** n eithin
**whinchat** n clochdar yr eithin
**whine** vb swnian crio, cwynfan
**whinny** vi gweryru
**whip** vb chwipio, ffrewyllu, fflangellu ▷ n chwip, ffrewyll, fflangell
**whiphand** n llaw uchaf
**whippet** n corfilgi
**whipping** n chwipiad, fflangelliad
**whir** vi chwyrndroi, chwyrnu
**whirl** vb chwyrlïo, chwyrnellu, chwyrndroi
**whirligig** n chwyrligwgan, chwyrnell
**whirlpool** n pwll tro, trobwll
**whirlwind** n trowynt, corwynt
**whisk** n tusw ▷ vb ysgubo; chwyrlïo
**whiskered** adj blewog, barfog
**whiskers** npl blew, barf
**whisky** n chwisgi
**whisper** vb, n sibrwd, sisial
**whist** n chwist
**whistle** vb chwibanu ▷ n chwiban, chwibanogl, chwît
**whit** n tipyn, gronyn, mymryn
**white** adj gwyn, can, cannaid

**whiten** vb gwynnu, cannu
**whiteness** n gwynder, gwyndra
**whitewash** n gwyngalch ▷ vb gwyngalchu
**whither** adv i ba le
**whiting** n gwyniad
**whitlow** n ffelwm, ffalwm, ewinor, bystwn
**whitlow grass** n llysiau'r bystwn
**Whit Monday** n Llungwyn
**Whitsun(day)** n Sulgwyn
**Whitsuntide** n dros y Sulgwyn
**whittle** vt naddu, lleihau
**whiz** vi sïo, chwyrnellu, chwyrlïo
**who** pron a, pwy
**whoever** pron pwy bynnag
**whole** adj cyfan, holl; iach, holliach ▷ n cyfan
**wholehearted** adj â'i holl galon
**wholemeal** adj â'r grawn cyfan, cyflawn
**wholeness** n cyfanrwydd
**wholesale** n cyfanwerth ▷ adj yn y crynswth
**wholesaler** n cyfanwerthwr
**wholesome** adj iach, iachus, iachusol
**wholly** adv yn hollol, yn gyfan gwbl, yn llwyr
**whom** pron a (y, yr)
**whomsoever** pron pwy bynnag
**whoop** vi bloeddio, banllefain · ▷ n bloedd
**whooping cough** n pas
**whop** vt ffusto, baeddu
**whopper** n un mawr
**whopping** adj mawr iawn
**whore** n putain, hŵr
**whorl** n tro, troell, sidell
**whortleberry** n llus, llusi duon bach
**whose** pron y ... ei, eiddo pwy? pwy biau?
**whosoever** pron pwy bynnag
**why** adv paham, pam
**wick** n pabwyr, pabwyryn, wic
**wicked** adj drwg, drygionus, ysgeler

**wickedness** n drygioni
**wicker** n gwaith gwiail
**wickerwork** n plethwaith, basgedwaith
**wicket** n wiced, clwyd, llidiart
**wide** adj llydan, eang, helaeth; rhwth
**wide-awake** adj effro, ar ddihun
**widely** adj yn eang
**widen** vb lledu, llydanu
**widespread** adj cyffredinol
**widgeon** n wiwell
**widow** adj gweddw ▷ n gwraig weddw, gwidw
**widowed** adj gweddw
**widower** n gwidman
**widowhood** n gweddwdod
**width** n lled, ehangder
**wield** vt llywio, rheoli; ysgwyd, arfer, trin
**wife** (wives) n gwraig, gwraig briod, priod
**wig** n gwallt gosod, perwig, wig
**wigging** n cerydd
**wild** adj gwyllt ▷ n diffeithle
**wilderness** n anialwch
**wildfire** n tân gwyllt
**wildness** n gwylltineb
**wile** n dichell, ystryw, cast
**wilful** adj gwirfoddol, bwriadol; ystyfnig
**wilfully** adj o fwriad
**wilfulness** (or u.s. **willfulness**) n ystyfnigrwydd
**wiliness** n dichell, cyfrwystra
**will** vt ewyllysio, mynnu ▷ n ewyllys
**willing** adj ewyllysgar, bodlon
**willingly** adj o wirfodd
**willingness** n parodrwydd
**will-o-the-wisp** n jacolantern
**willow** n helygen, pren helyg
**willowherb** n helyglys
**willowy** adj helygaidd, gosgeiddig
**willpower** n grym ewyllys
**willy-nilly** adv bodlon neu beidio, o fodd neu anfodd
**wily** adj cyfrwys, dichellgar

**wimple** n gwempl
**win** vb ennill
**wince** vi gwingo
**winch** n wins
**wind** n gwynt
**wind** vb dirwyn, troi
**windbag** n clebryn
**windfall** n lwc, ffawd dda
**windflower** n anemoni, blodyn y gwynt
**windless** adj di-wynt, llonydd
**windmill** n melin wynt
**window** n ffenestr
**windowpane** n cwarel
**windpipe** n breuant, y bibell wynt
**windscreen** n ffenestr flaen
**windscreen wiper** n braich law
**windward** adj tua'r gwynt
**windy** adj gwyntog
**wine** n gwin
**wineglass** n gwydr gwin
**wing** n adain, asgell; asgellwr (rygbi)
**wing-commander** n asgell-gomander
**winged** adj adeiniog
**wing-forward** n blaenasgellwr
**wink** vb wincio, cau llygad ▷ n winc; hunell
**winner** n enillydd
**winning** adj enillgar, deniadol
**winnings** npl enillion
**winnow** vt nithio, gwyntyllio
**winnower** n nithiwr
**winsome** adj serchog, deniadol
**winter** n gaeaf ▷ vb gaeafu
**wintry** adj gaeafol
**wipe** vt sychu
**wire** n gwifr, gwifren
**wireless** n radio
**wirepulling** n cynllwyn, dylanwadu, `tynnu gwifrau'
**wiring** n weiro
**wiry** adj gwydn, caled
**wisdom** n doethineb
**wise** adj doeth
**wiseacre** n doethyn, ffwlcyn

**wish** vb dymuno, chwennych ▷ n dymuniad
**wishbone** n asgwrn tynnu
**wishful** adj awyddus; **~ thinking** breuddwyd gwrach
**wishywashy** adj gwan, di-asgwrn-cefn
**wisp** n tusw
**wistful** adj awyddus, hiraethus
**wit** vb: **to ~** sef, hynny yw, nid amgen
**wit** n synnwyr; arabedd; gŵr ffraeth
**witch** n dewines, gwrach
**witchcraft** n dewiniaeth
**with** prep â, ag, gyda, gydag, efo, gan
**withdraw** vb tynnu yn ôl, encilio; codi arian
**withdrawal** n enciliad
**withe** n gwden, gwialen helyg
**wither** vb gwywo, crino
**withering** adj gwywol, crin
**withers** npl ysgwydd march
**withhold** vt atal, cadw yn ôl
**within** adv, n, prep i mewn, o fewn
**without** prep heb, di- ▷ adv, n tu allan
**withstand** vt gwrthsefyll
**witless** adj disynnwyr, ynfyd, ffôl
**witness** n tyst; tystiolaeth ▷ vb tystio
**wits** npl synhwyrau
**witticism** n ffraethair, ffraetheb
**wittiness** n ffraethineb
**wittingly** adv trwy wybod, yn fwriadol
**witty** adj arab, arabus, ffraeth
**wizard** n swynwr, dewin
**wizardry** n dewiniaeth, hud
**wizened** adj gwyw, crin, sybachog
**woad** n glaslys
**wobble** vi siglo, honcian, anwadalu
**wobbly** adj sigledig
**woe** n gwae
**woebegone** adj athrist
**wolf** (wolves) n blaidd
**wolfsbane** n llysiau'r blaidd
**woman** (women) n gwraig, merch
**womanliness** n rhinweddau benywaidd
**womanly** adj gwreigaidd, benywaidd
**womb** n croth, bru
**wonder** n rhyfeddod, syndod ▷ vi rhyfeddu, synnu
**wonderful, wondrous** adj rhyfeddol
**wont** vb, n arfer ▷ adj arferol
**woo** vt caru; deisyf
**wood** n coed, coedwig; pren
**woodbine** n gwyddfid
**woodcock** n cyffylog
**woodcutter** n torrwr coed
**wooded** adj coedog
**wooden** adj o goed, o bren; trwsgl, trwstan
**woodland** n coetir
**woodlark** n ehedydd y coed
**wood-louse** (-lice) n gwrach y lludw, mochyn y coed, tyrchyn llwyd
**woodpecker** n taradr y coed
**wood-pigeon** n ysguthan
**wood sage** n chwerwlys yr eithin, saets gwyllt
**wood sorrel** n surran y coed
**woodwind** npl chwythoffer pren
**woodwork** n gwaith coed, gwaith saer
**woof** n anwe
**wool** n gwlân
**woollen** adj gwlanog, gwlân
**woolly** adj gwlanog
**woolsack** n sedd yr Arglwydd Ganghellor
**word** n gair ▷ vt geirio
**wording** n geiriad
**wordy** adj geiriog, amleiriog
**work** n gwaith, gweithred, gorchwyl ▷ vb gweithio
**worker** n gweithiwr
**workhouse** n tloty, wyrcws
**working** adj yn gweithio, gwaith
**workman** n gweithiwr
**workmanlike** adj gweithgar, diwyd
**workmanship** n saernïaeth, crefft
**workshop** n gweithdy

**world** n byd
**worldly** adj bydol
**worldwide** adj byd-eang
**worm** n pryf, abwydyn; llyngyren ▷ vb ymnyddu
**wormwood** n wermod
**worn-out** adj wedi blino; wedi treulio
**worried** adj pryderus, gofidus
**worry** vb cnoi, baeddu, blino, poeni, poenydio ▷ n pryder, blinder
**worse** adj gwaeth
**worsen** vb gwaethygu
**worship** n addoliad ▷ vb addoli
**worshipper** n addolwr
**worst** vt gorchfygu, trechu
**worsted** n edafedd hirwlan, wstid
**worth** n gwerth, teilyngdod
**worthless** adj diwerth
**worthy** adj teilwng ▷ n gŵr o fri
**wound** n archoll, clwyf ▷ vt archolli, clwyfo
**wraith** n cyhiraeth, cyheuraeth
**wrangle** vb cecru, cweryla, ffraeo ▷ n ffrae, ymryson
**wrap** vt plygu, amdoi, lapio
**wrapping paper** n papur lapio
**wrasse** n gwrachen y môr
**wrath** n llid, digofaint, soriant
**wrathful** adj digofus, llidiog, dig
**wreak** vt tywallt, dial (llid)
**wreath** n torch
**wreck** n llongddrylliad ▷ vb llongddryllio
**wren** n dryw, dryw bach
**wrench** vt rhwygo ymaith, tyndroi ▷ n tyndro
**wrestle** vi ymgodymu, ymaflyd codwm
**wrestler** n ymgodymwr, taflwr codwm
**wretch** n adyn, truan; gwalch, dihiryn
**wretched** adj truan, truenus, gresynus
**wriggle** vb gwingo, ymnyddu
**wright** n saer

**wring** vt troi, gwasgu
**wrinkle** n crych, crychni ▷ vb crychu
**wrinkle** n awgrym, hysbysrwydd
**wrinkled** n crychiog
**wrist** n arddwrn
**wristband** n rhwymyn llawes
**wristwatch** n wats arddwrn, wats fraich, oriawr
**writ** n: **Holy W~** yr Ysgrythur Lân
**write** vb ysgrifennu
**writer** n ysgrifennwr, awdur
**writhe** vb ymnyddu, gwingo
**writing** n ysgrifen; ysgrifennu
**writing paper** n papur ysgrifennu
**wrong** adj cyfeiliornus, cam, anghywir, o'i le ▷ n cam ▷ vt gwneud cam â, niweidio, drygu
**wrongdoing** n trosedd, camwedd
**wrongful** adj anghyfiawn, ar gam
**wroth** adj dig, dicllon, digofus, llidiog
**wrought** adj: **~ iron** haearn gyr
**wry** adj cam, gwyrgam

**xenophobia** n senoffobia
**X-rays** npl pelydrau X
**xylophone** n seiloffon

**yacht** n llong bleser, iot
**yachtsman** n hwyliwr iot
**yap** vi clepian, cyfarth
**yard** n llath, llathen; hwyl-lath
**yard** n iard, buarth, cadlas, clos
**yarn** n edau, edafedd; stori, chwedl
**yawl** n bad mawr, cwch llong
**yawn** vi dylyfu gên, agor ceg
**ye** pron chwi, chwychwi; chwithau
**yea** adv ie, yn wir
**year** n blwyddyn, blwydd
**yearling** n anifail blwydd
**yearly** adv blynyddol
**yearn** vi hiraethu, dyheu
**yearning** n hiraeth
**yeast** n burum, berem, berman
**yell** vb ysgrechain ▷ n ysgrech, nâd
**yellow** adj, n melyn
**yellowhammer** n y benfelen,
    melyn yr eithin
**yelp** vi cyfarth, gogyfarth, cipial
**yeoman** n gwrêng, iwmon;
    amaethwr
**yeomanry** n meirchfilwyr
**yes** adv ie, do, oes etc
**yesterday** n, adv doe
**yet** conj, adv er hynny, eto
**yew** n yw, ywen
**Yiddish** n Almaeneg Iddewaidd
**yield** vb ildio, gildio, ymroddi,
    rhoddi ▷ n cynnyrch
**yoghurt** n iogwrt
**yoke** n iau, gwedd ▷ vb ieuo
**yokefellow** n cymar
**yokel** n lleban, gwladwr, taeog

**yolk** n melyn wy, melynwy
**yonder** adj acw, draw ▷ adv dacw,
    acw, draw
**yore** n y dyddiau gynt, y cynfyd
**you** pron chi, chwi, 'ch; chwychwi;
    chwithau
**young** adj ifanc, ieuanc
**younger** adj iau
**youngest** adj ieuaf, ifancaf
**youngster** n bachgennyn, plentyn
**your** pron eich, 'ch
**yours** pron eiddoch, yr eiddoch
**yourself** pron eich hun(an)
**yourselves** pron eich hunain
**youth** n ieuenctid, mebyd; llanc;
    **youth hostel** n gwesty ieuenctid
**youthful** adj ieuanc, ieuengaidd
**Yugoslavia** n Iwgoslafia
**Yule** n Nadolig
**Yuletide** n tymor y Nadolig

# Z

**Zambia** n Zambia
**zeal** n sêl, aidd, eiddgarwch,
    brwdfrydedd
**zealot** n gwynfydwr, penboethyn
**zealous** adj selog, eiddgar,
    brwdfrydig
**zebra** n sebra
**zenana** n gwragedd-dy, gwreicty
**zenith** n entrych; anterth
**zephyr** n awel dyner (o'r gorllewin)

**zero** *n* dim, diddim, gwagnod (o), sero
**zest** *n* awch, blas, afiaith
**zigzag** *adj, n* igam-ogam
**Zimbabwe** *n* Zimbabwe
**zinc** *n* sinc
**zip** *n* sip

**zither** *n* sither
**zodiac** *n* sidydd
**zone** *n* gwregys, cylch, rhanbarth
**zoo** *n* sw
**zoological** *adj* sŵolegol
**zoologist** *n* sŵolegydd
**zoology** *n* milofyddiaeth, sŵoleg